THE WRESTLING OBSERVER

Complete Collection By Dave Meltzer

1989
Part 2

Copyright © Dave Meltzer

Published by Titan Insider Press
contact@titaninsiderpress.com

With thanks to Dante Richardson (editor), Benjamin Richardson (cover design), Kenny McIntosh (compiler), Jessica Richardson (compiler) and Staurt Innis (compiler).

Designed and typeset by STK Design
Cover design by STK Design
Cover images: Howard Baum

First edition: 2023.

Printed and bound in the United Kingdom

Online: **F4Wonline.com**

Twitter: **@davemeltzerWON**

Twitter: **@WONF4W**

Email: **dave@wrestlingobserver.com**

www.insidetheropesmagazine.com

THE WRESTLING OBSERVER
Complete Collection By Dave Meltzer

1989

PART 2
JULY-DECEMBER

Dave Meltzer

CONTENTS

JULY 3, 1989

Topping things off this week is the retirement of the legendary Japanese wrestler Antonio Inoki. Inoki, 46, confirmed what had been reported a week earlier in several Japanese newspapers that he will be running for public office in Japan. Inoki announced his candidacy for a position in the House of Councilors on June 15th and when New Japan opened its most recent tour the next day in Tokyo, Inoki made a Live announcement to the wrestling fans and to the television audience. The election takes place on July 23rd, and I guess whether this is a temporary retirement to run for public office or a permanent retirement may be determined by the results of the election. Inoki's 30-year career in the ring has been one filled with many triumphs and failures and earned his the nickname within wrestling as "The Cat" since he seemingly had nine lives as every time it appeared his wrestling and management career within wrestling was history, he always rebounded, usually to return stronger than ever. What may have been his final coup was being in charge when the Soviets made their pro wrestling debut this past year and helped the New Japan business boom once again. Inoki, who owns roughly 47 percent of the New Japan stock, also gave up his presidency of the company to Seiji Sakaguchi, who also announced his retirement as an active wrestler in order to concentrate fully on running the company. Inoki will retain a position in the company as a member of the Board of Directors along with Takahira Nagasato (The TV director and representative of TV-Asahi which owns much of the rest of the stock), Tatsumi Fujinami, former pro wrestler Kotetsu Yamamoto (who is the color commentator on the television shows), Kantaro Hoshino, Mitsuo Yoshida (pro wrestler Riki Choshu) and Masanori Saito (Masa Saito). If Inoki doesn't return, it is expected that Choshu will be pushed as the top star within the promotion and win the World title before the year is out, although many expect that the superstars of the 1990s in this group will wind up being Koji Kitao (former sumo wrestler Futuhaguro who makes his pro debut on New Years Eve and is training right now with Lou Thesz), Keiji Muto (Great Muta) and Shinya Hashimoto.

We've got tentative Line-ups for both the upcoming NWA and WWF pay-per-view shows later this summer. The NWA's Baltimore Bash will be a two hour 45 minute show from 4:30 to 7:15 p.m. Eastern time on Sunday, July 23rd with the current Line-up being headlined by Ric Flair vs. Terry Funk for the NWA title (which will officially be announced on TBS Saturday afternoon), Lex Luger vs. Ricky Steamboat for the U.S. title in a no disqualification match with the winner getting both the title and the No. 1 contendership spot, Sting vs. Muta for the TV title with Eddie Gilbert in Sting's corner, a "War Games" match (two rings in a cage, members of each team enter in two minute intervals and the finish can't come until all 10 men are in the ring and the only way to win is by submission) with the Midnight Express & Steve Williams & Road Warriors vs. Samoan Swat Team & The Freebirds (Michael Hayes & v Terry Gordy & Jimmy Garvin), a yet-to-be announced singles match to determine the king of the two ring Battle Royals, Kevin Sullivan & Mike Rotunda vs. Rick & Scott Steiner in a tornado match, The Dynamic Dudes (Shane Douglas & Johnny Ace) vs The Skyscrapers (Sid Vicious & Danny Spivey managed by Teddy Long) and Brian pillman vs. Bill Irwin.

The WWF SummerSlam '89 will take place on August 28th from the Meadowlands. So far I've only got the top three matches officially which will be Hulk Hogan & Brutus Beefcake vs. Randy Savage & Zeus with Sherri Martel and Elizabeth in the corners; Andre the Giant & Akeem & Big Bossman vs. Demolition & Hillbilly Jim and Dusty Rhodes vs. Honky Tonk Man. I'm pretty sure they'll also have Rick Rude vs. The Ultimate Warrior for the Intercontinental title as the only championship match on the show. From that point on, we should be back to the routine and having roughly one PPV show per month, as the NWA will be back with a PPV in October, the WWF has the Survivor Series on Thanksgiving night from the Horizon in Chicago, NWA will be back for Starrcade which is tentatively planned for December 17th, then WWF will hold the Royal Rumble in mid-January and the NWA will probably have another show in either late February or early March and then we've got WrestleMania in late March or early April and on and on it goes.

The NWA opened its Bash tour on Thursday night at the Capital Centre and followed it up with shows in New Haven, Philadelphia and Pittsburgh before the weekend was out. The shows all did decent business. You can call it good taken in the context that there is no Ric Flair on these shows and in comparison to the crowds the NWA has been drawing all year. You can call it bad in comparison with the Bash crowds last year, but that really isn't fair since so much damage has been done to the NWA and you have to learn to walk before you can run and right now the promotion is just learning to walk. The Capital Centre card drew a $50,000 house, with New Haven drawing $35,000 the next night (with very limited walk-up business since Titan ran a Hogan vs. Savage match in nearby Hartford the night before which drew a $157,000 house), Philadelphia drawing approximately $50,000 on Saturday and Pittsburgh drawing slightly less than that on Sunday.

The NWA also debuted its Friday night prime time wrestling show, which didn't quite make prime time its first week since the Atlanta Braves game went long, as it always seems to do when wrestling scheduling is involved. The first show contained two notable surprises, one of which was the return of Gordon Solie to TBS and the other was the acknowledgement of other promotions during Solie's segment. The show, called the NWA Power Hour, featured three matches, all of which were entertaining; had a" Funk's Grill" with Missy Hyatt which came off pretty good; another interview with Ric Flair at home and the surprise segment with Solie reading off brief wrestling headlines of the past week, concentrating on the NWA and in particular the Lex Luger turn, but he also mentioned brief items on World Class, the Florida promotion (which Solie is heavily involved with) and the WWF, with a mention of the movie "No Holds Barred" which some took as a knock of the movie (saying it had mixed reviews and was falling in the ratings but still in the top 10), others took as a plug. As everyone probably knows, it violates all sorts of wrestling tradition to mention any other promotion to begin with, particularly when all the promotions mentioned in some form or fashion are competitors. I'm told this was Jim Herd's idea, and it was the leading topic of conversation this weekend with most calling not particularly understanding why it was done, but kind of liking it anyway. The plan is for Solie to weekly highlight wrestling news from both the NWA and other circuits and mention at least one brief WWF item on each show, which often will be news items concerning the WWF (such as this coming week with the mention of Jake Roberts' neck injury and surgery) that Titan itself won't acknowledge. Jim Cornette and Jim Ross host the show, and as a debut effort, it was a good show as both the matches and interviews were top-shelf. The key is whether or not they can retain this level of quality on a weekly basis, and also if the NWA can build this time slot into one with a sizable audience. As for the usage of Solie, I'm of the opinion that this is the correct usage of Solie, who still maintains a good deal of name recognition with long-time wrestling fans, notably in the South and also those who have had cable for many years as Solie hosted the TBS wrestling shows during their "glory days" in the early part of the decade.

In its third weekend, the movie "No Holds Barred" starring Hulk Hogan did $1.6 million at the box office in 1,327 screens (roughly $1,200 per-screen) which put it in the No. 7 slot for the weekend. As of last Monday, the movie had topped the $12 million mark in overall business. The split for the weekend was 75 percent for the theaters and 25 percent for New Line Cinema, and Titan's cut was a smaller percentage of that 25 percent. This past weekend and for the remainder of this week, the split will become 80 percent for the theaters and 20 percent for New Line, and if the

movie Lasts until June 30th, the split becomes 90/10. The movie was still in a good amount of theaters over this past weekend, although in most places it was now playing as part of a double-bill with "Pink Cadillac" and next weekend it'll mainly be on double-bills and the number of theaters should drop significantly (from 87 to 12 in Northern California for example). When all is said and done, the movie should fini. sh at around the $14 million mark in domestic gross sales. For a major summer movie, that would be considered a flop, but this wasn't really a major summer movie. For a low-budget film, which this was, $14 million is considered fairly successful although successful and profitable for Titan Sports are two different things because of the bad deals Titan had to make to get in this game. If they were to do a second film, which is at least a decent possibility, and it were to gross a similar amount with the same production costs, it would be a lot better of a financial deal all-in-all for Titan because they now have a track record as does Hulk Hogan as somewhat of a movie draw.

Speaking of NHB, comedian Richard Belzer, who hardly qualifies as an unbiased observer since he has a lawsuit out against Hogan stemming from an incident on his cable TV show back in 1985 where Hogan put him out with a front face lock, did a review of the movie in which he lambasted it pretty strongly on New York's Howard Stern radio show. Stern noted as Belzer was using every derogatory term in his vocabulary to describe the movie and Hogan's acting performance, that Belzer might be slightly biased since he hates Hogan to begin with. Belzer came back with a funny line: "Even if I was sleeping with Hogan, I'd still have to say the movie sucked."

By the way, the Ding Dongs, the NWA's answer to Hulk Hogan's performance on the silver screen, are supposed to be starting to work full-time on the Bash tour starting July 10th, mainly in matches against the New Zealand Militia (Rip Morgan & Jacko Victory). Anyway, the Ding Dongs are going to work a date in August in Hong Kong against some wrestler over there called King Kong. There have been a lot of people of late who have been saying that the stuff the NWA has been doing of late doesn't have any rhyme or reason, but at Least- now it has rhyme .

Pro wrestler and promoter Jerry Blackwell's health took a turn for the worst this past week, but luckily seemed to have stabilized as of week's end. As of last weekend, there was fear that one of Blackwell's legs might have to be amputated because of a staph infection, but luckily that wasn't the case. However, the 40-year-old Blackwell developed a condition of having fluid in his lungs and was in very critical condition as of mid-week but he finally started responding to treatment. Blackwell had similar problems three years ago while working for the AWA which pretty well finished him as a full-time active wrestler and for the past few years has wrestled on a part-time basis and heads up Southern

Championship Wrestling, an independent group based in Georgia.

For those of you who have attended Bash shows, the reason they've shot angles during the Battle Royals where Terry Funk attacks Sting with the branding iron and Sting winds up carried out on a stretcher and is unable to wrestle his scheduled singles match later on is because for the time being, the NWA is holding Funk out of action. Funk fractured his sacrum in the lower back this past Monday in Macon, GA and although he was willing to work his scheduled matches with Sting with the injury, TBS felt he should sit it out and let the injury heal, rather than risk aggravating the injury and threatening the PPV main event. Instead of sitting it out, they came up with the plan that has been put to use thus far in the Bash. From what I'm told, Funk will start back wrestling before the PPV show against Sting, but I'm not sure what date he'll be back in the ring but he'll be doing regular interviews and making all the shows.

There are a ton of rumors flying around concerning the future of Jarrett Promotions, both in regards to the Dallas and the Tennessee offices. For that matter, there are tons of rumors about the NWA going around as well. The only thing pretty well confirmed is that the Dallas group will shortly be changing its name from World Class Championship Wrestling to the United States Wrestling Association (USWA) and there is talk that when the name change takes place that the Tennessee-based CWA will become a part of the USWA as well. They have already been calling the World title that Jerry Lawler holds as the USWA title in both circuits.

Lawler met with the NWA this past Monday in Atlanta but no deal was reached but the door was left open for more discussion. Things that were discussed was an attempt by the NWA to use Lawler on a one-shot basis when it runs a card in July in Memphis in the main event against Terry Funk(currently the main event is scheduled as Funk vs. Eddie Gilbert and the advance for the show is poor, although Memphis is not an advance town) or even the possibility of the NWA using the Memphis circuit as a sort of minor league feeder system where it can send young wrestlers who need more seasoning and veterans who no longer can make it as headliners nationally but can help teach the younger wrestlers. But thus far nothing concrete has come from either of those ideas.

By the way, I forgot one match when I was running down the NWA's PPV card on 7/23. They will also have a tuxedo street fight with Jim Cornette vs. Paul E. Dangerously in which the object will be to tear off the tuxes.

A final comment on NHB. Whether the movie made money on domestic release for Titan, or does any overseas business, overall the doing of the movie has to be considered a positive for Titan. I've never seen so much talk about pro wrestling ever among the general public as there is right now with one exception, and that was the week of WrestleMania I. There was tons more talk about the movie than their was about any of the other WrestleManias, and I'm amazed as how "over" the WWF's characters have become, even more so of late, at least in this part of the country (they've been over" to a solid degree for years but I 've noticed a lot more widespread recognition of them and of wrestling in general). Now almost all of the comments regarding the movie are bad, but people still know and talk about Hulk Hogan, Randy Savage, Zeus, etc. and that bodes well for the PPV show in August. I don 't think there's any question SummerSlam will get the best buy rate of any PPV show for the remainder of this year because even if the NWA gets through this critical period and starts to turn the corner in time for Starrcade (and even optimistically, the end of this year is the earliest they can turn the corner because it take several months of strong television to rebuild the falling TV numbers), the Titan hype machine combined with the curiosity of Hogan and Zeus will do more than the NWA has the capability of doing even with a Flair-Luger first match with a hot build-up. I think everyone is pretty well convinced that ultimately it is Flair vs. Luger that is going to be the big money match in the NWA.

Since some of you will get this in time, the Morton Downey Jr. show on pro wrestling which includes Lou Albano, Larry Sharpe and many others debating whether or not wrestling should be regulated and whatever else came up will air either on Thursday or Friday night, depending on the market, of this week (June 29th or 30th). The show was taped several months back and got pretty heated although the discussion in typical Downey fashion degenerated mainly into yelling and screaming with little intelligent debate. Downey has been canceled already in most major markets but several of you may still get the show.

MEXICO

Here are last month's ratings in the various weight divisions in Mexico:

Lightweights: 1. El Hijo Del Black Shadow (WWA World champion) 2. El Hijo Del Santo (UWA World champion) 3. El Hijo Del Espanto 4. Hurricane Jr 5. El Hijo Del Diablo 6. El Matematico II 7. Estrella Blanca Jr 8. Pantera II 9. El Vengador Jr 10. La Mascara.

Welterweights: 1. Tornado Negro (WWA champion) 2. Negro Casas 3. Fuerza Guerrera (NWA champion) 4. Charles Lucero (UWA champion) 5. Yoshinari Asai 6. Americo Rocca 7. Ciclon Ramirez (Mexican national champion)8. Javier Cruz 9. Alcatraz 10. Ray Richard

Middleweights: 1. Super Astro (WWA champion) 2. El Dandy (Mexican champion) 3. Atlantis 4. Blue Panther 5. Leon Chino 6. Angel Azteca (NWA champion) 7. Kung Fu 8. Cuchillo (UWA champion) 9. Rocky Starr 10. Lobo Rubio

Junior Light Heavyweights: 1. Rey Misterio (WWA

champion) 2. Ringo Mendoza (UWA champion) 3. Gran Cochise 4. Pirata Morgan 5. Blue Demon Jr 6. El Rayo del Jalisco 7. Solar I 8. Kahoz 9. Super Muneco 10. Villano I

Light Heavyweights: 1. Lizmark (WWA champion) 2. Villano III (WWF champion) 3. Pero Aguayo 4. Sangre Chicana 5. El Gran Hamada (UWA champion) 6. Mogur (Mexican champion) 7. El Satanico 8. Anibal 9. Rambo 10. Fishman

Heavyweights: 1. Dos Caras (WWA champion) 2. Mil Mascaras (IWA champion) 3. El Canek (UWA champion) 4. Enrique Vera (WWF Mexican champion) 5. Konan 6. Angel Blanco Jr 7. Rayo de Jalisco Jr 8. Cien Caras 9. Pepitekus 10. Scorpio

AWA

The AWA ran a live card in conjunction with David McLane's Ladies Sports Club on 6/23 in Chicago drawing 600 fans. They taped two hours of television for the McLane group and another two hours for the AWA. The AWA portion aired live on local Chicago cable station Sportsvision. It was part of a big wrestling weekend in Chicago since Sam Decero's Windy City group, which is now a bitter rival of the AWA since Decero's former right hand man Alan Eppenstein left the group and took several of the wrestlers with him and went to the AWA, ran a show the next night with Col. DeBeers and Jim Brunzell, while the WWF was in with the Andre vs. Hillbilly Jim squad the next night drawing a $55,000 house.

The major angle on the McLane taping was they announced the signing of a match with Wendi Richter having a unification match for the World's ladies title (Wendi recognized as AWA champ) against McLane's champ who is going by the name of Tina Moretti (formerly Tina Ferrari with GLOW and Nina with POWW).

The AWA portion of the card saw Tommy Jammer pin Johnny Stewart in 3:09 * ½, Mike George (billed as WWA World champion) squashed Rockin Randy (substituting for no-show Bruce Hart of Canada) in 1:56 DUD, Paul Diamond (doing a Brutus Beefcake imitation) lost via DQ to Akio Sato in a good four minute brawl **, Ken Patera & Scott Norton beat Mike Enos & Wayne Bloom via DQ when Johnny Valiant interfered when Norton had one guy in the bearhug and Patera had the other in the full nelson DUD (really terrible match), Richter pinned Candi Divine in 3:30 DUD (both looked terrible) Chavo & Mando & Hector Guerrero beat The Texas Hangmen & The Executioner (Tom Stone) in a five minute squash *** (Guerreros did nothing but hot moves), Col. DeBeers pinned Derrick Dukes in that loser gets painted the color of the winner hideous angle match however DeBeers wound up with more black paint on him when Tommy Jammer ran in ** and Larry Zbyszko kept the AWA title going to a time limit draw with Greg Gagne which lasted 12:25, much of

which was taken up by Zbyszko doing the stalling *.

The next TV taping will take place on 7/8. in Rochester, MN with the matches announced having Zbyszko defending against Sgt. Slaughter, Gagne defending the TV title against Sheik Adnan El-Kaissey (if you want to try and estimate old Adnan's age, think of this, he competed in the 1952 Olympic games legit) , Norton vs. Valiant, Diamond vs. Sato, Dukes & Jammer vs. Tokyo Bullets plus Soldat Ustinov returns.

They are giving tickets away free to kids a Long with free photos and posters given away of Sarge (which for TV I've always thought was a good promotional - for example using the NWA as an example - when Flair finally returns, wouldn't it look hot on television for them to give away either posters or t-shirts of him and have a building filled with kids all wearing Flair shirts or holding posters – it would make it look to the general public that Flair, or Sting, or Steamboat or whomever is amazingly over which is what they are trying to get across in the first place).

CWA

The latest (this must be around No. 8) in the revolving co-host with Dave Brown slot on TV this past week was Local DJ Ron Jordan, who was terrible. Several wrestlers, including Action Jackson, who holds half of the tag team title and Frankie Lancaster were given notice by booker Jerry Lawler. Lawler on television issued a challenge to Ric Flair, Randy Savage and Hulk Hogan and Jerry Jarrett said that the CWA now has an open-door policy and challenged wrestlers from other promotions to come in and said that. NWA stars Al Perez and Black Bart have already accepted the challenge (forgetting that it has been years since Bart was in the NWA and Perez has been gone for several months).

Jackson & Billy Travis retained their CWA tag titles on TV, upsetting The Wild Side (Chris Champion & Mark Starr), who are said to be one of the best small promotion teams in the country.

They had a near riot this past Monday night in Memphis as Jerry Lawler beat Master of Pain to keep his title and as part of the deal, Ronnie Gossett had to give Lawler $1,000 which Lawler threw to the crowd. One fan was trampled on and got broken ribs and the ensuing riot to get the money and another fan was injured as well. Also on Monday, Black Bart beat Jeff Jarrett for the CWA title by hitting him with a branding iron after a ref bump; Bill Dundee beat Dutch Mantell via DQ in a match to determine the No. 1 contender for the CWA title when Champion & Starr ran in and Freddy (Tommy Gilbert) made the save while earlier in a single match with Starr vs. Freddy, Champion ran in to get Starr DQ'd and Dundee made the save. The D. I. is headed in to be the tag team partner of Spike Huber and they are working as heels. D. I. does a strong interview.

6/24 in Jonesboro, AK drew 300 as D. I. pinned Lancaster *, Dirty White Boy (Tony Anthony) went to a 15 minute draw with Huber * ½ (Huber was the heel here), Freddy (gimmick very much over) beat Master of Pain via DQ when Gossett interfered * ½, Jarrett beat Mantel 1 via DQ ** ¾, Travis & Jackson kept the tag titles beating Wild Side ** ½ and Bart beat Lawler via DQ when Lawler was caught using the chain Bart brought to the ring ** ½ in a match in which Lawler had won, he'd have gotten five minutes with Gossett.

The 6/26 card in Memphis was Don Bass vs. Lancaster, Dirty White Boy vs. Dustin Rhodes, Jackson & Travis defending the tag team titles against D. I. & Huber, Bart vs. Jarrett for the CWA title, Dundee & Freddy vs. Wild Side and the headliner is a six-man elimination tag match with Mantell & Master of Pain & Gossett vs. Lawler & Bam Bam Bigelow & Plowboy Stan Frazier (formerly Uncle Elmer of WWF fame).

WORLD CLASS

When this group changes its name to USWA, it will begin trying to syndicate three shows: USWA World Wide Wrestling; USWA Wrestling Challenge and The Best of USWA Wrestling which you must admit are imaginative names for wrestling programs. Action Media Group will handle the syndication which is an interesting twist since Action Media Group also sells the national ads for the NWA's syndicated package and the NWA isn't too happy over this.

6/23 in Dallas drew a sellout crowd of 3,000 fans at $4 per ticket as Jimmy Jack Funk beat Buster Fowler, Chris Adams beat Cactus Jack Manson, Al Perez beat Gary Young via DQ, Eric Embry went to a double DQ against P. Y. Chu Hi (Phil Hickerson managed by Tojo Yamamoto), Robert Fuller & Brian Lee won the World Class tag team titles beating Mil Mascaras & Jeff Jarrett, Kevin & Kerry Von Erich & Schaun Simpson beat The Blackbirds (Iceman King Parsons & Brickhouse Brown) & Harold Harris in a penalty box match and a wrestling bear beat Scandor Akbar and after the match Gary Young did a run-in and the bear chased Young around as well.

The 6/16 show did an $18,000 gate which is the largest gate in the Sportatorium in several months. They are raising ticket prices to $10, $8, and $6 for the 6/30 card which features Harris vs. Schaun Simpson in a 10 round karate gloves boxing match, Fuller & Lee defending the tag titles against Jarrett & Matt Borne, Young vs. Bill Dundee in a Texas death match, Blackbirds vs. Kevin & Kerry Von Erich with the loser of the fall leaving town (most likely Brickhouse), Embry vs. Chu Hi in a match where the last man left standing is the winner and anyone who interferes is fined '$10,000' and the headline match is Lawler vs. Adams for the USWA title.

They've got a holiday card on 7/3 in Fort Worth with a 20 man Texas Roundup (Royal Rumble style rules), Fuller & Lee vs. Kevin Von Erich & Adams, Chu Hi & Tojo vs. Embry & Percy Pringle, Borne vs. Young and Manson vs. Funk.

Eric Embry didn't even do one interview on the TV show that aired this past Saturday night. Perez, who has been a baby face, is now talking about accepting an offer to turn heel and join Akbar.

Lie of the week - Kerry Von Erich claimed that his brother Kevin has held more titles than any wrestler in the history of wrestling.

STAMPEDE

It looks Like the Dynamite Kid vs. Davey Boy Smith feud may never get off the ground.

While a singles match between the two this past Wednesday did a $25,000 house in the Northwest Territories, it appears the future of both guys within the promotion is in jeopardy although nobody really knows what is going to happen after a backstage blow-up between Bruce Hart and the Bulldogs which ended with Hart getting hurt.

6/24 in Edmonton drew 400 fans as Kim Scnau drew Goldie Rogers in 15:00 - **, The British Bruisers (Johnny Smith & Dynamite Kid) beat Sumu Hara & Ron Ritchie in 14:26 when Smith and Kid did a double simultaneous headbutt off the top rope onto Ritchie *** ¼, Davey Boy Smith pinned Bill Jodin *, Jason the Terrible beat Angel of Death via DQ when Larry Cameron interfered ¾ * and Chris Benoit beat North American champion Larry Cameron via DQ when Angel of Death interfered *. The main event was supposed to be Bob & Kerry Brown & Cameron against Benoit & Hart & Ricky Rice however Bob Brown was announced as suspended again, Kerry Brown wasn't there, Bruce Hart was injured so it wound up as a singles match.

Gary Allbright worked one match in Calgary two weeks back against Davey Boy Smith and was squashed.

A new tag team called the White Knights (Dale Veasy and the other Bob Brown) debuted on 6/23 in Calgary and lasted one night. They were going under the ring names Buddy Lee Parker and James Wright.

When Dynamite Kid "retired" a few months back (actually took time off for shoulder surgery) he gave Chris Benoit his wrestling boots and said that Benoit was going to be the biggest star in pro wrestling during the 1990s. Now in his interview since Benoit is wearing Dynamite's old boots and they are feuding, Dynamite claims that Benoit snuck into his dressing room and stole his boots from his locker and wants them back. With his crew cut and no teeth, Dynamite looks a lot like Butch Miller of the Bushwackers.

Jason the Terrible has miraculously learned to talk, but I'm not sure in what language.

PUERTO RICO

Some recent Saturday night line-ups: On 6/3 in Carolina:

Sadistic Steve Strong (DI Salvo) defending the Universal title against Invader #1 with Rufus Jones as referee; Rip Rogers & Abbuda Dein defending the WWC World tag team titles against White Angel (Curtis Thompson) & TNT with El Profe put in a cage above the ring, Miguelito Perez & Hurricane Castillo Jr. vs. The Battens for the Caribbean tag team title, Super Medico (Jose Estrada) defending the jr. heavyweight title against Jonathan Holiday and Victor Jovica vs. Mr. Pogo.

6/10 in Carolina had Strong vs. Invader in a lumberjack match for the Universal title, Dein (Rocky Iaukea) defending the TV title against TNT, Junkyard Dog vs. Rip Rogers (who is the booker), White Angel & Super Medico vs. Battens, Perez vs. Holiday and a mixed match with Jovica & Moon Akayo of Japan against Kensuke Sasaki & Eagle Sawai.

6/17 at Hiram Bithorn Stadium in San Juan (this card drew 8,000 fans) with Strong vs. Invader for the title, Dein vs. TNT for the TV title with two referees, Perez & Castillo vs. Battens, Rogers defending the Caribbean title against Kerry Von Erich, Junkyard Dog vs. Chicky Starr, Kareem Muhammad vs. White Angel, Super Medico vs. Mad Russian and prelims.

ALL JAPAN

The July tour begins on 7/1 in Omiya with TV tapings with the top matches sending Stan Hansen & Genichiro Tenryu vs. Jumbo Tsuruta & Isao Takagi (one guess who does the job here), Yoshiaki Yatsu & Kabuki vs. Tom Zenk & Jim Brunzell, Mighty Inoue & Isamu Teranishi vs. The Fantastics and Mitsuo Momota defends the PWF jr. title against former champion Joe Malenko.

7/3 in Takasaki is a TV taping with Hansen & Tenryu & Samson Fuyuki vs. Tsuryaa & Yatsu & Kabuki and Kenta Kobashi makes his TV debut teaming with Masa Fuchi against The Fantastics .

7/11 in Sapporo will be the first big show of the series with Tsuruta & Yatsu defending the PWF World tag team titles against Hansen & Tenryu, Momota vs. Dean Malenko for the jr. title and Fantastics vs. Brunzell & Zenk.

An interesting stipulation on the 7/11 card is that if Joe Malenko nobody wins the jr. title on the 7/1 show, he must defend it against his brother Dean on 7/11 and actually I expect that to happen. If that match was in Tokyo, it would sell out the smaller building by itself since that is the type of match-up that intrigues the Tokyo fans.

7/16 in Tokyo will be the Bruiser Brody Memorial card.

Baba is holding a tournament in July to give the younger wrestlers a chance for Tenryu's unified title as Akira Taue, Isao Takagi, Shun ji Takano, Samson Fuyuki, Toshiaki Kawada and Kenta Kobashi will enter and the winner gets the next title shot at Tenryu. Since the winner will almost surely be either Takano or Kawada, it creates the possibility of the Tenryu vs. Kawada dream match" and also the

Kawada vs. Fuyuki "Battle of the Foot Loose"match will take place during the month.

The 6/11 TV show with the Tsuruta vs. Tenryu and Sting vs. Spivey matches from Tokyo drew a 7.7 rating, while 6/18 with Dynamite Kid & Davey Boy Smith vs. Terry Gordy & Stan Hansen and Foot Loose vs. Dan Kroffat & Doug Furnas drew a 6.8 rating.

NEW JAPAN

The new series opened 6/16 before a sellout 2,050 fans in Tokyo's Korakuen Hall for an afternoon card (which aired on television the next day drawing a 4.7 rating as compared to the 8.1 rating the week before when Masa Saito vs. Salman Hashimikov was the main event) as Riki Choshu & Masa Saito downed Big Van Vader & Brad Rheingans when Choshu lariated Rheingans in 4:41 (Rheingans had a knee operation just three weeks earlier and wasn't in top form), Tatsumi Fujinami made Kokina the Wild Samoan submit in 5: 40, Jushin Liger (Keiichi Yamada) kept the jr. title beating Biff Wellington in 7:18 with a double-arm suplex into a power bomb finishing move (similar to the move Dan Kroffat uses in the All Japan rings) in what I'm told was the best match on the card, Kengo Kimura made Timur Zarazov submit to the boston crab, Super Strong Machine & George Takano beat Tatsutoshi Goto & Osamu Kido, Black Tiger (Mark "Rollerball" Rocco from England) pinned Kantaro Hoshino, Mike Kirchner (Corporal Kirchner) beat Black Cat and Shinji Sasazaki returned from Calgary and Memphis (where he worked as VietCong #2, Yang Chung and in Memphis as Samurai Senshe) to team with Hiro Saito & Kuniaki Kobayashi to beat Akira Nogami & Naoki Santo & Shiro Koshinaka.

Line-ups for the TV tapings for the rest of the tour are 6/22 in Saku with Vader vs. Fujinami, Cho shu & Masa Saito vs. Rheingans & Kokina, Riger & Koshinaka vs. Wellington & Black Tiger and Kido vs. Zarasov; 6/27 in Sapporo with Vader vs. Choshu, Zarasov vs. Rheingans, Fujinami & Kimura vs. Hiroshi Hase & Takayuki Iizuka (who missed the first week of the series because they were in the Soviet Union helping train the new Soviets who will turn pro plus Hase & Iizuka will come back having trained in " sambo" or submission style wrestling), Machine & Takano vs, Koshinaka & Kobayashi and Liger & Nogami vs. Sasazaki & Sano; 7/3 in Aomori with Machine & Takano vs. Choshu & Fujinami non-title, Masa Saito vs. Zarasov, Hase & Iizuka vs. Rheingans & Vader and Riger vs. Sasazaki; 7/12 in Osaka with the big show with Hashimikov returning from the Soviet Union to defend his title against Choshu, Liger vs. Black Tiger for the jr. title, Vader vs. Zarasov, Hase & Iizuka vs. Fujinami & Sano and Kido vs. Rheingans while 7/13 at the Tokyo Sumo Hall has Hashimikov defending against Vader, Liger defending against Sano, Choshu vs. Zarasov, Machine & Takano defending the tag titles against

Hase & Iizuka and Fujinami vs. Kido.

6/17 in Suwa drew 1,630 as Vader & Kokina beat Choshu & Masa Saito in 5:21 when Vader splashed Saito, Fujinami made Kirchner submit, Rheingans pinned Goto, Riger pinned Hiro Saito, Machine & Takano beat Wellington & Black Tiger, Zara sov made Kido submit, Kobayashi & Koshinaka beat Sano & Kimura and prelims.

6/18 in Fukushima drew 1,880 as Fujinami & Kimura beat Vader & Kirchner, Choshu pinned Kokina, Rheingans pinned Kido, Liger & Koshinaka beat Wellington & Black Tiger, Machine & Takano beat Masa Saito & Sasazaki, Zarasov beat Black Cat, Kobayashi & Hiro Saito double count out with Goto & Sano and prelims so as you can see without Inoki and Hashimikov, this group isn't drawing well on the road.

UWF

The next card is 7/24 so things are pretty quiet right now. Mainly the group is gearing up for an 8/13 big show at the 17,000 seat Yokohama Arena which will probably have a double feature with Akira Maeda vs. Yoshiaki Fujiwara and Kazuo Yamazaki vs. Masaharu Funaki on top.

JAPANESE WOMEN

The biggest news item is that Ttsuki Yamazaki of the Jumping Bomb Angels, who retired from the All Japan group on 5/14, showed up just two weeks later with the rival JWP joining another former All Japan star Devil Masami, who was Yamazaki 's original teacher in wrestling.

Linda Dallas and Kat LaRoux are working for the JWP right now, or I should say were up until this past weekend. Heidi Lee Morgan is in for JWP from 6/23 to 7/13. While most of the JWP shows draw around 1,000 fans; they had a crowd of 3,200 on 6/9 in Tokushima for the match between Yamazaki vs. Cutie Suzuki.

5/29 in Tokyo saw Devil Masami keep the UWA (Mexican promotion) Int. women's title beating Miss A before 600 fans while Yu Yamazaki won the JWP jr. title from Ozaki.

The All Japan group started its new series on 6/18 with Madusa Maceli. The series will feature a 19-woman round-robin tournament with the winner becoming the No. 1 contender for Lioness Asuka's World title and getting the title shot on 8/14 in Tokyo. They have a special show on 7/19 in Ota with Asuka vs. Maceli for the title and Ann Maria Tenkate of the Netherlands, a women' s kick boxer with a 25-0 record facing Toshiyo Yamada, who is the young girl who has the amazing facial resemblance to Chigusa Nagayo and because of that coincidence is going to be pushed as a major star with this group.

ALSO FROM JAPAN

New Japan announced the line-up for the tour after the current one concludes which will be 7/28 to 8/10 with

Soviets Victor Zangiev, Vladimir Berkovich, Wakha Eveloev and Timur Zarasov full-time plus U.S. wrestlers Dick Murdoch, Buzz Sawyer, Manny Fernandez and Rheingans plus a rookie from the U.S. said to be an amateur wrestling star and the return of Shinya Hashimoto.

Nord the Barbarian returns to Japan in October while Rheingans is trying to teach Wayne Bloom, Mike Enos and Scott Norton the Japanese style so that they can eventually tour for this group.

THIS AND THAT

Dustin Rhodes and Kendall Windham are feuding in Florida.

Chris Benoit will feud with Len Crazy Horse in Stampede. Owen Hart expected to start up with Stampede in late July or early August. He's still with Titan and over this past weekend did a job for Barry Horowitz in Chicago. Tom Prichard captured the CWF title from Wendell Cooley on 6/23 in Knoxville when Jerry Stubbs returned and put either on a towel and smothered Cooley with it after a ref bump. The Beauty (Terrence Garvin) is feuding with Miss Linda in CWF while Robert Fuller & Brian Lee are set to come in and have a tag team feud with Steve Armstrong & Tracy Smothers.

It was announced this past Saturday night on AWA TV that Wahoo McDaniel has retired from pro wrestling due to an eye injury suffered against Mike Enos & Wayne Bloom, although in reality Wahoo has taken the job as a road manager in the NWA. It is said that Wahoo still wants to wrestle in the NWA but management wants him strictly as a road manager.

Nathan Webb promoted a show on 6/19 in Atlanta drawing 40 fans as Jimmy Powell beat The Invader, Mr. Atlanta (Tony Zane) beat Steve Armstrong, The Nightmare (Ted Allen) drew with Scott Armstrong and Mr. Wrestling II beat Joel Deaton via DQ. The entire main event of Steve Lawler & Dino Minelli vs. The Bullet & Brad Armstrong all no-showed. CWF no-showed an entire city as they had a card scheduled on 6/20 in West Point, MS and nobody came and nobody informed the school that the show wasn't going to take place.

Congratulations to Observer reader Deborah McWilliams of Brooklyn who was one of the winners in the NWA's contest to win a trip for two to Baltimore to see the PPV show.

Got a Line-up for the summer-time Maritimes promotion on 6/1 in Halifax, Nova Scotia headlined by Harley Race (billed as King Harley Race) vs. Leo Burke, Ron Starr vs. Steve Pettipas, The Beast (who is a legend in that part of the world) vs. The Destroyer, The Cuban Commandos (Angel "Cuban Assassin" Acevedo & Jerry Morrow) against Paul "Butcher" Vachon & Wild Man Eddie Watts, Pat Brady vs. Paul Peller plus Buddy Lane and Frenchy Martin are working for this troupe.

Stan Hansen is to work a card in August in London, ONT against Austin Idol.

Back to the Maritimes, Leo Burke holds the International title while the Commandos, who are Cuban babyfaces, hold the tag team titles.

The lawsuit from several years back with Big Daddy (Steve DiBIasio) suing Dusty Rhodes when Big Daddy broke his ankle taking a bump over the top rope in a match against Les Thornton and Rhodes (the booker) ordered him to take the bump which he claimed ended his wrestling career. The suit will be coming to trial in September.

Those of you who aren't regular readers of Pro Wrestling Illustrated should check out the 100th anniversary issue which hit the newsstands this past week. There's lots of interesting statistical material when it comes to title histories, over the past decade, famous events etc. that even those of you who normally don 't buy wrestling mags would find worth your while.

Don Kernodle promoted a show on 6/2 in Burlington, NC before 1, 000 fans with the headline match having Kernodle & Sgt. Slaughter (who in the early 80s were just about the best tag team going) beating The Mod Squad, Sam Houston no contest with Nelson Royal, Robert Gibson beat Colt Steele via count out, Rocky Kernodle (Keith Larson) beat Chuck Coates and Rikki Nelson beat L.A. Stephens.

The big weekend match with Kevin Von Erich against Houston Post entertainment writer Ken Hoffman ended in an ironic fashion. Hoffman no-showed.

CWF Line-up on 6/24 in Rossville, GA had a 12 man blindfold Battle Royal, Jimmy Golden & Mongolian Stomper vs. Ricky & Todd Morton for the CWF tag team titles, Cooley vs. Stomper Don Harris, Danny Davis vs. Kevin Dillinger for the U.S. jr. title, Adrian Street vs. Lou Fabbiano and one more match. Ivan Koloff defeated The Phantom on 6/17 in Colonial Beach, VA to win the Virginia heavyweight title of the Virginia Wrestling Association. On the same show, Bobby Fulton & Robert Gibson beat the VWA tag champ Cream Team but didn't get the belts since Fulton wasn't scheduled as Gibson's partner.

Mike Graham was injured in a bar room brawl on 6/5 at PJ's in South Tampa suffering a black eye and injured knee. According to the newspaper article in the Tampa Tribune, Graham says he intends to file criminal charges and a formal complaint against Deputy Lon Atkins in a 1:45 a.m. fight. Graham claimed the deputy was being rowdy and he asked "What's your problem?" and he was decked for his trouble. The deputy told police that Graham threatened them and made the first move but the deputy beat him to the punch and Graham's head hit against the wall. Witnesses told police that when Graham was down and out, the deputy then continued to punch away at Graham. The police report said Graham was very intoxicated but Graham said he'd been drinking but denied he was drunk.

Ron Wyatt, Dennis Coraluzzo and Larry Sharpe are promoting a show 7/28 in Suffolk, VA with Joe Daniels (WWA champion) vs. Robert Gibson, Ivan Koloff vs. Russian Assassin plus Italian Stallion and Cruel Connection will appear.

WWF

Big news just in and it Looks as though the on-again, off-again Roddy Piper marriage with the WWF is on-again. Piper will start on 7/17 as the weekly co-host with Gorilla Monsoon on Prime Time Wrestling, replacing Bobby Heenan. The Monsoon-Heenan duo was a cult favorite and some credit it as one of the reasons prime Time has been the highest rated of the cable wrestling shows these past few months. Also, starting this coming Sunday, Hillbilly Jim and Gene Okerlund will become the announcing team for the All-American Wrestling show. Piper also has some weekend wrestling dates in July against Randy Savage booked including this coming weekend in Canada.

Elizabeth will start appearing this weekend in selected cities where Hogan faces Savage in the main events to counteract Sensational Sherri. In August, Elizabeth will work almost a full-time schedule and appear on the cards where Savage appears and work the corner of Brutus Beefcake or Jim Duggan, who will be Savage's main foes in August and of course be in the corner at SummerSlam where I expect a major angle to come out of the main event to set up WrestleMania VI.

They've got TV tapings this coming week in upstate New York and The Big Steele Man (Fred Ottman) will be getting his try-out on those shows.

Barry Windham's TV debut aired over this past weekend and they are calling him "The Widowmaker Barry Windham" so they are acknowledging he has a real name although they are disavowing his past and McMahon in his commentary made a strong point of getting across that he's an unproven wrestler.

The Hogan vs. Savage feud continues to draw hot gates out West. Officially, the 6/16 show in Los Angeles drew just under $190,000 for the sellout of 16,000 paid which is the second highest gate for wrestling ever in California (record is for the Live showing of Hogan vs. Bundy at WrestleMania II with high ticket prices).

Oakland on 6/17 drew $165,000 while 6/18 in Sacramento drew $100,000 and 6/19 in Pheonix drew $127,000. Hogan and Savage then worked in Hartford on 6/23 drawing the $157,000 house to counter the NWA show in New Haven the next night and followed in Bloomington, MN on 6/24 with an $80, 000 house and they were expected to draw more than 15,000 fans and nearly $200,000 on 6/25 in Detroit at the Palace in Auburn Hills which has turned into one of the WWF's hottest buildings of late.

Walt Disney productions wants Hulk Hogan for a movie since he now has a track record of being able to draw kids to theatres. Almost as impressive as these gates for the Hogan-Savage matches is that you can across the board add about 30 to 35 percent more in gimmick sales on each of these shows.

Lots of new marriages, which I assume they'll be shooting angles for at the TV this weekend, for the fall season. I don't: have the complete line-ups but do know that in August/September some of the matches going around the horn will include Savage against either Beefcake or Duggan; Andre the Giant vs. Ultimate Warrior (doesn't that sound like somebody's idea of a practical joke because legitimately as big and slow as these two are, they could actually hurt one another), Bushwackers vs. Powers of pain, Dusty Rhodes vs. Big Bossman (as the Dream gets his revenge back on all those who walked out on him), Demolition vs. Tully Blanchard & Arn Anderson (the only chance for a wrestling match during the fall), Jimmy Snuka vs. Honkeytonk Man, Red Rooster (Terry Taylor) vs. Greg Valentine (although they also have some Valentine vs. Badnews Brown matches booked as well) , and my favorite one of them all - Ted DiBiase vs. Hillbilly Jim.

Cable ratings from last weeks show Prime Time Wrestling on 6/19 drew a healthy 3.4 rating while All-American on 6/18 drew a below-par 2.8 but impressive 9.5 share.

6/22 in Hartford drew 13,200 as Lanny Poffo pinned Paul Roma, Rooster pinned Boreus Zhukov, Dino Bravo pinned Hercules, Demolition beat Twin Towers (great match), Snuka beat Rick Rude via DQ, Demolition (subbing for Rockers) & Tito Santana beat Rougeaus & Rick Martel and Savage beat Hogan via count out.

6/24 in Orlando drew 8,200 as Zhukov pinned Tim Horner ¼ *, Rockin Robin pinned Judy Martin * , Rooster pinned Brooklyn Brawler * ½, Beefcake pinned Valentine DUD, Rougeaus beat Rockers ** , Hercules beat Bravo via DQ when Ron Garvin came out and told ref Rick Hunter that Bravo had used the ropes for the pinfall ½ *, and Warrior beat Rude via count out ** ½.

6/19 in White Plains drew a near sellout as Bret Hart drew Mr. Perfect ** ¾, Warlord pinned Koko Ware DUD, Rougeaus beat Rockers Beefcake pinned Valentine ½ *, Dusty Rhodes pinned DiBiase * ½ and Duggan & Hillbilly Jim beat Andre & Haku -** . 6/16 in Lafayette, LA saw Barry Horowitz pin Zhukov, Robin pinned Martin, Paul Roma & Butch Miller beat Blanchard & Anderson when Miller pinned Anderson, Bravo pinned Hercules, Rooster pinned Brawler and Warrior beat Rude via count out.

In Portland, apparently the reason Buddy Rose isn't around is because he blew out his knee. They are doing an angle where Carl Styles needs a cornea (eye) transplant because Grappler blew the Kabuki mist into his good eye (he has one glass eye legit).

6/11 in Toronto drew 4,000 and $60,000 Canadian as Horner pinned Horowitz, Rougeaus beat Rockers, Beefcake pinned Valentine, Snuka pinned Zhukov, Duggan pinned Haku, Hart Foundation beat Powers of pain via count out, and Hillbilly Jim beat Andre via DQ.

NWA

Some notes that have been consistent from almost everyone reporting on the Bashes in each city: 1) The best matches every night have been the six-man tag matches with the Freebirds and the Lex Luger vs. Ricky Steamboat main events; 2) Scott Steiner pops everyone with this sequence where he does a unique type of backward suplex onto all three Freebirds in succession; 3) Luger gets the biggest crowd pop in every arena and it is a mixed reaction although in many cities he got a stronger face reaction than Steamboat. I hope they don't panic because Luger is their only legitimately hot property right now except for Flair upon his return as a face. Remember, Flair as a heel always was cheered by 30 to 50 percent of the crowd when he came out for his matches but until the recent destruction period, he also was a big draw; 4) Terry Funk's antics when he gets the forfeit win over Sting are better than most of the matches on the card; 5) Nobody knows what a Dragon Shi match is. When it is explained, nobody understands it, however Gilbert and Muta still get the crowd interested because the work in these matches is good. However, Muta in some cities was cheered more than Gilbert. In fact, last week in Center Stage when they did the angle where Muta blew red mist (to Look Like blood but they aren't allowed to use blood on TV) onto Gilbert's face, the crowd chanted, "Muta, Muta, Muta" after the TV cameras were off; 6) Road Warriors and Samoans still go to the double count outs brawling to the back but the matches are longer and better than they had been prior to the Bash.

TBS is going to broadcast "Wrestling's Greatest Hits" during the half hour between games of Atlanta Braves doubleheaders. This past Wednesday night they showed the Ric Flair vs. Sting match from the first Clash of the Champions. They do another match between games on Friday night and then have the regular Friday night show immediately after the wrestling. At least you have to give TBS credit for trying to expose their wrestlers with a new audience.

Sid Vicious & Danny Spivey are teaming up as The Skyscrapers managed by Teddy Long instead of Gary Hart. The idea of the Ebony Experience has been dropped since Ron Simmons didn't want to do it (and I don't expect he'll be pushed much because of it) and Butch Reed is on some sort of a suspension. Don't know the exact deal with Reed, but he was taken off all bookings through the end of July because he didn't sign his contract yet.

Tommy Rich debuted this past week at all three TV tapings

and since they were in Georgia, Rich got over very strong. He's dropped a lot of weight as he's been jogging and eating mainly a tuna diet (yeech) but still has a ways to go to get where they want him, but he should be in full-time in about a week or two. The Ding Dongs legitimately start full-time on 7/10 although nobody can give me an explanation as to why and have several matches booked against the New Zealand Militia.

This weekend on all the shows they'll announce the Flair vs. Funk match for Baltimore. The TBS show (one hour) for Saturday was taped this past Wednesday and Rich wrestles Bill Irwin and Flair does a Live interview along with the "press conference." I'm told the place went nuts when Flair came out.

They are doing a good job of late in getting Funk over as a killer as the TV bout with Ricky Santana (who is out of action with a blown out knee) was very good and he Piledrove half a dozen guys after the match. But as good as Funk works a crowd and as hard as they put him over, there is still a segment of the crowd which believes a man's wrestling ability is directly proportional to the amount of steroids he uses and in that case, well, you know what I'm saying...

Friday's TV show will have Gilbert & Rick Steiner & Steve Williams vs. The Freebirds and Sting vs. Simmons.

TBS on 6/17 drew a 1.6 rating with the show starting an hour later than usual because they had a two-hour track meet. From this point on the show will begin at 6:05 p.m. Eastern. As far as the 7/23 PPV show goes, my own thought is that until they can get consistent 3 ratings on the TBS shows, they have little chance of doing a two percent buy rate on PPV.

TBS has ordered a $1 million post-production facility for the wrestling company to use.

Italian Stallion is back as a TV jobber.

Tapings will be held for syndication during Bash shows on 7/3 in Columbia, SC and 7/4 in Fayetteville and TBS will be taped on 7/6 in Marietta.

Ken Resnick won't be coming in as an announcer so they are still Looking for one or two new announcers. Resnick has a full-time job with a Twin Cities car dealership and didn't want to give it up, thus couldn't devote the necessary time that TBS wanted him for.

6/17 in Harrisonburg, VA drew 500 as Norman the Lunatic pinned Steven Casey, Spivey pinned Santana (best match), Dick Murdoch pinned Rotunda, Midnight Express beat Reed & Simmons (without Teddy Long, who was with Norman), Gilbert beat Norman via DQ and Rick Steiner pinned Kevin Sullivan in a taped fist match.

6/16 in Johnstown, PA drew 556 and $5,325 as Norman pinned Casey, Rotunda drew Murdoch, Spivey pinned Santana, Midnight beat Reed & Simmons, Gilbert beat Norman via DQ and Steiner pinned Sullivan.

6/16 in Cleveland drew 1,500 as Brian Pillman pinned The Raider (Doug Gilbert) , Hayes & Garvin beat Scott Hall & Randy Rose, Dudes beat Militia, Gordy pinned Scott Steiner using the ropes, Williams pinned Irwin, Warriors double count out SST, Funk double count out with Sting and Luger pinned Steamboat using the ropes.

Jim Ross is no longer a member of the booking is committee but still putting together and producing the television show. The booking committee is basically Eddie Gilbert, Kevin Sullivan, Jody Hamilton, Wahoo McDaniel and Ric Flair.

NWA had a big meeting on Monday night before the taping in Macon with Jim Herd where it was stressed that everyone who is asked to do a job had better do the job or they would be fired. There was a problem with one of the leading wrestlers last weekend.

6/22 at the Capital Center in Landover, MD drew 4,200 and $50,000 as Bill Irwin pinned Joey Maggs, Dudes beat Militia, Norman pinned Casey, Midnight beat Simmons & Al Green (Green looked real bad here), Warriors double count out with SST, Sting won the 2-ring Battle Royal and Funk attacked him and they had to stretcher Sting out which cancelled the subsequent Funk vs. Sting match which Funk wins vis forfeit, Rotunda & Spivey beat Hal & Pillman, Muta beat Gilbert via count out in the Dragon Shi match when Gary Hart interferes so Gilbert can't beat the count, Freebirds beat Williams & Steiner brothers and Luger pinned Steamboat.

6/23 in New Haven drew either 2,500 and $26,000 (which would be pretty bad) or 3,500 and $35,000 (which at least would be decent) as Spivey & Rotunda beat Hall & Pillman when Rotunda pinned Pillman * ½, Norman pinned Casey * ½, Dudes beat Militia ** , Midnight beat Simmons & Irwin * ½, Sting threw out Hayes to win Battle Royal and was ambushed by Funk (good for a Battle Royal with a great finish) , Muta beat Gilbert via COR ***, Freebirds beat Steiners & Dr. Death *** ½ when Garvin pinned Scott, Warriors double count out Samoans ** ¾ in 5:22 and Luger pinned Steamboat using the ropes *** ½ (most cheered Steamboat but there were chants of "Steamboat sucks" and Luger supporters around).

6/24 in Philadelphia drew 4,000 and $50,000 as Irwin pinned Maggs (decent opener), Rotunda & Spivey beat Pillman & Hall (decent), Norman pinned Casey (nothing match but Long good at ringside), Midnight beat Simmons & Green in one minute, Dudes beat Militia **, Muta beat Gilbert via count out ** ¾, Battle Royal wound up with Rick Steiner in one ring and Sting in the other and they split the money and then Funk attacked Sting, Steiners & Williams beat Freebirds when Scott pinned Garvin in 15:00 ****, Warriors double count out SST *** ¾ and Luger pinned Steamboat.

6/25 in Pittsburgh drew 3,566 ($42,000) which has to be

disappointing since the AWA drew that we'll when they came in a few months back as Irwin beat Maggs, Rotunda & Spivey beat Pillman & Hall when Rotunda pinned Pillman, Dudes beat Militia, Norman pinned Casey, Midnight beat Simmons & Green in 45 seconds, Battle Royal came down to Sting in ring one and Steiners in ring two. Rick Steiner then eliminated himself leaving Sting vs. Scott and they wrestled before Scott missed a block and went over the top so Sting won the thing and then Funk did the ambush, Muta beat Gilbert in the Dragon Shi via COR, Steiner s & Williams beat Freebirds when Rick pinned Garvin, Warriors double count out SST and Luger pinned Steamboat (best match, crowd pro-Luger here).

THE READERS' PAGE

CLASH OF THE CHAMPIONS

I watched the Latest Clash and gave it a thumbs-up with a couple of qualifications. The Ding Dongs were outright embarrassing. Norman was far Less interesting in an actual match than he was in his videos and there were too many gimmick finishes, too many ref bumps and outside interferences. On the other hand, most of the actual wrestling was good and Ric Flair's interview was awesome. I've been getting really excited about the NWA Lately and hope they can keep up the momentum.

Maurice Forrester
Syracuse, New York

The recent Clash was very exciting. The NWA did an excellent job in getting their angles over and establishing their new key players. The Ric Flair interview was extremely well done. It Looked like it was a Barbara Walters special interview. The problem is that it might have been too classy. It seemed Like a halftime interview during a basketball or football game. My father, who knows absolutely nothing about wrestling, or for that matter basketball, walked in during the interview and commented that Flair looked too small to be a basketball player. This is the McMahon era where wrestling is completely separated from sports. Unfortunately, it appears that the majority of fans want to see the cartoon atmosphere. There is not much of a demand for two grown adults engaging in an intelligent conversation.

John D'Amato
Bellmore, New York

Clash rated a thumbs-up overall. For the most part, the heat was pretty good and the matches worked well. There were problems, but nothing major, such as: 1) Jimmy Garvin as the third Freebird. This was no surprise to anyone except Jim Ross who tried to convey both a sense of surprise and tried to act like he didn't recognize Garvin at first and made no mention of the fact Garvin & Hayes were a tag team in the NWA just Last year. Fans have a better memory than that; 2) The Ding Dongs. For a moment I thought I was watching the WWF. This is an idea whose time has not and will not ever come. Although counting the bells falling off their ring attire wasn't a bad way to kill time during a boring match, I'm not Looking forward to seeing this duo again; 3) Lex Luger's turn. This could have been done in any number of ways that would have shown some thought on the part of the booking committee, rather than an angle that wasn't badly enacted, but not original; 4) Gilbert throwing fire. I don't think the fans will buy Muta as a heel. Having Gilbert throw fire at him just diminishes Gilbert as a face.

Other than these minor quibbles, I thought it was a great show and gives me a good feeling about the future of the NWA. You can't go too wrong using Terry Funk as lead heel.

John Pelan
Seattle, Washington

Thumbs down on the Clash. They did too much dumb stuff. The Luger turn wasn't any good. Why turn one of your most popular guys? The Flair interview was excellent. Steamboat vs. Funk was 3 ½ stars. Didn't Like Freebirds vs. Midnight Express. Ding Dongs was the worst thing I've ever seen. Jim Ross and Bob Caudle were top rate as announcers.

Dan Reilly
New Haven, Connecticut

I gave the Clash two massive thumbs downs. It was enough to make me give up on the NWA for the time being for the following reasons: 1) Showing footage of the troops in Fayetteville, Jim Ross comments approvingly that these youngsters are doing something important with their lives, not wasting them partying at the beach. This is followed immediately by the first match, featuring the NWA's hot new team, the Dynamic Dudes; 2) Muta, the NWA's most interesting wrestler to watch is scheduled in a squash match, and even that was aborted. I can't say I enjoy watching wrestlers set fire to each other, either; 3) The Ding Dongs. Easily the stupidest wrestling gimmick since Jolly Cholly the wrestling Hobo in 1961. Who dreamed up this crap?; 4) I Loathe Rick Steiner's gimmick to the point I turn off the TV when he comes on. There are people in this world whose mental processes realy have been impaired by illness or accident; there are people with Tourette's Syndrome who really do bark uncontrollably in public. Watching Steiner and the NWA trivialize such things for a gimmick and watching fans bark along with him is right up there with watching George Steele eat turnbuckles; 5) Everything I said about Steiner goes double for Mike Shaw's gimmick. Mental illness as entertainment goes well beyond the limits of even pro wrestling's lack of taste; 6) Virtually every one of the tag team matches has basically the same type of finish. Apparently we don't need Dusty Rhodes for repetitive and unimaginative booking; 7) What a surprise the Luger turn was. The only major star not on the card and Jim Ross mentions repeatedly that he's in the building but won't come out here. Was there anyone who didn't expect him to show up in the Steamboat-Funk match?

I had really thought the NWA was on the verge of some real improvement, especially since the WWF is just about unwatchable. This card impressed me as a major step backwards, though.

Norman Antokol
Wheaton, Maryland

I'd give the Clash a B-. It was pretty good, but there were some definite negatives to the show. The Ding Dongs were awful and embarrassing. I can only hope they fade away fast. The Norman routine isn't my cup of tea and personally I find it in poor taste to use this gimmick and make fun of mental illness. Mike Shaw's act in Calgary was so much better. They totally wasted Muta even though the slow-mo of the fireball was very effective. The videos were a waste, and Sid Vicious should have been on the show. The Funk vs. Steamboat match was as good as expected and Luger came across a lot better as a heel this time. Gordy vs. Dr. Death was an okay match but the ending stunk. I got tired of all the army stuff real quick. It was like one big ad for the army and it got old. Overall, just a fairly good card.

David Williamson
Cleveland, Tennessee

THIS JUST IN

Robert Fuller will be back as booker for the CWF so he and Brian Lee will be there full-time and he'll finish up by dropping the World Class tag belts within a month. Dustin Rhodes was supposed to head to CWA full-time however with the new ownership in Florida, he's going to stay put so he won't be in Memphis after all. An idea not to try: The Japanese women tried a deal where they had two rings and matches going on simultaneously in both rings (kind of like a state level amateur wrestling tournament in the prelim rounds) on TV a few weeks back. Even though both matches were good, as a TV product it was horrible. The camera switching from one match to the other was distracting and made it so you couldn't enjoy or get into either match. Teddy Long getting rave reviews everywhere.

And finally: Since the year is half-way over, a lot of people have been calling here talking about the awards of late. Generally this starts happening' around now although one category is getting most of the attention and that is match of the Year. Usually the Wrestler of the Year is the favorite but this year, while maybe not good in some individual

categories, has been stronger than any I can remember when it comes to classic matches. Unless something amazing comes along, I'm sure one of the Flair vs. Steamboat matches will win, but have no idea which one it'll be. The Tsuruta vs. Tenryu match on 6/5 was of that calibre as was the December tag match with Hansen & Gordy vs. Tenryu & Kawada in the tag tournament finals and a few other matches involving Tsuruta & Yatsu vs. Tenryu & Kawada from around February. But most discussion is which of the Flair/ Steamboat matches will win.

Wrestler of the year is interesting as well. Flair has never finished lower than second, and his actual wrestling has been incredible most of the year, even against other foes than Steamboat. Maeda, who won last year, has been impressive once again due to the popularity of his promotion which drew two of the biggest gates in history without television. For all the reasons he won last year, he's got to be a favorite again. Both Hulk Hogan and Randy Savage have to be considered, if nothing else for their work outside of the ring. Tenryu has been amazing this year as well and is as important to his group, which is doing great business this year, as almost anyone is to their group. Most outstanding looks to be Flair, Steamboat and Tenryu as the favorites right now, but before the year is out guys like Muta, Jushin Liger and maybe Barry Windham and Kawada may be right in there. Best Babyface has to be Hogan and Ultimate Warrior; Best Heels are Savage, Funk and Rude with Luger having a good shot at winning by the end of the year; Best Tag Team to me Looks like Foot Loose, although Rockers may win the thing because it's hard for a Japanese team to win a category unless they are completely dominant. Actually this one is wide open with about seven or eight teams probably close. No runaway like Midnight Express the past two years. Unless things change in the Last six months, Cornette's several year domination of the best interview category is in jeopardy. Funk, Savage and Lawler look to me to be the favorites right now, but when he's on, nobody can top Cornette. There hasn't been a dominant manager this year like Cornette has been in the past. Akbar has gotten the biggest push and most heat, but really he can't hold a candle to the big boys (Cornette, Dangerously, Heenan, etc). Teddy Long may crack the top three as well. I'd say it's anyone's race. Jim Ross seems a lock for best announcer with Tony Schiavone being downplayed and Lance Russell out of Memphis. Really Vince McMahon is his only competition here in what has turned into a weak field. The Worst Announcer field is weaker as well with perennials like David Crockett and Bill Mercer gone. Got to be Ed Whalen in my book. Best TV show of late has been NWA's World Championship Wrestling and the All Japan show with WWF Superstars rounding out the pack. Of the smaller groups, Portland has been the most fun. I can't pick WWF for best wrestling promotion even though they are the best overall promotion, but where is the wrestling? New Japan has flourished with the Russians, but the best actual wrestling and also fan interest combined is All Japan and UWF. NWA just hasn't had the fan interest and WWF doesn't have the wrestling and New Japan's wrestling is nothing compared to past years even though the Russians have drawn big gates.

JULY 10, 1989

Not much in the way of major news this week. The Road Warriors did a job Sunday night at the Omni for the Samoan Swat Team, as in 1-2-3, when Samu used Paul E. Dangerously's phone on Animal and got the pin. It's not Like that's an everyday occurence and is surprising the heck out of everyone in the building. Even though the Road Warriors did gimmick jobs (the fast three count in New Orleans and the AWA tag title loss a few years back when half the world interfered), this was the closest thing to a loss the duo has done since probably around the summer of 1984 when they kind of stopped doing those type of things.

Of late, we've had the wrestlers-to-Hollywood syndrome, with several wrestlers getting small and a few substantial parts in Hollywood flicks. Is the next big thing going to be wrestlers-to-politics? As many of you know, Antonio Inoki retired from wrestling two weeks ago to run for the Japanese senate, and with the election on July 23rd, I'm being told he's got a legitimate shot at winning. Not to be outdone, Jesse Ventura has made waves throughout the Twin Cities media that he's thinking of running for mayor of Brooklyn Park, MN, a 50,000-person suburb of Minneapolis where he resides. Ventura says he's "seriously considering running in 1990" and will make his decision by Labor Day. When asked about whether he's qualified, Ventura brought up Ronald Reagen, Clint Eastwood (former mayor of Carmel, CA) and Sonny Bono (mayor of Palm Springs) as examples of celebrities who have gone on to public office. The mayor position is a full-time job paying $10,000 per year and Ventura said he'd use that income to hire a full-time secretary so he'd basically serve as a volunteer if he were to win. He said that his Titan commitments wouldn't interfere with prospective mayoral duties since his current schedule with Titan is mainly working one TV taping session every three weeks. If he were to get a movie part, which requires a more extensive time away from the job, he said he 'd know about it well in advance, that no movie he's been on has ever taken more than 10 weeks and it wouldn't be that big of a problem. The Minneapolis Star-Tribune had an article on this a few days back in which Ventura said he's 80 percent sure he's running and the only obstacle would be a scheduling problem. It also said that Ventura is in the running for a job as color commentator for the NFL's Tampa Bay Buccaneers this season. If he runs, Ventura would be taking on a 20-year incumbent named James Krautkremer and opposes the mayor for a variety of issues regarding development of the city. Ventura will run under his wrestling name of Jesse Ventura rather than his real name of Jim Janos.

"No Holds Barred" was No. 10 over the weekend of June 23-25, grossing $808,059 in 1 ,005 theaters for a total up to that point of $13,884,301. That would have been its last big weekend because it disappeared from most theaters this past Thursday. It's still around for a final week but its number of theaters will be a lot lower, as for example, it was down from 87 theaters in Northern California to 12 this past weekend. Over last week, the split between New Line Cinema and the theaters was 20/80 (New Line received 20 percent of the gross from the week with the theaters receiving 80 percent and Titan will wind up with about one-third of New Line's share). In the theaters where the movie remained this past week, the percentages were 90/10 in favor of the theaters. I've heard talk that Titan may try and push NHB later this year and tie it in with a PPV show. It would make sense to tie it in with Summer Slam since the first Hogan/ Zeus confrontation will be on that card, however my hunch is that is too soon and it may be tied in with maybe the Survivors Series on Thanksgiving . It's a solid marketing idea, maybe charging an extra $5 for a PPV of the movie and tying it in to a guaranteed two to three percent buy rate for the Thanksgiving show (movies on PPV are considered to be doing extremely well if they do a one-half of one percent buy rate) and it should easily get enough orders to make substantial money.

A few corrections from last week's Bashes. The actual gate in Pittsburgh last Sunday was $35,874, not $42,000 as I'd reported, and officially New Haven did 2,500 paid and $26, 000 (I had heard two figures, one of $26,000 house and another of $35,000). As far as New Haven goes, that's a disappointment, and in fact both shows have to be considered disappointing.

For this past week's Bash schedule, the NWA did a reported $33,000 in Raleigh on Monday; $30,000 in Greenville on Tuesday; $20,000 in Greensboro on Wednesday (all things considered, even considering the fact it was on a Wednesday and there was no Ric Flair, that is still terrible) and they were in Hampton, VA and Salisbury, MD on Thursday and Friday (no reports from either spot), Charlotte on Saturday did about $50,000 and the Omni on Sunday night did about 6,800 fans. For the most part, these shows did about as expected except the Omni was a little higher than I 'd figured and even though most folks who know the Greensboro situation told me in advance it was going to bomb, I really am surprised even on a Wednesday (historically, Greensboro has never drawn except on weekend dates) with that loaded of a line-up that they wouldn't draw better than that.

The NWA's television ratings for the weekend of June 23-25 really don't show much of a trend. The debut of the Friday night "Power Hour" show, which started 35 minutes late because the Atlanta Braves game went long, drew a

1.7 rating at 10:55 p.m. to 11:55 p.m. Eastern time. TBS is said to be happy about that number because it competed with the 11:00 news in the Eastern and Central Time zones and it was a debut of a new show, and drew double the rating "Night Tracks" draws during that same time period. In fact, its solid rating gave Night Tracks its best lead-in and Night Tracks had one of its best ratings in months following the wrestling show. The return of the Saturday World Championship Wrestling to 6:05 p.m. Eastern time drew a 1.8 rating, which is about what the show had been doing in its revolving time slot. Over the next few months, this is the rating to watch for improvement because fans should be able to get into the pattern of watching the show since it'll be at the same time each week. The Sunday Main Event show did a healthy 2.5 rating and 6 share, even more impressive since Dick Murdoch vs. Bill Irwin was the headline match and it did a lot better rating than the Braves game the same day. And finally, the replay of the 6/14 Clash of the Champions on 6/27 from 11:15 p.m. to 2:15 a.m. did a 1.9 rating which TBS was pleased to death with. In comparison, the replay of the New Orleans Clash did a 1.3. This rating was no doubt helped by its lead-in of the NBA draft covered Live on TBS, but if the NWA is looking to grasp for some positive news, the combined rating of the two airings of the last Clash (3.8 + 1.9 = 5. 7) was actually higher than New Orleans (4.3 + 1.3 = 5. 6) . That rating for the Clash replay, which wasn't pro-mo'd at all on the TBS wrestling shows, was also way up from the 1.1 that TBS normally would do during that three hour period on a Tuesday night.

Now I haven't seen this one yet, but I've been told that the match between the Foot Loose and Can-Am Express (Kawada & Fuyuki vs. Dan Kroffat & Doug Furnas) from the 6/5 Tokyo Budokan Hall show which aired on Japanese television two weeks back was the best match of this year. We've heard that a lot, and truthfully, I've never seen a year with anything close to the number of classic matches as we've seen since December, but those who have seen it said it was better than Flair-Steamboat or Tsuruta-Tenryu, so those of you who collect videos, I guess that makes it a must-see. I guess if the match was that good it also makes the 6/5 Tokyo card the card of the year" so far with Tsuruta vs. Tenryu and that match both being legit Match of the Years is any other year and Dynamite Kid & Davey Boy Smith vs. Terry Gordy & Scan Hansen and Sting vs. Danny Spivey both also being very good matches.

July ratings: 1. Genichiro Tenryu; 2. Ricky Steamboat; 3. Toshiaki Kawada; 4. Jushin Liger; 5. Barry Windham; 6. Dan Kroffat; 7. Nobuhiko Takada; 8. Jumbo Tsuruta; 9. Great Muta; 10. Shawn Michaels; 11. Arn Anderson; 12. Kazuo Yamazaki; 13. Naoki Sano;14. Akira Maedsa; 15. Ted DiBiase; 16. Tully Blanchard; 17. Curt Hennig; 18. Mike Rotunda; 19. Shiro Koshinaka; 20. Tatsumi Fujinami; 21.

Chris Benoit; 22. Terry Gorgy; 23. Johnny Smith; 24. Eddie Gilbert; 25. Bobby Eaton. Note: Ric Flair not rated due to inactivity since May. Tiger Mask and Terry Funk are not rated due to injuries.

More than any subject this year, more has been written and talked about within the newsletter community about the current and future status of the National Wrestling Alliance than anything else.

Even though the WWF has established itself as the pre-eminent force in wrestling and, as Paul Sherman wrote in the Letters page, in the general public's eyes, wrestling equals VMF, few will dispute that this is a country large enough to support more than one national promotion. Japan has five, three of which have done booming business at times during the year, and it's a country geographically no larger than California even though it does have several cities with huge population bases.

Whether the NWA can "beat" the WWF is no longer an issue. The issue is, can the NWA re-establish itself as a major league promotion and convince enough fans to make it profitable as an alternative promotion? That's the question TBS has to answer in the upcoming months, or years.

As a business standing on its own, World Championship Wrestling, Inc. must be operating deeply in the red. Its prime income source, house shows, have by and large been disastrous all year. Its pay-per-view events haven't drawn nearly what the company hoped, although nobody could have forseen the television ratings dropping to the levels they reached some weeks back, and that accounts for a lot of it. Depending upon who you believe, the company World Championship Wrestling is said to be losing $25,000 to $30,000 daily. It has between 35 and 40 touring wrestlers, five managers, one valet, a ref or two and even a television announcer (to do the 900 number fall-by-falls on most house shows) on the road daily. Approximately 25 of the wrestlers are under contract for between $75,000 and a reported $550,000 per year. Costs of taping so many television shows are high. And even those within the company who are optimistic don't expect major changes in this profit-loss picture until the winter at the earliest .

Under normal circumstances within this business, it would be about time to read the NWA its Last rites. Many are already doing so. And if these figures are correct, a potential $10 million in losses over the first year of the new company have to be a lot greater than even TBS bargained for.

I don't claim to have any inside knowledge as to what the real commitment TBS has in regards to wrestling. but I also don't believe those who are saying TBS wants to sell the company after this summer have any inside information either.

Even if World Championship Wrestling is losing money on paper, that can be deceiving. TBS, which owns WCW, is deriving millions of dollars annually in advertising income from its various pro wrestling shows . The wrestling shows still do better in their time slots than the "average" programming does on the station. TBS runs four hours weekly of what is now decently rated programming, which has a track record of being some of its highest rated programming. They run quarterly specials which bring in several hundred thousand dollars a piece in ad revenue, and TBS' share of the Nashville PPV show, for example, still should have been in the neighborhood of $750, 000.

In recent weeks, I've noticed what appears to be a greater commitment from TBS in regards to wrestling. They've given the wrestling company an additional hour, on Friday nights. They have given the Saturday show a stable time period which it has desperately been needing. The number of plugs during TBS programming for the wrestling shows is larger than ever before, and they group the wrestling show as part of "Super Sports Saturday", which is not the snide, snicker image other stations which do wrestling programming, Like ESPN for example, have chosen to take. They now run NWA updates between games of the Braves doubleheaders, and the Braves announcers have obviously been regularly instructed to talk wrestling and plug the wrestling programming.

This is encouraging. Some other things, like the TV ratings over the past few months and house shows, haven't been nearly as encouraging. Honestly, one had to expect that things were going to get worse before they got better and there have been some very encouraging signs, particularly the excellent PPV shows, from the company.

It's been said over-and-over but the NWA's biggest problem is exposure and perception. Product has little to do with it. The NWA can't survive as a nationally touring troupe if the public sees them as the feeder system for the WWF. And make no mistake about it, that is what the public sees them as. Over the past few weeks I've been put in a position, between sports talk shows through beach parties to meet or talk with literally hundreds of people who watch wrestling, don't read wrestling magazines, don't subscribe to newsletters, and probably for the most part their interest in wrestling at best would be the difference in TV ratings and maybe be the difference between the mild pop and the big pop at the big house show of the year or a PPV event. The public awareness of pro wrestling is higher than it has ever been, mainly due to the WWF. We can all knock McMahon for a lot of things, and he deserves a lot of them, but his marketing has been great for pro wrestling. If you look at the age group you need to be in, the people who pay to see Batman or Indiana Jones at the theaters, I'm amazed at just how well so many of them are when it comes to wrestling . Everyone knows Hulk Hogan. Most everyone knows Zeus, Randy Savage, Elizabeth, Andre the Giant and the Ultimate Warrior in that age group. Almost everyone also knows there is an NWA, knows Ric Flair, Dusty Rhodes, Lex Luger and

the Road Warriors. I can guarantee and this is in California, where if anything, TBS is weak, NWA syndication is weak, that Flair still has more name recognition than all but the top. three or four WWF wrestlers. However, people don't talk about Ric Flair vs. Terry Funk. Nobody does. People do talk about Jimmy Snuka vs. Honkeytonk Man. They know the NWA exists. They know the major names. But it's not the major league. Ric Flair is in some ways Like Herschel Walker must have been in the UBFL. Everyone knew Herschel Walker. Everyone knew he was just about the best running back around, give or take one or two Eric Dickerson's. But when he was in the USFL, nobody really cared who he was playing against or how he was doing. In fact, the most asked question about Ric Flair or Lex Luger is not about Flair's feud with Funk or Luger's feud with Rick Steamboat, but when will Flair, Luger, Road Warriors, whomever, go to the WWF? Nobody ever asks when Randy Savage will go to the NWA? That's why the losses of Tully Blanchard & Arn Anderson, and now with Barry Windham and Dusty Rhodes being on Titan's television, have been more damaging to the NWA than a press conference that was a little flat, or a screw-job ending of a big match, or the Ding Dongs on a TV special. The latter things get hardcore fans mad, but they will remain fans. To draw 10,000 people to cards, you have to draw people who aren't hardcore and it isn't that the NWN s product appeals only to hardcore fans, it's that the general public won't support what looks like the feeder system to the major league or a second-rate league. But you know what people ask about Hulk Hogan? They don't ask if he's going to the NWA of course, they ask about his matches with Zeus and Randy Savage. Vince has the public thinking what he wants them thinking. The NWA doesn't have the public thinking about all their feuds and angles, but about when their personalities will join the WWF.

Which puts the NWA at a day of reckoning. There are alternatives. Follow the current course and there is a chance. But only if Flair, Luger, Sting or whomever somehow can break in as media celebrities. To do this, you're going to have to buy a celeb and have them ride along in their coat-tails. Hogan was a great draw before Cyndi Lauper and Mr. T, but he wasn't a celebrity until he road on their coat tails, and established his own coat tails that Randy Savage, Liz, and everyone else have road on. The NWA doesn't have to be equal to the WWF in terms of media hype, but they have to be able to get enough media hype to where their top stars are at least slightly crossover celebs. They also have to bring in a major name from the other side. If people at least think the NWA is capable to taking a big name, they will be taken seriously . I agree it'll be a lot more beneficial when or if their syndication is strengthened to take advantage of a raid, but without a "dream" match, they aren't going to get any percent buy rates on PPV.

To look at promotional wars on a national level, you have to examine Japan. The country has had wars of this ilk for 20 years. Unlike here, where one side has network exposure and its competitors don't, no group has ever been able to totally dominate the country. But there have been times it looked like it could happen.

In the early 1980s, New Japan was more "over" to the general public, during the heyday of Inoki, Satoru Sayama and Riki Choshu, than the WWF is now, or probably ever will be. All Japan had a hard time competing, but were able to maintain a healthy audience by bringing in big name foreign talent. New Japan went down with a public scandal, and then when Choshu jumped in 1984, the tables were turned. Inoki, after the Choshu jump, was in almost as weak a position as the NWA is right now, maybe even weaker since almost every major drawing card left - they no longer could bring in Hogan because of the breaks with the WWF, Andre couldn't draw anymore because he was the pits, Sayama retired and went public with his complaints, and Choshu and all his allies went to the opposition. Inoki looked dead. So he raided Bruiser Brody, Baba's top drawing card, and was back doing huge gates. He didn't sit back and establish his own stars, because when you are the second-rate league, the best you can do is establish second-rate stars. Hey, in 1984, when Vince made his big push, he didn't establish one star on his own. He raided every star he could get his hands on. It wasn't until Vince had established himself as major league in the new areas of the country that had never seen Titan before the new era, that Vince was able to establish his own creations like Beefcake and Honkeytonk Man as stars. This raiding brings with it huge risk. It'll take a big money guaranteed commitment, and it may not work because the WWF may be like the NFL, and we've all seen what happened to its competitors.

They also can, come April, when these contracts expire, go the other route. Figure that they will run a regional promotion, not pay anything, keep costs down, and provide cheap programming for the station. Even scaled-down wrestling should do decent ratings on television. They'll have no potential to do huge houses, but they won't lose $10 million in a year either. This, without outside income from corporate sponsors, would never on its own be a money maker, because regional promotions haven't been able to make money for years. But to a company like TBS, with low costs, it won't Lose more than an amount which would be like a drop in the bucket. They'd also have to completely forget about PPV, because they'll lose the big stars.

Another alternative is to run mainly a television promotion. To do that, you'd keep maybe 20-25 wrestlers and primarily build up eight big shows a year (four PPV's and Clashes) and maybe do one or two national tours like the Roller Derby did in the late 1960s and hope to draw people twice a year as a novelty, rather than have the die-hard commitment that regular monthly ticket purchasing needs. An offshoot of this same idea would be to run maybe six or eight cities regularly on weekends in close geographic range and cater to those cities and build up a local following, and then tour. The most ironic part of this is the logic would be to base in Atlanta and tour the Carolinas, Georgia and Florida. Those also appear right now to be some of the most burned out places around to draw crowds for wrestling so that is a risk and running that five-state geographic promotion will lose money for a while.

The answer? There isn't an answer that will be a guaranteed success. But what the NWA needs to do immediately is decide what they want to be, both in terms of product as we've discussed in the past, but realistically in terms of whether they want to be major league and fight the big war, taking the huge money risks it'll take, or forget about being major league, forget about PPV, and just provide cheap programming with very little (comparatively) risks but no chances of any big rewards financially, either. When that decision is made, they've got to go all the way with it and give it a chance with the right people calling the shots.

If you want to go major league. Don't book anymore live specials in the summer in non air conditioned buildings. Don't book the Oak Ridge Boys on PPV. Don't put press conferences on television that don't look major league. And above all else, you have to hype the live shows and pay-per-view shows as good if not better than your competition, because the product in entertainment is hype . Product quality itself only becomes a factor when hype is equal.

WWF

Things fairly slow here right now as all the shows over this past weekend were held in Canada since Titan has made it a company policy to run as few shows as possible in the U.S. during summer holiday weekend periods. I believe they aren't running any shows through Wednesday, taking a few days completely dark.

Superstars taping took place 6/27 in NiagaraFalls featuring new characters The Big Steele Man (Fred Ottman) managed by Slick, who will certainly get the big push because of his size, and Mark Young, the same break-dancing Vince Young of NWA "fame" who is doing the same break-dancing. He did get booed in several cities on the road already when he started break-dancing after the matches, although one would think it's the kind of gimmick McMahon could get over to his fans a lot easier than the NWA could. But he's hurt by lack of size more here than he was in the NWA. Tully Blanchard & Arn Anderson made a challenge to Demolition for the tag team titles and the match will be taped on 7/18 in Worcester, MA as part of the Saturday Night Main Event (air date still 7/29) and it'll be two of three falls and since Demolition is in a six-man tag at SummerSlam you can read into this match what you want.

The main event on the SNME show will be Hulk Hogan & Brutus Beefcake vs. Randy Savage & Honkey tonk Man which will set up the angle where Zeus gets involved for Surnmer Slam. In a television match, Ultimate Warrior beat Haku via DQ when Rick Rude Piledrove Warrior on the title belt. Greg Valentine did a clean job for Dusty Rhodes in a television match, however Dusty had to put Ted DiBiase over when Virgil held his leg. They acknowledged Jake Roberts neck injury and Ted DiBiase gave him a golden neckbrace, so when Jake is able to return, they'll start that series up all over again. Barry Windham was referred to as simply "The Widow Maker" during the ring introductions at these tapings. In other matches in Niagara Falls, Beefcake beat Savage via DQ, Warrior beat Rude via count out, Demolition beat Twin Towers, Snuka pinned Honkeytonk Man, Hart Foundation beat Powers of Pain via count out.

Don't have complete details on Rochester on 6/28, but do know that Warrior challenged Andre to a match and that Rhodes did a run-in to save a jobber as Big Bossman tried to handcuff him. Steele Man worked with Tim Horner and Paul Roma as try-out matches but everyone was pleased with what they saw so expect to see lots of him.

6/24 in Chicago drew 4,300 and $50,000 as The Genius Lanny Poffo pinned Jim Powers, Snuka pinned Honkeytonk Man, Barry Horowitz pinned Blue Blazer (who was married this past Sunday), Hillbilly Jim beat Andre the Giant via DQ, Jim Duggan pinned Haku, Rick Martel pinned Tito Santana, Warlord pinned Bret Hart and Bushwackers beat Brainbusters.

They've got an interesting gimmick match booked come August in some cities with the Rougeaus vs. Rockers doing one hour marathon matches and the team that wins the most falls in the hour gets the win. Sounds like a Pat Patterson idea because many years ago (like 15 years), they had a similar match with Patterson and Don Muraco at the Cow Palace. The Japanese women had a match like that when I was there in 1987 and the heat when one team was down by a fall with three minutes to go was similar to a college basketball game where the home school is down by four with two minutes left. I wish they'd have someone other than the Rougeaus in it because I can sense 45 minutes of stalling which doesn't sound like fun.

6/25 in Cleveland drew 8,300 as Young pinned Sharpe ½ *, Barbarian pinned Jim Neidhart DUD, Snuka pinned Honkey ¼ *, Demolition beat Twin Towers via DQ **, Mr. Perfect (Curt Hennig) pinned Koko B. Ware ½ *, Badnews Brown pinned Paul Roma * and Hogan pinned Savage **. Elizabeth was in Hogan's corner during the match and the stuff between Sherri and Liz was said to be excellent. They do a bunch of spots together outside the ring and during the pin when Sherri tries to run in, Liz grabs her ankles and prevents it. As you can imagine, the heat is super for the women.

6/23 in Bloomington, drew 6,900 and $80,000 as Jim Brunzell pinned Mike Sharpe, Barbarian pinned Neidhart, Snuka pinned Honkey, Demolition beat Twin Towers, Perfect pinned Ware, Brown pinned Roma and Hogan pinned Savage.

Widow Maker will be booked in his arena debut matches during August with Roma everywhere.

6/25 in Wheeling, WV drew 4,119 as Tim Horner pinned Boreus Zhukov, Rhodes pinned DiBiase, Rockin Robin pinned Judy Martin, Beefcake pinned Greg Valentine, Hercules beat Dino Bravo via DQ, Rougeaus beat Rockers (best match), Red Rooster pinned Brooklyn Brawler and Warrior beat Rude via DQ.

CWA

Results from 6/26 in Memphis at the Mid South Coliseum saw Dirty White Boy (Tony Anthony) pin Frankie Lancaster, Action Jackson & Billy Travis kept the CWA tag team titles beating The D. I. & Spike Huber, Jeff Jarrett beat CWA champion Black Bart via DQ in a title match, Bill Dundee & Freddy (Tommy Gilbert) went to a no contest against the Wildside (Chris Champion & Mark Starr) and the main event was a six-man elimination tag match with Jerry Lawler & Stan Frazier (Uncle Elmer) & Bam Bam Bigelow beating Master of pain & Dutch Mantell & Ronnie Gossett. Mantell was pinned first, then Gossett hit MOP by accident with his shoe causing him to lose the second fall. It ended with the three faces against Gossett, who faked a heart attack for the second week in a row. This time Lawler gave him a fist-drop off the top rope, Frazier came in and used the leg drop and Bigelow finished it off with a head-butt off the top rope. Finally MOP & Mantell ran in and pulled Gossett out of the ring.

The 7/3 card in Memphis had all seats for $3 so they probably drew a good sized crowd as the main event had Lawler defending the USWA title against Kerry Von Erich. It was said by Gossett on a taped interview from his hospital bed that he would be managing Kerry, but Kerry denied it, or was supposed to deny it although nobody really understood what it was that he said so Dave Brown had to explain that Kerry denied it. Also Bart vs. Jarrett for the CWA title with Bart having a branding iron in the corner and Jarrett having an aluminium baseball bat; Wildside (who won the tag titles on 7/1 in Memphis at the TV studio) defend the tag titles against Travis & Jackson, Freddy vs. MOP and if Freddy Loses, he must unmask but if MOP loses, he gets tarred and feathered by the fans, D. I. & Huber vs. Dundee & Ricky Morton, Dirty White Boy vs. Dustin Rhodes (who is full-time and has left Florida), Chili B. Cool (a new wrestler who might be Botswana Beast without the make-up) vs. Mantell and Doug Gilbert vs. Lancaster . On the 7/1 tag title change, Jackson no-showed so Travis had to defend against both members of the Wildside by himself. Travis wound up doing his Tommy Rich juice imitation and the referee stopped the match and gave the belts to the Wildside. Jackson came on later in the show and said he arrived late because there was a major accident on the highway and they didn't let any traffic in.

Morton returned and was jumped on television by D. I. & Doug Gilbert who hit him with a chair.

Dustin Rhodes is in trying to talk like his father, unlike in Florida where he was low-key. He wound up getting into it with Bart & Dirty White BOY who were running down his father.

MOP tried to unmask Freddy on television but Freddy threw fire to chase him away. The Blackbirds (Iceman King Parsons & Brickhouse Brown) managed by Harold Harris are headed in next week full-time.

WORLD CLASS

The 6/30 card at the Dallas Sportatorium drew 1,500 with lots of interesting developments. In the loser leaves town match, Kevin & Kerry Von Erich beat Iceman King Parsons & Brickhouse Brown when Kerry pulled Harold Harris into the ring and pinned him, even though he wasn't a participant. It was then announced that since Harris owned the contracts for Iceman and Brickhouse and he was pinned and has to leave, they all have to leave. I guess that makes up for all those LLT matches where nobody left. Matt Borne & Jeff Jarrett won the World Class tag belts from Robert Fuller & Brian Lee, who are already history as Fuller has started back as booker for the CWF taking Lee with him. Eric Embry went to a double disqualification with P. Y. Chu Hi (Phil Hickerson) in a juice-fest and the main event with Jerry Lawler defending his title against Chris Adams ended in no decision. Ref Tony Falk was bumped, Lawler pulled out the chain and went for the punch, Adams used the superkick to beat him to the punch but no ref could count the fall. Cactus Jack Manson & Gary Young then hit the ref and beat on Adams & Falk. Under World Class rules, if it was a DQ, then the title changed hands, however they came up with this gimmick when Lawler and Embry had a similar no finish match two weeks earlier, that if the heels are interfering on behalf of Lawler, it's a DQ and title change but if they are acting on their own, it's a no contest and of course the heels will claim they were acting on their own.

The big story in this week's full-of-holes soap opera is the bidding war for the controlling interest in World Class wrestling. If you remember, three weeks back, Eric Embry beat Tojo Yamamoto for Yamamoto's "controlling interest" in World Class. Embry then played president for two weeks, allowing himself to take credit for an all seats $4 night on 6/23, then turned control over to Max Andrews, who in reality is the head of syndication. Going off on a

quick tangent, Andrews will still handle syndication for this group and Action Media Group will simply handle the ad sales, as they do with the NWA syndicated package. Anyway, somehow they'e forgotten all this and now they are saying that Andrews and Akbar are in a bidding war for the World Class stock and that Akbar has outbid Andrews but Andrews is trying to get the USWA to help him out to outbid Akbar to get the controlling interest and whoever outbids whoever will be announced this Saturday. I believe this is being done to explain why World Class will cease to exist and be replaced by the USWA, as USWA will buy controlling interest and hence they'll do the name change. With Fuller, Lee, Parsons and Brown leaving, this group has a heel shortage so they are going to turn Jimmy Jack Funk heel.

7/6 in Dallas has Embry vs. Chu Hi on top, Al Perez vs. Kerry Von Erich, Borne & Jarrett defending the tag titles against Young & Manson and Funk vs. Kevin Von Erich.

The TV taping this Saturday is going to be quite interesting, because things like freedom of speech and freedom of expression seem to be something that wrestling promoters can't deal with. There has been an ongoing battle, and this when it is all told, is going to sound like a wrestling angle, but it isn't, with Eric Embry against a small but vocal group of heel fans that sit in Section D at the Sportatorium each week. One would think this group would be thankful they have such loyal fans, but of course that isn't the case when they have the audacity to boo the booker. Of course, the more times Embry tried to taunt and shut up the group over the weeks, the larger and more vocal they became. Finally two weeks back, they roped off Section D and only let the wrestlers' wives and girlfriends and families sit in the section. So the "heel fans" were scattered, and somehow wound up right in front of the interview area. When Embry came out for his interview, he saw the fans right in front of him, grumbled a few words, dropped the mic and walked off and wouldn't do an interview on the TV show. This past Saturday at the taping, before it was time for Embry's interview, they kicked out two fans for no reason except they were cheering Scandor Akbar earlier in the show. When Embry did his interview, there were chants of "boring, boring" and Embry stopped again and asked whoever thought it was boring to raise their hand. Two guys did and the rest backed down. Embry then asked the rest of the crowd if they should kick them out and when the fans cheered, they proceeded to kick those fans out. Well, it turns out that the ACLU was contacted about this and is chomping at the bit to get involved in such an easy case since cheering Scandor Akbar isn't exactly sufficient reason to kick a fan out of the building.

Tojo Yamamoto & Scandor Akbar attacked Percy Pringle on television. Embry accidentally called Chu Hi, "Phil" in his interview, forgetting that the promotion has been trying to pretend Hickerson is a Japanese wrestler.

Jimmy Jack Funk and Kevin Von Erich started arguing over which family was the greatest family in wrestling (I'm not sure if they meant Von Erichs, Funks or Barrs) and I guess it didn't actually come off very well and TV announcer Mark Nulty (subbing for Mark Lowrance) said, when he thought his mic was dead and he was talking to the directors, "We gotta get out of this. It's going nowhere fast," except it went out over the air.

Al Perez officially signed with Akbar so he's back as a heel.

STAMPEDE

Things pretty shaky because of last weekend's backstage brawl involving Bruce Hart. I've heard about a million stories about what happened, but apparently Dynamite Kid sucker-punched Hart and broke his jaw and all sorts of stories about what would happen next ensued. Wrestlers were afraid that the promotion would be closed down and others felt that Kid & Davey Boy Smith would be history here but thus far nobody seems to know how it's all going to wind up. They have a "Super Summer Extravaganza" tour with dates on 7/15 in Edmonton, 7/21 at the Calgary Corral (8,000 seats as opposed to the 2,000 seat Pavilion), 7/23 in Vancouver and 7/25 in Victoria with Dynamite vs. Davey Boy on top in some cities and Dynamite Kid & Johnny Smith vs. Davey Boy Smith & Chris Benoit on top in others with Larry Cameron defending the North American title against Ricky Rice (they've been building this feud up on television for weeks). 7/1 in Edmonton drew 200 fans and $2,000 as Goldie Rogers pinned Bill Jodin DUD, Angel of Death beat Ron Ritchie ¾ *, Rice pinned Kerry Brown * ¼, Benoit pinned Sumu Hara * ¼ and Jason the Terrible beat Cameron via count out when Jason did the head-butt off the top rope and Angel of Death pulled Cameron out of the ring to get him counted out which saves the title * ½. The reason it was such a weak card is that many of the wrestlers were in Calgary for Owen Hart's wedding. Steve Ray from Kansas City is headed in. I saw him in February and he looked to have good potential.

JAPAN

Just a few brief notes. Bull Nakano captured the All Pacific title (Chigusa Nagayo held this title for a long time and retired with it) beating Mitsuko Nishiwaki for the held up belt on 6/18 in Tokyo. Also on the card, Madusa Maceli & Noriyo Tateno beat Lioness Asuka & Yumi Ogura. Baba has signed a 6-foot-9 ish American guy. Should have details but the magazines played it up big. UWF on 7/24 in Fukuoka will have Yoshiaki Fujiwara vs. Kazuo Yamazaki and Akira Maeda vs. Yoji Anjyo as the double main event. 8/13 in Yokohama will almost certainly be Fujiwara vs. Maeda on top. The Sting vs. Muta match in Baltimore on 7/23 is getting big play in Japan.

CWF

The 6/23 card in Knoxville, TN saw "Beauty" Terrance Garvin (of Beauty & The Beast tag team) pin The Star Fighter, Danny Davis kept the CWF jr. title pinning Cowboy Kevin Dillinger (Alan Martin), AdrIan Street pinned The Intern (Tim Fry), Stomper Don Harris pinned Ron Sexton, The Fantastics (Bobby & Jackie Fulton) beat Mike Davis & Lou Fabbiano, Tom Prichard regained the CWF title pinning Wendell Cooley when after a ref bump, Jerry Stubbs put chloroform on a towel and put Cooley out and Prichard got the pin, Jimmy Golden & Mongolian Stomper beat The Rock & Roll Express (Ricky & Todd Morton) in a cage match to keep the CWF tag titles in a juice-fest.

Ron Fuller was at the building and challenged Stubbs to a match.

The Fulton Brothers beat Stomper & Golden via DQ in a TV tag team title match on 6/9 in Birmingham.

Carl Fergie headed in as a jobber.

Sam Houston has been plugged as coming on television videos. . . Johnny & Davey Rich were back in to start a feud with Mike Davis & Don Harris.

OREGON

The 7/1 card in Portland drew a small crowd of less than 1,000 (part of the problem was the heat, no air conditioning and more than 1000 combined with the holiday weekend and an auto race that drew 50,000 in Portland head-up).

Carl Styles did a promo saying he has to undergo an eye operation and if he's lucky he gets the sight back in his good eye. They then announced there will be tournaments for both the Northwest singles and TV title as Styles held both of them. In the Scotty the Body vs. Steve Doll match which was supposed to have Scott Peterson handcuffed to Jonathan Boyd, Boyd instead was handcuffed to the bottom rope because Peterson wouldn't come out since Boyd has been carrying around a snake and Peterson is afraid of snakes. Doll pinned Scotty to win and as part of the stips, Ginger, Scotty's valet, became valet for Doll & Peterson. Then during Madril's Rose Garden, Boyd & Scotty come out with the snake and Doll & Peterson back off. Scotty grabbed Ginger by the hair and tried to make her kiss Boyd's snake (the reptile, this is family entertainment). This sets up next week's card with Doll & Peterson vs. Scotty & Boyd and if the faces win, Boyd has to get rid of the snake and if the heels win, Ginger has to come back. Top Gun wrestled Midnight Soldier in what was supposed to be a babyface match. Grappler came out and offered $1,000 to Top Gun if he could unmask Soldier (Brian Adams). Top Gun said No and Grappler kicked him from behind and said that Soldier did it. Top Gun then attacks Soldier who makes the comeback and Soldier wins via an over the top DQ ruling. Soldier tried to shake hands after but Top Gun wouldn't shake hands. Main event was Grappler vs. Billy Jack Haynes in a strap match. Ref Rex King checked Grappler and found gimmicks everywhere and TV commentator Scotty said that King must be a magician because he's planting all these foreign objects on Grappler. Haynes got the full nelson when Joey Jackson runs in and Grappler gets loose and Haynes destroys Jackson who does a stretcher job. Next week Haynes vs. Grappler in a stretcher match.

They were supposed to have a match with Beetlejuice vs. Al Madril and if Madril lost he'd have to dress like Beetlejuice and dance with the kids. Madril backed out of the match and agreed to pay for all kids tickets (Madril's been doing an "I hate kids" gimmick for months) this coming week in return.

OTHER NOTES

I've got to relate two stories I heard over the past week. The first came from Larry Sharpe of the Monster Factory who was talking about one of the students he was training came up to him and asked him that if he used one of the moves that Vince McMahon and Gorilla Monsoon call a patented move (ie Honkeytonk Man's shake, rattle and roll), can he be sued for it?

Last Saturday a friend of mine called up to tell me that his brother, who had attended a party on Friday night and wound up passed out on the couch, had this horrible nightmare. He dreamed he was watching wrestling on TBS when all of a sudden Gordon Solie was on, and he was talking about Hulk Hogan and No Holds Barred. Anyway, it wasn't a nightmare. TBS replays the "Power Hour" where Solie was on talking about Hulk Hogan and No Holds Barred last week at 4:15 a.m. here on the West Coast.

When Gong Magazine listed the 100 most famous matches in the history of Japanese wrestling in a recent booklet, matches since 1970 on the list were: 7/30/70: Dory Funk vs. Giant Baba for NWA title; 5/18/71: Billy Robinson vs. Karl Gotch; 12/9/71: Dory Funk vs. Seiji Sakaguchi for NWA title; 10/22/72: Baba vs. Bruno Sammartino; 7/9/73: Rusher Kimura vs. Shozo Kobayashi; 10/9/73: Baba & Jumbo Tsuruta vs. Dory & Terry Funk; 10/9/73: Mil Mascaras vs. The Destroyer; 10/14/73: Antonio Inoki & Sakaguchi vs. Gotch & Lou Thesz; 1/27/74: Jack Brisco vs. Dory Funk for NWA title; 3/19/74: Inoki vs. Kobayashi; 4/26/ 74: Inoki vs. Sakaguchi; 6/26/74: Inoki vs. Tiger Jeet Singh; 10/7/74: Mighty Inoue vs. Superstar Billy Graham; 10/10/74: Inoki vs. Kim 111; 11/20/74: Verne Gagne vs. Robinson; 12/2/74: Baba wins NWA title from Jack Brisco; 10/30/75: Baba vs. 111; 12/6/75: Dory Funk vs. Abdullah the Butcher; 12/11/75: Inoki vs. Robinson; 12/15/75: Baba vs. Tsuruta; 3 / 10/76: Gagne vs. Tsuruta; 12/3/76: Kimura vs. Gypsy Joe; 8/25/77: Tsuruta vs. Mascaras; 12/15/77: Funks vs. Sheik & Abdullah (this is the famous match where Funks become babyfaces in Japan); 7/27/78: Tatsumi Fujinami vs. Ryuma Go; 1/5/79: Tsuruta vs. Fritz

von Erich; 8/26/79: Inoki & Baba vs. Singh & Butcher; 2/8/80: Inoki vs. Stan Hansen; 4/2/80: Fujinami vs. Ashura Hara; 9/12/80: Harley Race vs. Mascaras; 1/18/81: Gagne vs. Baba; 4/23/81 : Satoru Sayama vs. Dynamite Kid; 4/30/71: Dory Funk vs. Terry Funk; 5/10/81: Hansen vs. Hulk Hogan; 9/23/81: Hansen vs. Andre the Giant; 10/8/81: Inoki vs. Rusher Kimura; 2/14/82: Hansen vs. Baba; 6/18/82: Andre vs. Hogan; 10/26/82: Sayama vs. Kuniaki Kobayashi; 4/3/83: Riki Choshu vs. Fuj inami; 6/2/83: Inoki vs. Hogan; 11/3/83: Choshu vs. Akira Maeda; 2/3/84: Davey Boy Smith vs. Kid; 4/17/84: Maeda vs. Yoshiaki Fujiwara; 8/2/84: Inoki vs. Choshu; 9/7/84: Sayama vs. Fujiwara; 2/21/85: Genichiro Tenryu vs. Choshu; 4/18/85: Inoki vs. Bruiser Brody 7 9/2/85: Sayama vs. Maeda; 10/21/85: Ric Flair vs. Rick Martel for NWA and AWA title; 11/4/85: Choshu vs. Tsuruta; 2/6/86: Inoki vs. Fujiwara; 4/5/86: Choshu vs. Hansen; 4/29/86: Maeda vs. Andre; 6/12/86: Maeda vs. Fujinami; 6/17/86: Inoki vs. Andre; 9/16/86: Inoki vs. Brody; 11/1/86: Hiroshi Wajima vs. Singh; 2/5/87: Tsuruta & Tenryu vs. Choshu & Yoshiaki Yatsu; 8/19/87: Choshu & Kengo Kimura & Fujinami & Super Strong Machine & Maeda vs. Inoki & Keiji Muto & Fujiwara & Sakaguchi & Kantaro Hoshino; 8/31/87: Tsuruta vs. Tenryu; 10/4/87: Inoki vs. Masa Saito; 10/25/87: Fujinami vs. Choshu; 11/19/87: Maeda & Nobuhiko Takada & Kido vs. Hiro Saito & Masa Saito & Choshu (" shoot kick" match); 11/22/87: Hansen & Terry Gordy vs. Brody & Jimmy Snuka; 3/9/88: Tenryu vs. Hansen; 4/15/88: Tenryu vs. Brody; 5/8/88: Fujinami vs. Big Van Vader; 5/12/88: Maeda vs. Kazuo Yamazaki; 7/22/88: Inoki vs. Choshu; 8/8/88: Inoki vs. Fuj inami; 10/28/88: Tsuruta vs. Tenryu; 12/16/88: Hansen & Gordy vs. Tenryu & Toshiaki Kawada; 12/22/88: Takada vs. Bob Backlund; 1/10/88: Maeda vs. Takada. That should stir some arguments with those of you who collect Japan tapes.

Southland Promotions on 7/4 in Cleveland, TN has Buddy Landel vs. Brad Armstrong, Pez Whatley vs. Kimala, Junkyard Dog vs. Tommy Rich, The Bullet vs. Mongolian Stomper, Moondog vs. Larry Santana, Mr. Wrestling I & II vs. Super D & Butch Mantell and Bambi vs. Peggy Lee Leather announced. Mitch Steinfeld promoted a show in Bound Brook, NJ drawing 158 fans on 6/16 as Tom Brandi beat Mike Kaluha, Misty Blue beat Comrade Orca, Don Muraco double count out The Mod Russian, Johnny Rodz beat Mondo Kleen (Kleen said to be huge), Cheetah Kid beat Tom Norton.

6/24 in Charlotte, NC saw promoter Greg Price draw 542 fans and $4,900 as Rick Link beat Super Punk Rocker, Brad Anderson drew Mitch Stallion, Vic Steamboat & Joe Savoldi beat Cruel Connection (Gary Royal & George South), Bambi double count out Peggy Lee Leather, Tommy Rich pinned Paul Diamond (sub for Tom Zenk), Ivan Koloff beat Russian Assassin (Dan Grundy) to earn five minutes with Paul Jones, JYD beat Manny Fernandez via DQ, Kendall Windham & Tom Prichard beat Johnny & Davey Rich and Nikita Koloff beat Barry Windham via DQ.

Nelson Royal's show on 6/20 in Monroe, NC drew 32 as David Isley beat L.A. Stephens, Ring Lords beat Tommy Angel & Rikki Nelson, Ken Shamrock beat Saoni, Sam Houston beat Colt Steele and Nelson Royal & Robert Gibson beat Mod Squad Spike & Brad Anderson. Ole Anderson and Masa Chono were to work for this group but never made it.

Chris Love folded up his promotion in Mississippi and lost his promoters license and has surfaced in the Midwest.

Ray Whebbe promoted a Rock & Wrestle for Shelter free card on 6/24 at Loring Park in the Twin Cities drawing 3,500 with theRussian Brute said to be 6-7, 350 (George Petrosky) plus Sharkey guys Johnny Love, Tommy Ferrera, Charlie Norris, Maximum Overdrive plus Tom Zenk and Baron Von Raschke. 6/21 at George's Sports Bar the PWA drew a full house of 350 and an interesting trivia note is that Jeff Warner of Maximum Overdrive did an interesting double that night. At 7 p.m. in a Twin Cities gym, he made his boxing debut knocking out Harry Baptiste in 26 seconds, and later that night won a wrestling match.

Speaking of boxers, former champ and current chump Leon Spinks had his mixed match against pro wrestler and former amateur great Wojo on 6/24 in Toledo. The thing ended when Wojo gave Spinks a backbreaker outside the ring and won via count out. Spinks wore gloves. I've still got nightmares of the finish of the Spinks/Inoki match in 1986. Spinks was supposed to get back suplexed and pinned, but when Inoki went for the finish, Spinks grabbed the ropes because he didn't want to take the bump so Inoki never got him off the ground. Then Spinks layed down and wouldn't get up. Inoki covered him and the ref gave the slowest count in the world to let Spinks kick out and Spinks wouldn't, then after the count, Spinks got right up like nothing had happened and it was riot city.

The AWA card in Chicago taped for Sports Channel last weekend may have had 500-600 in the building but the paid attendance was just 175.

There is an independent wrestler working outlaw shows in Puerto Rico who dressed up like Jose Gonzales (white mask, same pants,. etc.) and is using the ring name Murderer #1.

Kerry Von Erich and Rip Rogers worked a 40 minute draw at the Fathers Day card in San Juan.

Masa Chono and Shinya Hashimoto are wrestling for Otto Wanz in Austria. The top guys there are English wrestlers David Taylor and Steve Wright who are said to be outstanding. The only American there is Greg Boyd. I'm told everyone who works for Wanz earns at least $1,000 per week. Steele Man is coming in at the end of the tour to put Wanz over.

Masaharu Funaki bad-mouthed the UWF at a New Japan party which has caused a minor ruckus within the UWF.

WWF drew a 3.5 rating last week for Prime Time Wrestling (excellent for this time of year) and 2.8 for All-American.

Kendall Windham beat the now-departed Dustin Rhodes for the Florida title on 6/27 in Tampa.

Carlos Colon will be running the annual Anniversary card (equivalent to Starrcade or WrestleMania on the island) on 9/16.

Former WWF promoter Jon Gold of Elizabeth, NJ is doing independent charity shows in New York, Jersey and Pennsylvania. For more details call 201-354-4005.

In Florida, Jimmy Backlund is back wrestling under his real name (had been working as Jomo Kenya) teaming with Brett Sawyer (formerly Bubble Gum Kid) as heel tag team called "The Playboys. " Wayne Coulter, a friend of Gordon Solie's, is financing the continuation of the promotion. Apparently Dusty Rhodes never actually put up the money for the 60 percent interest and never actually bought the stock as he never signed the agreed upon papers. 7/1 in Orlando saw Ho Chi Winh beat Bill Mulkey ½ * , Brian Nobbs drew Sawyer -*** (Sawyer stalled for 11 minutes without a lock-up), Jerry Saggs beat Brady Higgins DUD, Nasty Boys double count out Sawyer & Rick Diamond ** ½ and Al Perez & Steve Keirn beat Winh & Sir Oliver Humperdink in a bloodbath ***. Dick Woerhle has a show 7/7 in Woodbury, NJ with Ken Patera vs. Nikolai Volkoff and Mike Sharpe and Bam Bam Bigelow announced.

NWA

Sting appears in an MTV-style video for Laaz Rock it. 6/26 in Raleigh drew 4,000 and $33,000 as Dan Spivey pinned Bobby Fulton (in for three days before Japan tour - good opener), Mike Rotunda pinned Brian pillman (bad), Norman the Lunatic pinned Scott Hall (real bad), Dynamic Dudes beat New Zealand Militia (bad), Midnight Express beat Ron Simmons & Al Greene, Great Muta beat Eddie Gilbert via count out in the Dragon Shi (fairly good), Sting and Steiners were left in the Battle Royal - Rick eliminated himself, then Sting wrestled Scott and Scott missed a crossblock and went out. Sting was beating on Teddy Long when Terry Funk came in leading to the stretcher job on Sting; Steiner's & Steve Williams double disqualification with Freebirds (excellent), Road Warriors beat Samoan Swat Team via count out (okay) and Lex Luger pinned Ricky Steamboat with his feet on the ropes (great).

NWA is close to closing up the deal to move the WPIX (Ch. 11) time slot in New York to 9 a.m. on Saturdays from its middle of the night VCR only slot in September. Most likely if that happens they'll start to promote live shows again in New York in November.

Nick Patrick is taking tons of abuse from fans everywhere concerning his legendary bump in the Michael Hayes vs.

Lex Luger match in Nashville. It was one of the worst to be sure, but check out the bump he took in the Steamboat-Funk match from Fort Bragg. I loved the NWA update they did between games of the Braves doubleheader last Friday night. TBS is showing a commitment and that segment looked first-rate professional.

Can't say the same about the press conference. With all the hype directed at it, the segment fell flat even with Flair. If this is the greatest wrestler of all-time (and if Flair isn't, he's no worse than second or third) and he may retire, you've got to at least make it look like the press cares even if in reality they wouldn't. But wrestling is fantasy and they ruined the fantasy of the importance of the press conference with no TV cameras (and geez, how far away is the entire CNN crew, couldn't they borrow something for five minutes), no wrestling press (pedicino, Ross, Russell, Apter, etc.), no tape recorders, no fake flashes going on, the whole scene was blown. Luckily Flair saved it with his interview on the TBS show but those who only get syndication must have been left flat.

6/28 in Greensboro drew $20,000 for a hot show as Pillman pinned Fulton (real good), Dudes beat Militia (good action), Spivey pinned Hall (bad), Steiners beat Simmons & Greene (average , Sting and Steamboat were left in the Battle Royal and they went at it for about five hot minutes before they both went out together and split the money and they did the Funk angle afterwards (very good Battle Royal, particularly the ending), Muta beat Gilbert via COR in the Dragon Shi (bad, mainly just hit each other with the stick), Midnight Express beat Hayes & Garvin via DQ when Gordy gave Eaton a DDT (good), Road Warriors & Williams double count out SST & Gordy (only five minutes but Gordy & Doc had an awesome brawl in the elevated ringside section which blew everyone's mind and Warriors and SST had to pick up the pace outside to follow suit - not much of a match but excellent brawl after), and Luger pinned Steamboat (good).

A local cable channel was advertising Ric Flair's return on the 7/23 PPV show one week before the press conference and the first NWA Friday show inadvertently in one of the matches had commentary announcing Flair vs. Funk eight days before the press conference. Mistakes, yes, but don't say Vince wouldn't have done it. He was advertising "Explosion of the Megapowers, Hogan vs. Savage" in Atlantic City one week before the NBC special where they did the break-up.

The commercial for the PPV (Summer in the USA, Baseball, Hotdogs, Apple Pie and NWA) is good if it only runs this week. The commercial mentions a War Games, but no participants (they show film of Warriors, SST, Midnight and Birds but don't actually mention anyone by name and the average fan doesn't read the Observer and realize that the guys they are showing are in the matchup), Flair vs. Funk and says also appearing are Sting, Muta, Steamboat

and Luger without mentioning actual matches. Hey, these guys "appear" for free three times weekly on television. Unless you give the matches, nobody is going to care. The newspaper ad also doesn't list any matches at all. Now that is something Vince wouldn't have done.

7/2 at the Omni in Atlanta drew 6,800 as D.J. Peterson had a try-out pinning Trent Knight with the belly-to-belly suplex (fans booed both guys, no heat, no recognition factor), Pillman pinned Irwin (real good), Militia beat Ding Dongs (Greg Evans & Richard Sartain - Ding Dongs not over in the slightest, tried comedy but nobody reacted), Norman pinned Steve Casey (crowd got into Norman - wears one tennis shoe and one wrestling boot in ring, lots of ringside fans brought keys to wave at him - this gimmick seems to be working - I think reaction initially wouldn't have been so negative if it hadn't been for the Ding Dongs fiasco earlier and the combination of the two made the Clash seem like a clown show), Skyscrapers (Dan Spivey & Sid Vicious) beat George South & Trent Knight (bad and one sided with highlight when Sid pressed South over his head and dropped him over the top rope where Spivey caught him and slammed him on floor), Terry Gordy pinned Dick Murdoch when Hayes distracted the ref and Garvin interfered (good match), Muta beat Gilbert via COR (Paul E. interfered but Missy came out and chased him away with the kendo stick - great match), Battle Royal ended with Sting and Steiners and you know what happens next, Steiners beat Sullivan & Rotunda in an elimination tag match that only went four minutes as Scott, Rotunda and then Kevin were pinned all within a one minute spot (Rick juiced immediately), Hayes & Garvin beat Midnight Express (Gordy DDT'd Eaton to set up the win - pretty good), SST pinned Road Warriors after a ref bump when Paul E. threw the phone in to Samu who used it on Animal for the pin (good match, Warriors sold great and Hawk did a flying bodyblock jumping from one ring into the other) and Luger pinned Steamboat in 19 minutes (good).

For those of you traveling to Baltimore for the Bash and are wondering about the 7/22 line-up for Philadelphia (many have asked about it), what I've got is a 10-man tag with Warriors & Williams & Midnight vs. Freebirds & SST, Steamboat vs. Luger for the U.S. title with no DQ, Gilbert vs. Muta in a Coal Miners Glove match, Rick Steiner vs. Sullivan in a street fight, Scott Steiner vs. Rotunda, Dudes vs. Militia and if Militia doesn't win in 10 minutes they forfeit $1,000 (that doesn't make any sense since Dudes always beat Militia anyway), Ranger Ross vs. Norman, Hall & Pillman vs. Greene & Simmons, Johnny & Davey Rich vs. Skyscrapers and Irwin vs. Murdoch.

The Friday show wasn't as strong in the second week as the first, but still an easy to watch hour. Still, from this weekend, my impression is the Friday show is simply what the Sunday show used to be and the Sunday show mainly shows "filler" material since TV main was Murdoch & Ross vs. Militia plus squashes with Pillman, Ding Dongs and Skyscrapers.

Skyscrapers as a name sounds way too much like Twin Towers and lots of people are feeling it's a rip-off. You know they are headed for a Road Warrior showdown in the winter.

Everyone loves Scott Steiner's blockbuster suplex. Hiroshi Hase in Japan does the same move and holds the bridge all the way over. Crowd pops whenever he does the thing with Terry Gordy.

Jobber Lee Scott takes awesome bumps for the SST including one where they throw him so high in the air that I'm afraid he's going into orbit.

THE READERS' PAGE

GREAT AMERICAN BASH

Luger vs. Steamboat at the Capital Centre bash was one of the best matches I've seen live. I can't believe how good Luger is now. At his size, it is incredible he can do the things he does. Steamboat was great as usual and sold big time. The crowd was about 50/50, although Luger played his heel role well and tried to get the fans to boo him more.

If not for the last two matches (Luger vs. Steamboat and Freebirds vs. Steiner Brothers & Dr. Death) this card would have been terrible. You are 100 percent right about fans perceiving the NWA as minor league. Tonight, however, they were minor league. Most NWA fans of a few years back felt that Dusty Rhodes, Nikita Koloff, Barry Windham, Tully Blanchard, Arn Anderson, Ron Garvin, Ric Flair and the Road Warriors were the NWA. Now, except for Flair and the Road Warriors, they are all gone and the fans feel that the NWA is dead. When they saw them all leave, and most to Titan, they feel the NWA is just a second rate promotion. The fans don't give the new guys like Pillman and Hall a chance. To them, they are minor leaguers because they are in the NWA. The major leaguers, with a few exceptions, are mostly gone to the WWF. Overhearing the NWA fans talking, they don't consider the NWA the big-time anymore. The WWF is the big-time. I think the only solution is what you have said. They need to steal someone big from Titan like Randy Savage or another top name .

Teddy Long is very good. I wish the NWA all the luck in the world because, unfortunately, they are going to need it.

Tom Mavrikes
Glenn Dale, Maryland

After attending the kickoff of the Great American Bash in Landover, I'm somewhat disappointed in the new NWA. Weren't no-shows, changes in the card, squash matches and screw jobs supposed to be a thing of the past. I sure thought so, but after an average card that was billed as a spectacular, I'm not too sure if the NWA has changed for the better.

It wasn't until the fourth match that there was any heat in the building. Of course Bill Irwin and Norman squashes with a Militia vs. Dudes match in between isn't much to cheer about. But you have to wonder how there can be heat in a lousy match where Al Greene replaced Butch Reed teaming with Ron Simmons against the Midnight Express. I've seen better on TV.

Luckily, next was the Road Warriors-SST going 5:17 of heat before the double count out. When this quickie was over, I'd realized that half the card was done and we'd only seen 10 minutes of wrestling.

Actually, the Battle Royal was worth four stars, but the reason for this was that two of the singles matches scheduled on the card actually took place in the Battle Royal. Dr. Death and Terry Gordy fought each other the entire time so they changed their scheduled singles match to a six-man tag later in the card. And since Sting did a stretcher job for Terry Funk, what was billed as the main event was given to Funk via forfeit since Sting was "taken to the hospital. " This really pissed off the fans. The Muta-Gilbert Dragon Shi match sucked for its four minutes. Muta hobbled around on a heavily taped leg and even though his injury is a legitimate excuse, you feel cheated when Muta doesn't do any high spots. Another Lousy match was Rotunda & Spivey vs. Pillman & Hall.

At least the card wasn't a total bomb as the Freebirds vs. Steiners & Williams was four stars. But the place got quiet as Luger vs. Steamboat didn't get the heat needed for a main event. In fact, many people left during the match. One mistake was booking a false finish with Steamboat winning because even more people left after that.

Despite the poor card, a hardcore WWF hater like myself will stay with the NWA, but the NWA has to worry about the fans next to me who commented that the WWF would have filled the place up. The guy was right and in his mind, the WWF show would have been better even though the matches would have sucked but the hype would make it seem like the guy got his money's worth.

Tim Harvey
Columbia, Maryland

I'm giving the Pittsburgh Bash a half-hearted thumbs up. While there were no dud matches on the card, there were no spectacular matches either. This was the third Pittsburgh Bash and it didn't compare with the previous two. The two ring Battle Royal was okay, but once you saw who was participating, or more importantly, who wasn't, it was easy to figure out who was going to win.

Ric Flair needed to make an appearence, even if just to wave to the crowd. While Funk was attacking Sting, everyone was chanting for Flair and not for Sting to make the comeback. Turning Luger was a big mistake. The crowd wouldn't buy it. No matter what he did, even the cheap finish, the crowd approved of. Steamboat was cheered when he was introduced, but couldn't rally support. A big problem is that all the teenage girls were screaming over Luger and couldn't care about Steamboat.

Muta was absolutely awesome. He didn't get over as big live as on television, but he was still pretty popular.

Andy Stowell
Pittsburgh, Pennsylvania

CLASH OF THE CHAMPIONS

Too many commercials. But it was basically a good show except for the Ding-a-lings and the missed camera shots. You'll never see the WWF missing a major shot. Fire is great, but only if you see it. It's absurd for even the most loyal wrestling fan to follow that Muta would be afraid of fire because his father was burned. At Least it was an attempt at something besides all those baby-heel switches that are out of control.

Name withheld by request

I have to give it a thumbs up. Overall, I enjoyed the card. It was well produced. The main thing that detracted from the show was the heat. The opening and early parts of the show had a very enthusiastic crowd so I felt it was a good site choice. However, as many began taking shirts off and Jim Ross was dripping with sweat, it made me hot and also the audience didn't react as well, I think because of the heat. The audience discomfort did hurt the card. Another lesson to be learned. Don't televise a card from a non air conditioned building.

Sharon Guillory
Alexandria, Louisiana

Although the NWA put a lot of effort into the Clash, it was just an average show. The worst thing was the Ding Dongs. They got the wrong kind of negative heat. The Dragon Shi demonstration was the pits. Not only did the camera miss Eddie Gilbert coming into the ring, it also seemed confusing after the fire was thrown. It wasn't until the replay that we even saw Gilbert get into the ring. There were also too many squash matches for what was pushed as a big show. The best part of the show was the Lex Luger angle. Steamboat really sold well and Luger Looked awesome. It was annoying how on every commercial they had a member of the army wishing the army a Happy Birthday. Hopefully the next Clash will be a better show.

Andrew Levy
Westminster, Maryland

I can truthfully say the best thing about the show, and the only good thing in my opinion, was the interview with Ric Flair. One bout had a ref bump. Another had the cliche ref distracted while there was outside interference. Another

saw two wrestlers simply leave the ring and walk away. And we can't forget the screw job finish of the tag team championship match. In recent months you've been saying the NWA is trying to upgrade its product, particularly the TBS product. If Clash of Champions is any example, then you 're dead wrong. As far as I'm concerned, it was an awful show.

Mike Wiener
Encino, California

In spite of the great Luger turn and the enjoyable Steamboat vs. Funk match, the show was a disaster. In addition to the many valid points you made on what was wrong (army overkill, Ding Dongs, Norman, bad camera work, empty seats during the key matches) once again the fans were treated to the usual NWA screw job finishes (ref bumps, DQ in the main event, too much outside interference in the tag team tournament instead of clean jobs). Once again, the WWF delivers real finishes and the NWA comes off with amateur-hour finishes.

Mike Omansky
Wyckoff, New Jersey

I gave the Clash a solid thumbs up. The matches that mattered were all good and Funk vs. Steamboat was fantastic. Terry Funk has always been one of the very best workers ever and it still shows. The match was a classic example of great 70s style wrestling as were the Flair vs. Steamboat matches, which is a style that has to become more prevalent in the NWA. I feel the Flair vs. Funk matches will top the Flair-Steamboat matches we've already seen for the match of the year honors.

Tom Hankins
Sepulveda, California

My opinion of the NWA has done a complete turn around. The NWA under Crockett and Runnels was the most boring promotion in the world. The NWA now is great entertainment and something to look forward to, But considering my present enjoyment of the NWA, I was really let down. First, the stuff with the army was way overdone. I thought the point of this show was to get wrestling angles over, but instead it came off as a commercial for the army with some wrestling interspersed.

The wrestling itself, when it fit in between the flag waving, was disappointing by recent NWA standards.

Who came up with the Ding Dongs? I've not seen an act bomb so bad since Vincent Young. As for Norman, Mike Shaw may have been hot in Calgary, but he came off as an out of shape oaf. Teddy Long is being wasted big time on this gimmick. Long has potential to be one of the best managers in the business but he's saddled with Norman. I believe Norman is destined for a big push. That's good for Long for whatever he can get out of it but bad in every other sense.

I don't want to hear this We Wrestle stuff and then come up with gimmicks like the Ding Dongs and Norman. The angle with Muta and Gilbert was pointless. Talk about Muta being wasted. I guess the point was that Muta is "afraid of fire. Hardly a phobia. I don't know anyone who wouldn't run if fire was thrown at him.

The Funk-Steamboat bout was amazingly disappointing. Maybe I was expecting too much. The Luger turn should have been done earlier in the show because it detracted from the main event. All told I give the Clash a reluctant thumbs down. Reluctant because I'm enjoying the NWA these days.

Jack Thompson
Salt Lake City, Utah

NO HOLDS BARRED

Speaking as someone who writes about movies, I think it should be emphasized that No Holds Barred has done very well at the box office. It was conceivable that it could have done a $1.5 million opening weekend and quickly dropped from sight. But its theater total didn't drop after the first week, and the 40 percent drop in business during the second week is average for an action-oriented picture. I think average is the key word here. The significant thing about NHB's performance at the box office is that it did mainstream movie business. It was not received as a fringe thing. It got over as mainstream. This must have thrilled Vince, because when he wants to make another movie, it will be easier for him to get a company to put up some of the money.

Besides, the movie is really almost like a loss-leader. It seems that Titan is neither going to lose nor make much money on the project, but even if they Lost a little, the experience is well worth it. Because of the combination of NHB/Hogan publicity and the Lite-a-mania commercials, the public's perception that pro wrestling equals WWF has never been greater.

I found your comments on Vince's appearence on Letterman to be funny. Though Dick Ebersole may have pulled strings just to get him on, what makes you think the NBC brass as a whole cares about Vince McMahon? I think it may have taken string-pulling to get him on because Letterman supposedly has an anti-wrestler bias. Roddy Piper was supposed to be on around the time of "They Live, and he even did a pre-interview, but his appearence was nixed. Piper had heard that Letterman had some sort of a run-in with Bobby Heenan and that Heenan tried to intimidate him in some way and that's why he didn't want any wrestlers on his show.

Paul Sherman
Brookline, Massachusetts

I was watching TV last week and while switching channels, happened upon a wrestling movie called "Hammer Head" Jones. I'm surprised other readers haven't mentioned it because the plot was identical to "No Holds Barred" and it was made three years earlier. Hammer Head Jones is the champion of the ACPW. Rip is WWF champion. Each movie has a sleazy promoter, except in HH Jones the promoter is the spoiled son of a recently deceased promoter so he's supposed to be Vince McMahon Jr. and not Ted Turner. Each movie has a monster heel and the ultimate opponent in the climactic battle. HH Jones' foe is Fred Ottman (Big Steele Man) as Zarak, the Prince of Darkness; Tiny Lister of course is Zeus. Rusty Brooks and Joe Mascaro choreographed the wrestling scenes which weren't that bad. The film features two very bloody death matches. The plot of the evil promoters in both movies is trying to force the babyface to face their monster heel and the plots are too similar to be coincidence. McMahon and Hogan apparently lifted the whole story from this 1986 movie and did it even worse.

Ronald Crook
Belmont, North Carolina

I saw No Holds Barred several weeks ago with a wrestling buddy. We agree it was bad, but we weren't expecting Citizen Kane. However, it wasn't the worst movie we've seen in the last 10 years. Rhinestone, Bo Derek 's Tarzan, Bolero, Death Wish II and Siesta were worse. In fact, any Sly Stallone movie since Rocky was worse. It was certainly not as bad as you described it and definitely better than Verne Gagne's stinker "The Wrestler". Yeah, Hogan was bad, but the writing was much worse. We purposely went to a 9:40 p.m. show to avoid the kids, but we were still the only age 40+ people in the audience.

Give the Clash a big thumbs down. Lousy matches and poor production. The crowd gets a thumbs up. There was more debris thrown into the ring than at the Boston Gardens. What a great place to hold a card. A temperature of 120 degrees and a crowd which could appreciate two guys pounding on one another. It reminded me of the crowd in Stan Hansen's joint in Ho Holds Barred, but with shorter hair. The Luger pearl-harbor job on Steamboat was no surprise.

Ron Hickey
Falls Church, Virginia

VIDEO GAMES

Where did you get your information on the Acclaim WrestleMania video game? In the first place, if you understood the current marketing situation vis a vis Nintendo, you would realize that the success or failure of a Nintendo-approved cartridge is basically pre-determined. The size of a run is dictated by Nintendo, they also sell the publisher, in this case, Acclaim, the chips to produce them, which artificially controls the market. The game is okay, but will in all likelihood not appeal to wrestling fans looking for a realistic simulation of WWF wrestling. For example, there are bonus icons, like Honkey's guitar and Hogan's crucifix, which literally float across the ring periodically so the wrestler can recharge himself. If you can find one, wrestling fans looking for a good action simulation should check out Nintendo's older program, Pro Wrestling, or PCI's upcoming World Championship Wrestling which uses an NWA tie-in and yes, they really do "wrestle" in this game.

But what stunned me was your comment that Titan isn't getting a percentage royalty on this game. Are you serious? If this is true, it is totally at odds not only with the entire licensing structure in the electronic entertainment industry but with Titan's own policy in every other project it's ever been involved with, including the computer game Microleague WWF wrestling which I was involved in designing. ML/WWF is a strategy game, not an action arcade game like WrestleMania and they do not compete in the market place so this isn't an attempt to sabotage a competitor.

Bill Kunkel

Woodhaven, New York

NWA

There has been a lot of debate lately as to what effect the constant raiding of talent has on the NWA's struggle to gain ground. Many say that Ted Turner should spend money to keep potential jumpers and steal a wrestler or two himself.

I disagree. There are few legitimate drawing cards in wrestling. Even when the NWA lost a great wrestler like Barry Windham, it didn't make one bit of difference at the gate. I believe Turner should keep his current pay scale as he must control his labor costs to turn a profit. The wrestlers don't draw the crowds Or TV ratings. Marketing does. Certain characters are used. Does it matter at the gate whether it was the Rock & Roll Express, Fantastics, Rockers or Dynamic Dudes? Which fat man is better? Bundy? Bigelow? Blackwell? Does it matter? The only example I can think of that doesn't subscribe to this theory is that no military man had the impact that Sgt. Slaughter had during his hayday.

The NWA needs to concentrate on the marketing aspect and slowly build a greater following. I believe that some NWA wrestlers could be promoted to being as big as Hulk Hogan is and that is what is needed to boost gates and TV ratings.

Once Turner has increased his market share and profit, then he should increase his pay scale to help raid and deter guys from jumping. The NWA has a long road ahead. Unfortunately, they will have to tolerate losing talent for the time being. They are doing a good job of bringing in new talent themselves right now. That is their best counter.

David McCormack

Saranac Lake, New York

Dave Meltzer: There are valid points here and I've heard a promotional theory identical to what you've written espoused by many. I've got to both agree and disagree. Certainly marketing plays the major factor, but to eliminate value placed on the individual performer isn't valid. Stars are not so easily created as just giving them a gimmick because I've seen too many guys pushed like crazy who never got over. It reminds me of two conversations I had with promoters who had lost their biggest star to other promotions, one to the WWF and another to the NWA. In both conversations, both promoters said that they had created the star from nothing and could create another one just as easy. The problem was, both of those same promoters had tried to create literally dozens of stars over the years, but these two clicked far more than all the others. The replacements didn't get over as well as the originals and in fact, both losses were key factors in each promotion going out of business before that year was out. While all the Rock & Roll teams you mentioned had similar gimmicks, the truth is only the Rock & Roll Express ever clicked as a major national drawing card. The Fantastics, who were better workers, never clicked to anything close to that level. The Rockers got "over" with the audience in the AWA, but since the AWA was perceived as minor league in most eyes at the time, they never drew any big houses. How many wrestlers in the last 20 years have been told to bleach their hair, act arrogant, do a rich playboy gimmick and got huge pushes by the promotion? How many Ric Flair's have their been in the last 20 years? I do agree that once you get past the top small echelon in each promotion, that the middle and low card guys are a lot more interchangeable.

CAN'T LET THIS GO WITHOUT COMMENT

For those who didn't have the pleasure of seeing it this past weekend, Titan did a skit with Dusty Rhodes as a plumber where he puts his hand in what appears to be you-know-what and in fact his arm is covered in it when he pulls his arm out. Shock value to be sure and it does get people talking. This is very similar to the angle which got the old Southwest Championship Wrestling show booted right off the USA network (which Titan benefitted from as it was its first national cable exposure in late 1983). Knowing Titan, I think aside from the shock value, Vince did it to flex his muscles once again, i.e. he can show something that got another promotion booted right off its national spotlight and nobody will even threaten to take him off the air. And they won't.

JULY 17, 1989

July 4th is not the best day to go driving in the wilds of Canada. As most of you recall, last year at this time wrestling suffered the tragic deaths of wrestlers Adrian Adonis, The Canadian Wildman and Pat Kelly. History came just a few feet from repeating itself this year.

Stampede wrestling babyfaces Davey Boy Smith, Chris Benoit, Jason the Terrible and Sumu Hara along with driver Ross Hart were in the van headed for Prince George, British Columbia when they had a head-on collision in Jasper, Alberta on a mountain road. Smith was thrown through the windshield and needed more than 100 stitches to close various wounds, suffered a cracked vertebrae in his back and spinal injuries. The first reports we had were that he would be out of action for a period which could be as much as a year, although first reports of this type are usually exaggerated. Jason (Karl Moffat) broke his leg in two places and it will probably be months before he can return to wrestling. Benoit suffered a twisted knee while Hart and Hara were both shaken up as well. Everyone in the van was considering themselves fortunate, however, as the van came just a few feet from going off the mountain road and it would have been a 1,000 foot drop off the side of the mountain.

Because of the injuries to four key faces, Stampede was forced to cancel its shows this past weekend, some of 'Which had excellent advances for a territory of that size because of the Dynamite Kid vs. Davey Boy Smith matches which were just starting up around the horn.

Jake Roberts, who has been out of action for more than a month due to neck problems, has had his list of problems added to. He was convicted this past week of assault and battery in a case stemming from an incident this past December. The five women, one man jury deliberated for less than two hours before bringing in the unanimous verdict against Roberts, who is being held without bond in Florida pending his August 14th sentencing, and from all indications, that may just be the beginning of Roberts' problems. Roberts was being tried for an incident where he was bar hopping with a non-wrestling related individual and the two started arguing about the merits of women in Daytona Beach and Roberts, the driver of the car they were traveling in at 4 a.m., was accused of stopping the car and punching the other guy out.

Another major story is that the long fight over the Pennsylvania State Athletic Commission appears to be over as this past week Governor Robert P. Casey of Pennsylvania signed a bill which would take most of the regulating power in regards to professional wrestling away from the athletic commission. Titan Sports lobbied strongly for this bill as they are attempting to remove pro wrestling around the country from athletic commission jurisdiction. Ironically, the main complaint from those in wrestling is over the tax money wrestling generates for the commission and gets little or nothing in return. Ironically, the bill that passed only increases that unfair situation. While McMahon and Titan had been pushing for a reduction in the state tax from five percent to two percent, the bill kept the state tax on wrestling to five percent which would go primarily toward funding of the athletic commission. The state will also earmark $350,000 annually to the commission which the commission will use, along with the wrestling income, to fund regulations on boxing. They established stronger health requirements when it comes to boxing, but the committee that wrote the bill wrote into law that wrestling was a show, not a sport. Physicians will still be required at ringside at all wrestling matches and an ambulance will also be required at all matches. Promoters must post a $10,000 bond and promoters are licensed by the commission. However, wrestlers no longer need to be licensed and no medical examinations of wrestlers are required. One of the biggest arguments in the state is that the commission had the power to appoint referees, timekeepers and ring announcers and even though all "played by the script" so to speak, Titan wanted to use its own employees in all roles since they were more experienced in doing exactly what Titan wanted. There was a real problem earlier this year when Titan taped a Saturday Night Main Event in Hershey, PA and wanted to use Howard Finkel as the ring announcer and its own referees and the commission wanted to appoint its own personnel. Titan wound up getting things the way they wanted it but not before the commission threatened to shut down the show. The Pennsylvania commission has been one of the most visible in the country, in fact, the most visible with the exception of Oregon, going back to the 1986 Great American Bash in Philadelphia when commissioner J. J. Bins threatened to shut down the show midway after the blade Wahoo McDaniel used in juicing became lodged in his forehead and Bins demanded no more blood on the card and a major blow-up ensued between Bins and then booker Dusty Rhodes backstage. At that point in time, the NWA's Philadelphia cards were jokingly described as "blood circus" since that was the method the NWA took in its war with Titan, and Philadelphia was drawing sizable crowds for both promotions at the time. Blood basically ceased to exist, although there have been exceptions, in Pennsylvania from that point on. The most interesting part of the bill is that the license of a promoter can be suspended or revoked if wrestlers self-inflict wounds to draw blood. That's probably a first, actually making the practice of juicing into something illegal.

Monday night features the return of Roddy Piper to Titan television as he'll start his new weekly job as co-host of Prime Time Wrestling replacing Bobby Heenan. I expect that an angle will run on 7/10 to set all of this up. What will also wind up happening is that Heenan will be getting his own weekly 30 minute show on the USA network called "The Bobby Heenan show" so it isn't like Heenan is being phased out at all. It should be interesting to see the contents of that show.

The NWA shot a major angle this past Thursday night in Marietta, GA which is scheduled for airing this coming Friday night (June 14th) on the Power Hour on TBS. It was scheduled as a Road Warriors vs. Samoan Swat Team cage match, however the SST didn't show up as the story goes and Jimmy Garvin & Terry Gordy took the cage match instead. As the match progresses with the Warriors gaining the upper hand, Michael Hayes attacks ref Tommy Young, who was guarding the door outside the ring, and gets the keys to the cage from him and opens the door and the Samoans come in as well. The whole group then proceeds to handcuff Animal to the ring ropes and does a heavy juice number on Hawk, finishing up with a stretcher job. Because of the heavy juice, I don't know how much of the post-match will air on TBS but was told the whole thing was pretty gruesome. This is to set up the War Games match on the 7/23 PPV show.

Over the past week, or really past weeks, I think a lot of questions have been answered as to what kind of commitment TBS has to pro wrestling. The showing of wrestling highlights between games of Braves doubleheaders was a move that shows that at this point, wrestling has become a major part of the TBS operation. Since then, we've seen wrestler Michael Hayes doing a commercial for Night Tracks (the Friday night rock video show on TBS); seen 15 minute special segments taped and aired at various times before and after baseball games giving updates on the NWA scene and hyping the PPV show; we've seen wrestling grouped in with the other legitimate sports such as baseball and track in the TBS Sports Saturday line-up on promos; and throughout this month, NWA babyfaces Ric Flair, Road Warriors, Sting and Rick Steiner will be taping national ads for St. Louis-based Kangaroo Athletic Wear. Most of the problems we've discussed in these pages remain and the NWA is a Long way from being where it needs to be for Long-term survival however these actions show that TBS doesn't appear to be in any hurry to call it quits at anytime soon as people have speculated. Besides, anyone who has followed the history of TBS, CNN and other Turner ventures has seen that things never looked good in the beginning but they have survived and become institutions. Of course, we could bring up the Atlanta Braves.

The NWA has announced the complete line-up for the PPV on its television shows throughout the weekend, so that problem has already been alleviated. Titan's SummerSlam PPV line-up looks to be taking shape as well. The top match of Hulk Hogan & Brutus Beefcake vs. Zeus & Randy Savage has been built up too although the official announcement of the match may not take place until after the Saturday Night Main Event from Worcester, MA (taped July 18th for a July 29th air date) which should include the angle that leads up to the match. We had incorrectly reported a six-man tag of Twin Towers (Big Bossman & Akeem) & Andre the Giant (called the Eiffel Tower in the build-up for the match) against Demolition & Hillbilly Jim, but actually Demolition's partner is going to be Jim Duggan. I've heard three other matches bandied about, one of which was pretty well announced at the taping in Rochester, NY with Tully Blanchard & Arn Anderson vs. Hart Foundation, plus probable matches of Dusty Rhodes vs. Honkeytonk Man and Ultimate Warrior vs. Rick Rude for the IC title. Tickets are scaled for a $378,000 house.

Entertainment Tonight will be doing a feature on the wrestling war, Ted Turner vs. Vince McMahon scheduled for a July 17th air date. It'll be interesting to see how they put the feature together since Titan has steadfastly refused to cooperate with any story that would make it seem like any other organizations exist in pro wrestling.

Raymond Schwartz, one of the two men accused in the murder of independent wrestler Jim Leon, will be going to trial on August 14th. Schwartz refused a deal in which he would plead guilty and the charge would be dropped to second degree murder. Schwartz and another gunman, Samuel Schellor, were accused of murdering Leon at his Baltimore home several months back. Scheller has since committed suicide

"No Holds Barred" is out of the theaters after basically a five-week national run in which the McMahon-produced film grossed just under $15 million. In its last week, which ended Thursday, business was non-existent and the number of theaters still carrying the movie was cut way down from the 1,000+ of the previous four weeks. Overall, Titan should be pleased that the movie did acceptable mainstream business and its gross is considered good for a low-budget movie. I'm not sure they should be as pleased with the content of the movie itself because its reviews, with only a few exceptions, were, well..scathing would be too kind.

OREGON

Top Gun (David Sierra) & Scotty The Body captured the Northwest tag team titles on 7/8 in Portland from The Southern Rockers (Steve Doll & Scott Peterson). Gun & Body are managed by Jonathan Boyd who brings a snake to ringside and every babyface is acting afraid of the snake. Top Gun turned heel on the 7/1 card during a match with

Boyd & Scotty against the Rockers interfered on behalf of the heels after a ref bump and Scotty gave Top Gun money on television after his interference. Stipulations for the 7/1 match were that whichever team won would get Ginger, who had been Scotty's valet. However, Ginger stayed with the Rockers anyway and Boyd chases her around the ring during their matches with the snake.

Nord the Barbarian returned on 7/8 and said he's back for good. During a match with The Grappler vs. Rex King, Grappler kept pounding on King and refused to pin him over and over again. Finally Don Owen came to ringside and got mad and yelled over the house mic for Grappler to quit doing this. Billy Jack Haynes then ran out and Grappler sprayed him in the face with the Kabuki mist. Nord than came out and Nord & Grappler were cleaning house on everyone when one of the security guys brought out Carl Styles, who had a patch over his good eye and is blind in the other eye (they are trying to get over that Styles is now blind in both eyes because of the angle some weeks back when Grappler spit the Kabuki mist into his good eye) and the security guy brought Styles to the ring and put his hand on Grappler's ankle and then Styles went wild because he could "feel" Grappler. Styles has gotten much bigger and more muscular since he left and looks like a monster now. They are building up to a double chain match with Grappler & Nord against Haynes & Styles which probably takes place on 7/15. This is similar to an angle done, I believe in 1979 in the old Mid South promotion when Michael Hayes "blinded" Junkyard Dog and they drew a then-record crowd into the Superdome of something like 25,000 to 35,000 fans for the "blind" JYD against Hayes in a chain match, and Len Denton was working Mid South at the time.

Al Madril finally faced Beetlejuice (Art Barr) in the match where if Madril lost, he'd have to have his face painted like Beetlejuice and dance with all the kids. If Beetlejuice lost, then Madril could ride him around the ring like a burro. Madril won the match pulling tights and put a sombrero on Beetlejuice and started riding him around. However, ref Sandy Barr was told that Madril used the tights and restarted the match and this time, Beetlejuice won with the sleeper and while Madril was out, they put the make-up on him and he got up and saw himself in the make-up and freaked.

They've got a tournament upcoming for both the Northwest heavyweight and TV titles, both of which were held by Styles before the "blinding" incident.

Roddy Piper has been in Portland for the cards every week except for 7/1 (when he was working for Titan in Canada), but never appears on television anymore, nor is his name ever mentioned on television, which I presume is part of his deal with Titan.

This last thing blew me away. On the 7 / 8 show, Apache Bull Ramos came out and did a babyface interview and was talking specifically about Boyd. Ramos, who was well known for being especially overweight during his wrestling days, was said to have not looked quite as overweight as in those days. Ramos was a major star, and in fact, the top heel in these parts during the early 1970s but his name hasn't been mentioned in regards to wrestling in many years.

CWA

The 7/3 Memphis show drew around 5,000 fans with all tickets $3 for the Jerry Lawler vs. Kerry Von Erich match for the USWA title. Ronnie Gossett (who is really funny to watch) was wheeled out at ringside since he's faked a heart attack the two previous weeks. Kerry told him that he could stay in his corner but not to interfere in the match. After the obligatory Jerry Calhoun ref bump, Gossett pulled out a chain and hit Lawler while Kerry was trying to revive Lawler so Kerry "didn't see it". Kerry then pinned Lawler to win the title, but not so fast. The fans started "telling" Kerry what happened and a few of the heels ran in to tell Kerry that Gossett hadn't interfered and one thing led to another and the heel s attacked Lawler and Kerry came to Lawler's rescue and helped run them off, and somehow out of all of this the match was ruled a no contest. In the other top matches on the card, the CWA tag team titles were held up in the Wildside (Chris Champion & Mark Starr) vs. Action Jackson & Billy Travis match when Calhoun was bumped and Frank Morrell ran in and there were simultaneous pins and each ref counted a member of the other team down plus Freddy (Tommy Gilbert) beat Master of Pain in a mask vs. getting tarred and feathered by the fans match but Pain tarred and feathered himself rather than let the fans do it. Dutch Mantell interfered causing MOP to lose and it appears that is the beginning of MOP turning as he had words to say about Mantells interference.

They had a Lawler vs. Gossett boxing match on TV on 7/8 which ended when MOP interfered for the DQ on Gossett. Gossett was blowing up something fierce, which if you 've seen him, wouldn't surprise you.

The 7/10 line-up in Memphis has Frankie Lancaster & Freddy vs. Iceman King Parsons & Brickhouse Brown managed by Harold Harris, The D. I. & Doug Gilbert vs. Ricky Morton & Bill Dundee, Wildside vs. Travis Jackson in a tag title match and if either member of Wildside loses they get their heads shaved while if either member of the Travis-Jackson team loses, they have to leave town (Jackson is Leaving), Jeff Jarrett & Dustin Rhodes vs. Black Bart & Dirty White Boy and the main event is Lawler & Bam Bam Bigelow vs. Mantell & MOP and if the faces lose then lawler gets tarred and feathered by Gossett but if the heels lose then Gossett gets tarred and feathered by the fans.

Spike Huber is gone already as is Chili B. cool.

7/9 in Nashville drew 700 as Brickhouse Brown double count out with Doug Gilbert in a battle of heels * ¼, Mantell pinned Cat Garrett ¾ *, Dundee beat D. I. by DQ when Gilbert interfered * ½, Rhodes pinned White Boy **, Freddy beat MOP via DQ in a mask vs. tar and feather match when Mantell interfered *, Wildside beat Jackson & Travis to "win" the tag titles (this switch will also take place in Memphis, Louisville, etc. this week) when the heels gave Jackson a double DDT in 4:00 of wild action ** ½, Bart beat Jarrett via DQ when Jarrett was caught using the baseball bat after Bart had used the branding iron first ** ½ and Lawler beat Parsons via DQ when Harris and Brown ran in and Lawler was triple-teamed, DUD.

7/10 in Jonesboro, AK drew 500 as White Boy pinned Jackson * ½, Dundee pinned Starr * ¾, Morton beat Bart via DQ when Bart used the branding iron **, Rhodes pinned Champion * ¾ (Champion is hurting pretty badly of late, either Leg or hip problems), Mantell pinned Travis *, Parsons pinned Jarrett ** ½, Brown pinned Lawler when Harris tripped Lawler ** ½, Wildside beat Jackson & Travis ** ¼, Blackbirds (Parsons & Brown) beat Morton & Dundee when Harris hit Morton with his ring (his gimmick) ** ½ and Lawler & Jarrett & Freddy beat Mantell & MOP & Gossett via DQ when the Blackbirds jumped in and Morton & Dundee followed * (all for the post-match antics, match was a DUD). Freddy gets the best babyface reaction of anyone on the circuit, including Lawler.

WORLD CLASS

The 7/7 card in Dallas drew around 1,000 as Corporal Braddock returned and pinned Nathan "Frogman" LeBlanc in the opener. I've been waiting for what happened next to happen somewhere. Scandor Akbar then came out as Braddock was doing an interview and asked him how much he made in the marines and Braddock said $363 a week. Akbar then told Braddock he'd give him $1,000 just to blow on the night if he turned and Braddock immediately turned. Anyway, to show his Loyalty to Akbar, Braddock held up his American flag and Akbar pulled out his cigar lighter and was about to burn the flag but of course Eric Embry came out to break that up. Then Chris Adams pinned The Masked Professional, Jimmy Jack Funk went to a no contest with Kevin Von Erich when Gary Young and Cactus Jack Manson interfered and attacked both men, Jeff Jarrett & Matt Borne kept the World Class tag team titles beating Young & Manson, Kerry Von Erich beat Al Perez via DQ when Perez brought a few chairs into the ring and Kevin ran out (you love the explanation for all this on television the next day) and finally Embry beat P. Y. Chu Hi (Phil Hickerson) but after the match Chu Hi and Tojo Yamamoto attacked Embry and Yamamoto held his Leg over the ropes and Chu Hi jumped on his leg several times and Embry did a stretcher job. Embry didn't appear at the TV tapings the next morning and it was announced that he had undergone arthroscopic surgery on his knee and he's not announced for next week's show either.

Funk is still doing face interviews and claiming that he isn't turning and he still wants the fans behind him and that he just has a problem with one wrestler, Kevin Von Erich, who has a super ego.

They had said they were going to announce this week the results of the bidding war for the World Class stock between Max Andrews and the USWA and Akbar but they said the bidding is still going on. The explanation for all this is that in the contract of the match in which Embry wrestled Tojo that the winner would get the rights to buy the stock at fair market value (the hype simply said beforehand that the winner would get the stock and in fact on the TV plot Embry acted as president of the company for one week and turned over control to Andrews before they came up with this new stipulation) and Yamamoto has raised fair market value. It'll most likely wind up coming down to another match again, anyway.

Chu Hi beat Embry for the Texas title on 6/30 in Wichita Falls, TX.

Braddock attacked Percy Pringle during a TV interview.

This group only plugged three spot shows over the next two weeks and is now trying to do shows at auto dealerships ala Blackwell's group in which fans could get in free and the dealership would underwrite the costs for publicity purposes.

Chris Adams completely lost control at the Saturday taping when one fan started yelling "boring" during his interview. Adams on TV threatened to beat up the fan and stormed off.

7/14 in Dallas has Perez vs. Mil Mascaras, Jarrett & Borne defending their tag titles against Chu Hi & Braddock, Kerry vs. Bam Bam Bigelow, Kevin vs. JJ Funk in a bullrope match and the Simpson brothers & Adams vs. Young & Manson & Akbar.

Saving this week's funniest interview for Last. Kerry was being interviewed about why Kevin interfered in his match the previous night with Perez and he said it was because Kevin saw that Perez was setting Kerry up for a move, which I believe he called the atomic brainbuster. They claimed this was a lethal hold that has been banned since 1952 when a wrestler named Stuttgart used it to kill someone. I think these guys have gotten so wrapped up into lying that they couldn't tell the truth if their lives depended on it.

ALL JAPAN

The latest tour opened on 7/1 in Omaya Before 4,100 fans as Stan Hansen & Genichiro Tenryu downed Jumbo Tsuruta & Isao Takagi in 16:30 when Hansen lariated Takagi, Kabuki & Yoshiaki Yatsu downed Tom Zenk & Jim Brunzell when Yatsu made Brunzell submit to the prison deathlock (similar to the old Indian death Lock used in the 60s), The Fantastics made their Japan debut beating Isamu Teranishi & Mighty Inoue, Joe Malenko captured the PWF

World jr. title pinning Mitsuo Momota in 14:10 (which sets up the match of Joe Malenko vs. Dean Malenko for the title on the 7/11 card), Kenta Kobashi won a Battle Royal, Toshiaki Kawada pinned Kobashi in 11:38 and Samson Fuyuki pinned Shun ji Takano in 13:46 in the Asunaro tournament (tournament with Kawada, Fuyuki , Kobashi, Takano, Akira Taue and Isao Takagi in which the winner gets a shot at Tenryu s "Triple Crown" title - PWF International and United National belts), Giant Baba & Rusher Kimura & Taue beat Haruka Eigen & Motoshi Okuma & Masa Fuchi, Big John Tenta & Shinichi Nakano beat The Terminator (Marc Laurinidas) & The Destroyer (Dick Beyer, now 58 years old), Dean Malenko pinned Yoshinari Ogawa and prelims. Nippon Television network, which broadcasts and owns All Japan, has declared July to be Bruiser Brody month and is airing 90 minutes of Brody's best matches in the early a.m. hours every Monday night during July.

UWF

The UWF has announced the Line-up for the 8/13 card at the 17,000 seat Yokohama Arena as Akira Maeda vs. Yoshiaki Fujiwara, Masaharu Funaki vs. Nobuhiko Takada, Kazuo Yamazaki vs. Yoji Anjo, Tetsuo Nakano vs. Minoru Suzuki and Shigeo Miyato vs. Tamura. I'm not sure if this is a guaranteed sellout, but it is guaranteed that this will do a huge gate with Takada vs. Funaki and Maeda vs. Fujiwara as " dream matches".

UWF will run a shot on the small town of Nagano on 9/7.

At the end of the year, the UWF will come up with a ranking system similar to the NWA's top ten but more Legit and all the matches on the cards will be for the ranking positions.

NEW JAPAN

This group got some good news as its TV show that aired on 6/24 (taped 6/22 with Tatsumi Fujinami vs. Big Van Vader on top) drew an 8.6 rating. The Fujinami-Vader match ended with Fujinami getting the win but Vader was beating on Fujinami after the match when Jushin Liger did a run-in and chased Vader away and they are actually trying to do a small feud between the two of them in order to get Liger (Keiichi Yamada) over as a fearless superhero as Liger is about 5-foot-4 and just under 200 pounds and Vader is about 6-4 and at least 330 or more pounds. The rating was particularly good news since it was achieved without either Antonio Inoki or the Soviets on the TV show. However, the house show crowds have still been pretty small this month without Inoki or the Soviets. 6/30 in Rumoi drew 1,480 as Fujinami & Liger & Shiro Koshinaka downed Vader & Black Tiger (Mark Rocco) & Biff Wellington in the main event when Liger pinned Wellington, Kengo Kimura pinned Samoan Kokina, Riki Cho shu & Masa Saito beat Brad Rheingans & Mike Kirchner (Corporal Kirchner),

Super Strong Machine pinned Shinji Sasazaki, George Takano pinned Tatsutoshi Goto, Takayuki Iizuka beat Black Cat, Kuniaki Kobayashi beat Osamu Matsuda and Naoki Sano pinned Akira Nogami.

7/1 in Hakodate drew 2,290 as Choshu & Saito beat Vader & Kokina, Fujinami beat Kirchner, Liger pinned Nogami, Kimura pinned Rheingans, Machine pinned Goto, Takano pinned Sasazaki, Koshinaka & Iizuka beat Black Tiger & Wellington, Tamal Zarasov pinned Kobayashi and Sano pinned Matsuda.

New Japan is trying to put together a major spectacular for New Years' Eve. There is talk that the card will be a combination boxing and wrestling card and will be held in two cities and closed-circuited back-and-forth (similar to the way the NWA ran Starrcade in 1985 and 1986 and the way WWF did the second WrestleMania) with the sites being Tokyo and Moscow, USSR which would be the first-ever international closed-circuit spectacular in pro wrestling history of this type. As you can imagine, there are so many headaches and roadblocks in putting something of this magnitude together so I'd bet the odds are less than 50/50 of it coming off in this form.

JAPANESE WOMEN

With the retirement of Chigusa Nagayo, the WWWA World tag team championship was returned to the commission as Chigusa & Lioness Asuka were the last champions. The Marine Wolves (Akira Hokkuto & Shizuka Minami) won the vacated titles on 6/18 in Tokyo beating heels Kumiko Iwamoto & Nobuko Kimura in a two of three fall match. Bull Nakano captured the All-Pacific title, which Nagayo also held, on the same card beating Mitsuko Nishiwaki. 7/1 in Furano drew 1,830 as Nakano & Iwamoto won two of three falls from Minami & Madusa Maceli and Hokkuto went to a 30 minute draw with Nishiwaki.

6/25 in Easashi saw Nakano & Iwamoto & Erica Shishedo beat the Marine Wolves & Maceli (who is working as a babyface and teaming with the babyface Japanese women unlike most foreigners who team with Nakano's group) plus Nishiwaki beat Kimura and Noriyo Tateno & Yumi Ogura beat Reuben Amada & Yumiko Hotta.

6/26 saw Maceli & Hokutto beat Kimura & Iwamoto, Tateno beat Ogura and Nakano & Shishido beat The Fire Jets (Nishiwaki & Hotta).

6/27 in Hakuro saw Nakano & Kimura & Iwamoto (who are now the top three heels in the group) beat Maceli & Fire Jets and Minami go to a double count out with Tateno. On the JWP side, Miss A captured the UWA International title from Devil Masami on 6/26 in Sapporo while Yu Yamazaki kept the jr. title beating Rumi Kazama via count out on the same card. Heidi lee Morgan from the U. S. is on tour with JWP.

NOTES FROM HERE AND THERE

The cards scheduled for this past weekend for Stampede wrestling which had to be canceled all had advances several days in of more than $10,000.

Stampede has the Calgary Corrall (8,000 seats) booked on 7/21 which was originally going to be the first meeting in Calgary of Dynamite Kid vs. Davey Boy Smith but that one fell through. I would guess they will go with Owen Hart vs. Dynamite as the main event as Hart is tentatively scheduled to start back up here on that date. Hart starts with New Japan on August 20th and will feud with Jushin Liger during that tour. With the injuries in the auto accident to Smith and Jason (out several months) and to Benoit (out maybe a few weeks) and Bruce Hart getting the broken jaw in a backstage brawl, this territory is almost totally devoid of babyfaces.

The Bruce Hart injury actually took place in Yellow Knife in the Northwest territories and not Edmonton as I'd reported. The report is that Bruce was talking with Davey Boy Smith, who had arrived at 10:45 p.m. for a 7:30 p.m. show along with Dynamite Kid and Dynamite punched Bruce a good shot.

Don Muraco beat Chavo Guerrero for the California Championship Wrestling ACCW title on 6/30 in Del Mar, CA before 500 fans.

Results from the Fathers Day card in San Juan on 6/21 which drew 8,000 fans and $45,000 were Rufus Jones pinning Jonathan Holiday, White Angel (Curtis Thompson) beat Kareem Muhammad (Ray Candy) via DQ, Kerry Von Erich went to a 30 minute draw with Rip Rogers, Invader #1 (Jose Gonzales) beat Steve Strong (DiSalvo) via count out, Jimmy Valiant pinned Chicky Starr, Super Medico beat Eric Embry via forfeit when Embry no-showed the card, The Batten Twins beat Hurricane Castillo Jr. & Miguelito Perez in a hair vs. hair match and TNT pinned Abbuda Dein.

Harley Race's "Homecoming" card in Kansas City on 7/6 drew 580 fans, however Race wasn't able to wrestle because his stomach incision from the operation last year popped open and he needed surgery after an injury suffered while working in the Maritime Provinces of Canada. Race appeared at the card and apologized for not being able to work. The main event was scheduled as Race vs. Col. DeBeers and Race told the fans that DeBeers was really Ed Wiskoski from St. Joseph and DeBeers freaked out and said he wasn't. Anyway, results saw Curtis Hughes & J.J. Cody beat Korchenko & Russian Brute (George Petrosky), Bobby Jaggers pinned Randy Rhodes (a copy of Dusty), The Black Harts (motorcycle tag team) beat T. C. Carter & Steve Sawyer, Akio Sato pinned Steve Ray, Butch Masters (billed as 7-2, 300) pinned DeBeers when Race hit DeBeers with a chair and Mike George went to a double DQ with Bob Orton.

Bruno Sammartino will be appearing on Ron Barr's Sports Byline USA show on July 19th which is broadcast on KSFO (560 AM) here in San Francisco area.

Dick Whoerle promoted shows on 7/7 in Woodbury, NJ and 7/8 in Wildwood drawing 130 and 350 respectively for main events of Ken Patera vs. Nikolai Volkoff.

FCW drew 103 on 7/9 in Orlando as Ron Slinker pinned Coconut Kid ½*, Nick Busick beat Rudy Diamond - *, Ho Chi Winh beat Mike Awesome DUD, Steve Keirn pinned Kendall Windham to win the Florida title ** and Nasty Boys beat The Playboys (Jimmy Backlund & Brett Sawyer) to keep the Florida tag team titles *.

Jerry Gray is promoting shows on a weekly basis in Apopka, FL billing wrestlers such as "Hammer Valentine, "One Man Gang" and "Macho Savage". Former pro boxing champ Leon Spinks' match with former amateur champ Great Wojo on 6/25 in Toledo drew 500 fans. Jerry Graham Jr. was in Wojo's corner, but Wojo still got a decent amount of crowd support since he's originally from Toledo and Spinks was mainly cheered as well. In the fourth round, Graham was decked by Spinks' wife, who used a purse, but the finish saw Graham hold Spinks by the leg outside the ring for the count out which pretty well upset everyone in the audience with the cheap finish. Others who worked the WWA show included Chris Carter, The Sensationals (Al Snow & Mickey Doyle), Kansas Outlaws (Sam Cody & Roger Ruffin), Tarras Bulba (known better in Canada as Johnny K-9), Bulldog Don Kent, El Brassero (Jose Martinez) and Muhammad Saad.

Nelson Royal's ACW drew 165 fans on 7/3 in Silver Valley, NC as Ken Shamrock beat Sioni, David Isley beat Len Waggoner, The Ring Lords beat Tommy Angel & Tommy Seabolt, Sam Houston won the ACW title from Colt Steele who was awarded the title that night when champion Don Kernodle didn't show up for the title defense and the main event saw Robert Gibson & Houston & Royal beat Basher of the Mod Squad, L.A. Stephens & The Ninja (John Savage).

Paul Diamond and Tracy Smothers were among those who worked an Ontario tour during the first week of July. The two worked as the tag team Bad Company, but the tour turned into a fiasco when on the Last night the police were called when the promoter allegedy disappeared with the money.

CWF running a show on 7/15 in Morristown, TN with a 12 man blindfold Battle Royal, Tom Prichard vs. Danny Davis, Wendell Cooley vs. Jiminy Golden, Adrian Street vs. The Beauty Terrence Garvin, Johnny & Davey Rich vs. Stomper Don Harris & RPM Mike Davis, Jackie Fulton vs. Kevin Dillinger and Jerry Stubbs vs. Todd Morton.

Jerry Blackwell (who was making progress from his bout with pneumonia at last report) and Nelson Royal are combining for a show on 7/15 in Cookeville, TN with Tommy Rich vs. Joel Deaton, Nelson Royal vs. Ninja Warrior (John Savage), Steve Lawler & Dino Minelli vs. The

Bullet & Brad Armstrong , Mr. Wrestling II vs. a mystery man, Jimmy Powell vs. The Invader, David Isley vs. L.A. Stephens and the Ringlords vs. Tommy Angel & Mitch Snow.

AWA held TV tapings on 7/8 in Rochester, MN drawing 1,500 (kids were free so paid was a lot less) as Larry Zbyszko beat Sgt. Slaughter via DQ in the main event. Finish saw Slaughter accidentally clothesline ref Gary "Juice" DeRusha and ref Tom Burton ran in and Slaughter wound up pinning Zbyszko, but after the match AWA president Joe "Stanley Blackburn" Blanchard overruled the decision and DQ'd Slaughter because he struck the official, plus Greg Gagne kept the TV title going to a double disqualification with Sheik Adnan El-Kaissey, The Destruction Crew (Mike Enos & Wayne Bloom managed by Johnny Valiant) beat Scott Norton in a handicap match and Derrick Dukes & Tommy Jammer beat The Tokyo Bullets.

Eric Embry is said to be out for around one month due to the gimmick with P. Y. Chu Hi and TOjo Yamamoto on 7/7 in Dallas.

How's this for a unique finish? In the tag team title change in Portland on Saturday night where Top Gun & Scotty the Body beat Steve Doll & Scott Peterson, the finish saw Peterson, who they are portraying as being deathly afraid of John Boyd's snake, back away from the snake and while backing away, hit the back of his head on the ringpost and was KO'd and was then thrown into the ring and pinned.

WWF

Minimal news from here since Titan didn't run any cards in the United States from 6/29 through 7/6. They ran a full crew in Canada over the July 4th weekend, which naturally isn't a holiday weekend in our neighbors to the North, and then didn't run any shows this past Wednesday. They still had a huge weekend with Ultimate Warrior vs. Rick Rude packing them in Denver and Los Angeles. Roddy Piper worked the previous weekend against Randy Savage in a few Canadian towns which bombed major drawing either 900 or 2,000 fans in Calgary depending upon who you believe and 4,500 in Montreal with Piper winning both matches via pinfall. It just shows that in this day and age with all the wrestling on television that someone, no matter how famous, if they aren't on television and if there isn't an issue between the combatants can't draw even if on paper Piper vs. Savage sounds like a match that would draw. WWF is planning another USA network special this fall from Europe, as they did last November with a taped show from France.

Titan will be placing WWF arcade video games in the lobby at the matches 7/10 at the Cow Palace in San Francisco so the kids can play the games rather than have to actually watch the wrestling matches.

Report's around the country consistently are that the Rockers vs. Rougeaus matches are the best matches running in this circuit right now. 6/17 at the Spectrum in Philadelphia drew 5,016 and $62 944 as Hillbilly Jim beat Andre the Giant via DQ and Jim Duggan beat Haku in the double main event.

Warrior vs. Rude headlines Philadelphia on 7/15 and the advance is weak for that.

Titan did make a mistake of sorts in this market as they've got a 7/10 SF card with Warrior vs. Rude and the advance was poor (all things being relative as any other promotion would be turning cartwheels for 3,000 tickets being sold in advance for a card) because they 've already announced an 8/8 Oakland card (same market) with Hogan vs. Savage with Zeus in the corner which has also sold 3,000 tickets. A lot of people are skipping SF that are regulars and instead going to the TV taping in Oakland which should draw another full house.

Madison Square Garden is scheduled to re-open on September 15th so the first wrestling event there of the fall won't be until after that date.

Elizabeth and Vince McMahon will be hosting Wrestling Spotlight when all the new announcing changes are completed.

7/9 in Denver drew 7,500 and $85,000 as Dino Bravo pinned Mark Young, Rick Martel pinned Tito Santana, Rougeaus beat Rockers (excellent match), Badnews Brown pinned Greg Valentine (Brown was babyface here), Dusty Rhodes pinned Ted DiBiase, Red Rooster (Terry Taylor) pinned Brooklyn Brawler (Steve Lombardi) and Ultimate Warrior beat Rick Rude via count out. The same basic crew worked 7/6 in Portland drawing 4,700 and $56,000; 7/7 in San Diego drew $63,000 and 7/8 in Los Angeles drew a phenomenal 12,500 and $147,000.

Mark Young (Vince Young in NWA) did the break-dancing on the first night of the tour in Portland to no reaction whatsoever and dropped the gig the rest of the way.

Hulk Hogan vs. Randy Savage drew a sellout on 7/6 in Spokane, WA with a $98,000 house.

6/24 at the Palace in Auburn Hills, MI drew 15,000 as Hogan pinned Savage, Demolition beat Twin Towers via DQ, Jimmy Snuka pinned Honkeytonk Man, Rhodes pinned DiBiase, Barbarian double count out with Jim Neidhart, Badnews Brown pinned Paul Roma and Mr. Perfect (Curt Hennig) pinned Koko Ware.

Both All-American and prime Time Wrestling did 2.7 ratings over the Holiday weekend.

NWA

The Road Warriors did another job for the SST in Charleston, SC over the holiday weekend.

The new state-of-the-art post production video facility is scheduled to open around November.

Terry Funk has been back in action this past week working

with Sting. He only takes one bump during the match but the matches are still good.

Butch Reed appears to be history.

The NWA canceled the 7/9 Bash at Brown University in Providence, RI due to no advance.

7/8 in Boston drew about 4,800 as Scott Hall pinned Bill Irwin, Dynamic Dudes beat New Zealand Militia, Mike Rotunda pinned Dick Murdoch, Norman pinned Steve Casey, Skyscrapers (Sid Vicious & Dan Spivey) beat Johnny & Davey Rich, Rick Steiner pinned Kevin Sullivan in a street fight that turned into a great brawl, Freebirds beat Steve Williams & Midnight Express (great), Great Muta beat Eddie Gilbert via count out in Dragon Shi match, Rick Steiner won the Battle Royal throwing out Rotunda to win; Sting beat Funk via DQ when Norman interfered, Road Warriors pinned SST and Lex Luger pinned Ricky Steamboat. Said to be a heated and good card from top to bottom.

6/2 in Salisbury, MD saw Brian Pillman pin Jack Victory, Hall pin Rip Morgan, Steiner brothers beat Ron Simmons & Al Greene, Hayes & Garvin beat Dynamic Dudes, Sting won Battle Royal and was attacked by Funk, Muta beat Gilbert via COR. Williams & Road Warriors double count out Gordy & SST and Luger pinned Steamboat.

Officially, the Bash in Philadelphia drew 4,107 paid and $54,070.

TV ratings over the July 4th weekend were encouraging: World Championship Wrestling on Saturday did a 2.2 rating and 6.1 share (best share for the Saturday show since December - rating, despite being over the Holiday weekend, was up from the past several weeks), NWA Main Event headlined by Murdoch & Ranger Ross vs. Militia drew a 2.4, the between games NWA Update show on Friday night drew a 2.1 rating which ironically was a better rating than either baseball game drew, and the Power Hour drew 1.7 starting at 11 p.m. Eastern time.

Pet Peeves for the week: 1) Gordon Solie's segment on the Friday night show. I don't care that they plugged the Warrior vs. Rude feud for Titan, but those Japanese segments either have to go or at least get the stuff right. Last weekend they talked about "Lord Alfred Blears" trying to set up a UWF promotion in Hawaii. Well, first off, there is no truth to that since Blears (and its Lord James Blears not Alfred Blears anyway) works for Giant Baba and if anyone, Solie should know Blears' name since Blears has been around wrestling even longer than Solie has; 2) This past week they talked about Inoki retiring because of shoulder surgery and he may run for office. Well, he announced his candidacy several weeks ago, and more so, the shoulder surgery he underwent was more than one year ago. 3) On Worldwide Wrestling they kept plugging that after the Ranger Ross vs. Luger match they would air a Ric Flair workout video and have an interview with Rick Steamboat. Well, the show ended, and even though both were plugged at least three times, neither

was on the show. By the way, Luger's mannerisms as a heel, particularly in the match with Ross, were just incredible. It's funny that half the crowd still cheers him and I don't think that will ever really change but that sneer and arrogance is awesome.

Two pop out of your chair moves for the weekend: 1) Scott Steiner's blockbuster suplex on the Bounty Hunter on Friday, even though their actual match was horrible, the finishing move was great; 2) The finishing move Brian pillman put on Bill Irwin in the 6-man tag (Pillman & Dudes vs. Militia & Irwin). Actually, the move itself was missed but pillman jumped from the apron onto the top rope in the middle of the ring, then springboarded over Irwin into a sunset flip, but either Pillman didn't take Irwin over right or Irwin's timing in going over wasn't right because the sunset flip part of the move was mistimed.

THE READERS' PAGES

FICTION VS. FACT

I've been wanting to write about the fictional marriage of Randy Savage and Elizabeth. While many people feel that their break-up is absurd because so many know the truth, I'm sure it is all part of Titan's strategy to ensure total control of all publicity rights. As you know, a producer owns all publicity rights in a fictional character. For example, Harrison Ford has no rights to the character of Indiana Jones. On the other hand, sports figures have all rights to themselves, unless they give them away to the player's union. So, by having a fictional break-up, if Savage and Elizabeth ever left the WWF, Titan could turn the screws by claiming ownership in these fictional characters.

This is also important in their battles to control the magazine market. As you know, Titan won a case against one of the magazines which included posters. The court rules that First Amendment rights to report news don't extend to posters, which are part of publicity rights owned by Titan. I can see a point in the future where Titan tries to claim that magazines don't even have the right to report news on fictional characters as it would be copyright infringement, similar to someone printing a movie script. I'm sure this is why every major addition to Titan has been brought in with a character, such as Widow Maker, Red Rooster, etc .

Jeff Hoster
Chicago, Illinois

SHAWN MICHAELS

Shawn Michaels is great. He's probably the best worker in the WWF and is developing a real following. I hope Vince realizes this before this talented wrestler decides to go elsewhere. On the opposite not Andre the Giant changed the atmosphere to one of a circus. It is really very sad. I was relieved to watch him lay down after his head-butt, chop and choke routine. I must also admit I was more impressed with Dusty Rhodes than I thought I would be. He did have Ted DiBiase working with him and Ted could probably make the Chinese Government look good, but Dusty was nimble and got a good pop from the crowd.

Peter Beutel
Bronxville, New York

NWA

After Lex Luger's incredible interview where he interrupts the VTR and the Clash of the Champions angle, it is obvious that he is the one the NWA needs to build around. You have to think McMahon would kill to get him right now.

Whenever the sad day comes when Ric Flair retires, Ted Turner should have Luger standing in the wings. The NWA should be prepared to spend big bucks to get his face all over the media. Can you imagine a guy of Hogan's stature with the backing of a huge corporation who can actually wrestle? If anyone could sway the WWF fan over to the NWA, it would be the combination of a heel/face guy like Luger, sort of like a counterculture anti-hero of sports in comparison with Hogan.

If all the fair avenues of trying to compete with the WWF don't work, the NWA should try something like what Randy Savage did in Memphis, forcing the media to take notice of the promotion.

George Maranville
Lexington, Kentucky

Just when I thought the NWA was finally getting its act together, as McMahon's concepts begin to fade into mediocre yuppie oblivion, with the hiring of Terry Funk, what do they do? They blow it. When Funk turned on Ric Flair, it was pro wrestling at its finest, and when Funk proceeded to destroy one jobber after another to be considered a top contender, everything was still on track. Then that one fateful Saturday came when Sting entered the picture, and Funk came out looking less than invincible. What for? As a wrestling fan, I hated this stupidity. Funk should appear indestructible, just like Hogan, if Flair is to be considered the top gun in late July. Not only should they have had Funk destroy every jobber that interfered in the first Sting confrontation, but Sting as well, who everyone respects and has accepted, should have taken the fall as well. Without Funk defeating Sting, Sting served no purpose other than just being a distraction. Funk should have devoured everyone and everything in his way for Flair's victory to have the necessary emotional impact and satisfaction. And if all of this wasn't bad enough, then came the Clash. Funk vs. Steamboat was all routine, although well executed. But what was the purpose of the match? To turn Luger? How stupid can they be? The purpose of that match should have been to have Funk pin Steamboat, the top contender and recent former champion who gave Flair himself fits. Instead, they had Funk retreating from Luger's ring entrance. Think of how scary a demented Funk would have Looked standing proud, crying gloating over Steamboat. That's the image I was waiting to see and the NWA stole it from me. If they wanted to turn Luger, or set up a Luger vs. Steamboat or Funk vs. Sting feud, fine, but the Clash was the wrong time and place to do it. I feel so devastated by the destruction of Funk's credibility that I'm ready to get in the ring myself with the morons who are making these decisions.

Zoogz Rift
Canoga Park, California

Even though the Lex Luger turn was done too early in the year, it will still turn out for the best. The run-in at the Clash was predictable, and the clothesline on Steamboat brought back memories of the Orndorff turn on Hogan in 1986, but it was still done to perfection. A few weeks later we have another classic skit where Luger potshots a TBS jobber, Lee Scott. This was by far the single best idea the committee has come up with in quite a while. Things like this could help the ratings for sure.

The eventual Flair vs. Luger matches may be the turning point if there is a turning point at all. Last year's matches drew decent, but they should draw better with the champion a face. It seems like a face champion is a must these days.

Mark Bennett
Jackson, Michigan

There is no doubt if the NWA can maintain its May pace there is no stopping them in terms of rebuilding. All they need to do is to actually get people to watch these shows as I have no doubt that people will get excited about the NWA if they are willing to tune in again.

You mentioned about wrestling arcade video games that needed correction on two accounts. First, you said all of them have been flops. Not true. The first one released, "Tag Team Wrestling," was very successful when first released and continued to be successful for about six months. The second one released, whose name I can't recall, was initially successful as well. All the rest were flops however. Interestingly, the most current game out in the arcades is called "Wrestle War. Even though the game has been out for a while, I still have to wonder what the Turner people think about the usage of the name. Second point to correct has to do with the games not using real wrestling characters. There is a women's wrestling game that uses Dump Matsumoto as a character.

Even though I'm rather late with this, I wanted to give my thoughts on two of three fall matches. I don't agree with all the resentment and opposition towards two of three fall matches. First, the idea that they get old rather fast is ridiculous. Two of three fall matches were prevelent for decades and they never suffered anymore from uncreative booking or predictability than one fall matches. Just because Dusty Rhodes and Vince McMahon booked two of three fall matches have been uncreative or that the matches in Mexico are usually predictable doesn't mean you have to use that as a benchmark for judging what any other booker could do. As was proven with Flair vs. Steamboat in New Orleans, two of three falls is an excellent way to pace a match.

Sean Ryan
Fairbanks, Alaska

I'll get right to the point. Lex Luger has for the past three weeks been the best heel in pro wrestling. He's been stunning during and since his turn at the Clash. His interview on the 6/24 TBS show was perfect. His tirade about little kids wanting his autograph was a riot. Hopefully his workrate will keep up with his attitude to make the Steamboat-Luger match in Baltimore the sleeper match of the card.

Ric Flair's total babyface return on the 7/1 TBS show was really hot. His match with Funk could very well equal one of the Flair vs. Steamboat matches this year. High expectations I realize, but hopeful none the less. Everything else about the NWA is exciting to me now also. The best thing is that the powers that be are apparently willing to allow the promotion go through this rebuilding period. All too often we see groups losing faith in bookers, wrestlers and/or fans too quickly and bailing out when the promotion could really take off. The CWF during Eddie Gilbert's reign as booker is a good example. The NWA is doing the right thing by giving these ideas a chance to grow.

The WWF is boring me to tears. Zeus will be a bomb in the ring and I think it 'll adversely affect the WWF. He can't wrestle. No Holds Barred was an insulting piece of filth that only deepened my distaste for the WWF. I can't blame McMahon or Hogan because they are giving the public what it wants but that doesn't mean I have to like it. But I 'm pulling for the WWF to survive with some decency so when they go the way of Schaun Cassidy, Pet Rocks and Atari, there will be something left with which to build a real wrestling promotion around.

Scott Hudson
Tifton, Georgia

Winning is not a sometime thing
  It's an all time thing
  You don't win once in a while
  You don't do things right once in a while
  You do them right all the time
  Winning is a habit
  Unfortunately, so is losing - Vince Lombardi
    I don't know what's more painful - watching Hulk Hogan do a love scene or following the NWA. Frankly, there's no

excuse for this huge morass they're in. Never have I seen so much mindless scrambling for position and to no avail. The entire NWA deserves negative six stars, never mind the Ding Dongs. I wonder what's next. Actually, I dread what's next, The Ring Dings. Actually it seems an appropriate name for those in charge, doesn't it. Panic has obviously set in because they are trying everything and have seemed to have lost track of what cohesiveness is all about. They have to re-examine the basics of running a successful wrestling promotion and following what Vince McMahon has done, rather than running down the promotion.

Shorten the TBS Saturday show to one hour. They've finally stabilized when the show will appear, but a two hour show is a bit much to take. If you can't present what you've got to present in one hour, you are giving away too much. Sometimes a little extra works against you. Plus, it detracts from the spectacle of a real two hour special like the Clashes. Short hot matches are the way to go when showcasing top talent on TV. Make the viewer beg for more, rather than try and make him digest too much. Never cut a match in progress in an attempt to think that people will tune in next week. Chances are they'll be so mad they won't. Don't anger fans with the shows, please the fans. Stop changing the hosts. Make a decision already, because all the changes are annoying.

Work hot 10-15 minute matches at the house shows. If they are good, nobody will feel cheated and since the average attention span is that long, you'll please more than you'll insult. Save to 30 to 40 minute matches for special occasions and only if the matches will be great. If you can't beat the WWF out of the gate, offer a better product with the same trappings. Quality can make you No.1 but only if you are perceived as a major league promotion.

Take a page from Vince. Raid. Raid. Raid. It's a matter of principle, not just acquisition. You keep McMahon unbalanced and not quite sure of what the next move will be. Had they tried harder, they may have gotten Roddy Piper which would have been a major acquisition both at the gate and on television, not to mention a headache for Vince. Here they could have had a potential wrestling cross-media celebrity, which is what we assumed they'd want. You have to pay for big talent. Don't take a "we'll develop our own talent" stance. Did Vince McMahon do that in 1984? No. He got the biggest names he could to build the promotion around. Later he developed some of his own. But when you are looking to turn things around you get name talent. Ric Flair can carry the promotion by himself while you experiment. He needs some support.

Why do you let your top attraction sit out for so long? You don't starve the calf to make the cow fatter . Flair/Funk was a good, but not an over-the-top angle to run on its own without both participants keeping the heat up and Funk isn't strong enough to carry the promotion. He should have feuded with Flair immediately after Nashville to perk up the house gates while developing a strong heel like Luger for Flair to feud with later in the year. Granted, Flair was overexposed, but two months isn't enough to kill overexposure, so you work within a good angle to bring up the heat. I wouldn't have given Steamboat the belt. There is something wrong with giving a mid-card guy from your opposition your World title, especially that quickly, without developing him so that people forget he was in the WWF. This is no reflection on Steamboat, just the perception problem. And in wrestling, perception is everything, don't change for the sake of change. Change only with a plan. Every time I watch the NWA, there is a new turn and a new angle. There's nothing wrong with excitement, as long as you don't do it at the expense of promotion. Committee booking obviously doesn't work because five frantic minds are worse than one. Either pick a guy like Gilbert, or if you want to build up slowly, rather than acquiring name talent, contact Len Denton.

They need character development badly. Scott Hall chasing around an alligator with a stick, which anyone can do, is stupid. Let him stick his hands in its mouth or forget about it. Nobody would have thought you could have done anything with Art Barr, but changing him to Beetlejuice did wonders. A little creativity is called for, and there's nothing wrong with coming up with characters kids can identify with. Owen Hart needs a strong gimmick like that because he doesn't talk well and the kids would love him with his moves and his size like he's one of them battling against the odds like kids feel in an adult oriented world. He doesn't need bells, just a good character. You don't have to stoop to the Bushwacker mentality .

Teresa DeMarie
Tuckahoe, New York

NEW ZEALAND

The weekly tabloids have been giving a lot of space to the WWF Superstars of Wrestling program which airs here. Several kids have been put in the hospital through copying, or trying to copy what they see on television and the tabloids have given these incidents considerable coverage. They also picked up on McMahon 's comments to the state athletic commission hearings and have regularly quoted a number of local experts, none of whom seem to be known by any of the local wrestlers, as saying WWF wrestling is all fake, but the WWF is still doing well in TV ratings. The newspapers here don't cover any wrestling except the WWF even though the letters to the editor columns often talk about issues within the NWA.

Frank Shanley
Upper Hutt, New Zealand

AUSTRALIA

Superstars of Wrestling is back on Ch. 10 on Monday and Tuesday nights at 11:30 p.m. or midnight. The current episode dates back around three weeks after SummerSlam 88. Wrestling Challenge appears to be gone forever as its time slot has been taken over by a show on the Rugby League. Challenge actually had been off the air for a long time before this in other states.

I'm now getting videotapes and have recently seen Starrcade '88, Chi town Rumble, Royal Rumble, the NBC special and am soon to get Survivors II. I enjoyed Starrcade the most as its consistently good matches kept my attention. I also enjoyed Chi Town Rumble, but didn't enjoy the Flair vs. Steamboat match as much as others did. What I actually enjoyed a lot more was the Clash V skit where Flair said the bit about helping the missus with the dishes. Now, that was fantastic.

Raymond Jennings
Woody point, Australia

Regarding the 5/27 SNME, I will agree that the suplex from the top of the cage was very impressive, but there appeared to be a bit of editing done while Hogan and Bossman were at the top to make it appear to be a more fluid move. Also, why was the crowd chanting, "USA, USA" during the Jim Duggan vs. Rick Rude match?

Tim Cousar
Burlison, Tennessee

The Red Rooster is the lamest gimmick I've ever seen in wrestling, and I 've been watching wrestling since the days of Bedlam from Boston. I hope Terry Taylor is very well paid for having to do the hair bit. I should think he'd be quite embarrassed about it.

Carl Gessner
Pluckemin, New Jersey

A lot of fans criticize Hulk Hogan. I don't want to defend Hulk Hogan, but I'd like to share the experience of a special occasion that I attended on May 31st as PS 158 in New York City. I witnessed first hand, with tears swelling my eyes, what Hulkamania is all about and it made a believer out of me. I believe the visit was a selfless act by Hogan and not a publicity stunt for No Holds Barred. There is another side of Hulk Hogan that not many fans get to see.

Name withheld by request

Dave Meltzer: This is not meant as a knock on Hogan, because he deserves credit for a lot of the stuff he does outside the ring, because a lot of it is done without any media attention. He does a great deal of stuff for the Make-a-wish society and really they don't use his work to hype his character so I consider that to be genuine charity work. There are a lot of other celebs, including one famous one (not a wrestler although he's been involved with the business) that has the image of being a frequent visitor to handicapped children that actually would never make such appearances unless there was media to give him to positive press from the visits. In fact, he's been known to frequently cancel such visits if the media publicity falls through. However, while I'm not doubting the emotion Hogan showed in the PS 158 thing as being genuine, when once does something of this type and tons of media is invited to watch, while it is charity work, it is not a selfless act and it is done, at least to some degree, as a publicity move since all the media attention on Hogan's appearence was tied to hype for No Holds Barred.

Dusty Rhodes is truly amazing in that introduction skit in the barn. It was a double-bladed sword in that it cut both ways. I can imagine Vince McMahon laughing at making Dusty shove "doo doo" to show the NWA's self-professed living legend as only worthy of such tasks in the WWF. When Dusty was saying, "Doo Doo is good for me, and Doo Doo is good for you, ish't he really saying, "I 'm in shit now, but this shit must be what you want. "

With the WWF being No. 1 and making tons of money, it must be what the public wants. Interesting that Dusty is being humiliated, but at least he understands it and told us why.

So many people and wrestlers are humliated for money in the WWF. In fact, it's the norm. Look at Koko Ware's hair, Terry Taylor's gimmick, Akeem, Slick, etc. When Vince uses you, he really makes sure to take all your pride away from you.

I saw No Holds Barred and it should have been called, No Cliches Barred. The one major thing I despised about the movie was the McMahon sense of humor. No, I don't think toilet jokes are funny. This contempt for the audience just shows once again that McMahon thinks wrestling fans are moronic kids who are struggling through puberty. So Hogan kissed a girl. I hope so. I'd hate to think he was kissing something else.

How about Zeus? He must have been given tapes of Andre the Giant vs. John Studd matches to study how to be a wrestler. I was surprised that in the movie, Hogan didn't use the leg drop as his finisher but instead used the polish Hammer. I suppose if you can't wrestle and need a new finishing hold, you might as well steal a move from another guy who can't wrestle. I did enjoy Stan Hansen, Jeep Swenson, The Duke Or Dorkchester and see the Masked Superstar gets pants to wear.

John Hitchcock
Greensboro, North Carolina

Watching wrestling today is not what it used to be, however going to mass isn't the same, either. I don't like the circus

that the WWF puts out. Running wrestlers in and out and seeing the same guy wrestle three times in a night ruins the mystique of pro wrestling. But in turn, wrestling is enjoyed by more people and talked about more than ever before. At least I can talk wrestling with more than two people. Lighten up and enjoy that wrestling hasn't gone the way of the USFL. I've been reading your comments concerning the NWA's television ratings. I have always watched the NWA every Saturday since our area picked up TBS, but a strange thing has been happening. I've been missing some shows. I can't blame it on time slot problems or the Atlanta Braves. The Braves screwed up wrestling every summer and I still never missed the show. The NWA is running in so many people and there are no real feuds to look forward to. They add so many people so fast that nobody really is set up to carry out a feud. The only thing I looked forward to with anticipation was the Flair vs. Steamboat feud. The NWA is trying to do too much. Tell the story but give it time to develop. They may wrestle, but their meat market is almost worse than the WWF's marketing.

Tim Stoecklin
Rockford, Illinois

JULY 24, 1989

Before getting into talking about Sunday's NWA pay-per-view card from Baltimore, let's update the two biggest stories from last week.

First off, as usually occurs in cases of this type, the early reports on the severity and recuperation times from injured wrestlers is usually exaggerated since wrestlers are used to working hurt to begin with and secondarily because they generally defy doctor's orders and return too soon after injuries anyway. Of the wrestlers injured in the 7/4 auto accident in Canada, Chris Benoit and Sumu Hara actually were back in action just days after the accident. Davey Boy Smith was hospitalized for two days and at last report was still on crutches, however there is talk he'll be back in action shortly. In fact, they are billing a Dynamite Kid vs. Davey Boy Smith main event for Calgary this coming Friday night and are talking like Smith will return this weekend. Jason the Terrible (Karl Moffat), at last report, was still hospitalized.

Jake Roberts was released from prison earlier this week after posting a $10,000 bond. Originally the judge had refused to grant Roberts bail stemming from his conviction last week on assault and battery charges stemming from an incident last December. Roberts will be sentenced on the charges on August 14th. The maximum sentence would be 15 years in prison, although the guidelines the state gives for first offenders in Florida are a prison sentence of 12 to 30 months. Titan is desperately trying to cover this one up because by sheer coincidence, they had been planning to start a television campaign for the kids to send get well cards to Jake (to help build up for the next souvenir bulk mailing), who legitimately is out of action due to recent neck surgery. However this could be a p. r. problem if word got out that they were having kids send get well cards to a wrestler who was in prison at the time. Roberts was convicted of punching John Bartlett, 27, a 5-foot-7, 160 pound man (Roberts is 6-5, 250) after the two were bar hopping earlier in the evening in Daytona Beach. Bartlett claimed that Roberts was driving as they were headed to an after-hours club at about 4 a.m. and Roberts made some nasty comments about women in Daytona Beach and Bartlett argued with him, Roberts stopped the car and punched Bartlett out. Roberts claimed he was acting in self defense. Bartlett suffered a broken cheekbone in four places and a broken bone around the eye interestingly enough, testifying on behalf of Roberts were Tully Blanchard and Bruce "Brother Love" Prichard, however the jury took less than two hours to come up with the verdict. Titan right now is trying to compile and get verified all the public service work Roberts has done in connection with their company over the years in hopes it will help come sentencing time. Since this was a first offense, even though the guidelines recommend prison, most offenders of this type get off with lengthy probation, however there is fear within Titan that Roberts' celebrity status may work against him here.

The biggest rumor of the week, and you'll have a chance to find out if it's true or not come Tuesday is that Bam Bam Bigelow is going to wind up in boxing. Bigelow told several friends that an announcement would be made on July 25th during George Foreman's fight that would begin Bigelow, the 390 pound tattooed-headed monster, as a pro boxer and he'd be built up for an eventual fight with Mike Tyson. This seems illogical for several reasons, mainly because Bigelow has no prior boxing experience that I know of (he does have amateur wrestling and martial arts experience). At the same time, Tyson has no legit boxing contenders, with the exception of Evander Holyfield and they are trying to keep from making that match for about two years so Tyson has to be kept busy against someone and perhaps Don King thinks he could market Bigelow as the ultimate monster, similar to the marketing Vince McMahon has done with Zeus.

Speaking of Zeus, tickets went on sale Tuesday for SummerSlam at the Meadowlands on August 28th. We'll have the complete line-up for the card elsewhere in this issue, but the show did a whopping 9,000 tickets and nearly $200,000 in first day sales alone which would be one of the largest first day sales in the history of U.S. wrestling. By Friday, 15,000 of the 21,000 tickets had been sold and it's a mere formality that the show will sell out live to the projected tune of $378,000. Titan is so enthused about this that there is optimistic talk that the PPV buy rate for this card could be on par with the six percent buy rate WrestleMania, and for the first time ever besides Wrestiemania, Titan will be closed-circuiting this show as well, although only in Canada (which has no PPV capabilities).

This points out an interesting facet of some of the biggest gates of this year around the world. They were accomplished by putting pro wrestlers in the ring against people who are not pro wrestlers. This has worked now in both the United States and Japan and created some of the biggest houses ever. The success of the first WrestleMania was primarily due to the appearence of Mr. T as a wrestler and Titan used Mr. T in the second WM (where he meant a lot less and by then, the most important matches were Hogan vs. King Kong Bundy and also a Battle Royal using several NFL football players including William ``Refrigerator'' Perry) as well. The biggest gates ever in Japan were both accomplished this past spring. New Japan drew a $2.8 million house at the Tokyo Egg Dome to see wrestlers face Soviet

Olympic wrestlers and Antonio Inoki clash with a former Olympic gold medalist in judo. The subsequent gates for the Soviet Olympic wrestlers all around Japan were huge, although I'm skeptical of the long-term effectiveness of the Soviets, but one can't ignore that the short-term success was nothing short of amazing. Just a few weeks later, the UWF drew a $1. 7 million gate using a sambo wrestler, Chris Dolman, against pro wrestler Akira Maeda, and even more impressive is that the UWF drew this house in Osaka without any television exposure. While in Japan they have used the gimmick of using non-wrestlers who were athletes in other sports as gimmick performers to draw huge houses, and it's consistently worked in the past with guys like leon Spinks and Muhammad Ali (the matches were disasters, but the TV ratings and box office results were record-setting), Chuck Wepner (a boxer), Mike Dayton (a bodybuilder), several kick boxing stars including Don Nakaya Neil sen (who wound up being the best actual worker of all the non-wrestlers), Monster Man Eddie Everett and Superfoot Wallace; with Titan, they've used actors, particularly black tough-guy actors to take advantage of the closet racism that a large percentage of the U.S. public really has when it comes to tough-looking blacks. Perhaps this is a lesson for the NWA. Inoki created his larger-than-life image in Japan by beating champions in judo, boxing and kickboxing and became a national celebrity. Hogan became a national celebrity originally from being paired up with a rock star and later being tag team partners with a famous actor. Maeda became a national celebrity beating kickboxers, karate guys and most recently a sambo wrestler. Since the vast majority of the public believes wrestling is a work anyway, these mixed matches, which the public isn't sure about, can have major curiosity appeal. Of course there is the down side. It is hard to trust people that you don't have full control over, and even though these matches generally work at the gate with an "over" promotion, they can hurt if things go wrong. Inoki vs. Ali nearly killed Japanese wrestling because neither would do the job and the match turned into a "shoot" with both guys fearing injuries to the point they never got near each other. Inoki vs. Spinks wasn't a disaster to the point it threatened the existence of Japanese wrestling, but the match itself was a disaster. Ditto the Roddy Piper vs. Mr. T boxing match. It would be almost impossible for this SummerSlam main event to turn into much of a disaster, even though Zeus (Tom Lister) will certainly be out of his league as a main event wrestler, even by Titan standards. But that's what Randy Savage is there for. To make sure Zeus isn't in the ring much and to cover for the other three in the ring. I'm convinced Brutus Beefcake is in the match to put Zeus over in a big way. And the interest Titan has been able to achieve in bringing this movie character into wrestling makes me almost certain the WrestleMania main event for next year will be Hogan vs. Zeus.

The last time the NWA did a pay-per-view show, back on May 7th in Nashville, it's generally regarded as the best PPV show in the four-plus years that wrestling events have gone nationally via this somewhat new technology. It also drew the lowest buy rate of any national PPV show with the exception of the AWA's Superclash show last December, which everyone knew well in advance didn't have much national appeal. Sunday's card in Baltimore could very well top Nashville as a wrestling card. It could also top Nashville on the negative side as well, with a low PPV buy rate once again.

First, let's look at the positives with this card - the action and card itself. On paper, this looks to be an excellent show. While nothing on the show may top the Flair-Steamboat matches in Chicago, New Orleans and Nashville, that is also an unfair standard for comparison, even though the natural comparison for the Ric Flair vs. Terry Funk main event will be with the three nationally - viewed Steamboat matches. Even with Funk's back injury and the chance Flair might be rusty with 11 weeks off, it is almost inconceivable that this won't be a great match. Steamboat and Lex Luger should also put on a great match as well. Even without blood, and guaranteed there will be people disappointed with that aspect of the War Games match, both the concept and the wrestlers pretty well guarantee an entertaining match and have a solid shot at being the best match of the show. Sting and the Great Muta are both the type of wrestlers who save their best moves for the big shows, as this is the big show. Jim Cornette vs. Paul E. Dangerously will be short, and it won't be a great wrestling match, but they'll probably make it entertaining. Rick & Scott Steiner vs. Kevin Sullivan & Mike Rotunda looks like a good match on paper; I pity the Dynamic Dudes against The Skyscrapers because the latter duo can only look good when destroying their foes and it looks like the Dudes are the next in line for destruction; and Brian Pillman vs. Bill Irwin should be a solid opening match. From top-to-bottom, this card Looks even more balanced than Starrcade '88, which was the best actual wrestling PPV show. Both the Chicago and Nashville PPV shows were carried by having a classic main event and having some good matches underneath, but Chicago had its bad matches as did Nashville. Starrcade's only "bad" match was the Russian Assassins vs. Ivan Koloff & Junkfood Dog , but that was at least kept short. This card, the only match that needs to be kept short is the managers match, although I'll assume the Skyscrapers match will be kept short as well because they are the type of team that needs short matches to maximize their effectiveness.

As far as promotion, TBS is getting things in gear and one has to be impressed with the short update shows hyping the PPV on before and in between a lot of the baseball games over the past few weeks. Still, the TV ratings for the wrestling shows, particularly in syndication, have been too low to get the two percent buy rate the NWA was hoping for when this card was first being put together. In that case, it wouldn't have mattered if everything on television was being done to perfection, because if people aren't viewing the television, they aren't going to get into the angles nor order the PPV. Of course, things weren't done to perfection. They spent so much time trying to get Terry Funk over as "crazy" that they didn't develop him as a legitimate contender for the title. While there will be tons of heat in the match to see Ric Flair return as a babyface, it doesn't seem like there is a question in anyone's mind over whether or not Flair will actually lose the title. And even though the interviews on both sides have been strong the past three weeks, my own feeling is that July 1st was too late to announce the main event for a PPV show that is three weeks later. While if you are a regular viewer of all the TV shows, you will know the entire line-up (with the exception of who is in the Triple Crown finals, which with one week to go, I don 't even know, and if nobody knows who is in it, it's useless to even have the match because it isn't selling any tickets if people don't know who is in it). However, it has never been tied together in one package strongly enough. The TV commercials list the War Games match without identifying who is in the War Games match (if you watch the TV you will know if you pay close attention, both the participants are still vague in many people's minds and they are also assuming more knowledge of what a War Games is than a lot of casual fans actually have - the actual concept of two men starting, the coin flip that the heels always win, the 2-on-1, 3-on-2 for the two minute intervals and finally the winning only via submission are points that haven't been hammered into the viewers' head this year as they were two years ago when the first War Games in Atlanta and Miami drew those huge gates). Next, on television this weekend, or just one week before showtime, we see Ricky Steamboat doing interviews challenging Lex Luger to a no DQ match and Luger not accepting. That's fine, if the card is a month away, not a week away. The entire card should have been finalized at least three weeks ahead and had all the stips down so they had a few weeks to hammer them home, not adding stips at the last minute. The TV commercials that aired all weekend still just listed Sting, Muta, Steamboat and Luger as "also appearing" rather than list their matches and explain the angles and stips for them. You can see those guys all just appear" on television for free several times each weekend. It's the matches that sell the show (that is, if at least people are watching the shows to begin with). The saddest part of all this is that this entire line-up, for the most part, was finalized several weeks back, but the line-up itself isn't being sold to the public. On the TV commercials that I saw during baseball, they didn't even mention the Flair vs. Funk match, just that Turner Home Entertainment was doing a PPV this Sunday. Nobody cares if Turner Home Entertainment is doing a PPV. They only care if there is a match, or preferably a few matches, that they desperately want to see enough to spend $15 to watch at home.

"No Holds Barred" is back in business again. It's playing around here at the $1 theaters and may be around for another week or two. This past weekend the flick did $300,025 in 420 theaters, although at this point, the splits are 90 percent to the theaters and 10 percent to New Line Cinema, which means Titan itself is seeing virtually nothing from this point on. As of last Monday, the gross was $15,238,653.

From a business standpoint, this wasn't the best week Vince McMahon ever had. Actually, if you are judging house shows, things were basically quite good. If you are judging the initial reaction to SummerSlam, things are excellent, but Titan was threatened with an advertiser boycott over the Dusty Rhodes skit where he pulled the crap out of the toilet. There has been a definite backlash over the skit and one company, Blue Ribbon Sausage, flipped out and is out of the game. Also, McMahon found himself backed into a corner so to speak and was forced to appear on "Entertainment Tonight" which was to air this past Monday night after he steadfastly refused to appear on any segment which would mention that there were any other wrestling promotions in this country. McMahon learned that while he is omnipotent when it comes to the pro wrestling business, when it comes to the television business, he is just a player, and really a bit player at that in comparison to the network hotshots.

I want to make a special mention here of something that has nothing to do with wrestling. One of our readers, Jeff Bukantz of New Jersey, captured the gold medal at the recent Maccabiah Games in Israel in men's fencing in the foil division. Bukantz beat Israel's Noam Katz, 10-7, to win in the Maccabiah Games, which is basically the Olympics for Jewish Athletes. Another of our readers, David Blackburn of California, represented the U.S. as a starting softball pitcher.

Titan has another winner in its Superstars of Wrestling video arcade game. The recently released game by American Technos is currently the No.1 video arcade game in terms of arcade business, right now doing about double the business of its nearest competitor, Double Dragon. The home video kit for the game is also No.1 right now, and the arcade game is also doing big business in Japan. As someone who played the game joked to me, the best part about the game is you can basically be the booker and make Hulk Hogan do jobs to the Honkeytonk Man if you want to.

I finally got the chance to see the Morton Downey show on wrestling that aired some two weeks back. Embarrassing. Actually, not everyone involved was embarrassed. But most were. The show was to argue whether or not pro wrestling should be regulated. Mort opened up saying they should dump the commissions and really tried to stand up for Vince McMahon(whom just about everyone on the show was criticizing) since the show was taped before Downey's $50,000 payday for ruining the Piper's pit. Then Mort later said that they needed to protect the wrestlers from unscrupulous promoters, which basically contradicted his earlier statements that nobody should be regulating wrestling. Anyway, it wound up with the silly real vs. fake issuer which isn't even an issue in reality when it comes to whether pro wrestling should be regulated with everyone, including Downey, all saying that wrestling was real but there were elements of entertainment, but even though every guest agreed, and in a sense, they were all fibbing since they all said that winners and losers weren't pre-determined (except in the WWF, of course, according to Captain Lou and several others but the NWA and AWA are real wrestling and Bruno Sammartino and Roddy Piper did real wrestling and you have no idea how much I loathe that hypocritical double-standard talk) they still managed to spend most of the show arguing over something that they all agreed on. The biggest argument was whether or not Vince McMahon admitted that his matches were predetermined. Albano insisted that he did, while several, including Downey, insisted Vince said nothing of the sort, only that his shows were both sports and entertainment, which of course ignores that it was in the New York papers that McMahon testified under oath in the Stossel case that he and his bookers determine the outcome of every match. And whether he does or doesn't, what does that have to do with whether the business of pro wrestling needs to be regulated?

PUERTO RICO

Got a couple of line-ups for major shows over the past few weeks.

7/1 in Caguas was headlined by Sadistic Steve Strong (Steve DiSalvo) defending the Universal title against TNT with Invader #1 handcuffed to Chicky Starr, Abbuda Dein (Rocky Iaukea) & Rip Rogers defending the WWC World tag team titles against The Invaders (Jose Gonzales & Johnny Rivera), White Angel (Curtis Thompson) vs. Kareem Muhammad in a no DQ match, Super Medico (Jose Estrada) defending the jr. heavyweight title against Chicky Starr and Miguelito Perez & Hurricane Castillo Jr. & Maelo Huertas vs. The Batten Twins & El Profe.

7/8 in Guaynabo had Invader #1 & TNT vs. Strong & Starr, Perez & Castillo vs. Dein & Rogers, Junkyard Dog vs. Muhammad, White Angel vs. Kendo Nagasaki, Medico & Rufus Jones vs. Battens and prelims.

STAMPEDE

With Davey Boy Smith out of action with injuries from the van accident last week, the group canceled shows 7/4 in Prince George, B.C. and 7/5 in Kamloops, BC. They were

back in action the next night, and on 7/7 in Dawson Creek, ALTA, Johnny Smith beat Chris Benoit for the British Commonwealth title due to outside interference from Larry Cameron. Benoit regained the title on 7/8 in Grand Prairie, ALTA and also won a Battle Royal on that card. Steve Ray from Kansas City and Jonathan Holiday, who most recently worked in Puerto Rico, debuted this past weekend. The card this Friday night in Calgary with Kid vs. Smith headlining has been moved from the 8,000-seat Corrall to the 2,000 seat Pavilion.

Owen Hart is scheduled to return this Friday. However, for those of you ready to start getting videos from this area and see "the old" Owen Hart back again, Stampede has decided that they are giving too much away on television and will no longer be taping the semifinal and main events on the Calgary shows (ie, all of Owen Hart's matches and most of Benoit's matches) in an effort to boost crowds which are at a Low point.

Also on the way in are Maximum Overdrive (Tim Hunt & Jeff Warner) from Minneapolis, Kensuke Sasaki of Japan, who most recently worked in Puerto Rico as Sasaki-San who is a decent-to-good worker and will form a team with Sumu Hara (Tatsumi Kitahara) who is well below the standard of most of the Japanese wrestlers who have worked this territory.

There is also talk that Barry Orton will be returning here as The Zodiac when he returns from prison, which could be shortly.

7/15 in Edmonton saw Benoit beat Johnny Smith, Cameron beat Hara, Steve Ray beat Goldie Rogers, Holiday beat Bill Jodin and Kerry & Bob Brown beat Ron Ritchie and somebody else.

Kim Schau, a prelim babyface, was also in the van accident last week but escaped pretty much unscathed.

Great Garna has returned.

CWA

The 7/10 card in Memphis drew 1,500 as The Blackbirds (Iceman King Parsons & Brickhouse Brown managed by Harold T. Harris) debuted beating Freddy (Tommy Gilbert) & Billy Travis *3/4, Bill Dundee & Ricky Morton beat The D. I. & Doug Gilbert * ½, Dustin Rhodes & Jeff Jarrett beat Dirty White Boy (Tony Anthony) & Black Bart via DQ **, Wildside (Chris Champion & Mark Starr) regained the held up CWA tag team titles beating Action Jackson & Travis in a match where the loser of the fall (Jackson) had to Leave the territory **, Jerry Lawler & Bam Bam Bigelow beat Master of pain & Dutch Mantell in a match where either Lawler or Ronnie Gossett would have to be tarred and feathered depending upon which team lost. Finish saw Mantell hold Lawler, who moved as MOP went for a big move, Mantell got hit and pinned. After the match Mantell and Gossett got into a big argument and MOP jumped Mantell and wound up tarring and feathering Mantell *3/4 (all for the post-match antics and Mantell's turn, match itself sucked) and the finale was a Battle Royal which came down to Lawler and Bigelow and Lawler wanted to split the money but Bigelow threw him out instead ** ¼ so both Mantell and Bigelow turned on the card.

On TV on 7/15, Bigelow slapped Lawler during a TV interview for not calling him Mr. Bigelow and calling him Bam Bam and now Bigelow is managed by Gossett.

Mantell & Dustin Rhodes are becoming a tag team. Wildside is still getting mainly cheers. Travis, Jackson and Frankie Lancaster are all gone from the scene.

7/17 in Memphis has Chris Champion vs. Lou Winston, Freddy vs. D. I. , Rhodes & Dundee vs. White Boy & Bart, Jarrett & Morton vs. Blackbirds, Mantell vs. MOP, Jackie Fargo (with Roughhouse Fargo who many of you may recall as former Mid Atlantic referee Sonny Fargo in his corner) vs. Gossett in a 10 round boxing match (bring out the stopwatches to see how quickly those guys blow up) and finally Lawler defends the USWA title against Bigelow. Bigelow and the Fargos worked most of the territory this week.

AWA

This group ran a show as part of the Platte County Fair in Columbus, Nebraska drawing 2,884 (this was a grandstand show - in other words, tickets were free with admission to the fair) as Mike George beat T.C. Carter, Tonya beat Shirley Black, Scott Norton beat Johnny Valiant via count out (all stalling), Akio Sato pinned Paul Diamond (good), Tommy Januner & Derrick Dukes beat Valiant & Wayne Bloom and Greg Gagne beat Larry Zbyszko-Gagne via DQ in the main event.

WORLD CLASS

Here's the latest on the changing of this group from World Class to USWA. It was announced on TV this week that the bidding war between the USWA and Scandor Akbar for the World Class promotion "had gotten out of hand" and so guess how they are going to settle it? How did you figure that out? There is going to be a match. Now they have already turned World Class into the heel promotion by saying that Akbar and Tojo Yamamoto represent World Class and that Eric Embry and Frank Dusek and Max Andrews (the syndicator, who they are portraying as the babyface member of the World Class board) represent USWA. Both groups this past week had their stockholders nominate a champion (now, isn 't Lawler already the USWA World Champion and thus, shouldn't he be the rep, but that makes sense doesn't it, and making sense makes no sense here). World Class picked P. Y. Chu Hi and USWA picked, surprise, surprise, Eric Embry. Now here's the catch. On the 7/7 card in Dallas, Embry was "injured" and had "major

Hall, the tag title match with Machine & Takano knee surgery" and is supposed to be out of action for six weeks (however, he was already doing run-ins and interviews all over the shows weekend) and Akbar has gotten this deal where the Embry vs. Chu Hi match for the control of the company must take place within 21 days so you know what's coming up next. 7/14 at the Dallas Sportatorium drew 900 fans as Kerry Von Erich beat Bam Bam Bigelow via count out to earn a shot at Lawler in a match where Mr. T (the one and only) was at ringside and yelled at Kerry to jump into the ring and beat the count so he got the win. Mr. T got virtually no reaction from the Dallas fans, surprisingly enough. Kerry did a funny television interview where he said that he and Mr. T stand for the same things, kids, Jesus Christ and wholesome living. Actually, they do stand for the same things. Mr. T did a funny interview as well, the highlight was when Mark Lawrance asked him to comment on Gary Young and Devastation, Inc. and T said he'd rather not make comment on that subject (like he had any idea what Lowrance was talking about).

The remainder of the Dallas card saw Matt Borne & Jeff Jarrett retain the World Class tag team titles beating Chu Hi (Phil Hickerson) & Corporal Braddock via DQ and all the heels jumped the faces after the match and Embry, on crutches, Limped down to ringside to make the save for the faces. Chris Adams pinned Cactus Jack Manson, but after the match the heels jumped Adams and he did a stretcher job, however he worked the next morning at the TV tapings, while also Mil Mascaras went to a double count out with Al Perez and the Simpson brothers & Jimmy Jack Funk beat Manson & Young & Akbar. The scheduled bull rope match between Funk and Kevin Von Erich didn't take place and I'll give you one guess as to why.

At the TV tapings on 7/15, Akbar signed up TV jobber Buster Fowler, who is now going by the ring name of Buster Blackhart. He also tried to sign up the Simpsons but Steve slapped him.

Action Jackson debuted on Saturday while they announced that Dutch Mantell was headed in.

7/21 in Dallas has Lawler vs. Kerry for the USWA title with Akbar and Kevin in the respective corners, Jarrett vs. Chu Hi in a street fight with Percy Pringle chained to Tojo Yamamoto outside the ring, Adams vs. Young in a death match, Akbar vs. Schauna Simpson and if Akbar doesn't win within 10 minutes he must forfeit "$10,000" (which makes no sense since shouldn't Simpson be the one who has to beat Akbar in 10 minutes or less?), Funk vs. Braddock and Manson vs. Steve Simpson. Killer Tim Brooks is running an opposition promotion every Tuesday night at the Longhorn Ballroom with himself, Brian Adias, Scott Casey, Jeep Swenson (billed as the star of the movie "No Holds Barred"), Johnny Mantell and John Tatum appearing and Killer Karl Kox serving as referee. They drew about 150 fans on 7/11.

Embry had a few fans kicked out of the building on Saturday at the tapings before doing his interview once again, while Adams lost control at the fans during his interview for the second week in a row.

NEW JAPAN

The 6/27 TV taping in Sapporo drew 3,750 as Big Van Vader (Leon White) beat Riki Choshu via count out in the main event but not before Choshu unmasked Vader, who did a heavy juice job. Also, Tatsumi Fujinami & Kengo Kimura beat Hiroshi Hase & Takayuki Iizuka, Jushin Liger (Keiichi Yamada) & Akira Nogami beat Naoki Sano & Shinji Sasazaki, Brad Rheingans made Soviet Chimur Zarasov submit, Shiro Koshinaka & Kuniaki Kobayashi pulled a major upset beating Super Strong Machine & George Takano, the IWGP tag team champs, in a non-title match when Kobayashi pinned Machine in 14:42, Wild Samoan interfered Kokina & Mike Kirchner (Corporal Kirchner) beat Masa Saito & Tatsutoshi Goto, Black Tiger (Mark "Rollerball" Rocco of England) beat Black Cat and Hiro Saito pinned Biff Wellington.

The next tour will be 7/28 to 8/10 with the final night being a big show at the Tokyo Sumo Hall. That series will be mainly composed of singles matches picked out of a hat with four teams competing to see which team gets the championship. The Russian team will be Salman Hashimikov, Victor Zangiev, Vladimir Berkovich, Chimur Zarasov and newcomer Efgani Altubin (don't know any background about this guy yet). The U.S. team will be Vader, Dick Murdoch, Buzz Sawyer, Manny Fernandez and Mark Haft. The Japanese "A" team will be Fujinami, Choshu, Masa Saito, Kimura and Osamu Kido while the Japanese "B" team will be Takano, Machine, Koshinaka, Hase and Shinya Hashimoto.

7/3 in Aomori saw a major upset as Machine & Takano retained their tag team titles beating Choshu & Fujinami in 14:21 when Machine pinned Choshu plus Vader & Rheingans beat Hase & Iizuka when Vader pinned Hase, Liger pinned Sasazaki, Masa Saito beat Zarasov, Kokina & Kirchner beat Goto & Kimura, Koshinaka beat Wellington, Black Tiger pinned Kobayashi and Sano pinned Nogami.

On the 7/13 card at the Tokyo Sumo Hall the tag title match with Machine & Takano vs. Hase & Iizuka was changed and Choshu will replace Hase in the match. Hase is taking time off to help Antonio Inoki campaign for senator with the election on 7/23.

7/6 in Ohmachi drew a sellout 2,330 as Choshu & Saito & Kimura beat Vader & Rheingans & Kokina, Machine beat Kirchner, Kobayashi & Koshinaka beat Kantaro Hoshino & Osamu Kido, Liger & Iizuka beat Sasazaki & Norio Honaga, Zarasov beat Black Cat, Black Tiger beat Hirokazu Hata and Sano pinned Wellington.

7/8 in Ito drew 1,220 as Vader& Rheingans & Kokina beat Choshu & Saito & Kimura as Vader pinned Kimura, Machine & Takano kept the tag title beating Koshinaka & Kobayashi, Sasazaki & Sano beat Nogami & Liger, Kido pinned Wellington, Kirchner beat Goto, Black Tiger beat Hoshino, Iizuka beat Hata and prelims.

For the most part, crowds for this tour without Inoki and Hashimikov were rather poor.

ALI JAPAN

7/8 in Kitami drew 2,350 as Stan Hansen & Genichiro Tenryu & Toshiaki Kawada beat Kabuki & Big John Tenta & Kenta Kobashi in the main event when Hansen Lariated Kobashi, Yoshiaki Yatsu & Akira Taue beat Jim Brunzell & Tom Zenk, Joe & Dean Malenko beat Masa Fuchi & Mighty Inoue, Giant Baba & Rusher Kimura beat Motoshi Okuma & Haruka Eigen, Isao Takagi upset and pinned Samson Fuyuki, The Fantastics (Tommy Rogers & Bobby Fulton) beat Shunji Takano & Yoshinari Ogawa, The Destroyer (Dick Beyer) beat Isamu Teranishi, The Terminator (Marc Laurinidas) beat Goro Tsurumi and Mitsuo Momotabeat Shinichi Kikichi.

7/7 in Obihiro drew 2,100 as Tenryu & Foot Loose beat Yatsu & Takano & Takagi in 27 minutes, Hansen pinned Tenta, Malenkos beat Brunzell & Zenk, Baba & Kimura & Kabuki beat Eigen & Okuma & Fuchi, Fantastics beat Inoue & Ogawa, Taue pinned KObashi, Destroyer beat Teranishi and Terminator beat Tsurumi. Jumbo Tsuruta injured his knee and has been out of action since 7/3.

OTHER JAPAN NEWS

The annual Itsuki Kajiwara Memorial card in Tokyo (Kajiwara was the creator of the animated Tiger Mask cartoon) took place on 7/2 with all forms of fighting from judo, karate, kickboxing, etc. represented. The highlight match on the show sent karate champion Seiji Aoyagi against pro wrestler Atsushi Onita, who was Baba's junior heavyweight star about five years ago and a protege of Terry Funk who most recently has been working in Mexico. The bout was a total bloodbath with Onita losing via DQ in the fourth round. JWP was represented with a tag match featuring Devil Masami, while Japan sent Kantaro Hoshino to beat Hirokazu Hata on the show. JWP's Cutie Suzuki continues to get a lot of non-wrestling press in mainstream magazines and poster books.

New Japan's 7/1 television show with Cho shu vs. Vader on top drew a 4.2 rating, while All Japan on 7/2 with Hansen & Tenryu vs. Tsuruta & Takagi as the main event drew a 6.3.

All Japan women on 7/8 in Himeji drew 2,020 as Lioness Asuka beat Yumi Ogura and Akira Hokkuto & Shizuka Minami & Mitsuko Nishiwaki beat Bull Nakano & Kumiko Iwamoto & Ericka Shishedo. 7/7's card saw Nakano & Iwamoto & Nobuko Kimura beat Hokkuto & Yumiko

Hotta & Madusa Maceli in the main event plus Minami drew Nishiwaki and Noriyo Tateno beat Ogura.

INDEPENDENT SCENE

Windy City ran a show on 7/1 in Berwyn, IL before 350 fans as Terminators beat Tokyo Bullets via DQ to keep the tag team titles when Buddy Rose & Doug Somers interfered to set up a new feud and Awesome Ondi Austin beat The Dazzler in the best match on the card and Steve Regal beat Rockin' Randy. Gate was $1800. Windy City will be bringing in Bam Bam Bigelow, Ken Patera, Jim Brunzell and Col. DeBeers to shows over the next month or so.

Scott Bednarski, son of pro wrestler Ivan Putski, who has wrestled a tad over the past few years under the ring name of Scott Putski, signed with the Houston Oilers this past week and will be attending camp that starts in a week or so. Bednarski was the starting fullback for Texas Christian University as a junior but didn't start much of his senior year because the coach was mad at him for remarks he made to the media after a loss.

The new Roller Games, which former Monday Night Football producer and ABC Sports bigwig Chet Forte is producing, is being programmed in syndication next season in most markets at 11:30 p.m. as the syndicated stations are hoping this campy deal will shave off some rating points of both Saturday Night Live and Saturday Night Main Event on NBC.

For Atlanta readers, the deal where the Home Shopping Network was going to buy WVEU (Ch.69, which runs the Saturday night wrestling block with Boni Blackstone) fell through last minute so the wrestling block, which was originally to be axed at the beginning of this month, is on without missing a week for the long haul. The station is now looking for a new buyer and the block could be in danger depending on the new owner, although it is the second highest rated show on the station so logically it appears to be somewhat safe. The only reason it would have been dumped was if HSN had completed the purchase then the station would become a 24-hour shopping network service.

Dennis Condrey is headed into the CWF as a babyface.

ACW appears on its last legs as the recent television shows have contained mainly repeated material from previous shows. Mike Golden is working for Southern Championship Wrestling.

An independent show on 8/12 in Waltham, MA is advertising Larry Zbyszko defending the AWA title against Kerry Von Erich in the main event plus David Sammartino, Vince Apollo, Lou Albano, Jules Strongbow (billed as Chief J. Strongbow) and Ken Patera are announced as well.

Ron Wyatt is putting together a show on 7/28 in Suffolk, VA with Joe Daniels defending the WWA title (Larry Sharpe's title) against Robert Gibson plus Ivan Koloff vs. Russian Assassin as a double feature.

7/8 in Wildwood, NJ promoted by Dick Whoerle saw Ken Patera beat Nikolai Voikoff via DQ, Bam Bam Bigelow squashed an Assassin, plus Tom Brandi beat Mike Sharpe.

Pro Wrestling Illustrated will be starting out a weekly newsletter in September.

CWF on 7/14 in Knoxville has Jimmy Golden & Mongolian Stomper defending the CWF tag team titles against Ricky & Todd Morton in a 2 of 3 fall cage match, Tom Prichard vs. Wendell Cooley for the CWF title, Ron Fuller vs. Don Harris for the USA title, Robert Fuller & Brian Lee defend "World tag team titles" against Steve Armstrong & Tracy Smothers.

Chris Love is headed to Oregon to work for Don Owen.

Bobo Brazil, Igor Zatkoff Man Mountain Jim Lancaster, Mickey Doyle and Rick O'Toole are among those working shows on 8/8 in Shiawassee, MI; 8/9 in Wayne County, MI and 8/10 in Huron, MI.

WALE talk radio 1400 in Fall River, MA is planning to put on a wrestling talk show by the end of July. I should have more details on the show in upcoming weeks.

Sika the Samoan put on a show on 7/9 in Pensacola, FL before just under 300 fans which included Bob Holly, Gator B. Long and manager Abdullah Farouk, Jr. The February 1990 issue of Playboy Magazine is tentatively scheduled to have a "Women of Pro Wrestling" feature featuring Magnificent Mimi as the focal point.

WWF

Don't have the complete card for SummerSlam after all. Bouts I've got so far are Hulk Hogan & Brutus Beefcake vs. Zeus & Randy Savage with Sherri Martel and Elizabeth in the respective corners, Demolition & Jim Duggan vs. Twin Towers & Andre the Giant, Tully Blanchard & Arn Anderson vs. Bret Hart & Jim Neidhart (which will almost surely be a WWF tag team title match), Rick Rude vs. Ultimate Warrior for the IC title, Dusty Rhodes vs. Honkeytonk Man and Rougeaus & Rick Martel vs. Rockers & Tito Santana.

Titan is negotiating for several non-wrestling PPV events over the next year.

When the WWF tapes its television in California, I believe the taping dates will be 8/8 at the Oakland Coliseum Arena and 8/9 in Fresno at Selland Arena. The first two hours will air prior to Sumner Slam but the third hour will air the week after the PPV event.

7/10 at the San Francisco Cow Palace drew 6,490 and $83,763 as Brooklyn Brawler (Steve Lombardi) pinned Jerry Monti in a battle of the biggest loser of the 80s against the biggest loser of the 70s, Dino Bravo pinned Mark Young (Mark Scarpa), Rockers beat Rougeaus (excellent match), Santana beat Martel, Bad News Brown pinned Greg Valentine (no heat at all during this match and bout was real bad as well), Warrior beat Rude via count out and Dusty Rhodes pinned Ted DiBiase in a match which got over huge locally. From what I understand, there was more attention during the prelim matches in the lobby where Warrior was posing for photos for $6 a shot and with the new video game (which fans were in line waiting to play rather than actually watch the matches). This was a rush-job card as they had a 10:30 p.m. flight out of town. Steve Blackman, who worked for Stampede wrestling, had a series of try-out matches but haven't heard anything on whether he's got a job or not. Sam Houston was in for 10-days simply to fill bookings that Owen Hart was originally scheduled for before he quit the promotion.

All-American Wrestling on 7/9 drew a 2.9 rating while Prime-Time Wrestling on 7/10 drew a 2.8, which are roughly the same as both shows would be expected to get at this time of the year.

7/14 in Baltimore at the Arena drew a sellout 14,000 fans as Randy Savage beat Hulk Hogan via count out (Sherri Martel was the entire match as Savage and Hogan didn't do much), Rhodes pinned DiBiase, Houston pinned Brawler (good match), Rougeaus beat Rockers (excellent), Dino Bravo pinned Hercules (terrible), Barbarian pinned Jim Neidhart (worse than terrible) and Jimmy Snuka pinned Honkytonk Man (normally terrible). This card got a ton of local publicity, which doesn't do the NWA any good with them running the big show nine days later. The Governor of Maryland was at the show posing for photos with Hulk Hogan (this wasn't Titan's idea, the Governor just wanted to get photos with Hogan since Hulk is such a big celebrity) and this made every newscast in the market. This was the WWF's first show in Baltimore since October and this was the closest date to 7/23 that the Arena would let them book a show so this show was loaded up primarily because of the NWA PPV event, even though as Vince would say, they aren't competition.

7/14 in Lakeland, FL drew 5,600 as Tim Horner pinned Barry Horowitz ** ½, Red Rooster (Terry Taylor) beat Badnews Brown via count out ** Boreus Zhukov pinned Jim Powers * ¼, Warrior beat Rude via DQ (before the match Warrior broke the arena's sound system during his ring entrance) ***, The Genius (Lanny Poffo) pinned Paul Roma - **, Martel pinned Santana DUD and Demolition beat Twin Towers * ½.

7/15 in Philadelphia at the Spectrum drew 7,226 and $90,014 as Warrior beat Rude via count out, Demolition beat Twin Towers, Snuka beat Honky Tonk, Santana drew Martel, Mr. Perfect (Curt Hennig) pinned Rooster, Bravo pinned Houston and Hercules beat Brawler.

7/16 at the Omni in Atlanta drew 3,500 and $42,000 as Horner pinned Horowitz, Barbarian pinned Neidhart, Rhodes pinned DiBiase, Hillbilly Jim beat Andre the Giant via DQ (no heat at all for this match), Rockers beat Rougeaus (good), Jim Duggan pinned Haku (horrible), Bravo pinned Hercules (worse than horrible) and Warrior beat Rude via

DQ. From what I'm told, the crowd wasn't even remotely the same as an NWA crowd although aside from Rhodes, there wasn't much of a reaction to the wrestlers. Vince McMahon and Elizabeth started doing Wrestling Spotlight over the weekend. Vince only lets Liz get a few words in. 7/8 in Edmonton drew 8,500 as Horner pinned Zhukov - * ½, Poffo pinned Roma - * ½, Brutus Beefcake pinned Greg Valentine - * , Bushwackers beat Tully Blanchard & Arn Anderson*, Snuka pinned Honkeytonk Man * and Hogan pinned Savage *.

Did you see the item in the news where the secret location for Bill Walsh's tryout for the NBC color analyst job was at the Titan Sports studios in Connecticut? Hogan vs. Savage drew a sellout $108,000 house in Birmingham, AL and a near $100,000 house in Houston over the weekend. Dino Bravo & Greg Valentine will be forming a tag team which should thrill everyone to no end and feud with the Hart Foundation.

TV tapings this week in Worcester, MA and Utica, NY including a SNME which will air on 7/29 will be taped in Worcester.

This has nothing to do with Titan Sports, but Chris Von Erich will be making his pro debut for World Class before the end of the summer. I'm trying to think of what is a more thrilling prospect, Chris Von Erich as a wrestler or Dino Bravo & Greg Valentine as a tag team.

7/1 in Halifax, NS drew 3,500 as Powers beat Zhukov, Genius beat Roma, Bushwackers beat Blanchard & Anderson, Bravo beat Heraules and Hillbilly Jim & Jim Duggan beat Andre & Haku plus don't forget the special appearance by Zeus.

6/29 in Brandon, Manitoba drew 4,000 as Mark Young pinned Brawler, Rhodes pinned DiBiase, Valentine made Horner submit, Warrior beat Rude via count out (Rude looked great carrying the match), Warlord pinned Neidhart and Demolition beat Twin Towers in a good match.

7/6 in Johnstown, PA drew 1,004 ($11,744) as Horowitz beat Biff Woods, Barbarian pinned Neidhart, Rhodes pinned DiBiase, Powers beat Megabum Magee, Warlord pinned Koko Ware and Demolition beat Twin Towers. Every match was awful except the main event which was only decent.

NWA

Marvin Hagler was at the NWA show in Boston and Teddy Long had to hold Norman back and they played quite a bit to Hagler.

Bashes keep rolling along. Mainly good shows, but not all. Crowds range from bad to decent.

7/10 in Springfield, MA drew 1,000 (the only television promoting the show was based in Hartford, CT and it: only had two weeks promotion time since it had been promoting the New Haven Bash for weeks before that) as Scott Hall pinned Bill Irwin *½, Dynamic Dudes beat New Zealand Militia *¾, Norman pinned Steven Casey DUD, Mike Rotunda pinned Dick Murdoch * ½, Great Muta pinned Rick Steiner ** ½, Sid Vicious won the two-ring Battle Royal throwing out Murdoch, Skyscrapers beat Johnny & Davey Rich ** (Skyscrapers are getting a huge push on TV and even though they are heels, they are being cheered in every arena), Midnight Express beat Terry Gordy & Jim Garvin via DQ when Gordy used a chair ** (too much stalling but some good action), Sting beat Terry Funk via DQ when Bill Irwin interfered in a wild brawl ***, Road Warriors beat Samoan Swat Team *** and Lex Luger pinned Ricky Steamboat *** ½.

7/11 in Chicago drew 3,042 paid and $39,165 in a harrowing night since inclement weather prevented several planes from coming in and there was fear nobody would arrive, but they actually put on an 11-match card even without Eddie Gilbert, Scott Steiner and Midnight Express & Jim Cornette not making it in. Results saw Dudes beat Militia when Ace pinned Morgan **, Hall pinned Irwin ½ *, Rotunda pinned Murdoch DUD (all stalling), Norman pinned Casey **, Skyscrapers beat Johnny & Davey Rich **, Steiner beat Muta via DQ when Muta used the green mist * ½, Steve Williams threw out Terry Gordy to win the Battle Royal, Hayes & Garvin beat Ranger Ross & Randy Rose *, Sting beat Funk via DQ when Norman interfered *** 3/4, Luger pinned Steamboat in the best match they've had so far ****3/4 and Warriors beat SST ** (they simply couldn't follow Luger and Steamboat and even in Chicago the Warriors didn't get that much heat) in 7:02 when Hawk pinned Fatu after the sandwich lariat.

Iron Sheik will be returning against everyone's wishes. Apparently the attorneys at TBS felt that Sheik had a legit gripe in saying he was unfairly fired, so they are going to bring him back as a jobber since George Scott had signed him to a one-year contract .

NWA will be running Syracuse, Buffalo and maybe Rochester, New York in September.

TV ratings for last weekend saw NWA Power Hour draw a 1. 7, World Championship Wrestling draw a 2.1 and NWA Main Event get a 2.2 which are all roughly the same as the July 4th weekend.

Flair has gotten very impressive reactions at the tapings when he comes out for interviews.

7/12 in Carbondale, IL drew 1,058 paid and $10,716 although there were 1,900 in the building.

Actually the Chicago crowd isn't too bad considering it was going head-to-head with the baseball All-Star game and Titan canceled all shows on Tuesday night rather than compete with the All-Star game.

They are loading up Chicago on 8/20 for the return with Flair vs. Funk, Luger vs. Steamboat, Sting vs. Muta, Warriors vs. SST in a cage match, Freebirds vs. Midnight for the tag

title, Williams vs. Rotunda, Steiners vs. Militia, Brian Pillman vs. Norman, Dudes vs. Bill Irwin & Al Greene (by the way, if ever someone had a last name that fit aptly), and Tommy Rich vs. Bill Irwin.

7/13 in Jackson, TN drew 1,200 as Hall pinned Irwin ½ *, Dudes beat Militia **, Rotunda pinned Murdoch DUD, Norman pinned Casey *, Skyscrapers beat Rich's 3/4*, Rick Steiner pinned Sullivan *, Muta beat Gilbert via count out in the Dragon Shi match ** ½, Gilbert won the Battle Royal throwing out Norman ** ¼, Sting double count out with Funk ***, Freebirds beat Williams & Midnight Express when Gordy DDT'd Stan Lane ** ½, (Doc & Gordy were really good brawling outside the ring but bout just okay inside the ring) Warriors beat SST ** ½.

7/14 in Memphis drew 2,500 as Hall beat Irwin ½ *, Dudes beat Militia *3/4, Rotunda pinned Murdoch DUD, Norman pinned Casey * ¼, Skyscrapers beat Rich's * ¼, Muta pinned Randy Rose ½ *, (they missed every spot) Rick Steiner pinned Sullivan *, Sullivan threw out Eaton to win the Battle Royal (explain that result in Memphis where Midnight Express was just about the most over act on the show), Freebirds beat Midnight & Williams ** (Gordy & Doc great outside the ring again, inside action was boring), Warriors beat SST **, Luger pinned Steamboat ** ¼ and Funk pinned Gilbert in a double juice brawl all over the place when Paul E. Dangerously hit Gilbert with the branding iron **** ¼.

7/15 in Richmond, VA drew 4,500 as Hall pinned Irwin, Shane Douglas pinned Jack Victory, Rotunda pinned Murdoch, Norman pinned Casey, Skyscrapers beat Rich's, Sullivan pinned Scott Steiner (good match, Rotunda gave Sullivan an object to use for the win), Rotunda won 2-ring Battle Royal, Freebirds beat Midnight & Williams (very good), Muta beat Gilbert via count out (pretty good), Rick Steiner beat Funk via DQ when Norman interfered (good), Road Warrior Animal pinned Fatu (short - Hawk was "injured" from the TV angle which played the night before) and Luger pinned Steamboat (excellent).

7/16 in Fort Worth drew 2,700 for a card in which every match advertised but one didn't take place as they switched it to a TV taping. Just about all squashes with no new angles. Best matches saw Gordy double count out with Williams in which Gordy was heavily cheered although Williams got the best pop on the card when he did a press-slam and Funk pinned Tommy Rich. No-shows were Muta (resting up for the PPV), Sting (given time off to move), Johnny Ace (broken cheekbone suffered in Memphis) plus Luger, Warriors, Flair and Steamboat weren't booked on the card so it was a watered-down show and Gilbert wasn't booked either but was there doing booking 7/5 in Charleston, SC saw Pillman pin Irwin, Militia beat Ding Dongs (Greg Evans & Richard Sartain), Norman pinned Casey, Skyscrapers beat Ranger Ross & Randy Rose, Steiners beat Rotunda &

Sullivan, Freebirds beat Williams & Midnight, Williams won Battle Royal, Muta beat Gilbert, Sting beat Funk via DQ, SST pinned Road Warriors and Luger pinned Steamboat.

Why are they still billing two-ring Battle Royals at the Bashes after the "triple crown finals" in Baltimore? Several Luger vs. Steiner matches after Baltimore since I don't believe Steamboat is working the first week of August and Scott Steiner has some openers against Pillman first week of August while they are scheduled to be taping a Tommy Rich vs. Eddie Gilbert babyface match for television on 7/18 in Amarillo, TX.

THE READERS' PAGES

DOWNEY SHOW

I'm not a Letter writer, but after the Morton Downey show on 6/29, I had to write. The whole show was stupid. Somebody ought to do something about Captain Lou as he's getting on my nerves. But what really pisses me off is that at the end of the show when the fans got a chance to speak, Joel Goodheart of the Philadelphia wrestling talk radio show said that the WWF stands for "Wrestling Was Fake". Well Joel, we all know pro wrestling is fake, so don't just say the WWF. Then Joel says something Like this - "The Philadelphia Spectrum (WWF) draws about 43 percent (which is probably true) and the fans are really getting ticked off. Well, if that's the case, why is McMahon still drawing about the same month-after-month. Then he goes, "The Civic Center (NWA) draws more fans than the Spectrum. Well, that's a lie. The last i've heard, the Civic Center has been drawing 2 000 to 3,000 a show.

Walt Marshall
Morrisville, Pennsylvania

The Downey show was even worse than his first wrestling segment. It got off to a good start with Dennis Coraluzzo, but as soon as Lou Albano came out, the rest of the show was reduced to a shouting match with Lou wanting the floor the entire show. I spent the rest of the evening shaking my head in disbelief as I couldn't understand a word being said. It was truly the ultimate in stupidity. I had to Laugh when Lou tried to put the NWA and AWA over as being real while saying the WWF is just show biz. He also again stated he never juiced with a blade. C'mon Lou, get real. After watching this fiasco, I wonder why anyone puts down Vince McMahon for making a mockery of wrestling.

Vincent Dipalma
Copiaque, New York

After seeing the Downey show on regulation, my personal feeling is that the main problem with wrestling is its image to the common person. When you ask anyone about wrestling the response includes Hulk Hogan, Macho Man, Elizabeth, singing, animals and movies. Nowhere is wrestling ever mentioned and this plays right into Vince and Linda McMahon's hands. They are trying to prove to all that wrestling isn't a sport, that it is family entertainment. If enough influential people agree with this, McMahon will take all the sport out of wrestling and have no regulations on him at all.

What the guys on Mort's show were trying to prove was that deregulation could allow anyone to come in as a promoter and do a screw job to the fans, wrestlers and the arena. What deregulating really means is there will be no attending physician at the matches, no guard rails separating the fans from the ring, no mats around the ring, no insurance for wrestlers, no guarantees of anything going correctly and no medical exams. My suggestion for a solution to the problem is to have state wrestling commissions. The commission should have two retired wrestlers, two commissioners and two members of the local wrestling promotion. This committee could agree and adhere to a set of rules and impose fines and penalties for infractions.

Bernie Bonner
Staten Island, New York

BEST WORKERS

I nearly levitated off the sofa when I read your PWI accolade. At least nobody can say that Apter doesn't have a sense of humor. As befitting your status as one of wrestling's 25 most influential people, I've been discussing with some friends who we think were the best workers from 1960 to the early 1970s. The era extends to our semi-smart and mark years, so although we're confident of our choices, Ray Stevens, Jack Brisco and Dory Funk, we'd like to know your opinion. By the way, might you ever do a Who Was Who book?

Jeff Levin
Norfolk, Virginia

Dave Meltzer: I'm not really the best person to ask about this, but of the wrestlers I've spoken with, more have said Ray Stevens was the best worker at least from the early through mid-1960s and I've probably heard Terry Funk's name more than any other for the mid-1970s. Dory Funk is generally regarded as the best of the World champions of that era for how he defended the title, etc. This sounds contradictory, but lots of people will say that Terry Funk was a better worker than Dory, but that Dory was a better World champion than Terry. As for doing a book, if I was to do one, it would be a behind-the-scenes book on pro wrestling today and how it evolved to where it now is, but frankly, I just don't have the time doing the Observer weekly to devote to doing a project like that of the quality I'd like it to be.

DAN SPIVEY

After watching the latest Japanese tapes as well as the last two weeks of the NWA product, it has become obvious that Danny Spivey is one rejuvenated wrestler. He may not be any better than the bland and slow wrestler we all know too well, but it seems that wrestling with Genichiro Tenryu in Japan has given him a new intensity that translates into making him a much better ring performer. His borrowing of Tenryu's power bomb makes a very effective finishing move. I also felt that Spivey was the lowest man in the Varsity Club pecking order, but his teaming with Sid Vicious brings him to the forefront as the leader of the team which has great possibilities.

The Foot Loose has securely claimed the spot of being the world's best tag team. They are a joy to watch and give 100 percent in every outing. Since the Midnight Express has returned to the NWA, they seem to have a lost a bit of the magic which made them the best over the last three years. Finally, when the NWA did the video previewing Mike Shaw as Norman, half of it featured Shaw talking like an intelligent person and then he would switch into his psycho character. Since he has shown up as a wrestler, all we see is a George Steele retread with a poor work rate to boot. Wouldn't Shaw be better used if he entered the ring as a sane individual and his transformation into a psycho was triggered by a bump to the head during the match?

Chris Zavisa
PIymouth, Michigan

AWARDS

While I enjoyed your run-down of mid-year award favorites, I feel you neglected several worthy candidates for Match of the Year, Best Wrestler, Most Outstanding and Rookie of the Year. Generally, I find you emphasize All Japan rather than UWF, while to my taste the UWF's spartan philosophy and distilled fundamentals is preferable to the power-packed but somewhat clumsy All Japan.

For match of the year, many readers will undoubtedly select one of the three Flair vs. Steamboat matches and I don 't know that I can disagree. Overall I favor the New Orleans match, although of Late I find myself once again revelling in the Chicago match's high spots. Two UWF candidates stand out as well. December's Osaka match when Nobuhiko Takada beat Bob Backlund was one of the tightest amateur style contests we ever see in pro wrestling. And of course, the January Budokan Hall match when Akira Maeda avenged in loss to Takada in 29 epic minutes, showcasing textbook chain wrestling and submission holds and bursts of Ninja-style destructive high kicks. Pro wrestling of this calibre, viewed by fanatical sellout crowds simply can't be ignored. The January match was the first bout ever close circuited in Japan and both matches were among Gong's Top 100 most important matches of all-time.

As for Wrestler of the Year, I'm sure we 're all pleased to see Flair in top form, and Maeda still may repeat based on the UWF's success for the rest of the year. But my personal choice is Takada, especially for the two matches out lined above plus his extraordinary matches with Kazuo Yamazaki. Is Takada the best wrestler in the world. Certainly he can stand on equal footing with Flair, Tenryu and Maeda. Likewise Takada is a perennial candidate for Most Outstanding, a triple threat with kicks, submissions and defensive wrestling prowess. But what about Yamazaki? His style of lightning fast escapes and kicks recalls his teacher, Satoru Sayama. I also feel Yamazaki's rivalry with Takada has produced matches every bit as exciting and diverse and Flair vs. Steamboat and Tsuruta vs. Tenryu. As for top babyface, with the intense devotion and reverence attached to both Takada and Maeda, neither can be ignored. The Japanese have also provided two top rookie candidates in Takayuki Iizuka and Minoru Suzuki. Suzukis matches with Yoshiaki Fujiwarar Yoji Anjo and Shigeo Miyato is schooling he couldn't have received in New Japan's clogged lower ranks. Also his signing by UWF was a PR coup, a political and image victory by UWF over New Japan.

Lastly, how about considering a card of the year. As a long-time fan of Gordon Solie's, I love the Wrestling News Network and TBS Power Hour shows. In Stampede in Late 1987, Hiroshi Hase was one half of the Viet Cong Express. Who was his partner? Is Lord Blears bringing the UWF to Hawaii? If the NWA returns to New York, which venue would they promote? I can assure you that the Nassau Coliseum would be a washout once again. It's nearly impossible for metropolitan area New Yorkers to access. The only sensible choice is the Meadowlands or Madison Square Garden.

Clinton Freeman
New York, New York

Dave Meltzer: Hase's partner in the original Viet Cong Express was Fumihiro Niikura, who suffered a heart attack while wrestling in Canada and was forced to retire. Later Hase & Shinji Sasazaki formed the Viet Cong Express. Blears isn't bringing the UWF to Hawaii. According to my records, Minoru Suzuki started working full—time in June of 1988 and Takayuki Iizuka in November of 1986, so neither would be eligible for Rookie of the Year awards this time out.

TWO OF THREE FALLS

This is almost meaningless mat trivia, but judging by the letters, a lot of people seem to care. Many of Buddy Rogers' NWA World title defenses in Madison Square Garden were two out of three falls. His last 2 of 3 fall defense in MSG was in December of 1962 against Dory Dixon. Dixon won the first fall is less than 30 seconds, which was his trademark in those days, and because of that demanded a one fall title match, won handily by Rogers in February of 1963. The significance of the rematch is that it repositioned title matches in the Northeast as one fall matches and Rogers next defense against Johnny Barend was also one fall. When Bruno Sammartino came along to win the title in May, two of three fall matches became mostly a thing of the past.

There were a few exceptions. Reader Rich Kraemer pointed out Bruno's MSG defense against Tank Morgan. While the alleged reason for this bout being 2 of 3 was Tank's manager, Wild Red Berry, didn't want Bruno to get away by taking a quick fall (so Bruno won two quick falls in a row), this was a rare MSG card taped for television. Morgan tied with Bull Ramos as Bruno's worst all-time opponent in major arenas. Bruno also had a two of three fall match in the mid-1960s in the climactic match against Cowboy Bill Watts after a year-long feud. Watts took the first fall, but "injured his neck" during the second fall and was thus forced to forfeit the final two falls. Another instance in Boston was a two of three fall tag team match with Bruno & Tony Parisi vs. Toru Tanaka & Mitsu Arakawa. The twist of this match was that Bruno's belt was on the line should he be pinned, which of course he wasn't. There may have been a few other rare instances. Bruno did venture to San Francisco for several matches with Ray Stevens and those were two of three fall matches.

Mike Omansky
Wyckoff, New Jersey

TYSON IS KIDS' FAVORITE
On a sad note, Hulk Hogan was ousted as the favorite athlete in the Kid's Choice Awards on Nickelodeon by Mike Tyson. Hogan had won this award for a few years. Now Mike Tyson, that's a real role model for kids, a wife-beating, violent, suicidal, semi-lunatic.

Teresa DeMarie
Tuckahoe, New York

NO BLOOD IN BALTIMORE
The Baltimore Bash card looks really good and I'm excited to see it, but Baltimore, land of no blood, so how can they have a War Games? To me, a War Games needs blood to seem somewhat realistic and without blood the match will come off as cheap. I've seen War Games and they've all been good and I feel with the people involved, this can be an excellent match.

I think people worry too much about gimmicks and feel that Norman is insulting only because they need something to worry about. This is pro wrestling. Everything is supposed to be silly. Look at Akeem, or Jim Cornette. Even though he's great, he's still silly. His clothes purposefully clash. Pro wrestling isn't meant to be taken seriously and therefore Norman shouldn't offend anyone. If wrestling was to be

taken seriously, we wouldn't be seeing Jim Cornette fight Paul E. Dangerously in a tuxedo match.

As for manager of the year, I feel Cornette has it locked-up. Dangerously is the next best and Bobby Heenan follows them. Cornette seems to have this quality about himself that Dangerously lacks. Cornette can make one laugh, cringe or stand up and cheer. He remains over as a face and yet when they revert back to being heels, I feel he'll be over more than ever before. Though Dangerously comes up with good lines, his performance is way too forced and I'm sick of his petty, childish whining on the NWA Main Event. Cornette can whine and still come off good but when Dangerously whines, he's atrocious. I think Teddy Long is too staged, but he does do a good interview.

Craig Stambaugh
Clariton, Pennsylvania

JULY 31, 1989

Before getting into the news of the Baltimore Bash Pay-per-view show, a quick note that Tully Blanchard & Arn Anderson did win the WWF tag team titles from Demolition at the Saturday Night Main Event TV tapings on 7/18 in Worcester, MA. The Brain Busters captured two of three falls, winning the second fall via disqualification (which should mean that the title doesn't change hands but the WWF has poetic justice to change its rules as it pleases whenever it pleases) in a match that airs on NBC-TV on 7/29. To correct a report that has been listed in several newspapers, Rick Rude has not lost the Intercontinental title to the Ultimate Warrior. At least not yet and he won't until the SumnerSlam PPV at the earliest. Titan has done one of its occasional gaffes in a few newspaper ads for announcement at one Live card for Warrior vs. Andre the Giant matches billing them as IC title matches. The NWA isn't the only one that makes mistakes Like that.

BALTIMORE BASH

Thumbs Up: 214 (97.7 percent)
Thumbs Down: 5 (2.3 percent)

Results of a survey of telephone recorded messages to the Observer on Sunday night and Monday. This is a record number of responses so quickly to any show, and while not by percentage, the most impressive thumbs up percentage thus far (Nashville's Music City Showdown PPV show on May 7th actually received 100 percent thumbs ups), any response of 90 percent or better has to be considered a phenomenal level of agreement. Some comments :

"It was the greatest show I've ever seen. The only flaw was the Terry Funk interview. It was the greatest collection of wrestlers and the greatest matches ever. Ted Turner is going to turn it all around as soon as they improve the syndication."

Steve Blitz
Minneapolis, Minnesota

"The show was the best one I've ever seen but Sid Vicious should have stayed home."

Ricky Poole
Pittsburgh, Pennsylvania

"The show was real good. With the improvements in production, they now put the WWF to shame in every category. The WWF had better react and improve their next pay-per-view card."

"A huge thumbs up. There wasn't a bad match in the bunch. Flair vs. Funk was awesome and the post match brawl was incredible. I loved it. I was also very impressed with Luger vs. Steamboat."

Scott Hudson
Tifton, Georgia

"Thumbs up for the execution. It did the job it was designed to do in establishing Flair as the focal point babyface of the promotion and elevating Sting and Muta to main event status. Technically, they still have to learn to use the overhead camera better."

Michael Tearson
WMMR Radio, Philadelphia, Pennsylvania

"One of the best cards I've seen in many years. " Someone who would never want their name in the Observer but is on pro Wrestling Illustrated's list of the 25 most influential people in pro wrestling today"

"Thumbs up, especially for the last three matches. Flair vs. Funk was great and the spots with the chair in Luger vs. Steamboat were great. The Battle Royal was good, but Sting vs. Muta had too confusing a finish as it was too obvious that nobody was pinned. Flair was just great. "

Bob Closson
Springfield, Ohio

"Thumbs up. I come out of it saying that I'd like to see their matches if they come to my town. I thought Dan Spivey was excellent but the War Games was underwhelming. The top three singles matches were all very good."

Jeff Bukantz
Livingston, New Jersey

"Resounding thumbs up."

John Arezzi
WNYG Radio, West Babylon, New York

"Everyone here gave it a big thumbs up. The angle at the end was incredible. We've lost all interest in watching this show. We liked Muta vs. Sting but the finish was the worst execution that anyone has ever done of that angle."

Skeeve
Brea, California

"Thumbs up. Flair vs. Funk was awesome, Luger vs. Steamboat was excellent and Sting vs. Muta was okay. The rest of the card was iffy but the last match was real hot."

Ron Lemieux
Altamonte Springs, Florida

"Resounding thumbs up. The last four matches were all very good. I really enjoyed the show.

Larry Lovell
Hillsville, Virg inia

"The best pay-per-view show of all-time. One of the best cards ever. Utterly fantastic. There were at least four matches on the card that were four stars or better.

Chris Zavisa
Plymouth, Michigan

"The best pay-per-view ever. Flair vs. Funk was five stars. It would have won match of the year in 1988. "

Jeff Bowdren
Plantation, Florida

"Give it a nine on a scale of one to ten. You have to deduct a full point for the Sting vs. Muta finish."

Jeff Steele
Jackson Mississippi

"Thumbs down. The show was too long and the War Games didn't interest me. Flair vs. Funk was very good. "

"Definitely an emotionally satisfying thumbs up despite a few glitches. I can't describe how great the whole thing was. The camera work in the Battle Royal was the only complaint. Flair's ring entrance was picture perfect. Flair vs. Funk wasn't as good as Flair vs. Steamboat but it was still very good. The angle at the end was great because it elevated Sting and Muta to the main event status they deserve. I watched the last two Starrcades and neither was close to this card."

Dr. Mike Lano
Alameda, California

"The show was five stars. It was the best big pay-per-view show ever. But the souvenir stand deserves a negative five stars. They were still selling Dusty Rhodes caps."

As I write this, I've yet to watch the televised version of the card but will be watching it later in the week. I attended the show live, and also an excellent NWA show the previous night in Philadelphia and will report on the card from a live-show perspective. From what I'm told from those who were there live and have already seen a tape of the show as well, both the Battle Royal and War Games matches were better matches live because there was so much action the camera couldn't get it all in. I was also told that the match with Rick & Scott Steiner vs. Mike Rotunda & Kevin Sullivan was a better match on television than live and that Ric Flair vs.

Terry Funk was also better as a television match than live, although it was an excellent match live as well.

As a live card, from a strictly action perspective, the card was excellent. It was a lot better live for action than the Music City Showdown. It also built better from beginning to end then Nashville and had far more heat. While I'd rate the Flair vs. Steamboat match in Nashville as a better match than any matches from Baltimore, the final three matches in Baltimore (Steamboat vs. Luger, War Games and Flair vs. Funk) were all better than any other match on either the Nashville or the Chicago PPV shows. Nashville did have better finishes. There were a few downpoints to the show, particularly the Sting vs. Muta finish which was never explained at all to the live crowd (and never touched upon or explained to the TV audience until the end of the show as well).

From a live show perspective, this was the first unequivocal success of 1989 for the NWA, as the show drew a sellout of 12,500 fans (11,500 paid) and $188,000, which is the biggest NWA gate since the 1988 Baltimore Bash (Flair vs. Lex Luger). The Baltimore Arena usually holds 14,000, however seats had to be knocked out due to requirements for televising a first-rate show. The show did sellout in advance, which is doubly impressive since Titan was in town one week earlier and sold out, plus for casual fans, a 4:30 p.m. Sunday afternoon starting time is traditionally death for wrestling. It's too early to gauge the PPV numbers, but the talk the night of the show was the card was projected to do a 1.2 to 1.3 percent buy rate out of a 12 million home universe, although PPV figures aren't exactly always reliable statistics. If those numbers hold up, TBS should be happy. Not overwhelmed, but happy, because there are a lot of reasons why it shouldn't have done so well. Let's hope they learn from the mistakes in promotion (not ever running the card down properly in TV publicity and especially newspaper and TV ads, not having enough lead time before the card before announcing the main events, etc.) and continue some of the positive strides (the pre, post and between baseball game wrestling specials and overall greater commitment to the wrestling product by TBS).The NWA even pulled a Vince McMahon, as it got an ad in in many (but not all) markets which carried the Prime Time Wrestling show the previous Monday, advertising the card, which is kind of poetic justice for Titan getting WrestleMania ads in during the two Clash of Champions specials which competed with the shows. If the show does a legit 1.2 buy rate, it would mean it would be a $2.1 million PPV show, which would be profitable, but the company was "hoping" for a 1.5 to 2.0 buy rate this time around. The current plan now for the remainder Of 1989 big shows is for a Clash of Champions on Sept. 13, tentatively slated for Columbia, SC (show hasn't been booked but don't be surprised to see a Flair & Sting vs. Funk & Muta tag match on top), a PPV show called

"The Halloween Holocaust" on Oct. 29 from Philadelphia (main events "discussed" have included Flair vs. Funk in a cage, Flair vs. Muta and a longshot of Flair vs. Sid Vicious), a November Clash of the Champions, possibly from St. Louis (which would be a bad idea because St. Louis won't draw on a Wednesday night) and Starrcade on Dec. 15, most likely from either the Omni in Atlanta or possibly the Greensboro Coliseum (best bets on top would be Flair vs. Muta or Flair vs. Lex Luger).

Before running down the matches, I've got to make a comment about the NWA concession stands. When Titan comes out here, they generally average about $4 per head in gimmick sales, which is well above their national average, but it still gives you an idea of the potential of correctly handled souvenirs. For this, the biggest money gate and largest NWA crowd of 1989, the selection of souvenirs was awful and the quality of them no better. I usually don't bother with this stuff but was asked to pick stuff up for friends, and was so embarrassed by the stuff I didn't get anything. They also didn't have any t-shirts in little kid sizes, and even though the NWA isn't particularly strong with little kids in comparison to Titan, there were plenty of kids around and kids are far more likely to buy gimmicks than adults (one of the secrets of Titan's marketing success) so to have nothing available in kid sizes is outrageous.

1. The card opened with a two-ring "King of the Hill" Battle Royal. The wrestlers, who were never announced individually (a major mistake for a big show - not everyone knows who every wrestler in the NWA is), came to the ring with either Harley Race style Imperial Margarine crowns or the cheaper Looking Burger King cardboard crowns. Stupid as it cheapened the match. Battle Royals are basically dead these days and two-rings is awfully hard to televise, but as a live match, this was very good as Battle Royals go. Everyone was working hard. The guys in this one were Scott Hall, Ranger Ross, Ron Simmons, Brian Pillman, Bill Irwin, Danny Spivey, Sid Vicious, The Steiner Brothers, Kevin Sullivan, Mike Rotunda, Steve Williams and maybe one or two others. It wound up with Pillman and Vicious in Ring One and Williams, Rotunda and Spivey in the second ring. Finally pillman missed a flying move and went over the top rope in ring two leaving Vicious alone. Williams threw out Rotunda and Spivey eliminated Pillman from the second ring. Williams was destroying Spivey when Rotunda tripped him. As Williams was distracted, Spivey clotheslined him over the top. With Vicious in Ring One and Spivey in Ring Two, the "Skyscrapers" split the "$50,000" and gave Teddy Long the cheap looking Burger King crown to signify the winner. Good heat for a Battle Royal. ***

2. Brian Pillman pinned Bill Irwin in 10:18 when he leaped off the top rope in one ring and flew to the other ring onto Irwin for the pin. Solid pacing and basically good execution. A good prelim match. ** ½

3. The Skyscrapers beat The Dynamic Dudes (Shane Douglas & Johnny Ace) in a 9:14 squash match which was the only bad match of the show. Even though it was bad as a match goes, it was interesting and got good heat because of the crowd reaction to Vicious. The guy has big star written all over him, even if his work, ahem, isn't of the level of the rest of the NWA stars. The crowd seemed to cheer the heels more than the faces early, but instead of switching, instead just reacted to Vicious. When he was in the ring, the place went nuts cheering him, even though he didn't do much in the ring partially because he was working on a very bad back. Spivey did lots of good offensive moves but neither big guy sold anything and really "squashed" the Dudes, which was hardly necessary for them to get over. When Spivey was in, the fans booed and chanted "We Want Sid. Everytime Sid tagged in the place popped. When Sid tagged out, they booed. Spivey finally pinned Ace after a messed up power bomb. *

4. Jim Cornette beat Paul E. Dangerously in the Tuxedo Street Fight in a marathon 6:22. Dangerously threw powder on Cornette and got the early advantage putting the phone to Cornette's bad knee (and his good one as well). Legitimately, Cornette showed a remarkable knack for timing by blowing out his knee the previous night and he wasn't even able to walk too well. Given that handicap, and the fact that neither of these guys are wrestlers and that they weren't supposed to do any wrestling maneuvers, this came off very well. It was good comedy and the crowd was into it, even though the match went twice as long as one would have expected, even if Cornette was able to move around. Finish saw Cornette, who was pounded upon most of the way with Dangerously walking around doing the Buddy Rogers' exaggerated strut and slapping him around, do the Hulk Hogan superman comeback. Funny stuff. Dangerously went for the powder again, Cornette kicked his hand, powder went into Dangerously's eyes, and Cornette ripped his pants off revealing blue underpants and Dangerously ran to the dressing room. *3/4

5. Rick & Scott Steiner won a tornado match beating Mike Rotunda & Kevin Sullivan in 4:42. They traded chair blows early. Rick Steiner and Sullivan picked up where they left off the previous night brawling all over the outside of the ring while Scott and Rotunda were wrestling inside. They did a new spot where Rick went for the sunset flip, Sullivan went to sit down on him, but instead Steiner head-butted him in the groin. Finish saw Sullivan have Rick up for a bodyslam, Scott came off the top rope with a flying press and both brothers pinned Sullivan. After the match (and I believe this

never aired on TV because they were doing a slow-mo of the finish and then interviews) Sullivan and Rotunda started shoving one another and Rotunda walked out on Sullivan, but I believe this was done more to distract the fans from the fact that heels lost than actually to foreshadow an imminent turn. ** ½

6. Sting and the Great Muta went to a no decision in 8:40 in a television title match. Sting opened with an incredible dive from one ring to another onto Muta. Muta made a quick comeback and did a dive on Sting outside the ring. This was a typical Sting match, a great beginning and great action at the finish but needs work around the middle part. Finish saw Muta try to blow mist, Sting ducked and it went into Nick Patrick's eyes. Sting then missed the Stinger splash and Muta hit the moonsault press as Tommy Young came out but Sting kicked out at two. Sting then used a back suplex and young counted three even though both men's shoulders were up. It was then announced that Sting was the winner and still champion, and moments later, Muta left with the title belt and none of this was explained to the live crowd. In reality, they are going to "hold up" the titles saying both men's shoulders were up (similar to a finish Terry Gordy and Dr. Death did a few years back on TV over the UWF title, but they did it better).***¼ (would have been rated higher except for the lack of explanation and bad execution of the finish)

7. Lex Luger beat Ricky Steamboat via DQ in 10:26 to retain the U.S. title. This was an excellent match, which is probably the only reason fans weren't really upset with the DQ finish even though the actual sequence of finish was excellent and popped the crowd like crazy. Four weeks ago on television it was announced that this would be a no DQ match, and the booking sheet all along listed this as a no DQ match. A few weeks later, Steamboat does a TV interview issuing the challenge for a no DQ, forgetting the fact that on at Least two occasions, the match was already advertised as no DQ. Luger continually refuses the no DQ, and on TBS the day before the show, it was announced it wouldn't be a no DQ but a regular rules match. Then, the ring announcer announces it was no DQ. Luger then grabs the mic and says if it's no DQ he would leave but if it was regular rules, he'd stay. Since this was originally also billed as No.1 contendership vs. U.S. title, Luger refusing the no DQ makes little genuine sense since he would have every bit as much to gain from the win. And if it was going to be regular rules with a DQ finish; which it was, then they shouldn't even talk about no DQ on television until after this match and use no DQ stips for the rematches (which they are apparently going to do). Anyway, Steamboat and promoter Gary Juster get talking and Steamboat agrees to a regular rules title match. The idea behind this is to make

Luger "back down" from the no DQ stip in an arrogant manner to get him heat from the crowd, but instead it makes the promotion look Mickey-Mouse on a show they can least afford to and at a time when that perception is what is killing them. Luckily, this whole tirade really is for naught because the match was so great that nobody has a right to complain about anything. Luger brought in a chair, but Steamboat used it on him for the DQ. The finishing spots where Steamboat held the chair over Luger as Luger begged (exactly the same but with roles reversed of the most emotional scene from the last Clash with an arrogant Luger taunting a begging Steamboat before hitting him with a chair) was incredible. Steamboat chased Luger all the way to the back with a chair, then Luger tried to jump Steamboat on the stage and Steamboat clobbered him once again with the chair. They worked at such a fast-pace, nearly flawless technically and did about 25 minutes worth of stuff in a 10 minute match. For pure work, you can't give Steamboat enough praise. The crowd started out pro-Luger but they turned during the match since Luger plays such a tremendous heel with his mannerisms. He seemed really upset at a section of fans at ringside who chanted "steroid faggot" at him. ***

8. The babyface fivesome of The Road Warriors & Midnight Express & Steve Williams beat the fivesome of The Samoan Swat Team & The Freebirds in 22:18 of a War Games when Hawk made Jim Garvin submit to a hangman hold. This was excellent live but heard it didn't come across as well on TV. All action all the way through with lots of stiff clotheslines, in fact, almost too many. Bobby Eaton opened against Jimmy Garvin and they did lots of bumps (well, Bobby did) and it was good action even though not a lot of heat because the crowd was waiting for the big guys to come in. Gordy came in next after the heels won the coin toss (how do they always manage to do that?) and Williams followed and press-slammed Gordy over his head eight times in succession for the awesome strength feat of the show. Samu and Animal followed, with Animal going on clothesline fever. Fatu and Stan Lane followed, with Hayes next until finally Hawk came in and went nuts. When Hayes came in, he DDT'd all four guys. Hawk did a dive from one ring to the other and nobody was even looking to get hit. Hawk just took off without his foes even ready for the thing . After the submission, the whole heel team trapped Animal in the ring and pounded on him until the faces made the save. ****

9. Ric Flair made his return to the ring after the second longest ring absence of his career and pinned Terry Funk in 17:23 to retain the NWA title. This was not your typical Flair match. In fact, it was simply a brawl both inside and outside the ring from bell to bell with double juice of the

heavy variety. The juice literally stunned the crowd into silence since this is Maryland and that stuff isn't allowed, however the NWA basically "challenged the commission" on its anti-blood position before the card and won. The commissioners actually left the show prior to the start of this match so they wouldn't have to actually be there for the carnage. Funk came to ringside with Gary Hart, which gave us scary thoughts but Hart really only got involved once. Funk broke a figure four by using the branding iron thrown in by Hart. Funk went for the spinning toe hold, Flair reversed it to the figure four leglock (shades of Jack Brisco vs. Dory Funk in the early 1970s), Funk caught the inside cradle (same sequence he won the NWA title from Brisco with in 1975 and that Steamboat beat Flair earlier this year in Chicago with) but Flair reversed it once again for the pin. After the match Muta ran out and spit the green into Flair's eyes and Funk and Muta doubled on Flair until Sting made the initial save but they doubled on him and Flair came back to save Sting and they wound up brawling with chairs all over backstage for several minutes in what was the best television brawl since the "Battle Of New Orleans" two summers back in the old UWF with Sting & Chris Adams vs. Eddie Gilbert & Terry Taylor. A lot of the crowd missed most of the brawl live which is why this match as a whole was better on TV than live. **** ½ (Note : I 'm told that if you include the post-match antics, that I couldn't see live, that this was a five star).

NOTES

Jason Hervey of "The Wonder Years" TV show was back and did the ring announcing for the Dynamic Dudes. He played Terry Funk's son on the old ABC-TV brief series "Wildside" in 1985 which had the misfortune of being put opposite Cosby and quickly disappeared. Ring entrances were first-rate and glitzy once again which is becoming part of the NWA's big-show package. On TV at the end of the broadcast it was announced that the title was held up between Muta and Sting. Lots of guys working at less than 100 percent. Johnny Ace suffered a broken cheekbone about ten days earlier. Terry Funk has been working on a fractured sacrum in the lower back and yet is still having excellent matches nightly. Vicious had the back injury. Cornette worked on a blown out knee. Even announcer Jim Ross' voice was dead before the show even started from calling so many matches per week for the last few months. I'm told that there were several spots where it appeared his voice would go, but his call of Flair vs. Funk rivalled the Flair vs. Steamboat Chicago match as one of the best "called" matches in recent memory. If the advertising and hype of these matches ever catches up to the action level, things will turn around. August is going to be interesting because most of the big shows have Flair vs. Funk, Steamboat Vs. Luger no DQ, Sting vs. Muta, Warriors vs. SST in a cage and

Hayes & Garvin vs. Midnight Express for NWA tag team titles as the headline matches.

Apparently there is at least a little smoke to the rumors of a possible mixed match with boxing champ Mike Tyson against pro wrestler Bam Bam Bigelow. At Least Bigelow has told friends that this deal is just about a lock, and as the story goes, the match would take place in the fall of 1990, probably at the Egg Dome in Tokyo. Tyson is over huge in Japan and the reason the match would be in Japan is to take advantage of several things: 1) Tyson is every bit as over in Japan as in the United States; 2) Pro wrestling is far more respected by the general public and even though it is fairly well known that the "sport" is a work, the wrestlers themselves are far more respected by the general public as great athletes; 3) Bigelow is very popular in Japan, however if he were to lose, it wouldn't hurt the wrestling business since Bigelow has done jobs for the upper echelon pro wrestlers in Japan as well. I do believe that Bigelow himself has been led to believe this is coming off since he's had his side try and settle legal differences with Larry Sharpe that he 'd been putting off. Supposedly, this would be a mixed match, and not a boxing match, but that Bigelow would have five or six tune up matches against boxing opponents" (the boxing term for jobbers) leading up to the big match, in which Bigelow would earn $500,000 (keep in mind not to believe money figures like that). I 've heard from the boxing side that talk of these type of "freak" matches with the likes of Bigelow, Mandarich and George Foreman are abounding because Tyson is in the position right now where the public doesn't believe that any "real boxer" stands a chance against him so they have to use "freak attractions" to get up the curiosity level. And don 't think Don King isn't well aware of the success Vince McMahon has had with Zeus, who is basically an outside freak attraction who isn't even a part of the wrestling business.

Speaking of Zeus (Tom Lister), the angle to set up SummerSlam was taped on 7/18 in Worcester for this Saturday's SNME on NBC. Randy Savage was wrestling Brutus Beefcake in a match said to be the best one Beefcake has ever been involved in. There were lots of near falls when Savage sent Sherri Martel back to bring in Zeus. When Beefcake gets the sleeper on Savage, Zeus interferes for the DQ and generally destroys Beefcake with one blow. Hulk Hogan makes the save and throws everything but the kitchen sink at Zeus, who doesn't sell a thing (similar to the television angle a few years back when Dusty Rhodes made Big Bubba Rogers) Everyone was pleased to death how the thing turned out.

Hogan is legitimately on the injured list right now, having missed matches in Indianapolis, St. Louis and Grand Rapids over this past weekend due to a pinched nerve in his neck and severe headaches. From what I'm told, Hogan in no way could work Indianapolis, but wanted to work St. Louis on Saturday but was talked out of it. This isn't a serious injury, but the last talk I 've heard is that it is expected the WWF will cancel Hogan's scheduled appearences this weekend in Reno, Nev. and Nashville and he go back to work the following weekend because Titan doesn't want to jeopardize SummerSlam. Give Titan credit for two things here: 1) Realizing everything revolves around the PPV and taking precautions not to hurt the show by having an injured Hogan have to work with an inexperienced Zeus; 2) In every city, Titan worked hard at informing the local media that Hogan wouldn't be there, posted signs outside the arenas and offered refunds at the building. Titan flew in Beefcake and Elizabeth, neither of whom were scheduled for the shows, to oppose Savage, which is most likely what will happen this weekend as well.

We've pretty well got the complete line-up for the SummerSlam show on 8/28 at the Meadowlands and on PPV: Hogan & Beefcake vs. Zeus & Savage with Elizabeth and Sherri in the corners; Andre & Twin Towers vs. Demolition & Jim Duggan; Blanchard & Anderson vs. Hart Foundation for WWF tag team titles; Rude vs. Warrior for IC title; Dusty Rhodes vs. Honkeytonk Man; Ted DiBiase vs. Jimmy Snuka; Rougeaus & Rick Martel vs. Rockers & Tito Santana; Mr. Perfect (Curt Hennig) vs. Red Rooster (Terry Taylor) and Hercules vs. Greg Valentine and probably there is a match or two left unannounced at present. It should at least be better than last year's show because a few of the undercard matches (Brainbusters vs Harts, Rude vs Warrior, DiBiase vs. Snuka, Rougeaus 6-man and Hennig vs. Taylor) at least have potential to be decent to very good. The last count I'd heard, which was as of Thursday of last week, was that 17, 000 of the 21, 000 tickets had been sold, so the show could very well be sold out before you read this.

"No Holds Barred" is still around at the $1 theaters and over the weekend of July 14-16 the movie did $195,275 in 285 theaters (split being 90 percent to the theaters and 10 percent to New Line Cinema which means Titan's cut of the entire weekend would amount to around $6, 000). As of July 17th, the total gross for the film was $15, 588,628. It's good for a low budget film to be sure, but those who are calling it a big success or a blockbuster are overstating things. The Robin Williams Dead Poet Society movie, which opened the same weekend as NHB and opened weaker, is now at $69 million for a comparison.

Also this past Monday was the debut of Roddy Piper as Gorilla Monsoon's co-host on Prime Time Wrestling, followed by the debut of the Bobby Heenan show. I've heard a lot of comments both positive and negative (mainly negative) aboutboth changes, but it appears the negatives are going to win out this time. Piper's PTW debut drew a 3.5 rating for the 90 minutes, which is very good. The Heenan show that followed did a 3.1 rating, which is still much better than USA generally did with the last half hour

of PTW. However, the powers that be in both USA and/ or WWF weren't pleased with the product mix and expect major format changes as early as next week. I didn't catch either Heenan show, but saw bits and pieces of both PTW's with Piper and as someone who enjoys Piper at least 90 percent of the time, found no chemistry there (I realize it is a very tough job trying to interact with Monsoon) and didn't enjoy Piper with the exception of a very few decent zingers.

The AWA and Bob Syres have come up with a team wrestling concept that they are trying to sell to independent TV stations similar to the proposed "American Gladiators" TV show that will be around in the fall. The idea is to do a 52 week schedule with teams of three male wrestlers, a male midget wrestler and a female wrestler competing in singles and tags for one hour shows and eventually have teams in a championship, etc. similar to the concept of Team Tennis. They've come up with the idea of at least three teams - Larry' s Legends captained by Larry Zbyszko; Team USA captained by Sgt. slaughter and the West Coast Waves captained by (don't laugh now) Roddy Piper. The idea is just to do syndication TV shows, no house shows, four pay-per-view shows in 1990 and six home videos. They are promising the stations that carry the shows cuts from the home videos and the PPV, and they are telling stations they could make $250,000 per year carrying the show so they may get some early clearences before the stations realize the scam. Anyway, Gagne and Syres sent four-page proposals to almost every independent station in the country looking for spots between 10 a.m. and noon on Saturday or Sunday or 4 to 6 p.m. on Saturday. They are planning on debuting this concept in eight weeks. Oh yes, the teams will have unlimited substitutions which of course would be necessary given the turnaround rate of the AWA. Gagne originally wanted to get the idea pitched to TBS. No way this concept can work because the basic lure of pro wrestling is mano/ mano combat, not teams, and as a one-time gimmick, like in Japan, team concept shows have done well (but remember the audience in Japan is more sportslike to begin with) but the promotions have always been smart enough not to overdo the concept .

Entertainment Tonight did a feature on the WWF vs. NWA wars last Monday night as its lead story. My own impression of the piece is that Vince McMahon came off like the schoolyard bully even though most of what he said as far as his competition's arena shows and TV ratings not being what they should be was totally valid. The piece really made the NWA look minor league in comparison with Titan, and in many ways, to an outsider, that is the impression that almost everyone would come up with. I don't know, but when I watched the piece it made the NWA 100k Like it was the USFL trying to tackle the NFL and made the promotion 100k like a dingy replica instead of trying to explain that in many ways the two groups present very much different products.

A quick correction from last time out. I mentioned that they are having Ultimate Warrior pose with kids in the lobby at the Cow Palace card out here for $6, but actually Polaroid has gotten involved with Titan and they let kids take pictures with an Ultimate Warrior cut-out.

We also attended an NWA show on 7/22 in Philadelphia before about 3,000 fans paying $39, 000. A humorous note. After the first match, ring announcer Joel Goodhart announced the next date for Philadelphia in August and then talked about the Flair vs. Funk match the next night in Baltimore and said how the promoters had signed the winner of tomorrow's match to defend the title against the loser of tomorrow's match" to virtually no crowd reaction. After the next match, Goodhart then announced the date again and said the main event would be Ric Flair vs. Terry Funk and the place went wild. I guess the moral of the story is you can't make things too confusing for wrestling fans or they won't understand them.

1. Big Al Greene & Ron Siltunons beat Scott Hall & Joey Maggs in 8:30 when Simmons pinned Maggs after a shoulderblock from the middle ropes. All four guys worked throughout, but there were plenty of missed moves and such.

2. Norman the Lunatic pinned Ranger Ross in 6:21. Actually live, Norman does pretty funny comedy. Ross came out with the American Flag and Norman then tied toilet paper to a stick and started waving his flag. The match itself was mainly Norman doing comedy. Ross got a big pop doing a bodyslam near the end. Finish saw Ross hit the combat kick and went for the pin but Teddy Long slapped him. Ross went after Long, Norman got him from behind and pinned him. ½ *

3. The Skyscrapers beat Johnny & Davey Rich in 7:40 when they used a double powerbomb on Davey. Davey took a 4200 flip after a clothesline from Sid Vicious just before the finish similar to the bump he took on the Friday Night Power hour from Sid. Basically a squash match and the crowd cheered the Skyscrapers as the faces. * (the star is strictly for the one bump)

4. Dynamic Dudes beat New Zealand Militia in 6:20 when Shane Douglas pinned Jack Victory with a cross bodyblock. Douglas was hit with a canteen before the match and took a hard bump on the floor. Fast paced good match.** ½

5. Mike Rotunda pinned Scott Steiner in a suplex match even though foot on the ropes during the pin in 5:38. ** ½

6. Kevin Sullivan pinned Rick Steiner in an incredible brawl for 5:10. Most of the match was outside the ring with them using tables, chairs, ring steps and everything else. Rotunda and Scott came out before the finish. Finish saw Rotunda throw in a foreign object, but ref Tommy Young intercepted the thing and as he yelled at Rotunda, Sullivan pulled his own object out and hit Steiner with it for the pin. Match would have been four-stars but too short. *** ½

7. Great Muta pinned Eddie Gilbert in 11:20 in a Coal Miners Glove match. This was a good match with an excellent finish. Paul E. Dangerously was at ringside with Muta and Gary Hart. I believe Dangerously threw in the kendo stick for Muta but Gilbert got it away and used it, then threw it so Missy Hyatt who chased Dangerously to the dressing room with it which was one of the high spots of the card for more than one reason. While this was going on, Muta sprayed Gilbert with the mist and got the glove. Gilbert tried to hit Muta, but instead KO 'd ref Nick Patrick. Gilbert used the glove and somehow when it was down and the ref was down, Hart then hit Gilbert with the glove and Muta rolled over for the pin. *** ½

8. Lex Luger beat Ricky Steamboat via DQ in 14:10 in a U.S. title match in a match that was even better than their PPV match. They did at least 25 minutes worth of moves and spots in 14 minutes, plus did lots of brawling outside the ring with chairs and tables. I can't describe how great this match was but to me it was better than anything in Baltimore. Steamboat shoved down the ref as he was pounding on Luger when Ron Simmons and Al Greene ran in and they tripled on Steamboat until the Dudes made the save, and they did the pull-apart brawl after it was over. Officially they DQ'd Steamboat for hitting the ref. Luger was the clear crowd favorite strongly during the match but the heat was incredible throughout and the crowd did slowly turn in favor of Steamboat, though not to the degree they did in Baltimore. ****

9. Sting beat Terry Funk in a no DQ match by pinning Bill Irwin in 14:35. Another fantastic match both inside and outside the ring. They used chairs and tables again and brawled on the table as well. I hate finishes of this type because they are rip-offs and it shows that this commitment to getting guys to do jobs has floundered. They had a no DQ match, but to appease egos or something, they still didn't have anyone lose. Obviously the day before the PPV, Funk should not have Lost but they seem not to want Sting to lose either, and if that's the case, they shouldn't vhave booked a no DQ match . **** (would have been rated higher except for the finish.

10. Road Warriors & Steve Williams & Midnight Express beat Freebirds & Samoan Swat Team in 16:15 of a Bad

Street match. Early in the match Terry Gordy threw a table at Jim Cornette and Cornette jumped down from the apron and blew out his knee and had to be helped to the dressing room. Road Warriors are using lots of Foot Loose moves now. Finish saw Garvin come off the top rope to hit Williams, who was being held by Gordy but Williams moved and Garvin hit Gordy, and then Williams cradled Garvin from behind. After the match the Warriors and SST brawled to the back. *** ¾

NOTES

Several that I talked with said that was the best Philadelphia card in about two years, which is amazing considering it was the night before an afternoon PPV show. Truthfully I expected everyone to go through the motions here, particularly with the small crowd, but not so in the least. No complaints about the action, but lots of complaints about the finishes of Scott Steiner-Rotunda, Kevin Sullivan-Rick Steiner, Luger-Steamboat (which apparently was advertised on TV as a no DQ match) and especially Sting-Funk. After watching Rick Steiner work both shows, I'm convinced that he can't be hurt, at least not by anyone else.

FLORIDA

The Nasty Boys, who held the tag team title, were fired on Tuesday when they refused to do a television draw with another team and the Star Riders are in temporarily to take their place. Dick Slater is returning while Frankie Lancaster is already in. Power Twins coming in August. The name PWF is now history and they are back to being called Florida Championship Wrestling (FCW). Steve Keirn is Florida champion feuding with 5 and previous shows approaching $10,000. Wayne Coulter is the majority (60 percent) owner with Sir Oliver Humperdink as booker. Jeff Jarrett is supposed to work some dates in August and they are working with Jarrett to bring in some World Class wrestlers. They drew about 200 on 7/22 in Ft. Lauderdale. Brett Sawyer & Jimmy Backlund will have already dropped their gimmick as "The Playboys" before you read this. Dallas Page does TV color with Gordon Solie and has a group of heel fans who cheer for him called "The Shade Brigade ". 7/23 in Orlando saw Sawyer beat Mike Awesome, Ron Slinker beat Dennis Knight, Lou Perez beat Rock Hard Rick, Windham beat Jeff James, Jumbo Barretta beat Lancaster and Keirn beat Ho Chi Winh. No—shows that night were Nick Busck, Dick Slater, Nasty Boys and Al Perez.

CWA

Jerry Lawler hosted the TV show this past weekend with Dave Brown on vacation and actually the announcing was the best it has been in a long time. The highlights of the 7/17 Memphis card saw Master of Pain beat Dutch Mantell when Ronnie Gossett threw in a foreign object, Mantell

intercepted it and used it but MOP still kicked out. Mantell went to the top ropes but Gossett tripped him and he fell off for the pin. They are billing this as a teacher (Mantell) vs. student (MOP) feud. The main event saw Jerry Lawler go to a double count out with Bam Bam Bigelow in a USWA title match with double juice that was said to be an excellent match. Newcomers to the area are Al Perez and Headbanger Ed, the latter of whom is one of Larry Sharpe's students.

They had an eight-man tag match on television on 7/22 with an interesting twist in that Doug Gilbert was on the heel side and Freddy (his father Tommy) was on the face side and they did meet at one point during the match.

The 7/24 card in Memphis had a tournament for the new Tennessee tag team titles which Jeff Jarrett & Ricky Morton won by beating The Blackbirds (King Parsons & Brickhouse Brown) in the finals. Other teams in the thing were Wildside (Mark Starr & Chris Champion), Headbanger Ed & Doug Gilbert, Lou Winston & Lou Fabbiano, Dustin Rhodes & Bill Dundee, Black Bart & Dirty White Boy and Freddy & Stan Frazier (Uncle Elmer). Also on 7/24 was a Mantell vs. MOP no DQ rematch and Lawler defending the USWA title against Perez.

7/16 in Jonesboro, AK drew 550 as Fabbiano drew Gilbert * ½, Mantell beat Champion via DQ when MOP interfered ** ½, Rhodes pinned White Boy ** ½, Freddy beat MOP via DQ when Gossett interfered *, Bart went to a no contest with Bigelow in a battle of heels CWA title match when both heels jumped ref Jerry Calhoun and Lawler made the save using a chair DUD, Jackie Fargo beat Gossett in a boxing match - **, as bad as anything you ever see) and Blackbirds beat Lawler & Dundee when Bigelow distracted the ref and Harris hit Lawler with his cane ** ¼.

ALL JAPAN

Genichiro Tenryu & Stan Hansen captured the PWF World tag team titles and PWF International tag team titles from Jumbo Tsuruta & Yoshiaki Yatsu in the main event on 7/11 in Sapporo before 3,800 fans when Hansen pinned Tsuruta after the lariat. The rematch with the two teams is set for 7/22 in Kanazawa. This makes Tenryu holding six different title belts at once which is probably an all-time pro wrestling record (PWF heavyweight, NWA International, United National, PWF World tag team, Int. tag team and NWA 6-man with Road Warriors) Also in Sapporo, Joe Malenko pinned Dean Malenko in 15:34 to keep the PWF World jr. heavyweight title, The Fantastics (Tommy Rogers & Bobby Fulton) beat Tom Zenk & Jim Brunzell when Rogers pinned Brunzell, Samson Fuyuki drew with Kenta Kobashi, Shun-ji Takano pinned Toshiaki Kawada, Giant Baba & Rusher Kimura & Kabuki beat Masa Fuchi & Motoshi Okuma & Haruka Eigen (who are now known as "The Wild Company"), Big John Tenta pinned Goro Tsurumi, The Destroyer (Dick Beyer) & The Terminator

(Marc Laurinidas) beat Akira Taue & Isamu Teranishi and prelims. 7/13 in Yagumo drew I,750 as Tenryu & Foot Loose beat Tsuruta & Kabuki & Taue, Brunzell, Hansen Baba inned Tenta, Yatsu & Takano beat Zenk & & Kimura beat Okuma & Eigen, Malenkos beat Shinichi Kikuchi & Fuchi, Fantastics beat Kobashi & Mighty Inoue, Destroyer beat Teranishi and Terminator beat Tsurumi. Fantastics are doing very well on the tour and it looks like a good shot that they'll be added to the December tag team tournament which looks right now to be a first-rate action tag team tournament with Tenryu & Hansen, Dynamite Kid & Davey Boy Smith, Dan Kroffat & Doug Furnas, Fantastics, Zenk & Brunzell, Foot Loose, Tsuruta & Yatsu and Terry Gordy & Danny Spivey as the teams. The latter combination is something NWA should consider since the tag tournament could overlap Starrcade (although usually it ends around 12/10). All Japan seems to have abandoned all finishes except clean pinfalls on the big Tokyo shows because of the influence of the UWF, and ironically, at the same time, this group has become the hottest promotion in Tokyo .

NEW JAPAN

The big Riki Choshu push started this weekend with Choshu capturing both this group's World heavyweight and World tag team titles. On 7/12 in Osaka, Choshu pinned Salman Hashimikov for the World title and the next night in Tokyo he teamed with Takayuki Iizuka to upset Super Strong Machine & George Takano for the tag team titles.

7/11 in Fukichiyama saw Choshu & Masa Saito & Osamu Kido beat Big Van Vader & Kokina the Samoan & Biff Wellington, Hashimikov pinned Corporal Mike Kirchner, Machine & Takano beat Kengo Kimura & Tatsutoshi Goto, Jushin Liger pinned Akira Nogami, Shiro Koshinaka pinned Shinji Sasazaki, Brad Rheingans pinned Kuniaki Kobayashi, Naoki Sano pinned Norio Honaga and Iizuka & Kantaro Hoshino beat Black Tiger (Mark Rocco) & Black Cat.

7/12 in Osaka saw Choshu pinned Hashimikov in 7:40, Liger (Keiichi Yamada) kept the IWGP World jr. title beating Black Tiger under European rules (rounds) when he used the Liger bomb (double arm suplex dropped into a power bomb) in 2: 53 of the fifth round; Machine & Takano beat Koshinaka & Iizuka, Vader pinned Chimur Zarasov, Rheingans pinned Kido, Sano pinned Nogami, Kimura & Masa Saito beat Kirchner & Kokina, Sasazaki pinned Wellington and Kobaya shi pinned Honaga.

7/13 in the Tokyo Sumo Hall drew a non sellout of 9, 950 as Choshu & Iizuka beat Machine & Takano for the tag team titles in 16:08 when Choshu pinned Takano after a lariat, Vader pinned Hashimikov in 8:45, Liger kept the IWGP jr. title going to a double count out with Sano in 13:55, Saito pinned Kokina, Kido & Kimura beat Rheingans & Kirchner, Kobayashi & Koshinaka beat Black Tiger & Wellington and prelims.

OTHER NEWS ITEMS

We've heard all sorts of conflicting stories on Davey Boy Smith. One is he's going to stay out of action for a while for insurance reasons, another that he'll be back in action in about one month. Owen Hart started back with Stampede wrestling this past Thursday and for right now all the cards are being headlined by Hart vs. Dynamite Kid. (Ch. 69) in Atlanta will carry the NWN s syndicated TV shows which is the first time the NWA syndicated TV shows have ever aired in Atlanta due to the exclusivity the local station WTBS wanted in the market. NWA has closed a deal with the Canadian CTV network and will start getting national TV coverage in Canada during September.

The UAWF's annual convention will take place Aug. 11-13 in Chicago. Dennis Condrey won the CWF title as a babyface from Tom Prichard on 7/22 in Dothan, AL, then turned heel later in the card. Bob Geigel is going to promote an 8/10 card in Kansas City with Mike George vs. Bob Orton in a taped fist match, Larry Zbyszko vs. Greg Gagne for the AWA title, Akio Sato vs. Paul Diamond. Robert Gibson's house was struck by lightning on 7/19 (which I also believe is his birthday) and the house was a gigantic mess when he got back in town two days later.

The "Shade Brigade" heel fans, who aren't plants, brought a home-made Russian flag for Comrade Nick Busick on 7/11 and were chanting, "Russia, Russia" during the TV tapings.

The Stud Stable is back in CWF with Robert Fuller, Jimmy Golden, Brian Lee, Sylvia and Downtown Bruno.

7/20 in Knoxville has a 10 man cage match with everyone on the undercard, Robert Fuller & Brian Lee defending the "World" tag team titles against Tracy Smothers & Steve Armstrong, Dennis Condrey vs. Don Harris for the CWF title, Adrian Street vs. Terrence Garvin, Tom Prichard vs. Wendell Cooley, Danny Davis vs. Mike Davis, Jimmy Golden vs. Ricky Morton and Todd Morton vs. The Storm Trooper.

Bob Raskin's USWA has a show 7/29 in Lansing, MI headlined by Sgt. Slaughter vs. Ivan Koloff and will also hold two cards in Virginia during August with Slaughter and Nikita Koloff as the top babyfaces.

Harley Race, The Beast, Steve Casey (from England), Ron Starr, Cuban Conunandos (Cuban Assassin & Jerry Morrow), Leo Burke, Eddie Watts, Frenchy Martin, Wayne Gillis and Phil LaFIeur (who I believe is Japan's Dan kroffat) are working in Nova Scotia this summer.

WWF

The 7/29 TV Guide has an article about WWF wrestling. Sherri Martel and Zeus were guests on Arsenio Hall on 7/21 with Zeus chasing Hall around the studio. Jake Roberts was getting a lot of personal harassment apparently since one newspaper in Georgia, in reporting on his legal problems, actually listed his home address.

Nothing major at the TV tapings in Worcester and Utica this past weekend aside from the SNME things already covered.

Hogan beat Honkeytonk Man after smashing the guitar on him and delivering the leg drop, Jimmy Snuka pinned Greg Valentine when Ron Garvin got involved, Ultimate Warrior beat Rick Rude via DQ in a good match. They brought in a jobber to 100k like Ric Flair at the tapings and another jobber from Tennessee was billed as "Bobby Jarrett. Another inside dig was in the Toilet Bowl sketch with Dusty several weeks back, in the bathroom there was an autographed photo of Rock Hudson signed to a prominent member of a rival organization.

Big Steele Man worked dark matches as a babyface at the taping but didn't get over at all as a face. In Worcester he beat Boreus Zhukov, but in Utica, did the job for Mr. Perfect in a match that nobody seemed to care about. All American Wrestling did its lowest rating of 1989 on 7/16 getting a 2.2 rating, which is actually Lower than the TBS Saturday show did for the firSt time in quite a while.

7/22 in St. Louis drew 8,700 and $89,000 as Badnews Brown pinned Sam Houston, Dusty Rhodes pinned Ted DiBiase, Demolition beat Twin Towers via DQ, Mr. Perfect drew Bret Hart (best match on card), Tim Horner pinned Barry Horowitz, Barbarian pinned Jim Neidhart and Brutus Beefcake pinned Randy Savage when Liz slapped Randy to set up the pin. They had to refund only 300 tickets in St. Louis and less than 50 in Indianapolis on 7/21 after announcing that Hogan wasn't going to be appearing. Indianapolis did a $107,000 gate for what was supposed to be Hogan vs. Savage while Grand Rapids, MI on 7/23 did a $57,000 house.

7/9 in Toronto drew 2, 500 as Jim Duggan & Hillbilly Jim beat Andre the Giant & Haku, Beefcake beat Savage. via DQ, Bushwackers beat Brain Busters, Mr. Perfect beat Hercules, Warlord pinned Koko Ware, The Genius pinned Paul Roma and Tim Horner pinned Mike Sharpe. No wrestling back in Toronto now until the closed-circuit showing of SummerSlam on 8/28.

7/10 at the Nassau Coliseum drew 5,800 ($80,000) as Horner pinned Sharpe, Warlord beat Ware, Hennig beat Hercules, Genius pinned Jose Luis Rivera, Duggan & Hillbilly Jim beat Andre & Haku, Roma pinned Sandy Beach, Beefcake beat Savage via DQ and Demolition beat Twin Towers.

The new domed stadium in Toronto seems to be the leading candidate for the next WrestleMania, but it isn't the lock that the newspapers in that city have been saying it is.

NWA

World Championship Wrestling on 7/15 drew a 2.4 rating and 6.7 share which is the highest share (but not rating)

that the show has drawn since the summer of 1987 when the ratings started going into the toilet when Dusty Rhodes turned the show into the 30 second squash/ 90 second interview format. The Power Hour show the night before was up to a 2.0 rating (it had drawn a 1.7 the previous two weeks).

NWA will move to an early morning Saturday time slot (I believe 9 a.m.) on WPIX in New York starting Sept. 16 so expect live shows in New York around November. .
Kangaroo Athletic Wear based in St. Louis will be coming out with a line of shoes called "Flair," "Sting" and "Luger" after the NWA wrestlers.

NWA cards earlier last week in both Amarillo on Tuesday and Lubbock on Monday drew sellouts. The only thing I know about Amarillo is they did a Power Hour match with Tommy Rich vs. Eddie Gilbert which went to a semi-scientific draw (and you should have heard all the fans in Philadelphia who thought they were smart telling everyone that Gilbert was going to turn on Sting at the Baltimore show - actually I thought it was a possibility as well). Amarillo drew 4,000 and I heard Terry Funk was a babyface in his match against Sting on that card until the finish with outside interference.

7/1 in Charlotte drew a $49,000 house as Brian Pillman pinned Bill Irwin, New Zealand Militia (Rip Morgan & Jack Victory) beat The Ding Dongs (Greg Evans & Richard Sartain), Norman the Lunatic pinned Steven Casey, The Skyscrapers beat Randy Rose Ranger Ross, Terry Gordy pinned Dick Murdoch when Jimmy Garvin interfered, Great Muta beat Eddie Gilbert via count out in the Dragon Shi match, Rick & Scott Steiner beat Kevin Sullivan & Mike Rotunda in an elimination tag team match, Rick Steiner threw out Norman to win the 2-ring Battle Royal, Sting beat Terry Funk via DQ when Norman interfered, Midnight Express beat Michael Hayes & Jimmy Garvin via DQ, Samoan Swat Team beat Road Warriors via DQ and Lex Luger pinned Ricky Steamboat in 22 minutes.

7/12 in Carbondale, IL drew 1,058 paid and $10,716 as Dynamic Dudes beat New Zealand Militia, Skyscrapers beat Johnny & Davey Rich, Rotunda pinned Murdoch, Muta beat Gilbert via COR in the Dragon Shi match, Steiner won the 2-ring Battle Royal, Steiner pinned Sullivan, Road Warriors beat Norman the Lunatic & Fatu, Sting beat Funk via DQ, Freebirds beat Midnight Express & Steve Williams when Gordy DDT 'd Stan Lane.

7/17 in Lubbock, TX drew a sellout 2,000 as Pillman pinned Irwin *, Militia beat The Bell Brothers (Ding Dongs) DUD, Skyscrapers beat Johnny & Davey Rich **, Norman pinned Shane Douglas DUD, SST beat Scott Hall & Steven Caey ** ¼, Steiners beat Sullivan & Rotunda ***, Sting beat Funk via DQ with Murdoch as referee **** and Midnight Express & Steve Williams beat Freebirds **** Steamboat's contract expires on 7/30. From all accounts it seems the

NWA wants him to stay and he wants to stay, but the new deal hasn't been reached.

There was a pretty major article in the Jackson, TN newspaper as Eddie Gilbert issued a challenge to kickboxer Anthony Maness. Maness is a kickboxer from Lexington, TN with a 7-1 record (only loss a TKO against World champion Bill Superfoot" Wallace) and the two went to high school together.

Ric Flair appeared on Ron Barr's Sports Byline USA show (the one I 've been on a Eew times) on Thursday night and Bruno Sammartino was on Wednesday. Thursday it wasn't carried here because the station it is on carries the A's games, but Bruno was pretty good on Wednesday.

THE READERS' PAGE

COMIC BOOKS

A quick note to bring you up-to-date on the Von Erich Warriors comic book. According to my best industry sources, the maximum number of copies that this thing could have sold is 1,200. I have no idea how many the publishing company printed, but the magazine was not well received in the comic market.

It had two things going against it. One was that no advanced advertising appeared in the trade publications. Second, it came from an unknown publisher, so retailers must have been extremely reluctant to take a chance on the publication at all. Considering the quality of the actual publication, in this instance, the instincts of the retailers was probably correct.

The WWF comic book from Blackthorne Comics sold in the neighborhood of 2,500 copies. Both of these publications were unprofitable, even though they were printed in the much cheaper black-and-white format. It is possible that they had other venues of distribution outside the comic book sales market which could have made them profitable, but inside the comic market both these titles bombed very badly.

Dave Olbrich
Newbury Park, California

"NO HOLDS BARRED"

I saw "No Holds Barred" with about 10 people in the entire theater. Two women in front of me were talking and asked me, "Clint Eastwood isn't in this, is he?" "No, he's not, I replied. "Well, what's this movie about. Do you know," she asked, It's about wrestling and Hulk Hogan is in it." "Oh," she replied. "I Like Hulk Hogan.

This is the difference between the NWA and WWF. Even people who don't have any idea about any aspect of pro wrestling know Hulk Hogan. Had I said the movie starred Ric Flair, they probably would have walked out of the theater. I think it's a shame that such a charismatic and entertaining performer as Ric Flair who works so hard night-after-night to make bums look good gets looked over and sidestepped by the general media and the general public.

Kevin Abernethy
Rockaway Park, New York

WRESTLERS EMBARRASSING THEMSELVES

What do the following people all have in common - Adam West, Joe Howard, Bob Bell and Red Skelton? Answer: They all made a damn good living by masquerading as characters whose appearance and/or behavior ranged from the silly to the ridiculous. West was TV's Batman. Howard was Curly of the Three Stooges. Bell as Chicago's Bozo the Clown for more than two decades and Skelton was one Of the wackiest comedians of all-time. And there are plenty more just Like them. Zanies, whose character portrayals served to entertain millions and enable them to succeed in their chosen field. Certainly, no one ever questioned their moral fiber. Which leads me to my point.

The raging concern that guys like Terry Taylor and Mike Shaw are embarrassing themselves to the point where they shouldn't be able to look at themselves in the mirror in the morning has really gotten out of control.

Now, I've never been an advocate of much of the havoc that Vince McMahon has wreaked upon pro wrestling, but developing appropriate characters for what is, or at the very least has become, an entertainment industry does not fall into that category. Harmless, cartoon-like characters like The Red Rooster and The Blue Blazer fill an important marketing niche that McMahon has oh-so-successfully developed. On the other hand, characters like Slick and Akeem that tread on tenuous moral grounds are a different story and do not, in my opinion, fall into the same category. Guys like Taylor and Owen Hart, who fill these well-paying roles, are doing nothing more than making sound business decisions.

As for those who remain in mourning for all the athletic ability that is going to waste, let's get serious. Like most of us, Taylor, Hart and Shaw and the rest are just trying to earn a living, not qualify for the Olympics. Batman and Curly may have been sensational athletes at heart, come to think of it, Moe saw to it that Curly took some awesome bumps, but athletic prowess just wasn't what their specific jobs called for.

As has been suggested on these pages several times before, Taylor does not need nor is he in all likelihood looking for the approval of a select group of fans who respect the work rate that he is genuinely capable of. Terry would rather build himself a handsome nest egg than win the Obsever's Wrestler of the Year award. Quite frankly, if my boss was willing to pay me $100,000 to put a red streak in my hair and crow at client meetings, I'd be at the barber shop this afternoon.

However, if those of you who are concerned about Taylor's self-image wish to put your minds at ease, look at it this way, it's not Terry Taylor who is making a fool of himself. It's his character. The Red Rooster. Terry's just the one who is cashing that nice fat paycheck.

Jeff Siegel
Evanston, Illinois

Dave Meltzer: The correlation between the actors and the wrestlers is a good one. In both forms of entertainment, and in most other forms as well, there are two sides to it. There is the performance and ego side and there is the pure business side. Most entertainers that I know, both in wrestling and other entertainment fields, the performance and ego sides is a lot stronger than the pure business side. This is what allows promoters to screw performers, which happens in every field, because the promoters are well aware that the vast majority of performers enjoy being celebrities more than they enjoy the money that comes with being a celebrity. In wrestling, there are those who are in it purely for the money and don 't care about performance at all. Others don't care about money, they just want to be stars and of course the vast majority fall somewhere in between the two, with the younger wrestlers generally more star-struck and the veterans who see the end of the line, looking more for how much I can make before the time runs out. In every entertainment field, there are clown roles, just as in wrestling. In most of these fields, however, the top-level performers, by both their own abilities and the ego drive which motivates one to be a top-level performer in their chosen field, usually don't play the more demeaning clown roles and if they do, are definitely embarrassed about it. Even Roddy Piper, who hardly qualifies as the world's greatest actor or an acting superstar is embarrassed about some of his early films. Adam West himself, who you brought up, has often over the past 20 years questioned whether his most famous role (Batman) typecast him to the point it destroyed his acting career. Mike Shaw, by his very look and size, is limited to what roles he can perform in pro wrestling. He'll never be an athletically gifted superstar so he has to get by using exaggerated character roles and doing strong interviews and getting his gimmick over. As for Taylor, only time will tell. For personal reasons, he pretty well was forced to go to Titan last summer and Titan wants its wrestlers to be obedient robots. He is making more money than ever before. Whether that is worth it to him is his own personal choice that he has to make. But I do know that most of my friends who are very casual wrestling fans or not fans at all, have seen him on the NBC specials and the first thing that has been said in public to me like on more that than occasion is just how depressing it must be to have to humiliate yourself in public like that to make one money. And I feel uneasy trying to justify it, because I realize

that to the average adult, that is what it looks like. What do you say? You say he's making a six-figure income? I don't know. The problem with a top worker playing these roles is psychological. I know enough wrestlers to say conclusively that there is a noticeable personality and drive difference and also pride difference between your top performers, mid-level performers and guys who coast through. The top guys pay way more attention to detail and every aspect and are more devoted to the profession. The same drive to be a top worker is the very antithesis of what having to play a cartoon-role where this ability that has taken years to learn is not allowed to be used. The paycheck may be worth it. Others may do it because they literally have no alternative, and in a few year, nobody may have any alternative if this becomes a one-promotion business in the country. But don't think for a second that a great performer who is not being allowed to perform doesn't get depressed about the aspect, even if he's being well paid to humiliate himself. If he didn't, he'd never have the drive to make it as a great performer to begin with. And in Owen Hart's case, at this stage of his life, he decided that being a great performer in Japan was personally more agreeable to him than being the blue blazer.

NWA

I have to agree with your comments concerning the NWA and the WWF. The NWA in my opinion represents the better wrestling show but the WWF is the better promotion. As a WWF fan for many years, my loyalty has switched of late to the NWA because I'd rather watch better wrestling. I'd faint if I ever saw a match the calibre of Flair vs. Steamboat in a WWF ring. The NWA has a long way to go, but I see them heading in the right direction. I just hope they don't sacrifice the product along the way when they improve the promotion, but keep the wrestling strong and improve the promotion.

Harvey Gampel
Baltimore, Maryland

Although the 7/8 Boston Gardens had no more than 5-6000 fans, it was an event that few of us who crave some action in this WWF dominated city will never forget. The crowd was special. A teen had an amateur wrestling headgear on and mimicked Rick Steiner's barks. Another youngster had on a jacket and painted his face up like Muta and he had two younger siblings with Muta face paint on as well. A bug guy had a Hawk haircut with the patented face paint. The place was loud for most of the card. I'm writing a letter in appreciation of Steve Nazro, the director of events at the Boston Gardens for letting the NWA in.

Tony Amara
Boston, Massachusetts

The Philadelphia Bash was like Dr. Jekyll and Mr. Hyde. The show was boring at the beginning and great at the end. When Terry Funk came out to do his antics it was the most heat ive ever seen live and that includes Hulk Hogan appearances at the Spectrum. Lex Luger tried hard as a heel but still basically got a positive reactions from the crowd. Luger is so much better now than two years ago as a heel. I could envision him as a world champion down the road. The NWA is so much more enjoyable to watch right now than the WWF in my opinion. The wrestling product is so much better, but they still have to learn to do more creative finishes in their big matches. Ric Flair should draw as a babyface but not as well as Hulk Hogan or Ultimate Warrior.

Chris Polus
Lansdowne, Pennsylvania

The Great American Bash was a disappointment to the Washington, D.C. fans. Being the first one and being at the Capital Centre, you would think they would have put on a good show. They brought in Scott Hall, Brian Pillman and the Dudes and nobody knew who they were. I sat next to a Japanese family who came to the U.S. three months ago and they are interested in Terry Gordy, Muta and the Road Warriors. They were on a downer because all the Warriors did was clotheslines and Muta only did one move. The Freebirds 6-man match was great but the Sting-Funk angle before the match killed the match. Steamboat vs. Luger has most of the fans cheering for Luger as his turn wasn't well known. The Bash has been special in the past because it meant Ric Flair every night and without Ric Flair, it was really bad. The NWA without Ric Flair would be in real trouble.

Robert Costolo
Gaithersburg, Maryland

Concerning the angle where Eddie Gilbert threw fire at Muta, suppose when they first started showing the angle when Muta spit mist at Missy Hyatt, they should have milked it to death ala Elizabeth on the Saturday Night Main Event last February. Every week they should have shown Missy making a step-by-step recovery. The WWF would have replayed the incident over-and-over for weeks including updates, visits to the Doctors office, etc. They should put Missy in an Elizabeth type role. Fans would them have gone for the revenge angle between Eddie Gilbert and Muta and at the peak of the feud, have Gary Hart appear to mislead and lie to Muta ala Snuka and Albano allowing Muta the opportunity to become a tremendous babyfac .

Name withheld by request

It is absolutely mind-boggling how the NWA promotes its house cards on the local syndicated TV shows. It is as if they don't want people to come to the live shows. For the past

several weeks on the Baltimore TV stations, when plugging the 7/23 Bash during Joe Pedicino Knows, they have never mentioned Flair vs. Funk or the War Games. They use a different beginning each week, then Pedicino says, "Let's run down the entire card" and the matches they announce are Sting vs. Muta, Cornette vs. Dangerously, a 2 ring Battle Royal, a World tag team title match plus Freebirds, Road Warriors, SST, Dynamic Dudes, Teddy Long's "Connection" (not even referred to as The Skyscrapers) and more. What an awful way to sell this big card to the local fans, and this line-up was still being plugged on TV one week before the show.

Instead, they should have run down the correct line-up with localized interviews each week. Not giving the entire card for a card this big is a joke, let alone giving an incorrect card. If the NWA can't perform a simple task such as advertising the right card on television, how in the world do they ever expect to compete with the WWF.

Name withheld by request

If there was ever any question in the minds of Boston wrestling fans about the NWA being minor league or a feeder circuit for the WWF, the Great American Bash answered it once and for all. No way. The action for the most part was very high calibre and most of the fans I spoke with said the WWF's cards in Boston and Worcester couldn't hold a candle to the NWA show. Regrettably, the crowd was rather small, but it was noticeably more vocal and enthusiastic than any WWF crowd I've ever seen at the Gardens. You can tell the NWA fans are true wrestling fans. The WWF fans simply routinely cheer for the faces, regardless of ability. The NWA fans cheer for the best moves and the best action. The Skyscrapers were over huge as faces, despite heel status. WWF fans cheering for the Brain Busters on the other hand would bring down a hail of napkins and paper cups from the no-minds that fill the stands.

Except for the Scott Hall vs. Bill Irwin snoozefest, the matches were Loaded with great moves, great bumps and sick out of the ring brawling (Steiner vs. Sullivan and Funk vs. Sting were masterpieces of brawling). There were not one, but two ring-to-ring aerial maneuvers that would top any move on any WWF card in recent months except for the Hogan superplex on Bossman. The only tactical mistake was not letting Kevin Sullivan win on his home turf and teasing the fans with the possibility of an SST turn on Paul E. Dangerously.

I suppose there is a good deal of truth in your observations about the general public perception of the NWA. While the cognoscente can certainly appreciate the superior quality of the NWA's product, the rabble are still into Titan's high-gloss, high-profile presentation. I can't understand why the NWA didn't try to do more of a tie-in with Terry Funk's recent film appearence in Road House, which was a hoot and much more satisfying a movie than the much-maligned No Holds Barred. It is that the NWA doesn't know how to exploit the star quality of its wrestlers. The NWA still has the greatest attraction in wrestling in Ric Flair. If you ask me, the Luger turn was necessary as they need his arrogance to balance out the namby-pamby goodness of the reborn Flair.

David Gionfriddo
Brookline, Massachusetts

ENTERTAINMENT TONIGHT
The segment on Entertainment Tonight was keen and quite penetrating. Having Mary Hart lead off the show with this story lent credibility to wrestling and zeroed in on the steep odds against the NWA and examined the basic dichotomies that position the WWF miles ahead of the NWA in virtually every category. In my interpretation, even Ted Turner conceded it was almost a lost cause. And Vince McMahon's closing remarks vis-a-vis a hypothetical match between the two entrepreneurs, as imagined by Terry Funk, were genuinely awesome. Vince, make no mistake, intends to keep suplexing, body slamming and pinning the NWA and Ted Turner every chance he gets. The saddest part of the piece was seeing those empty seats in Chicago.

I've only attended about five NWA shows this past year, three in Baltimore and two in Philadelphia. The period from Dusty to Turner has been so confusing. They can't decide on a game plan. They operate entirely too much on ad lib promotion and their TV schedule on TBS smacks of suicide. I wish the NWA well, but even their slogan of "We Wrestle" and claims of their superior wrestling smacks thin. Frankly, when the WWF can boast of and book talented workers like the Rockers, Demolition, Savage, Bret Hart and Curt Hennig, one must give proper credit. Finally, while they may not be great technicians, I admire Brutus Beefcake and Jim Duggan, especially in the case of Duggan, who is now clean.

Edie Bailey
Aberdeen, Maryland

BOBBY HEENAN SHOW
I know most of the hardcores probably wanted to kick in their TV's at "The Bobby Heenan show" but as television, I found it really funny. It reminded me very much of Martin Mull's talk show parody, "Fernwood 2Night," which had a big cult following in the mid-1970s. What they should try to do is develop running characters like "Fernwood 2Night" did and the nerdy character from the opening show should certainly be considered for such a part. Even when the guest isn't bad in the right kind of kitschy way (as was the case with the mother and daughter comedy team), Heenan is so good on-camera and his persona is so strong that he can keep the show afloat.

Of course, taking Heenan off Prime Time Wrestling has left the show with no chemistry. The Monsoon-Piper pairing has no spark and Piper's antics came off forced in his debut. He's such a great heel that I've always found his babyface schtick to be a little forced, and he was more interesting on PTW when he took an in-between sort of perspective like when he was saying that both Tito Santana and Rick Martel are good wrestlers. This approach is far more effective than having Piper be just another shill for the faces.

Paul Sherman
Brookline, Massachusetts

I just got finished watching "The Bobby Heenan Show." I can honestly say it's the worst thing I've ever seen masquerading as entertainment. At its very worst, TNT was 100 times better and that isn't saying much for TNT. Just how dumb does McMahon think his audience is? Does he really think that people are going to tune in each week to see the Oinkettes and cheap Raymond Babbit clones? It's a real testament to either my will or my stupidity that I watched the first show all the way through. I do have to give Vince credit for one thing. He has a real talent for making 30 minutes seem like 30 years.

As much as I like Roddy Piper, I don't think he fit in well on PTW. Piper needs space to get crazy and the show is far too structured for that. He seemed uncomfortable working with Gorilla Monsoon as well.

The piece on Entertainment Tonight. was interesting. McMahon seemed extremely hostile for someone who isn't concerned about having any competition. I'm in agreement with you that TBS is showing a firmer commitment toward wrestling. That's comforting, because the WWF is getting worse.

Michelle Johnson
Watertown, New York

I was really looking forward to Roddy Piper's return to the WWF, but after his first appearence on PTW, I can honestly say I wish he had stayed retired. He was so annoying I had to turn the show off after an hour. He added no insight, his jokes were terrible and his constant "on-ness" made him come off more like the Ultimate Warrior than Roddy Piper. The only good thing that can be said for him is he drowned out Gorilla Monsoon. Hopefully in the upcoming weeks he'll calm himself down a few thousand notches, or better yet, take a few lessons from Paul E. Dangerously on NWA Main Event or best yet, piledrive Elizabeth at SummerSlam or hit her with a coconut.

Andy Stowell
Pittsburgh, Pennsylvania

VIDEO GAMES

In response to Bill Kunkel's letter on video games in the 7/10 newsletter, Bill Kunkel obviously did not read what was written in the Observer a few weeks earlier about the new upright arcade video game from American Technos, Inc. a division of Technos of Japan.

American Technos has nothing to do with the Acclaim WrestleMania video game, nor the wrestling games produced by Nintendo. Both of these games are of poor quality and are television games. American Technos, in conjunction with the WWF, has produced an arcade game, for street locations, featuring most of the well-known WWF stars. It has three modes of play. One person can play against the computer, two players can play against the computer in a tag team or players can play against each other.

Players get to choose which WWF wrestler they want to be. Each wrestler is programmed with his own gimmick. Jim Duggan does the football stance. Honkeytonk Man does the Shake, Rattle and Roll. Ted DiBiase uses the sleeper hold. The game features bodyslams, backbreakers, flying kicks, punches, leg drops, piledrivers, etc .

The best thing about the game is that it allows players to "book" their own finish. If for instance, a kid is wrestling as Honkeytonk Man against another kid who is Hulk Hogan, Honkey can win if the kid is better at the game. That means that a kid can overcome Hogan and McMahon's egomania, even if nobody else can. In effect, you can make Hogan do a job for everybody.

American Technos has designed two of the top money-making games in the coin-operated video arcade industry, Double Dragon and Double I. The graphics are terrific in these games but the graphics in the WWF Superstars game are even better I've been in the coin-op video business for more than ten years and can say with certainty that the characters in the American Technos game are more lifelike and less cartoonish than in any video game in the market today.

Again, in no way does this game have anything to do with the Acclaim WrestleMania video game, or any other wrestling video game on the home video market. The upright WWF arcade game sells for $2,695 and is the top-rated game in America and Japan right now, making more money per location than any other game. It is also the top selling "kit" (at $1,495) in America and Japan, which means the buyer is only purchasing the control board and graphics and installing it in a used upright console. There is no home video version of this game.

Freddy Curtaz
Daly City, California

AUGUST 7, 1989

The top story of the week is that barring a last minute break of a negotiation impasse, that Ricky Steamboat's days with the National Wrestling Alliance will likely be over before you read this. Steamboat's contract with the NWA expired at the end of July and as of our last word, which was late this week, it appears both sides were far enough apart on terms and no move was being made to get together. The NWA was busy by mid-week making alternative plans for Lex Luger, while it appears that Steamboat wasn't nearly as likely to make any sort of a long-term deal as he had been.

There are several unfortunate things about this impasse, the main one being that my own impression is that it all could have been avoided. Maybe not, but at one point, the two sides were only $10,000 apart when it came to a yearly salary figure but that negotiations fell apart shortly after Steamboat agreed to certain terms that had been offered and then was told that the offer had been pulled off the table, and the two sides haven't been close since.

Last week in Baltimore the word out was that even if Steamboat didn't resign, that he would be working the dates advertised in August on a nightly guarantee, however by mid-week the NWA was already making plans to have other wrestlers (Tommy Rich and Steve Williams) fill the slots so my impression is that at least for the present, we've seen the last of Steamboat in the NWA.

What exactly does this mean? In the short run it hurts, since coming off of Baltimore, Steamboat vs. Luger was a hot issue and in its position in August, as second from the top of the card underneath a Ric Flair vs. Terry Funk headline match, it was a very strong match for that spot on the card. In the long run, it's not a killer. No loss of personnel by either major organization would be of major long-term significance except for Flair and Hulk Hogan. From a business standpoint, the loss is probably the same, or maybe a tad bit more significant than earlier in the year when the NWA fired Barry Windham, who was also a key headliner that a lot of time had been devoted to building to be a major star.

From a morale standpoint, both the NWA's wrestlers and its fans will see the loss as more major, because it comes across to the public as another in a long line of cases of what appears to the public as the NWA being unable to keep its top talent. Even though Steamboat wasn't the most popular wrestler in the NWA, he was a name star and held the group's World title for ten weeks this spring, not

to mention his involvement in the three most memorable matches in the United States of this and most other years. But overall, talking strictly business, the loss hurts some short-term, but over the long haul, whether the NWA turns it around or not, while Steamboat certainly would have been of help, whether he is with them or not isn't the significant factor as to what the future holds for the NWA.

Where the loss hurts the most is product quality, undeniably. Since his return to pro wrestling in January, Steamboat hit top form almost immediately and the consensus view of virtually everyone around is that with the possible exception of Flair, Steamboat night-after-night was the best worker in the business in this country overall this year. And my own belief is that the return of Steamboat is a major factor in how spectacular Flair has performed this year as well, and the effect is felt to some degree overall up and down the card. The top guys in the NWA don't like to be shown up on cards, and since the top guys aren't held back in order to not overshadow less talented guys getting a bigger push as in the WWF, it elevates the entire quality of the top matches to have a wrestler like Steamboat on the show. In a sense, as for show quality, it would have given the show two Ric Flair's. For a group whose sole advantage over its competition, and only real advantage, is its superior quality of actual wrestling action, the loss of someone of that quality, especially when I have to believe it could have been avoided, is unfortunate.

From the other perspective, one can argue that Steamboat wasn't a great drawing card, which is the same argument that can be made about every NWA wrestler this year since before the PPV Bash from Baltimore, the NWA hasn't had any truly outstanding houses all year. But it would be fair to say his popularity didn't quite match up to his work, which is more of a product of how wrestling fans have been educated towards this business (or more precisely, not educated) in this country, but it's also a fact in the present day. I don't know the salary figure that was being negotiated and asked for and offered by each side, so I don't want to call either side unreasonable. I do know that both sides were willing to accept a one year contract, in which Steamboat would agree to work roughly four dates per week, which would be less than some of the full-timers like Flair, Luger and Sting would work, but a similar deal to what the Road Warriors now have (and certainly nowhere near as Lucrative as the Warriors' deal).

BALTIMORE BASH FINAL POLL RESULTS

Thumbs Up:	457 (96.8 percent)
In the middle:	2 (0.4 percent)
Thumbs Down:	13 (2.8 percent)

This is from the results of telephone recorded messages and letters to the Observer during this past week. Phone messages which came after Thursday in California, Friday on the West Coast and Saturday everywhere else are not included because they could have been influenced by opinions in last week's Observer. Letters were accepted through Saturday. Of course, this is a completely unscientific poll with the margin of error being right around 97 percent.

A few notes to add to last week's comments:

*After watching the PPV broadcast tape a few times, my own rating for both the Sting vs. Muta match and Steiner brothers vs. Sullivan & Rotunda matches were too low. Even with the bad finish, I still can't give Sting vs. Muta any less than 3 ¾ stars and the Steiners match has to be three stars, even if it was too short.

*Television did not do justice to either of the two ring matches (The Battle Royal and the War Games). Both were significantly better live, even though the comments by Paul E. Dangerously and Michael Hayes at ringside was an added plus for the TV audience during the War Games. But TV viewers missed a lot of hot action in both matches.

*TV viewers also missed a highlight during the Steamboat vs. Luger aftermatch. While the TV audience was watching a replay of the finish, Luger attempted to sneak up from behind Steamboat on the stage, and Steamboat caught him with a chair blow or two and chased him away once again.

*Television never does complete justice to any Ric Flair match, because television never gives you the full impact of just how stiff the chops really are. However, with all the outside the ring antics, particularly after the match, this was one Flair match which was overall every bit as good on television. Still, even with the post-match antics, I'd give it 4 ½ stars.

*The natural comparison is going to be made between the Baltimore show and the Nashville show because overall they are the two best PPV shows in the four-and-a-half years of major wrestling events on PPV. Having been to both shows live, Baltimore was clearly the better house show. It also had more heat up and down the show. After being in Nashville and then watching the tape, I was blown away with just how good the show televised. In Baltimore, even throwing in the post-match brawl and the better overall quality of the matches, the PPV showing didn't blow me away. Part of that comes from being spoiled and quite frankly, several of those who voted thumbs down on the phone admitted that part of the view was being spoiled by the Flair-Steamboat matches at the two previous shows. But you can't expect a match that good every time out, nor can you have a World title change on every PPV card, so for that reason alone, in many people's eyes, both Chicago and Nashville did top Baltimore.

*The camera work was not good during the Battle Royal, but it must be difficult-to-impossible to try and do justice to two rings at the same time with 14 different competitors. From that point on, the camera work at least did justice to the show and didn't miss more than two or three key moves

(outside of War Games which once again has its inherent problem of too much going on at one time for a television broadcast) although some of the angles during the flying sequences particularly of Sting and Muta could have made the moves look even more spectacular. Overall it was the best of any show, with almost none of those annoying cutaways to the crowd, and none that I could recall in the middle of high spots, which had plagued the NWA on most big shows.

*The announcing was exceptional during the Flair vs. Funk and Steamboat vs. Luger matches, although it helps to have matches of that quality to call. Still, the preparation Jim Ross and Bob Caudle did in getting certain facts and intertwining them with calling the match added greatly to the match, particularly in comparing and contrasting the careers of Steamboat and Luger and their strengths as wrestlers. The commentary was good throughout except for the Jim Cornette vs. Paul E. Dangerously match. Ironically, one would have thought the only way to commentate on a match which before-hand looked to be a totally silly premise (watching them rip each other's tuxes off) would be to take the comedy approach, which they did. However the way the match went, with Dangerously going after the knee and Cornette obviously being hurt, should have forced the announcers to switch gears because until the final stripping of Dangerously's pants, this wasn't a comedy match after all. Toward the end the announcers changed gears, but there were too many cracks about the effeminate nature of both competitors after the match suddenly turned not only serious, but wasn't really even a badly worked match.

*Some will disagree on this, but I felt Gordon Solie was great in his role. Actually the only interview where Solie seemed to make a difference was the Ric Flair interview, a soft-spoken interview just before the match. Solie's questions were great, because in the context of the story line and if this was all legit, they were all the exact questions that should be asked.

*Will this show turn things around? It can't hurt, but being a major factor all by itself, no. First off, only 13 percent of the homes in the U.S. even had the capability of getting this show. Even if you figure that the NWA has a slightly stronger following among cable homes than non-cable homes because of its TBS exposure, you are still talking about a show that somewhere between 80 and 85 percent of the fans who would want to watch it probably wouldn't have had a chance to, at least not at their own home. Second, the buy rate, which depending upon which source you choose to believe was somewhere between 0.9 and 1.4 percent (probably not far off Nashville, but well below both Starrcade '88 and Chi-Town Rumble and slightly below the WWF's lowest PPV, the January Royal Rumble) which means the vast majority of viewers were the regular weekly TV viewers. A show of this type can expand your audience because the very nature of finding out about the show and the willingness to pay $15 for it in most cases limits you to fans you already have. My own impression, and every arena I've been to for the NWA seems to bear this out, is that to the "hardcore" audience which craves action, and to the serious wrestling fans, while they may complain about the NWA at times, they will support them whenever they present what looks to be an attractive product. The NWA's problems are the less serious fan, which by and large they don't attract and that's the fan which will make the difference in the long run if the company will ever become a profitable entity. The fans who quit watching the TV over the last year or so, very few of them most likely bought the PPV so it's not like a great show will win them back. With a buy rate of around one percent, you are hardly getting much in the way of casual viewers, so even if they would be entertained or blown away by the quality of the show, it's the more widely-viewed Clash of Champions shows and the week-to-week television antics that have to turn the business around. The PPV show will just be the financial windfall of the fruits of the labor if and when interest levels greatly increase, but PPV buy rates aren't going to go up until the television ratings are consistently up. It can't happen in reverse. As far as simple momentum for the company, the show should be a positive sign. But as far as the future of the NWA goes, I do believe we've seen the worst. But for things to get to where they need to be for the company to be profitable and stable will take a team effort, but right now there is far too much backstabbing and petty jealousy within the company which is slowing down progress.

The WWF ran Saturday Night Main Event on 7/29, taped on 7/18 in Worcester, MA. The main purpose of the show was to do the angle to set up SummerSlam on 8/28, and the angle couldn't have come out better. As for action, this show was nowhere near the level of the previous two, but they were two of the better SNME's since the show started:

1. Hulk Hogan pinned Honky Tonk Man in 6:00 to keep the WWF title. Hogan basically destroyed Honky at the outset until Jimmy Hart hit Hulk with the guitar to give Honky his first and only brief advantage. By the way, it was that guitar hit, which hardly looked as dangerous as that one Honky Tonk Man did in 1987 to Jake Roberts (and they showed a replay of it on this show and it's no wonder Jake's neck has never recovered from it) which is being blamed for Hogan's pinched nerve in his neck which has kept him off the recent house shows. The two worked at a decent pace, but the execution was awful on both sides. Honky hit his shake, rattle and roll finisher and strutted around rather than got the pin, Hogan made the superman comeback, hit Honky and Hart with the guitar, then used the legdrop for the pin. Basically awful. ¾*

2. Jimmy Snuka pinned Greg Valentine in 3:00. This match was just a backdrop for some sort of angle they are working with Ron Garvin. Before the match they had Jack Tunney announce that if Garvin got involved in any more unprofessional antics as a ref that he'd no longer be a ref. Valentine and Garvin argued, then Garvin punched Valentine, and Snuka flew off the ropes for the pin. In 1982, this would have been a great match, but it isn't 1982 anymore. ½*

3. Brutus Beefcake beat Randy Savage via DQ in a (surprise, surprise) great match. Savage had his working shoes on tight, and Sherri Martel at ringside worked harder than just about anyone in this organization. Beefcake wasn't bad either, in fact he was at his best, which means he was average. They went eight minutes before Savage ordered Sherri to go back and bring in Zeus (Tiny Lister on stilts, check out those boots they must have had four inches of lifts in them). After the commercial break, Zeus interfered when Beefcake got the sleeper on for the DQ. Zeus put Beefcake in the bearhug when Hogan came out and punched him to break the hold. Hogan threw a few haymakers at Zeus who sold nothing but laughed at him and put Hogan in the bearhug. Beefcake broke it and threw his haymakers and Zeus laughed at him as well. Hogan hit him with a chair and he didn't budge again. This was done so well it's scary, but Zeus is still an insult to anyone who understands or appreciates anything about pro wrestling. *** ¾

4. Brain Busters (Tully Blanchard & Arn Anderson) won the WWF tag titles from Demolition in a two of three fall match. For those of you who are trivia buffs, I believe Demolition's title reign was the longest in WWF tag title history, and also that Blanchard & Anderson would be the first team ever to hold World tag title recognition in both major promotions. First fall saw Smash pin Anderson with a hotshot in 5:00. Second fall saw Demolition get DQ'd at 5:00 for double-teaming. Third fall saw Andre The Giant throw in a chair which Blanchard used on Smash and Anderson pinned him in 3:00. The pacing was good throughout, but the match was nothing special and really wasn't as good as their bout on the last SNME. ***¼

For you trivia buffs, a few years back in Cleveland there was a SNME match with the British Bulldogs beating the Hart Foundation in a best of three fall match in which one of the early falls was via DQ and it was said that if there is a DQ in any fall, the title can't change hands. Not that consistency means anything in pro wrestling (with any organization, not just the WWF).

No announcement came forth this past Tuesday about Bam Bam Bigelow getting involved with the boxing world, so I'm tempted to believe that whatever was being talked about is far from being a sure thing. Anyway, nobody in boxing seems to know anything about this and I've heard nothing from Japan about it either, which normally would be the first place news of this type would break.

The WWF usually does a good job of satisfying its audience, with this past week at the house shows they didn't. On 7/27 in Tucson and 7/28 in Las Vegas, the main events were the first two U.S. meetings of probably the two worst main event wrestlers in the U.S., Andre the Giant and the Ultimate Warrior. It would have been the second and third meetings between the two (they actually met earlier this year in Switzerland, which nearly caused that country to abandon its neutral position and declare war on Connecticut) and there was a lot of fear going in because it's not like one could carry the other. Well, is Tucson, Warrior gave Andre a clothesline to the front, one to the back, Andre went down and 1-2-3 in five seconds. The fans were furious about a five second main event. In Vegas the next night, it took three clotheslines and 15 seconds before Andre layed down and the fans were hot once again. I realize that the fans should consider themselves fortunate that the match is over so quickly, but when you pay $15 to see the Warrior (who was the headliner and drew the houses both nights) and he's gone so quickly, without even a post-match posing routine, it leaves major bad taste. It won't hurt in Vegas, since Titan probably won't be back for another six months and everyone will have forgotten, but Tucson is a fairly regular city and usually they would take care of a market like that a little better.

Lioness Asuka, the current World Women's champion in the All Japan Women's promotion, retired from pro wrestling after this past Tuesday night's card in Tokyo's Korakuen Hall due to the mandatory age retirement rules. Asuka, whose greatest pro wrestling fame came as half of the Crush Gals tag team with Chigusa Nagayo (who retired in early May), was very much responsible for Japanese women's wrestling reaching such an incredible popularity level from 1984-88 and was the last main eventer linking today's women's wrestling with the glory days. Asuka announced her retirement after retaining her title on 7/19 in Tokyo beating Madusa Miceli in 28 minutes, and announced her final match would take place at the next Tokyo show six days later. Asuka turned 26 on 7/28. While in the past few years Asuka was pretty much in the shadow of Nagayo as far as popularity, she was the wrestler who set the women's attendance (and then, the gate record which has since been broken) record on August 22, 1985 for a match when he she challenged Jaguar Yokota for the World title before 13,500 fans at Budokan Hall in Tokyo. That match is generally considered the greatest women's match in history and arguably one of the greatest matches ever. Asuka said in her retirement announcement that she would like to follow in the footsteps of Dump Matsumoto and be a crossover entertainment celebrity in Japan.

PUERTO RICO

Got a couple of line-ups for recent shows. 7/15 in Caguas was headlined by Sadistic Steve Strong (Steve Di Salvo) defending the Universal title against TNT (Juan Rivera), Invader #1 defending the Puerto Rican title against Ivan Koloff, Jimmy Valiant vs. Kendo Nagasaki, Rip Rogers & Abbuda Dein (Rocky Iaukea) defending the WWC tag titles against Miguelito Perez & Hurricane Castillo Jr. , Junkyard Dog vs. Kareem Muhammad, Chicky Starr defending the WWC jr. title against Eric Embry and White Angel (Curtis Thompson) vs. EL Profe plus the Batten Twins against Super Medico (Jose Estrada) & Rufus Jones.

7/22 in Caguas had Strong defending against Invader #1 (Jose Gonzales), JYD vs. Muhammad in a dog collar match, TNT defending the TV title against Nagasaki, Perez & Castillo vs. Dein & Rogers for the tag team title, Starr defending the jr. title against Medico and White Angel & Jones vs. Battens.   Koloff won the Puerto Rican title from Invader #1 on 7/15 in Caguas, while Perez & Castillo won the tag team titles from Dein & Rogers on 7/16 in Mayaguez which makes them both WWC World and Caribbean tag team champs.

Starr won the jr. title from Medico, but don 't have a date on that one yet.

Carlitos Colon will return to action after several months on the sidelines on the 8/6 card in San Juan.

ALL JAPAN

Jumbo Tsuruta & Yoshiaki Yatsu regained the PWF World and International tag team titles beating Stan Hansen & Genichiro Tenryu on 7/22 in Ishikawa before 3,600 fans when Tsuruta pinned Hansen with a small package in 22 minutes. After the match Tenryu said in an interview that if he and Hansen don't regain the belts in a rematch that they wouldn't team up again. Also on the TV taping card, Joe & Dean Malenko beat Masa Fuchi & Yoshinari Ogawa, The Foot Loose (Samson Fuyuki & Toshiaki Kawada) beat Jim Brunzell & Tom Zenk, Kenta Kobashi upset Shunji Takano via count out to earn Kobashi a tie for first place with Takano, Fuyuki and Kawada in the Asunaro tournament (in which the winner is to get a shot at Tenryu's unified triple crown title). The four were to wrestle on 7/23 to determine the winner of the trophy. Also on the card, Giant Baba & Rusher Kimura & Kabuki beat Motoshi Okuma & Haruka Eigen & Akira Taue, The Fantastics (Tommy Rogers & Bobby Fulton) beat Mitsuo Momota & Mighty Inoue, Big John Tenta beat The Terminator (Marc Laurinidas), and Isamu Teranishi pinned Goro Tsurumi.

7/19 in Wakayama drew 2,100 as Hansen & Tenryu & Kawada beat Tsuruta & Yatsu & Kobashi in 19 minutes in what I believe to be Kobashi's first professional main event, Fantastics beat Zenk & Brunzell, Taue drew Fuyuki and Malenkos beat Takano & Teranishi in the top matches.

7/21 in Kyoto drew a sellout 2,700 as Tenryu & Hansen & Fuyuki beat Tsuruta & Kabuki & Taue in 21 minutes, Yatsu & Takano beat Brunzell & Zenk, Tenta pinned Terminator, Baba & Kimura & Kobashi beat The Wild Bunch (Eigen & Okuma & Fuchi), Malenkos beat Kawada & Ogawa, Fantastics beat Inoue & Teranishi and prelims.

7/18 in Otsu drew 2,450 as Tenryu retained his triple crown pinning Yatsu in 18:57 with the power bomb, Tsuruta & Kobashi beat Zenk & Brunzell, Hansen pinned Taue, Foot Loose beat Fantastics, Malenkos beat Inoue & Ogawa and Tenta & Takano beat Terminator & The Destroyer (Legendary Dick Beyer).

All Japan ran shows both 7/15 and 7/16 in Tokyo's Korakuen Hall, selling both out to the tune of 2,200 fans. On 7/15, the headline match saw Hansen & Tenryu beat Tsuruta & Kobashi (so I guess this was actually Kobashi's first main event) when Tenryu pinned Kobashi in 20:13, Malenkos beat Fantastics in 21 minutes (I've yet to see this bout on TV but from the magazine photos it looked like a really unique bout with lots of different moves) and Yatsu pinned Tenta to earn a shot at Tenryu's title on the 7/18 card in Otsu.

The 7/16 card was the Bruiser Brody Memorial card with both Stan Hansen and King Curtis Iaukea talking with the fans and giving speeches about Brody. This was the one year anniversary of the death of Brody and was part of Nippon TV's airing Brody matches for 90 minutes every Monday night during the month of July. Baba presented a card of unique matchmaking, with Hansen & Tenryu keeping the tag team titles beat The Foot Loose in 15:07 when Tenryu pinned Fuyuki (Foot Loose and Tenryu are normally tag team partners at the house shows so it is unique to have them oppose one another), Baba & Kimura & Tenta beat Tsuruta & Kabuki & Fuchi, Yatsu pinned Takano, Fantastics beat Zenk & BrunzelL and Malenkos beat Kobashi & Tsuyoshi Kikuchi which is also a unique match since Kobashi & Kikuchi have spent time in Hawaii being trained by the Malenkos.

The next series will be 8/19 to 9/8 with Abdullah the Butcher, Terry Gordy, Danny Spivey, Dan Kroffat, Doug Furnas, Johnny Ace, Shane Douglas (as the Dynamic Dudes) plus Shaska Whatley & Tiger Conway Jr. as the Jive Tones. This will mainly be tag team matches highlighting this tour with the Japanese regular teams, plus Jive Tones, Dynamic Dudes, Can-Ams (Furnas & Kroffat) and Gordy & Spivey working their first full series as a team to get ready for the December tag team tournament.

The 7/9 television show (Tsuruta-Yatsu-Kabuki vs. Hansen-Tenryu-Fuyuki plus Fantastics vs. Kobashi-Fuchi) drew a 6.9 rating, while on 7/16 (Tenryu-Hansen vs. Tsuruta-Yatsu, Joe vs. Dean Malenko, Fantastics vs. Zenk-Brunzell) drew another 6.9 rating.

NEW JAPAN

No word as yet on the results of Antonio Inoki's run for public office (the election was 7/23) but should have the results next week. New Japan hasn't run any shows since the 7/13 card at the Tokyo Sumo Hall. The new series runs from 7/28 to 8/10.

The main line-ups are 7/28 in Toda which has the Japan A team vs. Team USA in a battle of five singles matches, Shinya Hashimoto vs. Vladimir Berkovich and Jushin Riger vs. Akira Nogami.

7/29 in Tokyo at the Ota Ward Gym has a big show with the Japan A team vs. Japan B team, plus Manny Fernandez & Buzz Sawyer vs. Salman Hashimikov & Victor Zangiev (which I believe is the first time the Russians will work a tag team match), Big Van Vader vs. Chimur Zarasov, Dick Murdoch vs. Vladimir Berkovich and Riger vs. Shinji Sasazaki.

8/3 in Tottori has Japan B team vs. Team USSR, Tatsumi Fujinami & Kengo Kimura & Riger vs. Sawyer & Fernandez & Vader, and Riki Choshu & Masa Saito vs. Dick Murdoch & Mark Haft.

8/4 in Izumisano has Team USA vs. Japan B team, Choshu & Osamu Kido vs. Hashimikov & Zangiev, Fujinami vs. Berkovich and Riger vs. Hirokazu Hata.

8/5 is a big show in Nagoya with Team USA vs. Team USSR, Choshu & Takayuki Iizuka defending the IWGP tag team titles against Fujinami & Nogami, Super Strong Machine & George Takano vs. Masa Saito & Hashimoto and Riger defending the jr. title against Hiro Saito.

8/8 in Iwate has Japan A team vs. Team USSR, Hashimoto vs. Vader, Machine & Takano vs. Murdoch & Sawyer and Riger defending the jr. title against Iizuka.

The series ends on 8/10 in Tokyo with Choshu defending the IWGP title against Vader, Fujinami vs. Hashimikov to determine the No. 1 contender for the title and Riger vs. Naoki Sano.

The 7/8 television show (Choshu & Fujinami vs. Machine & Takano on top) drew a 5.3 rating and 7/15 (Choshu winning IWGP title from Hashimikov and Riger vs. Black Tiger) drew a 5.6.

The official announcement was made that on New Years Eve New Japan will try an ambitious promotion similar to the 1985 and 1986 Starrcades and the 1986 WrestleMania but even more so, with a live card to be held both at Budokan Hall in Tokyo and also in Moscow, USSR with it being satellited back from one building to the other. It is expected that besides using the Russians vs. Japanese vs. USA wrestlers on the show that it will also be the pro debut of Koji Kitao (former sumo star Futuhaguro) who is training in Virginia right now with Lou Thesz. From the reports we've got, Kitao is going to be quite impressive for a newcomer by the time December rolls around.

Riger vs. Black Tiger was awesome.

JAPANESE WOMEN

The big news is the retirement of Lioness Asuka.

They held a show on 7/19 in Tokyo at the Ota Ward Gym before 2,800 with Asuka pinning Madusa Miceli to keep her World title and after the match was the retirement announcement. Also on the card, The Fire Jets (Yumiko Hotta & Mitsuko Nishiwaki) winning the World tag titles beating The Marine Wolves (Shizuka Minami & Akira Hokkuto) in a two of three fall match, then female kick boxer Anne Maria Tenkate went to a five round draw in a mixed match against Toshiyo Yamada (theyoung girl with the amazing facial resemblance to Chigusa Nagayo which is why she's getting a major push) plus in an eight-girl tag, Bull Nakano & Kumiko Iwamoto & Nobuko Kimura & Ericka Shishedo beat Reuben Amada & Mika Toyoda & Yumi Ogura & Noriyo Tateno (formerly half of the JB Angels).

7/16 in Ueda saw Nakano & Iwamoto win 2 of 3 falls from The Marine Wolves in a non-title match, Nishiwaki drew Yamada and Asuka & Maceli & Ogura beat Hotta & Amada & Toyoda.

7/22 in Fukuoka drew 1,355 as Asuka beat Ogura by submission in the main event and The Fire Jets beat Nakano & Kimura.

OREGON

The tag team titles are now held up which means there are no champions in the promotion. Top Gun & Scotty the Body were champions, but they broke up as a team on 7/22 and are meeting on 8/5 in a Loser leaves town match, so Top Gun (David Sierra) turned face-to-heel-to-face in just a few weeks time, similar to Scott Peterson. And you thought the NWA was out of control with all the turns. Not only that, but it appears that Peterson is about to turn again which would make three turns within about two months which is totally out of control.

The singles and TV titles were held by Carl Styles, who was stripped of them when he left due to an "eye injury, but now he's back with no mention of the belts nor has there been any talk of late about a tournament for any of the vacated titles.

7/22 in Portland saw Rex King beat Al Madril in 20 seconds, Top Gun (as a heel) beat Joey Jackson in an impromptu loser leaves town match (made for fun television, Jackson had an interview saying he was tired of being a loser and from this point on was going to the top, Top Gun came out and challenged him and to make it more interesting, asked for a Loser Leaves town match which Jackson accepted and Top Gun beat him with a piledriver after a hot-shot. Then came a totally embarrassing skit. Al Madril was out with a kid dressed up with paint on his face Like Beetlejuice and started harassing the kid and wiping the paint off his face when jumping into the interview area came a guy in a Batman costume and in a campy scene right

out of the movie, Al goes up to him and says, "Who are you?" And trying to imitate Michael Keaton's voice, the guy in the costume says, "I'm Matman. Tell all your friends." Even in a building filled with kids, you could hear a groan come over the entire building. Matman, who was terribly green although he tried some flying moves, then beat the returning Moondog Moretti when Moretti head-butted Matman and was knocked out himself and pinned. To say this didn't get over would be giving it more praise than it deserves. Then came a six-man tag with Steve Doll & Scott Peterson & Beetlejuice (Art Barr) against Scotty the Body & Top Gun & Jonathan Boyd. Doll had Top Gun pinned when Scotty the Body jumped off the top rope onto Doll. Doll was supposed to move and Scotty was supposed to hit Top Gun leading to the pin but Doll didn't move and Scotty hit him, but Doll pretended he wasn't hit and pinned both Scotty and Top Gun at the same time. Top Gun and Scotty then argued and started fighting and Boyd attacked Top Gun and Doll made the save for him to set up a cage match the next week. The main event was Styles vs. Grappler (Grappler now has a patch in one eye because on 7/15 he somehow got the Kabuki-mist blown into one of his eyes) with Billy Jack Haynes and Nord the Barbarian in the respective corners inside cages to make sure they couldn't interfere. Grappler knocked down Haynes' cage, and one of the security guys named Ray who is Haynes' friend used a bolt cutter to let Haynes out of his cage and then Haynes took the bolt cutter to unlock Nord and they all went at it including all the guys on the undercard as well. Nord and Haynes got into it on an interview and they talked about signing a match between the two of them and hinted it would be on 7/29, but never actually said it and on 7/29, neither Haynes nor Nord worked the card but both were still talked about so they are apparently still around.

7/29 saw the only mention of Matman being an interview, and it was obvious it was Scotty the Body under the mask (it definitely wasn't the week before). The main event saw Top Gun & Doll beat Scotty & Boyd in a cage match but the heels beat up Top Gun after the match which led to the loser Leaves town challenge for this coming week. Top Gun asked Steve Doll to be handcuffed to Boyd in the LLT match but Peterson came out and said that Doll hurt his knee but he'd be handcuffed to Boyd, which was strange. Earlier in the card Peterson had played subtle heel in a babyface match where he beat Rex King, while Styles beat Madril and Beetle juice beat Grappler via DQ.

Grappler came out with a 2x4 with a picture of Haynes on it and jobber C.W. Bergstrom wrestled the 2x4 and gave it suplexes and such and pinned the 2x4.

The main angle on the show saw Beetlejuice throw coffee at Madril when Madril once again tried to wipe the face-paint off the same little kid but Rip Oliver showed up and beat up on Beetlejuice so Oliver is back in as a heel.

They are billing the 8/5 card as Roddy Piper Appreciation Night with all kids free. Crowds have been around 1,000 the past two weeks.

Former pro wrestler Bill Francis did an interview on television and from what I'm told he looks Like a monster now, 6'6 with a weightlifter body. When he wrestled, he was a tall, skinny kid. Francis is the brother of football's Russ Francis and son of former wrestler and promoter Edmund Francis. Bill Francis is now working as a sheriff but from what I'm told, with his Look and size could probably work for any promotion right now.

CWA

Things are pretty slow out here. From what I'm told, this promotion isn' t going to be closing down shop as has been rumored for the last month or two. I do know that several TV stations that carried this show were asked if they would agree to take the new USWA package in its place which is where the rumors got started.

Newcomers to the area now are Cousin Junior (Lanny Kean), Gary Allbright (who worked Stampede as Vokhan Singh, the half brother of Makhan Singh) and a guy called The Zombie, and Let's just say you can tell the fingerprints of booker Jerry Lawler.

The 7/24 card saw Jerry Lawler beat Al Perez via DQ when Ronnie Gossett interfered, Dutch Mantell and Master of pain had a pull—apart brawl and the tournament for the Tennessee tag team titles saw Ricky Morton & Jeff Jarrett beat The Blackbirds (King Parsons & Brickhouse Brown) in the finals but after the match the Blackbirds broke the trophy on the ringpost.

The 7/31 card has Doug Gilbert vs. Lou Fabbiano, The Wilds ide (Chris Champion & Mark Starr) defending the CWA tag team titles against Plowboy Stan Frazier & Cousin Junior, Freddy vs. The Zombie (a monster brought in by Gossett who they are going to bring into the building in a coffin) plus four cage matches——Blackbirds & Harold Harris vs. Morton & Jarrett & Robert Gibson, Black Bart & Dirty White Boy vs. Dustin Rhodes & Bill Dundee, Mantell vs. Master of Pain and Lawler defending the USWA title against Bam Bam Bigelow.

On TV on 7/29 they had a six-man tag match with Wildside & Doug Gilbert against Morton & Mantell & Freddy and once again the Gilberts went at it. Freddy (Tommy G) put the claw on Gossett during the match. They also held a new twist, a TV Battle Royal which went to a time limit draw because time ran out. They will re-start the Battle Royal with five guys left on television next week.

WORLD CLASS

This is the last week for this name, because as of Friday night, the promotion will no doubt be changed to USWA after the Eric Embry vs. P. Y. Chu Hi (Phil Hickerson) match at the Dallas Sportatorium for control and for the name of the company. The complete line-up for Friday night's card, which everyone is expecting will sell out since the Embry-Chu Hi battle for the company has been the main issue pushed for weeks, has those guys in a cage match, Gary Young vs. Chris Adams in a cage match, Kerry Von Erich vs. Taras Bulba (Juan Reynoso) and if Kerry wins, he gets ten minutes with Scandor Akbar, Jeff Jarrett & Matt Borne defending the World Class tag titles against Sheik Braddock (formerly Corporal Braddock) & Cactus Jack Manson, Percy Pringle vs. Tojo Yamamoto, newcomer Mr. Texas vs. Jimmy Jack Funk in a mask vs. mask match and Billy Travis vs. Buster Fowler.

The 7/28 card in Dallas drew a near sellout of 2,500 for the Jerry Lawler vs. Mil Mascaras match for the USWA title, which ended with Mascaras pinning Lawler, but after the three count, Akbar put Lawler's foot on the ropes. Lawler kept arguing that his foot was on the ropes but Mascaras had his hand raised and left with the title belt although there was no actual announcement of a winner or a loser. On television the next day, no reference was ever made to the match and Lawler was still referred to as champion. Also on the show, Young beat Adams in a first blood match when the two were brawling outside the ring, Manson came down but Adams got the chair from Manson and hit him with it and he juiced, but while this was going on, Akbar hit Adams with the riding crop and he juiced first although the blade job was way too obvious on television; Steve Simpson won a 20 man Texas Roundup (Royal Rumble) when he was left with Young & Manson but brother Schaun came in and helped Steve with the eliminations behind the refs back; Al Perez double count out with Kerry Von Erich; Jarrett & Borne kept the tag titles beating Braddock & Chi-Hi in 40 seconds when Jarrett pinned Braddock, Bulba pinned Tony Falk, Travis pinned Manson and Funk pinned Fowler. Interesting to note is that this card was nearly sold out without Eric Embry on the card and this contradicts the given wisdom that Embry is the reason that everyone comes to the matches.

Embry worked all the spot shows even though in Dallas and on TV they were claiming he was injured.

This group has just six shows booked outside of the weekly Dallas shows between now and 8/16, one of which will be at a flea market in Waxahachie, TX.

Kevin Von Erich has disappeared once again without mention.

Buster Fowler is back as a jobber so they've dropped the angle of two weeks ago when Akbar signed him to his side.

All the jobbers who worked the NWA show in Fort Worth on 7/16 haven't been allowed to work on the television tapings here again with the exception of Frogman LeBlanc, who was the best jobber they had and was the most popular with the boys since he was willing to do anything they wanted.

They did a television angle where Chu Hi jumped Mark Lowrance after Lowrance and Tojo were arguing. Chu Hi put Lowrance in a chokehold but Lowrance didn't sell the move one iota and of course Eric Embry made the save. The angle would have been good except Lowrance ruined all credibility by not acting the slightest bit concerned when a guy twice his weight was attacking him. After the incident, Percy Pringle did an interview and said that Lowrance was "one of the most respected announcers in the business." Well, in a promotion where Kevin Von Erich stands for clean living, anything that is said shouldn't surprise anyone.

A fan gave Chris Adams a 2 x 4 with a nail and a knife and Chris brought it out during his interview. I don't know about doing an interview wielding a knife as a weapon.

OTHER NEWS

The 7/21 card in Calgary which was supposed to be headlined by Dynamite Kid vs. Davey Boy Smith, but with Smith's injuries, they had Dynamite and Johnny Smith attack Davey Boy until Owen Hart made the save. Hart vs. Dynamite is headlining most of the shows for the next two weeks before Hart leaves for Japan, although there is lots of talk that Hart will be back in the WWF by the end of the year. Chris Benoit vs. Johnny Smith has also been on most of the cards.

Great Gama is in along with Biff Wellington returning from Japan and Maximum Overdrive (Tim Hunt & Jeff Warner) in from Minnesota.

Dennis Coraluzzo and Larry Sharpe's independent on 7/21 in Ocean City, NJ drew 850 with Joe Daniels & Sweet Daddy Falcone and Sonny Austin winning the main event over the Pit Bulls & Johnny Hot Body plus Tony Stetson beat Jungle Jim Mcpherson. The same duo is running a show on 9/16 in Cherry Hill, NJ at the Garden State Racetrack and word is out that it'll be the largest crowd for an independent show in 1989. Already booked are Stan Hansen, KimaLa, Nikolai Volkoff, Ken Patera and the main event is Larry Sharpe & Jerry Lawler vs. Daniels & Austin.

WALE Radio (990 AM in Providence, RI) is now running a nightly Monday through Friday pro wrestling call-in show from 7 to 8 p.m. Eastern time called "Wrestling Rap." Host Cody Boyns would like to hear from Observer readers across the country during the show and you can call 401-621-9253 to be a part of it. It's the only nightly wrestling call-in show that I know of.

Ken Patera is doing a daily three-minute 900 telephone message deal at 900-646-SLAM similar to what Bruno Sammartino, Lou Albano and several others do.

Congratulations to reader Jeff Bukantz, who followed up his Maccabiah Games gold medal in fencing with a bronze medal at the Olympic festival over the weekend in Oklahoma City.

Although as best I know this isn't definite, it is pretty well expected that Nick Bockwinkel will return to the AWA as a television color commentator. Verne wants him to come back as a wrestler as well, and who knows. Honestly , Bockwinkel, if he were to return, even after being out of action for nearly two years and being 54 years old, might still be a better worker than anyone in the AWA right now.

Pro Star Promotions in the Northeast ran a show on 7/20 in Elmyra, NY with Ken Patera vs. Nikolai Volkoff, D.C. Drake vs. Jules Strongbow, Cheetah Kid vs. Mike Incognito and Heidi Lee Morgan on the show as well. Drake is the promoter with Strongbow as the heavyweight champ and Incognito as junior heavyweight champ. Next show is 8/6 in Ledyard, CT with Sgt. Slaughter vs. Volkoff, Bam Bam Bigelow vs. Abdullah the Butcher, Drake vs. Larry Winters, Strongbow vs. Iron Mike Sharpe, Wendi Ricther vs. Heidi Lee Morgan and Cheetah Kid vs. Incognito.

I'll be appearing on Sunday, 8/13 on John Arezzi's phone-in show on WNYG in West Babylon, NY from 6 to 7 p.m. Eastern time taking phone calls from listeners and readers so if you've got a topic to discuss, give us a call.

Multimedia will be producing a demo tape this coming weekend in Las Vegas with Ken Resnick and Nick Bockwinkel doing voiceovers of the Tokyo Dome card trying to sell U.S. stations of the Soviets competing in pro wrestling as a selling device. Won't work.

For those interested in the Roller Games thing, they are taping the pilot show this coming weekend for a prime time nationally syndicated special in September. In most markets, this show will go head-on with Saturday Night Live (and in some weeks, WWF's Saturday Night Main Events).

Ed Faulk is running an independent promotion with five TV stations in small cities in Texas and Louisiana. One of his wrestlers, called The Rude Dog, is being praised as having real potential.

Scott Norton on the AWA shows has been issuing a $500,000 challenge to Hulk Hogan and Ric Flair for an arm-wrestling match. Since Norton is a World class arm wrestler, you know there won't be any takers.

Heard Sheik Adnan El-Kaissey attacked Verne Gagne on TV. Is Verne going to come out of retirement at the age of 64?

Woody Farmer is promoting some shows in Hawaii using mainly his students from California.

Ray Stevens promoted a card as part of the Antioch, CA fair with the AWA using Greg Gagne vs. Col. DeBeers on top plus the Guerreros, Alexis Smirnoff, Jerry Monti, Matt Moon and Local Earthquake Ferris on 7/29.

FCW ran a show on 7/30 in Orlando, FL before 138 as Rock Hard Rick beat Mike Awesome -* , Lou Perez beat Dennis Knight -*, Star Riders beat Playboys (Brett Sawyer & Jimmy Backlund) in a non-title match, Kendall Windham pinned Frankie Lancaster * ½ and Steve Keirn beat Ho Chi

Winh in a cage match * .

Playboys were given the Florida tag team titles after Nasty Boys were fired.

Ron Wyatt promoted a show on 7/28 in Suffolk, VA before 425 with Robert Gibson beating Joe Daniels via count out on top, Ivan Koloff beat Russian Assassin (Dan Grundy) via DQ, Tony Stetson beat Jungle Jim McPherson for the Southeastern title plus Italian Stallion worked underneath and there was a guy who wrestled as Batman (Jackie Fulton, younger brother of Bobby Fulton). Dennis Coraluzzo worked as a manager for the heels.

The Southern Boys (Tracy Smothers & Steve Armstrong) were given the CWF tag team titles. The last champs were Mongolian Stomper & Jimmy Golden but Mongolian Stomper is no longer with the group.

Dennis Condrey turned heel after winning the CWF title from Tom Prichard in a 10-man rage in a cage. Condrey was the only guy left from either team not handcuffed and was ready to uncuff his partners when Sylvia offered him "$10,000" to sell her the key. Condrey sold her the key and walked out while she unlocked the cuffs on the heels who beat up on the faces.

8/11 in Knoxville has Robert Fuller & Jimmy Golden & Brian Lee vs. Southern Boys & mystery partner, Condrey vs. Wendell Cooley for the CWF title, Doug Furnas vs. Tom Prichard for the Tennessee title, Adrian Street & Miss Linda vs. Beauty & The Beast (Mark Goleen came in dressed as a woman and attacked Adrian & Linda), Ricky Morton vs. Mike Davis and Danny Davis vs. Don Harris. By the way, this Don "Stomper" Harris is the same guy who worked in CWA last year as "Don Bruise" of the Bruise Brothers tag team.

Windy City Wrestling is running some shows as competition to Jon Gallagher's UAWF convention in Chicago. On 8/12 at DaVinci Manor they will tape TV with Steve Regal, Col. DeBeers, Ken Patera, Terminators, Debbie Combs and Buddy Rose & Doug Somers while 8/13 in Hegwish will be a rock & wrestling party featuring a wrestling card with Regal vs. Patera, Terminators vs. Rose & Somers, etc. Gallagher will be running the UAWF convention the same weekend in Chicago including promoting an AWA show with Larry Zbyszko vs. Derrick Dukes on top. For info on Gallagher's convention you can call 309-289-2662.

Virginia Wrestling Association had a card on 7/29 with Nikita Koloff vs. Russian Assassin in Blackstone, VA plus Buddy Landel vs. Mark Fleming.

Ivan Koloff, Rocky King and Kevin Dillinger (Alan Martin) have worked dates for Jerry Blackwell's SCW. Old-time wrestlers Big Bill Dromo and Rocket Monroe are billed on future shows for SCW along with Adrian Street and Linda and Tom Prichard and Ricky Morton.

WWF

Hulk Hogan remained out of action this weekend with the pinched nerve in his neck, but will return on 8/4. Hogan missed dates with Randy Savage this weekend in Reno, NV, Nashville, TN (which sold out) and Milwaukee.

No Holds Barred grossed $129,228 over the weekend of 7/21-23 in 238 theaters bringing its 50-day total to $15,812,920 but it wasn't expected to remain in the $1 theaters this week so the final gross should be just under $16 million when all is said and done.

7/29 in Greensboro drew a miserable $15,000 house as Barry Horowitz pinned Ken Shamrock DUD, Tim Horner pinned Megaman Tom Magee DUD (this shows Titan has finally given up on Magee after all these years), Red Rooster pinned Brooklyn Brawler, Rick Rude beat Jim Duggan via DQ (negative stars), Greg Valentine was awarded a win over Brutus Beefcake via forfeit when Beefcake didn't appear (he had to replace Hogan in Nashville instead), Dusty Rhodes pinned Ted DiBiase and Demolition beat Powers of Pain. Reader Larry Lovell said that was the worst wrestling show he's seen in 20 years as a fan.

7/28 in Las Vegas drew a heavily papered 4,500 as The Genius pinned Koko B. Ware DUD, Jim Neidhart beat Haku via DQ DUD, Jimmy Snuka pinned Honky Tonk Man *, Paul Roma pinned Boris Zhukov DUD, Rick Martel pinned Tito Santana in 4:30 *, Rockers beat Rougeaus ** and Warrior pinned Andre in 15 seconds.

For those in this area wanting to attend the 8/8 show in Oakland which are TV tapings, get tickets in advance because it will sellout well ahead of time. They had $100,000 in as of Friday and have huge ads in newspapers as far away as San Jose running regularly in both sports and entertainment sections.

7/23 in Omaha drew $54,000 as Horner pinned Horowitz, Rhodes pinned DiBiase, Barbarian pinned Neidhart, Demolition beat Twin Towers via DQ, Bad News Brown pinned Sam Houston, Rick Martel pinned Tito Santana, and Warrior beat Rude via count out.

There was talk of making Mark Young (Mark Scarpa) into the Blue Blazer but it was decided against doing that.

Barry Windham, as Widow Maker, is being groomed for matches with Hogan at the end of the year.

Roddy Piper has dates booked in September.

Don't expect the Bobby Heenan show to last more than a few weeks longer. USA network hated it from the first and wanted it pulled after the second week but Vince McMahon talked them into allowing him some time to gracefully make the change.

Most of the September shows will be headlined by Hogan vs. Savage with Liz touring; Dusty vs. Bossman (will be very interesting to see how well Dusty can draw because they are putting him in a position as a headliner which surprises me) and Warrior vs. Andre. Other new marriages include Demolition vs. Brain Busters, Ron Garvin vs. Greg Valentine, Jim Neidhart vs. Dino Bravo, Bret Hart vs. Bad News Brown, Akeem vs. Hillbilly Jim (which I guess means Akeem won't be turning at SummerSlam).

NWA

A late confirmation of the page one story is that Steamboat will be done before you read this. Will be interesting to see if Titan goes after him. There is bad blood there and those at Titan have said they wouldn't use Steamboat, but they said the same thing about Barry Windham and Dusty Rhodes.

7/27 in Tallahassee, FL drew 3,200 as Brian Pillman pinned Bill Irwin ¼ *, Dynamic Dudes beat New Zealand Militia ** ½, Norman pinned Steven Casey * ½, Steiners beat Kevin Sullivan & Mike Rotunda when Scott pinned Sullivan *** ½ (Sullivan & Rotunda did the break—up scene afterwards), Midnight Express & Steve Williams beat Freebirds when Eaton pinned Jim Garvin after Williams' hit him with a clothesline ***, Great Muta beat Eddie Gilbert via count out in a Dragon Shi match **, Eddie Gilbert threw out Norman to win a two-ring Battle Royal, Sting beat Terry Funk via DQ when Muta sprayed Sting ****, Road Warriors beat Samoan Swat Team when Hawk pinned Fatu after a flying clothesline ** ¾ and Lex Luger pinned Tommy Rich in 17:35 with a hotshot ***.

The George Michael Sports Machine on NBC on 7/23 ran highlights of both the Flair vs. Funk and Steamboat vs. Luger matches from the Baltimore PPV show.

7/28 in Orlando drew a SRO crowd of 6,500 as Pillman pinned Irwin ½ *, Dudes beat Militia ** ½, Norman pinned Casey *, Steiners beat Sullivan & Rotunda via count out in a Texas death match (this was billed as two singles matches in the advertising) *** ½, Williams & Rich & Eaton beat Freebirds when Williams pinned Garvin ****, Muta beat Gilbert via count out in the Dragon Shi match **, Scott Steiner threw out Norman to win the two-ring Battle Royal DUD, Sting beat Funk via DQ when Muta blew the mist — Dory Funk was there as well and got involved and they left Sting laying ****, Road Warriors beat SST *** ½ and Luger pinned Steamboat in 21 minutes (by the end, the whole place was cheering Steamboat) ****.

8/27 in New Haven has Flair vs. Funk, Luger vs. Williams, Hayes & Garvin vs. Steiners, Midnight vs. Skyscrapers (Spivey also booked for Japan at the same time), Pillman vs. Norman, Dudes (also booked for Japan) vs. Randy Rose & Bill Irwin, Rich vs. Al Greene, Road Warriors vs. SST in a cage and Ranger Ross vs. Phil Apollo. I can smell problems already if they are booking Midnight vs. Skyscrapers because Skyscrapers don't sell anything and you know Midnights will have to put them over if they are grooming them for the Road Warriors.

Two major glitches on TBS on Saturday. One, they had an interview with Rotunda challenging Dr. Death to a "scientific" match with no punching or kicking allowed, then did an interview with Doc, which apparently was supposed to air in two weeks, talking about the match as if it already happened and as if he was DQ'd for throwing the first punch. Then they had Sting come out, announced as TV champ, with the belt, then said that the belt was held up and had Gary Hart come out in an interview with the same TV belt moments later (the matches were taped before Baltimore, interviews taped in Baltimore).

7/21 in Dayton, OH drew 1,200 as Pillman pinned Irwin ** ½, Skyscrapers beat Johnny & Davey Rich * ½, Norman pinned Casey *, Scott Steiner beat Rotunda via DQ **, Williams pinned Garvin *¾, Vicious & Spivey split the money in the Battle Royal, Midnight beat Militia ** ¼, Road Warriors beat SST ** ½, Sting pinned Norman * ¾ and Luger pinned Steamboat *** ¾. No-shows were many -- Gilbert, Funk, Dangerously and the entire Dudes vs. Simmons & Greene match. Dudes were heavily pressured to cancel this Japan tour, but they are going, so expect an " injury" angle on television in the next week or two.

Cornette & Jim Ross are doing a great job on the Friday night TBS show

THE READERS PAGE

BALTIMORE BASH: GLORY DAYS

Thumbs up for the Baltimore Bash, despite the cheap ending in the Battle Royal. The Skyscrapers are terrible. Other negatives were Ricky Steamboat's ring entrance, a so-so tuxedo street fight and sound problems with Terry Funk's interview. Brian Pillman started a trend of guys jumping from one ring to the next. Sting vs. Muta was a minimum four stars, but did George Scott book the finish? The War Games was 4 ½ stars easy. Flair vs. Funk was five stars plus, four for the match and at least another star for the brawl at the end. It was the best booked match I've seen in 15 years as a fan and the post-match brawl was better than the 1987 Battle of New Orleans. Jim Ross was superb once again. Vince McMahon was right. Right now there is no competition. The NWA is the best promotion on this continent. We can talk ad infinitum about Vince's steroid circus, but why waste the space. But they can give the WWC very stiff competition for every "worst" award come December.

Paul Hanlin Jr.
Philadelphia, Pennsylvania

A big thumbs up to the Glory Days Bash. I really can't find anything to pick on. I thought the announcing was great. Jim Ross was totally into the show and it was great to see Gordon Solie. He added class to the show. Technically it was the best show they've done so far.

As for the matches, I don't go much for Battle Royals so

that was the weakest part of the show for me. I may be in the minority, but I don't care much for Teddy Long either. Brian Pillman flies better than almost anyone I've seen. The Dudes vs. Skyscrapers was good, but Sid Vicious' presence overshadowed everyone else. He's a marvelous monster.

Cornette and Dangerously worked their hearts out so you have to applaud them. Sting vs. Muta was a bit disappointing but Luger vs. Steamboat was great. The War Games was good for what it was although I

don't Like cage matches. Flair vs. Funk took brawLing to a new level . Five stars. It was a crowd pleaser and a show stopper. My request to the NWA and Ted Turner is please give us more of the same.

Karen Shehorn
North Hollywood, California

I don't have enough superlatives to say about the show the NWA put on in Baltimore. It was easily the best pay-per-view show anyone has done so far, even topping the May 7th card. The camera work was superb. The camera crew finally learned its lesson about those annoying cutaways to the crowd. The action in the ring is first and foremost. I especially liked Gordon Solie's dressing room interviews. They were similar to what the WWF does on its shows with Gene Okerlund, only much better. I was also amused at the sign of one fan which said "NWA No. 1, WWF stinks."

While the Flair vs. Funk match wasn't as good as the Flair vs. Steamboat classics, it did have enough action to keep my interest. Flair Looked a bit rusty but what happened after the match more than made up for any deficiencies. With each PPV show, the NWA keeps doing it better and better.

Vincent DiPalma
Copiague, New York

Despite the weak and uninformative ads, "Glory Days" was the best PPV event this jaded observer has ever seen. No one match stood out above the others because they were all so great. When it was over,

I was huffin' and puffin' like a racehorse, or more like the Ultimate Warrior after a leisurely stroll.

My favorite match was the Steiners vs. Sullivan & Rotunda which was virtually flawless. Come to think of it, I've seen more great Kevin Sullivan matches in the past six months than I've seen in his entire career. Maybe wrestling bookers aren't such a bad idea after all. Don't get any ideas, Pat Patterson.

Other highlights included the "WWF stinks" sign, the flashy and well-timed ring entrances, Flair's especially being hot and deservedly so, the successfully unpredictable booking that often befuddled even the smartest of fans, everyone taking their share of good bumps, a stronger crowd response to Steamboat and Luger in their proper face and heel roles and not a Ding Dong in sight.

Isn't it funny that non-wrestlers Jim Cornette and Paul E. Dangerously put on a better match than 90 percent of Titan's employees. Of course, most of them are non-wrestlers as well.

The NWA deserves numerous Barry Horowitz pats on the back for establishing the wrestling PPV event that all future cards will be judged against. Fifteen bucks were very well spent.

Steve Prazak
Atlanta, Georgia

I thought the Baltimore show was excellent. Fans watching on TV couldn't appreciate just how good the special effects were live. The turnout was great and the crowd was really up for a big show. Flair vs. Funk was a good match, but the angle after the match made it even better. Steamboat vs. Luger was great but the DQ finish was too predictable. Sting vs. Muta was a very exciting and fast-paced match but the finish was a big disappointment and another reason the NWA will never be at the level of the WWF. They would never have a finish like that. The War Games was the best match on the card. The only bad match was Dudes vs. Skyscrapers. On a major PPV show, you shouldn't look as bad as they did. On a scale of one-to-ten, I give this show a ten.

Robert Ferry
Philadelphia, Pennsylvania

The NWA continues to make a conscious effort to make entrances at major shows a special feature. Notable entrances were the Gong, for the Great Muta, the dragon procession (while not original, still memorable) for Steamboat and the Road Warriors appearing on the back of big hog motorcycles. Also great were Lex Luger doing movements out of bodybuilding shows, and after a solemn interview, Ric Flair led his company down the aisle with a cocky strut.

The tremendous ring-to-ring finishing move of Brian Pillman indicates why he's such an important addition to the NWA ranks. He combines true athletic ability, the agility of a gymnast with the ideal professional wrestling physique . Pillman, along with Sting and Muta, are the future cornerstones of the NWA.

The TV title match with Sting vs. Muta had the potential to be the best match on the card. It had some great moments but the ending stunk worse than the waste product of Rick Steiner's dog.

The visual sight of Dr. Death repeatedly overhead pressing Terry Gordy into the top of the War Games cage was brutally intense. The best match on the card was Lex Luger vs. Ricky Steamboat. I truly look forward to future Flair vs. Luger matches and it was great to see Steamboat finally get some well deserved crowd support.

Ric Flair vs. Terry Funk was a brawl in the best tradition of old Mid South and Memphis wrestling. While I understand why they did it, I must give a thumbs down to the heavy juice in the match. For a moment, I thought I was watching a match from Puerto Rico. I Loved the brawling, but truly believe Flair and Funk are good enough to have a tremendous brawl without heavy juice. I loved the match, but there was too much juice. The sight of Flair, the true king of wrestling, standing there with his crown prince and eventual successor Sting gives me hope for the future of pro wrestling as we know it.

Klon
Melbourne, Florida

Glory Days was an average show when you compare it to the other major PPV shows that the NWA has produced. The workrate was below what you would expect and the crowd really pissed me off. They really screwed up. On a national PPV it really makes the faces look bad when 90 percent of the fans are chanting 'We Want Sid.'

What surprised me was the pop Brian Pillman got on his way to the ring. The War Games match was excellent as all ten guys gave it their all.

As for Roddy Piper on Prime Time Wrestling, I thought it was hilarious. This show has the potential to break all ratings records for wrestling. On the other hand, the Bobby Heenan show was a total bomb.

Jim Papanou
Willowdale, Ohio

I have to give the PPV show an unequivocable thumbs up. It had a minimum of gimmicks and a maximum of wrestling action. There were no scenes of army life and no Norman and Ding Dongs. Everyone from Ric Flair on down worked their tails off. They certainly gave us our money's worth.

Elyise Zios
Union, New Jersey

In the past week, we've witnessed the best and worst of pro wrestling in 1989. The Bash PPV was outstanding. Truly one of the best produced wrestling cards ever. There were so many high points and great moments that I won't even try and list them. While philosophically I'm against blading, but I must admit it strengthened the Flair vs. Funk Match and made the show better as a whole.

The Bobby Heenan show is simply a waste. It's not a parody of talk shows with wrestling hype like TNT, it's just a bad half hour. I'd rather watch a match from Maple Leaf Gardens pitting Jose Luis Rivera against Johnny K-9.

Steve Gennarelli
Binghamton, New York

I thought the PPV was pretty good, except for the second

and third match. When Danny Spivey did the power bomb on Johnny Ace, Ace slipped. They should have done the ending over and different. The Pillman match sucked and Brian got hardly any heat. I hope to see him used better on the next card. The War Games was great. I'm glad Gilbert didn't turn heel. Everyone was expecting that. Sting vs. Muta was the best match on the card. I enjoyed Flair vs. Funk but it was too short. The juice added to the match and the brawl at the end was great.

Rob Feinstein
Longhorne, Pennsylvania

I enjoyed the show. I could find many things to be critical of but just because this was a PPV card doesn't mean it has to be perfect. It just has to be something which has special appeal and be a generally loaded card. Ric Flair's return, the War Games and a solid underneath card meets that criteria. It was well worth $20 for a live ticket, but not worth traveling across the country as the first Crockett Cup was.

I would presume the technical aspects went well judging by the large TBS crew. I didn't buy the last PPV and was sorry about it afterwards. I'll buy the next one, but to do so I have to go to a relative's house rather than suffer the abuse of non-fans.

I loved the way Sid Vicious got over and they didn't seem to know what to do with him getting a face reaction. Don't the powers in charge notice the kid from "Wonder Years" gets more boos than a lot of the heels? The Dudes match was too long with too many missed moves. Jim & Paul was too long although there weren't any moves. Can Brian Pillman talk? After so many years of too many interviews, now we get too few.

War Games are good on paper, but need juice to cover for the slow spots. The main event was the "worst" Ric Flair match I've seen but it was great as a brawl. To keep Flair's usual modus operandi match fresh, a match like this was welcome.

I 've gained a lot of respect for Lex Luger. He sells well, he's learned his craft and makes the loss of Barry Windham totally meaningless. Lex can sell tickets. Regrettably, Barry Windham can't.

Howard Kesner
Baltimore, Maryland

I really enjoyed the show. There were some weak spots here and there but overall I thought it was a good action-packed show and well worth $15. Thank God there were no Ding Dongs or Norman on the card.

The Battle Royal was okay, but nothing great. The Dudes vs. Skyscrapers wasn't too exciting but to me, everything else was good. Flair vs. Funk was great, as was Sting vs. Muta, the War Games and Luger vs.

Steamboat. The managers' match was fun and the Steiner's

match was good. I also liked Pillman vs. Irwin. As for the card, the NWA should be pleased because I know I was.

David Williamson
Cleveland, Tennessee

There was no need for a Battle Royal. The participants were less than top calibre and the winner got a plastic Burger King crown. Also, was I supposed to believe that Ranger Ross won one of these to get to the finals. And the guy who won almost every one of them, Sting, wasn't even in the match. I couldn't think of a worse way to start this card except have the Ding Dongs wrestle on it. The Pillman vs. Irwin match could have been eliminated as well as it served no purpose other than to kill time. At this point, I was very discouraged. A PPV should be all main events, not this crap. The next match sicked me. Dangerously vs. Cornette was as good as this sort of match could have been. Both worked well and I was pleasantly surprised we didn't see heart-covered underwear. The tornado match was good except for the finish. Early in the card Jim Ross claimed that no snakes are at ringside because in the NWA, they wrestle. Well, Steiner had a dog and Steamboat had a Lizard. Boy did Ross make a real idiot out of himself with that statement. Sting vs. Muta was great and the ref bump with the mist was creative. But the finish ruined the whole match and left a bad taste in my mouth. I've always hated that finish and it seems the NWA has made the finish the official finish of NWA PPV screwjobs.

I know why Steamboat isn't over. Fans respect wrestlers if they stand up for themselves and don't back down. Well, accompanied by his wife, son and lizard, Steamboat portrays the image of a family man and a pantywaist. I hate to say it, but this is how he's perceived. Then he shyly gives in to Luger's stipulations, showing he won't stand up for his rights. He is again seen as a sissy. For him to get over, his family must be kept out, the Lizard must be done away with and he must show the intensity he's shown on his recent interviews and the intensity he showed in the ring. The match was very good with a great finish. War Games was disappointing. The first War Games completely surpassed this one. The camera in the ring was bad because we only saw a small portion of the action. Also, if the match was so dangerous, why was a camera man in the ring? It took all reality away. I really missed the blood.

Flair vs. Funk was a solid 4 ½ stars. I loved Flair's brawling style and the blood was appreciated. But with all the blood, to make no mention of last year's screwjob finish is an insult to everyone's intelligence. The finish looked awkward, but was acceptable. The brawl after the match almost made up for every problem on the card. All four were incredible, make that five as Doug Dillinger was quite a hit as well. Flair's post-match interview was great.

Overall this card didn't meet my expectations and I

reluctantly give it a solid thumbs down. Reluctantly because Flair vs. Funk and the post—match brawl were great, but the negative aspects outweighed the positive. This card looked incredible on paper, but the early matches, the Burger King crown, the Sting-Muta finish and the War Games made it a step backwards. The announcers were a lot worse than usual and often sounded bumbling.

Craig Stambaugh
Claireon, Pennsylvania

After viewing the excellent PPV event from Baltimore, it should be obvious that the problems in the NWA do not originate with its booking committee. Eddie Gilbert, Ric Flair and Kevin Sullivan should be congratulated for one of the best cards I've ever seen and the best PPV event in history.

However, the artistic success of this card doesn't make red ink go away, nor will it add the necessary 5,000 or so customers to future arena shows. The easy way out would be to blame the booking committee and bring in someone who you hope would be another Hisashi Shinrna or Bill Watts. To do so would be wrong. While we can all find fault with some of the decisions in recent months, the NWA has the best wrestling and the most exciting scenarios in the country today. It is every bit as good as during the success period of the Dusty Rhodes reign or even during the Watts UWF.

The problem of not enough cash-paying customers will not be solved with a quick booking fix. I defy anyone to come up with more creative booking or to inspire the wrestlers to better matches than was evidenced in Baltimore. The real answer is going to be a Lot of hard work to re-establish a strong syndicated network and package that rivals the WWF.

The NWA must get their best syndicated program in every single major market. Get that program on in a good time slot and while the look of the product has vastly improved, they need to toss in a good bout or two on syndication. Ranger Ross vs. Rip Morgan as a main event isn't going to get anyone to change their social calendar to watch. They must vastly increase the amount of print advertising of house shows.

As a final suggestion, they should declare war on the WWF. Why not have Ted Turner back his champion in a million dollar challenge to Hulk Hogan? NWA fans should be urged to picket WWF house shows until Hogan and WWF accepted the challenge. That would surely generate a lot of needed media hype. The match of course would never be signed, but it would get the NWA some badly needed notoriety .

Chris Zavisa
Plymouth, Michigan

A few friends joined me for the Bash. We were all greatly

impressed. The Flair vs. Funk match was one of the grittier matches I've seen and the fact that there was no juice previously on PPV events made the effect of the blood much more primal. I wasn't particularly crazy about the branding iron playing so much of a role. I felt the competition was so intense that it cheapened the match by using the gimmick, but the post-match brawl was something.

Best moves of the day were in the first few minutes of Sting vs. Muta. The best line: "I live dangerously. I 've even hired Rob Lowe as a babysitter. Best ring entrance was Road Warriors on bikes. Worst interview was the too-subdued Ric Flair pre-match interview. Best change from Last year's card was no overwrought Precious psycho-drama and no Dusty Rhodes match.

Two of the group predicted every winner correctly. We all agreed that the Bash was the best start-to-finish PPV card and overall PPV production to date.

Mike Howell
Brook Line, Massachusetts

VIEW FROM ANOTHER COUNTRY

You say the NWA's lack of success and market penetration hangs on the perception of the group as minor league and also the quality of its hype in comparison with the WWF. I agree on these points and also on the Lack of any one figure having cross-media penetration like Hulk Hogan. But it strikes me from reading the Observer weekly and watching all the PPV's about a month later that there is another problem. The NWA's booking is too "busy." It's too complex for the casual interest market that they need to tap into. McMahon makes his wrestling "moron-simple" for the every-so-often viewer to keep up with the main issues, marriages and why's for the marriage. The NWA bookers jump all over. Look at the face team in the War Games. Road Warriors & Dr. Death & Midnight Express. Sure, it's like a dream team but is this a face team? Road Warriors have gone back-and-forth with no reason. Midnight turned face, left and came back as faces and Williams turned face after a tour of Japan. I regard this as symptomatic of the NWA's fundamental problem when it comes to reaching a wider audience. I agree that to attract this audience they also need top rate production values, top rate hype and some top name celebrity involvement (at least for a short time to get the ball rolling) but you've ignored a key element of the McMahon booking strategy which is to keep everything simple. With McMahon, you can watch five minutes of wrestling every three or four weeks and still know everything that needs to be known. Is this true of the NWA? I can 't keep up with some of the stuff they do. McMahon has succeeded in infiltrating the mainstream media mix of entertainment to the extent that people are aware that his wrestling is an ongoing part of the media mix. It will never be mass entertainment like Roseanne, but it is an entertainment option. The NWA is, in my opinion,

willfully cutting themselves off from this perception to their "too busy" booking pattern.

To the casual viewer, what is the No.1 NWA match? Flair vs. Funk? Luger vs. Steamboat? Flair vs. Luger? If a casual viewer caught the Nashville card, they were probably blown away by Flair vs. Steamboat and knocked out by the angle afterwards. I saw Funk's interviews after the card and his TV matches. That is the man the entire promotion should have revolved around until this PPV show, just like it used to around Dusty. That's what Vince would have done. After Nashville, all the emphasis should have been on Funk. I didn't care about anything else in the NWA after seeing the angle in Nashville, which should have been the correct viewer reaction.

Say the bookers slow things down. Say the production values improve. Say they improve the hype and they even manage to buy the participation of a few genuinely hot celebrities (and Titan never really has gotten that right with the exception of Cyndi Lauper) and work this right. Say it all comes off, which is a long shot I admit, but it's also essential if the NWA wants to be a major league force in the industry. What you would have then is two WWF's. What will be the difference and what could make them fierce competition? What even in the long run could give them the edge?

Strangely enough, it's the one area I don't think they've correctly exploited, and it's as plain as the logo on their face. 'We Wrestle'. The one thing they do inarguably far superior to the WWF. They have the better in ring product. It's an area you haven't mentioned and I'm surprised since you are obviously a sports fan is that the NWA, after everything else has been fixed up, if everything else gets fixed up, has the potential be tap into American sports market as a casual interest sport. This is a major difference in the NWA's favour and one they have only seemed to make a half-hearted effort to exploit. The WWF may have novelty and humour value to sports fans and the sports media, in the snide, parodic manner that is evidenced in various TV and press coverage of wrestling but my impression is the WWF doesn't have strong penetration with sports fans. The NWA could. It would mean a tricky balance of retaining the hype, the fun interviews and skits, but balanced with an exciting simulation of a physical contact sport with intensity. This isn't impossible. Lots of sports try to hype like wrestling but in a less full-goose fashion. Pro boxing hype has been similar. But if the NWA is to have a major league future, I can't help but think this is their 'niche'. In the long run they would have to pare down the wildest angles and characters, but in that context, a small push-and-shove during an interview or a 'weigh-in' or contract signing would have more effect than an attack in the parking lot which take things well out of the line of credibility. I think they came close in the Flair-Steamboat III match even with the aftermath brawl with Funk. I can't believe a sports crowd, if they were taught to understand wrestling, wouldn't show a lot of appreciation for a match with the action and commentary of that one. Think of a properly hyped Owen Hart vs. Keiji Muto feud as a showcase? That's why Norman the lunatic and the Ding Dongs are so gratingly wrong for their business. I like Mike Shaw and I like Teddy Long, but whether or not those angles are executed well, they can't be integrated with the direction the promotion needs to take for a major league future with its own niche. Colourful wrestlers and characters, absolutely. Low comedy, sometimes, and why not. That's part of baseball and football at times. But out-and-out cartoon characters will alienate your potential market case, and in the case of the NWA, the strongest part of the base and even if not, they will always look minor league in trying it since their opposition is acknowledged as far superior in that genre. I can't help but believe that the last straw to grab and run with to the limit is "We Wrestle."

Julian Licht
Melbourne, Australia

LATE NOTES

TBS is claiming that the PPV show from Baltimore did between a 2.0 and 2.1 buy rate, which if that is legitimate, would make it a tremendous success since the show would have grossed an estimated $3.9 million if those figures are Legit, but all PPV figures are works whether it be boxing, concerts, NWA or WWF.

The new Roller Games which starts in September already has cleared more than 140 stations which means this product coming from nowhere has more and a better syndication network than the long-established NWA. Titan has decided to use Big Steele Man as a heel, which is no surprise since he flopped as a face at the last taping.

No Holds Barred will be released on video on Oct. 19 with the asking price $ 89.95 and you get a Hulk Hogan doll free with every purchase. At that price they should throw in your own personal jobber.

Big Van Vader (Leon White) is trying to lease the rights to use the Vader gimmick in the United States. Currently New Japan has all international rights to the Vader name.

Luna Vachon underwent knee surgery.

NWA Bash on 7/30 in Miami drew a near sellout.

TV ratings for last weekend (7/22-7/24) are good for Roddy Piper but not good for anybody else. Prime Time Wrestling drew a 3.9 on 7/24, the second week of Piper, which is the highest rating for the show since 1985. However, the Bobby Heenan show that followed drew a 2.5, and even more substantial is the first 15 minutes drew a 3.0 and the last 15 minutes drew a 2.0 which basically means that they lost a huge portion of the wrestling audience by the 15 minute mark. Officially, the Heenan show will continue through Aug. 14 at which time a decision will be made, but I believe truthfully the decision has already been made. I don 't think too much stock should be put in the Prime Time ratings for another four to six weeks, because you knew the first few Piper shows would do well. If the numbers stay up, it'll be bad for Heenan since even though the Piper stuff hasn't been good with Monsoon compared with the Heenan stuff, for now Piper means a lot more in the ratings than Heenan ever did.

NWA had a terrible weekend, even with all the hype for Baltimore. The Friday night show fell to a 1.3 (down 40 percent from the previous week), Saturday TBS drew a 1.4 rating which is the all-time low (and they no longer have the revolving time slot to blame for bad ratings, although overall TBS had its worst Saturday ever so wrestling, compared with other programming did very well, the two shows prior to wrestling did 0.3 and 0.7 respectively) and Sunday did a 2.2, which went head-to-head with the PPV show.

WWF's AIl American wrestling on 7/23 drew a 2.5 rating.

There's talk of holding a Costume Battle Royal as part of the NWA's October PPV card. Please, say it ain't so.

AUGUST 14, 1989

The biggest news of the week is that legendary Japanese wrestler Antonio Inoki did win in his election bid for the Japanese House of Councilors (equivalent in U.S. terms to the House of Representatives) in the election on July 23rd. Inoki, who announced his retirement from wrestling five weeks earlier in order to start campaigning, had a close call and in fact, it wasn't known until 5:09 p.m. the next day whether or not Inoki would make the grade. Unlike in the U.S., the House of Councilors don't represent districts, but are all at—large seats, and there were 50 seats open in the election and Inoki finished 49th, which means he barely squeaked in with an "exciting-booked finish." This was very much a campaign centering on Inoki's involvement with pro wrestling, since his campaign manager was Hisashi Shinma, the former chairman of the board and booker for New Japan and former president of the WWF, while wrestlers Masa Saito, Riki Choshu, Tatsumi Fujinami, Hiroshi Hase and former pro wrestler and current New Japan president and booker Seiji Sakaguchi all stumped districts all over Japan for Inoki. Inoki was running as a member of a political party that he formed himself called "Sports Heiwato" (Sports Peace Political Party. and he's the only member. For Inoki to become an effective politician in the House, it is said he must affiliate himself with one of the major parties to have any influence, power and allies. Inoki will still be affiliated with pro wrestling, and in fact plans on using his political influence to help promote major shows including trying to put together a New Years' Eve spectacular which will be satellite transmitted with live events both in Tokyo and in the Soviet Union, plus Inoki has even talked of pioneering a pay-per-view wrestling card in the future for Japan (a first in Japan) which would emanate from the United States. Ironically, the UWF has also talked of doing a PPV event as well, and also would like the event to emanate from either Atlantic City or Las Vegas in the United States. These grandiose ideas of both promotions are interesting, because even though the live site gate isn't a major factor in PPV, no matter how big the event were to be, the Japanese wrestlers have almost no name recognition in the United States and you couldn't give enough tickets away to a show of this kind to have a respectable looking live house. While Inoki's political duties have taken him out of action as a day-to-day wrestler, there is talk Inoki may still work an occasional big show as a gimmick of being the wrestling senator. It is believed that this is the first pro wrestler to achieve this major of a political office. I do know that former Korean pro wrestler Kim Ill was a major force in Korean politics after his wrestling career was over, but I believe his position was as an adviser or a cabinet member equivalent in Korea, rather than as an elected official.

Aside from that, the two major news items of this week are really just extensions of stories from last week. There has been a ton of talk throughout pro wrestling of the situation where the NWA and Ricky Steamboat parted company. In fact, in a rare bizarre and almost honest approach, the NWA even acknowledged the parting of the ways on its Power Hour television show when Gordon Solie led off his news segment with the story about the split. Solie, and the NWA, are claiming the split wasn't over contract difficulties, but simply because Steamboat had a foot injury. The NWA even sent out a press release acknowledging that Steamboat was no longer with them, blaming the foot injury and personal reasons and saying the parting was amicable and that in the future they would like to bring him back. In truth, Steamboat does have a foot injury, but it was not an injury that would have led to him taking time off wrestling if contracts terms had been agreed upon. Virtually all wrestlers work daily with injuries of some sort, so that can always be used as an excuse, and this type of PR softening of the issue is not uncommon in professional sports, and I believe that among other things in Jim Herd's background was a stint in the front office with the National Hockey League's St. Louis Blues, which may be why Herd acknowledged Steamboat's leaving in press releases and on his own television show which, in contrast, is something the WWF would never have done. The WWF would have pretended that Steamboat never existed in the first place.

Steamboat was interviewed Sunday afternoon on John Arezzi's wrestling show on WNYG in New York and said the two sides had been negotiating for two months and agreed to contract terms a few weeks ago, but after agreeing to terms, the NWA tried to cut another $50,000 off his annual compensation and he felt insulted and serious negotiations broke off at this point. Steamboat said he wasn't ruling out eventually working for either the NWA or Titan Sports and expected some talks would begin with Titan, but that he wants to take the rest of the summer off at this point.

I want to be careful how I phrase these points but they have to be made. I don't want to pass judgement on either side here for two reasons. One is, I don't know what the money figure the sides were arguing over is, although the fact the sides were so close at one point makes me believe the figure wasn't unreasonable. I do pretty much have a ballpark estimate of the figure and it is basically in line with, or slightly below what similar-level NWA mainliners are earning right now. However, I don't know what kind of financial pressures Herd is under to try and balance the budget because obviously the wrestling company is operating deeply in red ink. While it is true that Steamboat doesn't have the popularity right now of, say Sting or Ric Flair, it is also true that there is an intangible not only because he's one of the two best workers in the United States and his presence to a degree elevates not only the quality of the card itself, but also can have a subconscious effect on others to work harder to be "in the flow" with the headliners. One NWA wrestler told me that having a wrestler of that calibre on the show elevates everyone's performance, and can, as the current situation with Lex Luger has shown, help significantly improve the work and experience of working for the guy he's regularly wrestling. Another point, and I want to point out that over this past week the phone calls from those in the business regarding this subject have been numerous, is that the NWA devoted the last six months to pushing Steamboat and making him a World champion and at a time when it needs stability for credibility, they lost him; and not to another organization. And while those at Titan have said they would never take Steamboat back, experience with Dusty Rhodes and Barry Windham indicates that isn't the case at all, since Windham left Titan on far worse terms than Steamboat ever did and Rhodes was one of McMahon s most bitter enemies business-wise for years (even if some would argue that in reality Rhodes was McMahon's ally all of that time, even if he wasn't trying to be). Additionally, Steamboat did everything asked of him, and more, during his six-month NWA tenure, he put over Lex Luger at all the house shows and did a clean job for Ric Flair when the time came to give up the NWA title, and there are several NWA mainliners who complain or won't do clean jobs that are making far more money. On the other hand, a case can be made that this is simply an economic decision, that Steamboat didn't draw in the amount of money that they would be paying him. That the "family unit" image hurt his popularity or that he simply didn't have the charisma of a Flair, Luger, or a Sting.

From the Titan side, that Zeus angle on last Saturday night which was played to death on all the shows this weekend was one of the great angles of recent times. From what I understand, when Zeus actually has to wrestle it may not be that much of a disaster, at least compared to what it could be. They are doing lots of practice sessions with him and in SummerSlam you know that Randy Savage will be in the ring 95 percent of the time anyway and the one or two minutes Zeus has to go in will be so well rehearsed and scripted that it will be passable. Eventually, when they get to the singles match with Hogan, it could be trouble because you can't do five or six minutes of "straight spots" with a green guy, especially when Hogan has to do the carrying, but I've heard talk that the first PPV match between the two of them may actually be a taped match in which case they can edit beforehand which eliminates a lot of potential problems and åt least guarantees it won't be a disaster.

How's this for an interesting note? The Bobby Heenan show on the USA network this past Monday drew a whopping 3.7 rating, which would make it one of the two or three highest rated shows of the week on cable television. USA had wanted the show off the air immediately after seeing the quality of the second show, and the second show also saw TV sets turn off en masse from the lead-in Prime Time Wrestling. But the sets didn't turn off, for reasons I can't even begin to explain, the third week. McMahon asked USA to hold off pulling the plug on the show until August 14th in order to have a "transition" and "explanation" built up for the abrupt schedule change. The last word I heard is that the show would be history after this coming Monday's episode, but I wonder if USA is changing its mind after seeing last week's ratings.

An interesting item made the national wires concerning former World champion wrestler Buddy Rogers. According to police and witness reports, Rogers was eating at a sandwich shop near his home in Lauderdale-by-the-sea, Florida, when Theodore Terhune, 30, burst into the restaurant and started swearing at the waitresses. Rogers got up and asked Terhune, 6'2 and 200 pounds, to quiet down. Terhune then called Rogers, listed at 68, an old man and challenged him. Rogers pushed Terhune, who picked up a chair and threw it at him and it hit Rogers in the mouth. Rogers then started pounding on the guy until he cried for Rogers to stop and Terhune ran out of the restaurant.

STAMPEDE

The Owen Hart vs. Dynamite Kid main event drew $20,000 gates in Calgary the past two Friday nights, with Hart's return on 7/28 drawing a sellout to the pavilion and the return match on 8/4 drawing just a few shy of a sellout. The 7/28 card saw Hart beat Dynamite via DQ, Great Gama beat Chris Benoit via count out, Larry Cameron pinned Ken Johnson, Maximum Overdrive (Tim Hunt & Jeff Warner billed as "Hunter" and "Warrior") beat Bob & Kerry Brown via count out, Johnny Smith pinned Jonathan Holiday, Biff Wellington pinned Kim Schau and Sumu Hara pinned Goldie Rogers. I was told both of the Hart—Kid matches were excellent and I know that the first match didn't air on television except for brief highlight clips in the local markets but perhaps the bulk of the match will air on the 90 minute TSN show in three weeks.

7/29 in Grand Prairie saw Hart beat Cameron via count out, Benoit beat Smith in a street fight, Bob & Kerry Brown beat Maximum Overdrive, Gama beat Wellington, Rogers drew Holiday and Hunter (Tim Hunt) beat Schau.

Steve Ray, Angel of Death and Ron Ritchie are all history.

As it turned out, because of Davey Boy Smith's injuries in the auto accident, the battles between Smith and Dynamite Kid were few. On 6/19 in High Level, ALTA, Smith won via DQ, on 6/21 in Hay River, Smith & Benoit beat the

British Bruisers (Dynamite Kid & Johnny Smith), 6/27 in Kelowna saw the same tag match go to a double count out, 6/28 in Williams Lake saw Smith & Benoit & Ricky Rice win an elimination tag match from the Bruisers & Cameron, 6/29 in Kamloops saw Kid pin Smith.

8/5 in Edmonton saw Hara pin Holiday with a Northern Lights suplex **, Smith pinned Schau with a Piledriver *, Cameron pinned Wellington *, Maximum Overdrive beat Goldie Rogers & Bulldog Bob Brown (generously described as a DUD, Overdrive was very green), Gama beat Benoit via DQ in a best of three fall match when Benoit got caught throwing Gama over the top rope after Gama had repeatedly done the same to Benoit *** ½ and Smith beat Owen Hart via DQ when Hart got the object from Smith but got caught using it ***.

Instead of weekly television tapings at the Calgary house shows as have been done in the past, they are now taping every third week in different arenas and doing three hours of television, so you won 't be seeing as many main event matches on TV and more squash matches.

This promotion wants to do a live TSN special sometime this winter.

Gama beat Benoit to win the Commonwealth title on 8/4 in Calgary.

Owen Hart Leaves for Japan in about a week. It was acknowledged in the program that Hart had been wrestling for the WWF but didn't say as the Blue Blazer. On television they said when Hart first returned that he had a contract with "The Wrestling Federation" in New York and they wouldn't allow him to wrestle in Calgary on 7/28 against Dynamite but he said he would anyway and this apparently is going to lead to a "worldwide suspension" for four weeks to explain his next tour of Japan. As of right now, it looks like the chances of Hart returning to Titan in the imminent future are very slim.

CWA

This group drew its largest crowd in a while at regular prices of nearly 4, 000 on 7/31 to the Mid South Coliseum (ironically just a few days before Titan came in with Hulk Hogan vs. Randy Savage on top) for a card topped off by four cage matches. In the main match, Jerry Lawler beat Bam Bam Bigelow via DQ when Ronnie Gossett (who was inside the cage) interfered. After the match Lawler threw fire at Gossett and another fireball at Bigelow, however Bigelow didn't sell the fire at all and started pounding on Lawler afterwards. Also on the card, Dutch Mantell beat Master of Pain in a cage when Gossett's interference backfired, Rock & Roll Express (Ricky Morton & Robert Gibson) teamed with Jeff Jarrett to beat The Blackbirds (Iceman King Parsons & Brickhouse Brown) & Harold Harris when Harris got pinned but after the match the heels got Jarrett locked up in the cage and starting beating on him, and in the other

cage match, Black Bart & Dirty White Boy beat Dustin Rhodes & Bill Dundee when Rhodes was handcuffed to the cage and the heels double-teamed and eventually pinned Dundee. In prelim matches, Freddy (Tommy Gilbert) beat The Zombie (really terrible, comes out in a coffin, can't work at all managed by a guy called The Undertaker) via DQ when Gossett and Undertaker interfered, Plowboy Stan Frazier & Cousin Junior beat CWA tag champs The Wilds ide (Chris Champion & Mark Starr) via DQ and Gary AIIbright pinned Doug Gilbert.

8/4 in Jonesboro, AK drew 430 as Starr pinned William "Freezer" Thompson ½ *, Bart kept the CWA title pinning Rhodes with his feet on the ropes and a match where they brawled all over the building including breaking the souvenir table where the Rock & Roll Express were selling their gimmicks ****, Freddy beat Zombie via DQ DUD, Lawler & Frazier beat Wildside via DQ **¾ (Frazier only in the ring for 15 seconds of a 17 minute match, mainly Lawler was beaten the whole way and Wildside did all their hot moves to him), Morton & Gibson beat Blackbirds in a match with no heat when they pinned the manager, Harris *¾.

The Battle Royal on television last week which wound up going to a TV time limit draw was re-started with the remaining participants, Ricky Morton, Champion, Starr and Gilbert starting out and Morton wound up winning.

8/7 in Memphis has Doug Gilbert vs. Ken Wayne, Wildside vs. Frazier & Mad Dog (Lee Boyd) for the CWA tag team title, Zombie & Undertaker vs. Freddy & Jason in a "horror" match (horror, as in short for horrible), Dundee & Rhodes vs. Bart & White Boy in an Australian Rules Football match in which two guys start with their partner handcuffed to the corner and a football is placed in the middle of the ring and whomever gets the football can uncuff the partner and make it two-on-one, Blackbirds vs. Rock & Roll Express and if the Blackbirds don't win in 10 minutes or less, Harris must forfeit $5,000 to the Rock & Roll Express, Mantell vs. MOP in a Loser leaves town, no time limit, no DQ, etc. match (One or the other is headed to Dallas) and Lawler vs. Bigelow for the USWA title in a coward waves the flag match with Eddie Marlin and Ronnie Gossett having flags and whomever waves the flag first, their wrestler Loses the match.

WORLD CLASS

The Dallas Sportatorium sold out to the tune of 3,000 plus for the match which ended the World Class era. Eric Embry beat P. Y. Chu Hi (Phil Hickerson) in the cage and by the terms of the match, the promotion is now called USWA and Embry tore down all the World Class banners all over the Sportatorium. Also, in another cage match, Chris Adams beat Gary Young via DQ when Cactus Jack Manson and Scandor Akbar interfered, Manson & Sheik Braddock won the World Class tag titles (which are now the USWA tag titles I suppose) from Matt Borne & Jeff Jarrett, Percy Pringle pinned Tojo Yamamoto and Jimmy Jack Funk beat Mr. Texas in a mask vs. mask match and Mr. Texas was unmasked to reveal TV jobber Buster Fowler.

They were supposed to have an Adams vs. Young hair vs. hair match at the TV tapings on 8/5, however, as the story goes, Percy Pringle went to Adams' condo to get him and Akbar's guys all beat up Pringle in the parking lot and he was hospitalized so Adams was in the hospital taking care of him so Embry wrestled Young instead and all the heels ran in and somehow Adams then got back and did the save.

For clarification of the 7/28 main event between Jerry Lawler and Mil Mascaras for the USWA title, what happened was that there was a ref bump, Lawler held Mascaras and Akbar went to hit him with an object, Mascaras ducked, Lawler got hit, Mascaras pinned him for a three count but Akbar put Lawler's foot on the ropes at the count of three and Mascaras left with the title belt but no announcement was made in the building and on TV the next morning, no acknowledgement was ever made of the match but Lawler was still mentioned as champion. The story is that ref Tony Falk saw "everything" and ordered the match re-started but Mascaras "didn't hear him" and left with the belt. So I presume Mascaras lost via count out. No, I'm told, no decision was made because Falk saw "everything." So then I presume Mascaras should have won via DQ because of the outside interference from Akbar, which in this promotion means a title change. No, I 'm guilty of trying to make sense out of professional wrestling, which is not supposed to make sense. If it did, why would a guy who hits a dropkick be able to get up right away but a guy who misses is always hurt even though they take the exact same bump? Or for that matter, if things made sense, why doesn't Lawler pull the strap down in the beginning of the match, rather than get his butt kicked for 15 minutes and when he wrestles Bigelow he can't hurt him with any move with the strap up, but after pulling down the strap, every single move hurts Bigelow. Speaking Of the CWA, they are doing the best job of using Bigelow of any promotion I 've seen since the last time Bigelow worked for them. They've got the guy over as the ultimate monster and crowds are picking up to see Lawler battle him, and the clips of the matches that they've shown on television look really good— the best Lawler stuff all year.

AWA

The new team concept isn't doing as well as they'd hoped for as far as clearing TV markets, but they have cleared Philadelphia, San Francisco, Pittsburgh and Tampa for the team show which is supposed to start airing the weekend of Sept. 18 and the first taping will be on 8/26 in Rochester, MN. The show that airs on 9/18 will announce the rules and

regulation for the new team format (teams will be five male wrestlers, a woman and a midget), on 9/25 they will have the drawing for the three proposed teams and the following week the actual weekly competition will take place.

The only new names thus far announced as far as coming in for the new series are Kokina the Samoan, The Russian Brute (George Petrosky) managed by Ox Baker, Kendall Windham, Ivan Koloff and possibly Big Van Vader depending upon whether or not Leon White can get the rights to use the Vader gimmick in the United States, although White has told others that if he gets the rights, he'd like to work in the NWA.

Matches announced for the Rochester taping will be Larry Zbyszko vs. Sgt. Slaughter for the AWA title, a two-on-three match with Baron Von Raschke & Scott Norton against Johnny Valiant & Mike Enos & Wayne Bloom, Wendi Richter vs. Judy Martin for the AWA Women's title, Paul Diamond vs. Col. DeBeers, Jonnie Stewart vs. Derrick Dukes, etc.

Contrary to what has been reported and said elsewhere, neither the Windy City cards for this coming weekend in Chicago have been canceled, nor has the AWA show in conjunction with the UAWF convention been canceled either.

PUERTO RICO

Carlos Colon's return from his shoulder injury suffered at the hands of Steve Strong took place on 8/5 in San Juan at one of the baseball stadiums drawing 10,000 fans (all tickets $5) and guess who won the Bunkhouse Stampede main event. How'd you guess?

WWC is trying to bring in some wrestlers from Stampede Wrestling for the anniversary show in September, but it is doubtful Davey Boy Smith will be back in action by then and Owen Hart will be in Japan so the only one with name recognition would be Dynamite Kid.

Midget wrestler Kid Chocolate (Hector Gonzales) who works here was sentenced to 11 years in prison in Guaynabo for selling cocaine.

7/21 in Manati had an interesting headline match with Invader #1 (Jose Gonzales) in a babyface match against Junkyard Dog. Also on the card was White Angel (Curtis Thompson) vs. Rip Rogers, Steve Strong vs. TNT, Maelo Huertas & Super Medico (Jose Estrada) against the Batten Twins, Kareem Muhammad vs. Kendo Nagasaki and Hurricane Castillo Jr. & Miguelito Perez vs. Abbuda Dein & Chicky Starr.

7/22 in Caguas had Strong vs. Invader #1 for the Universal title, Perez & Castillo vs. Dein & Rogers for the World tag team titles, TNT vs. Nagasaki for the TV title, JYD vs. Muhamrnad in a Dog Collar match, Medico vs. Starr for the jr. title and White Angel & Rufus Jones against the Batten twins.

UWF

The last card was 7/24 in Fukuoka drawing a sellout of 4,000 fans and $140,000 as Yoshiaki Fujiwara beat Kazuo Yamazaki in the main event in 29:09 when the referee stopped the match due to Yamazaki's profuse bleeding, Akira Maeda beat Yoji Anjo in 10:42 with a boston crab submission, Nobuhiko Takada pinned Shigeo Miyato in 10:43, Masaharu Funaki made Tetsuo Nakano submit in 9:04 and MacDuff Roesch of Florida went to a 30 minute draw in the opener against Minoru Suzuki.

The next show is 8/13 with Maeda vs. Fujiwara in the 17,000 seat Yokohama Arena.

The major UWF news is the story that they want to promote a card soon in either Las Vegas or Atlantic City in the United States.

ALL JAPAN

This group has its next card in Tokyo's Budokan Hall booked for 9/2 and Baba is trying to put together a main event of Stan Hansen & Genichiro Tenryu vs. Road Warriors on top, which would have a lot of interest since Tenryu and Warriors have been tag partners on the Warriors last tour and in the U.S. for the Clash in Cleveland and Hansen has never opposed the Warriors in Japan. Match not definite last I'd heard.

Baba and Gong Magazine, which have always gotten along, had a small rift. Baba was on a call-in show and a fan asked if the split up between Dynamite Kid and Davey Boy Smith in Canada would affect them coming in as a tag team in the future and Baba said that the two never split and the story in the magazines must be wrong. Gong then had to prove it wasn't making the story up by printing a photo of them opposing one another.

The last series ended on 7/28 in Kiryu before 2,350 fans as Jumbo Tsuruta & Yoshiaki Yatsu & Kabuki downed Stan Hansen & Genichiro Tenryu & Toshiaki Kawada in the main event in 19 minutes, Joe Malenko retained the PWF jr. heavyweight title pinning Masa Fuchi in 17 minutes, Shun ji Takano & Kenta Kobashi beat The New High Flyers (Jim Brunzell & Tom Zenk), The Fantastics (Tommy Rogers & Bobby Fulton) beat Samson Fuyuki & Yoshinari Ogawa (this match ended with two or three straight dives out of the ring), Giant Baba & Rusher Kimura beat Haruka Eigen & Motoshi Okuma, Dean Malenko beat Isamu Teranishi, The Destroyer beat Akira Taue, Big John Tenta pinned The Terminator, Goro Tsurumi pinned Mighty Inoue and prelims. Toshiaki Kawada wound up winning the tournament among the young wrestlers and will wrestle against mentor Tenryu during the next tour.

NEW JAPAN

New Japan announced its next tour from 8/25 to 9/21 which will feature Bam Bam Bigelow, Owen Hart, The Grappler (Len Denton), Patric Tanaka, Italian Stallion, David Peterson (D. J. Peterson), Kendo Nagasaki, Salman Hashimikov and Victor Zangiev. The final two nights of the tour will have big cards at the Osaka Castle Hall (13,000 seats) and New Japan's first card ever at the new 17,000 seat Yokohama Arena. Can't wait to see both Hart and Tanaka wrestle against Jushin Liger.

The new series opened on 7/28 in Toda before 2,020 as Team Japan beat Team USA 3—2 as Osamu Kido upset Manny Fernandez, Mark Haft upset Kengo Kimura, Masa Saito Pinned Buzz Sawyer, Dick Murdoch beat Hiroshi Hase and it came down to the finals as Riki Choshu beat Big Van Vader via count out. Also Jushin Liger pinned Akira Nogami to keep the junior heavyweight title (Liger is going to defend the title against six different foes this tour), Shinya Hashimoto returned and pinned Vladimir Berkovich, Salman Hashimikov beat Black Cat, Super Strong Machine & George Takano beat Kuniaki Kobayashi & Tatsutoshi Goto, Shiro Koshinaka & Takayykl Iizuka beat Naoki Sano & Shinji Sasazaki and prelims.

7/30 in Tokyo drew 1,860 as Vader & Fernandez & Sawyer beat Kimura & Choshu & Masa Saito, Murdoch & Haft beat Hashimoto & Hase, Zangiev pinned Kobayashi, Wakha Eveloev beat Akira Nogami, Liger & Iizuka beat Sano & Hirokazu Hata, Machine & Takano double count-out with Koshinaka & Kido, Chimur Zarasov beat Black Cat and prelims.

7/22 TV show (Choshu & Iizuka beating Machine & Takano for the tag title) drew a 5.9 rating.

OTHER JAPANESE NEWS

Atsushi Onita announced the formation of a new promotion called FMW (Frontier Martial Arts Wrestling) and at the press conference a karate star Masaji Aoyanagi attacked Onita and he juiced to set up the main event of wrestler vs. karate on 10/6 in Nagoya and they have their first Tokyo date booked on 10/10. The promotion will mainly pit pro wrestlers against karate fighters, plus will be the only promotion in Japan to book midget and Onita will bring in foreign wrestlers from Mexico mainly. Onita and Aoyanagi had a mixed match in early July as part of the Kajiwara Martial Arts Festival. Wrestling reporter Wally Yamaguchi is behind this promotion as well.

Lioness Asuka's last match in Kyoto drew 1,685 as she teamed with Mitsuko Nishiwaki to beat Bull Nakano & Ericka Shishedo in the main event.

OTHER NEWS NOTES

They had an interesting twist to a hair vs. hair match a few weeks back in Mexico City with El Dandy wrestling Emilio Charles, Jr (who are two of the best workers in Mexico). The match ended in a double count out, and both wrestlers wound up getting their heads shaved bald. El Satanico is turning babyface in Mexico. With that name?

Candi Divine has also worked in Mexico of late.

WMET (1150 AM in Gaithersburg, MD) is doing a weekly Thursday night phone in pro wrestling show.

ICW has a show in Parsippany, NJ on 8/19 with Tony Atlas, Bob Orton, Nikolai Volkoff and Mike Sharpe headlining.

In the AWA, Brad Rheingans won't be returning to the team with Ken Patera so Patera will pick a series of partners to defend the title against Destruction Crew (Enos & Bloom).

Even though Gordy Solie still owns 13 percent of the Florida Championship Wrestling promotion, he is no longer doing the telecasts and has been replaced temporarily by Oliver Humperdink until a new announcer can be found.

FCW drew 150 on 7/22 in Ft. Lauderdale with the top matches having Dick Slater beat Steve Collins and Steve Keirn beat Kendall Windham via DQ. 8/6 in Orlando drew 108 as Tim Parker beat Rock Hard Rick, Mike Awesome beat Dennis Knight, Nick Busick beat Coconut Kid, Brett Sawyer beat Blade of the Star Riders and Kendall Windham & Ho Chi Winh beat Al Perez & Keirn when Humperdink hit Perez with a loaded sock. No match better than one star, most matches a lot worse than that.

8/4 in East Baltimore, MD drew 150 as Nikita Koloff beat The Phantom (Johnny Ringo) who subbed for Buddy Landel. Sam Houston also worked the undercard.

Rock & Roll Express vs. Fantastics headlines 8/12 in Wildwood, NY which I believe would be the first ever meeting between the two teams.

Action Jackson is already gone from World Class and headed to Puerto Rico.

SCW has a card this week in Georgia (near Chattanooga) with this lineup listed: Chic Donovan vs. Steve Lawler, Mr. Wrestling II (Johnny Walker) vs. Nightmare #2 (Larry Clarke), Kevin Dillinger (Alan Martin) vs. Bobby Bennett, Joel Deaton vs. David Sammartino for the Southern Title (these are far and away the two best guys on the circuit) and tag champs Jimmy Powell & Ted Allen (Georgie Power) defending against Mike Golden & Mr. Atlanta (Tony Zane).

Bob Raskin's USWA drew 964 on 7/9 in Lansing, MI as Sgt. Slaughter beat Ivan Koloff in the main event.

Interesting trivia note for you baseball fans. Major League umpires Jim Mckean, Gerry Davis and Larry Young all had references to pro wrestling on their baseball cards. McKean said pro wrestling was his favorite TV show, Davis said he was a WWF junkie and Young said he's a big pro wrestling fan. Young and McKean work the American League, and are both avid readers of the Observer while Davis is a national Leaguer.

Dutch Mantell and Jeff Jarrett worked a wrestling match as part of Wichita State University's Percussion Ensemble on 8/1. The two wrestled each other with music playing in the background changing as the tide changed during the match.

OREGON

The 8/5 card in Portland saw Scotty the Body beat Top Gun in the loser leaves town match. There were about a million stipulations in this match besides the loser leaves. It was also a Coal Miners Glove match, John Boyd was to be handcuffed to Scott Peterson, the winner of the match got both tag team titles (the two had been Northwest tag team champions until they split up three weeks ago), plus no DQ, no time limit. It wound up with Grappler bringing down Boyd's snake which scared Peterson to death and while all this was going on, Grappler gave Scotty the loaded glove and he used it to win the titles and Grappler & Scotty are the new tag team champions. Also on the card, Steve Doll & Scott Peterson beat Grappler & Boyd, Carl Styles beat Col. DeBeers via DQ, Rex King pinned Al Madril and Beetlejuice went to a double disqualification against Rip Oliver.

NWA

Ric Flair is now chairman of the booking committee which basically means he's the booker with the final say, rather than have the committee vote and argue over what gets done. Eddie Gilbert and Kevin Sullivan and others still meet but Flair has the ultimate decision making power. It'll be interesting to see how this one works out. In one sense, it is good since every wrestler respects Flair (which is needed for a booker to get anything accomplished) but I hate to see anything that might take anything away from Flair, the wrestler, which is a full time job in itself (as in full time I mean 24 hours), not to mention that if the NWA ever is going to get anywhere, Flair is going to have to be marketed as a national celeb which means endless public appearances and there aren't enough hours in a week for what he would need to do in a day if he's booker, World Champion and celebrity and is to maintain this level of work.

8/6 in Omni in Atlanta drew 13,000 fans and $89,000 as the Dynamic Dudes beat Ron Simmons & Al Greene in 49 seconds, New Zealand Militia beat Ranger Ross & Steven Casey when Victory used the boomerang on Ross, Norman the Lunatic pinned Lee Scott and after the match, Rick Steiner, who was seated front row, gave Norman a belly to belly suplex; Tommy Rich pinned Bill Irwin in a match with no heat, Skyscrapers (Dan Spivey & Sid Vicious) beat Johnny & Davey Rich (crowd 75 percent cheering the heels), Eddie Gilbert & Scott Steiner beat Kevin Sullivan & Mike Rotunda in a Coal Miners Glove match when Gilbert got destroyed and juiced heavily courtesy of the glove, however Missy Hyatt tripped Sullivan when he was on the top rope and Gilbert did a major stretcher job afterwards; Great Muta beat Sting via count out in the Dragon Shi match for the TV title however the title remains vacant because of the count out as finish saw Gary Hart keep Sting from getting back in the ring (question – since the only way to win a Dragon Shi match is via count out, how can it be to determine a title if the title cant change hands via count out?) Lex Luger pinned Rick Steiner with his feet on the ropes (good, Luger almost 100 percent booed now), Ric Flair pinned Terry Funk in 14 minutes of a double juice bloodbath (great) and Midnight Express & Road Warriors & Steve Williams beat Freebirds & Samoan Swat Team in the War Games when Hawk made Hayes submit in 29 minutes of a major bloodbath.

7/30 in Miami at the Knight Center drew 2,800 as Brian PiLIman & Ranger Ross beat Militia * ½, Norman pinned Casey DUD, Sullivan pinned Scott Steiner *, Ross threw out Norman to win the Battle Royal (match was terrible except for Norman's comedy), Muta beat Gilbert via cor in the Dragon Shi ½ *, Williams & Tommy Rich & Eaton lost to SST & Terry Gordy when Samu pinned Rich * ½, Sting beat Funk via DQ when Muta sprayed Sting ***, Hayes & Garvin beat Dynamic Dudes * and Luger pinned Steiner ** ¾.

TV ratings for the last week. The Power Hour, which followéd a 17-inning Braves game and started about two hours late drew a 1.1 (better than Night Tracks does but well off what it had been doing), the World Championship Wrestling show on 7/29 drew a 2.3 (up 60 percent from it's all-time low the week before), The Main Event on Sunday drew a 2.4 and a Ric Flair vs. Sting match taped in Greensboro (Match of the Year in 1988) replay drew a 1.8 between a baseball doubleheader.

This coming weekend there is no Power Hour on Friday and no NWA Main Event on Sunday due to baseball commitments however on Saturday wrestling will air three hours straight from 6:05 to 9:05 p.m. Eastern time including a Fatu vs. Road Warrior Hawk match and Eddie Gilbert vs. Muta.

NWA VP Jim Herd was interviewed by John Arezzi (interview will air this coming Sunday on WNYG) to get his side of the story on Steamboat being gone. Herd said there was absolutely no pressure whatsoever to keep expenses down and no pressure to cut the payroll. Herd said the door isn't closed between the two and they would Like to get Steamboat back.

They taped three "amateur rules" matches between Steve Williams and Mike Rotunda in New Orleans on 7/31. In the first, Rotunda won via DQ when Williams punched him after Rotunda made all sorts of remarks about Williams' family (perceptive fans already know that ending since last week on TBS they mistakenly played an interview Williams did which was to air after the match where he mentioned the ending). The second match saw Williams come out with earplugs so he wouldn't hear Rotunda's insults, and pinned him. Third match saw ref Tommy Young bumped, Teddy Long comes out and as Williams is distracted, Rotunda gets

from behind him and pins him.

Tommy Rich will get Steamboat's spot and feud with Luger. They should have used the loss of Steamboat to force them to develop a new star to face Luger. Anyone, whether it be Sid Vicious (I realize Vicious vs. Luger isn't in the long term best interest since they want them both as heels, but still fans would find the match intriguing even if it would surely be terrible), Scott Steiner or even Brian Pillman could have been put in a hot angle to "elevate" them to main event status, unfortunately they already had booking plans for Pillman in a feud with Norman and Steve Williams (who may have been the best choice for one reason in that he's an established star) has the thing with Rotunda and the Steiners and Freebirds will be feuding now but I don't think Rich can cut it that high nowadays with a national promotion, and I'm even more sure he can't as a babyface.

They did a TV angle where Eddie Gilbert & Sting were facing the Militia when Terry Funk and Muta ran in and were beating on them and Ric Flair made the save and they brawled all over the place.

Also at Center Stage on 8/2 saw Rick & Scott Steiner have a tag match but Rick instead Sat in the bleachers eating M&M's with "Robin Green" while Scott beat both guys.

Gary Hart is now managing Funk on television. Why? Isn't that what set Funk apart from the other heels was he wasn' t part of a group?

The idea where the Ding Dongs came out with the polaroids was brilliant. Only wish it was used for Rick Steiner where it could have been of value. Actually, if they use Ding Dongs as squash guys who get creamed every week like the Mulkeys a few years back, they will get a cult following ala Momota in Japan, but if they try and push them on TV, they won't get over. NWA needs jobbers with personality to make the squashes more interesting, but they don't need jobbers being put over on television.

Idea for a Costume Battle Royal on the next PPV (please, no) is that the guys will be so dressed up in costumes that you don't know who they are and the wrestlers don't know who they are so anyone can fight anyone. Only problem is, aside from it making it look like a bunch of clowns out there, if the fans can't tell who is who, they won't care about it or root for their favorites, and besides, how can you disguise Sid Vicious?

Tom Zenk debuts at the Clash in September (9/12 out of Columbia, SC) as a masked wrestler called Mr. Z.

Ric Flair vs. Terry Funk in a cage in Kansas City in September with Harley Race as referee. Expect several Flair vs. Funk matches in cages around the horn around September and October.

Brad Muster of the Chicago Bears was asked to referee one as well, but don't expect it to happen since it would be during the football season.

8/5 in St. Louis drew 3,500 and $35,000 as Rich pinned

Irwin, Ace & Pillman beat Simmons & Greene in 58 seconds, Militia beat Ding Dongs, Norman pinned Casey, Hayes & Garvin beat Midnight Express due to outside interference of Terry Gordy, Luger pinned Rick Steiner using the ropes, Scott Steiner threw out Norman to win the Battle Royal, Road Warriors & Williams beat SST & Gordy when Williams pinned Gordy, Muta beat Sting via count out and Flair Pinned Funk in 15 minutes and they brawled all over the building for another five minutes after the match with double juice.

8/4 in Kansas City drew a $28,000 house for Funk & Gordy vs. Sting & Williams on top.

Talk of replacing Paul E. Dangerously as manager of the SST with Afa (Samu's father), and Dangerously will manage other heels.

WWF

Hulk Hogan returned from two weeks out with the pinched nerve in his neck on 8/4 in Memphis drawing 5,700 and $46,000 (largest house in Memphis for any promotion since the Lawler vs. Austin Idol hair vs. hair cage match in 1987) as Boris Zhukov pinned Mark Young, Koko B. Ware beat The Genius (Lanny Poffo) via DQ, Rick Martel pinned Tito Santana using the ropes, Ted DiBiase pinned Hillbilly Jim using the ropes, Jimmy Snuka pinned Honky Tonk Man, Jim Duggan pinned Haku and Savage beat Hogan via count out.

WWF coming to Anchorage, Alaska on 8/12.

The Nevada commission and WWF agent Arnold Skoal and had some major words after the 15 second main event on last week's card between Andre the Giant and Ultimate Warrior. They lengthened the match to 45 seconds in August, GA last week with Warrior winning again, and they almost had a riot at the box office from people feeling ripped off. Rather than change the ending, Titan apparently is insistent upon proving it can get away with anything. Now, they are moving them, even though billed as the main event, to an early match on the card and still doing the 15 to 30 second quickies with Warrior winning. Gates have been good for these matches as on 8/5 in Hartford, CT they drew $87,000 and 8/6 in Chicago drew $75,000.

Piper's third week on Prime Time Wrestling was good for a 3.8 rating, another winner. As mentioned, Heenan drew a 3.7 while the All American show drew a 2.6.

Los Angeles Coliseum and Toronto SkyDome are both making serious bids for WrestleMania VI.

WWF is adding a fifth PPV show for 1989 in Late December. I believe Hogan vs. Zeus will headline. It is thought part of this is booking shows on PPV in late November, late December and late January should flatten the market for the NWA's Starrcade (WWF is under the impression it'll be Flair vs. Luger which could do a decent buy rate if correctly hyped and they want to make sure that

a) companies don't even pick it up because three wrestling PPV's in three months is too many anyway; or b) if they do, their hype will pale by comparison and it'll flatten all shows, but they have the track record and can afford a few flat shows and if NWA trickles below one percent a few times, companies are going to be less enthusiastic about carrying future PPV events.

Hogan vs. Savage on 8/5 in Salt Lake City drew $115,000.

Roddy Piper will feud with Rick Rude starting in September.

No Holds Barred did $104,285 in 121 theaters the weekend of July 28-30 making the total $16, 001,563 after 57 days in release. At this stage of the game, that business, while Titan is seeing almost none of it (90 percent goes to the theaters), isn't too bad as the per screen average is decent for a movie out this long. However, in comparison with the other movies released at the same time, here's how it stands: Dead Poets Society has done about $75 million and was released the same weekend; Indiana Jones (a week before) has done $177 million and Scenes from the Class Struggle in Beverly Hills has done $2 million but it has been in very limited release (only a few dozen arty theaters and has a great per screen average). The business is good enough that if/when Vince decides to do a sequel, he probably can get others to completely finance it for him and he'll be able to make a better deal to almost insure he doesn't lose money the second go-around because he'll have a track record to point to.

7/23 in Grand Rapids, MI drew $54,000 as Genius pinned Jim Powers *, Mark Young pinned Bill Woods DUD, Bret Hart drew Mr. Perfect ***, Butch Miller pinned Tully Blanchard **, Warlord pinned Koko B. Ware DUD, Dino Bravo pinned Hercules DUD and Brutus Beefcake pinned Randy Savage ***.

The first 60 minute marathon match with Rougeaus vs. Rockers took place 8/6 in Chicago, with them ending in a tie and going into a sudden death overtime that the Rockers won. Somehow, even with an overtime period in, a match that was supposed to go 60 to start with, the time from start to finish was 45 minutes. Pat Patterson probably got this idea from Roy Shire, who on occasion booked this gimmick in the early 1970s and I recall seeing Patterson wrestle Don Muraco around 1974 in one of these which also ended in a time limit expired with each guy winning three falls and Patterson won in sudden death.

THE READERS PAGE

JAKE THE SNAKE

Once again I've gotten the inside scoop on an upcoming angle. Despite the current situation, the Great Muta will be turned late in the year. They will use the "To know America is to Love it" bit that was so successful in turning the

Koloffs. The mist will still be incorporated, however instead of spraying green mist, Muta will squirt red, white and then blue. This will allow Jim Ross to continue shouting, "How does he do that?" during every telecast even though Carl Styles will be able see how it's done. Unconfirmed reports claim he will wind up feuding with a masked man known as the Japanese Assassin (Giant Baba Victory).

On a more serious note, do you have any knowledge of whether the NWA has adopted the WWF's policy of contract stipulations whereby guys who want to leave are required to give several weeks notice in order to "job their way out?" That stipulation would certainly help discourage future jumpers and consider the difference it would have made to The Brain Busters and the Bushwackers, not to mention the Sid vs. Hogan match at WrestleMania 7.

Hey, isn't it wacky how life imitate art? Take for example, the incident whereby fictional character Jake Roberts attempted to help a friend get a better view of the women of Daytona Beach by moving his pal's cheekbone so it wouldn't obstruct his vision. You can't accuse Titan of not taking care of their own, though. First, they sent their finest character witness, Brother Love, to testify (I wonder if he called the judge "Brother Your Honor?") Then, judging by the televised hospital address to send Letters to Jake, they must have build a special medical wing in the WWF office building so that Jake's condition could be monitored regularly by Pat Patterson, a PHD (Phony Doctor) credited with saving lovely fictitious person Elizabeth from death after a bump from her non-husband.

Rumor has it that Titan is going to come clean about Jake's Legal problem, turn him heel and set up a feud with a former Stampede wrestling star who they will bill as "Legal Larry Cameron."

By the way, Las Vegas bookmakers are Laying five-to-one odds that Gordon Solie will describe the aftermath of the Ric Flair vs. Terry Funk match as a "Pier Six Brawl."

Ernie Santilli
Drexel Hill, Pennsylvania

Dave Meltzer: NWA contracts are for a specific period of time and don't automatically renew, while WWF contracts are originally for two years in duration, but automatically renew unless 13 weeks notice is given to be released from the contract (the 13 weeks being jobbed out of your mind time). The Brain Busters had contracts from Jim Crockett promotions which included promises of a certain money figure, which if not met by the payoffs, would have the difference made up in a balloon payment at the end of the contract term. When those balloon payments were reneged upon, it in a sense, made Tully & Arn free agents since their contracts weren't lived up to. While I'm not certain of this, I believe the Bushwackers never were contract performers in the NWA.

JESSE ON YANKEES GAME

Jesse Ventura appeared as a guest on MSG cable's broadcast of the 7/29 New York Yankees vs. Toronto Blue Jays baseball game. Jesse sat in with announcers Bobby Mercer and Tommy Hutton during the third and fourth inning. Jesse mentioned his meeting with George Steinbrenner on an airplane two years ago and said he always got George ringside seats for cards at the Tampa Sundome since then. This was Jesse's first time in Yankee Stadium and he said he enjoyed the fresh air as opposed to the Metrodome indoor games.

Greg Gumbel, Bryant's brother, another Yankee commentator made a snide remark Later in the game, that this was Ventura's first announcing skit where he didn't know the outcome of the event beforehand. Perhaps like his brother, he'd also rather watch Flair vs. Steamboat.

Steve Gennarelli
Binghamton, New York

HULK VS. TYSON

Apparently kids who watch Nickelodeon are better judges of athletes than one reader of the Observer. Someone heavily implied in a recent letter that Hulk Hogan would make a better role model for kids than Mike Tyson. Really?

Do we want more people around who "do their exercises, say their prayers and take their vitamins" while they accelerate their risk of developing skin cancer, heart, liver and kidney failure as they make total fools of themselves for a few dishonest bucks?

Tyson and Hogan can't even be compared as athletes, even though both are celebrities. Athletically, the difference between the two of them is greater than that of Ric Flair in his prime and the Ultimate Warrior in his grave. One guy is one of the best physically and aerobically conditioned athletes in any era in any sport. The other is a bleached blonde beefcake beach bump bass player and now a professional buffoon, whose greatest athletic feat is to bulge out his eyeballs and simultaneously puff his cheeks repeatedly in a bad impersonation of a goldfish half-way during his six-and-a-half minute main event matches.

At the personal level, I'm not so sure that the difference between Hogan and Tyson is all that great, although it would be safe to assume that neither would top Mother Teresa as a great human being. The common perception that Tyson is a "wife-beating, violent, suicidal, semi-lunatic" is more likely the product of the Big Apple commercial media and tabloids that concrete facts. With Tyson easily and repeatedly disposing of all opponents rather quickly, bored sportswriters had a field day with his ill-fated boxing-Hollywood marriage.

Neither Tyson, nor the sport of boxing, deserve any defenders. But considering that Tyson spent his childhood in jail, a correctional institute, he's done quite well for himself since being adopted by the Late Cus D'Amato. Not surprisingly, Tyson's well publicized problems began after D'Amato's death. Since being adopted by Vince McMahon Jr., Hogan has evolved into not only being a client, but also the president of the hair club for wrestlers.

Name withheld by request

Dave Meltzer: Actually, the letter on this subject was pretty much making fun of both Tyson and Hogan, who were the two recent winners in Nickelodeon's last two annual most popular athlete polls. I don't know of anyone who understands the two sports who would truly compare Hogan with Tyson as an athlete, but the question isn't who was the best athlete, but who kids admire the most. One would hope kids would have better sports role models than either Hogan, who many would claim isn't even an athlete in the truest sense of the word, or Tyson, even though he is absolutely an exceptional athlete.

BALTIMORE BASH

What a card! Yet another excellent PPV outing for the NWA. I do believe in getting my gripes out of the way first and here they are.

First, the King of the Hill Battle Royal — it has already been talked about at length about how meaningless this match was, yet they made matters even worse with the non-ending. If you really want to prove that in the NWA, "We Wrestle," why not let Vicious and Spivey go at it and come back two matches later as a tag team to show that squaring off in singles doesn't interfere with their mission as a team.

Second, I know that Lance Russell was doing the 900-number telecast, but he was in Nashville as well, and he did the interviews and he should have been doing the interviews here. Outside of the interview he did with Ric Flair, Gordon Solie didn't meet up to Russell's standards. A move like that just put Russell into the background and he's only been in for a few months.

Third, what was the ending of the Muta vs. Sting match? It might have worked with Steamboat vs. Flair in New Orleans, but here there was no question as to what happened. Sting had his shoulder up for the first two counts and had it down on the third count. How is that a three count? If you're going to give us an ending like this, at least get it right.

The only other problem was the audio in a couple of spots early, but that was soon cleared up.

The matches were excellent. Every guy on the card busted his butt from top to bottom. I don't see how anyone could walk away from the arena or the television set feeling that the NWA didn't give them their money's worth.

The Battle Royal was a decent opener despite the pathetic ending. Irwin Vs. Pillman was a well-worked match, albeit a little long for a bottom of the card match. I'm amazed at the height Pillman gets on those standing dropkicks. All sorts

of mistimed moves in the Dudes vs. Skyscrapers match but they tried to work as best they could. I love the fact that everyone wanted Sid in the ring. For someone so new in the business, he's going to be a tremendous heel draw in the future.

Cornette vs. Dangerously was fun and showed that the managers in the NWA work even harder than the wrestlers do in the WWF. Kevin Sullivan showed once again he is totally outclassed by the Steiners and Rotunda. This was a solid match, but Sullivan doesn't fit in with the other three, who are exceptional wrestlers. Sting vs. Muta was nothing from one injury—defying high spot after another. I'd give it three stars, but would have given it more outside of that lousy ending. Luger vs. Steamboat was the best match of the day. Well paced, great timing and you could sense a hatred between the two that was supposed to exist. The spot with the slingshot into the chair was awesome. On top of this, Luger was perfect in his backstage interview and pre-match histrionics on the no DQ clause. Taking everything into account, I'd give the match five stars.

War Games was good, but not as effective as it would have been with blood. I can remember the Omni War Games and how it was sheer brutality. Even without the blood, all ten worked a great match. I guess they had to sacrifice the blood for the next match. How about that entrance by the Road Warriors? Overall, three stars.

Flair vs. Funk was great. I was confused with Gary Hart's presence at first, but we all know where that led. It led to a superb post-match brawl. Flair's interview was exceptional before the match, as have all his interviews been since his return. Great interview at the end, and what a way to leave the telecast. I'd have given the match four stars, but with the brawl to top them all afterwards, it is five stars for sure.

Once again, the NWA has a great opportunity to capitalize on short-term success by creating a long-term trend. If the viewership was there and word gets around, we could see a bright future and a deserved reward for a patient TBS and Ted Turner.

Gabriel Daigle
Buena Park, California

One of the most impressive things about the spectacular Flair vs. Funk match was Flair's condition afterwards. With the blood, paint and sweat from a long fast-paced match and brawl, he visually looked like he was just in a helicopter crash. Yet, he was not breathing all that hard during his post match interview. He looked like he could have gone another hard 20 minutes when the rest of us were exhausted just watching the match. Sport or no sport, I don't believe anyone can deny that everyone on that card was an exceptional athlete.

Harry White
St. Louis, Missouri

Dave Meltzer: C'mon Harry, do you really consider Cornette an exceptional athlete? Well, if you consider talking a sport, maybe.

I thought the Bash was fantastic. The workrate was excellent and the entrances were well-done. The crowd was really into it. In my opinion, a new star was born , being Sid Vicious. He really was over with the crowd and I think singles matches with him against Flair will definitely be a PPV main event next year. Sting vs. Muta and Steamboat vs. Luger were both show stoppers, however Flair vs. Funk was sensational. The match wasn't as good as the Flair vs. Steamboat matches, but it still brought the house down. The finale brawl was great for the PPV audience, but kind of lost to the fans present live. A feud between Flair and Muta should be a real draw. I felt those both live and at home got their money's worth. Watching a replay of the card on PPV didn't do the show justice. I'm Looking forward to the October PPV. Although I have tickets, I can't say the same for Vince's SummerSlam.

Rich Kraemer
Lavallette, New Jersey

The Baltimore Bash was great. Of course, I wish they were all free, but this was the kind of a card I didn't mind at all paying for. Flair vs. Funk was an all-time classic brawl. The post-match action alone made the show worthwhile. Flair looked like a Christmas package with his face covered with blood and Muta's green mist. I think that Flair & Sting vs. Funk & Muta has the potential for being an excellent feud. Teaming Sting with Flair could be just what Sting needs to get over as the major he should be.

The ring entrances were great, especially those of the Road Warriors and Ric Flair. I'm surprised that the WWF didn't think of using the pyro first. It really makes for an exciting atmosphere.

The double ring set-up made for some really interesting situations. Sting's dive from ring-to-ring was incredible. I don't know how he does it, but I'm glad that he does.

As great as the show was, it did have a few flaws. It was an interesting idea to have the Skyscrapers as the last two in the Battle Royal, but the split-the-loot routine is overdone and cheap. The ending of Sting vs. Muta left a lot to be desired as well. Not only was it another dreaded screwjob, but it was never really clear what the referee's decision was and nothing was mentioned about it until the end of the show

Overall, the show was great and an encouraging sign as to what direction the NWA is going in. If they keep putting on great shows like this one, sooner or later somebody is bound to take notice.

Michelle Johnson
Watertown, New York

RODDY PIPER

Forgive me for asking, but of what relevance is the A&W Cream Soda Slam line on the NWA syndicated package? You are supposed to call up and vote yes or no and then what happens? Is this just to see who they can pawn $50 off?

From what I've seen of Roddy Piper on Prime Time Wrestling, he is far from funny and at times is even bothersome. Somebody should tell him to cut his hair.

Greg Roman
Ventnor, New Jersey

Dave Meltzer: I've been wondering all along if anyone really does call up those 900 numbers and vote yes or no on the A&W King of Slams.

I figured I'd give Piper at least a few shows to work things out before I'd offer any strong opinions on his work. Mind you, I've never liked Prime Time Wrestling and haven't watched it for years. The only reason I've been watching it is Piper. I'm certainly not watching it because of the Bobby Heenan Show, which at its best is moronic and more often than not is offensive. Every once in a while Heenan throws in a good one-liner, but you need more than that to carry a show.

As great a Piper fan as I am, I've got to be realistic here. Everybody has their fortè. Roddy's are skit work, interviews, interviewing, working live cards and being a heel. The highly structured disciplined format of Prime Time Wrestling requiring short, reasonably entertaining brain-dead patter about horrible matches and often silly angles between opposing (the WWF in all its wisdom violated a tenant of proper co-hosting here) co-hosts is not the kind of show Piper is going to be good at, particularly when he 's in a non-antagonistic role.

Piper's wrestling persona is hardly disciplined and structured, so he basically doesn't fit in with the format as it stands. Piper's a terrible shill. He's uncomfortable giving the WWF version of the truth and his distaste in doing so shows. He'd never make a good politician. He's coming across "too forced" as reader Paul Sherman pointed out, and that's unnatural for him. He's also trying too hard to mesh with Monsoon, when in fact, he should be antagonizing the goof. Monsoon is only bearable when he's being made sport of.

The best thing for Piper to do would be to turn heel on Monsoon. After three weeks of working with Monsoon, even the Pope would turn on him. While I realize Piper is reluctant to turn heel because of his acting career and for personal reasons, I don't think doing so would have as much of an effect on his outside endeavors as he thinks. If it isn't a possibility, he should work with Heenan.

Piper would be far more effective as a co-host dressed in regular street clothes as they mirror his personality better.

Save the kilt and T-shirt for ring appearances, where they work better. He looks fine with long hair, but it does need a serious trim, but it does look better lightened. While I realize the WWF is the land of the steroid God, Piper certainly could have stayed around his natural weight, which appears to be around 205 pounds, considering he never got over on size to begin with and he Looks far better at that weight.

Obviously the format has been shifted of late to having Piper take directions from Monsoon, to subdue himself and concentrate more on the angles that are laid out for him. It probably wouldn't be a bad idea to have Piper work from a script in this format, something he probably won't like but he's capable of doing and doing well . He needs to appear to be a little more prepared. At times he almost seems stuck for what to say, or more appropriately, what to say that's proper in the WWF scheme of doing things. To his credit, he's improved greatly from the first show to the third and I don't wince while watching him. I can see he may be good in a few more weeks if he continues this improvement, but he'll have to be far more subdued than wrestling fans are used to. With the current format, he will never be great unless he turns.

Teresa DeMarie
Tuckahoe, New York

NWA

Ever wonder why the NWA isn't doing better than it is, even though the product keeps getting better?

I recently went to a barbeque at my sister-in-law's house and in the course of conversation with two of her friends, I mentioned that I liked pro wrestling. Immediately I got the usual response, "Oh, I never watch that stuff. Can't stand it. How can you watch, etc." Then one of them said to me, "You mean you really watch that, Hulk Hogan, Macho Man and all of them?" Those were the names they knew. They weren't watching wrestling, but it was WWF wrestling that they weren't watching. They had never even heard of anything else.

Then in our local newspaper they had an interview with Ted Turner. He talked about his TV stations, about movies on television, about baseball, about ratings. Not once did he even mention that he owned a wrestling company. How committed to the success of the NWA can he really be when he won't even talk about it? Maybe that's why Vince McMahon claims they aren't competition."

Elyse Zois
Union, New Jersey

HOGAN VS. FLAIR

The arguments about whether or not the NWA can ever equal the WWF ignore the basic appeal of the McMahon promotion; an awesome looking champion. When Randy Savage was champion, the WWF lost a lot of its salability.

The man was a great worker with some incredible moves and he could talk up a storm, but he wasn't big enough to put the shows across. Only the Mega Powers and the eventual return as champion of Hogan got the WWF over again.

Ric Flair is a terrific technician and a hard worker, but when he stands next to someone of Hogan's size, he Looks like a junior heavyweight. No casual wrestling viewer, and that is where the big money comes from, will ever believe that Hogan could be beaten by someone the size of Flair. Making Ron Garvin or Ricky Steamboat as champion made the NWA look even wimpier by comparison. The answer is Lex Luger, Sid Vicious or maybe even Scott Hall. Luger and Vicious have better cut physiques and Hall is more handsome than Hogan and these factors matter in getting fans. Luger has some good moves, where Hogan has none. All three are much younger than Hogan and they all have full heads of hair. The flabby bald man could really be challenged by pushing one of those three. Save the high quality Little man Like Muta, Steamboat and Flair for the lesser titles and put somebody awesome in as World champion if you want to challenge the WWF.

Michael Burke
Houston, Texas

Dave Meltzer: While the point about Hogan's size being a major factor in selling him to the general public compared with Flair is valid, I don't buy the WWF lost much of anything in the year that Savage was champ. In fact, the three months prior to the last WrestleMania, with Savage as champ, had to be the best three-month run in the WWF's history when it comes to house show income. Besides, even when Savage was champion, the WWF left no doubt that the focal point of the promotion revolved around Hogan.

NWA PUTTING ON GREAT SHOWS

Having recently looked back over several years' worth of Observers, I noticed an overwhelming almost weekly preoccupation with the idea that the NWA has been a floundering group on its last legs all this time. Ups and downs aside, the facts are the NWA is still around, providing successful careers for many top workers and putting on consistently great shows, regardless of crowd size. It's called integrity, which one assumes is a quality not allowed in the WWF.

Mention the NWA and I think of Flair, Steamboat, Luger, Sting, Muta, Funk, Roadies, Midnight, Cornette and even Tommy Young and plenty more. Mention WWF and I can only think of Akeem, Duggan, Bravo, Beefcake, Hercules, Ultimate, Hillbilly Jim, Valentine, Bushwackers, Zeus and now Dusty Rhodes among far too many others.

This endless, constant NWA backlash can be attributed mainly to the great American tradition of clinging to winners and ignoring the underdogs, as well as a large ignorance factor. But it goes beyond marketing strategies, beyond the fact that we have two vastly different audiences (hype & glitz vs.

sweat & blood). If Titan's legion of 12-year-old children-of-yuppies really cared about action, they'd be talking boycott. But since Vince couldn't possibly appeal to a lower common denominator, he 's secure for the moment, so why should he care if the rest of the crowd gets ripped off?

Now that the NWA doesn't screw up. Too many titles. Too many confusing stipulations. The Ding Dongs. Everything involving two rings should be scrapped. It Looks like they 're trying to make up for something to beat the WWF, which is ridiculous at best. But for everything they do wrong, they do 20 things right, and that surely can't be said for Vince. My only complaint with the NWA is that with all the tremendous matches they've put on this year alone, particularly the Flair-Steamboat series, virtually everything else pales in comparison, and we're getting spoiled.

I was lucky enough to catch the annual Boston Garden NWA show in July. The fans were ecstatic, starved for great wrestling, which they got tenfold. The worst match on the card was easily better than the best of any ten years' worth of Titan shows I've seen in the same building, even without Flair on the card.

Since both groups give the fans what they apparently want, maybe it's time we start blaming ourselves, the fans, for any alleged public perceptions that arise. We are the public and we should stop kicking the NWA when it's down, stop nitpicking over these small and infrequent weak spots they are entitled to stumble onto. In much the same way that the mind can heal the body, my belief is that if we believe in the NWA and support them, they can give Vince a run for his all-too-ineffective money. Regardless of the continuous influx of fresh 12-year-oIds with cash, the rest of us can't put up with his drivel forever.

Joe Coughlin
Boston, Massachusetts

TWO OF THREE

There has been a lot of space in the readers' page section devoted to the topic of two out of three fall matches. Why? Why was this subject brought up in the first place? Does the topic really warrant any discussion? As I see it, two of three fall matches are no different than any other match with special stipulations, at least in this respect, if it's done right, it will work. If not, it won't. It's that simple. If you have good workers and good heat, then you have a good match, regardless of the stipulations. Don't overuse it and it won't die of overkill. You can't compare the merits of one type of match to another. Entertainment is subjective. Wrestling is entertainment. Everyone has their own preference. There can be no definitive discussion on the topic, especially

aspects of it. Some will like it. Some won't. Take the Tower of Doom match for instance. Even this match had some crowd pops. Not because the match itself was executed to perfection, but rather it involved some good workers and had a good deal of interest. So, due to these factors, a potentially disastrous situation came out okay.

Next, there was a report concerning an altercation backstage between Steve Williams and Hawk. You stated Hawk was lucky that some brave soul separated the two of them? Why? Is this strictly based on conjecture or do you know something we don't? I mean, I know Dr. Death is one of your favorites and all and I know he has an impressive athletic background, but why do you assume he is more formidable than Hawk? From what I know of Mike Hegstrand, he's no pushover. Does your assumption of the outcome stem from your disdain for roided-up gym-rat monsters. Which brings me to my next topic.

I don't remember who said it or what issue it was on, but the term "fake muscle" was used in reference to steroid use. What are fake muscles? I'm an avid weightlifter and follow the sports of bodybuilding and powerlifting, but I don't advocate the use or abuse of steroids. As a matter of fact, I often speak to potential users about their dangers and side-effects. Yes, a guy or gal can pump himself with all the anabolics he wants, but unless he hits the weights and hits them hard, all the juice in the world isn't going to build muscle by itself. And the muscle which is built, whether it be with the aid of drugs of without, is very real. Muscle fibers are muscle fibers no matter what methods aided their development. Steroids are merely a tool to help a person reach his or her goals quicker and easier. Yes, many consider it cheating. Yes, they are dangerous and illegal, but they also work. Guys like Ted Arcidi, Rich Gaspari and Jim Hellwig are very big, very strong and their muscles are very real. They put some real time and dedication in at the gym. You have to at least respect that. Now if you disagree with the methods they've used to achieve these ends, that's another topic.

How much of a bearing does heat have on the rating of a match? I mean, if Dynamite Kid in his prime and Randy Savage on his best night did a twenty-minute high spot match, would a dead audience and lack of heat make this a three star match instead of a five star match? If so, why?

Next, I 'd like to respond to the Letter of Teresa DeMarie on the 7/17 issue in which she lambasted the NWA and what she perceived as a lack of progress. Needless to say, this is one person's opinion. I think the TV shows have improved greatly both in content and format. Sure, the company still has structural problems and it shows from time-to-time, but nothing major enough for them to incur such a harsh condemnation. I think Ms. DeMarie and those who think as she does are missing an important point. The product we see is not made for the smart fans. It is made to appeal to the marks, or general viewers. People who tune in wrestling do not have a basic knowledge of the inner-workings of a promotion nor do they care. They just want to be entertained. If things are done right, they work and if they aren't done right, they don't work. Yes, some changes need to be made, but nothing happens overnight. Having owned a business of my own for three years, I have experience on a much smaller scale in trying to organize, develop and set in motion concepts and techniques. It is much easier said than done, especially by those on the outside looking in. Trying to be level-headed and comprehensive while in the thick of things isn't easy. I know, in retrospect, there is plenty I would have done differently. But all things considered, I think the NWA is moving in a positive direction, especially when compared to the reign of Virgil. Maybe there are too many cooks in the kitchen and not enough hands on management by the owners and maybe there isn't enough risk taking or thinking big, but the NWA is an infant company. Give them time to grow and mature. Don't chastise them while they are still green.

Rick Rude has to be the most improved worker of this season. His in-ring performance has upgraded tremendously lately and he's very exciting to watch. Let's hope he maintains his improvement and some other so-called wrestlers take notice.

Although I may sound argumentative and displeased with the Observer, that couldn't be farther from the truth. I eagerly await the arrival of each issue.

Scott Brooks
Philadelphia, Pennsylvania

Dave Meltzer: I would be foolish to insinuate that Hawk is any kind of a pushover because that's ridiculous, but Dr. Death is generally regarded by most in and close to the field as the toughest man in the business. As for Teresa DeMarie's letter, she was explaining why she felt the NWA wasn't gaining in popularity and TV ratings and house show numbers don't lie. While Flair's return will pop some houses now, there has been no steady indication of improvement in either TV ratings or gates since January, which shows NWA has lost interest and not gained interest among casual fans as a whole. I would hope the recent events may change that trend, but as an overall trend, the NWA's popularity on TV and at the house has been on the decline since January, and really, since the summer of 1987 when Dusty botched up the potential stemming from the UWF purchase.

WRESTLING VIEWS BY JEFF BOWDREN

Some random thoughts on the state of pro wrestling:

NWA: I think they should take a page from the Magnum T. A. push for Brian Pillman and have him win all of his matches in 20 seconds or so. Since they've been letting all their other television matches go longer, if one guy

continually wins short matches it makes him look more impressive to the casual fan. Two dropkicks and have him fly off the top rope and get him out of there. . . It's time for something to happen in "Funk's Grill" or the "Danger Zone. I think the last time one of them was used for an angle was when Paul E. was setting up Randy Rose for Secret Service Jack Victory. Yes, Lex Luger has been awesome since the turn. But don't you wonder if he really hasn't been so great simply because he's just being himself? What happened to the U.S. tag team title? The Midnight Express hasn't really done anything to excite me since their return. They seem to have gotten a half second slow all of a sudden. I don't know about you, but aren't you getting tired of waiting for the Road Warriors to get into this big, awesome money-making feud that everyone keeps waiting for? Didn't Bill Apter ordain these guys the greatest tag team in the history of wrestling? Where's the big feud, then?.... The Rick Steiner/ Robin Green stuff is excellent. It's the kind of thing that makes me want to tune in every week. It's so good because it is telling a story. It's not one of those infuriating angles that is done one week and then never followed up on. Steiner's antics are great. Either he really is stupid or he's a genius..... By the way, Scott Steiner isn't great yet, but he will be. He reminds me a little of Paul Orndorff during his Georgia and Mid-South days.

WWF: Like Muhammad Ali objected to Vietnam and refused to participate, I object to Titan and refuse to patronize. I realize that all wrestlers are in a sense, prostitutes, but watching great wrestlers like Ted DiBiase, Terry Taylor and Owen Hart have to humiliate themselves makes me ill. I'm surprised Vince saved the toilet cleaning for Dusty and didn't give it to Owen Hart, because they did everything else they could to humiliate him.

New Japan: I think this Russian thing is still a time bomb waiting to go off. What happens when the initial curiosity wears off? They may have set up a base for the next five years with that three million dollar gate, but they also may have shot their wad. . . I Love Keiichi Yamada 's new costume. I think this gimmick will get hot down the road and I'm already looking forward to his matches with Owen Hart .

All Japan: This is the stuff you look forward to the most when a tape arrives in the mail. The Foot Loose have become what the Midnight Express was last year, the state of the art when it comes to tag team wrestling, and every other team in wrestling gets caught copying their moves…... Dan Kroffat & Doug Furnas are going to both be a hot item in the United States soon, although I think the combination that would work the best in the States would be Kroffat & Tom Zenk. Furnas throws awesome dropkicks, which may be the best in the business and he does nice flying moves off the top rope, but he doesn't have the right babyface look. Even though he may be legitimately the strongest wrestler in the game, he doesn't have the powerhouse look that wrestling has programmed fans to look for like Lex Luger, Ultimate Warrior and the Road Warriors.

. Everything between Tsuruta and Tenryu has been done great. Do you realize the angle that started all this took place more than two years ago? That's called getting the most out of a feud. What's really amazing is that this group is so hot with one of its best wrestlers, Tiger Mask, out of action with injuries.

Japanese women: I saw the Chigusa Nagayo retirement show. It was well done, but I think the promotion should have done more. I would have liked to have seen some sort of a career highlight video, covering her career from beginning to end. Her final match with Lioness Asuka was confusing, with her getting pinned in two minutes, but the tag team match that preceded it, with the Crush Girls teaming for the final time against Mitsuko Nishiwaki & Akira Hokkuto was awesome. Chigusa threw every big move she ever used out there. I felt sorry for Asuka, who truly was and is great, but has been in Chigusa's shadow for most of her career and now will retire without anywhere near the Same fanfare as Chigusa.

Some thoughts on the best matches of the first six months:

December 1988: 1) Genichiro Tenryu & Toshiaki Kawada vs. Stan Hansen & Terry Gordy; 2) Ric Flair vs. Lex Luger at Starrcade '88; 3) Ric Flair & Barry Windham vs. Midnight Express from 12/7 in Chattanooga——even an inane finish couldn't ruin this one;

January : 1) Chigusa Nagayo vs. Lioness Asuka from January 29 in Tokyo, the last ever Battle of the Crush Girls; 2) Tenryu & Kawada vs. Jumbo Tsuruta & Yoshiaki Yatsu from January 20; 3) Flair & Windham vs. Ricky Steamboat & Eddie Gilbert on January 7 for Steamboat's triumphant return to the NWA;

February : 1) Flair vs. Steamboat February 20 in Chicago——one of the all-time greatest matches ever; 2) Rockers vs. Brain Busters from February 17 in Hershey, PA, best Titan match thus far in 1989; 3) Windham vs. Lex Luger in Chicago, somewhat underrated because it was a short match;

March: 1) Flair vs. Steamboat March 18 at the Capital Centre——many say this was the best match of the entire series; 2) Foot Loose vs. Tsuruta & Yatsu on March 29 in Tokyo; 3) Crush Girls vs. Yumi Ogura & Mika Komatsu March 4 in Tokyo;

April: 1) Flair vs. Steamboat April 2 in New Orleans, another true classic; 2) Tsuruta vs. Stan Hansen on April 16 in Tokyo where Tsuruta won all three major titles in Japan; 3) Foot Loose vs. Danny Kroffat & Tom Zenk on April 1 8 in Tokyo;

May: 1) Flair vs. Steamboat on May 7 in Nashville—— great match, great commentary and a great angle after the match; 2) Tenryu & Foot Loose vs. Kroffat & Doug Furnas & Danny Spivey on May 24; 3) British Bulldogs vs. Kroffat & Furnas on May 12;

June: 1) Tsuruta vs. Tenryu on June 5——destined to go down as one of the greatest matches in the history of Japan; 2) Foot Loose vs. Kroffat & Furnas on June 5; 3) Steamboat vs. Terry Funk in Fort Bragg.

AUGUST 21, 1989

The WWF rolled into town this past week for television tapings in Oakland and Fresno, drawing advanced sellout crowds in both cities. Oakland on 8/8 drew 14,000 fans (13,500 paid) and $169,000 while Fresno the next night drew 9,000 (8,800 paid) and $106,000. Both cities were sold out well before show time.

This is the third time the WWF has done a TV taping in the Bay Area and it was easily the most successful of the three. The first time, at the Cow Palace a few years back drew a sellout but it was heavily padded (2,500 freebies) and the show was pretty poor as entertainment went, with the fans booing both the faces and heels by the time the third hour of taping began and there was almost no heat for anything after the midway point of the second hour of taping. The second time around, in Oakland, was a better show although they only drew about 9 ,000 paid for Hulk Hogan vs. Big Bossman. The crowd wasn't as ugly as before, but generally seemed lethargic as the show drew on with the endless matches and didn't seem that pleased overall. This show was a marked difference. The crowd was hot for all three hours of taping and all the Prime Time Wrestling tapings as well, and very few people left early (a marked difference from the previous tapings) because of the anticipation of the Hogan vs. Randy Savage with Zeus in the corner main event. The enthusiasm for the entire show was impressive, considering the length of the show and the percentage of kids in the crowd. You can't expect good wrestling at a WWF taping (or any WWF show for that matter), so judging it on whether the matches are good is pointless, but there was one match out of 31 which was undeniably good and a few others were at Least passable. As for the rest, well. .

An interesting thing we all noted about the crowd reaction. With the exception of Hogan and Savage, who were over far more than anyone else on the card, it was almost hard to make a distinction as to who was over and who wasn't. The crowd reacted to almost everyone equally, as long as they had the accompanying music. For example, Mark Young, who has never been pushed on TV for Titan and nobody in the building knew who he was, still got about the same reaction as the Ultimate Warrior since the music was cranked up. Definitely Pavlov's Dog stuff here. Still, the crowd got into almost every act from start-to-finish which was an impressive sight.

Running down the show, which was mainly tapings for Superstars of Wrestling shows that will air August 19-26 and the first week of September, plus a few Prime Time Wrestling shots:

1. Boris Zhukov pinned Mark Young in the opener. Young got a big reaction and they popped for his break—dancing (they would have popped if he was picking his nose as long as there was musical accompaniment – whoops, I wish I hadn't said that because Vince will try and humiliate someone by making him do that at the next taping now). Young did some acrobatics but is slow getting into the moves. Zhukov must weigh around 320 pounds now. Way overweight. Young Looked as though he was trying to jump on the top rope and come off with a flying move, but slipped on the top rope and fell back on his head and Zhukov pinned him after an elbow drop. Give Young credit, the finish Looked Like a "mistake" so it appeared realistic. *

2. The Widow Maker (Barry Windham) beat Red Rooster (Terry Taylor) via count out. Windham has also gained a lot of weight on the special Titan diet, and looks around 290ish. In fact, his body and height reminds me of Bruiser Brody somewhat in the way he does the flying moves and moves around the ring. I was actually expecting a good match here but was watching the wrong promotion. Windham looked kind of lethargic with the added weight and the match was quite slow-paced. Everything they did was solid with the exception of some minor timing problems. Finish saw Taylor hold Windham in a headlock outside the ring and Windham go to shove him off into the ringpost, however Taylor didn' t go into the post but still wound up counted out of the ring. The bell rang out of nowhere and finish had no build-up whatsoever. ** ¼.

3. Ted DiBiase beat Jim Evans with the sleeper. The hold isn't over in the least. DiBiase is claiming to have ended Jake Roberts' wrestling career, and since he talked about Roberts before both his matches, it makes me think that Titan has a good idea Jake won't be serving any time when his sentencing comes about this week on the assault charges in Florida; Before the next match, they introduced Pepper Gomez to the crowd. Gomez was a headliner and a big draw here in the early 1960s feuding with Ray Stevens and worked on-and-off in the area through the late 1970s. Very few in the crowd seemed to know who he was which tells you about how much the wrestling crowds have changed in the past decade, although this crowd was hardly a stereotypical Titan yuppie crowd but more kids who probably weren't even born when Gomez had retired. A later mention on the card of Pat Patterson (the area's top draw from 1970-75) drew more name recognition and reaction, but still nothing like what one would expect from a regional legend's name.

4. The Rockers, who had Tito Santana in their corner, beat The Black Knight (Billy Anderson) & Tim Patterson. I guess Jesse Ventura and Vince McMahon can tell all the jokes about Tim Patterson being the illegitimate son of Pat Patterson like they did another time he worked a West Coast taping. The Rockers used a simultaneous double fist-drop on Patterson for the pin. Even though this was one of the more spectacular looking finishes, the crowd didn't pop for the finish since it wasn't an "established" finish. Rockers Looked great.

5. Koko B. Ware, with blonde and blue hair, pinned Greg Valentine. Ron Garvin came to ringside and when Valentine went for the figure four, he released the hold to argue with Garvin and Ware pinned him from behind. Huge pop for the "upset. " Nobody would have cared about the match except that Garvin came down and it appeared something was up.

6. Rick Martel, accompanied by the Rougeaus, pinned Jerry Monti with the Old Bombs Away kneedrop off the top rope. Martel is a lot better as a heel now then when he first made the turn. He's kind of getting the smug Jacques Rougeau act down.

7. Dusty Rhodes pinned Barry Horowitz. Rhodes now wears yellow spots on everything, his kneepad, his tank top and his trunks. This must be a rib because according to women's magazines, spots makes one look fatter than one really is and should be avoided by anyone who is even the slightest bit overweight. I don't know if it was the spots, but Dusty looked even fatter than before. He wears a policeman's hat and twirls around the knight stick that he stole from the Big Bossman. I don't know if this is intentional or not, but with the police hat and knight stick (instead of kendo stick), and the bleached blonde hair and grossly overweight frame, Dusty looks almost exactly Like Dump Matsumoto. Too bad he can't work like her. Dusty got a good reaction for his gimmick spots and a huge reaction to his entrance and exit music.

8. Brain Busters (Tully Blanchard & Arn Adderson) beat Stephan DeLeon & Louis Spicoli. Spicoli has a resemblance to Bobby Eaton. The Brain Busters won with a stiff piledriver.

9. Ultimate Warrior beat Steve Vega. The reaction for Warrior was no better than for everyone else. As the match got going, one of the Titan office guys was walking around us wanting to plant the gimmicks for the TV cameras to pick up. Unfortunately, one of my friends was wearing a TBS Sports cap so we didn't get any free Duggan foam rubber 2x4's. We didn't know at the time that we could have all got kicked out of the building for wearing such heinous apparel. They make Warrior carry the guy back that he beats, which is almost unfair because the guy can hardly walk without having a heart attack to begin with, let alone having to carry somebody to the back with him. After the match, Bobby Heenan and Warrior started an argument and Andre came up and choked Warrior out. Warrior stinks as bad as ever.

10. In a Prime Time Wrestling match, Curt "Mr. Perfect" Hennig went to a 20 minute draw With Santana. There were good armdrag spots and Hennig is easily one of the best workers they've got, but this was 85 percent restholds and the most boring match on the card. The last 10 minutes nobody was paying attention for the most part. The first half was actually better and it seemed the longer they went, the less heat they maintained. * ¼ (onLy because Hennig took some outrageous bumps).

Then came a Brother Love segment with Hulk Hogan and Brutus Beefcake and they cut Bruce's hair.

11. Widow Maker pinned Dan Brazil with a superplex. Apparently they must not have liked this match because they made Windham go out again two matches later, but this wasn't a noticeable disaster of a squash like the do-overs I've seen on other tapings.

12. Dino Bravo & Honky Tonk Man beat The Hart Foundation via DQ. Hart Foundation got the best introduction reaction thus far on the card with the possible exception of Virgil Runnels. Neidhart got caught using the megaphone at the finish. Match wasn't too bad since Bret Hart was in the ring most of the way. * ½.

13. Widow Maker pinned Spicoli. Fans were chanting, "Barry, Barry" at him. More heat and some cheers this time around.

14. Bushwackers beat Peter Ketchum & Don Stevens. All the kids do the Bushwacker walk. It's quite a sight to watch the crowd which is the best thing to watch because you know nothing is going to happen in the ring. They spent the match trying to get the Bushwacker hat over as a gimmick. The guy out of the ring wears the hat and they pass it back and forth when they tag in and out. Stevens used to do a wrestling bulletin about 20 years ago when his name was Don Alvarez.

15. Bad News Brown pinned Jim Gorman.

16. Jim Duggan pinned Ed Vargas, who those of you who have bad dreams that were reality may remember as former AWA superstar Rocky Mountain Thunder. Vargas got a

good reaction from the crowd due to his size (these people are definitely brainwashed to music and size).

Then came Gene Okerlund to tell the crowd to make noise as they were going to tape the "open" of the show (where they put the crowd making noise in the background as Vince & Jesse talk about the show). This was the loudest the crowd got the entire card with the possible exception of Hogan's entrance. Gene then got the fans to chant "Jesse, Jesse," which they did. A marked difference from the NWA in Baltimore when the ring announcer tried to get them to chant "Luger, Luger" but unfortunately for the NWA, their crowds aren't Pavlov's Dogs and they don't react that easily. As this was going on, there was a huge banner being walked around the building which said, "NWA #1." I only bring that up because of what happened next. The card stopped cold. We had no idea what was going on, but all of a sudden the card stopped. Several security officers and Tony Garea started chatting and then went into the crowd, and we started looking to see what the problem was but no fights in the stands or nothing. I kind of figured it out but the perpetrators of this heinous act were nowhere to be seen. It became obvious they were looking for the banner but couldn't find it, and they wouldn't re-start the card until they did. Luckily the WWF has no competition in this business and it was only a fictitious delay in the card trying to find a fictitious banner for a non-existent competitor. Finally, after a long delay, a few kids finked on the guys with the banner and they carted the guilty parties out of the building and ripped up the banner. I was truly amazed at all this. I don't mind them confiscating the banner, but to make such a fuss and hold up taping over something like this says more about Titan than anything anyone else can say. And after confiscating the banner to actually have the security kick the guys out of the arena was a bit much. By the way, this was all in the middle level of a huge building, so it's not like it would show up visibly on television Like it was at ringside.

17. Well, the delay was more exciting than the next match where Ted DiBiase pinned Hillbilly Jim on PTW. Almost all stalling till the finish. ½ *(because DiBiase took one really good bump off the top rope).

18. Rougeaus beat Jim Evans & Dennis Mirto. The Rougeaus song is a hoot.

19. Ron Garvin (newly reinstated as an active wrestler by Jack Tunney) used his dreaded NWA finishing move, the KO punch on The Intruder. Nobody cared about Garvin even with the angle earlier in the card and all the hype on TV for the past few months.

20. Jimmy Snuka pinned Mike Luka.

21. Haku pinned Riki "Power Bomb" Ataki. Haku gave Ataki a chance to show some stuff.

22. Warrior pinned Andre in about 20 seconds after three clotheslines. The only reason it took so long is because it took Andre a long time to get into position. The place popped like crazy at the finish, unlike in most other cities they've run this. My theory is that here everyone came to see Hogan vs. Savage and while this was advertised, it wasn't the main event as it is on the house shows and really nobody would complain about a short match when you were getting a nearly five-hour card to begin with. Besides, I was grateful it went as short as it did.

23. Bushwackers beat Blanchard & Anderson via DQ in a title match. The execution stunk but the "story" of the match with the near falls was good. Heels DQ'd for double teaming * ¾.

24. Brutus Beefcake pinned Chuck Hambone. Beefcake got a lot of whistles from the crowd. Unfortunately, the whistles were all from guys.

25. Demolition beat Zhukov & Jake "The Milkman" Milliman.

26 . Bossman pinned Bob Ellis (not the famous wrestler by the same name) After the match when Bossman was roughing up Ellis, in waddled the American Dream, with music (this taping seemed to be especially designed to see how many times they could play that song) and he used the knightstick on Bossman and ran him off and in the ensuing brawl, got a second nightstick from him.

27. Rick Rude pinned Tim Horner in a PTW match. Very good fast-paced match with good execution. Easily the best thing on the card and Horner was the best worker on the card. ***.

28. Hercules beat Darryl Nickel.

29. Powers öf Pain beat Tom Stone & Dale Wolfe (used to be Dusty Wolfe but nobody can be called Dusty here except for the Dream). The jobbers got the same reaction as Powers of Pain, who appear to be the deadest pushed act in the circus.

30. Rhodes pinned Bossman in five minutes after an elbow drop. Dusty was twirling two nightsticks. At least if it had been Dump Matsumoto this would have been a decent match. I pity the people who have to watch this match as a main event. No heat during the match, but they sure popped for that song at the finish. DUD.

31. Randy Savage beat Hulk Hogan via count out in eight minutes. Hogan was off but Savage and Sherri Martel more than made up for it. If it wasn't for the fact her interviews are weak, I'd say Sherri really should win manager of the year this year because nobody works better at ringside. Heat was deafening, even after midnight . Zeus is totally lost at ringside but they put him over great. Hogan kept running away from him, or I should say, backing away whenever he approached and showed fear. Typical Hogan match tho Savage was working hard but Hogan missed a lot of moves. Hogan bodyslammed Zeus after the match was over when it appeared Zeus had him caught in the corner. **

The NWA announced the line-up for its second annual "Fall Brawl, "a TBS "Clash of the Champions" special on 9/12 from Columbia, SC: Ric Flair & Sting vs. Great Muta & Terry Funk; Lex Luger vs. Tommy Rich for the U.S. title, Michael Hayes & Jim Garvin vs. Rick & Scott Steiner for the NWA tag team titles, Road Warriors vs. Samoan Swat Team, Steve Williams vs. Mike Rotunda, Brian Pillman vs. Norman the Lunatic and Sid Vicious vs. Ranger Ross plus the debut of Tom Zenk, who won't be coming in as a masked wrestler as originally planned according to the latest word I've received. Nobody can say that isn't a strong card for a free television special. Actually, it's probably too strong, since they are putting on television for free the basic headline matches at the house shows that they are running except the two headline singles matches are being put together in a tag team match. The PPV show will be 10/28 from Philadelphia, not the 29th as originally announced, so it's on a Saturday night.

STAMPEDE

Owen Hart pinned Dynamite Kid in the main event on the 8/11 card in Calgary which drew another near sellout of 1, 500 fans.

Kensuke Sasaki (Sasaki—san in Puerto Rico) is in, forming a tag team with Sumu Hara and I'm told they really look hot as a team. Interesting duo since Sasaki is contracted to New Japan and Hara with All Japan. The Maximum Overdrive team here isn't the same team as in Minneapolis. One of the guys is the same, Tim Hunt, but the other guy is Greg Sende. I was told the guys aren't green, they are chlorophyll.

They are going to be booking fewer dates over the next month since Owen Hart will be in Japan and Davey Boy Smith will still be out of action for a while. Smith is back in England at last report, recovering from the 7/4 auto accident. The group is really weak on the face side with Smith and Jason the Terrible (Karl Moffat) out of action from the auto accident and Bruce Hart not having wrestled since Dynamite Kid broke his jaw with a backstage sucker-punch.

8/12 in Edmonton drew 400 as Biff Wellington pinned

Jonathan Holiday in a babyface match * ½, Maximum Overdrive beat Goldie Rogers & Kim Schau ½ *, Larry Cameron pinned The Outlaw * ¼, The Samurai Warriors (Kensuke Sasaki & Sumu Hara) beat Bulldog Bob Brown and an unannounced rookie who was replacing Kerry Brown who is become a frequent no-show ** ¾, Johnny Smith beat Owen Hart via count out when manager Abdul Wizal held Hart's leg as he was trying to get back into the ring *** ¼ and Great Gama kept the Commonwealth title beating Chris Benoit in two of three falls when Wizal distracted the ref and Holiday (turning heel) threw water to revive Gama (who was out from a sleeper hold) and gave him a foreign object which he used to win the deciding fall. ** ½

USWA

There are no visible signs of any changes with the name change. In fact, the syndicated TV show is still being called World Class, although that will change.

8/11 at the Dallas Sportatorium drew 2,000 as Steve & Schaun Simpson beat The Masked Medics (two local jobbers), Billy Travis pinned Frogman LeBlanc, Kerry Von Erich & Jimmy Jack Funk went to a 15 minute draw with Taras Bulba (Juan Reynoso) & Al Perez, Eric Elnbry & Chris Adams went to a double count out with Gary Young & P. Y. Chu Hi (Phil Hickerson) and Matt Borne & Jeff Jarrett regained the tag team titles (I guess now the USWA belts) beating Sheik Scott Braddock & Cactus Jack Manson, who had won them the previous week. The main event was a Thunderdome cage match as heels Chu Hi & Braddock & Bulba & Young & Perez & Manson beat faces Travis & Adams & Jarrett & Borne & Funk & Embry and after the match was over and all the faces were handcuffed to the cage (this is the cage match where the object is to handcuff your opponents to the cage and when one team is completely cuffed, the other team can release all its members from the cuffs and beat up the helpless foes. Anyway, with all the faces cuffed, Tojo Yamamoto passed a kendo stick through the cage and Chu Hi used it to bloody up Embry.

8/18 in Dallas has Embry vs. Chu Hi with Embry putting up his hair and Chu Hi putting up the Texas title, Young vs. Adams in a match where each man has a kendo stick and can use it, Jarrett & Borne defend against Perez & Manson, Kerry Von Erich vs. Bulba in a Death match, Travis vs. Braddock and the three Simpson brothers (Steve—Schaun—Stuart) vs. Young & Manson & Scandor Akbar.

Chris Adams' wife Toni did some talking during a match and To jo and Chu Hi chased her away.

CWA

In the highlights of the 8/7 card in Memphis, the battle of the movie monsters saw Jason & Freddy beat The Zombie & The Undertaker. Jason had his hockey mask pulled off to reveal a skeleton mask, the Zombie got so scared he ran into his coffin and wouldn't get out of his coffin and Undertaker was double—teamed until Freddy finally beat him with the Freddy claw. I'm not making this up. Dustin Rhodes & Bill Dundee beat Black Bart & Dirty White Boy in the Australian Rules football match, Ken Wayne pinned Doug Gilbert, The Blackbirds (King Parsons & Brickhouse Brown) failed to pin the Rock & Roll Express (Ricky Morton & Robert Gibson) in 10 minutes thus had to forfeit "$10,000" however they only gave them "$142" instead, Master of Pain won the loser leaves town match from Dutch Mantell when Chris Champion and Mark Starr distracted the ref and Gossett sprayed green in Mantell's eyes, Rock & Roll Express won a Lights Out Match over Champion & Starr via DQ when Blackbirds and Harold Harris interfered and the finale saw Jerry Lawler keep the USWA title beating Bam Bam Bigelow in a Coward Waves the Flag match with Eddie Marlin and Ronnie Gossett in the corners. The finish saw Marlin beat up Gossett and wave his flag while hiding under the ring apron making it look like Bigelow, who was destroying Lawler, had given it up. Bigelow then beat up Marlin after the match and was "suspended" to allow him to leave for his Japanese tour. By the way, friends of Bigelow insist that Bigelow has a contract already signed to fight Mike Tyson, but nobody in the boxing world seems to know anything about it. New to the area is Texas Dirt, who is of course Dutch Mantell under the hood returning after losing the loser leaves town match. What a unique idea that has never ever been done before.

Buddy Landel has returned and they are calling him the No. 1 contender for Lawler's title saying he won a tournament in Florida and beat Mil Mascaras, Austin Idol, Super Destroyer, Steve Keirn, Kerry Von Erich, Al Perez, Dory Funk, Jack Briscoe Iron Sheik and Sgt. Slaughter to win the thing. As long as they were lying and bringing up names of dead wrestlers, retired wrestlers, braindead wrestlers and wrestlers with a dead act they might as well have said Ric Flair, Randy Savage, Hulk Hogan, Antonio Inoki and The Pope and the people would have believed it just as much.

Landel then wrestled Freddy on TV with Lawler at ringside and Freddy got the claw on when Wildside jumped in and Lawler & Marlin & Jason made the save. Jason tripped getting into the ring and fell on his face which is especially embarrassing for a monster out of the movies.

Gossett broke Marlin's glasses on television. Marlin had challenged Gossett to a match and took off his glasses and got into the ring when Gossett smashed the glasses and left.

8/14 in Memphis has Stan Frazier & Cousin Junior vs. Doug Gilbert & Gary Allbright, Dustin Rhodes & Bill Dundee vs. Black Bart & Dirty White Boy in a bunkhouse match, the mask vs. loser getting 10 lashes with Texas Dirt vs. Master of Pain, Marlin vs. Gossett and if Marlin wins, Gossett has to wear a diaper, but if Gossett wins, he gets to become the promoter of the CWA and matchmaker for one

week, Lawler vs. Landel for the USWA title and the main event is a War Games with Blackbirds & Harris & Wildéide (Starr & Champion) vs. Rock & Roll Express & Jarrett & Freddy & Jason.

JAPAN

Just a few notes this time out: New Japan's Jushin Liger (Keiichi Yamada) is starting to get over big-time with the kids, which was the goal in the first place to create a new Satoru Sayama. His work is incredible as well, as he's having four-star plus matches even with the likes of Shinji Sasazaki, who I never thought much of when he was in Calgary or Memphis but now is having awesome matches. The bouts to see appear to be Liger vs. Naoki Sano and the two met on 8/10 in Tokyo in a bout billed as "Junior War No. 2." Liger will defend his jr. title on the August/September series against both Owen Hart and Pat Tanaka. Unfortunately for you video collectors, due to TV-Asahi commitments for other sports programming, the wrestling shows will only air twice in the next five weeks so almost none of the matches in the upcoming series will ever air on television.

A quick correction from last week. When Antonio Inoki won his seat in the Japanese Upper house, he actually captured the 50th and last seat, not the 49th of 50 seats so the "finish" was even more dramatic than we thought. Inoki barely beat out an incumbent liberal democrat who had once served as vice minister of science of technology, which I guess aren't nearly as strong qualifications as being the only wrestler to make Andre the Giant and Hulk Hogan submit and to have pinned Lou Thesz and Karl Gotch.

New Japan drew a 7.1 rating on 7/29 while All Japan drew a 5.9 on 7/30.

From photos at the last UWF card on 7/24 in Fukuoka, it appears Masaharu Funaki once again kicked in the face of his foe, this time Tetsuo Nakano. The guy was bleeding from the nose and lips real bad. Funaki messed up Bob Backlund's face back in May, which I guess adds to the interest of a Funaki vs. Nobuhiko Takada match on 8/13.

Atsushi Onita did a major juice job from the mouth in that press conference on 7/28 when he was attacked by the karate guy to set up the new FMW promotion which begins in October.

Riki Choshu & Takayuki Iizuka kept the IWGP tag titles on 8/5 beating Shinya Hashimoto & Akira Nogami. It was originally to be Tatsumi Fujinami teaming with Nogami, however Fujinami has now disappeared from the New Japan wrestling scene.

After the 8/13 show, the next UWF show is 9/7.

The British Bulldogs as a team are being billed for the first week of September with All Japan.

New Japan drew 8,200 in Nagoya on 8/5.

Lioness Asuka's retirement card will be either 8/24 or 8/31 and Chigusa Nagayo will make an appearance at that show, probably to do a concert.

New Japan drew a 7.6 rating on 8/5 while All Japan did a 6.2 the next day.

All Japan women have created a new baby face tag team called "The Sweet Hearts" of Mima Shimoda & Manami Toyoda who will be getting a push from this point forward.

On the All Japan front, while the matches that involve The Foot Loose, or either member of the duo in there with Jumbo Tsuruta and Yoshiaki Yatsu are generally great, almost every tag match ends with the same finish of Tsuruta pinning one of the Foot Loose with the back suplex. Before the finish, the Foot Loose always get tons of near falls on Tsuruta, but in the recent matches the crowd pop hasn't been as great as it has been earlier this year. The reason is because everyone "knows" that neither Foot Loose will ever pin Tsuruta. If it were to just happen once, because of the action they provide, it would keep the feud going for another year.

THIS AND THAT

Rip Rogers & Abbuda Dein won the Caribbean tag team titles from Hurricane Caétillo Jr. & Miguelito Perez on 8/5 in San Juan. Perez & Castillo remain WWC World tag team champions having earlier beaten Dein & Rogers. Also, on 8/4 in Caguas, Super Medico (Jose Estrada) pinned Chicky Starr to regain the WWC jr. heavyweight title.

They had a Video Dealers convention earlier this past week in Las Vegas and only about a dozen or so readers called me with reports. Both Coliseum Video and Turner had booths, ironically on the same floor and almost next to one another. Even more ironic was that both Hulk Hogan and Ric Flair were there at the same time for autograph sessions. Both had long lines although the lines for Hogan were longer. According to those who were there, both sides spent too much time running down the other side (the guys from the video companies, not Flair and Hogan).

I'll be appearing on Eddie Schwartz' late-night program on WGN in Chicago this coming Friday night, 8/18 (720 AM) taking phone calls on pro wrestling, plus have upcoming shows booked on 8/24 on WALE with Cody Boyns in Providence, R.I. (990 AM) at 7 p.m. Eastern time and with Rich Mancuso and Jodi McDonald on WFAN in their 3 a.m. time slot on Saturday night/ Sunday morning on 8/26 to talk about SummerSlam and whatever else. For those in this area, the "San Jose Metro" newspaper will have an article about me sometime within the next week or so by Jon Vankin.

Edward Faulk promoted independent shows over the weekend drawing less than 100 in Shreveport, about 600 in Vivian, LA and around 250 in another Louisiana town. He's got television in about five markets, using mainly local talent including former lead World Class fan Freddie Fargo, who writes for Pro Wrestling Digest, as his heel manager and color commentator on the TV shows.

Dynamite Kid has a few dates booked in the Maritimes for Emile Dupree, working against Ron Starr.

The first-ever meeting of the Rock & Roll Express vs. Fantastics took place on 8/12 in Wildwood, NJ ending in a double disqualification. The Fantastics, who were Bobby & Jackie Fulton in this match, worked as the heels as they'll probably do a rematch somewhere in New Jersey during September. The main event on the card saw Bam Bam Bigelow beat Nikolai Volkoff.

There is talk of Multimedia now doing a women's promotion.

El Satanico beat Lizmark on 7/21 in Mexico City to win the Middleweight title down there and Satanico did turn babyface the next week. American wrestlers who are now working in Mexico from time-to-time are men Ken Timbs, Mike Stone, Rick Patterson and Steve Nelson along with women Candi Divine, Rhonda Singh (from Calgary; actually Canadian) and Diane Hoffman, who some of you may recall from about a decade ago in the states as heel Diane Von Hoffman.

Quick correction from last week, The Phantom who works for the Virginia Wrestling Alliance is Mark Fleming, not Johnny Ringo. I understand he's been doing really well for them as a headliner.

The card last weekend in East Baltimore, MD where he headlined against Nikita Koloff drew closer to 300 than the 150 we reported.

VWA has a show 8/26 in Blackstone, VA with Phantom vs. Ivan KoLoff on top and VWA also has a phone-in television show in Richmond, VA and over the next few weeks will have the likes of Lou Thesz, Ivan Koloff and Bobby Fulton as guests. Ron Wyatt and Bobby Fulton are promoting a show on 9/6 in Fisherville, VA with Fantastic s vs. Mod Squad, Ivan Koloff vs. Russian Assassin (Dan Grundy), Bambi vs. Peggy Lee Leather and Brad Anderson vs. Batman (Jackie Fulton).

8/5 in Maywood, CA drew 304 as Susan Sexton beat The Red Flame in the main event plus Mercenaries beat Steve Dalton & Alex Knight in the semi-final.

Emile Dupree's show on 7/27 in Halifax, Nova Scotia drew 369 as The Beast beat The Cuban Assassin, Ron Starr beat Leo Burke, Steven Pettipas beat Jerry Morrow, Steven Casey beat The Destroyer and Eddie Watts & Pat Brady beat Stompin' Paul Peller & Wayne Gillis.

Cowboy Woody Lee won a Battle Royal on 7/28 in Winamac, IN before 450 fans for Midstates Wrestling promoted by Shirley Dillon.

For area readers, we will be holding a party for SummerSlam here. For more info, contact us in Campbell.

NWA

Some names I've heard booked for future cards include

Dick Slater, Brad Armstrong and Tom Zenk, while I've heard Nikita Koloff (as a face) and Sir Oliver Humperdink mentioned as possible arrivals as well.

TV ratings for the past week saw the Power Hour on 8/4 draw a 1.5 rating at 10:30 p.m. after the Braves, World Championship Wrestling drew a 1.9 and the NWA Main Event drew a 2.0, which are all below par. Actually on Sunday the wrestling drew lower numbers than most of the rest of the programming which is unusual since traditionally the wrestling on TBS has drawn the best numbers for TBS.

After baseball season ends, the Power Hour show will be in a 10 p.m. Eastern and 7 p.m. pacific time zone weekly.

Keith Mitchell was hired as head of production. Mitchell was the production head for World Class during its glory days and was a pioneer in high production values of pro wrestling shows before the WWF.

TBS ran three hours of wrestling on Saturday, which is awfully long. The Power Hour show was one of the better ones with matches having Mike Rotunda beat Shane Douglas, Eddie Gilbert beat Great Muta in a no DQ match by pinning Gary Hart (boy do I hate that finish but I will say that Muta probably got over better by blowing the mist in Tommy Rich, Missy Hyatt and Eddie Gilbert's eyes than he would have had he just beat Gilbert) and Road Warrior Hawk pinned Samu by using Paul E. Dangerously's phone which began the break-up of the SST and Dangerously, or at least appeared to do so. Norman really put Brian Pillman over good at the syndicated taping in Baton Rouge going up for a body slam and a suplex near the finish.

The Funk's Grill with the Steiner brothers was probably the best Funk's Grill to date. It wasn't your typical heel vs. face animosity, in fact they all got along, but Rick Steiner's act is great, especially when he asked Funk if he went to high school with George Burns.

8/11 in Pittsburgh drew a $38,000 house as Greg Evans & Richard Sartain, without their Ding Dong outfits, beat Al Greene & Lee Scott; Ron Simmons pinned Curtis Thompson (back from Puerto Rico where he worked as The White Angel), Brian Pillman pinned Norman the Lunatic (Mike Shaw), Sid Vicious pinned Ranger Ross, Rick & Scott Steiner beat New Zealand Militia (Rip Morgan & Jack Victory), Great Muta drew with Sting so the TV title remains held up (very disappointing match), Lex Luger pinned Tommy Rich using the trunks (Luger carried it to watchable), Road Warriors beat Samoan Swat Team in a cage match when Hawk pinned Samu in about 15 minutes (three stars) and Ric Flair pinned Terry Funk in a star bloodbath brawl.

Steiners beat Michael Hayes & Jimmy Garvin in a non-title match on television and will be getting title matches upcoming.

The Dynamic Dudes were jobbed out on television in both singles and tags at the recent taping since they are headed to Japan. The official word is that Johnny Ace suffered a broken cheekbone (ironically, he really suffered a similar injury about a month back) when he was hit by the canteen in a TV match where the New Zealand Militia beat the Dudes.

8/4 in Kansas City drew a $28,000 house as Pillman pinned Bill Irwin, Militia beat Ding Dongs, Norman pinned Steven Casey, Dynamic Dudes beat Simmons & Al Greene in 24 seconds, Tommy Rich threw out Norman to win the two-ring Battle Royal, Muta beat Gilbert via count out in the Dragon Shi match, Hayes & Garvin beat Midnight Express when Terry Gordy interfered, Road Warriors beat SST in a match where falls counted anywhere in the building, Luger pinned Steiner and in the main event, Sting & Steve Williams beat Terry Funk & Terry Gordy when Williams cradled Funk. This finish defies logic if only because the main event on the next show has Flair vs. Funk for the NWA title. Funk's major problem as a heel is that nobody believes he has a chance to beat Flair and they only solidified that belief for the fans who presumably would be paying next month to see their match locally by having Funk get pinned by Williams. The finish might get a great pop for the moment, which it did, but what good is it if it hurts the gate appeal of the next card?

WWF

WWF will have tapings on 9/21 in Louisville and 9/22 in Cincinnati. The Cincinnati taping will be both Wrestling Challenge, and for the first Saturday Night Main Event of the fall season.

The WWF's added PPV show will be 12/27 which will be the movie "No Holds Barred" plus the first PPV match between Hulk Hogan vs. Zeus and one or two other matches. I'm not sure of this, but believe that the actual wrestling matches will be taped, rather than live, just to make sure Zeus doesn't totally blow it under pressure. This will give the WWF PPV shows in late November, late December and mid—January.

At the taping, a fan yelled at J.J. Dillon, "Who is the next guy you are going to get from the NWA?" and Dillon responded, "Who is left to get?"

No Holds Barred did $42,020 in 78 theaters over the weekend of 8/4 through 8/6 giving it $16,093,651 total.

Andre vs. Warrior drew 4,400 and $56,000 on 8/7 in Sacramento which is the lowest capital city crowd in more than a year but on 8/10 in Long Beach drew a sellout of 10,000 and $121,000 and on 8/12 in Anchorage (first WWF show there in years) drew something like $115,000.

The crowd in Sacramento stormed the box office because of the 15 second main event and heard Long Beach was pretty unruly about feeling ripped off by the short main event as well. They should be grateful Honky Tonk Man was on Arsenio Hall on 8/9.

WWF had a three-hour USA special on 8/13.

Bobby Heenan had a porno star guest this past week who took her shirt off and put her chest in Heenan's face and he "passed out"

8/13 in Miami drew $55,000 as Red Rooster drew Greg Valentine (best match on card), Jim Duggan pinned Haku, Brutus Beefcake beat Randy Savage via DQ, Paul Roma pinned Bore—us Zhukov, Ted Dibiase pinned Hillbilly Jim and Demolition beat Brain Busters via DQ.

8/7 in San Bernardino drew a sellout 3,000 as Barry Horowitz pinned Louis Spicoli, Bad News Brown pinned Hercules, Mr. Perfect drew Bret Hart, Demolition beat Brain Busters via DQ, Rooster pinned Brooklyn Brawler and Beefcake pinned Rude in a non-title match.

7/22 in Detroit saw Mark Young pin Bill Woods, The Genius (Lanny Poffo) beat Jim Powers, Jimmy Snuka beat Honky Tonk Man, Rooster beat Brawler, Rick Martel pinned Tito Santana, Rockers beat Rougeaus and Jim Duggan & Hillbilly Jim beat Andre the Giant & Haku.

8/5 in Salt Lake City drew $115,000 as Zhukov pinned Young , Genius pinned Koko B. Ware, DiBiase pinned Hillbilly Jim, Snuka beat Honky Tonk Man, Duggan pinned Haku, Martel pinned Santana and Savage beat Hogan via count out.

THE READERS PAGE

STEAMBOAT

After viewing the Baltimore Bash, I honestly thought that the NWA was turning things around, but now I'm not so sure. The departure of Ricky Steamboat only illustrates how the NWA can't hold onto their talent. They cannot compete with the WWF if they continually lose their talent to them, or just lose talent to nowhere. They keep making the same mistakes over and over again. For example, they don't hype the matches on their PPV shows well. They haven't improved their syndicated shows and the worst of their mistakes, they can't hold onto their main talent. Who is next to leave?

Richard Della Chiara
La Habra, California

Spoiled rotten. Ricky Steamboat got a lot of boos from a lot of folks since returning to the NWA in January. And people can be blamed for one thing. He spoiled us rotten. Is the NWA serious in trying to push Lex Luger vs. Tommy Rich? Who will watch that dud of a match after witnessing the match Luger and Steamboat put on in Baltimore? The NWA had a lot of potential with Steamboat. His work in the ring would have been great with guys like Muta, Sting, Pillman, etc. I'd like to thank the man for spoiling us rotten. Steamboat gave us an outstanding series of matches with both Flair and Luger.

Tony Amara
Boston, Massauchsetts

SATURDAY NIGHT MAIN EVENT

I thoroughly enjoyed the recent Saturday Night Main Event. I think you were a bit critical of the Hulk Hogan vs. Honky Tonk Man match. No, it wasn't wrestling at its finest, but Honky Tonk sold for Hogan well and made Hogan look like an unbeatable champion going into SummerSlam.

The Beefcake & Hogan vs. Savage & Zeus angle after the excellent Savage vs. Beefcake match was done to perfection. As much as it sickens me to think that with no experience, Zeus will be in the main event of a major show, I do think Vince is using him perfectly. It's been so long since there has been a real killer heel in any federation.

Is it just me, or is the NWA running way too many PPV shows? I know that each show has been better than the last, but the more shows they put on, the less important each one will become. They should follow the WWF's lead and come up with three or four shows a year, spread apart by about four months. Each show needs a specific name that stays the same each year. In the WWF, every fan knows when it is WrestleMania time, SummerSlam time, Survivors Series time and to a lesser extent, Royal Rumble time. The only event the NWA has like this is Starrcade. If the NWA continues to cram together its PPV shows without giving them any sort of importance, then all the quality wrestling that is being put on will be going to waste.

Sam Nord
Walnut Creek, California

Dave Meltzer: My own opinion as a fan is that the NWA isn't running too many PPV shows, but from a business standpoint I believe both the NWA and WWF are running too many. They've already ruined the "specialness" of the shows and the declining buy rates across the board for both groups is evidence of that. Since both groups will run five PPV's this year, I find it kind of funny that people are saying the NWA should copy the WWF and run less PPV shows, when both run the same amount. WWF has established WrestleMania as the biggie, and the NWA's equivalent is Starrcade, although not really established anywhere near as much because of the great job WWF has done for years in hyping WrestleMania with the celebrities. SummerSlam and the Bash PPV would be equivalent, so the comparisons would be Survivors and Royal Rumble vs. Chi-Town Rumble and Music City Showdown and my feeling is on a comparative basis, given the WWF's wider exposure, wider popularity and better job of hyping, that considering the comparative audience for both groups, that the NWA has done just as well or better with its shows when it comes to gaining interest. If the NWA tried a gimmick PPV headliner, Like an annual Survivors or a Royal Rumble, they, if everything went perfect, would do okay the first time and die the second time. With far greater popularity, WWF did well with the first Survivors (at a time when PPV wasn't oversaturated) and just fair the second time, while it did very well with Rumble as a TV special, but poorly with it as a PPV. I think in the long run, both sides would be better off concentrating on two or three PPV shows per year because they can maintain the "specialness" of the event, but with these almost monthly shows, the only event that has retained "specialness" is WrestleMania, although SummerSlam will sell this year because of the Zeus gimmick, but the rest aren't going to do any sort of sizable numbers and while they may be profitable at first and over the short haul, in the long run it'll drag everything down. But as a fan, I could watch NWA PPV's monthly if they maintain the show quality of the past four.

FUTURE PLANS

Generally, when a wrestler is brought into a territory, how far into the future is his push planned? For example, when Vince recruited Randy Savage, does he say, "Here's a great prospect. I'll bring him in, add his wife as manager, give him the Intercontinental belt, turn him, give him the WWF title, feud him with Hogan, etc. or do things get planned as they go along? Are carrots put in front of the wrestlers noses like belts and pushes? We hear so much about Vince calling all the shots and running the promotion with an iron fist but I can't understand why certain wrestlers would join Titan if they knew what they were getting into like Terry Taylor, Owen Hart and Ted DiBiase. Is the money difference that significant? Also, what is a wrestlers' contract like? Could it include gaining a title, thus making it legally binding?

David McCormack
Saranac Lake, New York

Dave Meltzer: Of course, this varies with both the wrestler and the promotion. For example, when Ricky Steamboat came to the NWA, much of his scenario with Flair was probably tentatively planning through winning and losing the title back, although original plans were for him to lose the title to Windham and those changed with the booking change. This explains the big push even though he really didn't turn out to be as popular or as much of a drawing card as the NWA had hoped for when he was brought in. Most, however, are brought in with tentative thoughts on their role, although the wrestlers generally aren't told as much as they should be. I think Titan brings guys in and has already determined how far they are going to push them, but things change. For example, when Butch Reed came in, Vince thought the gimmick of a black wrestler with blonde hair would make him the hottest heel in the business, but early along the way he realized this wouldn't work and changed plans. He thought that Honky Tonk Man

as a gimmick using music from the 50s and 60s would reach the audience that tunes into oldies on the radio and be a big hit as a baby face, but again he had to reverse his plans. With DiBiase, he gave him a push and went probably about as far with the gimmick as he could have gone, although when he tried the same with Curt Hennig, it didn't get over as well and he had to hold back the push. Carrots are almost always placed in front of wrestlers, particularly the big stars. That's the name of the game when it comes to bookers keeping talent under control. The carrot can be a belt, a push, an angle or simply more money but almost everyone but the top guys has some sort of carrot dangling in front of him in some way. As for contracts, the two major groups have two basic standard contracts. In the NWA, the contract specifies a certain amount of income per year, which depending upon the person, ranges from $75,000 up through more than $500,000. I believe Flair's contract may have provisions regarding the title as well, but none of the others do as far as I know. In the WWF, wrestlers are only guaranteed $50 for each time they work a television taping and the rest is at the discretion of McMahon, who basically pays them what he considers as fair (ie, hopefully enough to keep them pacified and happy and more than they could make elsewhere, but not enough to where they get so rich they can leave on the spot like John Studd did). DiBiase joined Titan for two reasons primarily, first, he didn't want to work for Dusty Rhodes and in hindsight, it was the wisest move of his career considering how Rhodes buried all the UWF talent to prove the NWA was superior after the purchase; and second, because he liked the gimmick and felt he could make money with it when McMahon came up with it for him. So he knew his gimmick ahead of time, including the black valet who would be named after Dusty Rhodes. Taylor had no choice at the time he made the move and had no leverage so he could either take it or leave it, and he couldn't afford to live on what he could make in World Class so the move was one of economic necessity, since the NWA wasn't an option since Rhodes was still booker when Taylor made his move and Rhodes had already buried him and tried to starve him into quitting, which he did. Hart came because of the opportunity, which never materialized, of being a "big star" in the "big time," but for whatever reason, those at Titan had other ideas. A lot of people talk about wrestlers going to Titan for guaranteed big money, but I've seen the standard contract, including one that one of the top-of-the-line stars has, and there is no guarantee of money, although that wrestler is making big money because he's been on top for a long time. But wrestlers know that as a general rule, and there are exceptions, but generally, a wrestler will make more money with Titan than they can make anywhere else, which is why most of them migrate there if they get the chance. Others, like Tully Blanchard or Arn Anderson, came in because of problems with the booker at the time, not because of a promise of a title belt or of more money, since neither was guaranteed (although the carrot was surely dangled in both cases) when the move was made, and since the NWA reneged upon the balloon payments in the contracts, they were technically free agents. Since most of the top talent is under contract to their respective groups and the NWA under Turner has yet to violate a contract as far as I know, moves like this happen less and less, although moves from one side to another aren't impossible even with contracts because a guy can get himself fired, thus be available to obtain work with the opposition, or even if the star is big enough, the two sides can get into a legal battle, and as other sports have shown, if the office tries hard enough, they usually can find a way to get them out of the contract. But neither side has yet opened up that can of worms by trying to "raid" a wrestler under contract.

BALTIMORE BASH
Regardless of whether or not the NWA survives, flourishes or declines as a promotion, 1989 will go down as a banner year for the product the NWA has put on, that of wrestling. The Ric Flair vs. Ricky Steamboat matches along with the subsequent emergence of Terry Funk and the unexpected push for an uncommonly gifted athlete in Keiji Muto adds up to Christmas arriving early for a serious wrestling fan. It may all fall by the years' end, but if the Baltimore Bash is any indication of what lays in store for the NWA, then things are looking great. Lex Luger is great as a heel and his reactions to the crowd are excellent. He has improved immensely since the oaf he was in Florida. Steamboat was the best wrestler on the card and Steve Williams was even effective on his interview. His appearance during Stan Lane's interview when he swam across the screen was the funniest moment of the year for me. With Michael Hayes back as a heel and Terry Funk being the true master of the interview, I can hardly wait for the return of the most amazing interview of them all, Zodiac Barry Orton. I only hope he joins the NWA in order for 1989 to be a banner year for interviews as well, even considering the decline of Jim Cornette. Funk & Muta as a team promises to be a fascinating juxtaposition of styles that can't fail to be entertaining.

Peter Schroder
North Altona, Victoria, Australia

I just finished watching the NWA PPV from Baltimore and it was the best card I've seen in more than 15 years of being a wrestling fan. Yes, there were a few minor problems, not announcing the entrants to the Battle Royal and not adequately explaining the Sting vs. Muta ending, but overall, it was terrific.

Also, I very much enjoyed the patriotic theme and in particular, the singing of God Bless the USA at the end. I do agree that during the summer months, the NWA should use only air-conditioned arenas.

Leonard Sims
Beckley, West Virginia

What can I say about the 7/23 NWA PPV show except it was great. It was the most exciting show I've seen since returning to the wrestling business after a 10 year absence and the best card I've seen anywhere since 1975. I got cold chills watching Ric Flair make his ring entrance and couldn't believe how good the aftermath of the main event was. Ted Turner should put this show on TBS in its entirety in prime time. It might cost him video cassette sales, but would be worth it in the long run by attracting new fans and bringing back some of those who have deserted the NWA in the recent past. The response on my radio show was 100 percent thumbs up. The NWA right now has a nucleus of talent that if promoted and marketed right will lead them back to many more Glory Days.

John Arezzi
Pro Wrestling Spotlight
West Babylon, New York

OTHER STUFF
The NWA should take a lesson from the late actress Jayne Mansfield, who in the 50s would walk down Hollywood Boulevard wearing a leopard-skin bikini and a snarling ocelot in tow, handing out autographed
photos of herself to everyone and anyone.

The NWA clearly has the superior product, but they can't compete with the WWF by relying mainly on word-of-mouth. They've made improvements in the hype department but they need to draw some serious attention to themselves. Maybe a major talent acquisition from the WWF isn't a bad idea. This wrestler wouldn't have to be one of the greatest workers as long as he has a good deal of recognition value. He must have enough recognition value to help get the NWA over with the general public. If they sent Jim Ross or Gordon Solie to the wrestlers' home to do a serious interview telling how McMahon holds his wrestlers back in the ring, how some wrestlers are humiliated to please the kiddies, just a hard, gritty interview without exposing the business and don't be afraid to show it a few times. When the competition is one network TV and their stars regularly appear on national talk shows, maybe it's time to put on that leopard-skin bikini.

Tony Duncan
Royston, Georgia

I attended the NWA PPV show in Baltimore on 7/23 and give the card a thumbs-up of course. The real highlight for me occured the morning of the show at the Missy Hyatt luncheon. The event was organized by Joel Goodhart of the

Squared Circle Fan Club. Missy was fantastic, although she has turned me off to all other women.

Although I understand those in the business being upset at your publishing a smart newsletter for marks, I feel strongly that the hardcore fans need somewhere to turn. I also realize that while they might publicly denounce the Observer, all the wrestlers read it. Deep down, everyone in the business is a Meltzerite.

Daniel Weisberg
Washington, D.C.

I've got some new ideas for Jack Victory. 1) Have him wheeled to the ring in a big box (Jack in the Box); 2) Walk out with a tool kit and overalls (Jack of all Trades) ; 3) Break a pumpkin over his head on Halloween and light a candle (Jacko Lantern Victory) .

David Press
Glenolden, Pennsylvania

One of the NWA's biggest problems with its syndicated shows has to be the match selection. Instead of showing its main stars (Flair, Luger, Funk, Muta, Road Warriors), they show arena matches with prelim wrestlers. Last week, while the WWF was showcasing the Ultimate Warrior, Brain Busters, Rick Rude and others in squash matches, the NWA Pro show had the Ding Dongs against the New Zealand Militia and Dick Murdoch & Eddie Gilbert against Bill Irwin and Norman the Lunatic. Except maybe for Gilbert, none of these guys sell tickets and have no reason for being pushed on TV. The average fan doesn't have a long attention span and is not likely to want to sit through ten minutes of the Ding Dongs. Not once during that whole show, except for interviews, which were mainly repeats from the previous week, did you see any of the main event wrestlers.

They also have a serious announcing problem. Jim Ross is doing way too many matches and he desperately needs a broadcast partner. Lance Russell and Bob Caudle are both old war horses and need their schedules reduced and shouldn't work together as it provides no balance. Paul E. Dangerously is the worst. On a weekly basis, he wears too thin. My suggestion is to replace him with Terry Funk when Funk becomes less active. Funk did a fine job with Ross during the Flair vs. Steamboat match at the New Orleans card. They should also consider using Joe Pedicino and Michael Hayes as a broadcast team.

Richard Wallner
Washington, D.C.

I've been going to WWF house shows since the 60s and I feel the major attraction in the Hogan era as well as the Sammartino era is seeing the Lead heel finally get pinned. It never diminished him in my eyes because I knew the cycle was over and he would be making his challenges

again, depending upon if he got a good crowd reaction. My favorite villain in the 60s was Bulldog Brower and it was fun to see him pinned after all the yelling and screaming on television. It's the same today with Randy Savage. Even though the NWA has a much superior product, the creative finishes leave me feeling cheated.

I've always been an admirer of someone with bad taste being able to pull it off, but I don't like seeing someone I've enjoyed over the years hit rock bottom. Roddy Piper used to be such an engaging personality and how he's just an absolute bore. I don't know who is at fault, but I hope the situation gets straightened out before all his appeal is gone. It's a shame to see him make a complete fool of himself and I for one can no longer watch him do a poor imitation of what he or Vince McMahon thinks his image once was. Bobby Heenan is a quick ad-libber and a terrific character, but he needs wrestlers to bounce off, not the collection of Morton Downey rejects thrown on his half-hour sketch. The concept is good, but the execution isn't. Maybe someone should tell Vince there are such things as comedy writers who could structure the thing to make it a good show, and possibly a cult favorite.

You've mentioned that the NWA would look a lot more credible if they were to sign up a WWF main eventer. My feeling is that the public would look upon anyone that the NWA would get as someone who has run out of steam. I can hear people saying about Savage that he must have lost it if he was in the NWA. The NWA is not a promotion to end up with, it's one to progress from. Again, I feel their product is much better than the WWF in terms of actual wrestling presentation, but it's all in the marketing.

Name withheld by request

We are the Oakland Coliseum 2. We are the fans who unfurled a banner reading "NWA # 1" at the 8/8 WWF TV tapings. We are life-long wrestling fans who had that banner confiscated by Tony Garea apparently on orders from Vince McMahon. Who are the fans who, totally unintentionally, brought the WWF TV taping money-making machine to a temporary halt because we dared to express an opinion that did not fit the WWF's official line for fans. We are the stone-sober fans with nearly 50 years of attending wrestling cards between us who were ejected from an arena for the first time for exercising a constitutionally protected right while drunken marks who were willing to cheer Ultimate Warrior as an exhibition of a wrestling talent remained.

Garea also stole another banner of ours which simply read, "Ric Flair" at the same time as our other sign was taken away. This banner was never displayed during the card and we kept it folded up under our seats. Upon being confronted by the police, whom we later called to attempt to get this sign back, Garea lied and said that he had put the sign back at our seats. We later learned from eyewitnesses that this sign had been destroyed.

Of course we can see why Garea had felt so threatened by the " Ric Flair" sign. As a former over-the-hill jobber for a promotion where wrestling talent is in short supply, he undoubtedly felt threatened by the very sight of the name Ric Flair.

As we were ejected from the Coliseum that night, we began to ask ourselves how a wrestling League whose heat depends so heavily upon Americanism, whose champion proclaims himself to be a "real American," whose major faces carry the Stars and Stripes to the ring, who call themselves "American Dream," could be ejecting fans whose actions were totally non-violent, didn't interfere with any fans enjoyment of the product and were clearly protected by our Constitution's guarantee of free speech.

Our discussion led us to a basic insight into the difference between the WWF and the NWA. It has also definitely answered for us the question of whether the NWA should copy the WWF's formula for financial success. After our treatment, we believe it should not.

What happened to us at the WWF card would not have occurred at an NWA card. At the house show for the NWA, the fan is the paying customer and, as such, is king. He has the opportunity for catharsis built up by hype. He has the opportunity to be silly, or even to be obscene. He can cheer for the wrestler of his choice or taunt him unmercifully .

McMahon and his crew have fundamentally altered this. The symbolic content of the WWF television shows is quasi-fascistic. While wrestlers have traditionally been skilled performers and athletes, the Titan champion is portrayed as a messianic superman. His Larger-than-life portraits dominate the arena and proclaim that "Hulk Rules." He issues "demandments" to his followers who are uniformed in red and yellow, who are referred to as an "army," and who engage in ritualistic salutes with souvenir giant hands.

This fascistic symbolism goes even deeper. The No. 2 face could easily serve as a model for a chemically engineered superman in fact called the Ultimate Warrior. Titan's invocation of Americanism is most disturbing because his brand of Americanism is clearly not democratic or patriotic, although it claims to be, but mere the mindless unreflective nationalism that is an essential component of a totalitarian philosophy .

But most importantly, McMahon's promotional philosophy has turned the relationship between crowd and performer on its head. In the WWF, house shows no longer exist as such. The shows that are put together without TV cameras are uninspired and boring and the wrestlers don't even work up a sweat.

When the cameras are present, the house show fans are subjected to hour after hour of meaningless squash matches for the sake of providing fodder for McMahon's TV shows. The audience that these shows thus become captive and

unwilling co-conspirators in the creation of the WWF product and expansion of the Titan empire.

Because TV cameras roll at these shows, the crowd must be regulated with military precision. The fans must cheer on cue and be quiet on cue. The younger fans are encouraged to run to the ring at the appropriate moment but they must move on cue, through the appropriate aisles that the cameras can cover and show the appropriate ardor for the correct wrestler. There is even a dress code for WWF fans, witness the fans a couple of months ago at a TV taping who were strong-armed into removing NWA T-shirts and wearing shirts with WWF wrestlers on them. Deviation from the party line can't be tolerated because it undermines the image that McMahon wishes to create, hence the destruction of our banner and our ejection from the building

We did nothing wrong. We were only carrying a sign that proclaimed our loyalty to the best wrestling promotion in the country and to perhaps the greatest wrestler ever as its world champion and standard
bearer.

The WWF represents a new mutant strain of sports exhibition. It is not the pro wrestling we have enjoyed since childhood. It represents many of the worst components of the darker side of American society: media manipulation of the public, intolerance and jingoisn. The NWA, to us, is the best expression of a combination sport and art form and is as American as baseball.

Our banner was neither a work choreographed by the WWF or engineered by the NWA. It was merely a spontaneous individual expression of our loyalty to the American style of pro wrestling. As such, it was an act that could neither be tolerated nor understood by the likes of Vince McMahon.

The Oakland 2

Dave Meltzer: As mentioned earlier in the issue, I was on the other side of the building and was a somewhat amazed spectator to all of this. All pro wrestling hype is based on symbolic propaganda and McMahon is only the worst from this standpoint because he's the best at doing it. I was neither surprised nor outraged that the banners were confiscated, but was shocked that Titan placed so much importance on it to hold up an already-long card and wouldn't let another match take place until the guys were kicked out and the banners destroyed. I wasn't surprised that they ripped the banners up, and by doing so, called more attention to the banners that the guys who showed them did in the first place, but was outraged that after destroying the banners they kicked the two guys out of the arena.

AUGUST 28, 1989

Two of the strangest, and almost inexcusable technical blunders occurred this past week with the National Wrestling Alliance. One, most of you already know—the Saturday World Championship Wrestling show on TBS that aired on 8/19 was the same program that had aired three weeks previous. The second, is that a major angle that was scheduled to air on the TBS show this coming Saturday was never taped.

What happened on Saturday, according to the best information I've been able to get, is that someone simply put the wrong tape in the box to air on Saturday and so the wrong show aired, complete with a match and interview with Ricky Steamboat talking about his upcoming no DQ matches with Lex Luger, and with promos for house shows that have already taken place. Actually, I consider this as a double mistake, and because of this, it's almost totally inexcusable. It took us all of five seconds to realize this was the wrong show being aired, so how come, after the first commercial break, they didn't realize something was wrong and make the necessary adjustments? To me, that's the real question, not this being just one of those unfortunate mistakes of someone putting the wrong tape in the box. I could go on and on right now about this being a critical time for the NWA and how, to the public, this type of mistake confirms what a lot of people that are fans are saying, but all this goes without saying right now.

To make matters worse, the previous Wednesday, the TBS tapings were held in Atlanta. They taped the show that was to air on 8/19, which never did, and to the best of my knowledge, never will, which was Ric Flair's first show as new booker and was to set up a couple of angles that were taped later and scheduled to air this Saturday. The major angle was a match between newcomer Dick Slater against Sting, which wound up with Great Muta and Terry Funk hitting the ring, followed by Ric Flair and Brian Pillman and during the ensuing melee, Flair got the branding iron that the heels had brought in and used it to "break Slater's arm." The show that was taped for 8/19 didn't air. The show that was taped for 8/26 will air, except that for some reason, somebody forgot to flip a certain "on" switch on the machines after a break and the last 20 minutes or so of the program, which included the match and angle, were never taped. They were holding an "emergency taping" on 8/22 in Greenville, SC and my guess is they will try and re-create some of this or at least do something similar and get it on the air in the 20 minutes of dead air time they have for this coming Saturday's TBS show.

There are a lot of things the NWA needs to do to become perceived as a major league alternative to the WWF. They do it on pay-per-views. They do it when it comes to providing action at the house shows. Sometimes they do it on television as some of the angles are very good, but sometimes there are weaknesses. But the same weaknesses they have in promoting house shows, and to a lesser extent ay-per-view shows, are still there. This has nothing to do with product quality, but the NWA needs to have its hype for both its house shows and PPV shows on the level of Titan, and really, exceed Titan, for a casual viewer to get interested in them as a legitimate alternative. Right now I see the NWA doing a great job in satisfying a small hardcore following of fans who are into pro wrestling for either the action or the brutality or maybe just into some of the NWA personalities. That core should consistently turn out in small numbers despite poor hyping of the house shows, simply because they want to see the product and they find it and find out when it is. To a more casual fan, and you need casual fans to draw six-figure houses, the hype, and by hype I mean localized interviews to get over the action in your hometown and talking about why the stipulations or matches are taking place and explain what will happen and what to expect; and graphics constantly running down the complete PPV shows, explain the background of these matches and get the ramifications of these matches over. You can watch the WWF every weekend and see all of these things done, the "secret formula" for promoting house shows on television is hardly a secret, but it isn't done. Titan doesn't do localized interviews per se, they do mass market interviews inserted into Sean Mooney's segment which appear to be localized, but they are so "over" at this point, plus run so many cards, that doing the old—style localized interviews isn't feasible. It would help the NWA to do it the way the WWF does it but it would help them more to do it the old way, because you can get over the show that you "missed" and explain to the audience why attending each live show in the city is important. It used to be that the house show was the most important thing and TV was used to set it up. Now, PPV is the most important, but in the Titan scheme of things, the house show is a close second but watching the NWA's television, the house show ranks a distant third (behind the PPV shows and all of the television shows).

The Universal Wrestling Federation of Japan had another in its long line of major successes this past Sunday night in Yokohama, Japan, drawing the fifth largest live gate in the history of pro wrestling of approximately $1,409,000. The show, which was the first men's pro matches at the new 17,000 seat Yokohama Arena (the first pro matches were actually held back in May when Chigusa Nagayo's retirement card set the women's gate record of more than

$500,000), which sold out well in advance, trails only the New Japan card at Tokyo's Egg Dome ($2,781,000) on April 24th of this year; The UWF's May 4th card in Osaka's Baseball Stadium ($1,714,000); the live WrestleMania V from Trump Plaza on April 2nd ($1,628 000) and the live WrestleMania III from the Pontiac Silverdome on March 29, 1987 ($1,599,000) in the all-time books. The main event on the card saw Akira Maeda defeat Yoshiaki Fujiwara via technical knockout from the five knockdown rule in 18:16. Other results from the card saw Nobuhiko Takada force Masaharu Funaki to submit in 12:00 with a camel clutch type of maneuver, Kazuo Yamazaki beat Yoji Anjyo, Tetsuo Nakano beat Minoru Suzuki and Shigeo Miyato beat Tamura. Even more impressive is that the UWF averaged an amazing $35-per-fan in gimmick sales, and even more revenue was derived for the wrestlers because of a sponsorship fee. Apparently, even though the UWF actual finishes are worked, unlike other groups, they have managed to maintain the image of legitimacy strong enough that they have gotten sponsors to put up extra "winner-take-all" purse money for the matches. In Maeda's match, the winner was to receive an additional $15,000; while both Takada and Yamazaki received an additional $7,500 for their victories on this card and the prelim wrestlers received an additional $3,750. Of the two established promotions in Japan, New Japan will try to run the same Yokohama Arena in late September. The fact that the UWF has been able to achieve such success without television is even more impressive, or that its "star" doesn't appear to be fizzling after more than a year of almost constant sellout business. It is expected that the UWF will get a network television contract in Japan by early 1990 as I'm told two different networks are bidding for them right now.

The WWF's big show of the sun-uner occurs on Monday night at the Meadowlands, "SummerSlam '88," featuring the main event tag team match with Hulk Hogan & Brutus Beefcake vs. Zeus (Tom Lister) & Randy Savage. In last week's issue of multi—channeL news, Titan exec Jim Troy predicted this would be the best-selling PPV event in history (somehow, that sounds familiar), predicting one million buys, which would be an eight percent buy rate. Troy was mentioning how the "advance buys" for PPV were ahead of anything they've ever done. While I don't know if that is true, I've heard that the advance is quite promising and that since PPV is very much a late buy business, Titan is optimistically hoping for a four to five percent buy rate legitimately which means the show could gross in excess of $10 million on PPV. The same issue confirmed what we had reported a few weeks back, that Titan has added a two-and-a-half hour PPV show on Wednesday, December 27th with show time at 2 p.m. Eastern time which would be the movie "No Holds Barred," a video piece concerning the making of the movie, plus two main events and the article

stated these would be live matches (our information was that WWF was contemplating making the two matches taped matches, since the main event could need serious editing). The article stated the main event would include a Hulk Hogan title defense, but didn't list Zeus (as I'm sure they don 't want that info out until after SummerSlam) as the opponent. The show will have a suggested retail price of $11.95.

Titan originally wanted a $14.95 retail price for the PPV show, but since movies traditionally go for $5, several major distributors balked and the price was dropped three dollars. Another interesting part of this showing is that they will run three repeat showings of the special (traditionally, PPV specials have one repeat) at 5, 8 and 11 p.m. Eastern time. The multi-channel news article also stated that Titan is bidding for the PPV rights to the Rolling Stones concert on Dec. 16 or Dec. 17 at Trump Plaza (Starrcade will be Dec. 15) although the last word I had is that Showtime seemed to have political advantage in getting the rights to the Stones.

In another PPV event announced this past week that really isn't wrestling related, except wrestling is in its title, Reiss Media Productions and IRS Media out of Los Angeles will do a mud wrestling PPV show hosted by Jessica Hahn on Nov. 10 with a $9.50 retail price, which will also include concert performers by several artists on the IRS label. This is the lowest price ever offered for a PPV event so they are hoping to use the low price as a lure.

Turner Home Entertainment's Steve Chamberlain announced that the July 23rd Baltimore Bash did its highest ratings of any PPV show it has done so far, so I guess they are learning from their competition about how to announce PPV figures. Chamberlain reported that the show did a two percent buy rate (ironically, TBS had reported the Flair vs. Steamboat PPV from Chicago did a 2.8). The reports we've got from cable systems indicated a buy rate of 1.4, and one NWA official gave me 1.5 as the legitimate figure and that the PPV grossed $2.3 million legitimately.

Because better movies are coming to cable and because of the NBA playoffs, wrestling events were way down in the list of the highest rated individual programs on cable for the second quarter of 1989. The highest rated wrestling show of the quarter was the Clash of the Champions from New Orleans (Ric Flair vs. Ricky Steamboat main event) which was the 17th highest rated show (traditionally, the Clashes have been in the top three to five for the quarter on cable). The NWA show trailed 11 NBA playoff games on TBS and five movies, two on USA, two on TBS and one on TNT. Editions of Prime Time Wrestling on June 12th, March 27th, June 19th, April 10th and an All American Wrestling show on April 9th all cracked the top 50 shows of the quarter on basic cable while the NWA's Clash of Champions on June 14th from Fort Bragg, NC finished in the No. 21 spot. Aside from the NBA playoffs, which dominated the top of basic cable for the second quarter, other sporting events in the top 50 included the NFL draft on ESPN (which tied with the Fort Bragg Clash at No. 21), the NASCAR Budweiser 500 on ESPN (tied for 36), a George Foreman boxing match on USA (36) and another Auto race on ESPN which finished in a tie for 44th, the NASCAR Transouth 500, which ironically, went head-to-head with both the Flair-Steamboat Clash from New Orleans and WrestleMania.

The sentencing of pro wrestler Jake Roberts on the assault charges stemming from an incident last December, was postponed for one month. Roberts was originally to be sentenced from the Daytona Beach case on Monday. Titan Sports is already advertising Roberts to return in October against Ted DiBiase around the horn, so they seem to be confident that Roberts won't serve any time stemming from his conviction on the charges in a trial last month.

Another Titan wrestler, Andre the Giant (Andre Rene Rousimoff) was arrested on 8/21 after an incident in Cedar Rapids, IA. Andre was charged with assault and criminal mischief when he accosted KCRG cameraman Ben Hildebrand after his 30 second main event with the Ultimate Warrior. According to the AP report on the case, Andre shook up the camera man, giving him a few bruises and knocking his back out of whack, and did $300 worth of damage to his camera when Andre thought the reporter was filming his match with Warrior. Hildebrand was told not to film the match, but was given permission by Titan to film crowd reaction shots during the match and the reporter claims he had his back to the ring when Andre attacked him.

Former pro wrestler and pro wrestling's leading color man Jesse Ventura is the leading candidate and "almost certain" to be named as the new color commentator for the NFL's Tampa Bay Buccaneers for this upcoming NFL season. Ventura, who has been wanting to branch out into other sports, had a try-out with the team and made a very favorable impression. Ventura has also received high marks from New York area sports TV critics for the job he did doing a Yankees game on cable on July 30th.

The UAWF held its annual convention Aug 11-13 in Chicago and the reports I've gotten on it were very favorable. The AWA card that was scheduled wound up being pulled, but the conventioneers instead attended a Windy City card promoted by Sam DeCero which was scheduled originally to be simply opposition to the UAWF convention. My own impression is the AWA never planned on running the show in the first place since they never mentioned the show on their Chicago TV outlet and several of the wrestlers involved were never given the date as a booking in the first place. John McAdam won the trivia contest this year and they inducted Gordon Solie, Paul Boesch, Bruiser, Crusher, Buddy Rogers and Nick Bockwinkel into the ring of immortals. A few dozen Observer were among those

attending and none gave me any negative feedback.

Special thanks to Jon Vankin of Metro Magazine for the great article on me in this week's issue (cover story, no less, and it was a great piece and I usually don't like articles about myself) and to Brad Muster for the mention of the Observer in the Chicago Bears yearbook. Also, a quick correction, I would like to thank the San Jose North Rotary Club for inviting me to speak on pro wrestling a few weeks back. Last issue I called it San Jose Rotary Club (which there is one of, and the two are apparently rival clubs). And if any of you on the East Coast are insomniacs or heavy-partiers planning on staying up late, I'll be on with Rich Mancuso and Jodi McDonald this coming Saturday night (August 26th) on WFAN (660 AM) out of New York talking about anything you want to talk about involving pro wrestling. The show will be at 3 a.m. Eastern time and they tell me because of its 50,000 watt signal and since it's on so late at night with little interference, the show can be picked up pretty easily in 28 states and parts of Canada as well.

I headed down to Chicago this past weekend (which was the main reason I missed the UAWF convention the week before) for the Bears game and the NWA show and to do a stint on Eddie Schwartz' radio show on WGN. You know what the first question I was asked was? What did I think of the Jim McMahon trade? Anyway, the show was fun and it went until something like 4 a.m. Since none of you want to hear about me getting lost after the game in Soldier Field or all the airline delays I had which got me home eight hours after scheduled arrival (which delayed this issue one day), we stick to the wrestling show, which was a good show with an excellent main event.

The NWA show at the UIC Pavilion on 8/20 drew about 3,600 fans and $43,000, which isn't bad considering that the TV didn't run in its scheduled time slot for the previous two Sundays prior to the card. It seemed the crowd was mainly the hardcores, who go out of their way to find the TV show and know about the live cards and seemed really pleased with the show itself.

1. The Ding Dongs (Richard Sartain & Greg Evans) beat Big Al Greene & Trent Knight in 7:45 when Ding picked up Dong and dropped him legdrop style onto Knight for the pin. Even though the Ding Dongs were the faces, the crowd taunted and booed them unmercifully. I was embarrassed a bit for the guys because they worked hard and really aren't that bad work-wise but the crowd hates the gimmick, and they didn't bring any bells with them. For work, it was a decent opener but the crowd didn't like it. *

2. Ron Simmons pinned Brad Anderson (son of former pro wrestler Gene Anderson) in 5:25 with Arn Anderson's spinebuster move. Good pacing and Simmons was quite aggressive playing the heel. Simmons is really improved. * ½

3. Brian Pillman pinned Norman the Maniac (no longer Norman the Lunatic, he's been promoted) in 5:05. Match was slow early with Norman trying to get his character over by throwing tantrums. Pillman did some hot moves with his comeback, particularly a dropkick off the top rope, a bodyslam and a suplex. After a missed dropkick, Norman took over with a crunch into the corner, then a splash and leg drop but Pillman kicked out and after Norman collided with Teddy Long, Pillman pinned him with a flying body press. After the match Long was slapping Norman around and the fans were wanting Norman to hit him back but Teddy held up the big keys and Norman backed down. They seem to be hinting at a Norman turn, but I don't think it'll be that soon.**

4. Rick & Scott Steiner downed the New Zealand Militia(Jack Victory & Rip Morgan) in 11:15 when Scott pinned Morgan. Some comedy, but mainly good wrestling. Scott does some amazing moves, the best of which is that flying headscissors type move that I recall Raul Mata used to use out here (but Steiner is three times Mata's size and does it just as well). Someone mentioned to me that the character the Steiner Brothers are playing is that of the Smothers Brothers, who were big TV stars in the 60s. ***

5. Steve Williams pinned Bill Irwin in 3:45 when Irwin tried to slam him into the ring but Williams fell on top for the pin. Action was fine but too short to be a good match. * ¼

6. The Freebirds (Michael Hayes & Jimmy Garvin) kept the NWA tag team titles beating the Midnight Express in 12:24. Cornette popped both guys with the racquet early. The body of the match saw them get heat on Stan Lane but the action was only so-so. Finally Bobby Eaton got the hot tag and things picked up but Garvin distracted the ref after a flapjack so he didn't do the count, and soon after, Garvin tripped up Eaton coming off the ropes and Hayes hit the DDT for the pin. ** ¼

7. Sting beat Great Muta via DQ in 9:11 in a match for the held up TV title, which with the DQ, is still held up. They did some nice spots during the match but considering the ability of the two involved and that it was a short match, it was pretty slow and disappointing. One nice sequence saw Muta work the left arm for a while, then Sting tried to make a comeback with the press-slam but the arm gave out and Muta fell on him for a near fall. Finish saw Sting have the scorpion on when Gary Hart interfered for the DQ finish. Sting chased them both away with a few clotheslines afterwards. * ¼

8. Lex Luger kept the U.S. title pinning Tommy Rich using the trunks in 11:15. Similar to their TV match but not as good. Luger got mainly cheers and vocal cheers when he came out but does a good job in turning the crowd. Nobody cares about Rich who couldn't rally any support but Luger has turned into a good enough worker to carry a match like this to being better than average and keeping complete audience reaction levels very high. ** ½

9. Ric Flair pinned Terry Funk in 18:58 to keep the NWA title in another incredible brawl. This was a better match than Baltimore. It was a lot bloodier and overall more brutal. Funk bled from the chest from the chops from the beginning, which I guess shows just how stiffly the two have been working nightly since Flair's comeback. The heat was incredible most of the way and they used chairs and rammed heads into tables and the post and the blood flowed like wine, or something like that. Flair bled really bad and Funk bled from the head and chest. Finish saw Gary Hart put the branding iron in the corner after a ref bump. Funk went to run Flair into it but Flair reversed it and Funk went into it for the pin. After the match the two continued to brawl all over the place until Muta came in, and of course Sting followed, and they brawled all over the building. **** ½

10. Road Warriors beat Samoan Swat Team in a cage match. It's impossible to follow a match like the previous one, but this was an action-filled 9:43 and good throughout, ending when Hawk pinned Samu after a clothesline off the top rope. Before the match, Paul E. Dangerously made a crack about Jim McMahon which got a ton of heat. Actually, his delivery was even better than the line, which was something to the effect of after one day in California, McMahon found out just how lousy Chicago really was. *** ¼

Special thanks to Steve Sims for putting up with me all weekend, which couldn't have been easy considering the Friday night radio spot lasted almost until dawn and Sunday we pulled an all-nighter, and he had just come off a similar weekend of the like with the wrestling convention. I also got to meet the amazing Wade Keller of the Pro Wrestling Torch for the first time and his friend Dennis Esperum of the Seattle area and Chris Zavisa from the Detroit area and Lance Levine of "Chokehold" and a few folks from Wisconsin and several Chicago-area readers. By the way, Sims was named as "Fan of the Year" by the UAWF. And Ray Whebbe, who does a wrestling radio show in the Minneapolis area was at the show, along with about a half-dozen members of the Chicago Bears including Muster, tight end Jim Thornton, defensive back Maurice Jackson and quarterback Jim Harbaugh (who is friends with Brian Pillman). Ironically, the next time the NWA is in Chicago on 9/17 with Flair vs. Funk in an old-style Texas Death match will be the same day as the Bears face division rival Minnesota Vikings.

PUERTO RICO

Got the line-up for the 8/5 card at Hiram Bithorn Stadium in San Juan which drew 10,000 fans and $50,000 headlined by Sadistic Steve Strong (Steve DiSalvo) defending the Universal title against Abdullah the Butcher, a 20 man Battle Royal which was won by the returning Carlitos Colon and included Jimmy Valiant and Kareem Muhammad besides those listed on the undercard, Invader #1 vs. Ivan Koloff for the Puerto Rican title (which Koloff won), TNT defending the WWC TV title against Kendo Nagasaki, Miguelito Perez & Hurricane Castillo Jr. defending the WWC tag team titles against Rip Rogers & Abbuda Dein and Kerry Von Erich vs. Kimala.

NEW JAPAN

The four team tournament that they ran and the recent series ended with Team Japan winning with a 3-0 record while the Team USA, Team USSR and Japan B team all had 1-2 records. The Japan A team consisted of Kengo Kimura, Osamu Kido, Masa Saito, Riki Choshu and Hiroshi Hase; USA team was Manny Fernandez, Buzz Sawyer, Dick Murdoch, Big Van Vader (Leon White) and Mark Haff, team USSR was Chimur Zarasov, Vladimir Berkovich, Wakha Eveloev, Victor Zangiev and Salman Hashimikov, while the Japan B team was Shinya Hashimoto, Shiro Koshinaka, George Takano B Takayuki Iizuka and Super Strong Machine.

Tatsumi Fujinami was out of action the entire series with a back injury and may not be back next month either. Shinya Hashimoto basically took his spot as the No. 2 Japanese guy behind Riki Choshu during the series.

8/10 in Tokyo's Sumo Hall drew 9,980 fans as Vader won the IWGP World title pinning Choshu in 10:04 after a flying dropkick. Vader has title defenses booked in Mexico and Europe and will also have a title vs. title match in Austria against Otto Wanz during September before returning to Japan for title matches on 9/20 in Osaka and 9/21 in New Japan's first card at the Yokohama Arena. In the semifinal, Naoki Sano captured the IWGP jr. title in a match billed as "Junior War II" beating Jushin Liger (Keiichi Yamada) when Liger was on the top rope ready to give a falling elbow and Sano climbed on the top rope behind him and gave him a backward superplex with both guys standing on the top rope to set up the pinfall. Also on the card, Hashimikov pinned Hashimoto, Masa Saito & Kimura beat Sawyer & Fernandez, Machine & Takano beat Koshinaka & Kuniaki Kobayashi, Kido upset Zangiev and Berkovich pinned Tatsutoshi Goto.

8/8 in Morioka saw Team Japan beat Team USSR to win the team series outright. Hashimikov pinned Kimura and Berkovich pinned Kido to give USSR a 2-0 lead but Japan "came back" with Saito pinning Zarasov and Choshu pinning Zangiev leaving it up to a Hase vs. Eveloev to decide the

thing and Hase made Eveloev submit. The undercard saw Vader beat Hashimoto via count out, Kantaro Hoshino & Sano beat Riger & Akira Nogami and Fernandez & Sawyer beat Takano & Machine.

8/5 in Nagoya drew 8,220 as Choshu & Iizuka kept the tag titles beating Hashimoto & Nogami plus USA beat USSR when Zara sov pinned Fernandez, Murdoch beat Berkovich, Hashimikov beat Haff, Vader pinned Eveloev and it came down to Sawyer vs. Zangiev and Sawyer "avenged" his defeat at the Tokyo Dome by scoring the "upset.

OTHER JAPAN NOTES

Antonio Inoki's first day in Japanese parliament was 8/7. Four days later Inoki appeared at a press conference in the Tokyo Hilton announcing he had struck a deal with the Soviet Union to help promote Soviet boxers going professional.

Six boxers from the Soviet Union, including two gold medalists from the Seoul, Korea Olympics and two of them had a public sparring workout the next day at a Tokyo Gym. Inoki is working hard at promoting a major New Years' Eve satellite show using both boxing and wrestling on the same bill and Inoki will probably wrestle on the card as well. It is right now expected that Inoki will work that card and maybe one or two others over the next year while serving public office and will have a major retirement card next spring at the Tokyo Egg Dome.

Danny Spivey canceled his Japan tour for the series that just began so Baba brought in Todd Champion to be Terry Gordy's new tag team partner. Quite a drop-off . Spivey told Baba he was going to the WWF, but in reality he canceled the tour because of pressure from the NWA and there was talk of bringing in someone like Kevin Kelly or John Nord to be a new Skyscraper if Spivey wouldn't give up his Japan commitments.

Atsushi Onita's new independent group debuts in October.

Ryuma Go is also promoting independent shows in Tokyo's Korakuen Hall on Oct. 26 and Dec. 24. Fumihiro Niikura will appear on these shows. Niikura was Hiro Hase's original partner in Calgary as the Viet Cong Express and was a great worker until being felled by a heart attack in early 1987 which forced him to retire.

The next I-JWF card will be 9/7 in Nagano with Fujiwara vs. Funaki as the main event, Maeda vs. Jumbo Barretta, Takada vs. Anjyo as the second and third from the top. This is obviously a lay low card to set up a major show later in the year.

USWA

The 8/18 show at the Dallas Sportatorium drew 500 fans as Billy Travis pinned Sheik Scott Braddock, Jeff Jarrett & Matt Borne kept the USWA tag team titles beating Cactus Jack Manson & Al Perez when Jarrett pinned Manson, Chris

Adams beat Gary Young via DQ in a kendo stick match when Manson did a run-in and the Simpson family made the save, Eric Embry captured the main event beating P. Y. Chu Hi in nine seconds in a match where Chu Hi lost the Texas title and Embry put up his hair, Simpsons beat Manson & Young & Scandor Akbar in a lights out match via DQ when Schaun was thrown over the top rope (this was all three Simpson brothers including Stuart Simpson who came in from South Africa) and Kerry Von Erich went to a double count out against Taras Bulba in a Texas death match.

Mark Lowrance quit as the TV announcer to become a preacher. I'm not making this up. His replacement was Toni Adams, the wife of Chris, and it only took one week before they shot the angle where Akbar and his crew started beating up on Toni and Chris of course went crazy.

CWA

Give this group credit for a lot of creativity and humor over the past week. It all started on 8/14 at the Memphis Mid South Coliseum with a match between Ronnie Gossett and Eddie Marlin and if Gossett won, he'd become promoter for one week and if Marlin won, then he would put Gossett in a diaper. Well, Chris Champion interfered and Gossett won the match and got to be promoter through 8/21. Also on the Memphis card, Dirty White Boy & Black Bart beat Dustin Rhodes & Bill Dundee when Rhodes was hung over the ropes by a bull rope and ref Jerry Calhoun stopped the match, Texas Dirt (Dutch Mantell) went to a double disqualification with Master of Pain, in a War Games match, the babyface team of Jeff Jarrett & Ricky Morton & Robert Gibson & Jason & Freddy beat The Wildside (Champion & Mark Starr) & Blackbirds (King Parsons & Brickhouse Brown) & Harold Harris when Morton pinned Champion. The main event saw Lawler keep the USWA title pinning Buddy Landel in a match with lots of near falls.

With Gossett as promoter for the week, the show opened with Wildside defending the CWA tag team titles against Lawler & Spike Huber (a heel) and Huber refused to tag in so Lawler got doubled on the entire match and finally ref Jerry Calhoun DQ'd Wildside when they gave Lawler a stuff piledriver Gossett then yelled at Calhoun and started calling him a lousy ref and then fired him as a referee. Then Blackbirds & Harris had a TV six-man against Freddy (Tommy Gilbert) and heel jobbers Rough & Ready who refused to help Freddy, but Freddy went wild and Jason the Terrible came in to help him. The new ref for the rest of TV was "Honest" Boss Winters, who manages Rough & Ready.

Gossett then announced he was bringing in a tag team to rid Memphis of Freddy & bringing in Frankenstein & The Wolfman. I hope Lawler doesn't spend too much time criticizing the WWF and calling it a circus with a stunt like this. Then Bart & White Boy wrestled Cousin Junior and a masked Super Destroyer, who also wouldn't tag in and they spent the whole match doubling on Junior and ended up beating him. Then Doug Gilbert, who has been working as a jobber, challenged Lawler to a loser leaves town match and Lawler accepted and reminded everyone how he beat Eddie Gilbert a few years back in the loser leaves town match which ridded the territory of Jimmy Hart. Gossett signed the match but then appointed a special referee, called Mr. Mystery Referee, and then Gossett said he had to go to the back to find the special ref he brought in, and then Gossett came out under a mask as the special ref. After the interview, Gossett came back out without the mask and asked Dave Brown if the special ref came out or not. When Brown insinuated what happened, later in the show Gossett fired Brown as announcer. Finally Gilbert & Gary Allbright wrestled Texas Dirt and jobber Rodney Napper and Napper never tagged in and they spent the whole match double teaming Texas Dirt. The next match saw Master of Pain team up with a midget wrestler with face paint called The Little Road Warrior against two jobbers and MOP destroyed one of the jobbers and had the midget pin him.

The 8/21 card in Memphis is billed as "Ronnie's Wrestling Riots" with Cousin Junior vs. Allbright, a "midget match" sending the Little Road Warrior against Bill Dundee (there is humor in this one if you think about it) with MOP as referee, Dustin Rhodes vs. Black Bart in a bullrope match with Dirty White Boy as referee, hair vs. hair with Dirty White Boy vs. Jeff Jarrett—if Jarrett loses, he has to get his head shaved but if White Boy loses, he has to shave under his arms (which he already does), then the circus match with Frankenstein & Wolfman against Jason & Freddy, a Battle Royal consisting of nine heels and Texas Dirt, then Master of Pain & Black Bart & Buddy Landel vs. Lawler and referees Jerry Calhoun & Frank Morrell, then a handicap match with the Rock & Roll Express against both Wildside & Blackbirds and finally the loser leaves town match with Lawler vs. Doug Gilbert with the Mr. Mystery Referee.

OREGON

The 8/12 card in Portland was headlined by a loser leaves town tag match as Scotty the Body & The Grappler kept the tag team titles beating The Southern Rockers (Steve Doll & Scott Peterson) when Peterson was pinned after Scotty hit him with a foreign object, Mat Man (now the guy is Pat Tanaka wearing face paint) & Beetlejuice beat Al Madril & Rip Oliver, Nord the Barbarian no contest with Carl Styles when Grappler interfered and all the faces came in to make the save and Nord & Grappler destroyed all the faces until finally Bill Francis (brother of Patriot tight end Russ Francis and a pro wrestler in the mid-70s) ran in to make the save and challenged Nord.

On 8/19, they had a going away party for Peterson which

Scotty & Grappler interrupted and messed up, but before the mess-up, Doll announced that Rex King was a new Southern Rocker so the two will form a tag team. They said that Peterson couldn't return for six months because of losing the match.

Also on the card Scotty wrestled Beetlejuice (Art Barr) and Madril kidnapped a kid at ringside who dresses up like Beetlejuice and finally Beetlejuice went after him and lost the match via count out.

Billy Jack Haynes vanished almost as quickly as he returned. We had heard during the brief time he was around, that promoter Don Owen used him so he would have to publicly apologize on television, but still hadn't really forgiven him and was only going to use him for a brief period.

Grappler canceled his Japan tour so he'll stick around.

OTHER STUFF

Lou Albano will have an MS benefit roast for himself in New York on 9/9.

ABC's "One Life to Live" soap opera has done a plot over the past two weeks using a pro wrestling storyline.

Ron West has talked of leaving pro wrestling which would give Robert Fuller just about complete control of the CWF.

Former pro wrestler Vladimir Petrov (Al Blake) has been released from prison and a halfway house and will probably be returning to the ring.

Ron Wyatt, who promoted an independent card in Suffolk, VA a few weeks back has sued Harvey Cobb of the Pro Wrestling Enquirer newsletter for $1,533 since Cobb, who was co-promoting the show and signed to put up a certain amount of guarantee money, allegedly came up $1500 short in the promised guarantee money.

Stampede Wrestling has entered into negotiations with ESPN for U.S. coverage.

An ICW TV taping on 8/18 in Parsippany, NJ drew 175 as Vic Steamboat beat Tony Atlas via DQ for Atlas' ICW title when Kendall Windham interfered and Nikolai Volkoff also worked the taping.

Tom Prichard was "injured" and has left the CWF to return home to Texas. On Saturday's CWF TV show they had Dennis Condrey give him a series of DDT's on a chair and he juiced heavily and was stretchered out.

Bob Geigel will promote a tournament on 8/21 in Kansas City with the Central States tag team titles at stake plus Mike George vs. Bob Orton and Destruction Crew (Mike Enos & Wayne Bloom).

The AWA tag team titles are held up after a match on 8/18 in St. Cloud, MN between Ken Patera & Baron Von Raschke vs. Destruction Crew, who ultimately will wind up with the belts.

8/18 in Calgary saw Owen Hart "injured" so he can tour Japan. Hart pinned Johnny Smith in the main event when Larry Cameron ran in and gave Hart a piledriver on the table which should set the two up for a feud when Hart gets back from Japan. Also on the card the Samurai Warriors (Sumu Hara & Kensuke Sasaki), who I'm told are a pretty good tag team, captured the International tag team titles from Bob & Kerry Brown.

You think these technical screw-ups only happen with pro wrestling, well, apparently over the weekend the Oakland A's and Minnesota Twins had a televised game out here and somehow the wires got crossed and for an inning or so the A's fans in the Bay Area instead heard the play-by-play by Twins announcers Ted Robinson and Jim Kaat.

The Jewish newspaper in Australia had a major story in the last few weeks about former pro wrestler Mark Lewin.

CWF on 8/25 in Knoxville has a CWF Showdown match with Tracy Smothers & Steve Armstrong & Jerry Stubbs (back as a face) against Robert Fuller & Jimmy Golden & Brian Lee with Stubbs and Golden tied together with a bull rope, Armstrong and Lee tied together with an Indian strap and Smothers and Fuller tied together with a chain. The undercard has Dennis Condrey defending the CWF title against Danny Davis, Stomper Don Harris vs. Wendell Cooley , Adrian Street vs. Terrance Garvin, The Beast (Mark Goleen dressed up like a woman) vs. Miss Linda and Todd Morton vs. Mike Davis.

The Fantastics (Jackie & Bobby Fulton) are set to work some AWA dates.

Pez Whatley, Brad & Scott Armstrong, Joel Deaton, David Sammartino, Kevin Dillinger (Alan Martin) and Tom Prichard have worked shots for Jerry Blackwell's Southern Championship Wrestling of late.

A group called the WWA had a three-show tour on 8/17 in Salt Lake City, 8/18 in Pleasant Grove and 8/19 in Ogden, UT. Card announced has Bam Bam Bigelow vs. Max Pain (Darryl Peterson), plus Tom Brandi underneath. Pain is also doing public service say no to drugs announcements.

The Detroit News is now running a new weekly wrestling column by M. L. Curly (you know, Moe, Larry & Curly).

Johnny K-9 promoted a show on 7/28 in Hamilton, ONT with Missing Link (Dewey Robertson) & Ricky Johnson double disqualification with K-9 & Dan "Bullwhip" Johnson on top plus Denny Kass (a former collegiate All-American from the University of Buffalo), Mickey Doyle, Wolfman Willie Farkas (a name wrestler in the early 70s), Taras Bulba and High Flyer Kurt Nile.

WWA in Toledo on 7/24 had former pro boxing champion Leon Spinks go to a double disqualification against the Great Wojo (former amateur wrestling great Greg Wojiechowski) in a rematch of an earlier match that Wojo had won via count out. Also on the card, saw The Sensationals (Mickey Doyle & Al Snow) beat Kansas City Outlaws (Sam Cody & Roger Ruffin), Jerry Graham Jr. double DQ with Chris Carter and Bulldog Don Kent of Kangaroo fame double dq with El Brassero (Jose Martinez).

Midwest Championship Wrestling promoted three fair shows on 8/8 in Flint, 8/9 in Belleville and 8/10 in Bad Axe. The latter of the three drew 1,500 fans. Among those working these shows included Doyle, Snow, Cass, Machine Gun Kelly, Dave St. Onge, tag team called The Flying Tigers, Man Mountain Jim Lancaster, Kurt Nile, Carl Rust, Brian Costello and legendary old-time wrestlers Bobo Brazil and Al Costello of the Fabulous Kangaroos.

A group started up in Australia promoting shows on 8/1 in Clayton and 8/6 in St. Albans in the province of Victoria (near Melbourne) drawing 1,200 and 1,000 respectively. Con lakovides and Mario Milano (a name in the WWWF during the late 60s) were headliners.

The biggest crowd I've heard all year at an independent show was on 8/16 in Nashua, NH of 4,800 fans promoted by Walter "Killer" Kowalski. The top matches saw Big John Studd beat Chris Duffy in 4:20. Studd was the big draw and the guy who drew the house, but just stood there in the ring and Duffy worked very hard in trying to carry things. Also Nikolai Volkoff pinned Mike Sharpe and David Sammartino pinned Johnny Valiant.

Former pro wrestler Bob Sabre died Thursday in Hoffman Estates, IL of cancer at the age of 60. Sabre, who also worked as a photographer for wrestling magazines, wrestled from 1952 through 1983, mainly as a jobber in the Chicago area. Sabre was billed as the commissioner of Sam DeCero's Windy City Wrestling in Chicago. He is most well-known in wrestling circles for his 1964 gimmick, which failed miserably, where he used the ring name "George Ringo, The Wrestling Beatle" shortly after The Beatles came to the United States and were all the rage. The other wrestlers hated the gimmick and they used to regularly bust his guitar in the locker room and he asked the promoters to quit within a few weeks. The Dubin Inquiry on steroid usage in Canada (brought upon by the Ben Johnson scandal) had a pro wrestling twist when Richard Lococo, who worked in the NWA briefly in 1987 as part of the Canadian Kodiaks tag team, said that steroid usage was prevalent in pro wrestling and "they're all taking them." Lococo gave up steroids for health purposes and said his weight dropped 60 pounds from 300 to 240. I believe the Lococo brothers were originally from San Jose, CA. Bob Raskin's United States Wrestling Alliance drew 2,189 on 8/16 in Manassas, VA as part of a grandstand show during the fair as Nikita Koloff beat Afa the Samoan in the main event on a card which included Misty Blue, Linda Dallas, Mike Kaluha, Larry Winters, Jules Strongbow, Ron Shaw and Cheetah Kid.

A similar grandstand show on 8/14 in Harrisonburg, VA drew 912 as Sgt. Slaughter beat Russian Assassin and Strongbow & Nikita Koloff beat Cheetah Kid & Tom Brandi.

NWA

Newcomers to the NWA include the State Highway Patrol (Dwayne Bruce & Dale Veasy), Cuban Assassin (David Sierra—Top Gun in Oregon) as mainly jobbers plus Brad Armstrong, Dick Slater and at the Atlanta tapings on Wednesday they had Kevin Kelly and Benjamin Frankl in Peacock (Botswana Beast – real name Ben Peacock) come in for tryouts. Peacock was supposed to be a jive-talking black wrestler but they booed him out of the place when he was trying to be a face and Kelly got little reaction, although that's not a fair evaluation since lots of guys don't get much reaction when fans don't know who they are. Tom Zenk and John Nord are supposed to be headed in as well before the end of September.

Cuban already did a job for Ric Flair on the Power Hour (taped in Charleston, WV on 8/14), while Armstrong did TV jobs for Flair and Lex Luger at the 8/15 taping in Cleveland.

It appears Sir Oliver Humperdink will be brought in as the manager of the Samoans or at least, he's the leading candidate. Paul E. Dangerously is staying with the promotion although I have no idea what his new role will be though it is rumored he will become Jim Ross' sidekick on the Saturday TBS show doing play-by-play and color.

Nikita Koloff hasn't committed yet to returning.

The Ding Dongs idea is finished as they were unmasked in Cleveland.

Butch Reed will be returning and will probably wind up as a tag team with either Mike Rotunda or Kevin Sullivan, while Iron Sheik & Ron Simmons & Cuban Assassin will form a top-level jobber trio.

Robin Greene will turn into Fallen Angel on television this coming weekend. There are many who are saying this is going to be a hot angle this fall when all is said and done and will lead to a natural rivalry with Missy Hyatt, which may be an out-of-the-ring rivalry as well.

TV ratings from last weekend were all 2.3's. The Saturday show, which was a three hour show (8/12) did a 2.3 in each hour so they kept the audience all the way through while the Sunday show also did a 2.3, which is pretty good since they had announced on TV that there wouldn't be a Sunday show, and due to some sort of a schedule quirk, it was put back at the last minute and it was all repeated matches.

Gary Hart will now manage Funk, Muta and Slater as the J-Tex (Japan-Texas) Corporation and they'll wind up feuding with Flair, Sting and Pillman (who is about to get a big push).

8/18 in Greensboro drew 8,500 as Bill Irwin & Al Greene beat Ding Dongs, Simmons beat Brad Anderson, Pillman pinned Norman, Steve Williams beat Mike Rotunda via count out, Steiners beat Militia, Freebirds beat Midnight Express, Sting drew Muta 20:00, Luger pinned Rich, Flair pinned Funk and Road Warriors beat SST.

The 8/19 card in Charlotte drew more than 6,000 with the same basic results. Report from Greensboro as far as match quality was about the same as Chicago except Sting and Muta was much better in Greensboro but told Flair-Funk was excellent all three nights.

8/12 in Norfolk drew 5,000 as Ding Dongs beat Al Greene & Lee Scott, Pillman pinned Norman, Sid Vicious pinned Scott Hall, Simmons beat Curtis Thompson (White Angel in Puerto Rico), Steiners beat Militia, Sting drew Muta, Road Warriors beat SST, Luger pinned Rich and Flair pinned Funk.

8/13 in Norfolk and 8/14 in Charleston, SC both drew mid-$30,000 houses.

8/15 in Cleveland drew 3,500 as State Highway Patrol beat Sartain & Evans without the hoods (they do a gimmick similar to Bossman except write tickets as a gimmick after the match), Bobby Eaton pinned Jimmy Garvin when Stan Lane interfered, Simmons & Cuban beat Eddie Gilbert & Tommy Rich when Sheik hit Gilbert with the flag for the pin (I believe Gilbert won't be traveling as much and concentrating on doing the detail work of asst. booker in the office since booker Flair will be on the road so much), Flair pinned Brad Armstrong in a face match (good match but crowd didn't get into the face vs. face stuff), Steiners beat Freebirds via DQ, Muta pinned Hall (Hall missing moves left and right), Flair pinned Funk (five stars--match not taped), Rich pinned Cuban (fans chanted "boring" unmercifully), Luger pinned Armstrong (excellent), Skyscrapers beat Ding Dongs and unmasked them, Steiners (with both Missy & Robin Greene—Robin in black, Missy in white) beat State Highway Patrol, Sting beat Muta via DQ (not good) and Luger pinned Rich.

WWF

WWF has got a cross promotion with Miller Lite and some guys will be involved in a stop or two of The Who's Summer Tour when WWF and Who are in town together.

Jim Powers out of action with a broken cheekbone.

All American Wrestling drew a 2.5 on 8/13 and the three-hour SummerSlam preview special drew a 3.3 that night and a 3.1 in the normal time slot on 8/14.

The Heenan show has already been dropped but they have Heenan and Rick Rude now in separate studios on Prime Time with Gorilla Monsoon and Roddy Piper in other studios and the interaction has been real good, far better than the wrestling matches. Expect a blow-up shortly and everyone expects Piper to be involved in Warrior winning the title at SurnmerSlam (if such a thing happens).

No Holds Barred finished its theater run at $16.1 million.

WWF jobbers are called "extras," like in movie terminology, not jobbers anymore.

Steve Blackman is coming in.

Crowds have been down with Summer Slam approaching, particularly over the weekend where Hogan vs. Savage, even in mid-sized markets, hasn't been able to sell out.

Hogan vs. Savage will have cage matches in late September.

8/19 in Philadelphia drew 12,145 ($140,936) as Hogan pinned Savage, Hart Foundation beat Dino Bravo & Greg Valentine, Rockers beat Rougeaus in a marathon match, Jim Duggan pinned Akeem, Widow Maker (Barry Windham) beat Paul Roma and Hercules double DQ with Haku.

WWF cards in the fall will be cut to seven or eight matches and supposedly longer length matches.

8/12 in Richfield Coliseum (suburban Cleveland) drew 1,500 as Widow Maker pinned Sam Houston ** ¼, Brooklyn Brawler pinned Dale Wolfe - ** ½ , Koko B. Ware pinned The Genius Lanny Poffo DUD, Bushwackers beat Powers of Pain via DQ DUD, Rick Rude pinned Jim Neidhart - *** , Rick Martel pinned Tito Santana ½ *and Dusty Rhodes pinned Akeem (sub for Bossman) DUD.

THE READERS' PAGE

NEWSLETTERS

I'm a fairly new reader of the Observer and sincerely appreciate the work it must take to put out such a great publication on a weekly basis.

In the late 1970s, most of the "good" wrestling newsletters thought it was smart to play along with the promoters and make believe wrestling was a shoot. Good publications put out by myself, Bill Hill, Terry Justice, Joe Shedlock and others would never dare admit that wrestling was nothing more than a work. In fact, most of the publications of those days just printed result after result of meaningless matches. Very dull reading.

In 1978 or 1979, I remember mentioning in one of my publications that wrestling blood might be fake (I didn't know about blading then) and many of the so-called legit writers in the business went nuts. How dare I print something that would question the legitimacy of the sport.

Things are so much healthier today. Instead of taking an Apter-like view of the wrestling world, we get the opportunity to learn about the wrestling business. It's much more interesting than finding out who beat who in Harrisburg, PA.

Sometimes when reading the letters section I get the feeling that many readers of the Observer feel that they are "smart" and can handle the facts of life about the wrestling business, but they feel that if the truth got out that others couldn't handle it and it would hurt the business and everything would collapse. This attitude makes me uncomfortable. I wish that everyone in the world knew what we know about the wrestling business. It would make the business far more enjoyable to the general public. Believing that pro wrestling is real is no more essential to your enjoyment of it than believing what happens on Miami Vice is actually taking place. If publications like Pro Wrestling Illustrated wrote like the Observer, their sales would skyrocket. I realize they can't do it because of a backlash from the promoters, but the WWF has already banned them anyway. Just as many publications on the newsstand enjoy overwhelming success by giving the inside news on the movie and TV industry, so would a newsstand wrestling magazine. 95 percent of the wrestling fans want to hear what's really going on, not some fantasy story from Vince McMahon.

Media coverage of wrestling is a joke. Newsstand publications act as nothing more than unpaid press agents for the promoters. The business needs a national magazine like the Observer to tell the whole world that even though pro wrestling is 99.99 percent pre-determined that it is still one of the best forms of entertainment available. I don't buy this line that newsletter readers are "smart" but that others can't handle the truth. That is such a narrow-minded and stupid view.

Gary Cubeta
Middletown, Connecticut

I take note of a growing and disturbing trend among newsletter editors, that of criticizing other newsletters. Did I say criticizing? That's putting it mildly. Savaging is much more to the point. Of all the counter-productive things a newsletter editor can do, this is the worst. It only creates bad feelings among a community that desperately needs togetherness and gives aid and comfort to the enemy, namely, the promoters.

The fact of the matter is that no newsletter editor has the right to criticize another unless it is a case of a newsletter taking pecuniary advantage of its readers. To do so otherwise is to cross the boundaries of good taste. If you have a criticism of another bulletin, simply write the editor of that bulletin. Do not blare it in your newsletter for the world to see, for while you may score a few quick points, the tide of public opinion will surely turn against you and your "victory" will have been a pyrrhic one. Does Time openly criticize Newsweek? Does Sports Illustrated criticize Sporting News? No, because they are competitors and it just isn't considered good taste. Tabloid newspapers often criticize each other, but they are notorious for bad taste, just read their headlines.

I've also heard the criticism that there exist too many newsletters. On the contrary, there aren't enough. Competition breeds excellence and right now, there are more excellent newsletters out there than ever before. Also, each newsletter has its own niche and no newsletter copies the other. Such newsletters as the Torch, Matwatch, Global Wrestling and the two I write for, Forum and Ringside Reflector are all different. Of course, all contain basically the same news. News is news, but each presents it in a different manner and style and adds extra materials to enhance the content. Instead of fighting, editors should encourage each other. When I was with Wrestling Eye, I was Fan Club Editor. I saw my role there as one to encourage bulletins and I never said anything bad about a bulletin. If I didn't like it, I may not have pushed it as hard as the Observer, but I never out-and-out trashed it in the column. The only advice I will leave you with is that of Voltaire's Candide: "We must cultivate our own gardens."

I would also like to comment on Jeff Siegel's recent remarks concerning the comparison of wrestlers and actors. I thought your point was very well taken and your position was solid, However, you left out one thing. Wrestlers, like actors, are subject to problems from typecasting. In the old days, when hoods were the rage, this didn't matter much. A wrestler could easily don a mask and start fresh, even in the same territory. In these days of cartoon characters and cable television, the dangers of being typecast are greater than ever. Sure, Terry Taylor is making more money than before, but it has a price. What happens when his push stops and the money isn't as abundant? In the old days, he could simply leave for another promotion. But his gimmick is so outrageous as to make that now impossible. With the penetration of the WWF on television, he is now and forever, the Red Rooster. He can't live that down. The only one who can help him would be McMahon, who has a great ability to recycle wrestlers. But if he were to go to another territory, this gimmick will have injured him to the point where he may never reach the necessary heights and pay to be fully compensated for leaving the WWF. McMahon has been known to cut salaries before and Taylor could very well find himself stuck and low paid.

Ed Garea
Irvington, New Jersey

Dave Meltzer: I decided a long time ago that it was best to not criticize other newsletters in the Observer, even though at times the Observer has been a favorite for criticism in other newsletters. However, I don't believe it's right to impose a standard like that for others. What makes newsletters is the free-flow of opinions, so long as they remain in decent taste and the arguments don't get personal and childish as happened last year in our letters pages. Also, I don't consider promoters as the enemy, even though promoters to a great extent do consider the Observer as the enemy. I do consider it my responsibility to criticize promotions that are dishonest and try and report on both the good and the bad within the business. If a promoter is honest and gives the fans entertaining shows that are well-run and creative, he deserves credit. If he treats fans like "marks" and is dishonest when dealing with them, he deserves criticism. By the way, I've seen TV commercials where U.S. News knocks Time or where Sporting News knocks Sports Illustrated (the cable spot where George

Brett is reading what is apparently SI and he says, "I like looking at girls in bathing suits as well as the next guy but when I want to read about what's really going on in sports I read The Sporting News"), which is similar to Jim Ross' occasional knocks at the WWF during Flair's title defenses. I completely agree that competition is the best thing, whether it be in the wrestling business or the newsletter business. The best thing for readers of every newsletter in the past year has been the advent of Matwatch, and to an extent, the improvement in Torch because it gives readers a greater variety of quality products and should force improvement in stagnant publications, just as competition should have been the best thing in the wrestling business because it forced improvement in stagnant promotions. It didn't turn out that way because in wrestling there was such a drive to put competition out of business As far as the criticism of newsletters in other publications, I agree with some of it, disagree with some of it, think some of it is in bad taste, but respect everyone's right to give their opinion.

ENJOYS BOWDREN ARTICLES
I very much enjoyed the Jeff Bowdren feature in the 8/14 Observer. As with his previous articles, Jeff's writing is both insightful and thought-provoking. My only complaint is his articles are few and far in between. We should have more of them.

In his article, Jeff offered an idea on how Brian Pillman should be pushed. As I stated in my 8/7 letter, I'm very partisan to Pillman. Much to my surprise, several well-known wrestling aficionados have publicly panned him. As the foremost wrestling expert, what do you see as his true potential? Do you see him as a face or a heel? Paul E. Dangerously is a big Brian Pillman fan and their combined efforts could make the Dangerously/Austin Idol/Tommy Rich triumvirate pale by comparison, especially if Eddie Gilbert is part of a new trio. Does the thought of Pillman against Muta, Sting or Ric Flair himself whet your appetite as it does mine or am I under some sort of delusion?

Klon
Melbourne, Florida

Dave Meltzer: I'm not the foremost wrestling expert, but I think Pillman has tons of potential. His athletic ability and his "look," particularly his physique, are already of main event caliber. He still lacks the experience of a polished main event worker, but my thoughts are that is mainly because he hasn't been in that kind of environment until his NWA start. In Calgary, there were a lot of great workers, but they were great athletic workers who were also inexperienced in comparison with a Flair or Steamboat, such as Owen Hart, Chris Benoit, Hiroshi Hase, etc. and worked a different style, based more on athletics and hot moves and less on psychology. Pillman has never worked as a heel, but I see potential there down the road but don't see a turn coming. Judging from the last TV taping, it seems Ric Flair is also quite high on Pillman as a future star, which means he will be getting his opportunity. His size can be a minor drawback, but if the charisma is there, his strengths, the right look, the physique and athletic ability and in time, I believe he'll be a top-class worker as well, should easily make up for it.

BALTIMORE BASH
Do you realize how much better the Baltimore Bash is on its second, third and fourth viewing? That has to be the best overall card from top-to-bottom that I've had the pleasure of witnessing. While the Flair vs. Funk match wasn't as good as the Steamboat vs. Flair match in Nashville, the card was much better than Nashville and I thought the Nashville show was great. Please initiate a Best Major Card award in the yearbook.

If I had to vote today, Flair is wrestler of the year, the Rockers are tag team of the year and Dangerously is manager of the year. Sherri Martel is incredible in her role. If WrestleMania VI is going to be Hogan vs. Zeus, they should do an angle to get Zeus over as a mean heel such as have Hogan and a bunch of kid actors doing some ultra-sentimental video and have Zeus come in and actually beat up a kid or just manhandle one of them. The run-ins following the Sting/Gilbert vs. Militia match was one of the best booked TV matches I've seen. I was jumping out of my seat waiting for Flair to involve himself. Piper is starting to grow on me on Prime Time but the Heenan show sucks. Whoever is responsible for letting Steamboat get away when they were $10,000 apart should be fired. While I agree with you that he wasn't a major drawing card, he still is the second best wrestler in the world and that should count for something. I'm enjoying the Rick Steiner/Robin Green angle, but can't figure out where it's going. I've got a sneaking suspicion SummerSlam is going to be better than we think.

Scott Hudson
Tifton, Georgia

After attending Bash shows in Philadelphia, New Haven and Baltimore, I can definitely say that while Philadelphia and New Haven were good shows, Baltimore was the best. I'd have attended the show even if I hadn't been a contest winner. By the way, both the plane ride and hotel room were fine, but the tickets given to the winners were in the loge section. Having already purchased ringside, I gave the tickets I won to a friend who wanted to attend the card.

The wrestlers worked really hard to put on a great show and the ring entrances were good. I really enjoyed the War Games. A War Games match is better when no blood is shed. Accolades should go to Bobby Eaton and Jimmy

Garvin who started the match. They looked exhausted at the end, yet continued to wrestle hard. There wasn't a dull match on the card. My only negative comment on the show was using the animals in the ring entrances. I felt it detracted from the overall quality of the show and hope it doesn't become a permanent fixture of the NWA.

I believe the NWA is capable of becoming a viable organization. They need to improve the advertising and promotion of both house shows and PPV shows. The NWA should have started promoting the Baltimore card back in May to the public. If I wasn't an Observer reader, I would never have called the Baltimore Arena as early as I did to get ringside tickets. The WWF always promotes its big shows two or three months ahead and the NWA should take a lesson and do the same. A positive step were the surveys done at the arenas in June and July. This allows the NWA to find out what the fans want to see and how they feel about certain things. Another positive step were the autograph sessions. One negative step was the introduction of the Ding Dongs. They remind me of a bad circus act and I hope they are sent back to oblivion.

Deborah McWilliams
Brooklyn, New York

STEROIDS

I totally agree with Scott Brooks letter in the recent Observer. I'm an avid lifter who belongs to FAD (Fight Against Drugs). These two hobbies intertwine. As a member of FAD, I, along with other students, travel to elementary schools and talk to kids about drugs. Being that I'm a lifter, the subject of steroids always comes up. I talk about Hellwig, Rood, Hegstrand and the like. People are always calling it "fake muscle." I have to explain that these guys are religious trainers. This is a common misconception. The heavy roiders do work hard in the gym. The question that must be asked is whether it is worth it. Hellwig may be dead soon and the others may have health problems and Rick Rude is already developing titties. It's a shame the wrestling business has taken this sad turn because of greed. I must ask, how can Vince McMahon live with himself?

Jonathan Mason
Roslyn, Pennsylvania

COMPARING WWF WITH NWA

You and your readers spend a lot of time comparing the NWA and WWF. This is like comparing Christmas with Labor Day, Johnny Carson with Pat Sajak and Disneyland with Knotts Berry Farm. You talk about perception, but why not talk about reality. Pro wrestling would be nothing without Vince McMahon. He's not perfect. Are you? He is to wrestling what The Beatles were to music and they weren't perfect either.

The NWA stars have to go to the WWF to make it big.

The WWF stars go to the NWA when it's over for them in the big time (JYD, Sheik and Reed) or when they can't cut it in the big-time (Freebirds; Bam Bam Bigelow, Missy Hyatt). In the WWF, Steamboat was the holder of the "B" title and he lost it.

In the NWA, he holds the "A" title and loses it. Flair vs. Funk was good, but Funk already had a series with Hogan and even lost once on national television to him.

When an attraction goes from NWA to WWF they continue to rise. Tully & Arn are now tag champs. One of the guys they beat used to work for the NWA and did real good with his move. Windham is going to get shots at Hogan. And there's Dusty. In the NWA he's a hero and many times world champion. In the WWF they use him for what he really is, an overweight bozo used for comedy. But he's headlining again and Vince doesn't pretend he's something that he's not like the NWA did.

The ship sailed for the Legion of Doom. These guys wanted to be big fish in the small pond and they choked on it. Would fans care if they left the NWA now?

Ric Flair should stay where he is for as long as he can because once he joins Titan, which he will, it's over for him. His one big push will be the eventual Hogan vs. Flair match at WrestleMania, which Flair will have to lose. The WWF champ has to beat the NWA champ.

The NWA is a fine alternative, but they can't compete with the WWF. They don't have the cable, they don't have NBC, they don't have the money and they don't have Vince McMahon's creativity and guts. Where would wrestling be without Vince McMahon? Where would this newsletter be without Vince McMahon?

Where would the NWA and AWA be without Vince McMahon? Dull.

Vince McMahon won't admit he reads the newsletter but we all know he does. So I'd like to thank you, sir, for pumping life back into our sport. You made the 80s great and keep it up in the 90s.

R.J. Dari
White Plains, New York

SUMMERSLAM

While I agree that SumrnerSlam's Hogan vs. Zeus angle is going over well, the reason why shouldn't be ignored. The whole angle is based on what Titan sees as the closet racism of the wrestling fans. If they did a demographic study of people who attend wrestling matches, you would find the people as white, rural and poorly educated. So what sells? A movie and subsequent promotion where their big white hero beats up a black neanderthal. Is there anyone who reads this newsletter who doesn't believe that long before Vince McMahon ever heard of Tiny Lister, he knew he wanted to cast a big black as Hogan's opponent? I'm not saying Vince is a racist, but I'm saying that he believes racism sells.

It's no secret that the reason there has never been a black World Champion in the NWA or WWF is because it's not what their overwhelmingly-white paying customers would have wanted. Would anyone cheer a black champion in Mooresville, NC, Waxahachie, TX or Shreveport, LA? Wrestling is more fantasy than skill appreciation and the sad fact is Hogan wouldn't have been a superstar if he wasn't white. Terry Bollea, if he was black, could have still made money in wrestling because of his size and charisma, but he never would have been a champion. He probably would have been like Ernie Ladd, spent most of his time as an underappreciated heel.

Vince uses blacks as either squash guys or clowns or heels. A black man hasn't held a title since Vince Sr. ran things. The NWA hasn't been any better, especially in the Virgil Runnels regime. Things seem to be changing now that Turner is running things but it's not likely a great worker like Ron Simmons will get out of prelims. Teddy Long and Slick are good managers but they are heels, and their men never hold any titles. Simmons and Butch Reed were both excellent babyfaces but have to work as heels to get over in major promotions. Obviously, somebody will point out Titan's use of Mr. T.

It was a breakthrough, but only worked because he was a TV star and was carried by a bigger and stronger white partner. In WrestleMania II, more people were cheering Roddy Piper, which helped Titan decide to turn Piper face afterwards.

Now we have SummerSlam. The big tag match between three white guys of some level of intelligence and a big, mean black neanderthal who is impervious to pain and beats on his chest like he's a gorilla.

How stupid. Yet, there I was at the Baltimore Bash listening to two guys say they couldn't wait for SummerSlam and watch Hogan "stomp the hall outta that big n***er. " Now I hear the card is going to make record money, which is a truly sad commentary. I hope Tiny Lister falls off his lifts on the way to the ring. Maybe only then will Vince stop insulting us.

Richard Wallner
Washington, D.C.

AND OTHER STUFF

I can't see why smart fans sit in the front row. I hate it. You are too close and all you see is a one-dimensional view of the action. In a big arena, I like sitting in the loge sections, higher than the ring. In a small arena, I sit in the back of the balcony.

To me, the biggest story of last week was that the least pinned wrestler in history was defeated twice in one week. Who cares if the fans were pissed off because the match was so short. Andre has been pinned very few times. Try thinking like a mark.

I've been watching a lot of Japanese wrestling lately and think the Japanese refs should count in Japanese instead of in English.

Steve Yohe
Alhambra, California

Dave Meltzer: Titan's audience isn't marks, it's primarily families with kids. Generally they attend to see "the star," either Hogan or Warrior (which is why crowds when either of those two are on the card are so much larger than when anyone else is on the card). They don't care that much about who wins and loses, since when Hogan lost to Savage on the last card, there was only a slight trace of negative heat with the verdict, nor was there anything but a smattering of heat when Windham beat Taylor or DiBiase beat Hillbilly Jim or other wins by a heel over a "name" face. The place did pop like crazy when Warrior beat Andre here, but it was also not the main event and the crowd came to see Hogan far more than Warrior. In cities where the crowd comes to see Warrior, to only see him for 15 seconds gets a lot of people upset they paid $15 for 15 seconds. As for me, I was glad to see them go so short. They use English when counting in Japan in wrestling, just like in baseball, because it's an Americanized form of entertainment. In the same way, in the U.S., during judo tournaments, the names for the "throws" and the counting is in Japanese because it is a Japanese form of sport.

I'd like to send a special thank you to some of the wrestlers who made the Denver fans invitational such a success, to Col. DeBeers for surprising us by being a very friendly, fun and witty guy who was even Captain, er, Colonel, of the winning softball team; to Dan Juan for showing us local spots like Whiskey Bill's; to Party Animal for helping us party and showing us how to shoot pennies; and to Charley Norris, Maximum Overdrive, Butch Masters, Mr. Outrageous, Cowboy Coltrell, Lord Littlebrook, Karate Kid and Chief Thunder Mug for joining in our activities and mingling with us. You all definitely made Denver the best convention ever .

Sharon Guillory
Alexandria, Louisiana

STEAMBOAT CONTRACT DISPUTE

One of the most talked about issues in pro wrestling over the past month has been that of the departure of Ricky Steamboat from the National Wrestling Alliance when his contract expired at the end of July. The story has pretty well been covered over the past few weeks here in the Observer, and in recent weeks both Steamboat and NWA Executive Vice President Jim Herd appeared as guests on John Arezzi's "Wrestling Spotlight" program on WNYG Radio in New York. In both cases, the interviews were a rare case of interviews dealing with the wrestling business being almost totally upfront and forthright, and for those reasons, I felt that readers would be most interested in the comments made by both parties, both in regards to Steamboat's parting of the ways with the NWA and the business of pro wrestling in general.

Ricky Steamboat: "Well, it wasn't (Leaving the NWA) because I really wanted to. We've been knowing that my contract was becoming due on July 31st so I approached Turner's people about two months ago and said let's get started on this thing and see if we can get something cooking for a year. They were happy to hear that and I was happy to offer it. I guess about a week before July 31st we had a set price that we had agreed upon and after two or three days I was informed that they had withdrawn the offer. Their comment was that they had their back up against the wall when it comes to salaries. I had come down a considerable amount to reach our final agreement. I had told them I wished to stay with the NWA and expressed my desire to help the NWA and I looked forward to doing business with them."

"I hope that I had something to do with the NWA getting back on its feet. After all, when Crockett Promotions sold out to Turner's people it was for an obvious reason, because they were so far in the hole. Coming back on the scene and maybe raising a few eyebrows and getting some of the interest back in the NWA, this is why I expressed my desire to Turner's people to stay on with them. By withdrawing their offer, it was something that was a shock to me because I had agreed on it and they agreed on it. After all, it was two months worth of negotiations going back-and-forth, talking to them whenever I went to Atlanta to do TV, talking to them countless times over the telephone and still expressing my desire to stay with the company and then to pull the withdrawl and then to call me a few days later and say 'Look, Rick, we'll sign you back up but we need for you to drop x-amount of dollars and if you want to know what x-amount of dollars is, it was in the neighborhood of $50, 000 off the salary."

(What the NWA has to do to remain competitive with the WWF): "They have to do a number of things. As you know in the last six months they have lost some big talent to the WWF. I think one of the major things they have to do is look for and continue to get a hold of top talent and keep them with the organization and put them in the spotlight and give them some attention. I think the NWA right now doesn't have the depth that the WWF has in terms of talent. I'm not talking about talent as it comes to wrestling, I'm talking about simply the number of people. The WWF has a big crew and they can run two or three cities a night and can split the talent up and still have a good wrestling card for the fans to come out to see and this is something the NWA is lacking. I also think that Turner's people should step up

their TV production a little bit although I think people have seen it and I've seen it in the last couple of months they are doing this, but I still think it needs to be stepped up a little bit to match the WWF. If they can get the same type of production as the WWF puts out and with a few more qualified wrestlers and top talent then the NWA can give the WWF a big run."

"I think at the present time I'd just like to cool it for the summer and just spend some time with my family, my little boy. I'm not saying I'd never go back to the WWF because never is a long time. If the workload would loosen up a little bit I might consider it if the salary and the money was right. Everybody may think that I'm just looking at the money aspect, well that does play a major role and I think anybody in the sports field or anyone that's out there looking for a job or a profession would have to consider that the money aspect would play a major part in the decision. After all, I'm going to be 37 and I feel real good about myself physically although in the mornings I don't quite get up the way I used to. My joints do bother me. And also with my son coming up, I'm looking at probably a couple of good years and I'd like to make my last couple of years my best years, and not go out like you've seen so many wrestlers who have been wrestling 20 or 25 years who used to be main eventers and now they're wrestling opening matches and people think of them as has-beens or people who used to be good. I've got a little too much pride within myself to go out of the sport that I've loved and put everything behind and I'd like to go out on top. Right now, I've done that but I'm not saying that I wouldn't go back if the right organization would approach me the right way."

"I really do appreciate these few minutes to talk with you (John Arezzi) and the fans on more of a one-to-one basis and let them know some of the inside things that they may never hear about. The business has grown so much in the last five years. It's taken off big-time. I wish to be with it for the next couple of years but if it doesn't happen, it doesn't, but if it does, I'd like to go in the ring with the idea I'm giving it my best shot and if it doesn't, I'd like to thank the fans for their support. They've been one of the major reasons why I came back to the business."

Jim Herd: (Why Steamboat wasn't signed): "No. 1, I think you're looking at it as a finality situation that doesn't really exist. Ricky Steamboat and I are still talking. We happen to think he's a fine gentleman in the pro sport that we're in and look forward to him wrestling for us in the near future. One of the things that has to happen in all business is we have to be fiscally responsible and we want to be sure that everybody doesn't get the wrong impression that Ricky wasn't signed because of pressure from above to keep expenses down. I think we prove that every day when you look at what we do, the money we spend on our PPV and Clashes on the Superstation."

(Does he think the failure to sign Steamboat might affect the confidence of some of the other NWA stars when their contract comes due): "I think they're going to reflect on the fact that Steamboat wasn't signed but I think they have to look at all different parts of contracts. There are all different parts of contracts and the monetary part isn't the only part, it has to do with travel, with days off, it has to do with a lot of things and I think one of the primary stumbling blocks in our inability to come to a reasonable situation with Ricky Steamboat is that he is a tremendous family man and this is not any kind of an act, it's a genuine love to be around his son and we do appreciate that but it does limit us to scheduling him a maximum of four days a week. That becomes difficult at times. When you look at what's happened, I don't think you can look at it from a monetary standpoint."

I think you have to look at it from all 36 pages that encompass a pro wrestling contract.

(wouldn't it have been good to show the public you are going all out to keep your most talented wrestlers by signing Steamboat): "There's no doubt that Steamboat represents one of the most talented wrestlers and we're in the public relations business to a degree, one of the reasons Ted Turner purchased this is because it was in trouble and I, as a responsible executive, don't; intend to jeopardize that by not doing what's reasonable as a businessman and I think most fans understand that. They have budgets. They have bills to pay. They have responsibilities at home and we have business responsibilities that have to be fulfilled."

(What must the NWA do to turn it around): "We had 10,300 in the Omni last time and 12,378 paid in Baltimore. Entertainment Tonight didn't have camera coverage on hand to shoot these shows because there weren't any empty seats to shoot. One of the things that happens when you become rather than a Southeastern regional wrestling promotion, you have to go and force the issue in a lot of cities that you haven't been in. You have to go in and gain the confidence of those fans and you have to tell them you're going to be back and you have to go back and once they understand that you're going to be a player, then they'll respond. We also had to mend a lot of fences that had been torn down by our predecessors as far as no-shows on cards and a lot of things that we don't approve of and we are mending those fences and we think we are doing a good job of it. The bottom line is that we are a player and will continue to be. As it relates to the WW, we are walking the fine line between wrestling purists and the hype that Titan Sports has made pay off handsomely. We don't intend to do what they do but one of the things that we have to do to create a sales atmosphere for television time and for merchandising is we have to add the necessary ingredients that attract the younger viewer, the kids."

(Fans who call the show continually say the NWA must raid a major WWF star to give the public the perception that they can do it since the WWF has signed so many NWA superstars): "I never say never, but one of the things that wrestling fans should look at is that a great number of the WWF stars are recycled from World Class, NWA and other venues under different names with different promotion."

"I happen to believe there is a tremendous amount of talent out there that can be developed the same way. However, never say never. There are some great wrestlers in the WWF like Bret Hart, Curt Hennig, Tully & Arn, those people can do what we do. I would be remiss if I told fans we wouldn't be interested in any of them if they were available but our primary thrust is going to develop our own stars."

(On McMahon publicly claiming the NWA isn't competition on Entertainment Tonight and elsewhere): "Well I think the one thing I would cite which makes what he said complete hype is he came in on top of us in Nashville the night before our pay-per-view. The next time in Nashville in September, we booked ourselves in with plenty of room on either side of the WWF dates and he once again added a date the night before us once again. It's certainly a predatory move if I've ever seen one."

(On NWA coming to New York): "In late September, our show moves to 9:30 a.m. Saturday on WPIX which will give us an operating base. We let that incubate for some time to see what kind of response we get viewer-wise and we make the necessary adjustments. We're going into Buffalo, Troy and just got a larger clearance in Boston on WLDI and we've going to make the necessary moves to come into the area. We get lots of cards and letters from fans daily saying they'd like to see the NWA in the Northeast. I think they understand it has to be done in a logical manner. Our next PPV will be in Philadelphia and we're looking forward to that. It's accessible to the whole Northeast."

(Future booking): "The belt, to us, is what we're going to push. Ric Flair is a great, great champion. There's no doubt in my mind who would win a match between Hulk Hogan and Ric Flair. What we have to do is listen to our fans and see how they perceive us and not worry about where the WWF goes."

(Future of NWA): "To project five years is foolish. I've worked for a lot of corporations that did five-year projections and they always wound up having to re-do it every year. Five year projections are silly. Six months or a year downstream you're going to see us in a nationwide perspective but gaining in popularity and hopefully preserving the image of the NWA as we go. One year from now we won't be in parity with the WWF because they have a huge head start but I would advise Vince McMahon and the rest of them what Satchel Paige said, 'Don look back or something might be gaining on you. You might remind people that Ted Turner hasn't lost any wars yet.'"

SEPTEMBER 3, 1989

The WWF's SummerSlam '89 was held 8/28 before a sellout crowd of approximately 20,000 fans paying more than $350,000 at the Meadowlands in New Jersey and a national pay-per-view audience. It certainly won't go down as anywhere near the best PPV event of 1989, but it was far from the worst and easily Titan's best PPV effort of 1989.

Really, this was a show saved by the booking, which was excellent from top-to-bottom as every finish was interesting. There weren't any great matches, but there were a few good ones and just a few stinkers. On a scale of one-to-ten, I'd give the show about a 6 ½, you would give Baltimore and Nashville NWA shows a 10 and WrestleMania maybe a 2 ½. Unlike the WWF's two previous PPV events, the show never really dragged once it got going although it did start slow and before the fourth match started, it Looked like a WrestleMania all over again.

The biggest shock and biggest story coming out of the show is that Zeus (Tiny Lister on stilts) did the job in the main event to Hulk Hogan's legdrop, which throws out every theory of a Hogan vs. Zeus match for WrestleMania next year. Although I don't have this confirmed, I still think they will try a Hogan vs. Zeus singles match in conjunction with the PPV of "No Holds Barred" on 12/27, but they won't get anywhere near the interest in that show as they could have because with Zeus no longer being invincible, there is nothing to sell with the guy. As for Zeus' performance, in comparison to other guys given major pushes in their debuts on big shows, he was decent. Overall, I'd call his performance real bad, but not embarrassing in any way. It wasn't a disastrous performance such as Andre the Giant in WrestleMania III (although it wasn't Andre's debut, he was crippled so bad he was beyond pathetic) or Mr. T in WrestleMania II or Raja Lion in a Japanese mixed match. He did less than Leon Spinks did in his mixed match back in 1986, but since he didn't screw up the finish like Leon Spinks did, overall he didn't come off as bad. Virtually all the Soviets that have debuted in the Japanese rings were far better in their first match and a comparison with Don Nakaya Neilsen (the karate fighter who had a pro wrestling mixed match against Akira Maeda in 1986) isn't even worthy of comment.

Technically it was a strong show overall. The lighting and picture quality was first-rate. They did a nice open interspersing scenes of WWF wrestlers with scenes of people enjoying the summer. The technical glitch which will go down in history was after the third match, Gene Okerlund was about to interview Rick Rude when the SummerSlam sign came down just as the interview started and poor Mean Gene uttered the immortal words "Fuck it" right on the air. They went back to announcers Tony Schiavone and Jesse Ventura who tried to cover for it before going back to the interview. Schiavone and Ventura, who had never worked together before, had a few rough spots when they seemed to step on each other's toes, but overall they were quite good and Ventura's quick wit was evident throughout the show. Another technical glitch was during the Rockers & Tito Santana vs. Rougeaus & Rick Martel match (technically the best match on the card) that twice before the finish somebody backstage hit the Rougeaus music which gave away who was going to win.

1. The Brain Busters (Tully Blanchard & Arn Anderson) won a non-title tag team match from the Hart Foundation (Bret Hart & Jim Neidhart) in 16:23. One thing about the WWF PPV shows that was evident here is that they get everyone so psyched up for the main event (or in the case of this show, the main event plus Warrior vs. Rude) that there isn't a lot of heat for the prelim matches. NWA ppv shows have more heat up and down, although almost every longtime promoter will tell you it's the main event you should emphasize and which should pop the crowd because prelim matches don't sell tickets, they should just be good enough to keep interest and maybe a little more. As an opener, this was fine but considering the talents of the four, quite disappointing since they aren't opening match wrestlers. Started slow with no intensity or continual action but the spots themselves were fine. Very slow-paced and all four didn't seem to show the spark that three of the four are quite capable of. Finish saw Neidhart powerslam Hart onto Blanchard, but when Hart went for the pin, Anderson came off the top ropes onto him and Blanchard pinned Hart. **

2. Dusty Rhodes pinned Honky Tonk Man in 9:36. Worst match on the card and a candidate for worst match on a big show of the year. Almost all stalling and restholds. At least Honky could have played the guitar behind his back during his ring entrance. Finish wag good, however. After a ref bump, Jimmy Hart got the guitar and went to hit Rhodes, who moved and Honky got a solid hit and Rhodes pinned him after the elbow drop. Honky pretended he had amnesia and thought he was Elvis in a post-match interview -** (that's giving it one star for the finish because it was negative three at that point)

3. Mr. Perfect pinned Red Rooster in 3:21 with the perfectplex. For such a short match, it wasn't the slightest bit hot. For a big show match with two guys of such talent, it was a real letdown. ½ * (only for one nice high spot early;

finish came out of nowhere and was a dud)

4. Rougeaus & Rick Martel beat Rockers & Tito Santana in 14:58. Love that Rougeaus entrance music. Jesse had a nice faux pas here. When he was talking about the Rockers double teaming he said that 90 percent of the Rockers double team moves are illegal. What are the other 10 percent? Legal? Early on Martel refused to face Santana. The early part of the match saw them try to get heat on Santana (getting heat as in business terminology for continually working him over, not actually getting heat from the crowd because it took several minutes before the crowd started reacting to the match). At about ten minutes, they actually started getting heat on Tito and they worked on him until 13 minutes when Shawn Michaels came in for the hot tag and looked about as good as anyone on the card. After twice starting the heels music too soon, with all six in the ring and the advantage going back-and-forth, Martel pinned Jannetty after Jannetty had Jacques Rougeau pinned and I've got no idea who the legal guy was. Finish was excellent and because of Michaels, this was the best overall match. *** 1/4

5. Ultimate Warrior pinned Rick Rude in 16:02 to win the Intercontinental title. This was the best match I've ever seen Warrior in, thanks to the booking and Rude because Warrior was terrible. Jesse asked at one point "What asylum did they let him (Warrior) out of?" and someone here said, "The Sportatorium." Rude took one great bump after another including being press-slammed and dropped on the floor for the first six minutes as Warrior kept trying to catch his breath, but his breath must have been moving too fast because he never did catch it. Warrior got crotched on the top rope and it was his turn to sell. That part of the match was pretty bad. Both wrestlers and the ref collided at 9:35, whereupon they went into a 6 1/2 minute finish. Rude got up first but no ref to count the pin. Warrior made the superman comeback at 11 minutes and clotheslined and power slammed Rude into oblivion but no ref. Piledriver by Warrior. No ref. Warrior goes for the splash but Rude gets his knees up. Rude then does a few finishing moves but Warrior kicks out. Roddy Piper finally shows up at 14 minutes and Rude does a few more finishers and Warrior keeps kicking out. Rude and Piper then argue for an eternity while Warrior is layed out from a piledriver. As Rude is on the middle rope yelling at Piper, Piper bends over, pulls up his kilt and basically tells Rude to kiss his ass. Warrior gives him a back suplex from behind, a flying shoulderblock and pins him for the title after a big splash and a press-slam. *** 1/4

6. Demolition & King Jim Duggan beat Akeem & Big Bossman & Andre the Giant in 7:23. It took two minutes before they (Akeem and Duggan) even touched. Finish saw

Smash slam Akeem and Bossman but Andre came in with a few head-butts and Akeem had Smash pinned but Duggan hit Akeem with the 2x4 and put Smash on top for the pin. Not good, but watchable. *

7. Hercules beat Greg Valentine via DQ in 3:08. This whole thing was to set up Valentine vs. Ron Garvin. Garvin was the ring announcer and it was a cute idea. At least it was different. Nothing much to the match, but it was faster-paced (and shorter) than one would figure from these two snails. Valentine got the pin with the feet on the ropes and Garvin announced Hercules as the winner. Valentine protested, Garvin said he made a mistake, talked to the ref, then announced Hercules had won via DQ because he told the ref Valentine used the ropes. 1/2 * (for the angle)

8. Ted DiBiase beat Jimmy Snuka via count out in 6:27. No heat here and fans were waiting for the main event. Snuka and DiBiase screwed up the patented leapfrog spot. Some decent action but no heat. Finish saw Virgil shake the ropes with Snuka on top, Snuka chased Virgil, DiBiase attacked him from behind and posted him and won via count out. After the match Snuka attacked Virgil and splashed him off the top rope. * 1/2

9. Hulk Hogan & Brutus Beefcake beat Randy Savage & Zeus in 15:04. Zeus was in more than I had expected but he did nothing but bearhugs and chokes, which did get old by his third time in. Savage did everything he could to make it hot when he was involved and carried the match for all four. Hogan was in for the first seven minutes with the heels trading off on him. Heat incredible throughout. Sherri Martel was great at ringside while Liz didn't do much until the finish. Beefcake lost the advantage when Savage hit him with Sherri's loaded purse when he had the sleeper on Zeus. Beefcake was beaten on until Hogan made the hot tag, but his comeback was thwarted when Sherri pulled his leg and Savage got the advantage. Savage did the elbow off the top rope and Hogan popped right back up without even a count this time. Finally Hogan and Zeus squared off at 14 minutes and Zeus started selling (not taking bumps, but getting the groggy look). Sherri tried to interfere but Elizabeth tripped her (the camera missed the entire sequence which led to the finish) and the loaded purse went into the ring and Hogan hit Zeus with the purse, bodyslammed and legdropped him and 1-2-3. After the match Hogan gave Sherri an atomic kneedrop and Hogan and Beefcake held her down while Beefcake cut off her ponytail. They really made Sherri look hideous in her outfit and make-up. The match was watchable and Savage and Sherri were quite good, but Zeus was terrible and Hogan and Beefcake were decent at best. ** 1/2

First night phone poll results were 47-22 thumbs ups for those who watched the show on PPV but 8-0 thumbs down for those who called and saw the show live in the Meadowlands or overall 47-30 or roughly a 61 percent thumbs up plurality. Virtually all callers gave it either marginal ups or marginal downs so even though the poll results were mixed, most everyone who called was in the same ballpark. The few who had strong feelings one way or the other mainly were positive on PPV and negative from the house show. Results from the week of phone calls and letters in next week's issue plus lots of readers' comments on the show. buy rate expected to be four to five percent. Should have a better estimate next week.

USWA

This promotion is turning into gimmick city right about now trying to revive crowds that are suddenly floundering once again. They had a big run prior to and immediately after the name change since fans had been led to believe that with the "new promotion" that things would be changing and there was considerable disappointment with the crowd when after a week of "new management" (which was really the same old management but fans were led to believe things would change) that everything was the same and the crowds the past two weeks in Dallas have dropped drastically.

8/25 at the Dallas Sportatorium drew 450 as Billy Travis pinned The Dog of War (Buster Fowler), Jimmy Jack Funk pinned Sheik Scott Braddock, Gary Young & Al Perez Lost via DQ to Matt Borne & Travis (the heels won the match and were announced as the winners, but later in the card it was announced that upon reviewing the tapes and seeing the interference of Scandor Akbar in the decision that the faces were the winners), Chris Adams vs. P. Y. Chu Hi (Phil Hickerson) never got started as Gary Young and Tojo Yamamoto did a run—in (well, Tojo did a walk-in) and Borne and Superman Eric Embry made the save, in the upset of the year, Tarras Bulba pinned Kerry Von Erich clean in the middle of the ring using the iron claw of all things which has to be the ultimate humiliation for Kerry, Embry pinned Cactus Jack Manson in a loser leaves town match in 12 seconds (Embry's two main event matches the past two Friday shows have lasted a total of 21 seconds—I guess we should nickname Eric, the Texas Ultimate Warrior) and the finale was a Thunderdome cage match which wound up being four faces against five heels and the faces (Borne & Embry & Travis & Funk) prevailed over the heels (Braddock & Bulba & Perez & Young & Chu Hi). Originally in the line-up, Travis wasn't supposed to be in this match and the face team was to include Adams and Kerry, however Adams was "injured" in his match which never got started and Kerry just didn't appear after losing earlier in the card.

Ironically, with no television, Killer Tim Brooks'

promotion at the Longhorn Bar in Dallas on 8/22 drew 750 fans for a group which includes former World Class wrestlers Brian Adias, John Tatum, Scott Casey and Johnny Mantell. A green newcomer called Bull Man Downs (comes in with a bullhorn and a ring through his nose) is said to be a green version of a Bruiser Brody type act and has a lot of potential.

Correcting a mistake from last issue, Mark Lowrance didn't quit as announcer. Lowrance is doing work as a preacher and missed a few tapings, but was back over this past weekend.

The 9/1 card at the Sportatorium has Jerry Lawler defending the USWA title against Embry, Adams vs. Chu Hi, Kerry vs. Bulba, Jarrett & Borne defending the tag team titles against Perez & Young, Travis vs. Braddock and Funk vs. Dog of War.

Manson is returning home to let his broken wrist heal after dropping the loser leaves town match over the weekend. He had broken his wrist during a scaffold match a ways back but kept working with the wrist, which is still in a cast, and the wrist never recovered properly.

The 8/26 television show set some kind of a pro wrestling record as during the two hour show there was only 14 minutes of wrestling and just two matches.

Coming to the area is a Ninja, who is supposed to come in as a face and be Adams' tag team partner, Ron Starr as a heel, plus Mexican star EL Halcon, who held the old American title for this group nearly a decade ago, is working a few dates.

The TV show this week consisted of four attempts to put on a JJ Funk vs. Chu Hi match. They tried three times and all three times, Adams ran in and chased the heels away in a maniacal rage (they keep airing the incident from the week before when Tojo and Chu Hi attacked Chris' wife Toni and ripped open her blouse). Adams also ran the same two heels off in the middle of an interview. Finally, on the fourth time they tried to put the match on, it was Adams wearing JJ Funk's Lone Ranger mask and outfit and when the bell rang, Adams pulled the mask off and immediately every heel on the card ran in and every face ran in moments later. Frank Dusek uttered a memorable line as Adams was coming to the ring in the JJ Funk outfit, "That's not Chris Adams, uh, I mean, that's not Jimmy Jack Funk."

They are running a Labor Day card in Fort Worth headlined by Adams & Embry vs. Chu Hi & Young in a Triple Dome of Terror match (or "Tripple Dome" as they spell it here), Perez & Braddock & Akbar vs. Borne & Jarrett & Dusek in a two-ring six-man tag team match, Bulba vs. Kerry, Tojo Yamamoto vs. Percy Pringle in a mud wrestling match, Funk vs. The Bounty Hunter in a bull rope match and an eight woman Lingerie Battle Royal.

Well, at least this promotion isn't pushing the religious angle hard anymore.

9/10 in Mesquite, TX has Chu Hi & Young & Yamamoto vs. Adams & Embry & Pringle in a scaffold match (just think about how cruel it really is putting a senior citizen like Tojo on the scaffold, but you know what is even more cruel, having to actually watch that match), Jarrett & Borne defending against Perez & Ron Starr, Braddock vs. HaIcon and if Halcon wins he gets five minutes with Akbar, Bulba vs. Kerry in a Dog Collar match and Travis vs. Dog of War.

CWA

Ronnie Gossett's week as promoter is over so Eddie Marlin returned and they are doing another week of gimmick matches as revenge for the faces, who lost just about every match on last week's card. In the bout in which they showed highlights of on television, Black Bare beat Dustin Rhodes when ref Dirty White Boy clotheslined Rhodes, midget Little Road Warrior pinned Bill Dundee in what was billed ag a midget match when ref Master of Pain refused to count every time Dundee had the midget pinned, and finally MOP clotheslined Dundee and put the midget on top and gave a fast count, Master of Pain & Buddy Landel (who supposedly will be sticking around here for a while) & Black Bart beat Jerry Lawler & referees Frank Morrell & Jerry Calhoun when the heels basically destroyed and pinned Calhoun. Jerry Lawler did beat Doug Gilbert in the loser leaves town main event with Gossett under a mask as Mr. Mystery Referee. I believe that Gilbert will be staying as a masked wrestler, maybe a replacement for Jason or one of the other movie monster characters that are running around the circuit right now.

On TV taped 8/26, The Wildside (Chris Champion & Mark Starr) defended the tag title against Lawler & Jeff Jarrett ending with the heels disqualified for throwing a snake, although they tried to throw it on Lawler, Lawler ducked and it wound up on Gossett who did the fake heart attack routine. Also Texas Dirt (Dutch Mantell) pinned Spike Huber on a TV match. Dirt challenged MOP to a loser leaves town match and Marlin said he had a special referee to work the match and went backstage and came back wearing a mask as Mr. Special Referee.

The 8/28 card at the Mid South Coliseum has Dale Mann vs. Super Destroyer, referee Frank Morrell vs. manager Nate the Rat, a handicap match with Dundee teaming with midgets Little John & Little Road Warrior vs. MOP (there was no explanation made why Little Road Warrior worked against and beat Dundee last week and also teamed with MOP on TV last week and why he's working as a face this week), Jason & Freddy vs. managers Boss Winters & Harold Harris, referee Jerry Calhoun vs. Buddy Landel with Landel being blindfolded, Rhodes & Jarrett vs. Bart & White Boy in a street fight with Freddy as referee, MOP vs. Mantell in a loser leaves town match with Marlin under a mask as referee, a handicap tag match with the Rock & Roll Express (Ricky Morton & Robert Gibson) facing both Wildside & Blackbirds (King Parsons & Brickhouse Brown) but in this match Wildside & Blackbirds will have their legs tied together with their partner (like the three-legged races some of you may remember from elementary school) and the headline match is a Lumberjack strap match with Lawler vs. Gossett with all the Lumberjacks being faces.

8/26 in Jonesboro, AR drew 400 as Doug Gilbert pinned William "The Freezer" Thompson DUD, Jarrett pinned Starr *, Lawler pinned Champion **, Dirt & Marlin beat MOP & Gossett *, Wildside beat Jason & Freddy DUD and the finale was Jarrett & Lawler vs. Blackbirds (don't have the result).

WWC

8/12 in Caguas saw Sadistic Steve Strong (Steve DiSalvo) defending the Universal title against Abdullah the Butcher in the main event, Carlitos Colon vs. Kendo Nagasaki, Abbuda Dein & Rip Rogers defending the WWC World tag team titles against Invader #1 (Jose Gonzales) & TNT (Juan Rivera), Miguelito Perez vs. Kareem Muhammad and Super Medico (Jose Estrada) defending the WWC jr. heavyweight title against Chicky Starr.

8/19 in Carolina had Strong defending the Universal title against Junkyard Dog, Colon vs. Muhammad, Dein & Rogers defending the tag title against Invader & TNT, Perez vs. The original TNT (I've got no idea who this guy is but obviously they are building it to a TNT vs. TNT match), Medico defending against Starr, White Angel (Curtis Thompson) vs. Nagasaki and Victor Jovica vs. EL Exotico (prelim heel doing a gay routine).

Dein & Rogers must have won the WWC tag belts from Perez & Hurricane Castillo Jr. earlier this month. Will try and get a date on it next time. Castillo was missing from both line-ups so maybe an injury angle.

NEW JAPAN

The new series opened this past weekend and they will have a series-long tag team tournament to determine the No. 1 contenders for the IWGP World tag team titles held by Riki Choshu & Takayuki Iizuka with the title match taking place on 9/20 at the Osaka Castle Hall (capacity 14,000). The teams in the tournament will be Tatsumi Fujinami & Akira Nogami, Masa Saito & Shinya Hashimoto, Osamu Kido & Kengo Kimura, Super Strong Machine & George Takano, Shiro Koshinaka & Kuniaki Kobayashi, Salman Hashimikov & Victor Zangiev from the Soviet Union and Owen Hart & David Peterson (D. J. Peterson). My guess is it'll be Saito & Hashimoto since it sets up Choshu against his mentor and long time tag partner in Saito and also the rematch with Hashimoto since Hashimoto beat Choshu at the Egg Dome card. Also on the 9/20 card will be Big Van Vader defending the IWGP World title against Bam Bam

Bigelow and Naoki Sano defending the junior heavyweight title against Jushin Liger (Keiichi Yamada).

The final night of the series will be this group's debut card at the 17,000 seat Yokohama Arena (where the UWF drew the $1.4 million house last week) and the only match announced is Sano defending the junior heavyweight title against Hart although most expect the headline match will be Vader vs. Choshu for the IWGP title.

Billy Jack Haynes appeared on this tour replacing The Grappler, who decided to stay in Oregon.

Vader will be defending his IWGP title in Mexico and Europe before arriving back in Japan for the Osaka card.

The first Liger vs. Sano match was another of those must-see matches. A lot of spectacular high spots and dives that would almost be commonplace with these two, including one dive where Liger dove through the ropes and twisted going through and landed on Sano. But two highlight moves I've never seen before, even in Mexico. One move saw Sano on the floor lying prone and Liger got up on the top rope and jumped off, did a flip in mid-air and landed neck first onto Sano. I don't see how Liger didn't break his neck with the move since he was falling from 13 feet or so but actually Sano took the move solid because he seemed "out on his feet" for about two minutes after the move and collapsed when Liger threw him in the ring and tried to do a high spot with him. Later in the match Sano did a move which almost equalled it, with Liger on the floor, Sano went to the top rope and came off with a dropkick which meant Sano had to take an insane bump onto his back.

ALL JAPAN

The new series began 8/19 in Tokyo's Korakuen Hall before a sellout 2,350 fans as Doug Furnas & Dan Kroffat retained the Asian tag team titles beating The Foot Loose in 13:12 when Kroffat pinned Kawada, Jumbo Tsuruta & Kenta Kobashi downed Genichiro Tenryu & Yoshinari Ogawa in a match where Ogawa was given his first chance to appear on television, Yoshiaki Yatsu & Kabuki beat Terry Gordy & Todd Champion, Abdullah the Butcher pinned Johnny Ace in 2:39, Sh ji Takano pinned Shane Douglas, Giant Baba & Rusher Kimura & Akio Sato beat Masa Fuchi & Motoshi Okuma & Haruka Eigen (The Wild Bunch), Big John Tenta pinned Goro Tsurumi, The Jive Tones (Pez Whatley & Tiger Conway Jr.) beat Isamu Teranishi & Akira Taue and prelims.

8/20 in Kanagawa drew 2,200 as Tenryu & Foot Loose beat Tsuruta & Kabuki & Fuchi in 22 minutes, Gordy pinned Taue, Takano & Yatsu beat Dynamic Dudes, Baba & Sato & Kimura beat Jive Tones & Abdullah, Can-Am Express (Kroffat & Furnas) beat Kobashi & Tsuyoshi Kikuchi, Tenta pinned Champion and prelims.

Champion appeared on the tour as Terry Gordy's tag team partner as a last minute replacement for Danny Spivey who decided to stay in the NWA (as the NWA pressured him that they'd replace him in the Skyscrapers tag team if he left for Japan). For some reason, Spivey told Baba that he couldn't come because he was about to sign with the WWF and Baba told the press that, which is where the rumors of Spivey going to the WWF got started. Baba was furious about the thing because he hates guys who lie to him and it is said that Baba will never use Spivey again, although you can never say never.

There will be a special "Giant Baba Night" on 9/30 in Tokyo's Korakuen Hall to commemorate the beginning of the 30th year of Baba's pro career as Baba's debut match was September 30, 1960.

They've got a big show on 8/29 in Osaka headlined by Tsuruta & Yatsu defending the tag team titles against Tenryu & Kawada (this would be the perfect opportunity to "make" Kawada by letting him score a pinfall because fans are losing interest in Kawada as a tag team title challenger since Tsuruta always pins him with the back suplex even though he "puts up a great fight") plus The Can-Am Express face Dynamic Dudes and Gordy & Champion vs. Conway & Abdullah the Butcher.

OTHER JAPAN NEWS

After the 9/7 card in Nagano, the UWF will try a few unique promotions. They are splitting the crew in half and running three matches on 9/30 and three more matches on 10/1, I believe both in Tokyo to see if they can sellout two consecutive nights in the same building, and then they'll probably be dark since they are planning on putting together a card at the Tokyo Egg Dome (capacity 55,000) late this year and try and break the all-time gate record set by New Japan when it ran the Egg Dome card. Perhaps they'll headline that card with Akira Maeda vs. Don Nakaya Neilsen. Japan Women's Pro Wrestling has five cards booked from 8/26 to 8/30 in Korea. The big show is 8/27 in Seoul with Miss A defending the International title against Devil Masami.

Another match some of you will find interesting was the Joe Malenko vs. Dean Malenko match in Tokyo. It was a total workout style match with smooth holds and counters and unique combinations of chain moves. The audience was almost library-like silent during the match but popped pretty big as they turned it on at the end. Both the Malenkos are among the best technicians to be found anywhere.

OREGON

Real life news sometimes does get in the way of wrestling characters. Art Barr (Beetlejuice) was arrested on 8/11 on charges of first degree rape in an alleged incident which occurred on 7/16 in Pendleton, OR. A 19-year-old woman told the police that Barr forcibly raped her after the matches that night somewhere in the armory building. According to a newspaper article that appeared in the Oregonian earlier this week, when Barr rode home to Eugene after the matches in Pendleton he told friends he had "messed around" with the woman but they hadn't had intercourse. Barr's lawyer has told him not to comment on the incident anymore. Barr's arraignment will be 8/30 in Pendleton.

Beetlejuice is the most popular babyface with the kids in Oregon and after the news, the crowd for the 8/26 card in Portland plummeted to around 300 with very few kids in attendance. The main event on the card saw Nord the Barbarian face Bill Francis which wound up with everything from metal suitcases to chairs and even football helmets brought into the ring. These guys work real stiff and brutal with each other but neither sells a lick which makes the matches not-so-hot as you hit people with every object in the book and they never go down. This week's card has the two in another rematch in which both will wear football gear and they each be awarded points for knocking the other down. Also on 8/26, the new Southern Rockers (Rex King & Steve Doll) beat Scotty the Body & The Grappler to win the Northwest tag team titles. Al Madril jumped Beetlejuice during a match and cut off a lot of his hair. Maximum Overdrive (Jeff Warner from Minneapolis) debuted and pinned C.W. Bergstrom in one minute doing three moves.

The card this coming Saturday will also have a 12-man tournament for the vacated Northwest title. Billy Jack Haynes will no longer be working here, even after Japan. Lots of problems during his brief stay including no-shows in main events on road shows.

Roddy Piper is on the Saturday night cards almost every week but never shows his face in public or appears on television. Piper was on a radio show in Portland plugging a celebrity golf tournament, griping about the local newspaper which he said never gives him any publicity even though he's a local celebrity (he griped because they had a story about all the stars in the "Love Boat Movie" that is being filmed and Piper is one of them and his name wasn't mentioned) and heavily plugged the Portland matches each Saturday. When the WWF was brought up, Piper tried to quickly change the subject.

WWF was in Portland drawing a $47,000 house with Warrior vs. Andre doing their 10 second match and it didn't go over at all. Fans were upset here as well.

Pat Tanaka was in for two weeks as Matman but has left for Japan. He's the third Matman they've used.

8/16 in Gresham, OR saw Carl Styles beat Grappler in a Dog Collar match, Beetlejuice & midget Coconut Willie beat Al Madril & midget Cowboy Lang, Scott Peterson beat Jonathan Boyd via DQ and Steve Doll beat Scotty the Body.

8/19 in Portland saw Doll beat Madril, King & Willie beat Boyd & Lang in a snake box match, Scotty beat Beetl juice via count out, Francis beat Nord via DQ and Styles beat Grappler in a Dog Collar match.

OTHER STUFF

The AWA held TV tapings on 8/26 in Rochester, MN which was supposed to be the debut of the new team concept, although I didn't hear of any of the team matches taking place. Only taping results I got were Paul Diamond going to a double disqualification with Col. De Beers, Wendi Richter beat Judy Martin, debuts of new wrestlers Kokina Maximus (Kokina the Wild Samoan from San Francisco), The Russian Brute (George Petrosky) who teamed with Derrick Dukes & Tommy Jammer and turned on them against Destruction Crew (Wayne Bloom & Mike Enos) & Johnny Valiant causing Dukes to get pinned while the finale with two refs saw Larry Zbyszko keep his AWA title beating Sgt. Slaughter via DQ with two refs when ref Tom Burton saw Slaughter use a foreign object that Zbyszko originally pulled out.

CWF taped television on 8/26 in Dothan, AL with the highlight being Jimmy Golden & Brian Lee winning the CWF tag team titles from Steve Armstrong & Tracy Smothers (The Southern Boys). Robert Fuller was doing the color commentary during the match when Downtown Bruno came down on crutches and Fuller said that Bruno had blown out his knee in an NFL camp (funny since Bruno must weigh 125 pounds at most). Anyway, Bruno tried to interfere and got clobbered and the crutches went flying but Fuller came in and hit Armstrong with the crutches and he was pinned. Also at the taping, Dennis Condrey retained the CWF title going to a double disqualification with Wendell Cooley; a cage match saw The Beauty (Terrence Garvin) & The Lady Beast (have no idea who she is) face Adrian & Linda Street with Todd Morton as the gatekeeper. The Lady Beast threw powder in Linda's eyes but Morton used one of his bandanas to wipe the powder off. Finally as the Streets were on the verge of winning, the male Beast (Mark Goleen) showed up and hit Morton with a bolt cutter and unlocked the cage and ran in and Beauty & Goleen held Linda's arm while the female Beast hit it with bolt-cutters to "break it." Also on the card, Jerry Stubbs & Southern Boys beat The Stud Stable (Fuller & Golden & Lee) in a cage match. On the TV that aired this past weekend, Condrey gave Danny Davis two DDT's on the table and Davis, like Tom Prichard the week before, did a heavy juice and stretcher job. It is said that Prichard will return in November to feud with Condrey and will do a tour of Japan and spend time at home in Texas during the interim.

The ICW will have a two hour special on Labor Day from 9 to 11 p.m. on the Sports Channel in New York.

Negotiations are underway to put Stampede Wrestling on ESPN and also to put it on television in the Minneapolis market.

Stampede Wrestling is closing down all operations for a few weeks, until Owen Hart returns from Japan.

Florida Championship Wrestling also looks in danger,

although they did have a new television show this past weekend, taped on 8/22 where the Nasty Boys returned and won the Florida tag team titles from The Playboys (Jimmy Backlund & Brett Sawyer). This group is no longer running shows in Orlando and Tampa.

Several of the CWA and USWA wrestlers are scheduled to appear in late September on a show in Delaware.

Eddie Sharkey's PWA in Minnesota drew a sellout 400 to George's Bar in Minneapolis on 8/16 as Ricky Rice turned heel. The main event saw Kenny Jay team with long-time photographer and referee Bruce Kreitzmann to beat Brett Derringer & The Creeper.

8/20 in Faribault drew 150 as Charlie Norris beat Rice via DQ and Nord the Barbarian & Jeff Warner (now in Oregon) beat The Wildman & Red Tyler.

8/22 in Shakopee, MN drew 500 as Tom Zenk double disqualification with Doug Somers as they brawled into the kitchen of the concession stand and Norris beat Rice via count out. Rice is billed as PWA champion as they say he won the title in a match in Edmonton, Canada from Larry Cameron.

Jim Shyman is in the process of putting together a movie called "Pro Wrestling Camp."

Several Mexican wrestlers including Arias Romero, Blue Demon Jr and Super Muneco appeared for an independent television taping on 8/27 in San Bernardino, CA.

An independent show headlined by Max Pain drew 150 on 8/17 in Salt Lake City. Pain was scheduled to wrestle Bam Bam Bigelow and Bigelow was there in the building signing autographs but never wrestled. The entire card lasted only 45 minutes.

Baseball umpire and wrestling fan Ken Kaiser has an annual celebrity dinner on Nov. 16 in Rochester, NY which includes Larry King, George Brett, Wade Boggs, Jose Canseco, Roger Clemens, Don Mattingly, Mark McGwire, Kirby Puckett, Kent Hrbek, Tim Raines and Frank Viola of baseball fame along with wrestlers Bobby Heenan, John Studd, Sting, Road Warrior Hawk and Gorilla Monsoon.

NWA

Lots of news from the television front. The two-hour TBS show which aired on 8/26 was one of the best in a long-time, featuring the change of Robin Green into the new Robin Green. The TV skit with Jim Ross and Rick Steiner where the change was made was one of the best TV wrestling skits I ever seen. Both Steiner and Ross were incredible playing their roles, and the interview later in the show where the new Robin Green was out with the Steiners and Missy Hyatt was another classic due to the antics of Rick. By the way, one reader wrote in asking if the name Robin Green is a spoof on Mike Tyson s problems (Robin Givens and Mitch Green) and I'm almost certain that is where the name came from. At least I'm certain that Robin

Green's similarity to Robin Givens is not a coincidence—I mean the name similarity.

The announcing with Jim Cornette and Jim Ross on that show was tremendous as well.

Last week I mentioned that they had lost the Sting vs. Dick Slater match and post-match angle, and lo and behold, it showed up on television. While this hasn't been confirmed for me yet, what I believe to be the case is that they lost the actual footage that was taped, but did have the actual film from different cameras and they re-edited the original footage back piece-by-piece and put on the original soundtrack (if you notice, the sound was about a half-second off the match the whole way but you had to listen close to notice any problems) and the match and angle aired. The commentary kept me interested the whole way and it was decent for television but Slater didn't look like anything special.

Tommy Edwards, the long-time director of the TBS wrestling shows, was the guy who was blamed for the snafu on the TBS Saturday show on 8/19 which was a replay of the 7/28 show. Edwards was suspended without pay and will no longer work in wrestling, but may be re-assigned elsewhere in the TBS empire.

They are already plugging the 9/12 Clash of the Champions hard. Ironically, the show will go head-to-head in most of the country with a two-hour syndicated debut of the Roller Games special which is going to get a lot of mainstream media hype as it approaches and one would think there would be a lot of crossover interest between the Roller Games debut and a major TV pro wrestling special.

I'm told TBS got hundreds of phone calls about the tape mishap last week. TBS did realize almost immediately that the wrong tape was airing and they scrambled everywhere to find the right tape and eventually did find the right tape, but not until about 45 minutes after the show was over.

8/24 in Raleigh drew 5,000 as Al Greene & Bill Irwin beat The Ding Dongs, Ron Simmons pinned Brad Anderson, Brian Pillman pinned Norman the Maniac, Rick & Scott Steiner beat New Zealand Militia, Steve Williams beat Great Muta via DQ (Sting no-showed), Lex Luger pinned Tommy Rich, Ric Flair pinned Terry Funk (best match on card, but only three stars) and Road Warriors beat Samoan Swat Team in a cage match which only went six minutes.

Ironically, the TV ratings for the Saturday show which was the rerun was a 2.0, which is better than some of the first-run shows they did and the audience actually grew until the end. The Power Hour on 8/18 drew a 1.6 (Braves game that preceded it did a 1.4) while the 8/20 Main Event show (Freebirds vs. Midnight for the titles) drew a 2.5.

The 10/28 PPV card from Philadelphia will be bucking at least two nationally televised college football games head-to-head.

This isn't a joke. On Friday I got a phone call from "The

Star" (one of the newsstand tabloids like the Enquirer) wondering if I could corroborate a story they had about Jane Fonda dating a pro wrestler, so you tabloid fans will probably see something like that around. I didn't answer the call, by the way.

How is this for organization? The NWA will be getting a decent time slot on WPIX in New York starting on Sept. 30. According to the NWA, the show will air at 9:30 a.m. on Saturday (in which case the last half hour will be head-to-head with the first half-hour of Titan's show on Fox), according to WPIX the show will air at 11 a.m.

8/25 in Baltimore drew 4,610 fans and $60,204 as Ranger Ross pinned Greene, Militia beat Ding Dongs, Simmons pinned Anderson, Pillman pinned Norman, Bobby Eaton went to a double count out against Danny Spivey, Steiners beat Freebirds via DQ, Sting beat Muta via DQ, Luger pinned Rich, Warriors beat SST in a cage match and Flair beat Funk in an old-style Texas death match when Funk was unable to answer the bell for the sixth fall after submitting to the figure four leg lock in the fifth fall.

Eddie Gilbert will be on the road part-time as a wrestler and in the office as a booking assistant most of the time since Ric Flair has to be on the road nightly.

As far as newcomers go, I haven't heard a peep about Benjamin Franklin Peacock (Botswana Beast as a face) so don't expect he's in the cards, Kevin Kelly is said to be up in the air, Nord the Barbarian is said to be coming in a month or two and Tom Zenk will start on the Clash of Champions. The Last word I've heard is Zenk will be called "The Z Man," but won't be wearing a mask, although I get conflicting stories on whether he'll be masked or not each day.

8/26 in Philadelphia drew 4,500 ($60,000ish) as Tommy Rich pinned Phil Apollo, Irwin & Randy Rose beat The Ding Dongs, Ross pinned Greene, Pillman pinned Norman, Skyscrapers beat Midnight Express (real good match), Freebirds beat Steiners via DQ, Sting beat Muta via DQ, Luger pinned Williams (Williams hurt his ribs during the match and had to miss the next night in New Haven), Flair pinned Funk and Warriors beat SST in a cage match.

8/27 in New Haven drew a $36,000 house (about 3,000) as Rose pinned Greene * ¼ *, Norman pinned Apollo ¼ *, Irwin pinned Ross DUD, Skyscrapers beat Midnight *** ½, Spivey pinned Eaton after a power bomb—Midnights sold great to make it the best match on the card), Pillman pinned Norman * , Sting beat Muta via DQ in 3:51 *, Steiner s beat Freebirds via DQ when Garvin hit Scott with the title belt *¾ , Luger pinned Rich *, Flair pinned Funk in 10:00 *** ½ and Warriors beat SST in a cage match *¾. By all accounts this was not a good card overall. Longtime wrestling photographer and longtime friend of ours Frank Amato refereed the prelim matches in jeans and a POLO shirt as a lot of the guys arrived late, including referees.

Chris Cruise (Brian Doble), who has prior experience with CNN and also with a military news service got a try-out as an announcer at the 8/14 taping in Charleston, WV and is said to have a good chance of getting the slot. He's got a good voice and he may be on the air by October once they train him the way they want him to announce.

TV taping on 8/22 in Greenville, SC drew a near sellout 5,000 fans.

They've already had three Steiners vs. Freebirds matches on television the past three weeks and have another scheduled for the Clash, and are also running the match at most of the house shows.

The Power Hour from Cleveland was a weak show since the audience looked comatosed during the three matches that aired and were loudly chanting "boring" during the Tommy Rich vs. Cuban Assassin (David Sierra) match. I felt sorry for Sierra because he was trying everything to get people interested and they just weren't buying anything. Those matches were taped very late on a marathon TV taping card.

8/14 in Charleston, WV at the TV taping saw the State patrol (Dale Veasy & Dwayne Bruce - billed as James Earl Wright & Buddy Lee Parker) beat the unmasked Ding Dongs (Richard Sartain & Greg Evans), Sting pinned Ron Simmons (good match aired on Power Hour previous weekend, Militia beat Scott Hall & Ross, Funk & Muta beat Evans & Sartain, Rotunda pinned Hall, Luger pinned Ross, Freebirds beat Midnight Express in a tag title match when Garvin pinned Lane after Lane "re-injured" his bad hand (Legit dislocated fingers suffered in the War Games in Atlanta), Sting beat Muta via DQ, Luger pinned Rich, Flair pinned Cuban Assassin and Flair pinned Funk.

8/23 in Bluefield, WV drew a sellout 2,000 as Dong pinned Greene, Rich pinned Simmons, Pillman pinned Norman, Ding beat Irwin via DQ, Steiners beat Militia, Freebirds beat Midnight Express, Sting beat Muta via DQ, Warriors beat SST in a cage and Flair pinned Funk.

WWF

The video of SummerSlam should be at your video store on 9/19.

Actually, the folks at Titan Sports were happy about the press coverage the Andre the Giant incident received over the past week. The thing made just about every newspaper around and got good play in the sports section because of the police quotes about Andre's size and how they were glad he didn't put up a fight.

8/26 at the Palace in Auburn Hills drew 6,800 and $82,000 as Tim Horner pinned Boreus Zhukov, Hart Foundation drew with Greg Valentine & Dino Bravo, Ultimate Warrior pinned Andre the Giant in 17 seconds, Brutus Beefcake beat Rick Rude via count out, Widow Maker (Barry Windham) beat Paul Roma with the claw, Mr. Perfect (Curt Hennig) pinned Hercules and Demolition beat Brain Busters (Tully Blanchard & Arn Anderson) via DQ.

Last word I've got on WrestleMania is that despite what everyone is saying, it is probable that the event will be in Toronto but the official decision has not been made and the officials at the Los Angeles Memorial Coliseum are expecting it will be held there as well. The card is slated for April 1, 1990 and who even has a clue now as to what will be on top.

Titan has dropped all Boston Gardens house shows from the New England Sports Network, This leaves only MSG cable in New York as showing house show matches. NWA could pick up some exposure and some money by trying to take the WWF spots on these cable stations, particularly in Philadelphia which they already run monthly and which Prism used to pay Titan almost as much money simply for the rights to broadcast the cards as the NWA is doing as a total gate in some months in Philadelphia.

Crowds overall have been a little down over the last week due to Summer Slam, although over the weekend Hulk Hogan's two matches with Randy Savage drew 6,000 in Richmond, VA and nearly 10,000 in Providence, RI, however his matches in smaller markets in mid-sized buildings in Binghamton and Glens Falls, NY drew respectably but not the expected sellouts.

USA Network didn't run a prime Time Wrestling show on Monday so as not to buck Summer Slam, unlike TBS, which has run its regularly scheduled TV shows head-to-head with its Sunday PPV shows.

I've received several newspaper clippings around the country decrying the Andre-Warrior matches as they've gone from city to city with the quickies. Rare real bad press for Titan.

8/20 in Lincoln, NE drew 3,712 as Tim Horner pinned Barry Horowitz, Perfect pinned Hillbilly Jim, Warrior pinned Andre in 28 seconds, Demolition beat Blanchard & Anderson via DQ, Rick Martel drew Tito Santana in 18 minutes, Rude pinned Beefcake.

8/18 in Wheeling, WV drew a sellout 7,800 as Widow Maker pinned Roma, Valentine drew Hart in 18:30 of a 20 minute time Limit, Haku pinned Hercules, Savage beat Hogan via count out (best match on card), Dino Bravo pinned Jim Neidhart, Jim Duggan pinned Akeem and Rockers beat Rougeaus.

8/21 in Binghamton, NY drew 5,400 as Widow Maker pinned Roma *** ¼, Hart Foundation beat Valentine & Bravo via DQ * ½, Haku pinned Hercules DUD, Hogan pinned Savage ***, Duggan pinned Akeem negative several stars and Rockers pinned Rougeaus *¾.

The two fans who were kicked out of the arena at the Oakland Coliseum Arena WWF taping on 8/8 for holding up the NWA banner are contemplating suing the WWF and the Coliseum for being kicked out without unruly behavior and for what they were kicked out for apparently constitutes some sort of a violation of freedom of expression.

8/12 in Anchorage, AK drew 7,957 and $114,000 as Mark Young pinned Horowitz *¾, Bret Hart drew Perfect **¾, Warrior pinned Andre in 10 seconds -*** (crowd reacted very negatively to this result and nobody for the rest of the card could get any heat as the fans felt ripped off and were in a sour mood the rest of the way), Bravo beat Hercules via DQ ¼ *, Bad News Brown pinned Horner ½ *, Rockers beat Rougeaus **¾, Jimmy Snuka pinned Honky Tonk Man ½ *.

The Village Voice in the 'Jockbeat' section ran a short on why Vince McMahon wound up doing the Entertainment Tonight segment even though he would have to acknowledge that there was opposition in the form of the NWA on the segment.

The shows with Dusty Rhodes vs . Big Bossman as the headline match are stiffIng at the box office.

THE READERS' PAGE

TITAN TAPING

I also went to the Titan taping last week in Oakland. I wasn't surprised that I was disappointed with most everything. The overall efficiency of the taping and Howard Finkel's delivery as ring announcer is flawless. These guys are pros at putting out a product and getting it right on the first try.

The highlight of the show was the Oakland 2, who I salute. They are the Dave Dravecky's of wrestling in a heroic way.

I would have never dreamed of paying for this card. I grew up on Los Angeles Olympic Auditorium and KCOP tapings, which I often attended with John Arezzi. I believe I experienced what everyone did from a good regional promotion. Anticipation that the show wasn't organized. That anything could happen. Any angle could happen at any time out of the blue that we'd never dreamed possible.

WWF tapings do away with all that. The potential in matches with Barry Windham vs. Terry Taylor and Curt Hennig vs. Tito Santana wasn't lived up to. The matches were boring exercises and it didn't even seem that anyone, even the workers, were interested. The show was so organized that the next guys were in the ring before the decision of the previous match was even announced and none of it was fun. You hit the nail on the head. As long as a guy had music, he got as loud a reaction as anyone on the card, even if the people didn't know who he was.

Anyone who remembers the Olympic Auditorium match between Ernie Ladd and Victor Rivera in 1972 will know what I mean about missing the fun of the unexpected that will never happen with Titan's flawlessly timed predictable angles. A masked man, fully clothed, appeared at ringside and distracted Ladd, who was pushed as an unstoppable monster heel, and Ladd was pinned and lost the Americas title. The masked man got Ladd to sign for a match before anyone figured out it was John Tolos, who had left the area several months earlier. I was tight with several in the promotion and they didn't even let on that Tolos figured in the angle. It was fun then and Titan just can't spark that in their calculated PPV angles.

Dr. Mike Lano
Alameda, California

OAKLAND 2

I would like to respond to the "Oakland 2." While I do believe they should not have been ejected from the arena, their response in the 8/21 issue to the event was unfair and reactionary.

First of all, the comparison of Hulk Hogan to I'Der Fuhrer" and Ultimate Warrior to the "Wunderman" is totally ludicrous. This is their gimmick and it makes them and the promotion money. I suppose Ted Turner chopped down a cherry tree and Ric Flair eats apple pie and drives a Chevrolet and Sting freed the slaves if you really believe your Nazi symbolism.

Secondly, you claim that at NWA cards you can taunt wrestlers unmercifully. Yes, as a matter of fact you can do that at any wrestling card, as long as no physical interaction occurs. However, you weren't taunting any wrestler, you were holding up a banner trying to be cute and smart and inside. You should have thought about using your responsibility as smart fans instead of putting on a spectacle.

Finally, you mention that wrestlers have traditionally been skilled performers. Yes, but if you weren't two nostalgic old men reminiscing about Lou Thesz, Karl Gotch, etc. you would realize what wrestling is and why it is the way it is. Six-to-eight year olds don't read the Wrestling Observer and to them, Hulk Hogan is a great role model. They have no conception of egomania or for that matter capitalism. Vince McMahon is a businessman, a self-proclaimed P.T. Barnum. You fail to face reality and that reality is that in 1989, pro wrestling is a business, not a sport. As Herbert Spencer, the social Darwinist would say, "business is a survival of the fittest." That is why you were removed from the stands.

I'm not condoning Vince McMahon's near-monopoly of his promotional techniques, but the Oakland 2 over-reacted, another common problem in America. I suggest these two carry their NWA banners to NWA shows, if indeed the NWA ever comes to the West Coast again.

Eric Krol
Orland Hills, Illinois

Dave Meltzer: The Dallas-based USWA promotion has already shown us that you can't taunt wrestlers unmercifully if you taunt the wrong wrestlers as they've kicked fans out for taunting the faces at television tapings. As far as the banner goes, a banner that reads "NWA #1" is hardly

"smart" or "inside." I was at a Chicago Bears game over the weekend and there were several very anti-Bears banners in the stands because of the Jim McMahon trade and this event was televised and nobody was kicking them out of the building or confiscating the banners. If the banners had read, "USFL #1, I think I'm safe in saying no banners would have been confiscated nor fans kicked out, either, yet the NFL is every bit as much a business as pro wrestling, and one with far more money at stake

Hats off to the Oakland 2. I hope that some kind of legal action will be taken against Titan for this. It's obvious that they are taking lessons from World Class, where if you boo the booker, you are taking a major risk.

It is getting very difficult for me to respect anyone involved with Titan Sports, from the wrestlers to the announcers right down to the fans. Vince McMahon obviously thinks the Constitution is something you line a bird cage with.

Paul Hanlin
Philadelphia, Pennsylvania

OTHER STUFF

The independent show here on 8/17 was advertised to start at 7:30. The first match didn't go on until 8:35 and the whole farce was over at 9:20. You're quick to bitch when McMahon has a 20 minute time limit match that only goes 18 minutes. What about an entire card that is over in 45 minutes? I'm forever more going to be torn between disgust and hilarity when someone writes to the Observer that McMahon doesn't give you your money's worth. I've never been to a WWF card that started 65 minutes late, consisted of three matches and was over in 45 minutes.

Jack Thompson
Salt Lake City, Utah

When Gordon Solie mentions the WWF on his wrestling news updates, he succeeded in one thing, making the NWA seem to be the equal of the WWF. We hear a lot about what the public perceives wrestling to be and if the NWA can make the casual fan believe they're the WWF's equal, they have a chance of being successful. That thought comes to mind after viewing the Entertainment Tonight feature. Did they mention the AWA or any other promotion? No. Anyone watching with only a slight interest in wrestling would perceive that the NWA and WWF were wrestling, so it helped give the NWA parity.

Greg Hatfield
Cincinnati, Ohio

I've been subscribing to the Observer since February, 1987 and I just want to extend a heartfelt thank you for the wonderful job you are doing.

I've reached the point now where I can't watch pro

wrestling without the Observer. In fact, I can't even imagine how I ever watched it in the first place without it. It would be like watching television without TV Guide or doing Carpenter work without nails or shooting pool without a cue. Your insights and penchant for telling what goes on in the wrestling world is uncanny as compared to the distortions the promotions try to present. The Observer has often been referred to as the New York Times of wrestling and I agree with this statement completely.

For Pro Wrestling Illustrated to select you as one of the 25 most influential people in wrestling is a truly unique honor and says much about the Observer.

Vince DiPaLma
Copiague, New York

I try to support the NWA in everything they do, but they make it very difficult with the mistakes they make like missing the 8/19 edition of World Championship Wrestling. The NWA has cut down on its mistakes from six months ago, but they still have a ways to go. I will say that the pay-per-view card from Baltimore was better than anything Titan could ever put on, but I truly believe the NWA has to steak a nationally-known Titan star in order to compete with Titan. There are only about a half dozen Titan wrestlers who could even cut it in the NWA right now. What is the NWA afraid of? It seems they are afraid to make the first move. Ted Turner wasn't afraid to sign big-name talent for the Atlanta Braves, who are still in the cellar. Is Turner satisfied with the NWA in the cellar? The NWA has great talent to build upon, but great talent alone won't turn a promotion around. There are a lot of people who think Warrior, Beefcake, Duggan, etc. are fantastic wrestlers who could beat anyone in the NWA. While none of them are great workers, the casual fans do see all of them as good wrestlers and great showmen who entertain with their gimmicks.

Roddy Piper has been getting better but it's hard to outwit Bobby Heenan, as he has a comeback for everything Piper says and makes Piper Look Like a fool.

Chris Poulos
Lansdowne, Pennsylvania

AWARDS FAVORITES

Yes, it's that time of the year again. Summer is just about ready to fly the coop and we've got a yearbook right around the corner. One of the main parts of every Observer yearbook is the annual awards, which have become almost an institution here. Each year we list awards in a few dozen categories, chosen by readership ballots in the month of December. And each week from now until December we'll be running down and reviewing the different categories that we'll be voting on. So it's time to get started.

WRESTLER OF THE YEAR: This category is supposed to be based both on workrate within the ring and impact upon the profession. I've got little doubt who will win the voting this year, since Ric Flair in the last nine years has finished first six times and second the other three, and he's had better matches and a greater variety of matches, plus has had more of an impact on the business this year than he has in other years. That's not to say there aren't any other deserving candidates, as there actually are several. Akira Maeda, last year's winner, is in my book even more deserving this year than last. For one thing, after 15 months of almost constant sellouts and phenomenal gates, whatever skeptics said about the UWF and the style being a flash-in-the-pan has been silenced. Last year, my main criticism of picking Maeda for the honor, which he still won handily, was that he hadn't wrestled for the entire year (UWF started up in May, Maeda had been fired by New Japan the previous November), which is no longer valid. It can't be overlooked that of the eight largest gates in the history of professional wrestling, the UWF has had three of them in the first eight months of the year and without any television exposure. In a business that is so clearly tied to television, the significance of that can't be stressed enough. Then there is Hulk Hogan. He is still clearly the man in pro wrestling when it comes to popularity and drawing power. If anything, his popularity has risen because of the hype coming off the movie, and he has, with the movie, further established himself as a cross-over celebrity. His drawing power can't be overlooked, although when a comparison with workrate is made with either Flair or Maeda, well no comparison can even be considered. Some would say that overall the best promotion this year is All Japan when everything is considered, and the key player on the All Japan roster is Genichiro Tenryu, who is probably the most popular wrestler in Japan right now and many would say the best worker as well. Another wrestler who must be considered is Randy Savage, who clearly carried Hogan through a summer's worth of matches and saved whatever was saved of the sorry skit that set up WrestleMania. Savage's interviews and heel persona was the best thing in wrestling in the early months of the year. While Savage doesn't have to take a back seat to anyone when it comes to ability, in truth, for night-after-night performance level, Savage is not in the top echelon. An awful lot of those who have discussed this category with me have also brought up the name Ricky Steamboat. Just for work alone, he accomplished a lot, and to be in what will for a long time be regarded as the best series of matches in recent memory, three of which were on national specials, makes him one of the key performers of the year.

BEST BRAWLER: The Bruiser Brody Award, listed in the name of the wrestler who captured the award in seven of the previous nine years. With Brody out of the scene, a lot of interest in this category has subsided. You really can't consider anyone in the WWF, because they simply don't have wild brawls there. Both Ric Flair, who is generally considered as a technician, and Terry Funk have had the best brawls I've seen in their recent matches. Funk and Sting also had first-rate brawls, which makes things look good here for Mr. Funk, but again he hasn't wrestled the entire year. The normal candidates, the guys like Stan Hansen, Dick Murdoch, Jerry Lawler and Terry Gordy haven't had the kind of memorable matches of years past. For sheer stiffness in his work, Tenryu has to be in here. Usually the smaller circuits, particularly in the South, bring out the best in the brawling, but this year the small promotions haven't had the quality of talent to put on those kind of matches as in years past. A very weak category this time out.

BIGGEST SHOCK OF THE YEAR: We haven't had anything like the deaths of major stars as in the past. Maybe the initial success of the Russians in New Japan, and in fact just the actual appearance of the Russians in the first place may be as good a qualifier as there is, I can't say the end result of the Jose Gonzales trial in Puerto Rico was any kind of surprise, even though there was considerable outrage with the verdict.

BEST BOOKER: One can go with success and talk about Vince McMahon and Pat Patterson In the WWF. The stuff is well planned out in advance and the story lines usually at least make sense within their context. Equally, it's hard to ignore Giant Baba, the normally conservative and staid head of All Japan, who made several changes this year in his normal philosophy by pushing so many "dream matches" on television and make creative tag teams like Tenryu & Road Warriors or the Tsuruta vs. Tenryu angle in Osaka which led to the record gate for their Tokyo rematch. For a promotion which earlier this year was clearly No. 3 in the country to make a comeback to the point where it can be debated that it is No. 1 once again is a significant accomplishment, especially since the increase in popularity wag achieved without adding any major "names" (Dan Kroffat & Doug Furnas hardly qualify as international superstars even if both have done some great work in Japan). Len Denton has been talked about in Oregon and he's revitalized a territory and done good television. Still, it's really hard to compare his product with the major promotions but his job of booking has been deservedly well-praised. One more name that I'll mention, which will surprise people, is Eric Embry. There is much to find distasteful about the former World Class promotion, but they did at least accomplish one thing this year, that is getting a solid core of fans to attend the Dallas matches weekly and the fans were as into the action and personalities as fans of any other promotion. For a promotion with weak personalities, the booker deserves credit because it was Embry's story lines, however

inconsistent and stupid they often were, that kept the ship afloat because they did minor miracles for a group which relied on the likes of Gary Young and Phil Hickerson as the top heels and revolved all the heat on a worn-out Scandor Akbar. Not to mention that the entire promotion revolved around the unlikely babyface star of Eric Embry, only a slightly better than average worker, not good-looking, awful physique and barely above average on interviews. If I were to pick one, it would be Baba based on his turning around a promotion which seemed to be stagnant through usage of smaller wrestlers (Malenkos, Kroffat, Foot Loose) which history would tell you that Baba wouldn't have pushed, not to mention his following the lead of the fans with Momotamania and with his own sudden increase in popularity with his tag team with Rusher Kimura as mid-card comedy. And those main events with Tsuruta and Tenryu against one another with various partners, in a feud that started years back, stayed interesting through the booking. Can't pick McMahon and Patterson any lower than second here, and maybe Denton next only because on principle the paranoia and pettiness of Embry's regime when it regarded fans who heckled him and the overreaction is something that has to be considered. The NWA booking committee booked some great live cards and some great television angles, and did entertaining television at times, but overall went in too many directions and wasn't focused enough because of too many people involved in the decision-making process and too many different ideas about which direction to go in. But I'm convinced booking the NWA is the hardest booking job in wrestling because of all the television shows and, in comparison with Titan, a smaller talent pool to draw from, and the ridiculous pressure of trying to put together ten (count 'em, ten) major shows between Clashes and PPV's during a calendar year.

SEPTEMBER 11, 1989

The NWA drew its largest crowd of the year for the Labor Day weekend card on Sunday night at the Omni in Atlanta. The crowd, estimated at a near sellout 15,500, was enhanced by a 'kids under-12 when accompanied by an adult would be admitted free' gimmick, so the gate was hardly record setting. But at this point, a crowd of that size, even if it was 20 to 25 percent papered (or more), has to be considered something of a positive sign.

This past weekend was also the start of NWA's running double shots on weekend dates. I'm not sure if this is an experiment for the month of September or something that will be taking place long term. For example, this coming weekend will have Memphis and Miami on Friday, Landover, MD (Capital Centre) and Palmetto, FL on Saturday and Greensboro and Fort Pierce on Sunday. Basically these Florida cards will be "B" shows. However, the following weekend they are running basically even split shows with St. Louis and Corpus Christi on Friday, Kansas City and Lubbock on Saturday and El Paso and Chicago on Sunday. While the NWA definitely has enough bodies to run two full cards per night, it is questionable whether they have enough wrestlers capable of headlining (when I say capable, I mean from a drawing card capacity, not capable of wrestling a headline calibre match) to pull this off. Because the NWA has so many wrestlers in its stable, and adding new names over the next few weeks, they have too many guys to just run one city per night and give everyone regular work. At the same time, they still haven't been able to consistently draw even with full cards with "all the stars," so it is unlikely they'll be able to pop any crowds right now with only half the big names on any given major city show.

SUMMERSLAM '89

Thumbs Up: 145 (55.3 percent)
Thumbs Down: 98 (37.4 percent)
In between: 19 (7.3 percent)

Results are from telephone responses and mail responses over the past week to the WWF's PPV card on 8/28. It's the best response to a Titan PPV since the Survivors Series last Thanksgiving, which got a better than 90 percent positive rating and was the first Titan PPV of the year to get any sort of positive feedback. Certainly, in comparison to Titan's previous PPV efforts of this year (Royal Rumble in January; WrestleMania in April), this was a hot show. At least it seemed the booking was well thought out and almost all the finishes popped the crowd. It was a marked contrast to WrestleMania, where it seemed like so much work had been put into the hype that very little thought was given into coming up with actual match scripts and as a result, it was a very dull show. Overall, it was hardly one of the great cards of all-time, not with two first-rate matches out of nine and three genuine stinkers, two more that would be classified as bad and two others as average or slightly better than average.

From a financial standpoint, it appears the show was a major success, which doesn't come as much of a surprise. PPV figures are all works and it is almost impossible to get accurate numbers, but the best we've been able to ascertain, it appears this show did right around a five percent buy rate, maybe just slightly under. At this point in time, I'd consider that as tremendous, given all the PPV shows that are around. It did better than SummerSlam last year, and that was during a time when there were very few PPVs, unlike this year when they seem to run just about monthly. If the show did a five buy rate, it probably means something along the order of 550,000 buys and maybe as many as 600,000, which at an $18.50 average price, adds up to in excess of $10 million, so this would easily be the biggest grossing overall show besides the past three WrestleManias. If you throw in closed-circuit from Canada and live gate from the Meadowlands, the show could conceivably have approached a $12 million total gate, although a realistic guess is in the $11 million range.

Before going on, here are some reader comments about the card:

"Five thumbs up. It was a great card."

Alex Marvez
Miami Herald

"A very hesitant thumbs down. The best match was Rockers & Tito Santana vs. Rougeaus & Rick Martel which I liked a lot. The finish of the match was excellent. Warrior vs. Rude was a crummy match but the finish alone was worth 3 ½ stars. The booking of the main event was atrocious. They killed off Zeus for no reason and I don't get into Hogan attacking women. The match itself was better than I expected and Zeus wasn't as bad as I thought he would be, but he was still far and away the worst wrestler on the card, followed closely by Andre. Valentine vs. Garvin, Rooster vs. Perfect and Dusty vs. Honky Tonk Man were all duds."

Scott Hudson
Atlanta

"I watched the show with 14 others at (WWF employee's) house. The consensus was it was a six on a scale of one-to-ten, which I guess means a marginal thumbs up. Warrior vs.

Rude was the best match. The finish of the Hogan match saved a bad match, but we were all perplexed that Zeus got pinned. That made no sense at all."

Ken McLaughlin

"Thumbs up slightly. If it had been an NWA card I'd have given it a thumbs down because it doesn't match up to what they are capable of, but for WWF it was all you can hope for. Worst match was Hennig vs. Taylor. Best match was Warrior vs. Rude. The best part of the card was the Gene Okerlund blunder. Was that incredible or what?

L.A. Roxx

"I attended it live and it was definitely a thumbs down. The crowd was up for some of the matches but the action left a lot to be desired and the main event was disappointing. After this card, fans may realize how Lacking the WWF is in talent."

Dan Weisberg
New York

"Thumbs down. What I saw was basically terrible. You can't knock the NWA for having bad taste after seeing what Gene Okerlund did."

Obin Johnson
High Point, NC

"I was there. The card wasn't spectacular, but I'd give it a thumbs up. It was good by Titan standards. Warrior vs. Rude was the best match."

Dave Kossr
New Jersey

"My favorite thing was the Gene Okerlund interview. Other than that the only thing I liked was the Warrior vs. Rude match. I can't give it a thumbs up or a thumbs down. It was just okay. DiBiase vs. Snuka was sad, Harts vs. Brainbusters was okay but not good, Rockers match was great. Dusty looked like a fat transvestite."

Fred Curtaz
San Francisco

"Thumbs down. The only worthwhile match was Warrior vs. Rude. Rude really did a nice job and his feud with Piper may be worthwhile. It's a little disturbing to see Hogan atomic dropping Scary Sherri. It was a pretty lousy example for kids."

Steve Ellenberg
New York

"Thumbs down. It made me embarrassed to think I was a WWF fan. It was so contrived it turned me off. I couldn't watch the thing. Tiny Lister was pathetic and it was sad

to see the WWF stoop to this Level. Tony Schiavone was terrible."

Richard Chemel
Los Angeles

"I saw it but I could have cared less when it was over. It wasn't bad, but it wasn't good."

David Olbrich
Moorpark, CA

"51-49 thumbs up. I was watching with a lot of casual fans and non-fans and they didn't like it one bit. I liked seeing Vince bury Zeus. It was a very surprising finish and very strange. Liz did well and Zeus was okay. But we could all see that Sherri was wearing a hairpiece so the haircut meant nothing. The only match I was interested in seeing beforehand was DiBiase vs. Snuka and it wasn't any good. Everyone else here gave it thumbs down, but this is as good as Titan is going to get so I gave it thumbs up."

Dr Mike Lano
San Francisco

"Resounding thumbs down. The only good thing on the card was Warrior vs. Rude. The fans live only cared about two matches on the card. Almost everyone left the building unhappy with the card."

Jeff Bukantz
New Jersey

"Minor thumbs up. It started off disappointing but finished up okay. Warrior was actually impressive and the crowd live popped big for Piper."

Mike Omansky
New Jersey

"I'd give it a thumbs up. Thought Warrior vs. Rude was the best match and I'd give it four stars. First half of the card was pretty good but the second half was real bad. The main event was interesting. When Savage was in, it was pretty good and when Zeus was in, it sucked. The six-man and Valentine vs. Garvin sucked and DiBiase vs. Snuka was only fair and Brainbusters vs. Hart Foundation was disappointing."

Ron Lemieux
Florida

"Thumbs down. It sucked. No doubt about it.

Ken Sabala
Chicago

"It was the best booked WWF show I've seen since WrestleMania III. The crowd felt a full range of emotions during Warrior vs. Rude and the Hogan tag match. Both endings were pleasant surprises which popped the crowd unbelievably. When Hogan took a beating the first six minutes the arena was in total disbelief that he couldn't overpower Zeus. I had no idea what we were in store for next. The Demolition match and Taylor match were kept mercifully short and Ron Garvin's ring announcing made that match somewhat interesting. The Rockers match was excellent. The show was well worth an eleven hour drive and ticket prices. A delighted thumbs up. "

Brian Dulik
Ohio

"Thumbs up. It was an excellent show. The second best PPV show this year, behind the NWA's Wrestle War The announcing was excellent. Tony Schiavone will get my vote for announcer of the year. Jesse was also excellent."

Walt Marshall
Pennsylvania

"Thumbs down. The finishes were terrible in virtually every match. The opener was good as was the six-man with the Rockers and Rude's individual performance. "

Tom Mavrikes
Maryland

"Thumbs up barely. Seeing the show live made me realize the impact the McMahon machine has on the masses. Unlike the NWA, whose main appeal lies with the hardcores, Titan appears to give the general public what it wants, Larger than life personalities, most of whom can't wrestle but seem to provide entertainment to the public. This is one well-oiled hype machine. Hart vs. Tully & Arn was passable, Rockers six-man was excellent, Savage and Sherri along with the surprise pin on Zeus saved the main event. Rude vs. Warrior was the best thing on the card. Was Ultimate much improved or did the McMahon magic cast its spell on me?"

Dan Reilly
Enfield, Connecticut

"I was all set to give it a thumbs up barely until seeing the Muta vs. Sting match on Power Hour. It wasn't bad, but for $20 on a big PPV, you deserve better than just watchable, you deserve something special. That was only delivered in one match, Warrior vs. Rude. After seeing the NWA put on a better match for free than anything on SummerSlam make me give it a slight thumbs down."

Brian Richardson
New York

A few notes about the card. Before the PPV telecast began, they did a live match with Dino Bravo pinning Koko Ware for the house crowd to warm them up and to allow them to start the card early and get fans in their seats for the first match. The Red Rooster vs. Mr. Perfect match didn't go completely according to the plans since Terry Taylor blew out his knee on the second leapfrog in the first and only high spot of the match. The finish was exactly as planned but the "body" of the match never took place because Taylor's knee was out. Taylor was to undergo arthroscopic surgery early this week and be back in action towards the end of the month.

I'd attribute the success of the card to two things, besides the excellent hype job done on the television shows:

1) All the movie hype set the stage for this card;

2) The angle on the Saturday Night Main Event was done to perfection. It's all very simple, when you have tons of media and a network time slot pushing your lead angle.

Lioness Asuka, real name Tomoko Kitamura, the last remaining major link of the All Japan Women's promotion with its glory days of 1984-86, retired on 8/24 before a sellout crowd at Tokyo's Korakuen Hall. Asuka, 26, was half of the famous Crush Gals tag team with Chigusa Nagayo (who retired this past May) and had announced her retirement about seven weeks back. Asuka was recognized as World champion by the All Japan promotion after defeating Nagayo for the title on January 29th. In Asuka's final show, she wrestled five minute exhibition matches against: Noriyo Tateno (formerly of the Jumping Bomb Angels) and Jaguar Yokota (the retired Legend Of Japanese Women's wrestling making her first in-ring appearance in three-and-a-half years).

On the legal side of things, Jake Roberts petitioned for a retrial in his recent assault conviction in Florida, claiming inadequate representation in the trial. A hearing on the motion was scheduled for late this past week. Roberts returned to the WWF doing interviews at the TV tapings on Tuesday and Wednesday night for his impending series of matches with Ted DiBiase, so apparently Titan is convinced Roberts won't be asked to serve any time for his conviction. In the Cedar Rapids, IA case involving Andre the Giant, which made national headlines, Andre no-showed at the hearing this past week and a preliminary hearing is to take place on Sept. 8. Ben Hildebrandt, the cameraman who is claiming that Andre roughed him up after a 30 second match in Cedar Rapids, did file a civil suit claiming back and neck injuries during this past week.

In an interesting note that may become a wrestling trivia question in years to come. What wrestler held World title recognition with two different federations in two different countries under two different names at the same time? The answer is Leon White, or Big Van Vader, who holds recognition in the New Japan promotion under the Vader gimmick as IWGP World Champion, and two weeks back in Austria, defeated Otto Wanz for the European version of the World title using the ring name "Bull Power White."

We'll be doing another poll for the NWA's Clash of the Champions special on 9/12 on TBS. You can call here and leave a thumbs up or thumbs down and a message or you can drop a letter or postcard with thumbs up/thumbs down and comments on the card as to what you liked and didn't like. If you are calling, please call by Sunday for inclusion in the poll and if you are writing, please mail by Friday because we'll be doing the poll rundown in the 9/25 Observer which will be completed on Monday the 18th.

STAMPEDE

Although there had been lots of talk that the promotion was going to close down for a few weeks while Owen Hart was in Japan, they have kept going on a fairly regular basis.

Johnny Smith has joined the Dynamite Kid working in the Maritimes in Eastern Canada.

Davey Boy Smith and Bruce Hart were scheduled to return to action from injuries suffered in the early summer over this past weekend. Smith, of course, was involved in the 7/4 auto accident, while Hart was injured a few weeks earlier when his jaw was broken by Dynamite Kid in a backstage punchout.

Owen Hart is to return in late September while Jason the Terrible (Karl Moffat) is to return in October from the broken leg he suffered in the auto accident.

Davey Boy Smith is scheduled to wrestle a guy named Mason, who is the bodyguard on Jonathan Holiday on the 9/8 show in Calgary. I think they are calling him Spike Mason and he's a green guy just starting out. Holiday is feuding with Chris Benoit while Owen Hart will feud with Larry Cameron when he returns which should draw good crowds, although I'm told not to expect Hart vs. Cameron to draw as well as Hart vs. Dynamite Kid drew in Calgary recently.

CWA

Crowds were really bad the past two weeks; with the Ronnie Gossett card of gimmick matches and all the gimmick matches where the faces got revenge the following week.

Texas Dirt (Dutch Mantell under a hood) won a Loser leaves town match from Master of Pain on 8/28 in Memphis. The headline match on that card saw Jerry Lawler beat Ronnie Gossett in a lumber jack strap match with only faces as lumberjacks.

Gossett got destroyed in the match, so he came back on television this weekend dressed up like the Joker from Batman and tried to laugh like Jack Nicholson did as Joker.

After watching recent tapes, this promotion has really hit an all-time low with all these movie gimmick creatures, none of whom are drawing although Freddy is over with the fans, but the rest are atrocious.

On television on 9/2, The Wildside (Chris Champion & Mark Starr) got disqualified and spray-painted the Rock & Roll Express.

Kerry Von Erich will be in next week.

The job guys are all getting torn up chests from working with Iceman King Parsons who is super-stiff on the chest blows.

Don Harris is in from CWF.

The 9/4 card in Memphis was headlined by Lawler defending the USWA title against Buddy Landel and Landel has to put up a car to get the title match. The undercard has Black Bart vs. Texas Dirt for the CWA title, Wildside vs. Rock & Roll Express in a no DQ match for the CWA tag team title, Master of Pain in his last match in town vs. Gossett in a mud wrestling match with Eddie Marlin as referee, Bill Dundee & Dustin Rhodes vs. The Blackbirds (Parsons & Brickhouse Brown), an eight girl lingerie Battle Royal, Freddy vs. Dirty White Boy, Spike Huber vs. Cousin Junior and Dale Mann vs. Don Harris.

Dundee's feud with the Blackbirds started on TV over the weekend when Jamie Dundee was "taking pictures" during a Blackbirds match and tried to prevent Harold Harris from interfering and then got attacked by the heels.

Harris moves around the ring great in his role as a manager. Gossett, on the other hand, while he can be funny because of how overweight he is, by putting him in the ring weekly it makes the promotion look sooo bad. They've built everything on the heel side around him and he doesn't have anywhere enough charisma to carry a heel side.

USWA

They came up with another ingenious gimmick this past weekend. On the Friday night card at the Sportatorium in the Jerry Lawler vs. Eric Embry main event, after Lawler repeatedly knocked down ref Tony Falk, Embry caught Lawler in the abdominal stretch and Lawler was screaming "I give, I give" when Falk got up, signalled for the bell and ruled Embry the winner via DQ and they announced in the building that Embry was the new "World" champion and had the celebration and everything. As they've done so many times, when television came on Saturday night, it was announced once again that Lawler was still the champion. Seems that in the switchover from World Class to USWA when they were writing the rules, one of the secretaries accidentally failed to transcribe the title can change hands via a DQ rule so therefore it wasn't in the books. That oversight has "now been corrected" but of course it means that Lawler is still the champ. The rest of the card, which drew only 450 fans, saw Kerry Von Erich beat Tarras Bulba via DQ when Gary Young interfered, Chris Adams went to a double disqualification with P. Y. Chu Hi (Phil Hickerson), Al Perez & Young drew with USWA tag champs Jeff Jarrett & Matt Borne, Jimmy Jack Funk beat The Dog of War (Buster Fowler) and Billy Travis pinned Sheik Scott Braddock.

The 9/8 card has Lawler vs. Embry in a rematch for the title, Adams vs. Chu Hi with the stipulations that if Adams wins, he gets five minutes with Tojo Yamamoto, but if Chu Hi wins, then Yamamoto gets five minutes with Chris' wife Toni Adams to "do whatever he wants with her" (on a TV angle Tojo ripped open Toni Adams' blouse), Kerry Von Erich & El Halcon from Mexico vs. Young & Bulba and Funk vs. Scandor Akbar in a bull rope match with Frank Dusek as referee.

Headed in is a masked newcomer called The Punisher.

On TV, Akbar lifted his bounty on Embry which should lead to some sort of an angle next week where it was all subterfuge and all the heels attack Eric and injure him once again.

During a Chu Hi squash, or actually before it started on TV, Adams came out with a chair and chased P. Y. and Tojo away and then beat up the jobber with the chair instead. Later in the show, P.Y. and Tojo challenged Adams to come down and Adams did and started beating on Chu Hi and Tojo attacked Adams but Adams got Tojo's kendo stick and was pounding on both of them and then beat up Braddock and Dog of War as well until a masked Super Zodiac came in (Gary Young under a hood once again) to turn the tide until the faces made the save.

The Toni Adams angle was a lot worse on videotape when you see it than it would seem if you just read about it here. It had the exact opposite effect of what an angle should have. An angle should try and get you to buy tickets for the upcoming shows. Instead, watching this angle, my gut reaction was to turn off the wrestling show because it was in such bad taste. Must have been a similar reaction to everyone since the crowds had been more than 2,000 per week and since the angle they haven't topped 500.

Killer Tim Brooks' independent show on 8/29 in Dallas drew 425 as Scott Casey beat Bullman Downs in a Lumberjack match on top when Brooks' interference backfired and Johnny Mantell pinned Brooks while John Tatum beat Batman (David Hinkle in the Batman getup).

NEW JAPAN
The latest tour opened 8/25 in Tokyo before a sellout crowd of 2,200 at Korakuen Hall. The biggest news wasn't a match, but the appearance of Koji Kitao (former sumo Grand Champion Futuhaguro who has been training in Virginia with Lou Thesz and Apollo Sugawara) at ringside. Before the main event (Riki Choshu vs. Bam Bam Bigelow), Bigelow started jawing at Kitao (who will debut tentatively on Dec. 31 and become a superstar in wrestling if he can pick up a decent amount of wrestling knowledge) and the wrestlers had to hold Kitao back and the thing made major news. Choshu then pinned Bigelow after two Lariats in just 2:48 in the main event and Choshu and Kitao shook hands in the dressing room for the newspaper photographers. The remainder of the card saw Super Strong Machine & George Takano upset Shinya Hashimoto & Masa Saito in

the tag team tournament when Machine pinned Hashimoto, Hiroshi Hase & Jushin Liger (Keiichi Yamada) downed Owen Hart & Pat Tanaka (wouldn't you love to see that match?) when Liger pinned Tanaka, Salman Hashimikov & Victor Zangiev of the Soviet Union beat Osamu Kido & Akira Nogami, Kendo Nagasaki & Billy Jack Haynes beat Tatsutoshi Goto & Kengo Kimura, Naoki Sano pinned Osamu Matsuda, Shiro Koshinaka pinned Italian Stallion, Kuniaki Kobayashi pinned Norio Honaga and prelims.

8/26 they were in Korakuen Hall again and drew another sellout with Bigelow pinning Hashimikov on top, Choshu & Saito beat Haynes & Stallion, Hashimoto beat Nagasaki, Kobayashi & Koshinaka upset Machine & Takano in the tournament when Koshinaka pinned Machine, Kido & Kimura beat Hart & Tanaka, Sano & Kantaro Hoshino beat Riger & Nogami, Zangiev beat Matsuda and Hase pinned Honaga.

8/27 in Kamaishi drew 2,080 as Choshu & Hashimoto & Kimura beat Bigelow & Stallion & Nagasaki, Saito pinned Haynes, Hase & Liger beat Koshinaka & Hoshino, Hart pinned Nogami, Sano pinned Tanaka, Zangiev & Hashimikov beat Machine & Black Cat and Takano pinned Goto plus prelims.

Before the tour began, Tatsumi Fujinami held a press conference to announce he wasn't going to participate in the tour, claiming a back injury, which is legit.

In the press conference, Fujinami made hints that he would be retiring if his back condition didn't improve because he didn't want to wrestle at less than 100 percent.

The next series will be 10/13 through 11/3 with Big Van Vader (Leon White), Kokina the Samoan, Tony St. Clair, Tom Prichard, Al Perez, Darryl Peterson (Max Pain) and Matt Borne plus the return to Japan of Masa Chono.

The 9/20 card in Osaka which has Vader vs. Bigelow and Sano vs. Liger in title matches will be taped for television, however the 9/21 card in Yokohama which has Hart challenging the winner of the Sano-Liger match for the jr. heavyweight title will not be taped for television.

ALL JAPAN
The 8/29 card in Osaka drew 4,050 as Jumbo Tsuruta & Yoshiaki Yatsu beat Genichiro Tenryu & Toshiaki Kawada in 23:04 to retain the PWF World tag team title. For those of you who follow this, you'll already know who pinned who using what hold without me having to write it, but Tsuruta pinned Kawada with the back suplex which is the same finish they always do when these teams go against each other. Also Terry Gordy & Todd Champion beat Abdullah the Butcher & Tiger Conway Jr. when Gordy pinned Conway, The Can-Am Express (Dan Kroffat & Doug Furnas) retained the Asian tag team titles beating the Dynamic Dudes (Johnny Ace & Shane Douglas) when Furnas pinned Douglas in 15:04, Big John Tenta pinned Pez Whatley, Giant Baba &

Rusher Kimura & Kabuki beat The Wild Bunch (Haruka Eigen & Motoshi Okuma & Masa Fuchi), Samson Fuyuki pinned Kenta Kobashi, Shunji Takano & Akira Taue beat Mighty Inoue & Isamu Teranishi, Goro Tsurumi pinned Akio Sato and Mitsuo Momota pinned Tsuyoshi Kikuchi.

Next series is 9/30 to 10/28 with Stan Hansen, Tiger Jeet Singh, Abdullah the Butcher, Dick Slater, Tom Zenk and the Can-Am Express (Kroffat & Purnas). Butcher and Singh will form a tag team to get them over as a combination for the December tag team tournament . This will be Hansen's 52nd tour of Japan which is an all-time record.

8/26 in Yoro drew 1,750 as Tsuruta & Yatsu beat Gordy & Champion, Foot Loose beat Dynamic Dudes, Baba & Kabuki & Kimura beat Butcher & Jive Tones (Whatley & Conway) and Can-Am Express beat Kobashi & Fuchi.

8/25 in Hirda drew 1,350 as Tsuruta & Kabuki & Fuchi beat Tenryu & Foot Loose in 24: 06, Baba & Kimura & Takano beat Butcher & Jive Tones, Can-Am Express beat Teranishi & Sato, Tenta pinned Champion and prelims.

8/24 in Takaoka saw Tenryu & Foot Loose beat Tsuruta & Kabuki & Taue, Butcher pinned Takano, Tenta & Yatsu beat Gordy & Champion, Can-Am Express double count out Dynamic Dudes and Jive Tones beat Sato & Teranishi.

8/21 they taped television in Baba's home town of Niigata before 2,550 as Tenryu & Kawada beat Gordy & Champion when Kawada pinned Champion, Tsuruta & Kobashi beat Dynamic Dudes as the headline matches.

They held a big card on 9/2 at Budokan Hall (capacity 15,000) with Tenryu vs. Gordy for the triple crown title as the main event and in a pre-match interview Tenryu said that he felt Gordy had surpassed Hansen as the best U.S. wrestler around.

OTHER NOTES FROM JAPAN

Several things relating to the United States are going on in Japan right now. Sid Bernstein, who was a famous rock promoter in the 1960s (he promoted the Beatles first concert in Shea Stadium in 1964) was in Japan and will be the UWF's United States promoter. Bernstein, according to Weekly Pro Wrestling issue that was released this past Friday, said he was going to promote UWF matches in New York in 1990. The UWF has now aligned itself with several rock acts in Japan and its crowd is similar to the rock concert crowd in Japan.

UWF wrestler Masaharu Funaki is now also working as a sports reporter for Ch. 6 in Tokyo because of his name recognition from his UWF stardom as the teenage heart throb. Funaki is currently on assignment in Europe reporting on different fighting martial arts forms that are popular in different countries.

A new women 's group called Ladies Pro Wrestling Association (LPWA) appears which will start up in the United States in November will be holding its first TV tapings on 10/8 in Tokyo's Korakuen Hall and 10/10 in Nagano. The president of the group is Tor Berg from Alaska and Vice president is Steve Edwards and it is affiliated with the All Japan women's promotion and Fuji network television in Japan. Not sure if the Japanese women will appear on the tapes or not, but it would seem to make sense in one way that they would, but not in another. Leilani Kai, Judy Martin, Velvet McIntyre and Desiree Peterson will be the top stars with the group built around Madusa Miceli, who is supposed to be working full-time in Japan for one year to improve her work. It is said that Nick Bockwinkel will be the television announcer.

The Lioness Asuka retirement card on 8/24 in Tokyo drew a sellout 2,200 at Korakuen Hall as Asuka had five minute exhibitions against Noriyo Tateno and Jaguar Yokota plus Mitsuko Nishiwaki won the Japan Grand Prix tournament pinning Miceli in the finals. It appears Nishiwaki will be pushed as the next top singles star in Japan with Asuka retiring. Also Reuben Amada from the Japanese title beating Erica Shishedo via DQ (titles changes via DQ in Japan), Toshiyo Yamada & Minami Toyoda beat Beastie from the U.S. & Bull Nakano. They are having a tag team tournament in All Japan women right now with Miceli & Nishiwaki as the top team.

JWP of Japan toured Korea at the end of the month with its top show drawing a hot crowd of 4,570 in Seoul, Korea as Miss A went to a double count out with Devil Masami for the UWA International title in the main event.

New Japan has the Tokyo Dome booked on February 12, 1990 while the UWF will run a Tokyo Dome card on November 29, 1989 with rumors of Akira Maeda vs. George Foreman being the main event. If that match actually occurs, it will shatter every live gate record set already this year.

Toshiyo Yamada & Etsuko Mita are billed as the new "Dream Orca" tag team for All Japan women. Yamaaa bears an amazing facial resemblance to a young Chigusa Nagayo (she's 19 right now).

The Budokan Hall card on 9/2 besides Tenryu vs. Gordy featured a dream match of Tsuruta vs. Yatsu, Baba vs. Butcher and a rematch of the Can-Am Express vs. Foot Loose.

TV ratings saw New Japan on 8/12 draw a 3.9 with the Japan A team vs. Team USSR while All Japan the next day got a 6.6 for the final night of the last series. New Japan drew a 5.7 the next week with Choshu vs. Vader and Sano vs. Liger while All Japan got a 7.0 the next week with the opening of the new series.

New Japan is trying to get All Japan to work with them for next year's Tokyo Dome card, which may be Inoki's retirement card and he wants to go out promoting a show with Americans, Russians and both major Japanese promotions.

Inoki, separate from New Japan, is talking with Tor Berg from Alaska to set up a promotion called the "Super Powers" promotion in the United States using the Americans who work regularly with New Japan plus the Japanese and Soviet wrestlers and want to get regular television starting in January in the States before actually starting to promote shows. I'm highly skeptical of this being able to take hold because it would need enormous television and media coverage, which it won't get, in order to compete with the two major existing promotions in the United States and Titan in particular.

OTHER NOTES

A few readers from Southern California checked out the Tijuana, Mexico show on 9/1 which was headlined by Yoshinari Asai & Tornado Negro & Kiss against Ricky Boy & EL SymboLo & Blue Panther. Supposedly Asai was out of this world. Asai must be good, because when he was part of a three-man team with Hirokazu Hata & Naoki Sano, Asai was considered the best of the three and Sano was good enough to return to Japan and become the hottest newcomer. Negro juiced like crazy like the way The Sheik did in the old days.

Southern Championship Wrestling has a show on 9/17 in Atlanta using CWA wrestlers Dustin Rhodes, Bill Dundee, Ronnie Gossett and Buddy Landel. Mike Golden & Mr. Atlanta won that group's Southern tag team title beating Jimmy Powell & The Nightmare (Ted ALIen).

Hasbro toys was expected to finalize a deal this week which would wind up with Big Van Vader as part of a Saturday morning cartoon series for kids and Leon White will do the voice. This will, of course, lead to Vader toys and dolls similar to Sgt. Slaughter with Hasbro. New Japan, which owns the rights to the Vader gimmick, was to be at the meetings as well and when the deal goes through, to promote the toys, White will have rights to use the Vader gimmick in the United States and will work either for the NWA or AWA. AWA appears the most interested of the two and would build around the Vader character for its team concept if he joins, but NWA offers far greater exposure. WWF would be out of the question if Hasbro owns the merchandising rights.

Bruiser Bob Sweetan was advertised for an independent show on 9/4 in Warner-Robbins, GA.

CWF in Knoxville on 9/1 has a tornado cage match with Jerry Stubbs & Southern Boys vs. Robert Fuller & Brian Lee & Jimmy Golden plus another tornado cage match with Beauty & The Beast against Adrian & Linda Street, Dennis Condrey vs. Wendell Cooley for the CWF title, Mike Davis vs. Danny Davis and Todd Morton vs. Lou Fabbiano plus manager Ron Wright is to make a special announcement.

Former pro wrestling promoter Mike London (real name Harold Anshutz), 80, died last weekend in Corrales, NM. London took the pseudonym in 1923 as a pro boxer, then went into wrestling in 1933, and began promoting in 1947.

Red Bastien taped six Lucha Libre TV shows before two

near full houses of 400 in San Bernardino, CA on 8/27. Among those appearing at the tapings were Bobby Bradley, Blue Demon Jr., Super Muneco, Boy, Lazartron (Hector Guerrero), Eddie Guerrero, Alex Knight, Ultraman II, Atlantis, Riki Ataki, The Mercenaries (Louie Spicoli & Dave "Angel of Death" Sheldon and another guy), Mario Valenzuela, Tim Tall Tree (son of former pro wrestler Tom Renesto and a good worker) and Arias Romero.

NWA

NWA and WWF will have two near head-to-heads in upcoming weeks. NWA has the Capital Centre booked this coming Saturday night while the WWF will run the D.C. Armory the next day. The following weekend, WWF has the Rosemont Horizon booked in the Chicago area on a Saturday night with Hulk Hogan vs. Randy Savage with Liz in the corner on top with nothing underneath while the NWA the next night has the Pavilion with Ric Flair vs. Terry Funk in a Texas death match and little underneath there as well (Sting vs. Muta, Rick & Scott Steiner vs. Danny Spivey & Sid Vicious, Scott Hall vs. Butch Reed, Dynamic Dudes vs. New Zealand Militia, Dick Murdoch vs. Cuban Assassin and Greg Evans vs. Tom Winters).

The 9/3 card at the Omni in Atlanta drew 15,500 (have no idea what the paid or gate was) with Muta winning the held up TV title beating Sting in one of the feature matches. They had a single hand-held camera taping the match so I assume the footage will be on TBS this Saturday. Complete card results saw Ron Simmons pin Tom Branch (Roberto Renesto), Brad Armstrong pinned Cuban Assassin (David Sierra), Brian Pillman pinned Norman the Maniac (pretty good), Skyscrapers double count out with the Steiner brothers (good match, the faces threw peanuts at Teddy Long; Skyscrapers sold for the first time, about 25 percent of the match mainly match consisted of the Scrapers getting heat on Scott), Muta pinned Sting (Sting was bleeding really bad. Not one of their better matches and nothing compared to the TV match. Gary Hart pulled the ref out of the ring after a bump and Muta went for the spray but Sting blocked the spray and had Muta beat when Hart came in and Muta got the riding crop and while Sting was attacking Hart, Muta got him from behind with the object for the pin), Freebirds beat Midnight Express in 18 minutes when Garvin pinned Bobby Eaton after Michael Hayes hit Eaton with the title belt (best match on the card), Lex Luger pinned Tommy Rich in 23 minutes clean in the middle (hard match to watch), Ric Flair kept the NWA title beating Terry Funk in a Texas death match when Funk couldn't answer the bell for the seventh fall after Flair piledrove him on a chair. Both guys juiced. Very good match but not as good as their previous Atlanta match and finally Road Warriors beat Samaon Swat Team in a cage match.

The new Pacific Coast Sports Network, a basic cable

sports channel service offered in Northern California which has the local sports teams on it and just began operation the beginning of this month has NWA wrestling on daily at 4 p.m.

The Road Warriors' Zubaz pants company is doing some significant business, particularly in the Minneapolis area.

Kangaroo Athletic Wear has taken out major full-page ads in sports trade publications which feature the Road Warriors, Flair, Sting, Steve Williams and Rick Steiner.

Williams is still out of action due to the injured ribs he suffered last weekend in Philadelphia. Originally I had heard that he wouldn't be back in time for the Clash of the Champions on 9/12, but others are saying he will be back by then. In the meantime, Mike Rotunda, who was to wrestle Williams on most of the NWA cards, has missed several big shows without an opponent so it comes off like two no-shows for the price of one.

Expect several angles at the Clash, and there had better be some good ones since the show needs to set up feature matches for the 10/28 PPV card.

NWA jobber Ray Lloyd is working as a junior high school football coach in his home town of Valdosta, GA.

As mentioned, the Clash will be going head-to-head with the Roller Games premiere on 9/12 and the Roller Games have several major stations around the country including Superstation WGN in Chicago.

Not a lot to comment on this weekend's NWA television. Sting vs. Muta has a very hot (four stars) television match on the Power Hour with Muta getting dq'd for the outside interference of Gary Hart. Ric Flair pinned Brad Armstrong in a World title defense on World Wide Wrestling. It was a good match and would have been even better if they had more time on a syndicated show since it was a babyface match which needs time to develop. After all that talk about a top ten and someone having to be in the top ten to get a title shot and then they do a title match with a guy who just the week before was pinned by Luger?

TV ratings for the previous weekend saw the NWA Main Event (headline match Bobby Eaton vs. Jimmy Garvin) as the top rated cable show of the week drawing a 2.8 rating (WWF's Prime Time Wrestling wasn't aired that weekend due to SummerSlam). The Power Hour on Friday drew a 2.0, which tied it's all-time best in the slot (ironically, it was the weakest Power Hour show thus far with the Luger vs. Armstrong headline match in front of a comatose crowd in Cleveland. Even more ironic is that the two-hour TBS wrestling show TBS show with Sting vs. Dick Slater, with the Robin Green angle, which was the best TBS Saturday show in a while, drew just a 1.9 rating, probably hurt somewhat because the show building up to it the previous week never aired.

WWF

Television tapings were held this past Tuesday and Wednesday after SummerSlam in Springfield, PA (Challenge) and Portland, ME (Superstars). At the Challenge taping on 8/29, Jake Roberts was there challenging DiBiase; Jim Duggan pinned Brooklyn Brawler (Steve Lombardi) who appears to be back to being a squash guy; Barry Windham (Widow Maker) pinned Tim Horner; Jimmy Snuka pinned Honky Tonk Man; Rick Rude pinned Paul Roma and after the match Rude went to kiss a girl who spit out the kiss; Roddy Piper then returned and pinned Barry Horowitz in 35 seconds, kissed the same girl and she fainted; Demolition beat Brain Busters (Tully Blanchard & Arn Anderson) via DQ, Ron Garvin beat Dino Bravo via DQ when Greg Valentine ran in and the two left Garvin laying and finally Hulk Hogan pinned Randy Savage.

The next night in Portland before a sellout 8,500 (some, but not a Lot of paper) saw Roma beat Zhukov in a dark match, Piper won a squash, Brother Love interviewed Roberts where he talked about DiBiase and made the classic quote, "I'll risk a jail term to get at DiBiase;" Demolition challenged the Brain Busters after a squash win; Randy Savage pinned Jim Duggan to become the new king of the WWF and Duggan did a stretcher job and Savage then beat up all the face jobbers who came in to save him to set up their feud for the fall (which will run on midweek nights mainly when Hogan isn't working); Hercules beat Akeem via DQ in a match as bad or worse than it sounds; Barry Windham went to a 20 minute draw with Tito Santana in a match which put everyone to sleep; Brother Love interviewed Piper and Piper sprayed Brother Love with shaving cream and toothpaste until Rick Rude made the save and they did a major number on Piper; Brother Love interviewed Andre, who now wears face paint and calls himself "Andre, the Ultimate Giant" and Warrior pinned Andre once again in less than 20 seconds and since it wasn't billed as the main event here, the crowd popped huge for it; they did the Savage coronation ceremony as the new King with all the heels; Demolition beat Anderson & Blanchard via DQ (okay), Snuka pinned Zhukov (Snuka was real brutal and gave hints both nights that he might be going heel later in the year), Dusty Rhodes beat Dale (formerly Dusty) Wolfe, they did a thing where Rick Martel claimed he was better looking than Brutus Beefcake so I guess they'll feud sometime soon and finally Hogan pinned Savage in seven minutes of a match with a lot of restholds and they let the women have the spotlight most of the way.

WWF set a new record for Prime Time Wrestling on 8/21 drawing a 4.0 to see Piper and Rick Rude and Bobby Heenan jaw at it. All American Wrestling drew a 2.7 on 8/20 and a 2.3 on 8/27.

The annual King of the Ring tournament will be 10/14 in Providence, RI.

At the taping in Springfield, Observer reader Dan Reilly showed up in the front row wearing a Pro Wrestling Illustrated T-shirt and Titan wound up giving him and his friends free T-shirts to wear over the shirt and free merchandise.

The first Madison Square Garden card in several months will be 9/30 and ringside ticket prices have been raised from $15 to $18.

Originally in the six-man tag at SummerSlam, John Studd was to team with Demolition and Titan forgot to replace Studd's name in most of the newspaper advertising for the card even though he had been gone from the promotion for months. Mark Ming, who worked as a jobber on the Fresno taping, played college football at Texas A&M, Cal-State Bakersfield and was a member of the spring squad at San Jose State when I was there but had back problems and didn't return for the season.

8/27 in Rochester, NY drew 4,000 as Bad News Brown pinned Mark Young (Young's breakdancing bit was booed here), Hart Foundation drew with Bravo & Valentine (very sloppy), Jim Duggan beat Ted DiBiase via count out (DiBiase carried Duggan, who looked awful), Warrior pinned Andre in 22 seconds (they kept the music blaring non-stop as a diversionary tactic after the match but it didn't work since there was a minor riot in the back of the building because of the brevity of the match), Akeem pinned Hillbilly Jim (terrible) and Demolition beat Blanchard & Anderson via DQ (entertaining).

8/14 in Albuquerque drew 4,689 as Young pinned Horowitz *, Rockers beat Rougeaus ** ½, Warrior pinned Andre in 25 seconds DUD, Bravo beat Hercules via DQ *, Bad News Brown pinned Tim Horner * ½, Mr. Perfect drew Bret Hart *** ½ and Snuka pinned Honky Tonk Man * ½.

FINAL NOTES

The NWA show on TBS on Saturday was delayed because a football game (which ended two hours earlier) went over and they ran the movie in full and delayed wrestling. This has caused a lot of questioning once again as to TBS' commitment to wrestling. We'll have to wait and see in future weeks since football will be on each Saturday and at some point in time, games will run over again.

Some of the fall Prime Time Wrestling shows will be pre-empted for tennis commitments on USA. Ironically, the wrestling generally does triple the ratings of the tennis.

The new Roller Games haven't even hit on television yet when we get word that a competing Roller league will be started up shortly, styled more after the old Roller Derby.

Titan is claiming a seven buy rate for SummerSlam, which means realistic figures are probably between 4 ½ and five percent.

Florida Championship Wrestling is still alive.

THE READERS PAGE

SUMMERSLAM

A group of friends from the old photographers and writers school and I watched SummerSlam. We all gave it a solid thumbs down. What a difference when Vince doesn't add his crowd soundtrack. We were quite depressed over the state of wrestling after viewing the so-called big show. Following this time-waster, I slipped in the tape of Ric Flair vs. Terry Funk match from Bash and we recovered from our depression and it saved our night. What a difference.

Finally, you've got to make mention of Jim Ross' comment about changing his pants after seeing Robin Green. Amazing they let that remark go through.

Brian Bukantis
Fraser, Michigan

I'm sure at SummerSlam everyone saw Jim Duggan's face painted up like the American flag. Does that mean Scandor Akbar would now have the constitutional right to throw fire at it?

SummerSlam gets a thumbs up from me. It was a far cry from being as good as the NWA's pay-per-view shows, but I wasn't expecting a good show when I ordered it, either. The main event sucked and Dusty Rhodes vs. Honky Tonk Man would sedate a rabid pitbull, but nothing else was painful to watch. The Rockers & Tito Santana vs. Rougeaus & Rick Martel was as good as Titan gets and Rick Rude's performance against Ultimate Warrior (who was blown up before the bell even rang) should lock Rude up as the most improved wrestler of the year.

John McAdam
Nashua, New Hampshire

The show was a tribute to the WWF's tireless efforts to prove that wrestling can replace valium and thorazine as tranquilizers. Jesse Ventura and Tony Schiavone didn't mix well. Jesse was uncharacteristically flat and Schiavone did his best to screech in the most annoying pitch possible at the end of every match. This is unusual for Schiavone, who is usually an excellent announcer. Must be taking Vince McMahon voice lessons. Sean Mooney was ridiculous throughout. As for the wrestling, not a genuine good match on the entire card. Could anything have been worse than Honky Tonk Man vs. Dusty Rhodes? Negative four stars as a match but I'd upgrade it a half-star for the amusing Elvis interview after being bashed by the guitar. Hart Foundation vs. Brainbusters, Hennig vs. Rooster and Rockers & Santana vs. Rougeaus & Martel were all disappointing. Santana should not have been the focus of the tag match and I got a lot of grumblings from friends watching it who wanted to see more of the Rockers. Ron Garvin tripped very badly over his lines and should have practiced more, as it could have been an amusing idea.

As for the main event, Zeus proved us all right in our estimation of his ability. He seemed not to be wearing his lifts, and he did try. There was a lot of poor camera work that night, in particular in the main event where they missed most of the outside the ring action with Sherri and Liz. A big surprise ending and if anything we should be grateful to Vince for not dragging Zeus on. Hogan atomic dropping Sherri was the low point of the match. Is it really necessary for him to appear to manhandle a woman less than half his size? It doesn't smack of heroism to me. Savage and Sherri get kudos for working hard.

Teresa DeMarie
Tuckahoe, New York

I thoroughly enjoyed the show. The only match I didn't like was Red Rooster vs. Mr. Perfect. The Ultimate Warrior vs. Rick Rude match was great. What I didn't like was Tony Schiavone, He screamed like a mad man every five minutes. It's a good thing Jesse was there to save the day.

Andy Levy
Westminster, Maryland

OAKLAND 2
In response to the letter from "Oakland 2" regarding their ejection from the Oakland Coliseum during a WWF taping, they are incorrect to say that the NWA customer is king at NWA cards.

At the 8/4 Great American Bash card at Kemper Arena in Kansas City, the fans were not free to yell what they wanted to and at whom they wanted without security hoarding around those persons doing so to be quiet. Front row ringside fans couldn't stand against the railing and cheer or boo for the respective

wrestlers entering or exiting from the ring without harassment from security. And when the front row ringside fans could not see the action taking place on the opposite side of the double-ring setup, causing back row ringside fans to stand in their chairs, security motioned those back row ringside fans to sit down. When objects were thrown into the ring, the perpetrators were never caught or escorted from the building. Instead the security hoarded around the entire section and treated all the fans like little children. Do you call the above royal treatment? Is the NWA customer really king?

There was no heat during the card. How could there be when the security killed it?

By its above action, the NWA has already ripped a page from the WWF's book of financial success, as has World Class, regarding treatment of the customer. One need not analyze the minor league vs.

major league perceptions as to why one promotion is super successful and another is struggling. One only has to look at the treatment of the customer in WWF, World Class and the NWA to conclude that wrestling is entering the Dark Ages.

Barbara Fick
Independence, Missouri

NWA
I'm surprised more wasn't written about the NWA television shows the weekend of 8/12. What made them so special? For the first time all year they started enough new 'stories' to encourage one to tune in the following weekend. Moreover, the events revolved around persons other than the headliners and were not simply brawls or turns. The soap opera has finally returned.

Granted, post-match fireworks are exciting but they have a few drawbacks as far as boosting TV ratings. For once the angle is televised, all you see are continual replays and that is hardly an incentive to watch subsequent broadcasts and all the different television shows. However, a slowly developed angle lends continuity to the weekly broadcasts helps develop undercard characters and lends a supercard aura to the ppv event when the feuding parties finally square off.

I agree that the next Clash card is too strong for a free television show in September. What I don't understand is if they are going to televise such a strong freebie, why not run it on SummerSlam night?

Ernie Santilli
Drexel Hill, Pennsylvania

Dave Meltzer: I believe right now, because of pressure put on by cable companies, that neither the WWF or NWA will counter a PPV event with a freebie on television.

The last time around in New Haven, the fans were treated to an autograph party from 7 to 8 p.m. Unfortunately, the session started late since the arena doors didn't open until 7:15 and it ended early. Fans were also treated to a Sting vs. Terry Funk main event which never happened due to Sting's 'injury' in the battle royal.

The spreading of goodwill toward the fans continued on 8/27, on what appeared to be the NWA's last dance in New Haven. This time around, fans saw a five minute Sting vs. Muta match, Steve Williams no-showing for a U.S. title match and ten minute long main events with Flair vs. Funk and Warriors vs. Swat Team in a cage.

We can rationalize and make excuses for the NWA all we want. We know that Funk was injured last time around. We also know that 8/27 was the last night of the Northeastern tour and the boys probably wanted to go home and were working before a small crowd in a town that they would probably never see again.

The sad thing is, despite all the excuses we can make, the bottom line is that just like the Nassau Coliseum in 1987-88, the NWA arrived in New Haven with a big splash and ran the town into the ground in just three shows, screwing the fans a little more each time around.

I'll pay to see the NWA live again simply because it's the only way to see real wrestling but I don't know if a casual fan in New Haven or New York would. The promotion has left a bad taste in a lot of people's mouths. In a time when public perception should be the NWA's top priority, the logic of a promotion repeatedly making the same mistakes and burning bridges behind it escapes me.

I can't express enough respect for Terry Funk. We saw him arrive at the arena and watching him walk from his car into the building was upsetting. Terry's knees and back were obviously bothering him and walking seemed to be an effort. Yet when he came out for his main event match, he looked healthy and showed no signs of age or physical problems.

Michael Hawkins
Massapequa, New York

I think the timing is right for the NWA in Rochester. The World Wide show popped up in the traditional Superstars of Wrestling slot on our local UHF station (very strong station) with Superstars moved back an hour. TBS is a very popular local cable station. Traditionally, the NWA PPV shows do extremely well here. If advertised correctly on TV and radio plus other stuff like live radio interviews with the stars or special guest appearances the day of the show, they could do a good walk-up .

Sean Hendrick
Rochester, New York

AWARDS FAVORITES

This is the second part of a series of rundowns on the various categories that we'll be voting on for the 1989 pro wrestling awards in the Observer yearbook that will come out at the end of the year. Each week from now until Thanksgiving we'll look at a few categories for the awards (which are technically to be determined from action in wrestling from December 1, 1988 through November 30, 1989). Voting will take place in December.

MOST OUTSTANDING WRESTLER: As opposed to Wrestler of the Year, in which outside factors should be factored in such as impact on wrestling and the like, this award is specifically for the guy who was the best worker and had the best matches during the year. There are really four wrestlers who stick out in my mind for this one. Ric Flair won this in two of the past three years (Tatsumi Fujinami was last year's winner) and as mentioned last week, if anything, he's been even better this year. His matches around the horn with both Ricky Steamboat and Terry Funk were probably the best matches all year in the United States, and some would say that his matches with Steamboat were the best night-after-night matches of the decade. Certainly all three of the nationally viewed Flair-Steamboat matches will be strong candidates for match of the year, and if it weren't for those matches, some of the Flair vs. Funk matches would be possible winners as well, and a match which everyone has probably forgotten but was another classic was Flair vs. Lex Luger from Starrcade. It takes two to tango, and Ricky Steamboat is also a strong candidate here. Enough has been written this year about his matches against both Flair and also his recent matches with Lex Luger. Here is a guy who came out from nearly a year out of the sport and was immediately shoved to the forefront, yet responded by doing more than anyone could have asked for. A late choice, but one who in my book could be a legitimate winner is Jushin Liger (Keiichi Yamada). His matches week-after-week have been tremendous of late. He's having four star matches with opening match wrestlers and making them look better than they've ever looked before. Even though Liger will never match up to the "legend" of Satoru Sayama (just as many would have compared Sayama unfavorably with a guy like Argentina Rocca because you remember things as a lot better than they really were), if you watch his matches, he's all-around a far better worker than Sayama ever was. The fourth guy is Genichiro Tenryu. He's had a series of outstanding matches and is as hard a worker as there is, because in terms of true athletic ability, I wouldn't rate him with a guy like Steamboat or Yamada or Flair, yet because of desire, his work and his matches don't take a back seat to anyone. About the only other wrestlers I'd consider here for this year would be Toshiaki Kawada, and maybe Dan Kroffat or Shawn Michaels as longshots that people wouldn't think about but deserve credit. The Great Muta just isn't consistent enough to crack the elite here, even though at times he's one of the most spectacular around.

BEST FLYING WRESTLER: Owen Hart will need a late surge to even be considered to defend this crown. In North America, there is no doubt in my mind that the Great Muta did the widest variety and most outstanding flying maneuvers around. Atlantis is still great, even with the choreographed style you have to respect the ability he has to pull the things off. Still, for flying in the context of a match and a wide variety, my pick is Liger. Naoki Sano has been great since he's returned to Japan. Brian Pillman is good, but has kind of been held back and hasn't done the real bizarre high risk stuff like Liger.

MOST DIGUSTING PROMOTIONAL TACTIC: Boy, theres a lot of promotions that worked hard to get here this time. I really can't see how anything can top the return of Jose Gonzales as a triumphant hero in the World Wrestling Council. The trial itself was bad enough. It really leaves a bad taste in a lot of people's mouths. An awful lot of World Class stuff would be in here as well, but the incident where Eric Embry threw up in the ring was pretty low class and the endless hospitalizations and loser leaves towns where nobody left is exactly the most honest methods of promotion. How about the Col. DeBeers vs. Derrick Dukes angle with the winner painting the loser black or white. In this day and age, it's a shame to think people think that this gets over with even a small segment of the audience. Judging by the crowds, nobody cared about it anyway. Personally, that bit where wrestlers try to get more money from the audience for immediate rematches is pretty low-rent as well. The WWF skit with Dusty and the toilet for shock value was pretty low since it was from a group that doesn't have to resort to such levels, but does anyway.

PROMOTER OF THE YEAR: Both Vince McMahon and Giant Baba deserve consideration for the reasons that were laid out last week in the booker of the year thing. Another candidate would be Akira Maeda and the UWF. It says something for the promotional ability of someone to draw three of the biggest houses in the history of the business (including a closed-circuit major success) without any television. The UWF's success of 1988 has grown into where it deserves a strong footnote in the history of the pro wrestling business.

September 18, 1989

We're getting to that time of the year when we are going to be inundated with major shows, as if it doesn't seem like we've got one every third week already. The NWA's latest Clash of the Champions, which is its most-hyped Clash since the first one, will have taken place before you read this. My guess is the show will have set up angles leading to the 10/28 PPV show from Philadelphia. After that, the NWA will come back with another Clash card on Nov. 15 to Lead up to Starrcade '89 sometime in mid-December. Not to be outdone, the WWF has the third annual Survivors Series on Thanksgiving night, Nov. 23 and a special PPV show again on Dec. 27 which will be a one or two match card combined with an airing of the movie "No Holds Barred." The UWF in Japan is attempting its biggest undertaking thus far on Nov. 29, with a show at the Tokyo Egg Dome at the same time the other two groups will be in the midst of their annual tag team tournaments.

Not a lot is known yet about what will actually take place on these cards. We should have the line-up for Philadelphia next week, and the main event should be set up from something in the tag team main event from the Clash on Tuesday night in Columbia. I do know that the original plan for the Starrcade main event was to be Ric Flair vs. Great Muta, but that was a ways back and things like that could easily have changed. We also know that Dec. 27 was originally going to be headlined by Hulk Hogan vs. Zeus, but we're not as yet sure of Zeus' future in the WWF.

I have a line-up, or at least a semblance of a line-up for Survivor Series, although that line-up also is scheduled to be finalized early this week. The line-up I was given lists a main event between "The Hulkamaniacs" and "The Million Dollar Men." The matches will be eight-man elimination matches instead of the ten-man matches of the past two years since Titan doesn't have as many wrestlers on its roster as at this time over the past two years. The top match would have Hulk Hogan & Demolition & Jake Roberts vs. Ted DiBiase & Zeus & Powers of Pain, which goes to show you just how highly Titan really must think of DiBiase's work rate and experience to guide a trio like he's teaming with. Two other matches will be a team captained by Randy Savage against a team captained by Jim Duggan and a team captained by Bobby Heenan against a team captained by the Ultimate Warrior. Now, this line-up was from before the SummerSlam, and one has to question whether Zeus figures in the plans after he did the job in the SummerSlam

main event. The most reliable word I've got is that he still does, and Zeus was at the last set of TV tapings but never showed his face to the crowd, nor has his name even been mentioned on the WWF broadcasts the past two weekends. Perhaps in their own world of fantasy the belief is that if he isn't mentioned, that he never existed, or perhaps the ignoring of his name is because if they never mention the job he did at SummerSlam, people will forget he ever did it and they can pretend he didn't when they need to push him for the next two PPV cards.

The original Starrcade date for the NWA was Dec. 17, but I 'm now told the card will occur earlier in the week. Dec. 17 would have put the card head-to-head with NFL games, not to mention just ten days before Titan's show. I was given Dec. 13 as a tentative date earlier this week, and no live site has been officially announced other than word is they would like to hold it somewhere other than the South to break the image that they are a Southeastern regional outfit. Jeez, the Last two PPV's going into Starrcade will be in Baltimore and Philadelphia, so they almost are due for a PPV show out of the Carolinas or Georgia as they've yet to hold one there.

The World Wrestling Council is holding its "Anniversary" card this coming Saturday night (Sept. 16), which is the Puerto Rican version Of a Starrcade or a WrestleMania. The line-up for the card this time out is Sadistic Steve Strong defending the WWC Universal title against Carlitos Colon in the main event (almost every year at anniversary has seen Colon regain the Universal title on top), Ivan Koloff vs. Invader #1 (Jose Gonzales) in a chain match, TNT vs. The Original TNT, Kerry Von Erich vs. Abdullah the Butcher, Abbuda Dein & Rip Rogers defending the WWC tag team titles against Mark & Chris Youngblood, Super Medico (Jose Estrada) defending the WWC junior heavyweight title against Jeff Jarrett, Kareem Muhammad vs. Jimmy Valiant, Invader #3 (Johnny Rivera) vs. Manny Fernandez, Hurricane Castillo Jr. & Miguelito Perez vs. The Samoans (Afa & Sika) and Junkyard Dog vs. Paul Jones.

Last week we reported that there was talk that the headline match on the UWF's Tokyo Dome card could be Akira Maeda vs. George Foreman in a mixed match. The last word from Japan was that Maeda would probably face a big-name karate star, possibly Don Nakaya Neilsen, who Maeda had a famous mixed match with back in 1986. The opponent hasn't been announced as of the latest word, but my gut feeling says that the Foreman thing just can't happen. For one thing, if Foreman were to face Maeda, and naturally do the job for Maeda, it would kill any chance he would have for a future massacre against Mike Tyson. It would also detract totally from Foreman's somewhat publicized boxing comeback if he were to get involved, Let alone do the job, for a pro wrestler, and mess up plans for a boxing PPV with Foreman against Gerry Cooney in January. So while on paper, the idea of Maeda vs. Foreman would spell big business and a probable all-time live gate record for pro wrestling, the reality is that politically this appears to be a difficult one to pull off.

California state senator Richard Floyd's bill to deregulate pro wrestling in California passed the state house of representatives 62-2 earlier this week, which puts the bill in the hands of the governor who will decide the fate of the state athletic commission when it comes to regulating pro wrestling. There was no debate and virtually no opposition to the bill in the state senate.

There will be meetings held this week in regards to ESPN airing Stampede. Wrestling, as has been mentioned in the past. A lot of production value upgrading would have to be done with the Stampede show for this to take place, but one can't think that ESPN is thrilled with the ratings the AWA is now getting and that contract is apparently due for renewal in the near future. I'd say ESPN probably isn't thrilled with the quality of the shows but in reality, I doubt they would even know a good quality wrestling show from a bad quality show, but do probably realize that there is very little interest on a national basis in the AWA. I'm not sure Stampede would do any better, and at least in Nick Bockwinkel, the AWA does have a first-rate color commentator and if the Stampede duo of Easy Ed Whalen and Bulldog Bob Brown was ever visible to the U.S. public, well batten down the hatches.

This is not going to become a newsletter dealing with Roller Derby or Roller Games or any of the various incarnations of such that will be popping up over the next year. Nevertheless, I've had a lot more phone calls over the past week regarding the debut of the new syndicated version of the Roller Games than I've had about pro wrestling. The first show is set for a two-hour debut special sometime this coming week, at different times in different markets but in many markets it was to start on Tuesday night, head-to-head, with the NWA's Clash. The show has a lot of strong affiliates and about 140 stations, a comparable number of stations as the NWA's syndicated package but generally stronger clearances, particularly in the major markets. Many of the stations are using the new show as counter-programming for pro wrestling, and more particularly, the WWF, since in many places it's set for 11:30 p.m. Saturday slots (to counter the Saturday Night Main Events and Saturday Night Live on NBC) and in many other markets it is directly opposite the local WWF syndicated shows. There have been those in wrestling who have speculated that if it hits, it could put a major dent in the wrestling business. Even though I would tend to agree that the old Roller Derby/Roller Games, which were very popular in the late 60s and early 70s in some regions of the country drew a similar demographic audience and similar audience in general to what pro wrestling did in those days,

my feeling is that is an overreaction. Roller Games at best are going to only have a minor affect on the pro wrestling audience, and more likely, virtually no affect at all.

Apparently, a major corporation from Australia, which is more financially well-heeled than TBS, and not even in the same solar system, financially as Titan Sports, is behind the selling of the game. That's why it got such strong clearances with a product which has basically had no sustained appeal anywhere since 1974. Bill Griffiths, who headed up the Roller Games (as opposed to Roller Derby, two groups that differed in style similarly to the difference in style and promotion of the WWF as compared with All Japan) is behind this new group. The TV shows, which were filmed in an airplane hangar in Southern California, were supposedly done for $700,000 per episode, which is roughly ten times as much money as Titan spends per episode of its syndicated shows, or in other words, these things should be slick beyond belief. They've shot 13 weeks worth of shows and will wait to see how the response is before starting to film a second set of 13-week shows. Even though a lot of money is behind this thing, that is hardly any guarantee of success. For one thing, unlike Vince McMahon in 1984 when he was able to make several major media breaks for pro wrestling, this is a "sport" with no major established group of fans as a drawing base. There is also no deep grass roots history of anything remotely resembling this thing except in a few cities Like San Francisco and Los Angeles, and any real popularity in those markets is really from another generation. But maybe the time is right for a rebirth of a Roller Derby type deal, which like wrestling, has always had somewhat of a cyclical spurt of popularity and semi-dormancy. Certainly the so-called rebirth of wrestling, and the claimed and legitimate PPV numbers and merchandising that Titan has done was a catalyst in getting this thing going. Even before the first show has aired, I've already heard two plans of competitive groups to try and syndicate in opposition to the Griffiths league. Another Los Angeles based group called World Roller Federation, which has talked with Patrick Schaeffer about syndication (Schaeffer was involved with Global Wrestling in Florida and later Pro Wrestling this Week) and supposedly headed up by John Hall, who for years was Griffith's major star as coach or general manager of the Los Angeles T-Birds. We've also heard talks of another group using a lot of the skaters from the glory days of the Roller Derby, many of whom skated in a local league here from 1977-85. Actually when the idea for this group came around, the local league was in the running for the big syndicated slot and Griffiths supposedly got the slot since he promised that his women skaters would be babes instead of old hags. Griffiths had in the early 80s tried to revive the Roller Games based around a babyface team of pretty blonde women, chosen for looks and not for skating talent and continued to operate, but never made any serious dent in national popularity. The group running out of the Bay Area, which stuck to the traditional approach, didn't get any farther due to an inability to develop new stars and the fact the established stars were all aging, plus they didn't tape enough television shows to keep syndicated stations happy. Anyway, there is some connection with wrestling being that Bill Apter is going to be heading up the official magazine of this new Roller Games group, there is going to be a lot of glitz (and little emphasis on actual talent) in the new group which makes it similar to Titan Sports and supposedly this group is going to give the skaters wrestling-type names, there will be wrestling-style interviews and no doubt many of Titan's marketing concepts will attempt to be copied. Another show similar to wrestling and advertised heavily on various wrestling shows this weekend, "American Gladiators," based on a popular Japanese game show which Dump Matsumoto frequently appears on, debuted over the past weekend. They also have the characters similar to wrestling chosen apparently by looks and physique, given wrestling-type names and doing pro wrestling style interviews. This outfit is given less of a chance to survive than the Roller Games, mainly because there is, a generation back, and a generation before that, history of a Roller Skating style pseudo-sport that achieved a good deal of popularity.

OREGON

Scotty the Body (Scott Levy) won the tournament on 9/2 in Portland to become the Northwest champion. The title had been held up for several months since Carl Styles Left the area temporarily due to an "eye injury." Scotty won the tournament beating Styles in the tournament finals when The Grappler interfered.

First round matches in the tournament saw Beetlejuice (Art Barr, who is still being pushed as one of the lead faces particularly to kids) go to a double count out with Steve Doll and Beetlejuice won a coin flip to advance to the second round, Al Madril beat Maximum Overdrive (Jeff Warner) via DQ, Scotty beat John Boyd via forfeit when Boyd was paid off by "Scotty's mother" not to wrestle, The Grappler pinned Moondog Moretti, Styles beat C.W. Bergstrom and the returning Midnight Soldier lost via DQ to Rex King. In the next round, Madril and Juice were both DQ'd, eliminating them both while Styles beat Grappler via DQ and Scotty beat King via DQ which led to the finals. Also on the card, Bill Francis beat Nord the Barbarian in a match where both guys wore complete football gear and Doll beat Scotty via count out in a Lights out match. They ran an angle where heels Nord, Grappler and Brian Adams (Midnight Soldier, who was unmasked in his tournament match against King) attacked TV announcer Don Koss and "injured him."

STAMPEDE

TSN is in the process of becoming on basic cable throughout Canada which should give this group wider exposure.

Angel of Death has returned while a tag team called The Black Hearts and a tag team from Minnesota trained by Eddie Sharkey of the Derringer brothers are headed in.

Also back in the area is K.Y. Wakamatsu (Ichimasa Wakamatsu) as a heel manager which is another in the long line of Calgary heel managers who can't do interviews.

Maximum Overdrive tag team (Tim Hunt & Greg Sende) have left while Larry Cameron, who holds the North American title, has also left the area but word has it he'll be returning in one month to feud with Owen Hart.

Tom Nash from Florida will be starting back up this week while Jason the Terrible (Karl Moffat) still has the cast on his leg, which was broken in a few places in the July 4th auto accident and his October return may be premature.

Johnny Smith has left for Nova Scotia while Dynamite Kid is still in the Maritimes.

Davey Boy Smith returned over the weekend as did Bruce Hart. Smith is desperately trying to return to the WWF.

9/9 in Edmonton drew 220 as Goldie Rogers beat Ken Johnson, Angel of Death beat Steve Gillespie, The Samurai Warriors (Tatsumi Kitahara & Kensuke Sasaki, who are one of the best tag teams in North America on the small circuits) beat Kim Schau and Drago Zhiavago, Chris Benoit beat Jonathan Holliday via count out, Davey Boy Smith pinned Skull Mason (a rookie from the Hart family training camp) and Great Gama beat Bruce Hart via DQ.

Holliday is being billed as the Doctor of Disco and his gimmick in his matches is basically to run away from his opponents all night, which doesn't make him the most popular guy in the territory to work with right now.

CWA

Texas Dirt (Dutch Mantell) captured the CWA title from Black Bart on 9/4 in Memphis. In other major matches on the card, the Jerry Lawler vs. Buddy Landel main event for the USWA World title ended with both guys colliding head-on and getting knocked out and it was ruled that the first guy to get to his feet would be the winner and Lawler climbed up, pulling himself up with the ropes to be declared the winner. It was announced that Landel had put up his limo against the belt which is why he got the title shot. Then on television, Lawler said when he got the limo he found out it was a rented limo and then he got stuck with paying for it. Lawler confronted Landel on TV and demanded $40,000, which Landel had claimed in pre-match interviews, that the limo was worth. As Lawler grabbed Landel and started shaking him when Spike Huber attacked Lawler and hit him with a chair and Lawler juiced heavily.

Also on the Memphis card, they held a Lingerie Battle Royal won by Dirty White Girl Girl (Kim Wolser, same girl who accompanied Dirty White Boy in Alabama) when Dirty White Boy hit Donna Shepherd in the face and eliminated her. Shepherd showed up on television over the weekend with a bruised up face to make it look even worse.

Also The Wildside (Chris Champion & Mark Starr) downed the Rock & Roll Express when Champion hit Robert Gibson with a chain thrown in by Ronnie Gossett.

Gossett also announced on TV that he was now managing Huber. Gossett wasn't dressed up like The Joker this week.

On television they had a match with The Blackbirds (King Parsons & Brickhouse Brown) against Dustin Rhodes & Bill Dundee. Harold Harris didn't show up so the heels were managed by Boss Winters. Winter put ether on a towel and put Rhodes and Dundee out with it and then all three heels beat up Jamie Dundee (Bill's 18-year-old son) and put him out with the ether on a towel and then put a dress and lipstick on Jamie Dundee.

The card for 9/11 in Memphis has Jeff Jarrett vs. Don Harris, Bambi vs. Peggy Lee Leather in a women's match, Dirty White Boy & Dirty White Girl vs. Freddy (Tommy Gilbert in a Freddy Kruger outfit) & Donna Shepherd, Texas Dirt defending the CWA title against Black Bart and Bart put up a pick-up truck in order to get a title rematch, Rhodes & Bill & Jamie Dundee vs. Blackbirds & Harris, Wildside defending the CWA tag team titles against Rock & Roll Express with Gossett handcuffed to Jarrett and the main event has Lawler & Kerry Von Erich vs. Huber & Landel.

USWA

The 9/8 card in Dallas at the Sportatorium drew the same 450 ish that they've done the previous two weeks. See if you can pick up a pattern when the finishes are run down: Kerry Von Erich beat Tarras Bulba via DQ when Scandor Akbar interfered and they tied Kerry by the hand to the ringpost and Bulba kept head-butting his right hand and they "broke the claw hand;" Chris Adams pinned P. Y. Chu Hi (Phil Hickerson) and by virtue of the win got five minutes with Tojo Yamamoto. Tojo threw salt at Adams right away and had the advantage for the first three minutes before Adams made the comeback. Adams then held Tojo and his wife Toni (who was attacked by Tojo a few weeks back) slapped Tojo twice until Chu Hi came back in and attacked Chris Adams for the DQ; Al Perez & Ron Starr & Sheik Scott Braddock beat Matt Borne & Jeff Jarrett & Billy Travis when Starr pinned Borne after hitting him with a foreign object; Jimmy Jack Funk (Jesse Barr) beat Akbar via DQ in what was advertised as a bull rope match but turned out to be a chain match when Gary Young did a run-in; Travis beat Young via an over-the-top rope DQ; Perez went to a 15 minute draw with Borne and the main event saw Jerry Lawler pin Eric Embry to keep the USWA title. After a ref bump, Embry had Lawler pinned and when Eric tried to help ref Tony Falk up, Lawler snuck up from behind and cradled him for the victory.

9/15 in Dallas is headlined by a 10 man Battle Royal with the winner to get a title shot at Lawler, Kerry & Adams with Toni Adams in the corner against Bulba & Chu Hi with Tojo in the corner in what is billed as a Mexican Death match which means that each side gets to bring a weapon of their choice to ringside and there is a coinflip before the match and whichever side wins the coin flip gets to have their object put in a box on top of a pole and whomever climbs the pole can use the object; Jarrett & Borne defend the USWA tag titles against Starr & Braddock; Embry defends the Texas title against The Masked Punisher (I'm not certain of this, but I believe the guy will turn out to be the Master of Pain who lost a loser leaves town match in Memphis Last week), Funk vs. Young and Travis vs. The Texas Battleship.

Adams, in his interview, hinted that the object he was going to bring was his wife Toni's .357 magnum. Real family entertainment here.

Starr stole the tag belts at the TV tapings on 9/9. Starr & Perez went to a TV time limit draw against Jarrett & Borne and when the match ended Starr grabbed the belts and took off.

NEW JAPAN

Antonio Inoki will return to wrestling to headline cards on 12/6 in Osaka and 12/7 at the Tokyo Sumo Hall. I believe those will also be the final two nights of New Japan's tag team tournament. Inoki will apparently work a few major shows this year while serving in the Japanese House of Councilors (the upper house in the Japanese Parliament) and is expected to have a major retirement card sometime next year, perhaps at the February Tokyo Dome card.

Seiji Sakaguchi (New Japan booker) is in the United States as I'm writing this and has a meeting scheduled with Vince McMahon to attempt to book WWF talent. The price would be exorbitant and Sakaguchi has to know that, but he probably can see that the box office magic of the Soviets has worn off and they'll need a new gimmick to pop crowds. I'm sure they are looking to book Hogan at the Tokyo Dome.

9/2 in Iwaide drew 1,770 as Riki Choshu & Masa Saito & Shinya Hashimoto beat Bam Bam Bigelow & Billy Jack Haynes & Kendo Nagasaki in the main event, Salman Hashimikov & Victor Zangiev beat Hiroshi Hase & Kengo Kimura, Naoki Sano & Norio Honaga & Kantaro Hoshino upset Jushin Liger (Keiichi Yamada) & Akira Nogami & Osamu Matsuda in 16:19, George Takano double count out with Shiro Koshinaka, Owen Hart pinned Kuniaki Kobayashi, Super Strong Machine pinned Italian Stallion, Osamu Kido beat Pat Tanaka via submission and Tatsutoshi Goto beat Black Cat.

9/3 in Yonago saw Choshuu & Machine beat Bigelow & Nagasaki, tag team tournament matches saw Hashimoto & Saito beat Koshinaka & Kobayashi and Hashimikov & Zangiev beat Hart & Tanaka, Hase & Sano & Hoshino beat Liger & Nogami & Takayuki Iizuka, Kimura beat Goto, Kido beat Stallion and prelims.

Former New Japan wrestler Higo Hamaguchi (wrestling name Animal Hamaguchi, was famous as Riki Choshu's tag team partner in the mid-1980s) placed seventh in the recent Japanese bodybuilding championships.

It was announced that Hashimoto will get the main event title shot at the IWGP champion Big Van Vader at the 9/21 card in Yokohama.

ALL JAPAN

The 9/2 card at Tokyo's Budokan Hall drew 13,800 fans, which would mean another gate well in excess of $500,000. One of the "secrets" in the "revival" of All Japan's popularity in Tokyo is that in every match there is either a pinfall or submission on the big shows after years of doing so many double count out finishes. Baba learned from the success of the UWF which has nothing but clean finishes.

Main event saw Genichiro Tenryu retain the triple crown pinning Terry Gordy in 12:12 with the power bomb; Jumbo Tsuruta earned the next title shot at Tenryu by pinning Yoshiaki Yatsu, his normal tag team partner with the back suplex in 16:24; The Can-Am Express (Dan Kroffat & Doug Furnas) retained the Asian tag team titles beating The Foot Loose (Samson Fuyuki & Toshiaki Kawada) in 19:56 when Furnas made Fuyuki submit to the over the shoulder backbreaker; Giant Baba pinned Abdullah the Butcher in 14:37, Johnny Ace pinned Kenta Kobashi, Big John Tenta & Kabuki beat The Jive Tones (Pez Whatley & Tiger Conway Jr.), Shunji Takano & Shinichi Nakano beat Shane Douglas & Todd Champion, The Wild Bunch (Haruka Eigen & Motoshi Okuma & Masa Fuchi) beat Rusher Kimura & Mighty Inoue & Isamu Teranishi (who used to be three of the four top stars of the Long defunct IWE promotion in Japan), Akira Taue upset Goro Tsurumi and Akio Sato & Yoshinari Ogawa beat Tsuyoshi Kikuchi & Mitsuo Momota.

It's questionable whether Dick Slater or Tom Zenk will appear as scheduled for the October series since both have NWA commitments during that time. There is much heat between the two groups, who really could have worked together for mutual benefit but couldn't put the deal together, because it has cost All Japan a lot of wrestlers they were using regularly since the NWA is signing guys up to keep them from wanting or needing to go to Japan to earn top dollar. I believe this is Johnny Ace's last tour as well as he was offered an NWA contract (reportedly for $100,000) and it wouldn't allow him to make future Japan tours.

Baba is running a card on 9/15 in Tokyo without any foreign wrestlers with Tenryu & Foot Loose taking on Baba & Kimura & Fuchi (fans will sellout the building to see Baba wrestle The Foot Loose and Tenryu since they never meet on normal cards for obvious reasons), Tsuruta & Yatsu vs. Kobashi & Kabuki, Takano vs. Nakano (usual tag team partners against one another) as the top matches.

I believe the only NWA wrestler who is going to keep up future Japan tours will be Gordy, with the exception of the Road Warriors who may work an occasional week here and there in Japan but I doubt they'll work full tours.

OTHER JAPAN NOTES

Jimmy Backlund from Florida is going to work for Atsushi Onita's new promotion in October. Onita is going to try something different by booking a lot of Mexican wrestlers, plus book women on the same cards as men (which doesn't happen in Japan as they appeal to different audiences) and also book midget wrestlers, who don't appear in Japan or haven't for many years.

There was an incIdent in a recent Korakuen Hall match where Hashimoto faced Nagasaki and Nagasaki sold very little for the "new star" and made him look bad and Hashimoto was taunted by the fans saying things like "How can you expect to wrestle Vader when you can't even take out Nagasaki."

Akira Maeda was asked about a future match with Koji Kitao, who is expected to be New Japan's star of the future and Maeda and is supposedly the toughest of all the Japanese pro wrestlers in many fans' eyes who see sumos as the ultimate in Japanese toughness. Maeda said he wanted to wait until Kitao Learns more wrestling before considering it.

Got to see some recent tapes and a few things stood out. The tag team title match in the women s promotion where The Fire Jets (Yumiko Hotta & Mitsuko Nishiwaki) beat the Marine Wolves (Akira Hokkuto & Shizuka Minami) was first rate and given a little more time in the spotlight, these two teams will be capable of having the classic matches the Japanese women were famous for before all the big names retired. Madusa Miceli has improved her workrate tremendously here and can keep up with the Japanese for stamina, but her biggest problem is she completely lacks grace and fluidity in her moves. In other words, it looks like she misses every move she does, even if she doesn't miss, and her high spots don't look graceful even though she doesn't mess them up. When she returns to the States she'll be much-improved, but even with a year in Japan I just don't know if she'll be a smooth worker.

Jushin Liger (Yamada) is working with a serious shoulder injury, which is why the second Liger-Sano match wasn't at the level of the first. In a television tag match, Liger & Akira Nogami (who is one of the most improved wrestlers of the year) faced Sano & Hoshino and Nogami worked virtually the entire match. One noteworthy move was when he did a dive through the ropes at Sano and Sano moved and Nogami went flying headfirst into the guardrail, forehead on the top of the rail and came up with juice. A psychotic bump if ever I've seen one.

They had a televised six-man tag with Liger (5'4, 195) on one side and Vader (6'4, 340) on the other side and the two worked so well together it was amazing. Liger actually worked spots with Vader which looked legit when he did hot moves and got advantages and Vader sold what needed to be sold and also "crushed" Liger when he needed to be crushed. Liger is far and away the best working small man in the business and Vader has improved to where he may be behind only Bigelow as the best working high spot big man in the business (by big, I mean bigger than Terry Gordy who is still easily the best working 300 pounder around).

OTHER U. S. NOTES

The Cleveland rock band called "The Bastard Squad" has written a song called "If I only had a brain" and when they perform it, they dedicate it to Kerry Von Erich . Seriously.

Scott Norton has disappeared from the AWA. There are rumors flying around that he's NWA-bound, but nobody in the NWA has confirmed them. Norton signed a two-year contract with the AWA and the NWA doesn't seem to want to open up the can of worms by signing wrestlers under contract to other promotions so we'll have to see what happens.

The AWA will hold a tournament for the vacant tag team titles on 10/1 in Rochester. Everyone expects Destruction Crew (Mean Mike Enos & Wayne "The Train" Bloom) to win, since they are the only tag team currently in the AWA. Enos & Bloom are two hard workers who are both, particularly Bloom, awfully good considering their level of experience. Actually, with the exception of Dustin Rhodes, I'd consider Bloom the best rookie I 've seen this year.

Bobby Fulton promoted a show on 9/5 in Fisherville, VA with The Fantastics (Bobby & Jackie Fulton), Mod Squad, Russian Assassin (Dan Grundy), Ivan Koloff and others.

Larry Sharpe and 6'7, 450 pound protégé 'Hoss' will appear in a Piggly Wiggly commercial in the Carolinas and Virginia.

Manny Fernandez and Johnny & Davey Rich scheduled to work some dates for Angelo Gavoldi's ICW.

Nothing new on the AWA's team concept, which I had originally heard was set to debut this month but as far as I know, they haven't even started doing any tapings.

Both AWA and NWA are making noises that they are close to deals with WGN in Chicago.

Stampede Wrestling is trying to put together a deal to book Ric Flair for one shot against Owen Hart.

Afa the Samoan is promoting a card on 9/27 in Bethlehem, PA with Afa vs. Nikolai Volkoff and Ken Patera vs. Mike Sharpe.

CWF is trying to bring in Sam Houston and the Rock & Roll Express.

Former pro wrestler Edouardo Perez, who wrestled in Florida in the 1960s and early 1970s, died on 9/7 after a lengthy battle with cancer.

Despite rumors to the contrary, Florida Championship Wrestling is still alive and now has four managers, believe it or not, for a minor circuit. Blackjack Mulligan has shown up seconding his son, who now goes by the ring name Kendall Wayne Windham, as a heel. Also around as heel managers are Diamond Dallas Page, Sir Oliver Humperdink and Sonny King. King is managing The Terminator (Marc Laurinidas) and Comrade Nick Busick.

9/9 in Nassau in the Bahamas was headlined by Tyree Pride vs. Busick in a chain match, Windham vs. Steve Keirn in a bull rope match and The Playboys (Jimmy Backlund & Brett Sawyer) vs. The Nasty Boys for the Florida tag team titles.

Former karate star Benny "The Jet" Urquidez worked a wrestling match on 8/26 in Brooklyn for Johnny Rodz in Queens, NY beating Cuban Savage #2. Also on the card, besides Rodz, was Cousin Luke (Gene Lewis) and Misty Blue. Urquidez was a full contact karate legend and was the trainer of Don Nakaya Neilsen. Urquidez worked a karate match on the UWF's card Last summer at the Ariake Coliseum in Tokyo.

The deal between Leon White and Hasbro and New Japan wasn't finalized this past week for the Big Van Vader dolls. Negotiations are still going on mainly between Hasbro and New Japan before finalizing the deal.

Bob Raskin's USWA promoted a show on 9/9 in Maplewood, NJ drawing 550 as Sgt. Slaughter beat Nikolai Volkoff. Volkoff tried hard, but couldn't do anything. Slaughter didn't try and at, even though there isn't much he can do either. Cousin Luke, Afa the Samoan, Cheetah Kid, Larry Winters and Ron Shaw also worked the card.

Lou Albano was roasted on 9/9 in a M.S. benefit which raised nearly $20,000 at the Yonkers Raceway. Roasting Capt. Lou was boxing coach Lou Duva (who trained Roddy Piper for that classic boxing match with Mr. T), wrestling magazine publisher Bert Sugar (who tried to be funny, but wasn't) and Bruno Sammartino (who tried to be funny, and was, and also was quite eloquent in praising Albano). An MS spokesperson at the show claimed that Albano, through Ugly Bartender contests, had raised $35 million for MS over the past six years. Both Albano and Duva were recently elected to the Italian-American Sports Hall of Fame. Albano and Sammartino are both about to get involved in a pro wrestling trivia 900 number while Sammartino has an autobiography that is due out in 1990.

Edward Faulk 's IWF in Louisiana drew 700 fans in Vivian, LA without any major names, while 30 miles away in Shreveport, the USWA (formerly World Class) ran a show the same night (9/9) and drew 70 paid and wound up cancelling the card and sending all the boys home. Brickhouse Brown and Iceman King Parsons have four dates this week for the IWF while Nightmare Danny Davis is coming in for several shots in October as the group has 17 shows booked in October. Freddie Fargo, who does the heel columns in Pro Wrestling Digest (which is disbanding as editor Dennis Brent is doing all the writing of the NWA's new color program), works as heel manager for the group and wrestled Faulk on the Vivian, LA card.

The Northwest tag team titles are held up as on 9/9 in Portland, the match with Rex King & Steve Doll (champs) against Scotty the Body & The Grappler ended with a double pin.

Johnny Valiant is now managing Johnny Stewart in the AWA.

9/2 in Clinton, IA drew 400 as Mike George beat Curtis Hughes, Stewart no contest with Mighty Thor, Col. DeBeers pinned Derrick Dukes, Baron Von Raschke beat Larry Zbyszko via DQ and Paul Diamond & Tommy Jammer beat Wayne Bloom & Mike Enos.

Big John Studd teamed with Ricky Morton to beat The Samoans via DQ on 8/26 in Hagerstown, MD and Ken Patera beat Kimala via DQ in a co-feature.

CWF on 8/25 in Knoxville, TN saw The Southern Boys (Tracy Smothers & Steve Armstrong) team with Jerry Stubbs to beat Robert Fuller & Jimmy Golden & Brian Lee via count out, Dennis Condrey beat Danny Davis, Wendell Cooley pinned Davis, Terrence Garvin beat Adrian Street, Miss Linda no contest The Beast and Todd Morton beat Keith Hart.

Los Brazos captured the 6-man titles in Mexico. There is talk of putting together a title unification match for the heavyweights in Mexico between Dos Caras (WWA champ) and El Canek (UWA champ). Blue Demon Jr. won two mask vs. mask matches, beating EL Rayo De Jalisco Sr., who turned out to be Max Lineras, and beat El Matematico (Ruddy Garcia).

Negro Casas has appeared a few times Lately on the Galavision TV show from Mexico City.

NWA

Terry Funk's physical ailments continue. Just got word Funk suffered a staph infection in his left elbow and was forced to miss his Texas death matches with Ric Flair over the weekend and was replaced by Dick Slater. As I write this, it is touch-and-go whether Slater will have to fill in for Funk in the Clash match-up on Tuesday night.

Steve Williams returned to action this past week from his rib injuries.

Sting is working nightly with a very bad ankle, which is why several of his recent matches with the Great Muta have gone less than five minutes. Actually, almost everyone is

banged up right now because of the physical style.

The Omni card on 9/3 drew between 10,000 and 11,000 paid and $95,000, although there were nearly 15,000 in the building because kids under 12 were admitted free with a paying adult.

Flair vs. Funk Texas death drew $24, 000 on 9/4 in Nashville.

Lee Scott is turning into one of the best jobbers in the game. Certainly the craziest bump-taking jobber around.

NWA has done a terrible job getting over to fans what exactly a Texas death match is.

Besides Washington, D.C. and Chicago which I mentioned last week in having NWA vs. WWF cards head-to-head, there were also head-to-heads in Nashville last weekend, Greensboro this weekend (WWF booked nearly Winston-Salem with Hogan vs. Savage the day after NWA booked Greensboro) and West Palm Beach. At the beginning I thought this was a coincidence, but obviously that isn't the case.

TV ratings for last weekend saw NWA Main Event with Steiners vs. Freebirds draw a 2.7 rating (that match drew a 2.9) while World Championship Wrestling, delayed about 20 minutes, drew a 1.5 which is the second lowest rating in the history of the Saturday show and the Power Hour did only a 1.3, which had the Sting vs. Muta hot match.

Even though we've made a big deal about the Clash competing with the Roller Games debut, the real competition for Clash is the season opener of "Roseanne," which goes head-to-head with its second hour, and that is the single toughest competition on television.

Bobby & Jackie Fulton are headed in as The Fantastics.

Tommy Rogers is working another job and didn't want to come in full-time and is content to work only in Japan.

10/8 at the Omni in Atlanta has the first Road Warriors vs. Skyscrapers match. The main event is Flair vs. Funk in an I Quit match, while the rest of the show has Muta vs. Sting for the TV title with Gary Hart in a cage, Lex Luger vs. Williams for the U.S. title, Freebirds vs. Steiners for the tag team title, Dynamic Dudes vs. New Zealand Militia, Tommy Rich vs. Norman, Eddie Gilbert vs. Brian Pillman and Tom Zenk vs. Bill Irwin. Part of the reason the NWA is drawing so much better in Atlanta than anywhere else is because they are doing specific promos for the cards on TBS, plus airing localized interviews for the Omni matches on Ch. 69 in Atlanta, which carries the two syndicated shows.

NWA World Wide Wrestling aired on 9/9 on WPIX in New York at 11 a.m., will be pre-empted the next two weeks in that slot for Roller Games, then on 9/30 moves into the slot permanently, although the NWA has been telling people the show will air at 9:30 a.m.

NWA on TV is advertising a debut card in Syracuse, NY on 9/29, but the tickets being sold are for a card on 9/28, so who knows?

NWA lost the Capital Centre as the building cancelled all future cards and is bringing the WWF back in. I pretty much expected that would happen all along since the NWA wasn't strong enough when it got the building to sustain the size of crowds the building would be satisfied with when it kicked WWF out.

Samoan Swat Team is taking one month off I believe after this upcoming weekend.

Prelim wrestler Dale Veasy, whose gimmick, ironically is of the State Patrol tag team, was arrested this past week for theft and extortion in trying to intimidate a witness in regards to his arrest in August on a charge of selling steroids.

How come the NWA never booked a date in Amarillo when Flair vs. Funk was running? That sellout was a gimmee.

9/8 in Memphis drew 6,000 as the Militia beat Scott Hall & Ranger Ross, Eddie Gilbert pinned Ron Simmons, Williams drew Mike Rotunda, Skyscrapers double count out with the Steiner brothers, Sting beat Muta via DQ, Luger pinned Gilbert and Flair beat Slater in a Texas Death match.

Same card with same results on 9/9 at the Capital Centre before 2,500 except Luger pinned Tommy Rich there.

NWA will promote future D.C. cards at the DC Armory.

9/6 in Alexandria, LA drew 1,978 as Simmons drew with Brad Armstrong , Brian Pillman pinned Norman, Danny Spivey double count out with Scott Steiner, Sting beat Muta via DQ, Freebirds beat Midnight Express, Luger beat Rich and Flair beat Funk in a death match when Funk couldn't answer the bell for the seventh fall and Road Warriors beat SST in a cage match.

9/2 in Monroe, LA drew 3,500 as Bill Irwin beat Alex Porteau, Skyscrapers beat Hall & Steven Casey, Pillman pinned Norman, Steiners beat Freebirds via DQ, Luger pinned Dick Murdoch and Flair pinned Funk after a piledriver.

TV highlights for the weekend: Power Hour had an eight-man tag as Steiners & Warriors beat Freebirds & SST (mainly clothesline spots but a lot of action); Saturday TBS had Sid Vicious beat Scott Hall (one of the worst matches of the year, so bad that they had to insert crowd footage several times during the match over the actual action to cover up missed moves and messed up stuff) and Pillman pinned Gilbert with Gilbert's foot under the ropes (Gilbert played very subtle heel, match got over what is was supposed to but never got sustained action). Only thing I'd call "must see" was Pillman's line calling Norman "400 pounds of raw sewage" and an excellent TV match with Flair vs. Bill Irwin on Worldwide.

9/8 in Miami drew 1,100 as Lou Perez beat Powerhouse Parker, Murdoch beat Cuban Assassin, Kevin Sullivan pinned Armstrong, Jim Cornette beat Paul E. Dangerously, Pillman pinned Norman, Armstrong & Bobby Eaton beat Freebirds via DQ and Warriors beat SST in a cage. Armstrong subbed for Stan Lane in all three Florida shows

as Lane is allergic to the state of Florida right now.

Ricky Santana should return in about one month after major knee surgery.

No Power Hour this weekend.

WWF

Only newcomer is "Tugboat Tyler" who is Fred Ottman (Big Steele Man) as a babyface so that's the role they decided for him.

Hillbilly Jim, Jim Neidhart and Bad News Brown will be taking temporary short-term leaves in a few weeks. Hillbilly wanted to be taken off the road because his mother had a stroke.

The new $18 top ticket price for Madison Square Garden is also for all other New York area major shows. The first MSG on 9/30 has Ultimate Warrior vs. Andre the Giant for the IC title, Brain Busters vs. Demolition for the tag titles, Roddy Piper vs. Rick Rude, Jimmy Snuka vs. Honky Tonk Man, Ron Garvin vs. Greg Valentine and Red Rooster vs. Mr. Perfect.

The long-delayed trial in the lawsuit of former pro wrestler Steve DiBlasio (Big Daddy) against Dusty Rhodes when Rhodes was booking Florida begins this week. DiBlasio claimed that Rhodes ordered him to take a bump over the top rope in a match against Les Thornton in 1983 and a broken ankle from the bump ended DiBlasio's career.

Steve Blackman worked some upstate New York dates.

The Hart Foundation and Rockers had a match at the Springfield, MA TV tapings ending in a no decision with the Rockers interfering. Heard it was a *** ½ star match and the crowd was 70 percent pro-Hart Foundation.

St. Louis on 9/30 has Hulk Hogan vs. Randy Savage in a cage match. It's the only place I've heard of the match being booked, probably to make up for Hogan missing the previous St. Louis card due to his pinched nerve in his neck.

WWF has shows in Paris and London this fall.

WWF is still in the running to promote the PPV of a Rolling Stones concert in mid-December. No musical act has ever done business on PPV yet, for example the Sammy Davis, Frank Sinatra, Liza Minelli concert and a Grateful Dead show both did barely any better than the AWA's Superclash show. The Who on PPV bombed a few weeks back as well. The Stones should do better than any of them no matter who promotes it, but it's not like this will do the kind of business a major wrestling event on PPV does.

Correction from a few weeks back. Jim Powers is out of action because of a bad ankle, not a broken cheekbone as we'd reported.

Another wrestling album is due in mid-December with cuts by the Rockers, Koko B. Ware, Rougeaus (that song still cracks me up), Jimmy Snuka, Dusty Rhodes, Hillbilly Jim and Roddy Piper. I guess that means another Slammy's for this year as well.

King of the Ring tournament will be 10/14 in Providence, RI.

9/9 in Boston Garden drew 6,000 as The Genius Lanny Poffo pinned Koko B. Ware ½*, Bad News Brown pinned Hercules DUD, Warrior beat Andre in 33 seconds, Rick Martel beat Brutus Beefcake via DQ ** (started very bad but very good finish), Akeem pinned Hillbilly Jim —**, Greg Valentine double count out with Ron Garvin * ½ (lots of stiff chops, very little movement), and Rockers beat Rougeaus in a marathon match three falls to two which lasted 65:30. Didn't lock up for ten minutes and the first half hour was nothing great but turned into an excellent match. The stips weren't over with the crowd because when the first fall ended, about half the fans left the arena so they missed the best action of the night. When they announced the Warrior vs. Andre rematch for 10/7, there was no pop at all.

9/9 at the Met Center in Bloomington, MN saw Tugboat Tyler beat Brooklyn Brawler (Steve Lombardi), Dino Bravo pinned Mark Young, Tito Santana pinned Haku, Dusty Rhodes beat Big Bossman, Jim Duggan beat Ted DiBiase via DQ, Rick Rude double count out with Roddy Piper and Demolition beat Tully Blanchard & Arn Anderson via DQ.

Andre no-showed his matches with Warrior in Houston and Dallas last week.

All American drew a 2.7 rating on 9/3 while Prime Time was pre-empted in its regular slot by tennis and they just had Monsoon do a late-night version of the show.

THE READERS' PAGE

WORKMAN'S COMPENSATION

I recently had the opportunity to attend the UAWF convention in Chicago. During the convention, Nick BockwinkeL spoke at a fans' press conference. One fan asked Bockwinkel about medical and disability benefits available to wrestlers who are injured while wrestling.

I am an attorney in Chicago. I represent many football players as both an agent and as their attorney in workers' compensation claims. At the recent NFLPA meetings in Chicago, I was asked to work with the NFLPA in workers' compensation claims. I asked Nick the follow-up question of whether any wrestlers had made claims for workers' compensation benefits with the WWF. Nick was not aware of any claims having been made.

Workers' compensation laws differ from state to state. In general, an employer need not provide workers' compensation insurance for an independent contractor. The government agency that administers workers' compensation claims in Illinois is the Industrial Commission. The Commission will bend over backwards to find that a claimant was actually an employee rather than an independent contractor. Although many factors are considered in determining whether a

person is an independent contractor or an employee, the factor given the most weight by the Industrial Commission is the degree of control maintained by the employer. A wrestler working a one-shot deal for an independent promoter would probably be classified as an independent contractor, whereas a wrestler under contract to Titan or World Championship Wrestling would most likely be classified as an employee under Workers' Compensation Act. The fact that a wrestler and promoter might stipulate in the contract that the wrestler is an independent contractor is merely one of many factors the Industrial Commission would consider in determining whether that wrestler was an independent contractor or an employee.

Are you aware of any claims filed by wrestlers for workers' compensation benefits? Have any wrestlers been able to obtain their own workers' compensation insurance as they move about the country as independent contractors? Did Adrian Adonis make a claim against the AWA when he broke his ankle?

Raymond Asher
Chicago, Illinois

Dave Meltzer: I'm not aware of any wrestlers filing workers' compensation claims. Because wrestling is so politically-based when it comes to push and the like, nobody would risk the ire of the promotion or the fear of other promotions for something prior, to actually make a claim I would think against a major. There are wrestlers who have their own insurance but they are in the minority. I do know that the NWA wrestlers under Crockett had an insurance plan but don't know if they do under Turner or not, but there were stipulations and I think ring-related injuries weren't part of the plan. Adonis either was going to file suit, or had filed suit against the AWA for his broken ankle, just before his death last summer.

NEWSLETTERS

This letter is in response to Ed Garea's in the 8/28 issue, concerning newsletter criticism. I feel Garea was referring to my bulletin Chokehold, but for some reason, didn't mention it by name. For those unfamiliar with the situation, I recently ran an article criticizing the newsletters of Tom Burke and Harvey Cobb. I did so because I was fed up with people putting out half-assed publications and not caring about their readers too much. Global Wrestling News Service and Pro Wrestling Enquirer both feature bland, outdated news, poor spelling and grammar and outrageous prices. That sums it up without repeating my entire article.

Garea must live in a castle if he refers to wrestling promoters as "the enemy." Whether we do inside sheets or not, promoters are the ones who financially back the performers that make wrestling go around. I hardly think of them as enemies. According to his letter, "No newsletter editor has the right to criticize another." I wonder if there is a provision about this in the Constitution which excludes newsletter editors from the Freedom of Speech amendment. Yes, I have criticisms of other newsletters and I'm going to speak up about it. Would it be better for all newsletters to report the same news without any concern for putting out a quality product? Should we all peacefully make no waves and be happy about people who claim to care about the business but can't take the time to simply proofread their own newsletters? No, it is my right, and everyone else's right, to speak my mind. Why have a newsletter if you can't say what you honestly feel?

As for your analogy that Time doesn't openly criticize Newsweek, you assume all the bulletins are competing with one another. I don't consider PWE and GWNS either as rivals or competition. I simply made statements criticizing them. And putting the spelling and grammar of PWE in the same league with Time could land one in prison for slander.

When you reviewed bulletins in Wrestling Eye, you say that if you didn't like a bulletin, you still didn't say anything bad about it. Why? Many unsuspecting readers would send money to people like Cobb, based on your so-so-review, and unfavorably decide what wrestling bulletins are apparently all about based on his, and blow off excellent publications Like the Observer and Matwatch. I suppose if someone did a one page newsletter in crayon with stolen material and charged $10 an issue, you'd still condone a nice plug for them because the more bulletins there are the better.

Lance Levine
Chicago, Illinois

I've been an avid subscriber for three years and have not written a letter yet, but I feel it is time to voice my opinion. When I first began subscribing, the newsletter contained many stories about what goes on behind the scenes of wrestling. There were things that you could only learn from reading your newsletter. About a year ago, it began becoming something different. You started leaving ends open. Nothing from behind the scenes. It was disappointing. I feel the newsletter began to lose its substance at that point. In the last few months, it has become a letters page. Pages and pages of letters from people praising the Baltimore Bash. Who cares? What do most readers really care about what Sally or Joe in Wherever, USA think about the Baltimore Bash? The endless letters which repeat what you say are nothing but birdcage liner. Let's get back to what made me wait by the mailbox on Saturday for more information.

Another thing I'd like to address is your obvious bias against the WWF. It might be difference of opinion but I think there is no comparison. I attended the 8/11 NWA show in Pittsburgh and I was very bored. I just can't get interested in Tommy Rich against Lex Luger. And the Flair vs. Funk match that everyone raves about was no big deal.

Fifteen minutes of rest holds and ten minutes of action is no big deal. A week later, I attended the WWF show in Wheeling. I sat front row for both cards. Wheeling was jammed and the fans were psyched up for every match because they knew the wrestlers and the matches meant something. The Hogan-Savage match was fantastic. I agree booking has a lot to do with it but the people were into it. For Flair vs. Funk there was no heat. The Hogan vs. Savage was fast-paced with good moves and very entertaining.

One last thing I'd like to comment on is the Oakland 2. I was glad they were thrown out of the building. It was the correct thing to do. In a sold out building where the environment is one of a good time, they shouldn't let two malcontents ruin everything for everyone else. You blame Vince McMahon for stopping the show and putting the place into a lull, but you have to remember that Vince pays a lot of money to fly the TV equipment and cameraman to put out a first-rate product. It was written in the 9/3 issue that was not smart, you are right, it was smart-ass. If they wanted to show their sign, they should have protested outside the building where there weren't any cameras. But they violated whatever rights they had by coming inside and trying to get on camera. The Oakland 2 were the ones who tried to ruin everyone's good time by delaying the show. I don't think anyone would have bothered them outside the building.

Walter Kurelis McKees
Rocks, Pennsylvania

FANS' BEHAVIOR
I had front row seats for the Springfield taping with four other friends. I was wearing a Pro

Wrestling Illustrated T-shirt and a buddy of mine was taking pictures while I took notes on the card. After the first hour, I was asked by a WWF official to please take one of their T-shirts instead of my PWI shirt to wear. I didn't argue, but asked for all five of us to get shirts. They complied and also gave us WWF Ice Cream bars, Bret Hart sunglasses and Hacksaw Duggan 2x4's. They asked if we were taking photos for commercial usage and we said no, and they said okay. They were very friendly, and so were we, but they are a paranoid bunch.

Dan Reilly
Enfield, Connecticut

Last week a New York TV station reported a story on fans being ejected from Yankee Stadium for carrying derogatory banners and/or wearing shirts or caps that stated "George Must Go." A Yankee security guard interviewed stated that these signs were causing profanity and rowdy behavior among the fans. Like the confiscated NWA signs at a recent Titan taping, these anti-Yankee management signs in reality caused no disturbance at all, other than a WWF-

Like paranoia among the powers, er, egos in charge of the company. Unlike the WWF incident, the ACLU got wind of these illegal ejections and have threatened to take action against the Yankees if something like this happens again. Should Vince's Gestapo continue their tactics of sign removal, we might see WrestleMania VI featuring the ACLU against the WWF and the ACLU is a tag team that doesn't do jobs.

Steve Gennarelli
Binghamton, New York

SUMMERSLAM

SummerSlam may have been the WWF's best PPV effort to date. It at least rivalled the 1988 Survivor Series as the best. It looks as if Titan is learning how to put on good shows from the NWA. The production was slick, most of the wrestling was good and Tony Schiavone and Jesse Ventura worked well in the broadcast booth. I think if they added Gorilla Monsoon and made it a threesome it would have worked better because Ventura could have directed his barbs as Monsoon, who is quicker with his replies.

A major reason why the card was so successful was because it was held in the Meadowlands where there were real wrestling fans, unlike at Trump Plaza. If I had to rate the show on a one-to-ten basis, I'd give it a solid eight. If McMahon really believed what he said on Entertainment Tonight, I don't think he would have bothered to spend the time to put together this good of a show.

Vincent DiPaLma
Copiague, New York

Why do I persist in giving the WWF a chance to prove itself with its PPV shows? Yes, I watched SummerSlam. Yes, it was terrible. Yes, it was even worse than last year's fiasco. Both Nashville and Baltimore kicked tail on this show. Not only was the action better, but so was the announcing, the graphics, the camera work and the ring entrances. Now if the NWA could only label their tapes properly.

SummerSlam had a few good moments. Hennig fileted the Rooster, they gave DiBiase a win even if it was a cheap count out. Honky Tonk's case of amnesia was priceless and Ron Garvin's ring announcing was hilarious. The highlight of the card was the Warrior vs. Rude match. This was near a Flair/ Steamboat match by standards although that just goes to show the quality of the matches Vince offers. Rude showed why he can be one of the best in the business. In the ring, he was superb and both his interviews were excellent as were Heenan's histrionics after the loss. I must admit, I feared for Warrior's health at the 15 minute mark but he probably had the best match of his life. By the way, was he speaking English during his interview?

As for the bad, which I'll limit, Dusty does look fatter than ever. Andre can't even walk, let alone wrestle. What happened to Tony Schiavone? During the Warrior and Hogan matches he sounded more like Vince than Vince.

We knew Zeus couldn't wrestle and he proved that. We knew Savage would work and he did. We thought Beefcake would take the pin, which he didn't. We knew Hogan had the biggest ego in wrestling which he reassured us of.

For weeks, I've been reading letters about how erratic the NWA's booking is. Wake up. That Hogan finish is the worst booked finish I've ever seen. How could they build up a guy as a superhuman for four months, get him over Like crazy, and then destroy it all in one night?

Gabriel Daigle
Buena Park, California

DUSTY RHODES

All my life one of the performers I've enjoyed the most has been Dusty Rhodes. I never tired of watching him even when it was in to participate in Dusty bashing. Dusty Rhodes and Tully Blanchard gave me the impression that not only did they hate each other as wrestlers but deeply hated each other as people, which made their matches more interesting. The Rhodes character was a classic and I never tired of watching and collecting videos or memorabilia on him. I bring this up because I want to express my concern over the sorry treatment of the Dusty Rhodes character since coming to the WWF. The Rhodes character used to come across natural and believable on interviews and skits. Now it's forced. It's painful to watch him try and act live a jive, jolly, effeminate fat man. I can't believe this version could be more popular than the real Rhodes character. I wonder if the decision to have him act like a buffoonish slob doesn't have so much to do with marketing ideas as much as people wanting to humiliate former competition. I can't blame Virgil Runnels because a job is a job and you've got the bills to pay but I miss the character I've enjoyed for years and I'll still support him as a way of saying thanks for years of entertainment. I know a lot of people hate him and that's sad. The man spent years giving everything to this sport and whether you agree with his methods or not, you don't survive that long without having something going for you. When people like Ted DiBiase, Terry Taylor, Barry Windham, Ray Traylor and others entered the WWF, Vince rebuilt them from the bottom up. Dusty still had enough clout to enter with almost the same character and go right into the matches. A topic of conversation was at the local card, people were talking about the upcoming Warrior vs. Andre match. I felt sorry for the fans who were carpooling all the way to Long Beach to see the match since I was aware of how short it would be. But it just proved how Vince can get over talentless guys. The fans in my section were calling Tully Blanchard "Too Boring" Blanchard. So many things about this sport I love yet I hate that the majority think Warrior is an unbelievable wrestler while a tremendously entertaining and hard-working wrestler like Blanchard is viewed as boring.

Dan Cerquitella
Redlands, California

TSN WRESTLING CENSORS

I'm writing to comment on an incident which recently took place on TSN wrestling. Ed Whalen was interviewing Larry Cameron and Camerson became enraged when the fans started chanting, "Owen, Owen, Owen," and Cameron responded by saying, "That is the thing that pisses me off most." I was shocked and disgusted not only with the language used but by Mr. Whelan's irresponsibility in not pulling the mic immediately on Cameron or censoring the interview later. He didn't even flinch. How such a well-respected and responsible community-minded person like Mr. Whalen could let this profanity, aswell as such poor grammar, go on air is beyond me. I will seriously consider not letting my little girls watch the show again.

J.Z . Travis
Woodstock, Ontario

SEPTEMBER 25, 1989

The steady stream of big shows continued this past Tuesday night with the NWA's Clash of the Champions card from Columbia, SC on TBS.

While the show left a lot of people with some positive emotions, because for the most part the action was top-notch and it was a good live television special, not to mention it delivered surprisingly strong ratings, I think people who are thinking that this was a turnaround for the promotion are being quite premature. The promotion is months away from a turnaround in its fortunes, and that's provided that the occasional steps forward aren't negated by steps backward which always seem to follow.

Before getting into the NWA news, and there's a lot of it this week, we rundown the Clash show:

1. The Road Warriors beat the Samoan Swat Team in 6:46. The Warriors opened early doing a lot of clotheslines to gain the early edge until Hawk missed a shoulder block and went flying to the floor. Hawk was then pummeled after a groin shot on the guard rail. The SST got heat on Hawk. One interesting thing I noted is that when they had the near falls on Hawk and he kicked out, that there was no crowd "pop." Yet every other near fall situation on the card where the babyface was down, the crowd popped for the kick out. This is where that invincibility works against you. People don't believe there's a chance of actually seeing that pinfall, so it makes it hard to build up heat by long-term selling. Animal tagged in three minutes later and they went to the four-way leading to the finish. Paul E. Dangerously threw the phone in to Samu who went to hit Animal. Hawk clotheslined Samu and hit Fatu with the phone after it dropped. Animal then lifted Fatu up on his shoulders and Hawk gave him the flying clothesline off the top rope to set up the pin. After the match, Paul Ellering punched Paul E. Dangerously (which the cameras missed, and it wasn't like this was the only shot of the night that the cameras missed) and Ellering then destroyed the telephone, stomping it into oblivion. The SST then walked out of the ring without Dangerously. They had been hinting for weeks that the break-up of Dangerously and the SST would occur, and it figured to be on this card. It wasn't much of an impact-making break-up, which my impression was, because they didn't want to focus on this because they were getting ready to phase out Dangerously. I'm not sure if this was the plan, but it turned out to be the end result. Solid work throughout with a good finish to end the feud. *** ¼

2. The Z-Man (Tom Zenk) beat The Cuban Assassin (Dave Sierra) with the sleeper in 3:36. This was the only match on the card that didn't have good heat, and that's hardly an unexplainable phenomenon, since nobody "knew" Z-Man and he just showed up out of nowhere with no build-up. This was the one match on the card where I didn't care for the commentary as Jim Ross and Jim Cornette pulled a Vince McMahon "Who is he?" routine. While I'm sure that a great number of fans didn't recognize Zenk since it's been two years since he's been with the WWF (and so few people watch the AWA), the bottom line is a great number of fans did recognize who he was and it made the announcers look like they didn't know the business they were covering. In the WWF, that's fine, because that's part of the gimmick, but in the NWA, that's pretty insulting to your audience and hurts the credibility of your announcing and production team as "experts" in the field when the fan thinks he's either being insulted, or knows more than the guy who is telling him what's going on knows. Zenk mainly used armdrags. It was too routine a performance for a debut match and the sleeper isn't too spectacular of a finisher nowadays. My own belief on Zenk is that he has the potential to be a star here, but only if he's spectacular in the ring, because he's so similar in look and physique to Brian Pillman and Scott Steiner, both of whom can be spectacular performers and on this night he came off a distant third. ½ *

3. Sid Vicious destroyed Ranger Ross in 1:08 with the power bomb. Basically a squash match but they did the "right thing" in keeping Sid as a killer and also they didn't give Sid long enough to screw up any moves. ½ *

4. The Freebirds (Michael Hayes & Jimmy Garvin) retained the NWA tag team titles beating the Steiner brothers in 10:27. This match began at exactly 9 p.m. Eastern time since the Clash was going to buck "Roseanne," the highest rated show on television, and it was felt they needed a strong match to start at this time so as not to lose too much audience. As it turned out, this worked perfectly, since the show's ratings held up during "Roseanne," which is something that couldn't be said for the Roller Games debut show in the markets where it competed with "Roseanne". The Freebirds came in with only one tag belt because the other one was stolen somewhere on the road. The NWA frantically tried to get two of the three old six-man belts from out of Minnesota that the Road Warriors held with Tenryu to be brought in as new belts but they must not have arrived on time. The Steiners dominated early doing their hot moves until Rick missed a dive into the corner and they started pounding on him. There was tons of heat at the finish, particularly when Scott made the hot tag at

10 minutes and did the Mata head-scissors move on both Freebirds. As Scott came off the rope, he was tripped up by Robin Green and Hayes used the DDT to finish him. The camera missed Green tripping Scott, which was planned as they wanted to put mystery on which woman (Missy Hyatt or Robin Green) did the tripping and Scott claimed Robin did it while Rick claimed Missy did it. *** 1/2

5. Brian Pillman pinned Norman the Maniac in 3:38 with an arm and leg crucifix takedown. While short, this match was excellent for the time it was on. Easily the best both guys have looked since they came to the NWA. Norman was told beforehand to work like he worked in Canada and surprised a lot of people, since his work ability had been subdued in trying to play a Lunatic. Pillman did a flying crossbody onto Norman onto the floor and his springboard off the top rope clothesline. As Pillman went after Teddy Long, Norman crunched him from behind and went to work on him. Norman missed a crunch into the post and Pillman got the advantage back until he was caught in mid-air on a flying press and was power slammed. After kicking out of two near falls, Pillman hooked the arms and legs for the pin. After the match they had an argument with Norman and Teddy Long. Too short to be a three-star match but too good to be anything less than three stars.

6. Steve Williams pinned Mike Rotunda in 7:04. Williams did five press-slams in succession on Rotunda early. Both guys worked hard and solid here. Finish saw Williams try to stampede Rotunda who held onto the ropes and fell on top but Williams reversed it and got the three count. Rotunda attacked Williams after but Williams managed to run him off. ***

7. Lex Luger pinned Tommy Rich in 10:36 in the surprise match of the night. Not that the result was a surprise, but the quality of the match was. This was a fast-paced excellent match with both guys shining here. The finish was kind of weird as Rich "hurt his hand" punching the post, but got the sleeper hold on with Luger outside the ring and Luger dropped down and Rich caught his throat on the top rope and was pinned. ****

8. Ric Flair & Sting beat Dick Slater & Great Muta via disqualification in 19:16. The match itself was excellent but the angle afterwards has turned into one of major controversy. All sorts of good moves, some of which the cameras actually caught. Heat was incredible. They did one excellent false finish where Gary Hart hit Sting with a foreign object and it looked like a sure fall but Sting kicked out. Flair bled at the 17 minute mark and the ref wound up on the floor. Terry Funk, who came out of the hospital specifically for this angle, put a plastic bag over Flair's head

and "tried to suffocate" him. At the same time, Slater hit Sting's ankle several times with the branding iron and the faces were both Left lay ing and 'out'. **** 1/4

The show itself drew a 4.7 rating as a composite which means 2.4 million homes and approximately 5.3 million viewers. The rating itself was the best for any Clash since the third Clash from Albany, GA last year with Barry Windham vs. Sting on top with John Ayres doing the run-in. As for the number of viewers, it was actually the most number of viewers (since TBS is available in more households this year than last year) for any Clash except the very first one opposite WrestleMania IV. The show opened strong with a 3.9 rating for the Road Warriors vs. SST match and stayed at that level and grew slightly during the first hour. It popped up to a 4.9 rating for the Freebirds vs. Steiner brothers match, which was opposite "Roseanne" in most of the country. It was thought going in that this was the second hottest match on the card, and judging from the ratings this was a correct assumption. In contrast, the Roller Games in Los Angeles dropped 63 percent when "Roseanne" came on for their two-hour special on KTLA. The ratings dipped slightly (4.5) for Pillman vs. Norman and showed a slight increase (4.8) for Williams vs. Rotunda. The Luger vs. Rich match drew a 5.3 rating while the show peaked for Flair's tag match which drew a 5.8 rating and a 9.1 share or three million homes and million viewers which made it the second-most watched match in NWA history behind the Flair vs. Sting match at the first Clash. Overall, these numbers have to be an encouraging sign, since every Clash this year had seen ratings dip, and this Clash was facing tougher competition with first-run network prime-time than any of the previous Clashes of late, particularly in "Roseanne," and the much hyped Roller Games debut in several markets which was figured to draw a similar demographic. It is expected that this will be the highest rated show of any kind on cable television for the month of September and it will probably be the highest rated wrestling show on cable television for the year of 1989, including Titan Sports shows.

There was a lot of good with the show and some bad. The work-rate was basically excellent throughout with six of the eight matches being good-to-excellent, one other lasting just one minute and being a kill job and one match which wasn't too good, but it was at least short. The crowd enthusiasm was superb, particularly considering the live crowd was only 2,600 in Columbia, yet they made more noise and showed more enthusiasm than the 20,000 at the Meadowlands on Titan's PPV show two weeks earlier. The lighting was quite good, although the camera work left a lot to be desired. In fact, many people disliked the show particularly because of the camera work, which missed several key shots, and because of that, when they were "supposed to" miss a shot in the finish of the Steiner brothers match, it made them look even more inept because they'd been missing shots all night, including key shots (Paul Ellering belting Paul Dangerously and breaking the phone, one or two totally telegraphed spots during the Warriors match, too many crowd shots again at inopportune times during the show, and unforgivably getting bad shots of both dives out of the ring by Sting and Muta in the main event, plus showing Flair with a bag on his head while they were doing the angle to explain Sting's ankle injury, not to mention missing Terry Funk's run-in, he was all of a sudden in the ring without any explanation). The NWA's camera work had been showing improvement at the recent PPV shows and this was a major step backward. The announcing was basically very good, particularly in the Rich vs. Luger match where Jim Cornette managed to use a lot of background info to tell a story and make Rich seem like the legitimate contender that nobody else has been able to put him over as to this point. It helped that the two put on a hot match. The lone complaint with the announcing, and my guess is this was a decision by the higher-ups, was it made the announcers look bad to not know anything about Tom Zenk, since at least a decent percentage of the fans knew who he was and he had appeared on ESPN not all that long ago.

As far as the changing of the announced main event, there were a lot of complaints about this registered to me. There was nothing they could do about that because Funk legitimately was hurt. He had a severe staph infection in his elbow and the blood poisoning had spread and he underwent surgery about a week before the Clash. The television promos were all taped beforehand and the final TBS shows before the Clash were taped beforehand. The injury was actually so severe that the doctors said if Funk hadn't had it treated for a day or two longer that they would have been forced to amputate the arm. Still, Funk came out of a hospital bed to do the run-in on the show. However, to the public , Funk was fine on Friday night's Power Hour and people saw it as a cheap way to change a main event that had been pushed for weeks. The problem here is the basic lack of trust a lot of fans have for the NWA because they've been burned so many times with no-shows and changing of announced matches at house shows. A promotion that had been totally honest with its public, and even though that is a lost art today in this country, it can be done and you can promote successfully being honest as people like Giant Baba, Paul Boesch and Sam Muchnick showed and all three were successful for decades, could have done the same scenario with no complaints because people would have believed the scenario. Ironically, this scenario was totally legit, the changing of the card was completely excusable, but people have been burned so many times with bait-and-switch from the NWA dating back for the last few years that many saw this as another cheap angle. This could have all been avoided if on Saturday's shows or the late promos they

spent a few minutes doing a new voice-over and promos, and may even have cost them a few viewers on Tuesday (but it wouldn't have been a significant number) but overall my opinion is they have to bend over backwards to regain the trust of the fans, and even then it will take at least 18-months to two years to do so. I'm not holding my breath because the current business regime doesn't appear to believe that keeping fans up-to-date about the house show line-ups is an important priority.

As for the bag over the head during Funk's run-in - own personal opinion when watching the show was I didn't think anything of it, just saw it as a different type of run-in and given what is coming up and given that Funk had to do something given the current circumstances with the promotion since the injury suffered in the fans' eyes would complete Flair's revenge on Funk, the run-in finish was the only finish that would be correct for this. After all, it was a free television show, not a PPV, and every other match on the card had a pinfall, and only one of which had even the slightest bit of controversy. However, I've heard far too many complaints and those complaints are valid about the bag over the head. Pro wrestling is a combination of sports and entertainment, and attempted murder is neither sport nor entertainment. The announcers came back from the most inopportune commercial break and talked about how during the break Brian Pillman had to give Flair mouth-to-mouth resuscitation and that is pretty strong stuff. Don't say Titan wouldn't have done it, because they did an Andre heart attack and the Randy Savage/Steamboat angle where they had to cut a hole in Steamboat's throat so he could breathe, and the bag over the head has been used in other promotions, and in fact last summer I saw Jim Cornette and the Midnight Express use it as a gimmick against The Fantastics in several cities and nobody complained about it then, but I can see the point.

From our readers poll, the show was considered an aesthetic success:

CLASH POLL

Thumbs up: 311 (88.6 percent)
Thumbs down: 35 (10.0 percent)
Undecided : 5 (1.4 percent)

I should mention a few more things before getting into readers' comments on the show. They did two skits on the show, one, "The World According to Theodore R. Long," was basically Teddy Long doing his DJ voice and making some comments about cards in future cities over the next few weeks. It was just a way to plug upcoming house shows on what turned out to be the highest-viewed show of the year and one which the regular house show plugs weren't running on. They also had a segment with Missy Hyatt and Robin Green going shopping, with Robin getting Rick

Steiner's American Express card and buying a $1200 dress and a $998 piece of jewelry and renting a limo for the day, trying to portray Robin as "using" Steiner to set fans up for the finish of the tag match. The skit and the ensuing tag match finish went hand-in-hand, and in that way, the skit was fine in the context of the show. The actual execution could have been better, and the few lines Missy Hyatt had were out of character for her, but it served its purpose in the overall story.

Readers opinions on the Clash:

"Thumbs up. The main event was less marvelous than expected without Terry Funk but it was still pretty well done. Luger worked a good match and overall a good show."

Joel Lerman
Stanford, CA

"Thumbs up. Terry Funk's interview from the hospital bed alone gave it a thumbs up, let alone all the great matches."

Bill Johnson
Reading, PA

"Big thumbs up and easily the best Clash they've ever done. Matches were good-to-excellent except for the Z-man which was a Zzzzz. Couple of glitches in the camera work. It was incredibly dumb for the announcers to plug the 900 number and ask people to turn off the TV audio and listen to the telephone audio. The Funk run-in was too predictable but overall the show was absolutely excellent".

Mike Omansky
Wycoff, NJ

"Resounding thumbs down. The bookers must have had their own heads in a paper bag because of that angle. Sid Vicious and Brian Pillman got over good and Jim Cornette did an excellent job in the Rich—Luger match and Rich worked real well himself".

Jeff Bukantz
Livingston, NJ

"Thumbs up. Even though Funk was hurt they handled it really good. Zenk sucked. They did a good job with Sid. The best match was the main event. Rich-Luger, Steiners-Freebirds and Warriors-SST were all good and the finish with Steiners and Robin was good. Ironically, I think Funk not wrestling on the card will help the next PPV. Thank god there are no fat transvestites in the NWA, although Norman certainly qualifies as being fat".

Freddy Curtaz
Daly City, CA

"Thumbs up but a lot of people were upset at the bad camera work. They missed Paul Ellering punch Paul E. Dangerously. People were also mad that Funk didn't wrestle. Good Halloween Havoc commercial."

Dave Rubin,
Island Park, NY

"Great from start to finish but I kept going to the store to buy Twix candy bars from all the ads on television so I missed half the show and gained two pounds."

Harry White
St. Louis, MO

"Thumbs up, no question but who was directing? They missed too many shots. They were too tight on Sting and Muta's dives. The angle with Robin Green was perfect. The paper bag over Flair's head was a little disgusting but it was effective. Cornette's comments that they went too far came off as a shoot. There are a lot of ways to do an angle but I don't think suffocating someone should be one of them. That's a criminal offense and not entertainment. Pillman vs. Norman was fantastic, Warriors vs. SST pretty good, Steiners vs. Freebirds was excellent, Loved Missy and Robin shopping and Ross and Cornette did the best announcing job I've ever heard on a big show."

Mike Kachel,
Rockville, MD

"Pretty good but the camera work was atrocious, but the wrestling made it a good show."

Mike Wood
Sacramento, CA

"Excellent show. Much better than SummerSlam. The only bad thing about the show was Tom Zenk's match. Overall the best Clash since the first one."

Floyd Perry
Stockton, CA

"The last match was fabulous. Big time thumbs up."

Peter Thiele
KSTP radio, Minneapolis, MN

"Very good show. The ending with the plastic bag was a bit too much but overall it was a great card."

Bob Verhey
Denver, CO

"Thumbs down for two reasons. The main event promised wasn't the match you got and this was possibly the worst camera work I've ever seen. Too many crowd reaction shots. The camera work ruined the whole show. What was there was good when you could see it, but there was no payoff in the main event."

S.C. Dacy
Hollywood, CA

"Thumbs in the middle, or maybe just a middle finger for the camera work. The main event was really a great match but boy did they screw up the camera work something awful. If Mean Gene was announcing, he'd have said it several times during the show."

Skeeve
Brea, CA

"Thumbs down. The camera work was terrible and the show wasn't up to NWA standards. They didn't set up enough for the PPV."

Dan Weisberg
New York, NY

"Thumbs up. The matches were all good with some great angles, especially when Funk put the plastic bag over Flair's head. Ross and Cornette were good as usual on commentary."

Sid Brooks
Tifton, GA

"Thumbs up. The action was non-stop throughout the show. On the negative side, Jim Ross kept on telling us to call the Wrestling Hotline. Once or twice would have been okay, but it seemed like he told us 100 times."

Rich Slovarp
Fargo, ND

"Overall very good. The action level was high the whole card and I was very surprised to see Flair and Sting get destroyed like that in the main event. The only bad points were Jim Cornette's constant talking and those irritating Twix commercials. Give it a 7 out of 10. "

Chris Walker
McLean, VA

"Easily the best Clash to date. I thought it surpassed the last two PPV cards and overall it was good enough to be a PPV card. The matches were fast-paced and the bumps were great. Road Warriors vs. SST was the best match. The final match was a big disappointment. I was expecting Terry Funk and got Dick Slater. It took too much of the excitement away. I also expected more from the angles. The SST and Paul E. angle never materialised and I expected more of an angle out of the main event. It should have been Muta putting the bag over Flair's head. Flair as a babyface can be another Hulk Hogan in popularity."

Vincent DI Palma
Copiague, NY

"The matches were all entertaining and the main event was great. Luger vs. Rich was better than I expected. Although Funk not wrestling bothered me, Slater did a good job. Considering it was a free show, what more could anyone ask for? My main complaint is it was too obvious Funk was going to run- in. On the other hand, the Steiners vs. Freebirds finish was great with the whole camera angle gimmick."

Bruce Colon
Chicago, IL

"Thumbs up because overall the action was quite good. There weren't too many problems although the camera shots of the audience were annoying and some hot moves were missed altogether. None of the matches were really bad, although The Z Man's match was off. I didn't like the plastic bag act and Slater didn't belong in the ring. When Ross informed us that Pillman revived Flair with mouth to mouth resuscitation I had a flashback to Fritz Von Erich's bogus heart attack. That plastic bag went a little overboard. Praise goes to Luger for carrying Rich."

Tony Amara
Boston, MA

"Marginal thumbs down. Ross and Cornette were great together and most of the matches were good. The finish of the Flair match left me with a bad taste about the show. Trying to make Funk a challenger to Flair's title by having him try to suffocate Flair was too much to take"

Frances Delauretis
Shoemakersville, PA

"By allowing himself to take a beating the way he did, Flair did the same thing Akira Maeda did last year, put the promotion in front of his own ego. Flair and Sting were the most popular NWA tag team in years, but they didn't play supermen and made it look legit. The plastic bag kept me interested. The video with Missy and Robin was hysterical. The ending of the Steiners-Freebirds didn't work. I was so inspired by the main event that I'm attending the next PPV show and I've never traveled anywhere for a card."

Andy Stowell
Pittsburgh, PA

"Hang Keith Mitchell at high noon, and make sure the angle is shot properly. For God's sake, no crowd shots. The guy did more for Tommy Edwards' credibility as a wrestling director than Tommy ever did for himself. How could they miss so many shots? Really, they made a tremendous main event look bad on television. At least he got the Steiners-Freebirds ending right. The wrestling itself was about par for the NWA and once again showed their in-ring superiority over Titan. Pillman and Luger's matches were both watchable. Luger made Rich look pretty darn good."

Gabriel Daigle
Buena Park, CA

"Overall thumbs up. Too many crowd shots. Great preparation work by the announcers. Enough quality matches to offset the bad ones. A very respectable show, especially for a freebie. The tag matches all cooked. The singles matches were flat except Pillman vs. Norman. Loved the overhead corner shot when Lex went to splash Rich. Hated missing the dives by Muta and Sting."

Ernie Santilli
Drexel Hill, PA

The next big one up for the NWA will be the Halloween Havoc PPV show on 10/28 from the Philadelphia Civic Center. I've still yet to get any kind of an adequate explanation as to why they are even running a PPV show this close to Starrcade (which by the way, has been finalized for December 13th at the Omni, which is a Wednesday, which makes it awfully difficult for people who want to travel to see the show). Anyway, the line-up I've been given for the show has Flair & Sting vs. Funk & Muta in a cage match on top; Luger vs. Pillman for the U.S. title; Road Warriors vs. Skyscrapers; Freebirds (with Terry Gordy) vs. Steve Williams & Midnight Express; Z Man vs. Mike Rotunda.

A few notes on the WWF's Survivor Series PPV on Thanksgiving night from the Rosemont Horizon. The main event we listed last week has been confirmed to me as the actual main event, with Hulk Hogan & Demolition & Jake Roberts vs. Powers of Pain & Ted DiBiase & Zeus. Zeus in fact will then be facing Hogan on live shows throughout much of December leading to the PPV. Since the PPV show is on a Wednesday afternoon, that makes me think that the Hogan vs. Zeus match has to be taped because I can't believe they'd run a live house show match on a Wednesday afternoon. I don't have the complete line-up for the Survivor Series, but do know that Randy Savage's team (which includes Barry Windham) will face Jim Duggan's team; Ultimate Warrior's team faces Bobby Heenan's team; Rick Rude's team faces Roddy Piper's team and Dusty Rhodes has a team as well and I'm not sure who they are facing but I think Bossman & Akeem are on the opposing team. All the matches will be eight-man elimination tag team matches. I also know that Jimmy Snuka will be on Roddy Piper's team and a lot of people are already forseeing a turn at this point.

Lots of big names on the injury list right now. Besides Funk, who was "suspended indefinitely" by the NWA on the TBS show Saturday for his actions with the plastic bag on Tuesday's Clash (my guess is the suspension will be lifted just a few weeks before the PPV and the PPV show will be Funk s first match back, however I believe Funk will still

appear on his television spots doing interviews and Funk's Grill), others out at present include Roddy Piper, Sting and Brian Pillman. Piper was rushed to the hospital this past Monday night and originally it was thought he was going to have to have his gallbladder removed, but it turned out he was suffering from fractured and bruised up ribs and he'll be back in action roughly about the time you read this. For now, Jake Roberts is starting back early to take his place. Sting had been bothered by a bad ankle for several weeks, which is why many of his house show matches with Muta had been disappointing. The bit on television during the Clash where Dick Slater pounded his ankle with the branding iron was to explain the arthroscopic surgery he was undergoing and he'll be out until early this coming week. Pillman was hospitalized over the weekend when he was coughing up blood. It has never been fully explained on the NWA TV although Jim Ross constantly hints about all the obstacles Pillman has had to overcome, but one of the ones is probably around two or three dozen operations to his throat going back to childhood.

The WWF's annual King of the Ring tournament on 10/14 in Providence, RI has a pretty disappointing line-up. The non-tournament main event sends Dusty Rhodes vs. Big Bossman, while the tournament itself has these first round matches: Red Rooster (Terry Taylor,) who is scheduled to return to action this week at the WWF's TV tapings in Louisville and Cincinnati following arthroscopic knee surgery when he blew out his knee at SummerSlam) vs. Haku, Jimmy Snuka vs. Konga the Barbarian, Jim Neidhart vs. Hercules, Brutus Beefcake vs. Akeem, Rick Martel vs. Hillbilly Jim, Warlord vs. Luke Williams and Butch Miller vs. Widow Maker (Barry Windham).

The biggest out-of-the-ring story of the week is that Paul E. Dangerously officially was fired on Thursday, after the TV taping in Atlanta. The firing occurred after a backstage argument between Dangerously and Ric Flair over a number of things, but most particularly because Dangerously was uncertain about his future role with the promotion. Actually I believe this had been brewing for about three weeks although I'm not sure why. The original plan was for Dangerously to stop managing after the Clash temporarily as the Samoans were going home to San Francisco for about a month and the Samoans and Dangerously had never gotten along from the start. He was to continue to do television work and then return sometime down the line in a managers' role again, but after watching the way the break-up was handled on Tuesday night, it appeared the writing was already on the wall. The final straw was Thursday, when according to one side, Dangerously didn't do what he was told to do on the Danger Zone, and according to the other side, he wasn't given any direction in the first place and the ensuing argument resulted in the firing. I'm really not sure of the legitimate reasons for all this because it had been brewing for a while and whatever happened on Thursday seems more like an excuse to do something that was eventually going to happen anyway. But in a promotion where Gary Hart is managing the top three heels, this hardly seems like a move that makes any sense from a business standpoint. People can say what they want about Dangerously, but nobody can accuse him of not being as good a manager as Gary Hart. Additionally, it is a valid point that the highest rated wrestling show on TBS for almost this entire year has been the Sunday show with Dangerously as host, and it has never been that way in the past with more than 10 years of pro wrestling history on the station on both Saturday and Sunday.

Governor Carol Campbell of South Carolina was on the Clash show and proclaimed Tuesday as "Ric Flair Day" in the state of South Carolina. Most of the time when politicians do these things they come off as stiff and phony because the politicians generally aren't familiar with what is going on in wrestling and it's easy to see they are just doing it to get their faces on television. Not the case here. Campbell, who I'm told has been a big wrestling fan way back, was both enthusiastic and came off as knowledgeable in his announcement including saying how many people consider Flair as the greatest pro wrestler of all-time.

The AWA has announced the teams for its proposed new team concept promotion and television show which will have its first taping on 10/1 in Rochester, MN. Last week on television when they did a press conference to announce the three captains (Larry Zbyszko, Sgt. Slaughter and Baron Von Raschke), they had names on the board as possible entrants to the promotion including Tully Blanchard, the Rockers and Ricky Steamboat, which was a pretty classless act. Anyway, Zbyszko's team will include himself, Ken Patera, Akio Sato, Wayne Bloom, Mike Enos, Bob Orton, Ivan Koloff, Kokina Maximus (Kokina the Samoan) and Jake Milliman plus female wrestler Magnificent Mimi (Mimi Lessos) and manager Johnny Valiant. Slaughter's team has Col. DeBeers, Jerry Blackwell (sure), Bobby & Jackie Fulton (this is only the third promotion in the last week that claims to have these guys), Johnnie Stewart, Pat Tanaka, Tom Stone, The Unknown Soldier and female wrestler Wendi Richter. Von Raschke's team (and just the fact he's a captain dooms this concept from the start) has himself, Mike George, Paul Diamond, Big Van Vader, Todd Becker, Derrick Dukes, Tommy Jammer, Russian Brute, The Trooper, girl wrestler Candi Divine and manager Ox Baker.

The story about Bam Bam Bigelow getting into boxing was reported in the Tokyo newspapers last week. The newspapers reported that Bigelow signed a contract with Ray Parker, who is the boxing manager of George Foreman. The story of a proposed boxing match against Mike Tyson in Tokyo was explored, and Bigelow claimed in the article that Don King told him that he would get a fight with Tyson

in one year after they had him beat six opponents during the year. This doesn't confirm that this story is true, only that it has been reported elsewhere.

I was in Chicago over the weekend for no apparent reason although there was the Bears-Vikings game and both NWA and WWF wrestling in town over the weekend. I wound up missing the WWF show on Saturday night because nobody that I knew wanted to attend (they drew more than 12,000 fans to the Horizon and $148,000 for Hogan vs. Savage on top with a very weak undercard). The NWA show was one of the worst ones I've seen live all year, officially drawing 1,859 paid with 2,522 in the building (I don't know where they were hiding them because it sure didn't look Like that many) and $23,658.

1. Greg Evans pinned Larry Williams with a Randy Savage elbow drop off the top ropes in 8:15. DUD

2. Cuban Assassin pinned Richard Sartain in 6:00 after a backbreaker. ½ *

3. Dynamic Dudes beat New Zealand Militia in 9:00 when Rip Morgan had Johnny Ace picked up for a bodyslam and Shane Douglas dropkicked Ace's back and he fell on top for the pin. **

I missed the first three matches because of traffic getting out of Soldier Field but got reports on the matches from Steve Sims, Lance Levine and John Henricksen.

4. Butch Reed pinned Scott Hall with his feet on the ropes in 11:00. I can't describe how bad Hall looked in this match. The guys worked hard but everything looked terrible, including a messed up finish and having to go back and try a similar finish again. – ½ *

5. Rick & Scott Steiner went to a double count out against the Skyscrapers (Sid Vicious & Danny Spivey) in 15:21. There were some cheers for the Skyscrapers here. The match itself was mainly clowning around and stalling in between spots, but the finish was pretty intense. The highlight was both Steiners standing on the same turnbuckle and diving simultaneously with flying shoulder blocks on each member of the heel team. Scott Steiner did do his Mata headscissors move on Spivey (you didn't think he 'd try it on Sid, did you?). Sid is going to be a big superstar of the 90s but he sure looked bad here. Scott did a german suplex on him near the finish and Sid wasn't too happy about it either. The finish saw Spivey crack a chair over Rick's head hard and the chair bent but Steiner didn't sell it at all and they fought outside until both were counted out. * ¾

6. Lex Luger pinned Tommy Rich in a match that wasn't

scheduled on the card to begin with but they brought the two in for the show to hopefully pacify the fans because Terry Funk and Sting, two of the guys in the top two matches, weren 't going to be there because of injuries. Everyone booed Rich and cheered Luger here, even more so than in any other arena. This match was every bit as bad as Tuesday night's match was good. Mainly headlocks and armlocks with Luger yelling at one section of the crowd which did chant stuff like steroids and the like at him. He got good heat from that section but the remainder of the fans were all comatose and there were cries of "boring." Finish saw Rich try to suplex Luger in the ring but Rich's leg was hooked in the rope and Rich tripped and Luger fell on top for the pin in 13:39. ½ *

7. Dick Murdoch beat Great Muta via DQ in 5:30 in a TV title match. All restholds, mainly a long short-arm scissors by Muta. Neither guy did a thing. Finish defied all logic. Gary Hart ran in for the DQ. Murdoch subbed for Sting, but surprisingly, nobody really seemed too unhappy about it. ₋ ** ½

8. Ric Flair kept the NWA title beating Dick Slater in a deathmatch when Slater couldn't answer the bell for the sixth fall in 18:33. When Slater and Hart came down the aisle for the match, they might as well have been two security guards or two fans because nobody either cared or noticed, or both. Flair got the big pop. It was announced at the beginning of the card that Funk wouldn't be there and Slater was taking his place and the people booed that one loudly. Nobody cared about Slater, but from about the four minute mark on, most of the crowd was on its feet. Slater wasn't bad or anything and it was a pretty good match. Flair bled four minutes in and Slater won the first fall when Hart held a chair in the corner and Slater ran Flair's head into it. Slater won the second fall with the neckbreaker. Flair won the third fall with the figure four leg lock and the fourth fall with the figure four while on the floor. There were a lot of low blows by both guys throughout the match. Finish saw Hart throw in a chair and Slater go for the piledriver, Flair reverses it and gives Slater a piledriver, then during the rest period between falls behind the refs back, Flair hits Slater in the head with a chair once again and Slater can't answer the bell for the next fall. By the standards of Ric Flair matches that I've seen in 1989, this was disappointing and nothing compared with last month's match with Funk, but they still brawled up and down the aisles using chairs and tables and had about three-quarters of the crowd on its feet for about ten minutes straight. *** ½

NEW JAPAN

Senator Antonio Inoki returned to wrestling during the middle of this week as a special referee for Big Van Vader's

title defenses on 9/20 in Osaka against Bam Bam Bigelow and 9/21 in Yokohama against Shinya Hashimoto. Inoki will wrestle in Osaka and Tokyo in December on the last two nights of the tag team tournament.

Hashimoto is getting a major push as the new tag team partner of Masa Saito. The two won the tag team tournament, beating Salman Hashimikov & Victor Zangiev in the finals on 9/15 in Nagahama before 2,210 fans. By virtue of the tournament victory, the two got the shot at IWGP World tag team champions Riki Choshu & Takayuki Iizuka on 9/20 in Osaka and captured the title as well when Hashimoto pinned Iizuka in 18:52.

I believe that Owen Hart will capture the IWGP jr. heavyweight title on 9/21 in Yokahama from Naoki Sano.

Seiji Sakaguchi went to the United States to try and meet with Vince McMahon about booking Hulk Hogan on the February 10 date at the Tokyo Dome but Vince wouldn't meet with Sakaguchi. Even though it is virtually impossible that any kind of a double-cross would occur should Hogan wrestle in Japan, Titan is in the position where it really can't afford and doesn't need to take the risk. Sakaguchi did meet with the NWA and Ric Flair in Memphis but I believe the only NWA wrestler he was able to book for the Tokyo Dome card was the Great Muta, who if he returns on that show, will get a huge push since he's been able to go to the top of the NWA.

The TV show for this group has been pre-empted throughout most of this series due to other sports programming so the only show aired on 9/2 with Hashimoto & Saito vs. Zangiev & Hashimikov as the main event and did a 3.9 rating.

JAPANESE WOMEN

JWP set some records on its tour of Korea. They drew a paid attendance on 8/28 in Seoul, Korea of 4,750 which is a recordfor the group, then had a free show at the Olympic Stadium in Seoul, Korea on 8/29 which drew 37,000 fans, which may be an all-time record for women's wrestling, but it was a free show.

Madusa Miceli captured the vacant IWA World Women's title beating Beastie on 9/14 in Kumamoto before 3,000 fans. Chigusa Nagayo had held this title since winning a tournament in Calgary last year so this is actually the Stampede wrestling version of the World's women's title.

Speaking of Nagoya, her first concert since her retirement as a pro wrestler was about a week back in a Tokyo music hall and it was considered successful since it both got good reviews and drew a sellout crowd.

Her recently retired tag team partner Lioness Asuka is taking a different road, as she has become a professional auto racer and had her first race on 9/16.

Also in Kumamoto, The Fire Jets (Yumiko Hotta & Mitsuko Nishiwaki) retained the World tag team titles beating Kumiko Iwamoto & Nobuko Kimura.

UWF

The 9/7 card at the Nagano Gym drew a sellout 4,500 fans and $140,000 as Yoshiaki Fujiwara made Masaharu Funaki submit with an achilles tendon submission in 14:15, Akira Maeda made Johnny Ballete (Jumbo Baretta) submit with a chicken wing cross face in 6:49, Nobuhiko Takada beat Yoji Anjo with the sleeper in 8:59, Kazuo Yamazaki knocked out Minoru Suzuki in 11:09 and Shigeo Miyato beat 'Keiji Tamura with the chicken wing crossface in 5:40. This was considered an "easy show" because none of the matches, with the exception of the main event, had any real doubt about the outcome of who would win or lose however it still sold out in a small city and the fans went crazy for Maeda, Takada, Yamazaki and Funaki.

Koji Kitao was at the card and had photos of himself and Akira Maeda all over the newspapers the next day. Even though it had been reported in newspapers beforehand that Kitao was going to challenge Maeda at the show, the two had an amicable meeting and Maeda asked Kitao if he wanted to become the Japanese Hulk Hogan and Kitao said yes. Maeda then invited Kitao to attend the next UWF shows on 9/30 and 10/1 in Tokyo.

UWF is trying another experiment with these shows as they are booking three match cards, again with matches where every fan knows who will win and lose ahead of time, on consecutive nights to see just how little they can give on the matchmaking and still sellout and save the "big" matches for the major cards. The 9/30 Tokyo show has Takada vs. Tetsuo Nakano as the main event, Fujiwara vs. Norman Smiley and Anjo vs. Tamura. The next day in Tokyo has Maeda vs. Miyato, Yamazaki vs. Bart Vail and Funaki vs. Suzuki. 10/25 in Sapporo has Fujiwara vs. Takada and Maeda vs. Funaki in the first time either of these matches will take place with the new UWF.

The Tokyo Dome card in November looks to be headlined by Maeda against a karate fighter. Speculation from here is that it will be Rob Karmen, who beat Don Nakaya Neilsen recently in the WKA World title match in Tokyo. Maeda was at ringside and was the first person in the ring to raise Karmen's hand after he knocked out Neil sen in the third round.

ALL JAPAN

Giant Baba's 30 year anniversary special card commemorating his professional debut in 1960 drew an easy sellout of 2,350 at Korakuen Hall on 9/15. Results of the card saw Genichiro Tenryu & The Foot Loose beat Baba & Rusher Kimura & Masa Fuchi in the main event when Tenryu pinned Fuchi; Jumbo Tsuruta & Yoshiaki Yatsu beat Kenta Kobashi & Kabuki; Shunji Takano pinned Shinichi Nakano; Akira Taue pinned Akio Sato; Motoshi Okuma pinned Haruka Eigen;

Mighty Inoue pinned Goro Tsurumi and Mitsuo Momota pinned Yoshinari Ogawa.

Ironically, that was the second pro card of the day in Korakuen Hall as JWP ran a Friday afternoon card in the same building and drew a sellout of 2,070 paid to see Devil Masami beat Shinobu Kandori via knockout in the main event plus Miss A kept the UWA International title beating Eagle Sawai.

Tenryu's long-awaited triple crown defense against often-time tag team partner Toshiaki. Kawada of the Foot Loose, stemming from Kawada winning the tournament a few months back to get the shot, will be on 10/8 in Korakuen Hall.

Baba's next big show will be 10/11 in Yokohama headlined by Tenryu defending the triple crown against Tsuruta; The Can-Am Express (Doug Furnas & Dan Kroffat) defending the Asian tag team titles against Kobashi & Joe Malenko and Kawada & Stan Hansen vs. Yatsu & Takano.

The tour begins on 9/30 in Okinawa with Tenryu & Hansen vs. Tsuruta & Kabuki on top, and the next night on the same island will have Tenryu & Kawada vs. Tsuruta & Takano as the main event.

TV ratings have been strong of late as the 8/27 TV show drew an 8.2 rating (Tenryu & Kawada vs. Terry Gordy & Todd Champion on top); 9/3 drew another 8.2 (Tenryu & Kawada vs. Tsuruta & Yatsu for the tag team title) and 9/10 drew a 7.9 (Tenryu vs. Gordy for the triple crown).

STAMPEDE

The 9/16 card in Edmonton saw Biff Wellington pin Drago Zhiavago with a DDT * , The Black Harts managed by Hugo Hart beat Steve Gillespie & Ken Johnson * ½, The Samurai Warriors (Kensuke Sasaki & Tatsumi Kitahara) beat Skull Mason (a rookie from the Stampede camp) & Goldie Rogers *, Chris Benoit pinned K. Y. Wakamatsu (former Japanese manager Ichimasa Wakamatsu) * ¼, Davey Boy Smith pinned Angel of Death ½ * and Great Gama kept the Commonwealth title beating Bruce Hart via DQ.

9/15 in Calgary saw Kim Schau beat Gillespie, Dr. Bee Gee Holiday (Jonathan Holliday, proclaiming himself the Doctor of Disco and claiming to be single-handedly reviving this somewhat dead musical form) beat Benoit via count out, Angel of Death beat Ken Johnson, Samurai Warriors beat Rogers & Zhiavago, Smith pinned Mason and Bruce Hart beat Gama via DQ.

Owen Hart returns on Friday night's card in Calgary.

The Black Harts are billed as relatives to the Hart family, like nephews or illegitimate sons of Stu Hart, I'm not exactly sure of the gimmick but they are heels. I believe the two are Tom Nash & David Heath from Florida who do a lot of double-team hot moves but are pretty green while their manager, Hugo Hart, is the same guy who worked here earlier as manager Ronald A. Trump (Ben Ryan).

USWA

The 9/15 card at the Dallas Sportatorium drew 400 as Billy Joe Travis beat Texas Battleship, Eric Embry beat The Masked Punisher (Master of Pain) via DQ to keep the Texas title, Kerry Von Erich & Chris Adams beat P. Y. Chu Hi & Tarras Bulba in a Mexican Death match (foreign object on a pole), Ron Starr & Sheik Scott Braddock won the USWA tag team titles beating Jeff Jarrett & Matt Borne when Starr hit Borne over the head with a chair and Eric Embry won a Battle Royal to get a title shot at Jerry Lawler on the 9/22 card.

It was announced on 9/22 that the Lawler vs. Embry title match would be a Lumberjack match and Embry would pick the lumberjacks and he picked Jarrett, Borne, Travis and Adams. It appears that of the four, it will be Travis who turns heel and costs Eric the World title since at the TV taping on 9/16, as Travis was getting pounded on by the Punisher, Embry ran in to make the save and caused Travis to lose via DQ and Travis was "upset" as Ernbry and claimed he didn't need the help. The semifinal is Adams vs. Chu Hi in a cage match and if Chu Hi wins, then Tojo Yamamoto gets a date with Toni Adams. Pretty sick stuff.

They aired a video of the Rock & Roll Express on television as coming in.

Starr is Looking very good and is said to be the best worker on the circuit right now.

9/10 in Mesquite, TX saw Embry & Adams & Percy Pringle beat Chu Hi & Gary Young & Yamamoto in a scaffold match when Young took the big plunge, Jarrett & Borne kept the tag belts beating Starr & Al Perez, Kerry beat Bulba via DQ in a dog collar match, Jimmy Jack Funk beat Braddock which gave him a five minute match with Scandor Akbar while Funk won via DQ when Braddock and Young interfered and Travis beat Cowboy Tony.

The Labor Day card in Fort Worth on 9/4 saw Embry & Adams beat Chu Hi & Young in the Triple Dome of Terror match which could only end when one man was knocked out and Young did the job, Borne & Jarrett & Frank Dusek beat Perez & Braddock & Akbar, Travis beat El Grande Colossor Pringle beat Yamamoto in a mud wrestling match with Mark Lowrance as referee, Kerry beat Bulba via DQ in a lumberjack match when Perez interfered and Funk beat Bounty Hunter.

CWA

A couple of title changes to report. The CWA title went back-and-forth this past week with Black Bart beating Texas Dirt (Dutch Mantell) to win the CWA belt on 9/11 in Memphis, however Dirt regained the title on the 9/18 Memphis card. The Rock & Roll Express (Ricky Morton & Robert Gibson) won the CWA tag team titles from Wildside on the 9/11 Memphis card when Chris Champion was about to throw powder in Morton's eyes, Morton

kicked his hand, the powder went into his own eyes and a double dropkick finished the job. They had a tag team title rematch on the 9/16 television studio show ending in a pull-apart brawl with lots of juice. Later in the show, the heels jumped Morton as he was doing an interview. Also on TV, Dirt faced Buddy Landel which ended in a DQ on Landel when Bart interfered and used the branding iron to give him "injured ribs" leading to the 9/18 title match. On the 9/11 Memphis card, Bill & Jamie Dundee & Dustin Rhodes beat King Parsons & Brickhouse Brown & Boss Winters when Jamie Dundee pinned Winters with a flying bodypress off the top rope.

Mike Davis is back forming a tag team with the Dirty White Boy.

The 9/18 card was billed as a benefit for wrestler Jerry Bryant who is in real bad shape right now because of Lou Gehrig disease. Buddy Landel even did an interview on television praising Bryant which made him come off as a face because he was out of character.

The 9/18 line-up had Stan Frazier vs. Spike Huber, White Boy & Davis vs. Jason & Freddy (I believe Jason is now Doug Gilbert), Blackbirds vs. Bill Dundee & Dustin Rhodes, Lou Winston (Bryant's old tag team partner as The Memphis Vice) vs. Landel, Bart puts up the CWA tag title and allows Dutch Mantell to return against Texas Dirt, who if he lost would have to unmask and get his head shaved), Jeff Jarrett vs. Ronnie Gossett with the loser getting powdered up and having to put on a diaper, Rock & Roll Express vs. Wildside in a two of three fall match and Lawler defending the USWA title against Kerry Von Erich on top.

Lawler & Von Erich beat Huber & Landel in a tag match in the main event the previous Monday and split up once again after the match. On TV, they showed a tape of the excellent match the two had at Superclash where Lawler played heel using a foreign object and Lawler said on his interview that he was going to wrestle Kerry like he does in all the other cities, which basically acknowledges that he's a heel everywhere but the CWA area.

9/10 in Jonesboro, AK drew 260 as Donna Shepherd beat Vicki Lynn ½ *, Freddy beat Gossett via DQ when the Wildside interfered DUD, Morton & Gibson beat Blackbirds ** , Dirt beat Bart via DQ when Dirty White Boy interfered * ½, Morton & Gibson beat Wildside via DQ ** ¾ and Lawler beat Landel via DQ n a 20 minute match for the USWA title on top ** ¾. An interesting note on the card is that Morton grabbed the house mic before the match with Wildside and said, "These boys (referring to Wildside) worship the devil and if you cheer them you're going to hell with them. He said that because all the young kids cheer Wildside instead of Rock & Roll Express.

Highlights of 9/18 saw Kerry beat Lawler via DQ when Kerry pulled out a foreign object but Lawler got it away from him and was caught using it; Morton & Rhodes (subbing for "injured" Gibson) beat Wildside via DQ in a two of three fall match, Dirt beat Bart to regain the title and Jarrett beat Gossett who was powdered up and put in a diaper.

OTHER NOTES

Larry Sharpe and Dennis Coraluzzo promoted an independent show on 9/16 in Cherry Hill, NJ and drew 2,700 fans in the rain (I was told they had actually sold 5,500 tickets for this show) as Sharpe & Jerry Lawler beat Joe Daniels & Sonny Austin in the main event ** and Stan Hansen beat Kimala via DQ in a match where they brawled all over the place and Hansen threw mud (outdoor show at a race track) all over Kimala and ended up breaking the nose of the referee who slipped in the mud **** while Nikolai Volkoff and Jim McPherson appeared in prelim matches. The same group is looking to promote a Hansen vs. Abdullah the Butcher match soon.

A combination USWA/Memphis show will now be set for November somewhere in the Northeast.

Chris Love is starting up an independent in the Carolinas.

Rex King & Steve Doll won the held up Northwest tag team titles on 9/16 in Portland. The finish, in the match against Scotty the Body & The Grappler, saw Jonathan Boyd come to ringside with the snake and chase King back to the dressing room. The heels then were doubling on Doll and had him beat when King came back down the wrong aisle from the dressing room and got into the ring and rolled— up Grappler from behind, just as he had Loaded his boot and was about to kick Doll.

9/2 line-up in Caguas, PR saw Carlitos Colon vs. Nikolai Volkoff on top, Invader #1 (Jose Gonzales) & Junkyard Dog vs. Sadistic Steve Strong & Chicky Starr, TNT vs. Original TNT, Miguelito Perez vs. Rip Rogers and Hurricane Castillo Jr. vs. Kareem Muhammad.

Titan's Survivor Series was the first PPV card ever held in Puerto Rico although I'm told the NWA blew it there because the NWA wrestlers are more well known in Puerto Rico than the WWF wrestlers. Colon was scheduled to have PPV for the first time ever for the 9/16 anniversary show.

Bobby Fulton and Ron Wyatt promoted a show on 9/6 in Fisherville, VA drawing 410 as Ivan Koloff threw out Spike ofthe Mod Squad to win a Bunkhouse Battle Royal when Bambi hit Spike with a chair, Fantastics beat Mod Squad, Ivan Koloff beat Russian Assassin (Dan Grundy), Bambi beat Peggy Lee Leather, Batman (Jackie Fulton) beat Brad Anderson (managed by Gene Anderson— Gene Anderson also managed The Mod Squad).

9/7 in Chatham, VA drew 480 as Batman won a blindfold Battle Royal, Ivan Koloff & Bobby Fulton beat Mod Squad via DQ when Russian Assassin and Gene Anderson interfered, Peggy Lee Leather beat Bambi, Ivan beat Russian Assassin, Batman beat Brad Anderson.

An indie on a Naval Base in Long Beach, CA. included The Beast (a Mexican wrestler who looked very impressive) beating Mando Guerrero, Eddie Guerreron beat The Centipede (great match), Jay Strongbow Jr. (Don Giovanni) beat Jack Armstrong, Susan Sexton beat Reggie Bennet and a co-ed Battle Royal won by The Beast.

8/26 in Caguas, PR had Strong vs. JYD, Abbuda Dein & Rip Rogers vs. Invader #1 & TNT for the WWC tag titles, White Angel (Curtis Thompson) vs. Original TNT, Perez vs. Muhammad and Super Medico vs. EL Exotico.

NWF drew 1,000 in Indio, CA as Sgt. Slaughter beat Krusher Krugenoff, Wendi Richter beat Susan Sexton, Cousin Luke (Gene Lewis) beat Armstrong plus The Mercenaries (Billy Anderson & Louis Spicoli) on the card.

10/11 in Patrick Air Force Base, FL has Sika the Samoan vs. Bugsy McGraw in a chain match plus Bill Mulkey, Bambi, Rusty Brooks, Bob Cook and Tommy Wright on the card.

WWF

Al Perez and Nikolai Volkoff are headed in during October. Perez is working as an opening match babyface while Volkoff will be a heel and reforming the Bolsheviks tag team with Boreus Zhukov as Titan is short on heel teams right now.

Titan will be airing another Election Night special on the USA network that will be taped in either England or France in October. The first WWF card in London, England is 10/10 with Hulk Hogan vs. Randy Savage on top and the card has already sold out.

Group W cable in Chicago ran Titan's SummerSlam PPV for free last week.

John Studd appeared at a Las Vegas video game convention signing autographs and the folks there were under the impression he was appearing for Titan Sports. Don't know the real story or if that's the case, but it does sound strange. Speaking of Studd, all of Titan's newspaper ads for SummerSlam listed Studd in the six-man tag match instead of Jim Duggan even though Studd had left the promotion months earlier.

9/17 in Toronto drew 9,000 as Hulk Hogan pinned Randy Savage and after the match Savage and Sherri were beating on Hogan until Jimmy Snuka made the save, Snuka beat Honky Tonk Man, Brutus Beefcake beat Rick Martel via DQ, Widow Maker (Barry Windham) beat Mark Young, Lanny Poffo beat Koko B. Ware and Paul Roma pinned Barry Horowitz.

Hogan's other appearances over the weekend drew a sellout and $180,000 house in Los Angeles on 9/15 against Savage and the 12,500 and $148,000 the next night at the Rosemont Horizon.

Hogan has some matches booked in October against Bad News Brown and in November against Mr. Perfect which are just "easy" wins before Zeus in December and I expect Windham the early part of 1990.

Hogan vs. Savage in a cage on 10/6 in Miami.

Next tapings after this will be in Wheeling, WV and Toledo, OH.

Jesse Ventura did get the job as radio color analyst for the Tampa Bay Buccaneers.

The first Andre-Warrior rematch after the 30 second matches was 9/17 in Tuscon, AZ and drew just over 3,000 fans.

9/10 at the DC Armory in Washington, DC drew 8,200 as Akeem pinned Hillbilly Jim, Bad News Brown pinned Hercules, Beefcake beat Martel, Ron Garvin beat Greg Valentine, Rougeaus beat Rockers via DQ and Hogan pinned Savage.

Prime Time Wrestling on 9/11 drew a 2.9 rating, which is the lowest rating since Roddy Piper returned. The major factor in the drop is that this was the first week the show went head-to-head with regular season NFL games. All American on 9/10 drew a 2.7 rating.

OTHER NOTES

Steve Keirn beat Kendall Windham to win the Florida title on 8/24.

Giant Baba is wanting to promote four shows in the United States in 1990.

Buck Robley is starting up an independent promotion in Louisiana and Mississippi in January.

Ron West, who has been general manager of the CWF under David Woods, left the promotion because Robert Fuller has basically taken over and is going to start his own opposition group in October using Pez Whatley, The Fantastics and Ivan Koloff as the top draws.

Cactus Jack Manson will be headed to the CWF when his wrist heals up while Ron Fuller will make some spot appearances and Kerry Von Erich is booked on 9/22 in Knoxville.

Edward Faulk's IWF had three small town shows in Louisiana over the weekend drawing two crowds of 400 and the other of only 100. Freddie Fargo had his first pro match in a tuxedo street fight against promoter Edward Faulk on the card.

NWA

The actual crowd at the gate for last week's show at the Capital Centre was 4,000 and $45,000 (I had reported 2,500 last week) and it is the NWA's last show in the building. The WWF insisted on exclusivity or they wouldn't come back. The NWA also will no longer get the one Bash date each summer that they had in the past as Titan insisted on total exclusivity this time around.

Titan also booked Worcester, MA two days before the NWA's debut show there in October.

The NWA's debut show in Rochester, NY has a weak advance as of last report.

The PPV card in Philadelphia has sold 2,000 tickets and $30,000 even though no line-up has been announced.

The 11/12 Clash of Champions card will be at the 5,800 seat RPI Fieldhouse in Troy, NY. Don't ask me why. All I know is the powers wanted the show in the Northeast because they are so subconscious of the Southeastern regional image. Unfortunately, the Southern crowds are the wildest and most heated and the show comes across better because of it.

Jim Cornette is now the adviser of the Dynamic Dudes and they are setting up a Dudes vs. Midnight Express feud down the line. Cornette is also the newest booking assistant which has some of the veterans unhappy since wrestlers, particularly veteran wrestlers, don't like to take orders from someone who wasn't a veteran wrestler and Cornette is in his mid-20s and isn't an athlete. Others say that Cornette has possibly the sharpest wrestling mind around and even though he's never been a full-time active wrestler, he's choreographed matches with the Midnight Express and put together finishes for years that have been top-notch.

Big Van Vader was interested in coming in but the deal isn't going to happen. NWA doesn't want to use wrestlers with hefty Japan commitments, plus Vader is close to signing a merchandising deal with Hasbro and the NWA is going to have a merchandising deal in 1990 with a rival toy company.

The first Ric Flair vs. Great Muta and Lex Luger vs. Sting matches will take place on 10/14 in Baltimore.

Kevin Kelly said on KSTP in Minneapolis that he was NWA-bound, although nobody in the NWA is confirming that, nor has there been any recent talk about Nord the Barbarian headed in.

The SST returns in mid-to-late October and it is still uncertain whether or not Sir Oliver Humperdink will be coming in as manager for them, but the NWA is under the assumption that is the case. Tom Zenk starts full-time the first week of October. There is talk that when the SST returns, it will be as a three-man team with Tonga Kid/Islander Tama who is Fatu's brother, as the third member of the team.

Notes from the TV tapings on 9/18 in Roanoke, VA. Scott Steiner came out for his matches all black and blue in the face. I'm not exactly sure how this all transpires however the angle with Robin Green turning heel will air this weekend on TBS and the shows taped here air afterwards. Somehow it comes down to Rick Steiner asking Robin Green to marry him, Scott tries to investigate something and gets beaten up by four guys with masks. The Dudes, seconded by Cornette, beat the Militia, Muta pinned Murdoch, Freebirds went to a time limit draw with The Dudes in a tag team title match, Flair and Slater had an impromptu television brawl, The Midnight Express won a squash match and the Birds interfered and were beating on them when the Dudes made the save and Cornette left with the Dudes and left the

Midnights in the ring while Skyscrapers double count out with Steiners and Luger pinned Rich and Flair beat Slater in dark matches.

Gilbert vs. Pillman rematch on TBS this weekend.

On 9/16 in Kansas City, which drew about 2,500, the Flair vs. Slater main event with Harley Race as referee wound up with Muta attacking Race. I believe they will bring Race back for one match to team with Flair against Muta and Terry Funk in November, although I'm not certain of that but those in KC for the card appeared to think that was the case.

9/15 in St. Louis drew 2,809 and $28,944 as Greg Evans beat Larry Williams, Cuban Assassin beat Richard Sartain, Dudes beat Militia, Butch Reed pinned Scott Hall, Steiners double count out with Skyscrapers, Luger pinned Rich, Muta pinned Murdoch and Flair beat Slater in a Texas death match.

Robin Green will wind up managing Reed & Sullivan as a tag team so expect them to face the Steiners at the PPV card.

Gordon Solie will be used as co-host on NWA Main Event with Jim Ross since Dangerously is gone. They are thinking of using either Teddy Long or Michael Hayes in the spot down the line. It appears that when Chris Cruise starts up as host of Worldwide (leaving Jim Ross just on TBS), his co-host will be Terry Funk.

9/10 in Fort Pierce, FL saw Lou Perez beat Powerhouse Parker, Murdoch beat Cuban, Cornette pinned Dangerously, Bobby Eaton & Brian Pillman beat Freebirds via DQ and Road Warriors beat SST in a cage match.

9/15 in Corpus Christi, TX drew a sellout 3,000 and $30,000 house with Warriors vs. SST in a cage with Wahoo McDaniel as ref on top plus Freebirds vs. Midnight and the same card was expected to sellout in Lubbock, TX the next night.

Power Hour on 9/8 set an all-time record with a 2.2 rating with the 8-man tag (Warriors & Steiners vs. SST & Freebirds), while World Championship Wrestling got a 2.3 and NWA Main Event dropped to a 2.2 in its first week opposite the NFL.

On the Bears vs. Bengals game on NBC on 9/9, when Brad Muster caught a pass, Dick Enberg and Bill Walsh started talking about the NWA and Ric Flair and Terry Funk, which couldn't have made Titan happy since it was on their network.

THE READERS' PAGE

DOING JOBS

When I hear about so many of these guys today refusing to do jobs, I have to laugh. It wasn't too long ago that this wouldn't have been tolerated within the business. These so-called superstars putting themselves and their self-serving egos above the good of the wrestling business can only hurt the business in the long run. When Sam Muchnick promoted in St. Louis, nearly every single big name did jobs when asked to. The result? Decades of packed houses in St. Louis. It is true that a large ego is a basic trait that is necessary to anyone who rises to the top of the wrestling business, but they're going way too far into fantasy land when they themselves start believing the bullshit and thinking they are really indestructible. There are very few, if any, who really are.

Tom Hankins
Sepulveda, California

PRO WRESTLING PLUS

I watched Pro Wrestling Plus for the first time in a long time. Ed Whalen now shows Calgary, Winnipeg and Tomko action as his only up-to-date stuff. His other "current" action included Steve Constance and Tim Ashley as a tag team from 1984, "A Deep South match from Georgia" which was actually a 1986 Kansas City match and announcer Rick Stuart even said "Welcome to NWA All Star Wrestling" at the beginning.

He also talked about Andre's recent arrest and how Andre was really a nice guy who couldn't live a normal life because of his size. What a shame that people eat this up. The fact he tries to pass all this old stuff off as current really bugs me.

Jeff Zinger
Woodstock, Ontario

SUMMERSLAM

SummerSlam was pretty lame. I was expecting a much better card with matches like the Hart Foundation vs. Brainbusters, but as usual, I was bitterly disappointed. Bret Hart did get in a few good moves but he didn't spend enough time in the match. Of course, as one of the best workers on the card, he also was one of the few who did a fairly clean job.

The main event was everything that I thought it would be, long and boring. I guess it could have been worse. It could have put me in a coma. Hogan's matches are getting progressively less believable. It was funny that the only one who can hold Zeus back is the referee. I wasn't particularly fond of the angle where Sherri got turned upside down wearing a skirt. I wasn't offended by it, or Roddy Piper's angle, but to me they are just two more examples of Vince McMahon's contempt for his viewers. Vince seems to think that his audience can only be entertained through cheap humor. In the WWF, if someone isn't fishing through a toilet, then they're taking off their clothes.

Michelle Johnson
Watertown, New York

I thought SummerSlam was the second best PPV event the

WWF has done, behind only WrestleMania III. I believe you were a bit too critical of the Ultimate Warrior in his match with Rick Rude. Warrior gave a good effort and did some things I didn't think he was capable of. Yes, Rude was great, but give Warrior credit, I gave the match 4 ¼ stars. It was an extremely intense and exciting match. The Rockers are without question the most exciting tag team in the country right now.

Chris Poulos
Lansdowne, Pennsylvania

FAN BEHAVIOR
Being from Canada, I'm sure some things differ from the United States, but not much. Last year, the

WWF came to a nearby city. On the card was Curt Hennig and a guy at ringside held up a placard reading "Curt Hennig is the real AWA champion." Well, you never guess who came over to confiscate the sign.

Nick Bockwinkel. At least they didn't throw the guy out. The guy quite willingly surrendered his sign. I really hope the Oakland 2 launch a lawsuit and make as big a stink out of this as possible. Why is it you can go to matches and rag on a wrestler and swear and spit on each other but you can't carry a sign expressing your thoughts?

Kathy Prescesky
Maymont, Saskatchewan

First, I'm only a mark and a WWF fan to boot. I also believe that Hulk Hogan is not a member of a fascist organization out to deprive me of my Civil Rights. Being of such unsound mind, I totally believe the Oakland 2 weren't out to disrupt the TV taping. You were only carrying a banner proclaiming the NWA to be No. 1 to show your enthusiasm for the sport and not to embarrass the WWF. You carried a Ric Flair sign solely to show your respect for a great wrestler, which Flair is, and had no intention whatsoever of displaying the sign at an inopportune moment. Not being born yesterday however, the WWF officials didn't see it quite that way. Were you deprived of your right to freedom of expression? Maybe. Did the WWF act wrongly? Perhaps. Would the NWA ever stoop to such low actions? Of course. If you don't believe me, try attending an NWA card carrying a "Hulk Rules" banner. If this is too blasphemous for you, then sit in the front row wearing a Macho Man T-shirt on a TV taping. I'll be watching for you on TV, but won't be holding my breath.

Elyse Zois
Union, New Jersey

Dave Meltzer: I've got to comment on this because it does explain a basic difference between the two groups.

At least a dozen times this year alone, including at a live Clash special from Cleveland, I've seen NWA tapings with fans wearing WWF T-shirts in the first two rows. By those actions alone, obviously nobody is trying to pressure people into changing clothing because of paranoia of being afraid people will realize there is opposition. Ironically, it is the NWA, on its own TV, which acknowledges WWF on Power Hour and in media interviews while the reverse is not true, the WWF pretends there is no such thing publicly, while privately try and book dates in the same cities in competition.

AWARDS FAVORITES
We missed running down the categoriese last week so we've got some catching up to do. Each week between now and Thanksgiving we are running down the different categories that readers will be voting on for the 1989 pro wrestling awards in the Observer yearbook. The voting itself for the awards will be done by the readers during the month of December and results will be released in the yearbook inJanuary.

BEST BABYFACE: This category is to be judged by heat generated at the show and box office appeal. Hulk Hogan is the obvious winner. Nobody gets more babyface heat than Hogan. Nobody draws more than Hogan. I suppose one could make a good case for Akira Maeda as being Hogan's equal as a drawing card, but in a sport environment, they don't really have babyfaces and heels, so therefore I can't consider Maeda or any UWF wrestlers here, even though they are all over tremendously. Ultimate Warrior gets second place. The guy is over tremendously no matter what one might say about his lack of skill and utter lack of conditioning. As for third, Ric Flair, since his switch, has been over huge for the NWA and has contributed to somewhat of an increase in NWA crowds of late and he gets the best reaction of all the NWA wrestlers. Roddy Piper may also be a contender. We have to see what the long-term value of him turns out to be at the box office, although working with a heel like Rick Rude should certainly help him out. Sting can be considered as well as he's been popular throughout the year, but it seems to be that the Sting fervor has died down a lot since last spring when the guy was really on fire. He still gets a good reaction, but it seems something is missing from before. With the retirement of Chigusa Nagayo and the weaknesses of the smaller promotions in the U.S. , there really isn't anyone else to consider. Eric Embry? Don't make me laugh.

BEST HEEL: Four candidates jump immediately into my head here. Randy Savage was awesome the first part of the year leading up to WrestleMania. He did the best interviews around and successfully turned from a very popular wrestler into a legitimate major heel on the prime time Main Event special. The other WWF candidate is Rick Rude, whose arrogant mannerisms has kept him as a major pushed babyface going on his third year. The NWA's top candidates are Terry Funk and Lex Luger. Funk is much better at getting heat at the live shows and in that way, is the best in the business right now. He's also been given the chance to do more devious things. Luger's arrogant mannerisms are great, but unlike the other names mentioned, Luger has the problem that he gets cheered everywhere. There really isn't a lot he can do about it and he's got a bad rap as to being a failure as a heel because of it, but the truth is that the hardcore fandom of the NWA is going to cheer who they feel like cheering and they feel like cheering Luger, just as they felt like cheering Ric Flair and the Road Warriors when they were heels.

MOST OVERRATED: The Ultimate Warrior, for obvious reasons. While Hulk Hogan, to the general public, is vastly overrated in terms of being perceived as a "great wrestler," he is certainly passable. Warrior's lack of ability remains a joke, but his lack of conditioning is even more of one. He does have a ton of charisma, which is the be all and end all of getting over, but there are people who believe he's a good wrestler and nothing could be farther from the truth. On the other hand, Eric Embry's big push is more of a joke and he's got to qualify for the Dusty Rhodes booker award of building a whole promotion around himself. In this day and age, I think Jerry Lawler is overrated, at least as a face in Memphis. He can be a great worker when he's motivated, but for a guy with such a rep as a worker, how come most of his matches aren't any good? Randy Savage was actually overrated in terms of being a worker when you compare reputation with actual output, but in the past few months he's turned on the steam again. Larry Cameron is another guy that I just don't see anything in, but he gets a big push. He seems more like a poor man's Allan Coage. While he does a decent interview, his ring work is pretty poor and he can barely get a decent match out when put in the ring with a top-notch worker like Chris Benoit and his matches with anyone else if they go more than five minutes are generally unwatchable without the fast-forward button. Akira Maeda is a great wrestler, but not as great as his reputation. Riki Choshu is pushed as the No. 1 guy in New Japan, and a few years back I could see why but the guy has nothing but his reputation going for him today. He's a decent wrestler and can have a good match, but everyone else in the promotion is just as good as he is. In the NWA, when it comes to working, Sid Vicious is far and away the worst, but since he's got the necessary size and charisma to be a superstar, few notice. Even though Dick Murdoch can be great, I dread watching him in U. S. rings.

MOST UNDERRATED: You can look at this one in a few ways. There are guys that people just don't know about. There are guys who could get over more than guys ahead of them but just don't get the right pushes from the promotion. And there are guys who are great workers but don't have the right charisma to be main eventers and thus wind up getting buried. Bret Hart is a good wrestler, who can be a great wrestler, with the right charisma to be a bigger star than he is, although he's a legitimate star, but certainly could be bigger than any babyface in the WWF except for Hogan and Warrior with the right push, which he hasn't really gotten. Brad Armstrong is a great worker which nobody will deny, but he's not the type to sell tickets. To some extent, to many fans, I would call Ricky Steamboat underrated even though he was pushed as a World champion because a lot of people never realized or understood just how great a worker he really was. Almost every young wrestler in New Japan works hard and has a lot of hot moves, so you could make a case for many of them. Dan Kroffat is underrated because nobody sees him. Toshiaki Kawada is a little underrated, but is getting more of a push as time goes by. Chris Benoit may be the best worker on the small promotions in North America right now, but he is getting his share of magazine publicity these days.

BEST COLOR COMMENTATOR: We all know that Jesse Ventura will win big, and he deserves it if simply because he's both professional and good and he's been doing it all year. Jim Cornette can be every bit as good as Ventura. Ventura has the edge because he's got a better voice but Cornette has Ventura beat because he's got a quicker mind and also an amazing understanding and recollection of the business. But Cornette hasn't been doing it all year, either. As for others, Lord Al Hayes is bad, Bobby Heenan is okay but predictable, Paul E. Dangerously can make a bad match entertaining but comes off so strong in his commentary that he dominates over the match while Scotty the Body is good as well, but unpolished. Bulldog Bob Brown is hideous, and that's being kind, and I don't even want to discuss Frank Dusek.

BEST GIMMICK: Of the new ones this year, the two that pop into my mind because they got over were Beetlejuice in Oregon and Jushin Liger in New Japan. I'm partial to Liger since he's such a great worker. But it's amazing how they got Art Barr over to such a big deal, since he was just a prelim wrestler and is so small. Freddy got over in Memphis, but they went and ruined it by bringing in Werewolves and Zombies and the whole thing made the promotion look like a bad freak show.

WORST GIMMICK: Terry Taylor as the Red Rooster is one of the sadder sights around. It's just so degrading. Still, one bad gimmick sticks out above all others, that is Phil Hickerson as P. Y. Chu Hi in World Class and trying to actually pretend that a redneck from Tennessee is actually

Japanese. I don't know what is worse. The few people who actually buy that it's the case, or the promotion for actually believing that more than a few people could ever believe something that ridiculous.

OCTOBER 2, 1989

Before getting into the news I want to apologize about last week's issue. We had computer problems here with the mailing which made it impossible to get the mailing labels out until Monday, which means the issue wasn't mailed until the day before this issue presumably will be mailed out. I'm sincerely sorry about this problem, because in retrospect I should have had alternatives in case of a computer failure and still be able to get the issue out, and I just didn't foresee the problem and wasn't prepared for it. Well, we've got back-ups now and this won't happen again. It was really frustrating from this end because after getting back from a weekend away from home, I had to pull two almost all-nighters between gathering information and writing the issue to get last week's done on time and it was one of the best issues of the past several weeks.

We've got plenty of news to hit this week as well. The biggest story, and one with a lot of potential ramifications is that Tully Blanchard and Arn Anderson gave their notice to the WWF at the TV tapings on Wednesday night in Louisville and will be leaving after the Survivor Series on Thanksgiving night to return to the NWA. If nothing else, this is the first time in recent memory that the NWA has actually raided the WWF for main-line talent and been successful. Truthfully, this has been a year without raids on either side as with the exception of the WWF signing up Tony Schiavone, a television announcer, neither side had raided the other for talent all year despite all sorts of rumors that constantly float around.

While between now and Thanksgiving gives Titan plenty of opportunity to downplay Blanchard & Anderson, and I would say it is almost a certainty that unless they are persuaded to change their minds and stay, that the belts will be taken from them at the next set of television tapings, they will still leave the WWF as main-line talent, not top drawing talent but still as recent champions. While the loss won't hurt the WWF at all, except from the standpoint of front office headaches of trying to put together and market a few new heel teams (the Rougeaus are also leaving the WWF and the loss of both teams does leave the WWF with a sizable void in the heel tag team department), it should help fan perception of the NWA.

Certainly it would cause some fans to, at least question, the NWA as minor league in comparison when the NWA can raid the WWF's tag team champions, or when it comes to pass, recent ex-champions away.

But to me, the raiding of Blanchard & Anderson is really a minor point in this story. The real story is what will happen next. I do know that Blanchard & Anderson had signed contracts with Titan when they arrived last year. The standard Titan contract for all newcomers is for two years, automatically renewable for a third year unless notice is given. Blanchard & Anderson have only been in the WWF for just over one year. While Blanchard & Anderson may have signed a different contract from most of the recent Titan signees, sources close to the situation have said that they do, in fact, have time remaining on their current contract and believe that because the contract doesn't guarantee any money, with the exception of $50 every television taping they appear on, that it isn't a binding contract. If this is the case, the ball is in Vince McMahon's court and several wrestlers are watching.

In recent months, the salary structure within Titan Sports, at least for the middle of the card wrestlers, has been lower than in the past, with the speculation being that the wrestlers no longer had any viable alternatives so there was no point in keeping the money up to the previous levels when the NWA was considered a viable alternative. I do know that most of the WWF wrestlers didn't consider the NWA as a viable promotion since most of the information they were getting was that the organization was on its last legs, since brainwashing propaganda of the boys has been a long-time tool of management in many promotions probably since the beginning of time in the business. With Blanchard & Anderson leaving and claiming that it was because they would make significantly more money in the NWA, all of a sudden a lot of people who didn't consider the NWA an alternative financially will be taking notice as to how Vince McMahon handles this situation. Will McMahon ignore it, figuring that he's on top and is so far on top that this is nothing more than a minor inconvenience Will he try and take legal action and force Blanchard & Anderson to fulfill their contract, because by not doing so it would seem to signal a green light for any Titan wrestler who wants to renege on their contract? Will he try and "gain revenge" by trying to raid a key NWA name, and at that point, will the NWA's contracts, which do guarantee specific amounts of money in them, be able to hold up? If the NWA contracts don hold up, then why does the NWA even bother to sign these guys up, so one would figure the NWA has these guys under contract specifically to keep them from jumping and therefore maybe the contracts would hold up. Will the NWA try more raids of Titan talent, or is this a single isolated instance?

From the NWA standpoint, presuming they are able to gain the services of Anderson & Blanchard for the Starrcade show, expect a re-uniting of the Four Horseman, with the new quartet for 1990 consisting of Anderson, Blanchard, Ole Anderson (who replaced Eddie Gilbert on the booking committee this past week and presumably will have an on-camera role as Lex Luger's manager) and Lex Luger, all of whom will feud with Ric Flair. It's something different and still something the same as a few years ago. It should create interest and presumably up attendance a tad, but the problems the NWA has with drawing at house shows are such that acquiring a few wrestlers is only a small part of the answer. Of course Anderson & Blanchard are two of the best workers around and at the very least should improve the quality of the cards and give an added hot match on the big shows.

I don't have anything new on the WWF' s PPV show on Thanksgiving, other than Zeus will be used in a greater role than I had expected down the road. His character looks like it will last in 1990 after all, although I don't see him getting too many matches with Hulk Hogan after the PPV runs its course.

The NWA's "Halloween Havoc" PPV show from Philadelphia on 10/28 has these matches that I know of, and this sounds like a fairly complete card: Ric Flair & Sting vs. Terry Funk & Great Muta in a Thunderdome cage - a cage with a top on it and the match continues until one team can't continue; Lex Luger vs. Brian Pillman for the U.S. title; Freebirds vs. Dynamic Dudes for the NWA tag team title; Road Warriors vs. Skyscrapers, Rick & Scott Steiner vs. a new tag team which will be called something like "The Team of Doom" or "War and Doom" but it'll be Butch Reed & Ron Simmons managed by both Kevin Sullivan and Robin Green; Midnight Express & Steve Williams vs. Samoan Swat Team & Tonga Kid (Sam Fatu) managed by Oliver Humperdink and The Z Man (Tom Zenk) vs. Mike Rotunda. It has been reported elsewhere that Bruno Samnartino will be the referee for the main event match, and I'm told Sanunartino has been contacted but my best sources say that Sanunartino, who is on vacation at this writing, had not agreed to do so before leaving. I had heard the NWA was interested in using Sammartino as a referee on cards in Philadelphia and Pittsburgh to hype crowds in those two cities and presumably bring back long-time fans who no longer attend matches in both those cities.

Hurricane Hugo got the better Of the World Wrestling Council on 9/16. The WWC was planning its anniversary show, an outdoor spectacular in Juan Lobriel Stadium in Bayamon and I'm told the advance sales for the show were in the 25,000 range, however the hurricane forced cancellation of the card. The last word was they would try and; reschedule the card for sometime in the next two weeks, but apparently the island of Puerto Rico and the San Juan area in particular were devastated by the Hurricane and it wasn't known how quickly it would be feasable to reschedule the show.

A correction from something reported here a few weeks back. Karate Legend Benny "The Jet" Urquides did not appear on a Johnny Rodz card in Queens as a pro wrestler. Apparently it was someone else using the wrestling ring name of "Benny the Jet" and I was given incorrect information that it was the famous karate star.

As for the various injury reports on the top guys who have missed dates of late, Terry Funk should be back in action this coming weekend as they will announce Saturday on TBS that his suspension has been lifted. Sting returned to action this past weekend after missing about 10 days with minor ankle surgery, while Roddy Piper also returned to action this past weekend, although there are still some concerns about Piper' s condition. If Piper's ribs don't heal properly over the next few weeks, then they will have to perform an operation, in which case, Piper would be out of action for a significant period of time, but for right now, Piper is out.

Dusty Rhodes missed some dates this past week because he had to appear in Florida because of the Lawsuit against him by former pro wrestler Steve DiBlasio (Big Daddy) stemming from an incident during the summer of 1983. DiBlasio contends that his wrestling career was ended after a match against Les Thornton in West Palm Beach when booker Dusty Rhodes ordered him to take a bump over the top rope for a DQ finish. DiBlasio contended that he had never taken a bump before, let alone one over the top rope and didn't want to do it but Rhodes threatened to fire him if he didn't. Rhodes told him to hook the rope on the way over the break the fall, which DiBlasio claimed he did, but at 450 pounds, the rope broke and DiBlasio crashed onto the floor and his ankle bones were crushed. Rhodes, along with Championship Wrestling from Florida (now defunct), the National Wrestling Alliance and the city of West Palm were sued. Rhodes first claimed that pro wrestling wasn't choreographed and was a sport so DiBlasio claims were false. The final (outcome) in all matches is the two men in one-on-one competition, Dusty wrote in the pretrial statements. "Pro wrestling matches are not choreographed." But during the trial under oath, Rhodes was forced to admit something different, calling the matches "100 percent show business" and comparing the story lines and choreography to a soap opera. Also in the trial, lawyer Mike Nipon for DiBlasio asked whether the scars on Rhodes' forehead were from purposely cutting himself with a razor blade to bleed during the matches and Rhodes had to admit that this was the case. DiBlasio claimed that when he told Rhodes he was afraid to take the bump that Rhodes threatened to blackball him out of the business. In typical Rhodds fashion, when asked about DiBlasio, "He had no athletic ability, no charisma, which you have to have. He was as dry as a piece of bacon. I'm the most charismatic guy you've ever had sit in this room here. Rhodes' attorneys tried to have the suit dismissed by claiming that DiBlasio was a professional athlete and the injury is the risk he assumed when he stepped into the ring. DiBlasio's attornies countered by saying that DiBlasio was not a professional athlete, but an actor playing the role of a professional athlete. An actor would be allowed to sue if he was injured performing in his role.

A couple of interesting notes on how the promotions handled some of these missing main eventers during the week. In Portland, OR on Sunday night, Rhodes missed his semi-main event match, but fans were not informed of this, nor were refunds offered, and Hercules, who worked earlier in the card, took Rhodes place against Big Bossman without any mention of Rhodes, a replacement, or anything. This was in contrast to the policy Titan showed back in August when Hulk Hogan missed several dates with a pinched never and Titan went to the local media to report that Hogan wouldn't be there, had posters outside buildings, flew in both Brutus Beefcake (who was scheduled elsewhere) and Elizabeth (who was at home) to replace Hogan and ran shows and offered refunds. Saturday night in Richmond, VA, the NWA ran a show and nine of the wrestlers (Ric Flair, Lex Luger, Tommy Rich, Freebirds, Road Warrior Hawk, Midnight Express and Terry Funk) couldn't appear because the Charlotte airport was closed due to Hurricane Hugo. No posters were put outside the building. In fact, as it turns out, the show had a huge walk-up and was the biggest crowd of the year in Richmond (Flair vs. Funk was still billed as the main event on television that afternoon even though Funk was " suspended" the week earlier although there was one voiceover during the show the last week which said if Funk was suspended that Gary Hart may have to put someone else in his place). Fans were told about the no-shows and told they could get a refund, which thousands did, but the refund line was an hour long and it left a bad taste in a lot of fans' mouths because they could have saved everyone hours of time if they had just put posters in the lobby telling fans that most of the main eventers weren't going to be there.

A few notes on the various incarnations of skating leagues. The big Roller games two-hour debut special has aired just about everywhere. The show, which I believe was called "Rock and Roller Games," featured a few rock acts including Deborah Harry (who was a big star as "Blondie" some years back) and a couple of other name acts and a couple of Roller Derby like games with new-fangled rules. The production quality of the show itself reminded me of a Vince McMahon NBC special. Slick. Good graphics. The outside the ring vignettes looked professional. Watching that show, of a product that has no base audience to speak of, and is coming from nowhere with no participants have any kind of national name or appeal and being able to pull off a special so slickly really made the NWA's syndicated shows look even worse by comparison. Here is a group with no base audience which already has a better syndicated package than the NWA and has better syndicated television, when it comes to look and production. Quintex from Australia is sinking big money into this. Whether this will

make it or not is another question. Those I've talked with in promotions and television seem more negative about it. Make it financially? I don't see how it can be profitable, but if Quintex is using it for a tax write-off, it doesn't have to be, just as the NWA doesn't have to be if Turner doesn't care if it's profitable (although most feel that TBS cares a great deal that the wrestling outfit becomes profitable). The production for each show is allegedly $700,000, which sounds awfully high, but even if it's only half that, where would the income come from? Neither the NWA, nor WWF are able to pay for their television production expenses simply through sales of TV ads, and both are spending far less on television, and each has house show revenue to back it up. Of course, the NWA and WWF pay a considerable amount for talent, whereas in the Roller Games, even the top skaters are only making $125 per game and as of yet, they aren't doing live show appearances although-one assumes that won't be far down the line. They were already talking about merchandising gimmicks like with Titan, but when watching the show, I felt they were painfully lacking in charismatic performers to market. It looked more like a bunch of anonymous skaters, and anonymous folks don't have the charisma to sell record albums and lunch boxes or T-shirts. The skating product itself didn't look good. Part of the problem was the skaters themselves only had one month to practise on the new figure-eight track. The rules were also far too confusing and the track was too big for television purposes. Because the owners didn't want problems from the older skaters used to skating the old, basically defunct game, most of the "name" skaters and "best" skaters were not allowed in this new incarnation which hurt the quality of the pool of skaters, although most on the track looked experienced. Still, only a few seemed to have genuine talent. I expect the long-term of this is similar to when most of these same people and the same promoter got on ESPN about four years ago. It drew very good ratings for the early shows, the novelty wore off, and it wasn't long before it disappeared from sight. I expect good ratings early here and the stations have committed them to 13 weeks. My guess is the second run of 13 weeks will be ordered but the shows will wind up moved from good time slots to fringe time slots and it'll slowly disappear from there, just Like GLOW, which started fast and faded just as fast. A competitor, called the World Roller Federation, was to have taped a television pilot in Irvine, CA over the weekend, which was to be more like traditional Roller Derby, although there was in-fighting amongst those in charge who wanted it either like the old Los Angeles Roller Games (bad skating, lots of gimmicks), Philadelphia Roller Games (stronger skating, lots of character development) or traditional San Francisco Roller Derby (few gimmicks, solid skating, little character development). This pilot would be attempted to be sold to stations in January. Anyway, the one point so painfully clear in watching the Roller Games special is how far superior the show was, from a technical standpoint, to the NWA and how they, with no product or base audience can do something like that in their first shot.

OREGON

Rip Oliver has switched to babyface after an incident on 9/9 in Portland. Rip's brother Jerry Oliver, who had his leg amputated in an auto accident, was out doing an interview and The Grappler kept insulting him and they argued back and forth until Grappler picked up a chair and went to hit his good leg and Oliver made the save and the two brawled all over the building. On the 9/23 card, Oliver came out in street clothes and chased Grappler away during a Battle Royal and they got into another unscheduled brawl later in the show, which leads to their main event match on the 9/30 card.

TV announcer Don Koss was also attacked on the 9/9 show by Grappler, Nord the Barbarian and Brian Adams. He showed up on 9/16 wearing a neck brace and saying he had injured ribs from the attack, but by the 9/23 TV show, he came out appearing just fine.

The 9/23 Battle Royal was won by Carl Styles, who is now being billed as "Country" Carl Styles wearing overalls, a cowboy hat and he carries a pig with him to the ring. After the match Nord attacked Styles and Adams came in with a kendo stick and Bill Francis came in and also got destroyed until he got his football gear and made the save at that point. The 9/30 card has Styles & Francis vs. Nord & Adams in a match with football gear and a kendo stick on a pole.

Beetlejuice (Art Barr) was "injured"' a few weeks back by Adams' full nelson and they said he had a broken neck, which many felt was just a way to write him out since his was arraigned on a rape charge, but he returned with no mention of the neck injury this past week and is back feuding with Al Madril.

Rex King pinned Northwest champion Scotty The Body on the 9/23 card in a non-title match and stole the belt.

USWA

The 9/22 card at the Dallas Sportatorium drew another small house as The Punisher (Master of Pain wearing an outfit similar to that of The Spoiler) pinned Jimmy Jones, Jeff Jarrett & Matt Borne downed USWA tag team champions Sheik Scott Braddock & Ron Starr when the tapes were reviewed and it showed that Starr's foot was on the ropes after the pinfall, so the title belts have been held up pending a rematch this coming Friday, Kerry Von Erich beat Taras Bulba via DQ when Punisher interfered Gary Young pinned Jimmy Jack Funk after hitting him with a foreign object, Jerry Lawler pinned Eric Embry in a Lumberjack match with all babyface Lumberjacks to keep the USWA title when Billy Joe Travis was holding Lawler

and Ernbry went to throw a punch, Lawler ducked and Embry hit Travis. Travis then hit Embry with a chair and Lawler pinned him. Don't have a result of the P. Y. Chu Hi vs. Chris Adams match where if Chu Hi won, then Tojo Yamamoto would get a date with Toni Adams (Chris' wife) but apparently Adams won the match.

Travis claimed on a TV interview that he was sorry for what happened in the Lawler-Embry match and that he acted on a spur of the moment and apologized, however Embry on his interview said that his family (the fans in Dallas) told him that it was no accident and he refused to accept Travis apology.

The 9/29 card in Dallas has Embry & Kerry Von Erich vs. Bulba & Punisher, Chu Hi & Tojo Yamamoto vs. Chris & Toni Adams with Toni Adams being allowed to use a kendo stick as an equalizer when she's in the ring, Funk & Frank Dusek vs. Young & Scandor Akbar and Borne & Jarrett vs. Braddock & Starr for the held up tag team titles. Al Perez is already gone even though it's still a few weeks until he starts with the WWF.

Uncle Elmer (Stan Frazier) is headed in. 10/1 in Fort Worth has Embry vs. Bulba, Kerry vs. punisher, Starr & Braddock vs. Ricky Morton & Robert Gibson, Adams vs. Chu Hi and Young vs. Funk.

10/21 at Mesquite Speedway they will be holding a wrestling card and also have a Demolition Derby with the wrestlers as drivers.

CWA

Ronnie Gossett didn't appear on television this week as he was embarrassed about being powdered and diapered at the Monday night matches in Memphis.

They showed a video of Dutch Mantell taking Texas Dirt (who had been Mantell under a hood) back to Texas and Mantell then came out with the CWA title that Texas Dirt had won on Monday night in Memphis from Black Bart. However Eddie Marlin told Mantell he couldn't keep the title because Texas Dirt was the champion, not Dutch Mantell, and if Mantell were to admit he was Texas Dirt than he's have to be suspended for wrestling after losing a loser leaves town match, so they will be holding a tournament for the CWA title probably next week.

Buddy Landel accused Jerry Lawler of "taking a powder" in one of their recent matches, so Lawler came out and dropped a bag of powder all over Landel's head.

Tommy Gilbert wrestled without the Freddy gimmick on television as a heel teaming with Spike Huber against the Rock & Roll Express, and then in the next match on television Gilbert wrestled as Freddy teaming with Dustin Rhodes against The Wildside.

Because of the Mid South Fair, there was no wrestling at the Mid South Coliseum this yeek, but they ran a card at a downtown gym in Memphis that held 2,500 fans and didn't come close to filling it on 9/23 as Stan Frazier beat The Executioner, Dustin Rhodes pinned Spike Huber, Wildside (Chris Champion & Mark Starr) went to a double count out with Jason & Freddy, Jeff Jarrett pinned Mike Davis, Dutch Mantell pinned Dirty White Boy, Jamie Dundee beat Harold Harris via DQ when The Blackbirds interfered and the Rock & Roll Express made the save, Rock & Roll Express beat Blackbirds to keep the CWA tag team titles and Lawler beat Landel to keep the USWA title.

OTHER NEWS NOTES

Bruno Sammartino appeared on WALE radio in Providence, RI and as usual in these settings was pretty vehement about the WWF, but surprisingly was somewhat praising the NWA, saying that he liked "95 percent" of what they were doing although he thought the plastic bag over the head at the clash was going too far. He praised the talents of NWA wrestlers Steve Williams, Scott Steiner, Mike Rotunda and Ric Flair saying they were as good as the wrestlers of his era. Larry Sharpe and Dennis Cora-Luzzo's independent show at the Cherry Hill Racetrack on 9/16 drew a near-$40,000 house, which is one of the two Largest independent houses in the U.S. this year. It might be the Largest, although Killer Kowalski promoted a show in New England that drew in excess of 5,000 fans a few months back.

The Central States tag team tournament was scheduled for this past Thursday night in Kansas City, however the show was canceled due to a non-existent advance.

Despite rumors of Scott Norton being NWA bound, word we get is that Norton is working full-time in construction and is history when it comes to Pro wrestling. Norton never officially quit the AWA, just stopped showing up. In a way to embarrass him, the AWA had Larry Zbyszko accept Norton's arm wrestling challenge just after Norton left the promotion, so now it will appear that Norton backed out when someone accepted the challenge.

Ron Fuller will be returning to the CWF, billed as USA champion.

Kensuke Sasaki, who is half of the Samurai Warriors tag team that holds the belts in Stampede Wrestling, will be leaving for West Germany in October.

New Japan will probably be sending their younger wrestlers more to Europe because immigration problems in the U.S. combined with the weakness of the smaller circuits and inability to work with NWA and WWF have made the U.S. a less viable option.

Yoshinari Asai wanted to return to Japan (from Mexico) and work on Atsushi Onita's Frontier Wrestling Alliance shows in October but he was threatened by El Gran Hamada that if he went to Japan for those shows that he would no longer be able to find any work in Mexico so he had to back out. A quick correction on the Roller Games magazine. Craig Peters is the guy doing the magazine, not Bill Apter, although it is coming from the same publishing company.

Boris Malenko and Tommy Rogers (of The Fantastics) are opening up a wrestling school in the St. Petersburg area.

Jerry Gray's Southern Wrestling Federation has been running fairly regularly of late, particularly doing fair shows and have used the Rock & Roll Express, Kendall Windham, Bugsy McGraw and Blackjack Mulligan on recent shows.

CWF had a show 9/22 in Knoxville with Brian Lee & Jinuny Golden defending the CWF tag team titles against Tracy Smothers & Steve Armstrong, Dennis Condrey defending the CWF title against Kerry Von Erich, Ron Fuller defending the USA title against The Black Barbarian (Bill Tabb), Wendell Cooley vs. Bill Dundee (who I believe is returning here full-time), Robert Fuller vs. Jerry Stubbs, Adrian Street & Todd Morton vs. Beauty & The Beast, Downtown Bruno vs. midget wrestler Butch Cassidy, a loser leaves town match with Linda Street against The Baroness (who used to be the female Beast) and Danny Davis vs. Lou Fabbiano. Jerry Lawler has been announced as coming in for a few dates.

The AWA will be holding the debut of its Team Challenge at its TV tapings on 10/1 in Rochester, MN plus will also hold a one-night tournament for the AWA tag team titles. The six-team tournament will have these first-round pairings: The Texas Hangmen vs. The Tokyo Bullets, Greg Gagne & Paul Diamond vs. Johnnie Stewart & Akio Sato, Destruction Crew (Wayne Bloom & Mike Enosi vs. Sgt. Slaughter & Baron Von Raschke. Other matches announced are Larry Zbyszko vs. Derrick Dukes and Wendi Richter vs. Candi Divine.

Verne Langdon is opening a Slammers Wrestling Gym in Sun Valley, CA with the Fabulous Moolah as head wrestling trainer. They had a party on 9/22 for the grand opening which included Moolah, ACCW promoter Joe Palumbo, Mike Mazurki (former wrestling star and later acting heavy), Gene LeBelle and others.

Congrats to Observer reader Bill Hanrahan on his marriage next month and to Dr. Mike Lano on his recent wedding.

And not to forget Brad Muster scored two touchdowns Sunday in the Bears win over the Detroit Lions.

NWA

Before starting on the NWA news, I've got to comment on the skit they aired involving Scott Steiner on the TBS wrestling show this past Saturday. The story line is that Rick Steiner asked for a TV camera crew to be there when he was to ask Robin Green "the big question." Rick hadn't arrived, but Scott was there with the crew when Robin rides up in a limo and invites Scott into the limo and when he gets in, three guys beat up Scott and throw him out of the car onto the pavement and one of them (who is obviously Kevin Sullivan because of his tree-trunk thighs) kicked Scott in the ribs several times. This may have been the biggest piece of garbage I've ever seen from a national promotion. How this was ever even let on the air is beyond me. It's not so much that the idea itself was bad, but the product that went out over the air was worse than bad. I really didn't think that plastic bag thing at the Clash was as big a deal as a lot of people are making it out to be, however I got so many phone calls and letters about it from NWA hardcore fans and realized that it probably wasn't the right thing to do. But this was a whole lot worse. It was the first time in more than a year that I turned off an NWA TV show in disgust in the middle of a show (and with a Piliman vs. Gilbert match and Flair interview still to come). And this is someone who never once turned the Heenan show off in disgust. I don't even want to bring up why they would air something which looked like a criminal offense, and why there would be two cameramen there to film it and just quietly observe the procedings and then fail to show the faces of the guys involved (all we saw was a massive leg kicking Steiner in the guts) even though most who called up could tell it was Butch Reed & Ron Sinunons. If they could tell, why didn't they show the guys who did it. If they were going to have film to prove it happened, why do the film guys not try to do anything about it? Why don 't they film the face of the guy instead of just his cowboy boot kicking Scott? And do they really think this crap is going to sell tickets? It never worked in Florida or San Antonio or any of the places they went to these Lengths and it's not about to work for a national promotion. World Championship Wrestling on 9/16 did a 2.1 rating while there was no Power Hour or NWA Main Event on TBS over that weekend. A replay of the Clash on 9/17 did a 1.5 rating which was a major disappointment, particularly since the Flair main event match only did a 1.9 rating.

The management of the Richmond Coliseum was very upset with how the NWA handled the no-shows on Saturday night. The NWA was forced, because of Hurricane Hugo, to cancel the Sunday night card at the Charlotte Coliseum which will be rescheduled for 10/29, the day after the next PPV event.

Terry Punk's suspension will be lifted this coming Saturday and he'll be headlining most shows against Ric Flair in October.

Also on TV this Saturday will have Brian Pillman challenge Lex Luger to set up the PPV match and they get into an impromptu brawl and Luger takes a powder. Clash won't be the highest rated cable show in September as the USA network movie "Fire and Rain" did a 5.3 rating.

The New Fantastics debuted in Roanoke, VA on Monday night losing to the Freebirds in a television match. Jackie Fulton was really green. Made me realize just how great a worker Tommy Rogers really is.

The NWA will be running in competition with its own

PPV show. The second hour of the TBS show on 10/28 will go head-to-head with the first hour of the Philadelphia PPV show. In addition, while I don't have this confirmed, I believe that Titan has Madison Square Garden booked the same night and the MSG cable network will run the card Live which is only competition in a few markets, but still competition.

NWA has gotten Elvira to do TV commercials for "Halloween Havoc, and I believe they will have Vineent Price do some commercials as well for the show.

If Bruno Sammartino does agree to referee on the card, expect David Sarnmartino to be given a job.

Missy Hyatt will no longer be accompanying the Steiner brothers and will no longer be appearing on television. Eddie Gilbert is still around but is. being phased out. Gilbert lost via count out on syndication and by pinfall on TBS to Pillman this weekend.

9/16 in Kansas City drew a $20,000 house as Cuban Assassin pinned Richard Sartain, Dynamic Dudes beat New Zealand Militia, Butch Reed pinned Scott Hali, Steiners double count out with Skyscrapers, Lex Luger pinned Tommy Rich, Dick Murdoch beat Great Muta via DQ and Ric Flair beat Dick Slater in a deathmatch with Harley Race as referee when Slater couldn't answer the bell for the fifth fall.

9/23 in Richmond, VA for the skeleton card with the no-shows because of the hurricane wound up with Ron Simmons pinning Scott Hall, Gilbert pinned Cuban, Shane Douglas pinned Rip Norgan, Norman the Lunatic pinned Johnny Ace, Steve Williams drew Mike Rotunda, Z-Man (Tom Zenk) beat Dick Slater and Sting returned to action and beat Muta via DQ.

Correction on a result from last week in St. Louis, Murdoch beat Muta via DQ, not Muta pinning Murdoch as I'd reported.

9/10 in Greensboro drew 5,000 (WWF was in nearby Winston-Salem the next night with Hogan vs. Savage drawing 2,500) as Simmons pinned Gilbert, Militia beat Hall & Ranger Ross, Rotunda drew Williams, Steiners double count out with Skyscrapers, Sting beat Muta via DQ, Luger pinned Rich and Flair beat Slater in a death match.

WWF

Officially, to the best of my knowledge, the only wrestlers who have given their notices are the Brain Busters and the Rougeau brothers. I've been given five other names of wrestlers who I've been told will very shortly and a few others who are taking a "wait and see" attitude. None of the names are Randy Savage or Roddy Piper but all are name wrestlers. If the others don't reconsider, it will leave the WWF in a depth problem but they'll survive with a minimum of headaches, but may have to cut down to two shows or quickly add about six or seven newcomers to fill the slots.

They need to create at least one new heel team, however. It's very interesting to see how Vince McMahon will handle all this. Of the nine names that are either officially leaving or strongly discussing leaving, six would be NWA-bound and I've got no idea what the other three (two of which are the Rougeaus) are planning as their next move.

Prime Time Wrestling did a 2.5 rating (lowest in eight months) and All-American fell to a 2.3 on 9/18 and 9/17 respectively. Basically the fall in both shows can be attributed to going head-on with the NFL, which as it turns out, has been costing the WWF between 25 and 40 percent of its audience both in syndication and on cable, at least on opening weekend. Over Labor Day Weekend, the WWF's syndicated package fell to a 7.8 rating (usually it's around a 10) with most shows bucking college football and the like, while the NWA did a 7.2, which ironically, is a point higher than they normally do.

Not much at the new TV taping. A newcomer appeared called Earthquake Evans, managed by Slick. I was told he was a huge guy, but didn't look impressive.

Fred Ottman is now being billed as Tugboat Thomas instead of Tugboat Tyler, but no name is definite until he works television with the name.

Highlights from the taping of SNME and syndication: Lanny Poffo will be the new valet for Curt Hennig and basically follows him around and admires him for being so perfect. Hennig also challenged Hulk Hogan and they'll meet in November around the horn. When King Savage and Elizabeth did an interview (and they now have Lavish ring introductions as the King and Queen of the WWF), Savage doesn't let Sherri talk. In SNME matches, Savage pinned Jimmy Snuka when Sherri freely inter-fered, at the finish she distracted Snuka and Savage rolled-him up from behind and after Snuka went to splash Sherri but Savage pulled him out, Rick Martel DDQ Tito Santana when all the lumberjacks ran in for a free-for-all, Warrior beat Andre in 24 seconds and Hogan pinned DiBiase. Zeus and Jake Roberts were in the corners and Jake used a snake to keep Zeus from interfering (you know the stereotypes about blacks afraid of snakes). Virgil stole the snake, Zeus held Hogan, Hogan ducks, Ted punches Zeus, Hogan pins Ted and afterwards they double on Hogan until Jake & Damien make the save. They crowd was nearly 12,000 paid and 14,000 total (not a sellout, but the $136,000 house is a city record for wrestling).

Earlier that day, Savage appeared in the Reds' broadcast booth with Joe Nuxhall and Marty Bennaman to do a guest shot. Reds owner Marge Schott was furious about this and immediately sent word to Brennaman that if he didn't get Savage out of the booth immediately that he was fired. Schott took a royal ribbing in the press for her overacting to Savage's appearance.

9/24 in Portland, OR drew 4,000 and $44,000 as Boris Zhukov pinned Mark Young, Widow Maker (Barry Windham) beat Koko Ware, Demolition double DQ with Blanchard & Anderson, Hercules pinned Haku, Hercules pinned Bossman (this was to make fans happy since fans were upset about Dusty not being there), Badnews Brown pinned Bret Hart and Warrior beat Andre via DQ.

The same crew in Denver the previous night drew $71,000.

9/23 at the Palace in Auburn Hills drew 12, 500 as Tim Horner pinned Barry Horowitz, Paul Roma beat Bill Woods, Mr. Perfect drew Beefcake, DiBiase double count out with Duggan and Hogan beat Savage in a cage and afterwards Hogan beat up Savage and held Sherri so Liz could deck her.

9/24 in Montreal drew 9,000 as Hogan beat Savage, Duggan beat DiBiase, Ron Garvin beat Greg Valentine, Bushwackers beat Powers of Pain, Perfect beat Jim Neidhart and Dino Bravo pinned Beefcake.

9/19 in Utica, NY drew 1,500 as Roma beat Horowitz, Snuka beat Honkeytonk Man, Widow Maker beat Richard Charland, Warrior beat Andre in 21 seconds, Rockers beat Rougeaus, Poffo beat Ware and Martel beat Young.

9/16 in San Diego drew 5,000 as Zhukov beat Young, Hart drew Perfect, Warrior beat Andre, Demolition beat Brain Busters via DQ, Bravo beat Neidhart, Akeem beat Hillbilly Jim and Dusty pinned Bossman.

9/18 in Grand Rapids, MI drew 2,500 as Widow Maker pinned Brian Costello * , Roma beat Horowitz **, Warrior beat Andre in 30 seconds DUD, Snuka beat Honkey *, Martel beat Young *, Poffo beat Ware * and Rockers beat Rougeaus **. The local newspaper panned this card because of the 30 second main event with complaints from fans at ringside.

9/15 in Los Angeles drew a sellout 15,000 and $180,000 as Horner beat Zhukov, Bravo beat Neidhart, Akeem beat Hillbilly Jim, Garvin double count out Valentine, Duggan beat DiBiase, Demolition beat Brain Busters via DQ and Hogan pinned Savage.

Piper vs. Rude drew 4,000 in San Antonio on Saturday.

THE READERS' PAGE

OAKLAND 2

I read the letter from Walter Kurelis in the 8/18 issue and I was also glad the Oakland 2 were thrown out of the building as it was the correct thing to do. But as the correct thing to do, both you and Mr. Kurelis should have also followed the correct policy when it comes to his letter. One of the highlights of my week is Thursday when the Observer arrives. My feeling getting the Observer is one of a good time. Why should a malcontent letter writer ruin my fun and everyone else's fun by having a different opinion? Like Vince McMahon, you should do the correct thing. You shouldn't run letters like that. Not only shouldn't you run letters like that but you should immediately cancel that man's subscription and not offer a refund. After all, he himself said it was the correct thing to do.

If people have a difference of opinion, let them protest outside the wrestling arena, or better yet, Let them write letters and not mail them so nobody can see. Mr. Kurelis violated whatever rights as a subscriber he had by trying to get his Letter in print and he tried to ruin my good time by getting me mad this week when I read the Observer.

Now, seriously. Vince McMahon charged admission to the TV taping here. He encourages people to voice their opinions and to wear wrestling related merchandise. But when the opinions don't jive with his, or the merchandise isn't what he's selling and from a non-existent competitor, all of a sudden that's forboden. If Mr. McMahon was to pay his arena crowds like extras in the movie, which is what they really are at TV tapings, then he should have 100 percent right to determine what they wear and what opinions they express. When they are paying him admission to view his product, like a baseball game or a hockey game, they have the right to express their opinion. in either signs or any other way even if it doesn't follow the party line. If Mr. McMahon wants to be able to control his audience because it is a television taping, he should either pay them as extras, or at least more feasably, not charge admission. just as real television shows don't charge admission for tapings for the very same reason that it gives them the right to control their audience.

Glen Johnson
San Lorenzo, California

DON'T BLAME NWA
I don't like the NWA getting unjustly knocked (Readers' Pages 9/11/89). Barbara Fick indicated that the NWA didn't treat customers well at the 8/4 card in Kansas City. Her complaint should be against the Kemper Arena and not the NWA. Every arena's security personnel handle wrestling crowds differently. Some don't care if you throw ice. Others throw you out for it. Some let quite a bit of standing go on while others tell you to sit down as soon as you rise. The things she described are controlled by the security people and/or the policies of the arena, not the NWA.

To compare what security did in Kansas City to the Oakland 2 incident or World Class throwing out Freddie Fargo is totally unfair.

Sharon Guillory
Alexandria, Louisiana

DUSTY RHODES
I disagree with Dan Cerquitella's letter in the 9/18 Observer concerning Dusty Rhodes. Mr. Cerquitella states that he can't believe the "jive, jolly, effeminate fat man," that Rhodes is currently portraying could be more popular than the "real"

Rhodes character. What Mr. Cerquitella doesn't understand is that in a profession that embraces great athletes and/or musclemen as the most powerful performers like Ric Flair, Sting, Great Muta, Owen Hart, Hulk Hogan, Lex Luger, etc. that fans will not respect a fat, out-of-hape, non-athlete in the same manner they respect the above mentioned people. The problem with Dusty Rhodes in the NWA is that he tried to make himself out to be a serious contender for the World title while even the most idiotic fan. realized Dusty had no place being in the ring with the serious main eventers.

The character that Rhodes plays in the WWF fits him perfectly. Dusty is a performer, not a serious wrestler. His current role gives him the chance to emphasize his comedic talents instead of his wrestling ability. In fact, when Dusty's common man skits ended, I began to lose all interest in him.

Sam Nord
Walnut Creek, California

The letter from the Oakland 2 was the perfect description of what is wrong with pro wrestling today.

But the Letter from R.J. Dari was one of the most outrageous things I've ever seen in the Observer.

Naturally, everyone is entitled to enjoy whatever promotion they want. But to imply that the NWA somehow deserves a second-rate status because it doesn't have millions of dollars to spend is callous and unjust.

R.J. says Vince isn't pretending that Dusty Rhodes isn't anything he's not? So I can assume that Dusty Rhodes is really a pizza deliverer and walks through women's apartments with shit all over his arms? Vince then also must not be pretending that the Ultimate Warrior, Andre the Giant, Zeus, Powers of Pain or Hulk Hogan are anything they're not, either?

As to the motion that those who jump to Titan continue to rise in stature, look no farther than Terry Taylor, Curt Hennig, Owen Hart or Ted DiBiase.

Why assume that people like Ricky Steamboat and Terry Funk were in the NWA for some unseen circumstance? Why should great workers like these two be refused to get their chances to show their wares and shine because someone wants to push only steroid freaks who can't wrestle?

It's an unfortunate catch-22 situation for the wrestlers. Everyone wants the money and fame of being in the WWF. But once they get there, they put themselves in Vince's hands and he can destroy their image and leave them with no future. Even the most gullible mark couldn't possibly think that anyone poses a threat to Hulk Hogan. WWF fans don 't buy tickets to be surprised. They buy tickets because they know the outcome.

I seriously doubt we will ever see a Hulk Hogan vs. Ric Flair match at WrestleMania. If Flair ever jumped, Vince would put him in another pathetic chicken outfit or something equally degrading to downplay his talent and he'd probably never get anywhere near a match with Hogan. And yes, the Road Warriors would be sorely missed if they ever left the NWA.

The clincher was the line about Vince McMahon being to wrestling what The Beatles were to music.

A far more appropriate analogy would have been the band "Kiss. They used make-up, costumers and a lot of high-gloss special effects to cover up an enormous lack of creativity and talent.

UNKNOWN

ARRESTS

Let's put things into perspective. Which is worse, putting the wrong tape on television or having one or your main eventers arrested? The Andre story was carried by all the major newspapers. While the NWA looks like a League that isn't very organized, the WWF Looks like a league that is made up of criminals and drug users and toilet cleaners

I don't think the NWA should raid the WWF or needs to. Butch Reed, JYD and Iron Sheik didn't draw and I don't think Dino Bravo, Honkeytonk Man or Ted DiBiase would either. Ricky Steamboat is a great wrestler but he didn't draw either.

The NWA lost a great promotional opportunity with Terry Funk and the movie "Road House. I would have had a lot of hype on the movie on NWA shows, do on-set interviews, clips and interviews with cast members. Instead they talked about Funk and Stallone, which happened years ago.

The NWA needs to take risks. Have Steve Williams appear at a WWF live PPV and challenge Hulk Hogan. Sign Leon Spinks to fight Ric Flair. That will get some media coverage. The NWA needs to book small and mid-sized cities instead of going to Chicago and competing with concerts, football games, etc.

Rick Murphy
Leavenworth, Kansas

Dave Meltzer: The Andre story only got publicity because of the size gimmick and because he was in the WWF. If an NWA wrestler, even Flair, have done the same thing, it wouldn't have gotten one-one hundredth the publicity even though it would be the exact same thing. Titan wasn't unhappy about the publicity either because it put them on page one of sports sections around the country and helped get over Andre's heel image. It's not fair to say the WWF is made up of criminals, or in that regard, any different from the NWA, AWA or other organization. It's just that if something happens involving a WWF name wrestler, because of greater mainstream name recognition, that unless Vince can squelch the story (which happens frequently and the same goes for the NWA if one of its top names were to get into trouble that often the story gets squelched and never makes the papers), it would be reported. In a lot greater

detail than the same exact incident with wrestlers from another organization. Nobody has ever suggested signing Bravo or Honky Tonk would be a good move for the NWA, and for that matter, very few thought Reed, JYD or Shiek would help the NWA (although somebody at the NWA must have because they were all brought in). When people talk about raiding the WWF, they mean only the big names - Savage and Elizabeth or Roddy Piper for gate appeal or guys like Anderson, Hart, Blanchard, Hennig, etc. who wouldn't make an immediate difference in the gate but could work up to NWA standards and be pushed in meaningful angles down the road.

TERRY FUNK

When I was in Memphis in July, the two NWA Bash cards I saw were disappointing, saved only by Terry Funk. He's really the only reason I still watch the NWA shows. He had a fantastic Line directed at Missy Hyatt prior to his match with Eddie Gilbert in Memphis. He said, "This is no place for a lady, or even for a slue like Missy Hyatt." You could "hear a collective "ooohh from the crowd when he said that. I saw Funk at the airport and you can tell the years of abuse on his knees as he walks. This guy is my idol in wrestling, he is what this business is all about and he is still giving to this sport which is why no matter how good people may say Lex Luger has become, he is still only out for himself and not the business. I don't think people have realized the impact Funk has had in getting the NWA back on its feet, despite the fact that he could have been pushed a Lot smarter.

SMM
East Coast

I feel a major problem with current NWA booking is they feel anyone who watches their TV will be thrilled to see people like Tommy Rich, Terry Funk and Dick Slater. What they don't seem to understand is that anyone who has heard of these people already buys tickets. Everyone else, if they saw something exciting, might buy a ticket but sees these guys as either old or out-of-shape.

As for the Oakland 2, these fans went not to see wrestling, or whatever it is that the WWF promotes, but to cause trouble. They got their trouble. Why are they upset? If I owned a restaurant and someone walked around with a sign saying "Eat at Joe's," I would throw him out, free speech or not.

Johnny Black
Philadelphia, Pennsylvania

Dave Meltzer: Outside of the South, I haven't noticed any interest in Rich, while I haven't noticed any for Slater either, although he was pushed to the top without any time for the fans to get interested in him. But I don't see him as a main eventer nowadays. As for Funk, he drew the three largest houses of the year for the NWA and got more heat at house shows as a heel than any heel they've had in years, so his interviews must be making up for the fact that he is old. Can't buy the restaurant analogy because they are two different things. If you were to call your waiter a easel really loud at a restaurant, you'd be kicked out. At a wrestling match, you are encouraged to be and express your opinion.

LIGER VS. SANO
One of the things I like most about the Observer is that it whets your appetite for watching the top matches, almost like coming-attraction trailers at the motion picture theater. After reading your description of the Liger vs. Sano match, I couldn't wait to see it.

After finally seeing the match, I was awestruck. You didn't exaggerate the death-defying nature of these incredible high-risk moves. Both Yamada and Sano should get high marks for taking the sport to a higher plateau. It's a good thing I have two VCR's since one is about to be worn out by my repeated rewinding and SL-MO-ING Yamada's suicidal flip and Sano's dropkick from a height higher than a basketball rim. Both moves are destined to be discussed for a long time. If you ever did a -List of the most amazing moves in wrestling, both would earn a high spot on the list.

This brings to mind other startling moves over the years, the kind that when first seen elicit expressions of disbelief. Snuka's two great dives from the top of the cage in New York against Bob Backlund and Don Muraco in the early 1980s would qualify. Many Of Satoru Sayama's dives, his elevated double bridge and great acrobatic sequences, particularly with Steve Wright, were also great. Yamada's shooting star press takes your breath away as does Tiger Mask Misawa's amazing flip-dive over the ropes onto the chest of an opponent. Who could ever forget Lioness Asuka holding Jaguar Yokota high aloft the top turnbuckle and then throwing her face first into the center of the ring. How both didn't fall to the arena floor and kill themselves is a miracle. The first time I saw anyone dropped face first over the top rope to the arena floor was when Davey Boy Smith did it to The Cobra in February, 1984 and even though it has been done many times since then, it is still an amazing feat. I guess the Randy Savage-Ricky Morton table-top piledriver in Memphis would make a lot of fans' lists and I seem to remember a piledriver involving Eric Embry and Bobby Fulton from the middle rope in San Antonio about five or six years back that was unbelievable. What other moves would you place in this category?

Chris Zavisa
Plymouth, Michigan

Dave Meltzer: A real interesting topic. A lot depends on when you saw the move. The first time I saw Scott Irwin

do the superplex in the U.S. (the first guy I actually saw do it was Ashura Hara in Japan but at that point in time they were always three to five years ahead on hot moves) blew me away, but now the move is almost commonplace. A lot of Sayama's dives were incredible at the time, but now you see lots of guys doing them, even in the U.S. The real high dropkicks off the top rope, such as the one Dynamite Rid did on Cobra when Davey Boy Smith used to have him up on his shoulders were incredible at the time. For sheer craziness, moves that stand out to me are Sayama and Cobra (Takano) used to do something they called the space-flying-tiger-drop which began like Muto's handspring elbow, but instead of ending Like an elbow drive they flew over the top rope and splashed onto the foe. Dynamite Kid once did a move where Bruce Hart was in the aisle by the second row of seats, Kid climbed to the top rope, then put his one foot on top of the ringpost and balanced on the foot and flew Off with a diving head-butt, landing sprawling on the concrete floor. Owen Hart tried similar moves but it was never quite that incredible, Hogan's superplex of Bossman was incredible when you consider the size of Bossman. A lot of the stuff Atlantis did in Mexico the first time I saw it when incredible. When Savage was younger, he used to do elbow drops off the top of cages a lot higher than the one Snuka jumped off of. I believe Owen Hart and Pillman did splashes similar to Snuka's in cage matches in Canada that were never televised. Fatu did that splash off the top rope onto the floor on Tony Super not all that long ago on NWA TV. Once in Japan one of the girls gave Akira Hokkuto a piledriver off the top rope and legitimately broke Hokkuto's neck, a move made more awesome because it was in the second fall of a two of three fall match and Hokkuto actually worked the third fall holding her head up with her hands and actually worked the fall even though it was almost one year before she could return to wrestling after the move. That move where Akira Nogami missed the dive through the ropes and purposefully busted his head against the guard-rail and juiced was pretty amazing. Even though this wasn't amazing in the sense of the other moves we've talked about here, unforgettable would be the description of chair blows by Bobby Eaton on The Fantastics during a contract signing in Mid South back around 1984. Moves by Dynamite Kid and some of the Mexican wrestlers are probably the nuttiest of them all.

CLASH OF THE CHAMPIONS
The Clash was a dynamite show. Several four-star matches. It was a thumbs up to be sure, but for all its entertaining moments, it failed in some key areas.

First of all, and this has been commented on before, the TV direction needs a lot of improvement.

It seemed every crowd shot caused us to miss a key moment during a hot match. And a number of camera angles failed to tell key stories such as Muta's yellow spray couldn't be seen or blew an opportunity to highlight why the NWA blows the WWF away from an in-ring product standpoint as neither Muta or Sting could be seen actually flying over the top rope during that incredible back-to-back dive sequence. The one bright spot, and this was done to perfection, was the Robin Green reverse angle shot. This was further enhanced by the commentary of Ross and Cornette.

I can't ever recall a better tandem at the mike during a big show. Two weeks ago, when Cornette was doing color on TBS, I actually watched the entire two hours instead of fast-forwarding through the squash matches. The reason? Cornette was so good, I was afraid I'd miss something. As a play-by-play man, Ross is without peer. And now with Cornette, he is complemented with the perfect sidekick, a guy who is not only entertaining but insightful with regards to ring tactics in the same way John Madden is during NFL games.

The show was much too much fun and two well booked to nitpick minor points to death, but I do want to comment on one other thing. The Ric Flair suffocation thing was in poor taste. I realize that something was needed at the time to take the feud to a more intense level, but with so many options available, why stoop to that? While brawls and chairs and branding irons are acceptable as foreign objects that get used in the heat of the moment, what we're talking about here is premeditated attempted murder, a criminal offense punishable by life in prison in some states. As much as I like watching pro wrestling and Ric Flair in general, I think I'd have a hard time letting my kids watch that sort of thing.

Ryan Clark
Rockville, Maryland

Thumbs up barely, but I expect more from the NWA. Tom Zenk's match was a dud. The Vicious-Ranger Ross match will just about kill the Ranger from ever getting any kind of a push. Freebirds vs. Steiners match was okay but the angle with Robin and Missy will be interesting. Thought Pillman looked great against Norman. The main event ending could have been better. Muta wasn't emphasized enough during the match. Luger looked great and had to work hard against Rich. I expect more from the PPV.

Ken Capps
St. Louis, Missouri

CLASS ACTS
Let's not forget Ivan Koloff, Lex Luger, Sting, Ric Flair, Rick Steamboat, Jim Garvin and Precious, Magnum T. A. , Ricky Morton, Robert Gibson, Baby Doll and Sam Houston for appearing with Nikita Koloff at Nikita's Gym in March to give a hand at a benefit for Mandy Koloff's medical expenses. Since the major promotions in this country are officially oblivious to everything that happens outside their promotion, I commend everyone above because they came from several different organizations to help a fellow wrestlers' family.

Honorable mention goes to Ron Simmons for refusing to partake in the Ebony Experience angle. Unfortunately, pro wrestling still perpetuates ethnic stereotyping well into the 1980s. Simmons gets a Class Act award because he risked losing a major push, if not his job, to maintain self-respect and to somewhat draw a line for professional decency within the NWA, an organization with historically deep roots in the deep South. Simmons' refusal overshadows his would-be partner's willingness to parade himself as "The Natural" for the WWF.

Tom Amara
Boston, Massachusetts

AWARDS FAVORITES

It's time to look at a few more of the awards that we be voting on for the yearbook. Voting takes place in December for the annual Observer awards with the results of balloting being released in the yearbook in January.

FEUD OF THE YEAR: This is a tough one because it encompasses many different aspects - a) heat and interest, particularly from the box office standpoint; 2) quality of the matches. My guess is that Ric Flair vs. Ricky Steamboat will win because those were the best matches, night-after-night, in years. One could argue that it didn't have the box office appeal to be a winner, although last year the Midnight Express vs. Fantastics, which won for having the best matches nightly, hardly drew the kind of money as the second place Randy Savage vs. Ted DiBiase feud, which was no slouch in the ring for the most part. A lot of others to consider. From the gate perspective, both Hulk Hogan vs. Randy Savage and Hulk Hogan vs. Big Bossman should qualify. Ric Flair vs. Terry Funk was well set-up and it was the best drawing series that the NWA had all year and headlined its best PPV show and the matches were excellent. Ironically, as good as the matches were, it'll be hurt in the balloting because of the Flair vs. Steamboat quality of matches. In the WWF, nobody had better matches this year than the Rockers vs. Brainbusters. There was really nothing on the smaller circuits that got heated enough to compete with the big stuff mentioned. In Japan, a surprise feud for quality of matches would be Jushin Liger vs. Naoki Sano, which should have one or two more chapters before the year is out. And another strong candidate, well into its fourth year, is Jumbo Tsuruta vs. Genichiro Tenryu, which is as hot today as it was when it first started brewing, and provided a lot of high quality wrestling and will lead to a lot of positive comments on the All Japan promotion in general.

BEST PROMOTION: Again, the same old debate. Do you pick the WWF because of its success, and ignore the quality of work? Do you justify the quality of work as saying that's what the public wants to see, which is somewhat unfair since unless the competitors had the same sized front office, the same syndication the same area access and NBC, you really don't know head-to-head what the general public would want to see since the general public had little or no knowledge of outside groups. After all, tons more people buy the National Enquirer than the New York Times. Tons more buy Wrestling Eye than the Wrestling Observer. Do those facts really mean anything? The NWA has its bad nights at house shows, but has put together an incredible string of excellent PPV shows and several good Clashes in 1989 to boot. But so much disorganization on promotion end makes it hard to justify picking them first either. UWF? The Stats speak for themselves. They'll have done three $1 million live show gates before the year is out and have done two closed-circuit spectaculars to boot. All with no television and only a handful of wrestlers and two front office employees. But in a lot of peoples eyes, their live cards really aren't that great, but again, the style works for the fans and it is a style you have to respect. Best all-around this year to me is New Japan. Television is almost always good and often-great. The big house shows have been good, and the June 5 show in Tokyo may very well have been the best card of the year. I saw what was described as the worst match in the card and it was three stars, and there were two five star matches and match of the year candidates on the card (Tsuruta vs. Tenryu, Can-Ams vs. Foot Loose. Strong product, strong business, no gimmicks, no frills, lots of respect from everyone involved, a promotion that follows the fans when it comes to its angles and creative booking particularly in Tokyo shows has taken a group which has been stagnant for years and put it back to forefront of Japan at a time when it looked like the Russians in New Japan and Maeda in the UWF were on the verge of it.

WORST WRESTLER: Last year's winner as the Ultimate Warrior, who is far from the worst guy around today, although he's still pretty embarrassing to watch. The worst of the worst are Giant Baba, Rufus Jones, Hillbilly Jim, Junkyard Dog, Andre the Giant, Stan Frazier and since he was portrayed as a wrestler, Zeus. I almost hate to say this, but another guy who belongs on the list is Jim Duggan, because even though he was once a great brawler, he is terrible to watch and doesn't seem to work in the ring. Warrior is terrible, but he's not crippled like Andre and he does at least try and they save him by putting him in with good workers who can carry him through to decent and even good matches. If I had to pick one, it would be Andre. Completely un-carryable, even when he was matched with Randy Savage.

MOST EMBARRASSING WRESTLER: This is the answer to the question that when friends are around who aren't wrestling fans and this guy shows up on the screen, who embarrasses you most to be a wrestling fan. I suppose seeing Joe Gonzales get cheered in Puerto Rico would be the ultimate, but we don't get Puerto Rican tapes (the stations that carried it in the states dropped the show when Gonzales returned and that wasn't coincidental). Since it's happened on more than one occasion, the Red Rooster gimmick has to be mentioned, not the wrestler, but the gimmick. When he's been on Saturday Night's Main Event, it embarrasses me to be a wrestling fan. The Ding Dongs didn't embarrass me, but boy were they stupid. Andre is pretty embarrassing. Baba would be, but they keep him off television. All those monster creatures in Memphis should be high on the list. In fact, The Werewolf, Zombie, Frankenstein and the Undertaker all tie for the win here. When I saw the tape, I erased it immediately. I didn't want to stick it in the machine by accident when anyone was around because it was the ultimate in garbage. The WWF has never even approached that level.

OCTOBER 9, 1989

Most of the talk this week continues to center around the apparent return of Tully Blanchard & Arn Anderson to the NWA after Thanksgiving. While rumors run rampant about wrestlers who "definitely will" follow or those who "may" follow, to the best of my knowledge as of press time, nobody else, with the exception of the Rougeau brothers, who aren't NWA bound, has given notice to Titan. It is expected, even within Titan circles, that one or two more wrestlers may follow, but no names are definite. I do know the NWA has talked with at Least one and maybe more semi-major name, but to say anyone else is on the way would be presumptuous.

The wrestling rumor mill (and keep in mind whenever wrestlers' salaries are discussed here that figures are probably worked) has it that Blanchard & Anderson will more than double their present WWF pay by making the jump, with the rumor mill saying they would be receiving a $250,000 per year deal with the NWA. That figure sounds high on the surface, and even those in Titan admit that Blanchard & Anderson would never be able to earn that kind of money in the WWF. While nobody questions Blanchard & Anderson as workers or as a quality-tag team, whether they will mean that much at the box office is open to a lot of debate. It depends on how they are used, and more likely, depends on so many circumstances and variables beyond their control that while the money sounds way high, maybe their return can be the building blocks of something. Of course, the way things are going right now, it's going to take some major turns before that's the case.

Blanchard & Anderson's final card for Titan, pending a late change of mind on their parts, would be the Survivors Series from the Rosemont Horizon on Thanksgiving night. A complete line-up for that card is now available. The headline match will send the Hulkamaniacs (Hulk Hogan & Demolition & Jake Roberts) vs. The Million Dollar Team (Ted DiBiase & Zeus & Powers of Pain). The remainder of the show will consist of the Warriors (Ultimate Warrior & Jim Neidhart & The Rockers) against The Heenan Family (Andre the Giant & Haku & Anderson Blanchard); Roddy's Rowdies (Roddy Piper & Jimmy Snuka & Bushwackers) vs. The Rude Brood (Rick Rude & Mr. Perfect & Rougeaus); The 4x4's (Jim Duggan & Ron Garvin & Hercules & Bret Hart) vs. The King's Court (Randy Savage & Greg Valentine & Dino Bravo & Widow Maker); and The Dream Team (Dusty Rhodes & Brutus Beefcake & Tito Santana & Red Rooster) vs. The Enforcers (Big Bossman & Akeem & Honkeytonk Man & Rick Martel). The elimination tag team matches will be preceded by a singles warm-up match which won't be part of the PPV card. The plan, as Titan has done earlier this year in Houston for the Royal Rumble and in the Meadowlands for Summer Slam is to announce a starting time of 15 minutes prior to the time the PPV starts to the crowd in the city the show originates from. That way, you don't have the empty seats in the building when the show starts and have people filing in during the opener.

The first card in Madison Square Garden in several months (MSG was closed down over the summer because of remodelling) took place this past Saturday night before a sellout crowd with the double main event of Warrior vs. Andre and Rude vs. Piper. With tickets raised $3 across the board, the gate was probably in the range of $285,000 for the show, which would be the third largest live show gate for Titan this year (behind the Summer Slam and WrestleMania shows) and also the third largest gate ever at MSG for wrestling (behind WrestleMania I and last year's SummerSlam). Ironically enough, the next MSG card will be on Oct. 28, or the same night as the NWA's PPV card from Philadelphia. My guess would be these MSG dates are arranged months in advance so this head-to-head would be coincidental (and the overlap of homes which get MSG cable and have PPV availability is relatively few), and Titan hasn't loaded up the card (Warrior vs. Andre and Duggan vs. Savage as the double headliner). Of course, if a special winds up on the USA network that night, that's another story.

The NWA is mainly gearing up for its PPV card from Philadelphia, and on television this weekend the announcement was made that Bruno Sammartino would referee the main event. To make a correction on what we reported last week, apparently Sammartino had agreed to referee the main event before leaving the live ticket sales in Philadelphia for the card, which already had been doing well without any matches announced. I don't see the name as having any kind of an impact on the PPV buys, however. The line-up was listed here last week with the exception of the opener (Tommy Rich vs. Dick Slater). On paper, it looks like the weakest NWA PPV event since the Nassau Coliseum fiasco in early 1988. That doesn't mean it won't be an action-filled card, because it probably will be. But it's hard to get excited over this show.

There is a lot that can be said about the current state of the NWA, but the emotion I keep hearing from those who follow the promotion is more and more one of frustration. A lot of the problems are nobody's fault. There are certain things, like the Hurricane last weekend which destroyed the show in Richmond and forced cancellation of Charlotte that is out of everyone's hands. Perhaps if the NWA had created better relations with its audiences and been more honest over the last two years about no-shows at the house shows, maybe the public would accept the occasional unforeseen and unavoidable problems such as the hurricane. Maybe not, but one would think so. Injuries are bound to happen when the style of wrestling is so hard-hitting and the schedule has such few days of rest. That has to be accepted as part of the game if you are one who wants a Gough style of wrestling. Over this past week, the NWA was plagued with no-shows once again, one from an injury, another from a wrestler who had a tree through his house from the hurricane, another whose girlfriend was savagely attacked in an apartment burglary and on and on it goes. The promotion can 't be blamed for any of this, but the promotion continues to suffer negative consequences from all of it because it results in disappointed fans at house shows. Following the promotion on television this weekend continued this frustration, some again, which the promotion isn't responsible for but still that doesn't help them, and some which they are responsible for. On Friday's Power Hour show, much of the show hypes the upcoming television shows over the weekend. For most of the show, they were talking about a series of matches for Sunday that actually appeared on the previous Sunday. It wasn't until late in the show that the mistake was realized and they began plugging the "right" Sunday show, which as it turns out, never aired anyway. For the Saturday show, we were promised a Ric Flair press conference, a Dan Spivey vs. Dick Murdoch match, an interview with Robin Green and Flair & Sting in a tag team match. The press conference never aired, although there was a report by Gordon Solie saying that Terry Funk had been reinstated (and that Ric Flair had paid Funk's $100,000 fine in order to get him back in the ring-please) and an interview with Flair that followed lasted about five seconds before it suddenly ended, there was a bunch of dead air, and the football scoreboard show aired. Flair & Sting never teamed although Flair did appear in the television opener in a singles match. I don't even want to talk about the interview with Robin Green since it reminds me too much of that angle they did the previous week. Throughout the show they plug a Ric Flair vs. Dick Slater match for Sunday, which had also been plugged on Worldwide Wrestling the previous week for this weekend but instead Worldwide consisted mainly of matches that had already aired on previous cable shows. Sunday, through absolutely no fault of the NWA's, the Braves once again go into extra innings (at least it was their final game, of the season) and NWA Main Event never airs. To make matters worse, after sitting through a baseball game, hoping it would end and we'd see at least some of the wrestling show, when it does end, they air a commercial talking about the wrestling show and the Flair vs. Slater main event coming up next, and then they go to a movie instead Of the wrestling show. This is not to blame TBS either, because I'm sure at this

point that the movies are drawing better TV ratings than wrestling but between all the glitches on Saturday's show, this was one frustrating weekend to follow the NWA.

A couple of notes from last week in the lawsuit by former pro wrestler Steve DiBlasio (Big Daddy) against Dusty Rhodes As mentioned several times here, DiBlasio is charging that his wrestling career was finished when Rhodes told him to take a bump over the top rope and when the 450-pound DiBlasio took the bump, the rope broke and he broke his ankle on the fall. The key points this past week were DiBlasio having to admit that when he claimed that Rhodes told him "that it was my way or the highway" in reference to taking the bump over the top rope for the DQ finish in a 1983 match against The Masked Professional (Les Thornton) that he was paraphrasing and Rhodes never actually threatened to fire or blackball him if he didn't do the move, just that he assumed that would be the case. When Rhodes was under oath and asked if he ordered the move, Rhodes said that he had told the wrestlers that he wanted an over-the-top-rope DQ finish and that he didn't care which guy went over the top at the finish. Rhodes claimed that DiBlasio was the one who volunteered to take the bump.

California Governor George Deukmejian signed the bill to deregulate professional wrestling which means that in this state, as of Jan. 1, wrestling is no longer under the auspices of the state athletic commission.

STAMPEDE

The Black Harts, a masked tag team which allegedly consists of relatives of Stu Hart that are mysterious heels managed by Hugo Hart (Stu's evil nephew) captured the International tag team titles from fellow heels Kensuke Sasaki & Sumu Hara (Tatsumi Kitahara) on 9/29 in Calgary. The title change took place among other reasons because Sasaki is leaving for West Germany. The Black Harts are actually Tom Nash from Florida (a Malenko protege) and Red Tyler from Minnesota (a Sharkey protege), although the original team was Nash & David Heath but Heath left the promotion after just a few weeks.

Among those headed in are The ArchAngel (Curtis Thompson, who will use a similar gimmick to the one he used in Puerto Rico) as a heel, Tom "Beef" Burton from Minnesota, plus Dynamite Kid, Johnny Smith and Bulldog Bob Brown returned from the Maritimes since the season ended there while Owen Hart and Larry Cameron are set to start back this Friday and headline the cards.

They did an injury angle with Chris Benoit and he's out for two weeks.

Bruce Hart has been feuding with Great Gama on top.

Jonathan Holiday was injured, actually quite badly, in a dressing room brawl at the 9/29 card in Calgary. I don't have complete details on the attack, but it was apparently quite brutal and some are speculating that criminal charges will be pressed regarding the beating. I'm not exactly clear as to why, but I'd been hearing for weeks that Holiday had heat with some of the boys. From a fan reaction standpoint, he was the most "over" heel in the promotion but the faces hated working with him since his antics as Dr. Bee Gee Holiday, the Doctor of Disco consisted of him mainly running away from his foes (mainly Benoit) which doesn't make for much of a great technical match.

CWA

The tournament for the vacant CWA titles takes place on 10/2 in Memphis. The title was vacant when Texas Dirt held the title and tried to give it to Dutch Mantell (who he really was) but Eddie Marlin wouldn't allow it and Mantell couldn't say he was Texas Dirt since that would be admitting that he was wrestling in the territory after losing in a loser leaves town match.

The first round matches in the tournament send Dustin Rhodes vs. Kevin Dillinger (Alan Martin), Chris Champion vs. Freddy (Tommy Gilbert), Mike Davis vs. Plowboy Stan Frazier, Mark Starr vs. Robert Gibson, Ricky Morton vs. Iceman King Parsons, Bill Dundee vs. Brickhouse Brown, Jeff Jarrett vs. Dirty White Boy and Mantell vs. Buddy Landel. The winner of the tournament on that night was also to get a shot at Jerry Lawler's USWA title.

Lawler did an interview about the card and talked about how that everywhere in the country that he wrestles with the exception of Tennessee that he's a heel and the fans hate him and he's prepared to wrestle the same way at the card if one of the faces like Rhodes, Dundee, Morton or Gibson win the tournament. All four came out during the interview and said they'd love to get a shot at Lawler's title.

This week Ronnie Gossett came out in army fatigues and claimed he was declaring war and all the faces.

At the 9/30 television tapings, Lawler beat Landel via DQ when Landel clotheslined ref Jerry Calhoun; Mantell & Freddy beat Blackbirds via DQ when manager Harold Harris interfered and Rhodes & Dundee beat Wildside via DQ when the heels used the flagpole as an object and got DQ 'd. None of these matches were as good as they sound on paper from what I was told.

"The Soul Taker", a 6-foot-7 inch black giant who is "a better worker than Zeus" (what a compliment, huh?) will be starting here next week managed by Larry Sharpe to feud with Lawler.

USWA

This week they blinded Eric Embry as if they haven't done everything else. It all happened at the 9/29 card at the Dallas Sportatorium which drew only around 300 fans. The main event was Embry & Kerry Von Erich against Taras Bulba & The Punisher (Mark Calaway/Master of Pain under the hood) and it ended when Billy Joe Travis came down with

a white cup and gave it to Scandor Akbar who threw it in Embry's face. They had all the faces and even the fans try to rub water in Embry' s eyes and they had him carried cut on a stretcher and the whole works. At the TV tapings the next day they said that Embry has only 40 percent vision in his left eye and that they were concerned he was going to lose his right eye and they were claiming that it was ammonia that they threw in his eyes, although it looked more like Sprite. Before the TV show was over Percy Pringle announced that Embry would still appear in every show he was booked in and he was advertised in a main event rematch in Dallas on 10/6. In other matches on the card, Jeff Jarrett & Matt Borne captured the USWA tag team titles which were held up after last week's match by beating Ron Starr & Sheik Scott Braddock, Chris & Toni Adams beat P. Y. Chu Hi & Tojo Yamamoto and the opener was to send Jimmy Jack Funk & Frank Dusek against Gary Young & Scandor Akbar, however Dusek no-showed (in fact, there was no sign of him the entire weekend nor any mention of his absence so he may be history here) and was replaced by Travis. Young threw Travis out of the ring and he got up like he jammed his knee and limped to the dressing room leaving Funk against both guys and he was eventually pinned. Later in the card Travis limped to the ring to talk with Pringle, however when Travis came out for the run-in in the main event, he sprinted to the ring to complete his turn. Lots of speculation this group will lose its stranglehold as the main promotion in Dallas. Killer Tim Brooks' promotion, which runs on Tuesday nights at the Longhorn Bar in Dallas (three blocks from the Sportatorium) on Tuesday nights was up to around 550 fans this past week. Those working for Brooks include John Tatum, Scott Casey, Botswana Beast, Skip Young (Sweet Brown Sugar), Johnny Mantell and Brooks (who has lost nearly 60 pounds from when he last worked for World Class.

Brooks' promotion starts on television in Dallas on 10/14 with a weekly Saturday night show on Ch. 39 (for years the flagship station of World Class) at midnight.

10/6 in Dallas has Kerry & Embry against Punisher & Bulba on top, Jarrett & Borne vs. Starr & Braddock in a loser of the fall leaves town match (expect Starr to leave as he never stays in any territory for a long period of time - he's about the best worker in this territory but didn't get over with the fans), Funk vs. Young in a taped fist match and Chu Hi vs. Adams with Tojo Yamamoto in a cage and Toni Adams getting the key to the cage.

Kerry Von Erich did an interview where he said that Embry was just like one of the family and that teaming with him was just like teaming with David, Kevin or Mike. I'd hate to even speculate what that means. The Saturday morning taping had a good match with Adams & Funk beating Chu Hi & Young which was the best television match this promotion has had in quite a while. Toni Adams was at ringside with a kendo stick to keep Tojo from interfering but Tojo stole Toni's high heel shoes and on camera wiped his butt with Toni's shoes.

AWA

Destruction Crew captured the AWA tag team titles in the tournament on 10/1 in Rochester, MN before a crowd which started out at 1,500 but was closer to 200 by the time the title match took place. Destruction Crew (Wayne Bloom & Mike Enos) won the final match over Greg Gagne & Paul Diamond when Sheik Adnan El-Kaissey and Kokina Maximus beat up Gagne and Kokina splashed Greg's often-injured knee leaving Diamond by himself. Diamond was doing well until Bloom used a foreign object on him for the pinfall. The tournament, scheduled for six teams, only wound up with four teams as Diamond & Gagne beat Mike George & Jonnie Stewart and Destruction Crew beat Sgt. Slaughter & Baron Von Raschke via DQ in the semifinals.

Ken Patera and Derrick Dukes both quit the promotion this week. Dukes was scheduled to wrestle Larry Zbyszko in the main event on the card for the title but Dukes wouldn't do a clean job and quit the promotion just before the match was to take place so they announced Dukes had left the building , Zbyszko did a speech about the young wrestlers not having the guts when their chance comes and Zbyszko was just awarded a win via forfeit so he never even wrestled at the taping.

Newcomers at the taping were The Trooper (Del Wilkes) who is a babyface and hands out plastic badges before the match and The Unknown Soldier, who pinned Mike Enos in an undercard match. The Soldier was supposed to be David Sammartino, to set up a feud with Zbyszko, but Sammartino wasn't there and we 've got no idea who was under the mask to take his place.

They had two interesting gimmick matches at the taping. In one, they had a two of three fall match with The Tokyo Bullets (as faces) against The Texas Hangmen (Rick Gantner & Mike Richards). The rules were that whichever team won the first fall, that team could have both members of the team in the ring at the same time while the other team had to tag in and out. Naturally the heels won the first fall, but at the disadvantage, the Bullets won the second fall. Third fall, which was actually a tornado match since both teams got to have both guys in the ring ended in a time limit draw the other was a match where Stewart, Trooper and Kokina were all in the ring at the same time winner-take-all. It wound up with Stewart getting pinned and Kokina getting counted out (in a lumberjack match because Kokina was so heavy the lumberjacks couldn't pick him up and get him in the ring on time to beat the count) so Trooper won. They announced on TV that in case of a wrestler leaving the promotion in the Team Challenge that among those listed as "possible replacements" were The Rock & Roll Express, Ricky Steamboat, The Guerreros, Greg Gagne, Bam Bam Bigelow, John Studd and Nikita Koloff. Why didn't they just say Hulk Hogan and Ric Flair as well? Mike George is now doing a gimmick called "Timekeeper Mike George" in which, before his match starts, he sets a time on an alarm clock and tries to beat the guy before the clock. He set two minutes for a jobber and beat the guy in 90 seconds.

The matches with Soldier vs. Enos, a Wendi Richter beating Candi Divine via DQ, the two of three fall tag team match and the three-man lumberjack match were all taped for the Team Challenge show, which should debut within a few weeks.

NEW JAPAN

This group finished its recent tour with a couple of subpar crowds for the big shows during the last two days.

9/20 at the Osaka Castle Hall drew 8,180, which is the largest crowd for wrestling in Osaka in a few years, but that's mainly because all three groups run at the Puritsu Gym (7,000 seats) rather than Castle Hall (14,000 capacity). The headline match on the card saw Big Van Vader (Leon White) retain his IWGP World title beating Bam Bam Bigelow after a powersLam in 11:32 with Antonio Inoki serving as special referee. After the match Bigelow body slammed Inoki and Vader started daring Inoki to fight back. Masa Saito & Shinya Hashimoto captured the IWGP tag team titles beating Riki Choshu & Takayuki Iizuka in 18:52 when Hashimoto pinned Iizuka after a DDT, plus Naoki Sano retained the IWGP jr. title pinning Jushin Liger (Keiichi Yamada) in 18:23, Salman Hashimikov pinned Italian Stallion, Owen Hart pinned Tatsutoshi Goto, Osamu Kido & Kengo Kimura beat Billy Jack Haynes & Kendo Nagasaki, Super Strong Machine & George Takano beat Shiro Koshinaka & Kuniaki Kobayashi, Kantaro Hoshino pinned Pat Tanaka and Akira Nogami beat Osamu Matsuda.

9/21 saw the series end before 4,220 fans in Yokohama as Vader used the powerslam to keep the title pinning Hashimoto in 10:08 with Inoki serving as referee once again, an interesting tag team semifinal saw Hashimikov & Choshu team up for the first time beating Saito & Bigelow when Hashimikov pinned Saito with the Northern lights Suplex in 9:03, Sano pinned Hart in 13:31, Liger & Nogami & Iizuka beat Koshinaka & Kobayashi & Hoshino, Kido & Kimura beat Machine & Takano, Hiroshi Hase pinned Stallion, Nagasaki made Haynes submit to the boston crab, Norio Honaga pinned Tanaka and Goto pinned Matsuda. This card wasn't taped for television.

9/15 in Nagahama drew 2,210 as Hashimoto & Saito beat Hashimikov & Victor Zangiev in the main event when Saito made Zangiev submit to the Boston crab. Zangiev was reportedly hospitalized after this match and missed the rest of the tour because of a leg injury suffered from Hashimoto s heavy kicks. Also Bigelow & Haynes beat Choshu & Goto,

Koshinaka pinned Sano in a non-title match, Hart pinned Tanaka, Liger pinned Nogami, Kimura & Kido & Hase beat Kobayashi & Machine & Takano, Nagasaki pinned Stallion and Iizuka pinned Matsuda.

OTHER JAPAN NOTES

Terry Gordy's nephew Richard is currently in Japan training with the All Japan wrestlers until the end of the year and will turn pro next year. Tiger Mask (Mitsuhara Misawa) has begun training for his comeback after reconstructive knee surgery and should be back in action in December.

New Japan TV announcer Kotetsu Yamamoto (the bald-headed color commentator) was the special ref for the JWP card on 9/15 in Tokyo for the Devil Masami vs. Shinobu Kandori main event.

JWP and UWA jr. champ Yu Yamazaki returned the titles due to knee surgery and on 9/15, Prime Mariko became the new champion beating Cutie Suzuki and Marumi Ozaki in a tournament.

Akira Maeda's opponent for the 11/29 card at the Tokyo Egg Dome was announced this past week. I don't know the name, but I believe it is an American who was an NCAA champion wrestler in the early 1980s who has never wrestled professionally.

OTHER AREA NOTES

Downtown Bruno is now the CWF jr. heavyweight champion after beating midget Butch Cassidy on 9/22 in Knoxville. The midget was beating on Bruno until a ref bump, then Robert Fuller interfered and piledrove the midget for the win. Also on the card, The Southern Boys (Tracy Smothers & Steve Armstrong) lost to Jimmy Golden & Brian Lee (CWF tag team champions) via DQ when Armstrong got the kendo stick that Sylvia was using and was caught using it on the heels, Kerry Von Erich went to a double DQ with CWF champion Dennis Condrey, Ron Fuller pinned The Black Barbarian (Bill Tabb) and unmasked him to keep the USA title, Bill Dundee beat Wendell Cooley via DQ, Adrian Street & Todd Morton beat Beauty & The Beast via DQ, Miss Linda beat The Lady Beast or The Baroness as she's now called in a loser leaves town match, Robert Fuller pinned Jerry Stubbs and Danny Davis pinned Lou Fabbiano. Want to know about a sick angle that you won't be seeing? Fuller wanted to do an angle with Linda Street where they would say Linda was pregnant and during the sixth month, Fuller would attack her and cause her to lose the baby. Saner heads prevailed and you won't be seeing this one.

Mark Tendler is promoting a show on 10/29 in Paterson, NJ with Ken Patera vs. Nikolai Volkoff, David Sammartino vs. Larry Zbyszko and Dominic DeNucci vs. Davy O' Hannon.

Mick Karch ran a poll on television in the Twin Cities asking fans to vote for their favorite and least favorite wrestler. Interesting results. Ten most popular, in order, were: 1. Ric Flair; 2. Road Warriors; 3. Hulk Hogan; 4. Sting; 5. Curt Hennig; 6. Lex Luger; 7. Ricky Steamboat; 8. Larry Zbyszko; 9. Rick Steiner; 10. Ultimate Warrior.

The ten most unpopular, in order, were: 1. Hulk Hogan; 2. Andre the Giant; 3. tie between Terry Funk and Eric Embry; 5. Randy Savage; 6. Honky Tonk Man; 7. Greg Gagne; 8. Ultimate Warrior; 9. Jim Duggan; 10. Dusty Rhodes.

Koji Kitao will be training in Hamel, MN with Masa Saito and Brad Rheingans after finishing his training with Lou Thesz and prior to his Japanese debut.

Here's the latest on Bam Bam Bigelow as a boxer. What the deal is that some boxing promoters are trying to put together the match. Bigelow will first get some tune-up matches and then they will try and sell Tyson's people on the viability and marketability of this match in Japan. It's far from a sure thing, but there is some substance to the rumors.

The independent wrestler in New York who has been using the "Benny the Jet" name will no longer be using it as former kick boxer Benny Urquidez had the name trademarked.

Buck Robley will tape his first television show for a proposed promotion to open next year in Louisiana and Mississippi on 10/5 in Jackson, MS with Fantastics (Fulton brothers) vs. Rock & Roll Express billed as the main event plus Bob Orton and Abdullah the Butcher announced.

Big Van Vader will work some dates in Mexico in November.

Speaking of Mexico, the masked wrestler who goes as Konan the Barbarian is actually an American according to Viva La Lucha, a newsletter covering Lucha Libre. Another interesting fact is that Steve Nelson who works in Mexico is the son of former pro wrestlers Gordon Nelson and Marie LaVerne and grandson of former wrestlers Bobby Pico and Ann LaVerne.

There was talk at a New Orleans convention on sponsoring live events (in all forms of entertainment) that one promoter is working with the ICW on doing a PPV show out of Atlantic City or Las Vegas. Sweet dreams.

Speaking of PPV, some changes are in the offing in the cable industry as a company called TCI is trying to buy out a lot of systems. The end result of this is there is talk that perhaps as soon as next spring, the number of addressable homes for PPV may top 20 million, or about a 60 percent increase over the current total. In other words, if all things were to stay the same, big PPV events would gross about 60 percent more money next year than they do this year with roughly the same costs of putting the events together. This could happen in time for next year's WrestleMania which would virtually guarantee it setting every wrestling PPV record for total revenue and total orders, even with a lower buy rate than previous Titan PPV events.

Playboy Magazine in this month's issue previewed for next month it will have a feature on the women of pro wrestling. I believe the feature will center around some of the GLOW and POWW girls, particularly Mimi Lessos (Magnificent Mimi).

When I was running down the worst gimmicks of last year, I inadvertently forgot to mention the Ding Dongs. How could that be forgotten?

An independent show at Henderson's Arena in Atlanta drew 300 on 9/17 as Mike Golden & Mr. Atlanta (Tony Zane), billed as The Peach Street Mafia, went to a 15 minute draw with the new Fantastics . TV announcer Randall Brown turned heel and cost John Michaels a match against Cowboy Kevin Dillinger (Alan Martin), Mr. Wrestling II beat The Nightmare (Ted Allen), they had a match where two girl wrestlers wrestled against a guy wrestler and manager Samuel Kent and Joyce Grable pinned Kent, Randall Brown turned back babyface by the end of the night and the top matches saw a pair of double count out brawls with Dustin Rhodes vs. Randy Rose and Dutch Mantell vs. Joel Deaton. Earlier that same day in Alpharetta, GA, David Sanunartion beat Joel Deaton for the Southern title for Southern Championship Wrestling.

A show booked for early November in Medina, OH has this interesting Line-up: Kerry Von Erich vs. Paul Orndorff, Brian Blair & Jim Brunzell vs. Larry Zbyszko & Buddy Landel, Jerry Lawler vs. Kimala, Steve Regal vs. Sam Houston, Ivan Koloff vs. Paul Jones, Fabulous Moolah vs. Heidi Lee Morgan and Manny Fernandez vs. Iceman King Parsons. Don't bet on these matches actually taking place as for political reasons it's hard to believe Von Erich, Lawler and Zbyszko would work the same card (Jarrett and Verne Gagne have lawsuits pending over the distribution, or I should say lack of distribution of income stemming from Superclash last December) plus Orndorff hasn't worked one wrestling date since his retirement some years back and he's told everyone who has asked in the interim that he's not interested in ever returning, including the Japanese.

Jerry Lawler defended his USWA title last week in Dothan, AL against Wendell Cooley, I believe on 9/23. Finish saw a ref bump, Cooley bulldogged Lawler. Dennis Condrey runs in with an object to hit Cooley, who ducks and it hits Lawler. Cooley superkicks Lawler and has him pinned but before the ref could make the count, he dq'd Lawler for the outside help. Kerry Von Erich beat Condrey via DQ on the same card.

9/28 in Hazel town, PA promoted by The Samoans saw Samoans beat Volkoff & Russian #1 on top, Mike Sharpe drew with Cheetah Rid, Ken Patera beat Tonga Kid (Sam Fatu) and Patera won a Battle Royal plus Mike Kaluha, Tom Brandi and A. J. Petrucci worked underneath.

Don't expect a deal between Stampede Wrestling and

ESPN.

Florida Championship Wrestling is now running weekly in Tampa on Saturday nights and drawing about 250 fans per show. Blackjack Mulligan is back in the ring teaming with son Kendall Windham as a heel team feuding with tag champs The Nasty Boys on top. Diamond Dallas Page is a babyface managing Steve Keirn. There is talk that this group is trying to put together a deal where its stock would go public.

10/1 in Fort Worth for USWA saw Jimmy Jack Funk & Matt Borne draw with Billy Joe Travis & Gary Young, Rock & Roll Express beat Ron Starr & Sheik Scott' braddock, Chris Adams beat P. Y. Chu-Hi when Tojo Yamamoto interfered for the DQ, Jeff Jarrett pinned Tarus Bulba and Kerry Von Erich double count out with The Punisher. So Eric Embry did miss at least one show with his "blindness".

Correction on the 9/23 results from Portland. I reported that Carl Styles won a Battle Royal, when in reality the Battle Royal was won by Nord the Barbarian'. Results from 9/30 saw Rex King beat Johnny Boyd, Beetlejuice beat Scotty the Body via count out when King came to ringside and waved the Northwest title belt (which he stole from Scotty after winning a non-title match on 9/23) and Scotty chased him for the count out loss, Steve Doll pinned Al Madril, Bill Francis & Styles beat Nord & Brian Adams via DQ and Rip Oliver went to double disqualification against The Grappler.

The World Wrestling Council is scheduled to start up action this week after being closed down since the hurricane hit the island.

Ron West's rival promotion to the CWF is scheduled to start up this coming week with a TV taping on 10/8 in Chattanooga with these matches announced: The Bullet (Bob Armstrong) vs. Ivan Koloff, Pez Whatley vs. Kimala, Brad Armstrong vs. Jimmy Golden (it will be very interesting if this name is Legit as Golden is the cousin of Robert Fuller and half of the tag team champs in the CWF), Bambi vs. Peggy Lee Leather plus The Fantastics (who are appearing for almost every independent in the South), Mr. Wrestling II and Terry Gordy (who has no scheduled return date for the NWA that I know of as they pressured him to give up Japan and obviously he wasn't about to do so).

Southern Championship Wrestling is advertising that Junkyard Dog, Ivan Koloff, Fantastics, Rock & Roll Express are all coming in.

9/23 in Maywood, CA before 379 saw The Mercenaries (Billy Anderson & Tim Patterson & Louie Spicoli under hoods) keep their six man titles beating Steve Dalton & Alex Knight & The Beast (who I believe works as Konan in Mexico).

A recent movie video to a flick 'No Safe Haven' features former wrestling announcer Bill Mercer as a football announcer, while a video release "Midnite" features Tom Lister (Zeus) as a Security guard named Tiny.

NWA

Expect some changes in direction (again?) at TV tapings in a few weeks. What direction, who even knows.

Dick Slater left for Japan until the PPV.

Terry Funk started back on Wednesday even though the announcement of his suspension being lifted wasn't until TV on Saturday. At the house shows they said that the suspension was lifted on Monday, however Funk was being billed for cards every-where when he was still announced on TV as suspended.

Missing in action this week have included Jimmy Garvin (a tree went through his house during the hurricane), Brian Pillman (his girlfriend was stabbed four times by a burglar and was hospitalized, Road Warrior Hawk (personal problems) and Lex Luger (injured) although Hawk and Luger were back in action by the weekend.

NWA has five PPV events planned for next year. While an argument can be made that is too many, and it is certainly too many for them to remain special (just as they did too many for each to be a special event this year), PPV is one area the company is profitable in, and if the number of potential homes increases by as much as people are saying that it will, it makes being profitable in PPV that much easier. First one of the new year will be on February 25 and billed as Wrestle War '90.

Newspaper and TV Guide ads for the PPV event on 10/28 include the names Ricky Steamboat and Paul E. Dangerously. Dangerously's name is at least understandable as he's been gone just a few weeks, but Steamboat's been gone since 8/1. These ads to have to be placed ahead of time, but changes and last minute editing can also be done a lot farther in advance than two months.

A memo went out to the bookers that TBS wants no more blood or heavy unnecessary violence on its television shows, although the PPV shows will have no such restrictions. I guess this is why Jim Ross said on TV that parental discretion is advised on the PPV show. My own belief is they should have a Lot freer reign on a PPV show because an audience is specifically buying the show and expecting grudge matches and heavy violence while the TV show is watched by a lot of casual people and they should limit stuff that the general public would find repulsive (I guess that means Vince should make Dusty wear a shirt while he wrestles as well).

9/27 in Worcester, MA drew a horrendous $7,000 house (Titan drew a nearly as bad $25,000 house two nights earlier in a more expensive building to book) Eddie Gilbert pinned Cuban Assassin, The Z-Man (Tom Zenk) pinned Norman the Lunatic, Steve Williams pinned Mike Rotunda, Skyscrapers beat Dynamic Dudes (fans cheered Scrapers about 80 percent), Tommy Rich pinned Jacko Victory, Bobby Eaton pinned Michael Hayes when Cornette hit Hayes with the tennis racquet, Road Warrior Animal pinned Rip Morgan, Sting beat Great Muta via DQ when Gary Hart interfered and Ric Flair pinned Terry Funk in 12:12 of a good match but shorter than one would expect.

Ratings for last weekend saw Power Hour on 9/22 draw a 1.6 rating (the Braves game that preceded it did a 1.2), World Championship Wrestling on/23 with the Scott Steiner angle did a 2.0 while NWA Main Event on 9/24 with mainly repeat matches did a 2.1.

TBS is apparently serious about the heavy violence being a no-no as promos were shot for last week's Power Hour showing the plastic bag stuff and none of them ever aired.

The November PPV from Troy, NY is being called "New York Knockouts" and I'm afraid that meaning could be quite literal and not what they mean.

The debut card in Troy on 9/28 drew just 1,300 fans and the crowd was "cold" for most of the show (except for Flair vs. Funk) and the lighting in the building is terrible so they are going to need a major overhaul to make the crowd seem into it and the lighting up to big show standards. Results saw Gilbert pin Cuban ½ *, Z-Man pinned Norman *, Skyscrapers beat Dudes * ¾, Rotunda pinned Williams ¾ *, Lane pinned Hayes when Cornette used the tennis racquet ** , Warriors beat Militia ** ¾, Sting beat Muta via DQ ** ¾, Luger pinned Rich * and Flair pinned Funk *** ½. Told the main event saved an otherwise lacklustre show.

Earlier that day, Flair did a stint as a guest DJ on a Local radio station in Albany with callers asking him wrestling questions. He did really good and the DJ's plugging the show kept saying Flair was the real World champion and how he'd beat Hogan like it was nothing, but Flair really didn't want to comment on that subject. There were two interesting calls, however. One was from Jeff Blatnik, the Greco-Roman gold medalist in the 1984 Olympics and an avowed pro wrestling hater, but he was quite complementary to Flair and said that "Flair was a true wrestling champion, " and another caller asked Flair if he would do a unification match and Flair and the DJ's assumed the caller was talking about Hogan and Flair said he'd love to, but the caller said that he meant Lawler. Flair said that he was upset that anyone would even consider Lawler or his title comparable to Flair and his title and the normally diplomatic Flair finished off saying, "Jerry Lawler is a disgrace to professional wrestling. No idea what that's all about, but my guess is Flair doesn't take too kindly to all of Lawler's interviews where he claims to be the only World champion and calls Flair nothing more than a company champion.

Fantastics are already through.

Robin Green is now referred to as "Woman" and Butch Reed & Ron Simmons will be known as "Doom" for their feud with the Steiners.

Speaking Of the Steiners, the interview they did over the weekend about the limo angle was about the most effective one I've seen them do, particularly Scott. That closed eye was pretty darn graphic as well and visually effective. Originally they wanted to use make-up for that effect like in the movies, but make-up runs when you sweat so if he wrestled with it on, it would look totally goofy, so he had Rick haul back and punch him right in the eye to shut it. I know most of you still won't believe that but it really is true. Brings up a few questions. What kind of (guts/ insanity) does Scott have to Stand there and take a blow like that without flinching? What kind of damage could Rick do if he actually was mad at someone? In the old days, before blading was popular, in some of the smaller circuits they occasionally did hardway blood in a similar manner, trying to throw Legit bare-knuckle punches to the forehead to open it up. As one ex-wrestler once told me it wasn't so bad, except when the first punch didn't open the forehead and you had to take two or three more to get the job done.

The actual skit which was supposed to have done the damage did have an explanation for the silliness and bad camera work. You can hear in the background the camera man say, "I 'm going to get help" and he put down the camera which is why the lens didn't pick up Sullivan's face, so that was the explanation. Only problem is, almost nobody who saw the piece heard the camera man. Lots of comments on it this week. Vast majority didn't like it. Some liked it a lot, but even those who did like it thought it was a waste for the Steiners to be doing a program with Simmons & Reed.

WWF

Vince McMahon had personal meetings this past week with both Hulk Hogan and Randy Savage to make sure the key stars aren't considering making a move. Actually, neither of those names had even been mentioned by anyone, although either would be a key acquisition. I'd figure Hogan would be impossible to get. Savage would be very hard because he's got long-term plans here, but money talks and never say never.

As far as anyone leaving, I've talked to a few sources close to the "action" backstage and their comments are: 1) One or two more might go but no more than that; 2) A few more are expected to go but as long as it isn't Hogan, Savage or Piper, none would be major losses; 3) Five to seven more are going but they haven't given notice; 4) Don't believe that anyone else is going. With TV tapings on Monday and Tuesday night of this week in Wheeling, WV and Toledo, OH, we should know a lot more next week.

Tapings are one week early because several of the major stars including Hogan and Savage will be touring Europe next week. The London debut on 10/10 sold out a 12,000 seat arena in just one week for Hogan vs. Savage on top.

The WWF video game by American Technos was voted the best video arcade game of the year at the convention two weeks back in Las Vegas. John Studd, Jimmy Hart and Honky Tonk Man all attended the convention as reps for Titan. Studd's name sounds strange in that company since he quit Titan, but I guess is still doing promotional work for them.

9/25 in Worcester, MA drew 2,000 as Paul Roma pinned Barry Horowitz, Dino Bravo pinned Jim Neidhart, Mr. Perfect pinned Tim Horner (best match) , Bushwackers beat Powers of Pain via count out, Greg Valentine pinned Ron Garvin, Jim Duggan beat Ted DiBiase via count out and Brutus Beefcake pinned Randy Savage when Duggan distracted Savage and Beefcake cradled him from behind.

Titan pulled off WLDI in Boston which it had been on since the beginning of time because that station started airing NWA shows just before the Titan shows.

Prime Time Wrestling did a 2.4 on 9/25 which is the lowest in more than one year (the week before was the lowest rated of 1989, so the NFL is doing a number on PTW, with or without Roddy Piper) while All-American, which started Late due to USA network sports commitments, did an 0.9 on 9/24 against the NFL which is its lowest rating in history.

MSG results from 9/30 saw The Genius (Lanny Poffo) over Koko Ware, Jimmy Snuka beat Honkeytonk Man, Perfect beat Red Rooster, Mark Young beat Horowitz, Warrior beat Andre via DQ, Demoliton beat Brain Busters via DQ, Valentine pinned Garvin and Roddy Piper double count out with Rick Rude.

9/30 in St. Louis drew 8,800 and $97,000 as Widow Maker beat Horner, Dusty Rhodes beat Big Bossman, Haku double count out Bret Hart, Rick Martel drew Tito Santana, Power s of Pain upset Bushwackers, Badnews Brown pinned Hercules and Hogan beat Savage in a double-juice cage match.

CNN did a personality feature on Jesse Ventura.

9/23 in Sacramento drew 5,000 as Boris Zhukov pinned Young, Brown pinned Hart, Widow Maker pinned Ware, Snuka pinned Honkey, Hercules pinned Haku, Demolition beat Brain Busters via DQ and Warrior beat Andre via DQ.

Randy Savage should send a thank-you card to Marge Schott for all the free publicity.

Hogan vs. Savage did $145,000 at the Bradley Center in Milwaukee for a cage match on 9/29.

THE READERS' PAGE

INDEPENDENT CONTRACTORS

I probably don't know as much labor law as Raymond Asher (9/18 Observer) but I'd Love to argue with him whether even a one-shot jobber is an " independent contractor" or an "employee" (who would be eligible for worker's compensation). The traditional test is whether the worker is subject to the control of the superior as to the details of his work.

Almost by definition, then, even one-shot jobbers are

employees. If they weren't subject to direction as to the details of their performance, the effect of the wrestling show would be seriously undermined. "Independent contractor" describes the relationship between the arena operator and the wrestling promoter. The arena doesn't care what goes on in that building, as long as it's lawful, as long as the bills are paid. Further, the fans perceive that even one-shot jobbers are "representatives" of the promoter. Fans do not understand that some are under contract and some aren't. Consequently, if a one-shot jobber injured a fan at ringside, I believe it is uncontroversial that the promoter would face automatic Liability because the jobber is the representative of the promoter. By contrast, the arena owner would not automatically face liability for the promoter's negligence (although the owner might, under legal theories other than the employer-employee theory).

Chuck Shepherd
Washington, D.C.

AWARDS
With the obvious emphasis this year on huge mega shows, PPV cards and cable clashes, I feel an additional award is needed: Card of the year. This year provided many big events, but to me these were the best: 1) UWF 5/4 Osaka Baseball Stadium; 2) New Japan 4/24 Egg Dome; 3) UWF 1/10 Budokan Superbout Maeda vs. Takada; 4) NWA New Orleans Clash of the Champions; 5) UWF 8/13 Yokohama, not to ignore NWA Chi town Rumble, Nashville Wrestle War, Baltimore Bash, 6/5 ALI Japan Budokan Hall.

Biggest shock of the year: 1) The Great Muta's immediate acceptance, push and success in the NWA. Few would have believed one year ago that Super Black Ninja would have this potential; 2) Intense disappointment in the Hogan-Savage feud. When Hogan fought Savage in Dec. 1985 and Jan. 1986 at Madison Square Garden, those were Hogan's two best matches ever in New York. While their 1989 matches are better than most of the WWF matches are, which isn't saying much, one would have thought that Hogan's regaining the belt would have created a lot more "excitement. Perhaps in retrospect, the Wrestlemania V finish was a mistake, especially since we now have ZZZZeus as the Leading contender; 3) Flair's overwhelming popularity as a face. The NWA got at least one scenario right when Flair was turned face with the title win against Steamboat.

Match of the year: 1) Maeda vs. Takada 1/10 Tokyo; 2) Steamboat vs. Flair New Orleans; 3) Yamazaki vs. Takada 5/4 Osaka; 4) Steamboat vs. Flair 2/20 Chicago; 5) Steamboat vs. Flair Nashville; 6) Fujiwara vs. Funaki 5/4 Osaka; 7) Jushin Liger vs. Naoki Sano; 8) Muta vs. Sting Baltimore; 9) Flair vs. Funk Baltimore; 10) Maeda vs. Fujiwara 8/13 Yokohama; 11) Spivey vs. Sting 6/5 Tokyo; 12) Fujiwara vs. Yamazaki 7/24 Tokyo; 13) Sting vs. Muta

Greenville, SC

Clinton Freeman
New York, New York

LETTER TO VERNE GAGNE
(Editor's Note: About six weeks ago in Pro Wrestling Torch, editor Wade Keller interviewed Verne
Gagne about a variety of subjects. When the name Bruiser Brody was brought up, Gagne responded that
Brody "probably got what he deserved." Needless to say, we've gotten a lot: of letters on that statement)

Dear Verne,
So Bruiser Brody probably deserved what he got? Several inches of lethal metal twisted into his stomach wall, his blood forming thick pools around his furred boots, his hands futilely attempting to hold in the intestines from spilling forth their fluids. According to you Verne, that cold slab in a dirty Puerto Rican morgue was reserved for Frank Goodish. That urn that holds his ashes sits right where it belongs.

Each year the various wrestling sheets give out awards for the most disgusting or obnoxious event in wrestling. Almost always the ignominious honor goes to a promoter or booker whose angle crosses the boundaries of what even by wrestling standards passes for good taste. Well Verne, this year it's a lock. It has probably been a long time since any award had your name on it but I would bet the ranch on this one. If your comments had been within the context of an ill-planned angle designed to draw cheap heat and stir controversy for your TV show, they would have been judged as stupid and in poor taste. Fans would have shaken their heads saying "Verne has gone too far this time". However, your comments were given in total seriousness to a writer. They were not staged or contrived but were obviously what you believe to be true. This makes it many times worse than some offensive angle gone wrong.

Verne, you have worked hard over the decades to craft an All-American squeaky clean reputation. There is Verne Gagne, the babyface champion of all that is good and just. I remember the Verne Gagne of the early 1960s hustling something called "Protein Power Pack Formula" that you promised would help build strong bodies and healthy minds. Now you are justifying cold-blooded murder. That's quite a jump. What did Frank Goodish ever do to justify his fate? You probably saw him as a mean, self-centered sob who changed finishes and refused to take your advice and direction. Even if Frank personified everything that was wrong with a wrestler, does that justify his murder? I guess you think so.

Part of your image is that of Verne Gagne, the family man. There can be no doubt that you do take care of your own. Your son has the body of a swimmer, yet you make him a wrestler. Despite his limited ability, you push him beyond all reason and even shower him with a variety of titles. But he is your son and it is your promotion and you can do whatever you want. Your daughter works in the front office. Her husband is made your World champion. Forget that his glory days were at the beginning of this decade and we are approaching a new decade. It's your family, your promotion and you can do as you please. But you've been stripped of your family man costume. The only family you care about is your own. Other people's families, the concept of a family, doesn't mean a thing to you. Why don't you knock on Barbara Goodish's front door. Tell her that Frank probably deserved what he got. Why don't you talk to her son. You can't miss him. He's the little boy without a father.

One of the things I do for a living is teach psychology. We know that as people age, they tend to look back on their lives with a sense of judgement. If they like what they have seen they develop a sense of integrity and their senior years tend to be mellow and satisfying. On the other hand, if they look back and see broken dreams and unfulfilled promises, they can turn into cranky old men. Maybe that's the problem. The game has passed you by. You were once a World champion. You had more fame and fortune than most and would be considered very lucky by most people. But look at the last decade. Hulk Hogan is the hottest thing in wrestling and you had him. He was packing arenas for you. The money was flowing Like water. But you blew it. You couldn't keep him happy when you should have, and now the initials WWF are mass marketed throughout the world while the initials AWA are a trivia question.

Every once in a while enjoy watching the first minute of your TV show. The AWA logo comes on and then the words, "the major League of wrestling. That's funnier than a whole season of Saturday Night Live. That's what the AWA has become. A big joke.

Chris Zavisa
Plymouth, Michigan

NWA

I'm quite pleased with the line-up the NWA has given us for their first show on 10/1 here in Rochester.

The only problems so far are the local spots with Joe Pedicino plugging the card are pretty weak . Only one plug per show. Also, the tickets are priced the same as Titan. If scaled down, they could grab borderline buyers. Anyway, the ball is in the NWA's court on how they promote, execute and wrestle on this show, and if they ever return. My gut feeling right now is that they will be lucky to draw 2,000 fans.

I truly hated the deal with the plastic bag with Flair and Funk. It was in very poor taste. Dick Slater and Gary Hart both belong in a minor circuit. They just don't fit in well in the big time.

Sean Hendrick
Rochester, New York

I have mixed emotions with the NWA right now. First off, losing Ricky Steamboat was a big mistake. I Loved the way Steamboat carried Lex Luger in Baltimore and to see Luger vs. Tommy Rich is a big disappointment. Nobody in Baltimore cared about Rich or thought he had any kind of a chance at all. Baltimore is a hungry town for wrestling as the WWF comes in about four times a year. The NWA gives no localized interviews and we don't even get the line-up for the cards until two weeks before the card, which results in weak advances.

When the NWA first came to the Northeast, Baltimore stood alone in supporting them. The reason was we received localized interviews and knew the entire card a month in advance. I've never missed an NWA card and have always given them my hard-earned $15 monthly for ringside tickets and feel they must go back to the old routine of giving the fans a right to feel important.

Many fans come to me at the matches complaining about things like no blood in cage matches. There used to be a day when blood in cage matches was a formality .

Fred Creutzer
Baltimore, Maryland

Dave Meltzer: I also think the NWA needs localized interviews and the line-ups announced farther in advance at its house shows. However, the blood in cage matches it out of their hands. The commission doesn't allow blood (made an exemption for Flair-Funk, but it is a commission ruling) in Maryland and both promotions have to work around the guidelines issued.

RANDOM COMMENTS

After reading recent Observers, I feel I've got to write. Although it 's hard for smart fans to swallow, the WWF will always be the No. 1 promotion. They know who to push and how to push them. I see constant complaints about Hulk Hogan throwing Sherri Martel around. That may not be tolerable in real life, but that's what the audience wants to see. For every ten people apalled, there are 100 that Love it. Money is the bottom line. An NWA star told me, F that We Wrestle, the WWE' is making a million dollars. " He also told me, "I don't want nobody making fun of me, but money is the name of the game." Also, the Ultimate Warrior is by no means the worst wrestler in the business. Tom Magee, JYD, Honky Tonk Man, Superfly Snuka, Dusty Rhodes, Andre the Giant, Akeem, Greg Valentine, Dino Bravo, Jim Duggan, Tommy Rich, Scott Hall, Kevin Sullivan and numerous small promotion wrestlers are just as bad or worse. Which one of the above could have had as good a match with Rick Rude as Warrior did?

I've talked with many mainstream Titan stars who were extremely unhappy with Mr. Lister's push. As far as wrestling goes, the WWF has the best two working tag teams in America in the Rockers and Brain Busters and Bobby Heenan is the best all-around manager in the business right now. Paul E.

Dangerously and Jim Cornette are super talented, but neither is in an effective role right now.

The NWA is my favorite promotion, but the Oakland 2 were wrong in what they did. Titan did overreact in throwing them out.

I think the NWA needs Steamboat back, because in my opinion, he's not a total performer of the quality of Ric Flair, but he's the best actual pro wrestler in the world.

I don't think the Big Van Vader gimmick can get over in the United States. I also think your statement that Jushin Liger was a better worker that Satoru Sayama may be the result of someone spiking your grapefruit juice.

Name withheld by request

CLASH OF CHAMPIONS
The Fall Brawl was great. The action was so stiff it hurt to watch. People like to say that pro wrestling is fake, but there is nothing fake about the bumps they were doing. The injuries can become a big problem with the NWA as time goes on.

Theodore Kumlander
Rochester, New York

For the first time in five or six years, I forgot that pro wrestling was worked when watching the Clash. I was completely irritated and agitated at the actions of Terry Funk. It was quite a thrill and really a job well done on the NWA's part.

Steve Ellenberg
New York, New York

Overall I'd give the Clash a thumbs up. All the matches were entertaining and the main event was great. Luger vs. Rich was better than I expected. Although the angle with Funk bothered me, Slater did a good job and considering the show was for free, what more could anyone ask for? My main complaint is it was too obvious Funk was going to do a run-in. On the other hand, the Steiners-Freebirds finish was interesting with the camera angle bit.

Bruce Colon
Chicago, Illinois

AWARDS FAVORITES
We've got a few more categories to Look at for the awards that will be voted on in the yearbook. The awards balloting, which technically is for the time period from December 1,1988 through November 30, 1989, will take place during the month of December and the results will be in the yearbook published in January. A complete listing of the categories will be in the Observer in November and December.

TAG TEAM OF THE YEAR: Unlike in previous years, this is a category that is really hard to pick a winner in. Over the past few years, there usually is one or two teams that are so far above the rest of the pack that their positions at the top are pretty clear-cut. Not so this year. The Midnight Express, which has dominated this poll for three straight years, isn't a contender this year as they have been relegated to mid-card and uninteresting feuds since their NWA return. There are quite a few good teams this year, but it's hard to pick one team that: has been consistently excellent all year long. The Foot Loose comes the closest to being consistently excellent, but no Japanese team hag ever won this award and there have been some awesome teams in the past (Riki Choshu & Yoshiaki Yatgu, Dynamite Kid & Davey Boy Smith when they worked in Japan are were really hot, Akira Maeda & Nobuhiko Takada, Stan Hansen & Bruiser Brody) that have been hotter than the Foot Loose. The best teams in the U. S. seem to be The Rockers and the Brain Busters. When matched with each other, either team could have and should have been a leading contender, but: since their early year feud, they haven't had the excellent quality matches. On the NWA side, the Steiners haven't teamed together for long enough, Freebirds just aren't good enough, Road Warriors are like Rockers and Brain Busters in that they are often good, but not always. Samoan Swat Team is awesome against jobbers but didn't work well with the Midnight Express. Over in Japan, the only duo pushed hard besides The Foot Loose as a team in All Japan has been Jumbo Tsuruta & Yoshiaki Yatsu, who can be good with good opponents, but Yatsu holds the team back right now and Tsuruta is hot-and-cold. Doug Furnas & Dan Kroffat have had a few excellent matches, but really it is Kroffat who is a super worker and Furnas who can execute a few good high spots, but oftentimes looks Lost in the ring. Super Strong Machine George Takano in New Japan are a good team, but certainly not a great team. Rockers, Brain Busters and Warriors look as good as any in the States with Foot Loose probably being the best, but having the least chance to win.

BEST TELEVISION SHOW: Again, not a standout, although in my book All Japan Pro Wrestling is the winner here. Good matches and sometimes great matches on a weekly basis . Of all the weekly shows, it also has the largest audience (due in part to being on a network). WWF Superstars of Wrestling is a great show. Sometimes, actually often, it gets somewhat heavy-handed, but it accomplishes what it is supposed to, although one can certainly argue the quality of wrestling is rarely even decent. The TBS packages have varied throughout the year. At times they've been excellent and at times they've been poor. The lack of consistency (both in product quality and also consistency in when the shows themselves will actually air) has hurt the audience for the shows. New Japan is good, excellent when the junior heavyweights are in the ring and usually at least decent with the heavyweights, although about those Russians - well at least they do wrestling moves but those transitions are non-existent. The smaller promotions have been really bad this year. CWA and Stampede have declined greatly from last year. The Eric Embry show doesn't have any top-flight wrestlers and the angles that are designed to make you interested seem to make people embarrassed to be watching instead. Portland Wrestling has good angles and is the best of the small promotion TV shows in the U.S., but the quality of the wrestlers can't compete with the major leagues.

WORST TAG TEAM: Usually there is one tag team that gets pushed somewhere that is so bad this award becomes a formality. That's why I'm hoping the AWA gives the tag team titles this weekend to Sgt. Slaughter & Baron Von Raschke because if they don't, I'll have to think long and hard about this one. Of the WWF teams the Powers of Pain stand out (actually stand still) as being the least talented. Actually, I can't come up with many pushed tag teams in the smaller groups that are particularly bad. The duo of Bob & Kerry Brown held the tag team titles in Stampede for a long time and they were awful. The only other team I can come up with, and they may actually be the worst and probably are, just they almost never appear on television, the Baba 's comedy tag team of Baba himself and Rusher Kimura.

CARD OF THE YEAR: A new category and one that people have been begging me to include. With the big show concept becoming more and more prevalent both in the United States and in Japan, and with increasing technology, this trend should get even stronger. There have been some outstanding big shows this year, both in terms of success and in terms of quality shows. The UWF has drawn some Of the biggest live gates in pro wrestling history this year and has already done two closed-circuit shows. Wrestlemania speaks for itself in terms of revenue, but it speaks very softly in terms of quality. SummerSlam was a good show and made a ton of money. The NWA has had many excellent shows this year. The card in Nashville drew an incredible 100 percent thumbs up in the Observer POLL which is something I would have never thought was possible, while the big shows in Norfolk (Starrcade), Chicago (Chi town Rumble), New Orleans (Clash with Flair-Steamboat 55 minute match), and Baltimore all drew greater than 90 percent favorable responses. Baba's 6/5 card at Budokan Hall may have been the best, but I've only seen five of the ten matches and won't judge a card that I haven't seen ail of against full shows live the NWA's PPV shows. New Japan's Egg Dome card was a great success drawing 53,800 fans and setting the gate record of $2.8 million, but that says nothing for quality. If I had to pick one show as the best one of the year, I'd go with the Bash from Baltimore. Nashville would be second and third would be tight between either Starrcade (for overall show) and Chicago (for better production and a memorable main event).

OCTOBER 16, 1989

The expected change of the WWF tag team titles took place this past Monday night (10/2) at the TV tapings in Wheeling, WV as Demolition regained the titles from Tully Blanchard & Arn Anderson. The change was expected, of course, since Blanchard & Anderson gave notice to the WWF at the previous set of tapings and will be headed to the NWA after the Survivors' Series on Thanksgiving night. The match itself was taped for the " Superstars" show and will air in a few weeks, and lasted just 5:24 before Ax pinned Blanchard using the Demolition's normal backbreaker/ elbow drop combination finisher. There was controversy in that technically Anderson was the legal man in the ring, but my guess is that was just a way to get Blanchard & Anderson to do the finish and that won't be acknowledged when they put the commentary track on the match in upcoming weeks.

Since much of the talk within wrestling of the past few weeks has been who, if anyone, will follow Blanchard & Anderson is switching from the WWF to the NWA and if so, what, if any, retaliation will the VMF take, that there is little new to report on the subject. While several names have been thrown around, nobody gave notice at the tapings this week. While wrestlers in both the WWF and the NWA have mentioned to me that Bret Hart would be following Blanchard & Anderson as switching, the reports I've got are that saying that any deal has been reached would be premature. Supposedly the NWA and Hart are stillnowhere near agreeing on a money figure, and there are still political reasons why I'd be surprised to see Hart make the move. As far as other names that have been rumored to be making the move, and may have even talked about making the move, apparently there hasn't been serious negotiations on the NWA side with any of them.

A few new things have been added to the main event at the NWA's pay-per-view show on 10/28 in Philadelphia. The Thunderdome cage match with Ric Flair & Sting vs. Terry Funk & Great Muta will have an "electrified" cage and each team will have a "terminator" in their corner. The only way for the match to end would be if a team's terminator were to throw in the flag for that team. The mild surprise is that Ole Anderson will be the terminator for the face team, with Gary Hart as the terminator for the heel team. With Anderson as a face, and Anderson was out on interviews at the 10/4 TV tapings in Atlanta (which start airing this weekend on TBS) with Flair & Sting, it makes me think that Arn Anderson & Blanchard will arrive in the NWA as faces

and set up a feud with Flair & Arn & Tully vs. Funk. & Muta & Sting. One would expect that eventually some or all of the remaining faces will turn on Flair in 1990.

As many of you already know, the verdict came in about a week ago in the lawsuit filed by Steven DiBIasio (Big Daddy) against several parties, most prominent being Virgil Runnels Jr. (Dusty Rhodes) over an injury suffered in a match with DiBIasio vs. The Professional(Leslie Thornton) on June 13 1983 in West Palm Beach. Technically, DiBlasio both won and lost the case although the reality is one would have to consider that he lost the case. The verdict of the jury was that the city of West Palm Beach and the National Wrestling Alliance were not negligent in DiBlasio's injury. DiBIasio's attorney, Mike Nipon, felt that the case against the city was the strongest part of the case since the injury occured when DiBlasio, who was then 440 pounds, took a bump over the top rope and hooked the rope on the way over to lessen the shock of the fall, but the rope broke and DiBIasio landed hard and shattered his ankle. While DiBIasio did make an attempt at a comeback in wrestling, his mobility, limited to begin with, was destroyed and the comeback was short-lived. The jury did find

Rhodes negligent in "designing a dangerous script, however no monetary damages were awarded in the case against Rhodes. The fact that Rhodes was found negligent in booking a dangerous script is precedent setting. The key in the case was that the jury ruled that DiBlasio "assumed the risk of injury" by agreeing to take the bump and by competing as a pro wrestler, just as an athlete in any competitive sport assumes the risk of injury. In Florida, as in most states, the assumption of risk is a complete defense. DiBlasio was, however, awarded a $317,000 verdict against Thornton and against Championship Wrestling from Florida, but in reality that means nothing since nobody knows the whereabouts of Thornton, who was Last heard from somewhere in Alberta, Canada trying to run a short-lived independent promotion. Championship Wrestling from Florida went out of business and no longer exists, although DiBlasio may make a motion to try and get damages from the new promotion in Florida since they run out of the same office in Tampa and have many of the same stockholders, Mike Graham in particular. DiBlasio has filed a motion for a new trial and the motion will be heard within the next two weeks. If granted a new trial, the trial will take place within six months. If the motion is denied, DiBIasio will have thirty days to decide whether to take his case to a Florida appellate court. DiBlasio is attempting an appeal on the grounds that the judges' instructions to the injury about "assumption of risk" is not applicable to professional wrestling. In the past, the assumption of risk defense has been limited to contact competition sports and DiBIasio's attorneys are contending that pro wrestling is a show, not a sport, and that distinction applying to professional wrestling is inappropriate. In the actual jury verdict, the jury ruled that DiBIasio was 85 percent responsible for his injury and that Rhodes was 15 percent responsible, however the judge overturned that verdict saying that if DiBIasio assumed the risk in performing the stunt, then assuming the risk absolves Rhodes of all monetary negligence. The reason this case took so many years to come to trial is that in 1986, DiBIasio was awarded a verdict against Rhodes and company for all the defendants disregarding court orders and showing disrespect for the courts. However an appellate court overruled the original verdict and sent it to a trial court.

We are sorry to report the death of television commentator Rick Stuart this past Thursday night. I don't have complete details on this, other than Stuart was in his late 20s and had been announcing for several of the smaller promotions beginning in 1980 with Southeastern (now Continental) Championship Wrestling. Stuart also had stints announcing for Southwest Championship Wrestling out of San Antonio, Central States Wrestling out of Kansas City, Southern Championship Wrestling from Georgia and most recently, Atlantic Coast Wrestling run by Nelson Royal. Most of the time Stuart worked as an announcer in areas where Buck Robley had come in to book. Apparently Stuart had suddenly taken ill early in the week. The only national attention Stuart ever received as an announcer was as one of the voices doing commentary at Starrcade 86.

Japan's Universal Wrestling Federation has announced several combat sports athletes from other sports as participants on its next spectacular on 11/29 at the Tokyo Dome. The event will almost certainly draw one of the two or three largest gates in the history of pro wrestling, as it is being held in the same site where New Japan set the gate record of $2,781,000 on April 24th, and UWF has sold out every show but two that it has promoted since re-opening in May of 1988 and Tokyo is its hottest city. The recent show in Yokohama, a city about 60 miles south of Tokyo, drew $1.4 million without any "outside" participants. None of the matches were announced yet, but participating in the show will be Willie Willenheim of the Netherlands, who is a former gold medalist in the European judo championships; Morris Smith, the current World Karate Association World heavyweight champion (who is the best bet to face Akira Maeda in the main event); Duane Koslowski (not sure of spelling) who was an NCAA and AAU amateur wrestling champion from Minnesota and I believe competed in the Olympic games; Glen Belegu of the Netherlands, who is the country's heavyweight boxing champion (Belegu had a mixed match with Yoshiaki Fujiwara in 1988 that went to a four round draw on a martial arts card) and Chris Dolman, the former World champion in sambo wrestling that Maeda worked with and defeated on May 6th in Osaka's Baseball Stadium, which drew a $1, 714,000 gate, which is second only to the New Japan Tokyo Dome card and slightly ahead

of Wrestlemania V in the history of pro wrestling.

Originally, it was assumed that Maeda's opponent at the Tokyo Dome would be Don Nakaya Neilsen, a kick boxer from the United States who Maeda faced on October 9, 1986 in the most "memorable" and exciting" mixed match ever with Maeda winning via submission in the fifth round. Although it was Neilsen's debut in a pro wrestling atmosphere, he put on an exceptional performance, and followed it up in the New Japan rings in 1988 with victories over Keiichi Yamada (now Jushin Liger) and Fujiwara in exciting matches as well and it was expected he was being "set up" to put over one of New Japan s big stars and do a big gate. There were also constant rumors of a Maeda vs. Neilsen rematch on the UWF mat, but that the rematch couldn't take place until late in 1989 because of the Neilsen vs. Rob Karman "Dream match" that was going to take place in the karate world. To "set up" the dream match, Neilsen had a match on May 14 in Tokyo against WKA Super heavyweight champion Kevin Roseyear, and it was believed that Neil sen would win to help hype the dream match, however Roseyear overpowered Neilsen throughout and scored an easy knockout. Because of his injuries, including a broken ankle, suffered in that match, the bout with Karman scheduled for June, was postponed until September 5, and that match was also quite one-sided with Karman easily knocking out Neilsen who showed very little, thus there is no interest in Neil sen among wrestling fans but Karman is now in the spotlight. Karman will have a mixed match on October 21 in Tokyo against Caswell Martin, who has wrestled in the past in both New Japan and the old UWF, and who I believe has wrestled extensively throughout Europe. An interesting thing in viewing the Neilsen vs. Karman "shoot, is that the kicks and stiffness in a "real" fight didn't appear to be as stiff as the kicks thrown during the UWF matches this year.

There has been a lot that has gone down over the past few weeks in regards to how graphically violent should professional wrestling be allowed to be. The two incidents in the NWA that have fueled the debate were Terry Funk placing the plastic bag over the head of Ric Flair during the Clash of the Champions on 9/12, then a few weeks later the "mugging" skit where three "unknown" assailants beat up Scott Steiner as the TV cameras rolled. While these two events have stirred up a lot of controversy, particularly since the NWA is owned by TBS and TBS wants to promote to the mainstream, neither of these incidents are things that have never occured before in wrestling, and there was never an outcry, or at least as much of one, when they had in the past. Plastic bags have been used at least a few times that I'm aware of, including last summer at several house shows in the NWA during the Midnight Express vs. Fantastics bunkhouse matches. Skits of "on the street" beatings have been a part of wrestling in the south in many promotions, particularly when they get desperate, but I can recall two incidents right off the top of my head similarly involving Ole & Arn Anderson a few years back, with Magnum T. A. and Dusty Rhodes respectively. And what about the incident a few years back when Rhodes tied Jim Cornette up by the neck to the back of a truck and had Baby Doll drive out of the arena with him? This is not to defend any of these incidents, just to say things like this have occured within this promotion for years. This is not a new trend. If we start talking about Southwest Championship Wrestling and the old CWF promotion when Kevin Sullivan was booker, we can find even more extremes, particularly the Hangman's Noose matches with Sullivan vs. Blackjack Mulligan where the only way to win was to hang your opponent, and theoretically "kill" him, and angles to set up the match were shown in which both men attempted, on television, to hang the other but were always saved by other wrestlers. At one point, Sullivan stabbed Mulligan in the heart with a spike during that same feud. Keep in mind that Southwest Championship Wrestling went out of business partially because of its ridiculous level of blood and violence, and while this is a debatable subject because many causes can be given, there are those who believe the beginning of the end of the famous CWF promotion came because so many "mainstream sports fans" were run off by the hardcore and ridiculous nature of the hangings, heart attacks, devil worship and stabbings during that era of Florida Wrestling.

How much is too much? When is this fine line broken? Pro wrestling has always relied on violence as one of its drawing points. In the upcoming weeks, I expect the NWA to issue some strict guidelines and I've already heard that TBS is unhappy with the double entendres that the announcers, particularly Jim Ross and Jim Cornette have done in regarding to comments on Missy Hyatt and later Robin Green, or whatever we are supposed to be calling her, and doesn't want any suggestions of "death" or "killing" no matter how heated the feud gets.

From an economic perspective, being that pro wrestling is a business, the answer to how much is too much in theory at least, should be determined when the number of fans "turned off" by the brutality and bloodshed and graphicness exceeds the number of fans turned on. Of course, it is almost impossible to determine when that is the case, short of a major gain or plunge in TV ratings, neither of which has happened in the last few weeks. Listen, I've heard all the theories about red turning to green and all that for years now, and even though you could never convince someone who isn't a hardcore wrestling fan that the practice of blading isn't anything short of sick and barbaric, I do believe that blood in its proper context can add to the drama of a wrestling match or angle. Too much blood is a turn-off, as every promotion that has gone the blood city route has crumbled in recent years eventually. Too much blood

also hurts when attempting to market wrestling outside of a hardcore audience. I can't tell you how many times. I've personally experienced this, as far as having friends start to get into wrestling and then they see a bloodbath and never want to watch it again, and in most cases, I myself enjoyed that bloodbath. We've already seen that the most popular promotions in the world and the hottest ones, WWF and UWF, almost never use blood, but during the rare times they use it, the usage is effective because it is done so sparingly.

There will always be a hardcore audience that wants blood. But it is the lure of blood that turns the audience on, not the blood itself. It is similar to sex in the movies. There is no question at all that sex sells in the movies, and the hardcore "X" movies do get an audience because they are still around. But they do no mainstream business. The sex that sells to the greatest number of people is softcore, subtle and subliminal rather than hardcore right in front of you. Maybe that's one reason why the most over female on the U.S wrestling scene is Elizabeth, even though there are women just as good-looking, and in fact even better looking on the scene today, but why they don 't gain the foothold of popularity (aside from better marketing which can't be overlooked) is because they are portrayed in a sleazier atmosphere and environment.

The reason I'm bringing this subject up now is because a philosophical explosion when it comes to the direction the NWA is taking is being sensed by a lot of people close to that scene. The plastic bag incident has drawn a ton of ire, not only from those who complained to TBS, but from those at TBS itself, to the point that some promos which featured the plastic bag were pulled from the air a few weeks back. In addition, a promo package for the 10/28 PPV show for advertising on local cable stations, which also included the Terry Funk attack, was redone not to include the attack. Apparently several PPV companies were quite unhappy about the "parental discretion advised" being said for the next PPV show to the point that at least one threatened to drop the show. I had assumed the 10/28 show would be a bloodbath, at least in the main event, and with an electric cage, coward throws in the flag stips, it basically is promising blood and no matter how exciting the match itself is, there will be those who feel ripped off if the match doesn't contain blood. However, recent events makes me wonder, what with the pressure that is now on the booking committee because of the recent furor over the direction getting too violent. Even Jim Herd of the NWA was quoted in last week's "Matwatch" that: "It (Scott Steiner angle) sure was too far and so was the bag. And you can quote me that we 're going to bring these things under control at TBS. This is going to be a family show. That's amazing in itself, having the guy running the company publicly coming down on a direction his company has gone in. I look at this as a sports analogy of a general manager publicly saying that his

Coach has implemented the wrong game plan or is starting the wrong quarterback. While the GM may privately feel that way, when something like that goes public, you sense the Coach's days aren't long. And in wrestling history, it is a very rare occasion when a booker is replaced that he stays on with the same promotion as an active wrestler. Those are points I don't even want to bring up, but emphasizes the potential seriousness of what I hope won't happen if these problems aren't ironed out.

As I've written here before, I had no adverse reaction when watching the plastic bag thing but enough phone calls came to where I knew the angle hit a nerve with a lot of people. I was furious at the Steiner angle, more because I thought it was such bad television than anything else. At the same time, there are people who are trying to put together a PPV show when there are no match-ups built up to the point where a big show is ready to happen and when there just have been too many PPV shows. To make matters worse, after this show, there has to be enough heat coming out for another show less than six weeks later, which being Starrcade, should at least in theory, be the biggest show of the year. On one hand, one would say they need a big angle. On the other hand, they've already done so many "big" angles that turned out to not be big and have been so hardcore that they've gone as far as they will be allowed to go in that direction.

CWA

Dirty White Boy (Tony Anthony) won the tournament 10/2 in Memphis for the vacated CWA championship. First round in the tournament saw Dustin Rhodes beat Cowboy Kevin Dillinger (Alan Martin), Chris Champion pinned Freddy (Tommy Gilbert), Mike Davis beat Plowboy Stan Frazier due to outside interference from Downtown Bruno, Robert Gibson beat Mark Starr, Ricky Morton beat Iceman King Parsons via DQ when Brickhouse Brown interfered, Bill Dundee beat Brown, Dirty White Boy went to a time limit draw against Jeff Jarrett (10 minutes) and White Boy won the coin flip to advance and Dutch Mantell beat Buddy Landel via the over-the-top rope DQ call.. The second round saw Rhodes beat Champion, Davis pin Gibson after hitting him with a chain, Morton and Dundee went to a time limit draw and Morton advanced via coin flip and White Boy beat Mantell via DQ when Mantell used a chair. Semifinals saw Rhodes beat Davis and White Boy pin Morton and White Boy beat Rhodes in the finals when the Dirty White Girl (Kim Wolser) gave DWB a foreign object. The winner of the tournament was then going to have a unification match with USWA champion Jerry Lawler and it ended when Landel interfered and hit Lawler with a foreign object and White Boy pinned Lawler but the decision was reversed and Landel and White Boy beat up on Lawler after the match and left him laying.

At the TV tapings on 10/7, the Wildside faced the Dream Warrior (a newcomer billed as the younger brother of former wrestler Norvell Austin) & Freddy and when they tried to unmask Freddy, Lawler and Rhodes interfered for the DQ. The Blackbirds (Parsons & Brown) came out and introduced their new manager, Reggie B. Fine, to replace Harold Harris who is gone (some sort of legal problems) and in a six-man match, Lawler & Rhodes & Freddy beat Dillinger & Davis & Spike Huber when Huber tried to hit Lawler, but instead hit Dillinger and Lawler pinned Dillinger and after the match Dillinger and Davis beat up on Huber, who is now a babyface.

New to the area is the Soul Taker managed by Larry Sharpe. Sharpe did a good interview getting the guy over, and he's about 6-7 and was quite green, but has only been training a wrestler for around four months. He looked aggressive on TV and beat two guys in 52 seconds.

Don't expect Sharpe to be around for long since he's got business interests and promotes shows regularly in the New Jersey area. 10/9 in Memphis has Huber vs. Davis, Freddy vs. Dillinger, Soul Taker vs. Tommy Montana, Wildside vs. Dundee & Mantel 1, Rock & Roll Express vs. Blackbirds for the CWA tag team titles, Landel & White Boy vs. Lawler & Rhodes and the main event is a non-title match with Lawler vs. Soul Taker and I presume Lawler will put the guy over big to create a new "monster" Heel.

STAMPEDE

It looks like nobody wants the tag team titles here. The Black Harts hold the titles, however the members of this masked tag team are changing on a weekly basis. It was first Tom Nash from Florida with David Heath from Florida. Heath left, and they put Red Tyler from Minnesota in the spot, but Tyler lasted all of two days before they put a local trainee Jason Anderson in the spot, but they felt he was too small for the gimmick, so right now they are once again looking for someone.

The Derringer brothers from Minnesota have come in and they mainly do comedy.

Owen Hart hasn't returned, so Larry Cameron is feuding with Davey Boy Smith over the North American title.

Ed Whalen's wife is running for mayor of Calgary.

Expect at least a few guys from here to head to Puerto Rico since word up here is that Leo Burke (who has often worked here) and Cuban Assassin (Angel Acevedo) are supposedly going to help book Puerto Rico. Jerry Morrow is headed to Puerto Rico as well.

Curtis Thompson is in as heel Arch Angel managed by Hugh Hart (Ben Ryan), a similar gimmick to what he had in Puerto Rico.

Tom Burton from Minnesota was coming in to play heel ref, but not sure the status of that right now.

Steve DiSalvo (Steve Strong in Puerto Rico) has moved

back here. Last word I had, DiSalvo held the WWC Universal title and since the big anniversary card in which he was to defend the title (and most likely lose it) against Carlos Colon didn't take place until this past Saturday, I guess he walked out on the place without doing the job. DiSalvo is talking that he's going to real estate school during the week and only wants to wrestle on weekends, but hasn't started with the promotion yet.

Dynamite Kid and Johnny Smith are in town, but haven 't started back up yet either, but should be wrestling shortly.

Heritage Championship Wrestling: This is a new promotion that started up on 10/5 with a television taping in Vicksburg, MS . Thomas Parker is the promoter, Jack Curtis Jr. is the general manager (long-time employee of Bill Watts) and Buck Robley is the booker). The TV taping featured The Fantastics (Bobby & Jackie Fulton), Bob Orton, Mr. Olympia (Jerry Stubbs), Abdullah the Butcher and The Rock & Roll Express. Television shows were taped in a 30 and 60 minute format and the plan is to televise "hot" 30 minute shows and try and syndicate them, particularly in Mississippi, Louisiana and Arkansas and eventually to run a territory similar in geographical size to the one Watts used to run. Spike Huber and Tommy Lane also worked over the weekend.

While the original plan was for this to become a full-time promotion in January, they have 15 dates booked in November and 22 dates booked in December and will be running bi-weekly TV tapings out of Vicksburg, MS for the time being.

Next taping is 10/25 and will include Terry Gordy, Paul Orndorff, Dustin Rhodes and Sam Houston.

They already have a promotional motto on their souvenir T-shirts, "More wrestling. Less talk."

From all accounts, the first tapings went quite smoothly.

WWC

They finally got the "Anniversary" show off on 10/7 at Juan Lobriel Stadium in Bayamon (the show was originally scheduled for Sept. 16 but had to be postponed due to the hurricane). Some of the matches had to be changed because of the changing of the date. I'd heard the original show sold about 25,000 tickets, but haven't heard what the crowd was at the Stadium for the replay, although this was the WWC's first PPV show as well with the card available throughout Puerto Rico. The main event saw Carlitos Colon win the Universal title from Steve Strong (Steve DiSalvo), so Strong did return to Puerto Rico to do the final job and drop the strap. The match was in a barbed wire cage with Chicky Starr and Redbeard in the corners of Strong and Colon respectively. Starr sprayed something in Colon s eyes and Strong pinned him, however Redbeard (apparently Colon s original trainer) pulled the spray can away from Starr and showed it to the ref and they restarted the match and

Colon scored the pin with a cross bodyblock after ducking a clothesline. Other results saw Invader #1 regain the Puerto Rican title beating Ivan Koloff in a Russian Chain match, TNT beat Starr in 4:57 with a karate thrust kick in a match where TNT put up his name and the right to paint his face while Starr put up his hair, so Starr had his head shaved (the match was originally to be TNT vs. Original TNT for the right to the name, but original TNT has already left), Mark & Chris Youngblood became WWC World tag team champions once again beating Rip Rogers & Abbuda Dein (Rocky Iaukea), Kevin Von Erich pinned Ron Bass (sub for Al Perez who went to the WWF who was subbing for Abdullah the Butcher who had to cancel his appearence because of a commitment in Mississippi), Jimmy Valiant pinned Kareem Muharunad (Ray Candy), Manny Fernandez pinned Invader #3 (Johnny Rivera), Super Medico (Jose Estrada) retained his WWC jr. heavyweight title beating El Gran Mendoza and The Mercenaries (who worked in Stampede as the Cuban Commandos - Cuban Assassin & Jerry Morrow) captured the Caribbean tag team titles from Miguelito Perez & Hurricane Castillo Jr. The original card had Medico defending against Jeff Jarrett and Perez & Castillo against Afa & Sika the Samoans but both changes were made on television because of the date change.

USWA

Frank Dusek is out. I don't have the details on what happened but he was fired by Jerry Jarrett and no acknowledgement has been made about him on television.

The 10/6 card at the Dallas Sportatorium drew another small crowd, estimated at 250, as Billy Joe Travis pinned Tony Falk, The Headhunter beat Steve Williams (not Dr. Death but a rookie trained by Chris Adams whose real name apparently is Steve Williams), Gary Young beat Jimmy Jack Funk when Travis inteffered, Sheik Scott Braddock & Ron Starr beat Jeff Jarrett & Matt Borne in a loser of the fall leaves town match when Borne was pinned, which was a big surprise, Chris Adams pinned P. Y. Chu Hi (Phil Hickerson) when Tojo Yamamoto gave Chu Hi salt, but Adams kicked it in his face and got the pin but after the match The Punisher threw Toni Adams into the penalty box cage (which was there for Tojo's interference) and Tojo, Chu Hi and Punisher all beat up on Chris Adams until Kerry Von Erich made the save, and the main event saw Kerry & Adams beat Punisher & Taras Bulba.

Eric Embry did sit out a week and returned at the tapings on 10/7 with make-up over his eye because of the ammonia burn from the week before.

New to the area were three Headhunters, two of which were Chief Tio & Prince Tapu (Tio & Tapu Taylor, a father-and-son Samoan tag team) and no idea who the third guy was.

Terry Gordy returns on 10/21 for a card billed as

"Wrestlewreck", because before the matches, the wrestlers will participate in a Demolition Derby while Bill Dundee also returns for that card.

The 10/13 card in Dallas is headlined by the all-time classic main event of Jerry Lawler defending the USWA title against Uncle Elmer (Plowboy Stan Frazier), Plus Embry vs. Travis, Kerry vs. Punisher, Jarrett vs. Starr, Adams & Funk vs. Chu Hi & Young and Braddock vs. Williams.

Killer Tim Brooks' card at the Longhorn Ballroom on 10/3 in Dallas drew 550 and the first TV taping for the group is 10/10 (two weeks worth of tapings) which starts up on 10/14 at midnight on Ch. 39 in Dallas with John Tatum, Johnny Mantell, Botswana Beast, Steven Casey, Scott Casey, Brooks, Steve Cox (who is now working for Eagle Brand Potato Chips) and Brian Adias.

ALI JAPAN

The latest tour began on 9/30 before 2,750 fans in Okinawa as Genichiro Tenryu & Stan Hansen downed Jumbo Tsuruta & Kabuki in 16:47 when Hansen lariated Kabuki, Shunji Takano & Yoshiaki Yatsu beat The Foot Loose in 15:37, Doug Furnas & Dan Kroffat & Ken Shamrock (a rookie trained by Nelson Royal who was a top-notch amateur wrestler) beat Joe Malenko & Kenta Kobashi & Shinichi Nakano when Furnas made Nakano submit to the over the shoulder backbreaker in 18:26, Dick Slater & Joel Deaton beat Akira Taue & Akio Sato, Mighty Inoue pinned Isamu Terahishi, Giant Baba & Rusher Kimura beat Haruka Eigen & Motoshi Okuma, Masa Fuchi pinned Goro Tsurumi, Mitsuo Momota pinned Yoshinari Ogawa and prelims.

They are holding a round-robin tournament to determine the No. 1 contender to the PWF jr. title (held by Malenko) with the winner getting a title match on the last night: of the tour.

UWF

UWF promoted two shows on Successive nights in Tokyos Korakuen Hall, both drawing sellout crowds of 2,300 fans and $80,000 houses with mainly what would be considered squash matches. The first night saw Yoji. Anjyo beat Kiyoji Tamura in 8:34, Yoshiaki Fujiwara knocked out Norman smiley in 6:57 and Nobuhiko Takada made Tetsuo Nakano submit with an armlock in 10:21, so the entire card contained only 25 minutes of wrestling. The show was 9/30. Don't have results of 10/1, but obviously promoting shows like this shows they are getting rather cocky.

OTHER NOTES

Got a first this week - a wrestler calling to complain because a star grade for a match was too high. Complained because what he said was no more than a one-star match (all walking and talking) got two stars here.

MTV filmed a segment at Larry Sharpe's "Monster Factory" last week which aired over the past weekend. .

Johnny Rich is now road manager for the CWF.

As expected here, on 10/9 in Memphis, Sharpe's protege The Soul Taker beat Jerry Lawler clean in the middle with no controversy in a non-title match in Memphis.

Ricky Steamboat is back in the ring working an independent show on 10/10 in Peru, IN and another show on 10/21 in Baltimore for Cystic Fibrosis.

The Steve DiBlasio case was covered on Monday night on "Inside Report". Florida Championship Wrestling has changed its name to Professional Wrestling from Florida (PWF) and on television this past weekend prominently mentioned that Eddie Gilbert and Missy Hyatt were coming in. Word I get is that isn't the case, since both are under contract with the NWA through February (more on that in NWA section). They are promoting a big show on 10/27 in Tampa with Lawler vs. Bam Bam Bigelow for the USWA title, Steve Keirn vs. Kendall Windham for the Florida title and Nasty Boys vs. The Terminator (Marc Laurinidas) & Jumbo Baretta for the Florida tag team titles plus Lou Perez, The Fantastics (Fulton brothers) and Wendi Richter.

Alexis Smirnoff is promoting a card on 10/21 in Manteca, CA with Smirnoff & Rex Farmer vs. Earthquake Ferris & Jim Gorman on top with Ray Stevens as guest referee. Apparently they will do something to set up a Smirnoff vs. Stevens match down the road.

The ICW has added a lot of television on cable stations such as Pacific Sports Network in Northern California.

Diamond Dallas Page (as a babyface now) and the legendary Coach John Heath are doing play-by-play for the Florida group.

Masaharu Funaki apparently broke his arm recently, perhaps on the 10/1 UWF card in Tokyo but not sure if it was in a match or in practice. The CWF's next card in Knoxville will be the last one because of a dispute between Ron Fuller and David Woods. Fuller claims that Woods has never paid him in full for the USA territory that Woods bought more than a year ago. Fuller and Local promoter Bob Polk have talked with the NWA and are planning to bring them in starting in November.

Chris Love, who now goes by the name "Sweetness" promoted a show on 10/5 in Benson, NC drawing 280 fans and $1,152. Only name I know of on the show was Ali Bey, the Turk, who if it is the same guy, used to work the small circuits in the early 80s. Love's first area show was 9/23 in North Wilkesboro, NC drawing 212 paid.

USWF ran a free show on 9/16 in Lima, OH drawing 1,000 - 1,500 headlined by Nightmares beating Flying Tigers.

Rob Russen sent out a press release that he's starting a new promotion called International Wrestling Association and planning on running shows coast-to-coast. Listed as a talent roster were Jerry Lawler, Bam Bam Bigelow, Ricky Steamboat, Nikolai Volkoff, Mike Sharpe, Manny Fernandez,

Jules Strongbow, Sgt. Slaughter, Hillbilly Cousin Luke, Pat Tanaka, Ricky Rice, Abdullah the Butcher, Derrick Dukes, Nikita Koloff, Ivan Koloff, Stan Hansen, Kimala, Ken Patera, Jim Brunzell, Teijo Khan, Soldat Ustinov, Baron Von Raschke, Cactus Jack Foley, Austin Idol, Larry Cameron, Sam Houston, Col. DeBeers, David Sammartino, Missing Link, Brad Rheingans, The Fantastics, Rock & Roll Express, Nasty Boys, Terminators, Samoans, Guerreros, Mod Squad and basically everyone who is working independently right now.

WWF

WWF is currently on a tour of Europe with Hulk Hogan vs. Randy Savage headlining cards in both Paris and London. They also have seven more dates booked, I believe with Jim Duggan as the headliner.

Besides the tag team title change, also at the 10/2 TV tapings in Wheeling, WV before a sellout 7,800 fans saw the return of The Bolsheviks (Nikolai Volkoff & Boreus Zhukov) as a tag team and the creation of Bobby Heenan's new tag team of Andre the Giant & Haku, who will challenge Demolition for the belts at the house shows down the road. Dino Bravo is getting a renewed push and they did an angle with him to set up a feud with the Ultimate Warrior for the TV title later this fall (I'm not making this up). Anyway, Dino the Dinosaur comes in and does push-ups with Jimmy Hart on his back and Gene Okerlund isn't impressed, since Hart doesn't weigh much. They pull a guy out of the stands who weighs 440 pounds (Big John Tenta from Japan) and Bravo does a few push-ups with Tenta on his back. Then Warrior comes in and Tenta says he's afraid to sit on Warrior's back, but Warrior okays him and starts to do the push-ups but Tenta splashes on him and he and Bravo and Hart all beat up on Warrior. They never gave the "fan out of the audience" a name except "John". By the way, Tenta had worked the previous taping as Earthquake Evans managed by Slick in a dark match, so I guess they've already given up on that character. The jobbers are also doing stretcher jobs for Bravo's new deadly finishing maneuver, The bearhug. It's funny that I'm always told by WWFers that the NWA pushes simply on who is friends with the booker and they push on who can draw money. Like Dino has all this charisma and great ability to draw money in comparison to the guys not given a push? Al Perez debuted as a babyface but got no reaction. Greg Valentine had Red Rooster (Terry Taylor) beat with a figure four when Ron Garvin ran in for the DQ, which shows where Rooster is headed. Mr. Perfect (Curt Hennig) pinned Bret Hart in 17 minutes in a match taped for Prime Time Wrestling which I'm told was a 4 ½ star match, Rick Rude beat Roddy Piper via DQ with the new finish they've been running everywhere where the ref gets bumped, Piper knocks Rude out of the ring, the ref counts to 10 like he's counting Rude out, then DQ's Piper

for no apparent reason, Warrior beat Andre in 25 seconds and Hulk Hogan beat Randy Savage in a double juice cage match.

10/3 at the Challenge tapings in Toledo saw the only "competitive" match for TV had Tito Santana beat Honky Tonk Man via DQ when Big Bossman interfered and Dusty Rhodes made the save. Dark matches saw Blanchard & Anderson keep the tag titles (that they had lost the night before, but titles don't change hands until the match airs on television) going to a double disqualification with The Bushwackers, Rude beat Piper via DQ, Warrior beat Andre in 25 seconds and Hogan pinned Savage with a Leg drop.

Fred Ottman is now working as Tugboat Thomas, the act isn't getting over a bit, although that isn't really fair to say since until an act appears on television, it's impossible for it to sink in with the fans anyway. He goes "toot, toot", throughout the match but his work is pretty bad.

Rick Martel is now being called "The Male Model" for his feud with Brutus Beefcake. A correction here. The 10/14 card at the Spectrum in Philadelphia is being headlined by Warrior vs. Andre and Piper vs. Rude and the advance is incredible. I'd heard the advance was going crazy and assumed it was Hogan vs. Savage, since that's really the only match drawing huge crowds anywhere right now, but from what I'm told, Piper's return means a lot more in the Northeast than anywhere else as his match from the crowd reaction seemed the match the fans came to see at Madison Square Garden last week when they sold out as well. Told the Spectrum will have a near sellout and a gate in the $200,000 range which would be the largest crowd for the WWF in Philadelphia (or for anyone, for that matter) in nearly three years.

Jesse Ventura is getting good reviews for his work as color commentator for the Tampa Bay Buccaneers NFL team's radio network.

Prime Time Wrestling did a 2.6 on 10/2 while All-American did a 2.3 the day before, which are both well below "normal" but up from the week before. WWF in syndication did a 7.6 rating the weekend of 9/23, which is an all-time low, although still beat out NWA's network which did a 5.4 although WWF had 250 stations to the NWA's 163 as Of that weekend. 10/6 in Miami drew 8,000 as Haku pinned Jim Neidhart, Greg Valentine pinned Ron Garvin, Bravo pinned Rooster, Rockers beat Rougeaus, The Genius (Lanny Poffo) pinned Koko Ware, Jim Duggan pinned Akeem and Hogan pinned Savage. The same crew drew 6,000 in Tampa the night before.

The 10/28 Madison Square Garden card won't be televised on MSG cable until the next night because of Ice Hockey commitments by the MSG cable network so it won't be competing on cable with the NWA's PPV show after all.

10/7 in Boston drew 8,473 as Paul Roma pinned Barry Horowitz * ½, Widow Maker (Barry Windham) pinned Tim

Horner *** , Jimmy Snuka pinned Honky Tonk Man DUD, Rude beat Piper via DQ * (tons of heat before the match started but died after two minutes because the match wasn't any good) , Bushwackers beat Power of Pain -** (rating for the match, if you include the finish negative 10 as Fuji threw in the cane and Butch was supposed to use it on Barbarian, which he did, and throw it out so the ref couldn't see it in the ring, unfortunately Butch is no Dan Marino and threw it into the ropes and it bounced back in and the ref had to not turn around and Fuji had to make the save by jumping into the ring and pulling out the cane before the ref turned around making it about the most botched up finish imaginable), Hillbilly Jim beat Zhukov DUD, Rick Martel pinned Santana * ½ (decent work but no heat) and Warrior beat Andre via DQ (pathetic match but lots of heat) ½ *. Return on 11/11 With Savage vs. Duggan and DiBiase vs. Roberts.

10/9 in Tulsa drew 1, 700 as Tugboat pinned Horowitz (terrible), Valentine pinned Garvin, Bushwackers beat Power of Pain via count out, Beefcake pinned Martel, Rude beat Piper via DQ and Rhodes pinned Bossman.

9/29 in Milwaukee drew 12,000 as Widow Maker pinned Horner, Martel drew Santana, Rhodes beat Bossman, Hart double count out with Haku, Badnews Brown pinned Hercules, Bushwackers beat Powers of Pain via DQ and Hogan beat Savage in a double juice cage match.

10/1 in Hartford, CT before 9,500 saw Mark Young beat Horowitz ½ *, Genius beat Ware DUD, Rude beat Piper via DQ **, Garvin pinned Valentine -**, Demolition beat Blanchard & Anderson via DQ ** ½, Perfect pinned Hart **** and Warrior beat Andre via DQ*

10/1 in Johnstown, PA drew 850 as Roma pinned Bill Woods, Bravo pinned Neidhart, Snuka pinned Honky Tonk Man, Rhodes pinned Bossman, Tugboat pinned Brooklyn Brawler, Duggan pinned Akeem, Rockers beat Bolsheviks.

Roddy Piper's "They Live" video was awarded the most popular sci-fi video of 1989 while Coliseum's WrestleMania tape was awarded the most popular sports video and the Video Software Dealers Association's convention in Las Vegas.

NWA

The next two weeks worth of TBS shows were taped on 10/4 at Center Stage in Atlanta. The only non-squash match saw Great Muta beating Bobby Fulton. Lex Luger did a run-in during a Brian Pillman match and the two brawled to the dressing room while The Freebirds ran in during a Dynamic Dudes match and Jim Cornette went back to get the Midnight Express to help but they came in really slow and by the time they got to the ring the Dudes had run the Freebirds off by themselves.

Teddy Long was abusing Norman the Lunatic more and more and it seems the babyface turn is in the works.

Ole Anderson debuted in front of the cameras that night and did interviews with Ric Flair and Sting for the PPV show.

The main angle is they continued the Dudes-Cornette-Midnight bit, finishing up on the 10/21 show where Lane and Cornette get into an actual argument and Cornette says something like, I've been with Bobby for six years and he's on my side and Bobby instead sides with Stan and they walk off on Cornette. I expect the Midnight vs. Dudes match will take place at the 11/15 Clash from Troy, NY.

10/1 in Rochester, NY drew 2,900 as Eddie Gilbert pinned Cuban Assassin, Z-Man (Tom Zenk) pinned Norman, Danny Spivey pinned Johnny Ace, Steve Williams pinned Mike Rotunda (and the fans in Rochester did chant that nearby "Syracuse sucks"), Road Warriors beat New Zealand Militia (great), Lex Luger pinned Tommy Rich, Freebirds beat Midnight Express and Ric Flair pinned Terry Funk (excellent).

Those Elvira commercials for the next PPV are awesome. I don't think it'll help the PPV do business too much but they do put together great commercials for these events on TBS. Nice to see so much mention of Paul Ellering on the commercials simply because he's the only guy in the promotion whose name rhymes with Sting.

To answer all the questions and quell all the rumors, here's the status of Gilbert, Missy Hyatt and Paul E. Dangerously. Gilbert and Missy are under contract through February and since these are six-figure deals, they would be foolish to walk out on them, even though Hyatt's last actual NWA appearence aired on TBS Saturday and she won't be around at all and Gilbert will be used to put over the top guys on TV and work prelims at the house shows.

Dangerously was also under contract, but worked out a release of his contract with Jim Herd. Officially they wouldn't make any offer to him (despite rumors of him already having signed with WWF) until they saw the NWA contract release because of tampering and anti-trust problems if they go after someone with a valid contract with their competitors. The carefulness they've displayed in this deal tells me that there is no way, at least right now, they would try and steal anyone with a valid NWA contract unless the NWA lets the guy out of his contract.

Brian Pillman's girlfriend is "okay physically" after the stabbing attack on her in her apartment about 10 days back. Apparently the assailant turned out to be the maintainence man in the apartment.

Jack Petrik, the president of World Championship Wrestling, was promoted to the TBS board of directors.

10/7 in Pittsburgh drew 3,760 and $44,000 as Ranger Ross pinned Brad Anderson, Z-Man put Bill Irwin to sleep, Norman pinned Rich using the key, Dudes beat Militia, Pillman pinned Cuban, Steiners beat Freebirds via DQ, Sting beat Muta via DQ for blowing the mist, Skyscrapers beat Midnight (fans cheered Skyscrapers) , Luger pinned Williams and Flair beat Funk in a Texas Death match *** ½ when Funk couldn't answer the bell for the seventh fall after 24 minutes. It was one of those "Flair's match saves the show" cards with the underneath stuff lackluster.

10/8 at the Omni in Atlanta drew 9,000 as Dudes beat Militia, Norman pinned Rich using the key (fair, lots of stalling between spots), Z-Man beat Irwin (missed a move and everyone knew it and never got intense heat after), Pillman pinned Gilbert (disappointing), Skyscrapers beat Warriors via DQ (got heat on Hawk for six minutes, Animal came in with hot tag and quickly Teddy Long and Paul Ellering interfered and Ellering was DQ'd for hitting Sid with the key ** ¾ mainly because of excellent heat), Sting to a 20:00 draw with Muta with Hart in a cage above the ring *** ¾ (started slow, ended up as an excellent match with lots of hot moves at the end-after the match Sting got on the house mic and called Muta and Hart "dipshits"), Luger pinned Williams (no crowd reaction or interest in the match but up close the work was solid), Steiner's beat Freebirds via DQ ** ½ when Garvin hit Rick with the title belt and Flair beat Funk in 25:20 of the I Quit match *** ¾ but the ending really pissed off the fans. Flair juiced heavy and heat was incredible. Finish saw a ref bump, Flair put Funk in the figure four but no ref to bring the house mic into the ring to see if Funk would quit. Ole Anderson ran in with the house mic and he and Gary Hart started fighting and Flair and Ole ran Hart and Funk off. If Funk "quit", nobody in the building heard it or thought he did so fans felt ripped off with a count out finish of an I Quit match.

TV taping 10/9 in West palm Beach drew 2,598. Chris Cruise debuted working with Jim Ross on World Wide Wrestling. Samoan Savage (Tonga Kid, Sam Fatu) debuted managed by Sir Oliver Humperdink. Shane Douglas didn't work and had his arm in a sling. Ricky Santana and David Sierra were doing commentary in spanish and NWA is going to try and put together a spanish network and they were building up the usage of Friar Tormenta from Mexico on a card in Corpus Christi (he's the preacher in Mexico who wrestles to benefit the orphanage) and supposedly they have signed a major Latin star as well. Major matches at the taping saw Muta beat Gilbert, Steiner's double count out Skyscrapers (terrible), Zenk & pillman beat Militia, Sting beat Irwin, Sting beat Muta via DQ and Flair beat Funk in 18:00 ***.

They announced that inside the Thunderdome cage on the PPV will be spikes and chains and that the entire cage will be electrified so if you hit the cage in any form you get shocked.

They need to get Bruno Sanunartino to do some taped interviews for TBS and especially the syndicated shows before the PPV.

9/26 in Beckley, WV drew 1,800 as Militia beat Gilbert & Rich, Norman pinned Brad Anderson, Rotunda drew Williams, Stieners beat Simmons & Hayes, Sting beat Muta via count out.

9/29 in Syracuse, NY drew 1,500 as Gilbert beat Cuban, Z-Man beat Norman, Spivey pinned Ace, Rotunda pinned Williams clean (Doc played heel but got cheered when he did his spots, Rotunda was a complete face however in Syracuse), Warriors beat Militia, Luger beat Rich, Sting beat Muta via DQ, Freebirds beat Midnight (best match on the card), and Flair pinned Funk (very good).

Sid Vicious hurt both Ace and Douglas working with him over the New York weekend by potatoing Ace and re-injuring his face (although I don't think he had to miss work) and dropping Douglas wrong and nearly breaking his arm (he did miss a few matches and his arm is back in a sling again after he worked mid-week).

Ricky Steamboat will apparently be suing the NWA over usage of his name and photos of him in the print ads for the 10/28 card in Philadelphia. While an argument can be made in that these ads may or may not have been taken before Steamboat left the NWA, a valid point for Steamboat is that at no time was he ever under contract past July 31st and thus until they had him re-signed, his name shouldn't have been used in advertising a card late in October.

Power Hour on 9/29 drew a 2.1 rating (second best yet) while WCW on 9/30 drew a 2.2.

SOME DERBY NOTES

With the extra space, I thought I'd run down some skating news. Patrick Schaeffer taped a TV pilot on 9/24 in Irvine, CA for a game more like the traditional Roller Derby. There were arguments about the product style, whether it would be old Los Angeles Roller Games style (as John Hall wanted), Philadelphia Roller Games style (as Buddy Atkinson Jr. wanted) or Derby style (as Joan Weston wanted), but Hall apparently won the power struggle and he was in charge of bringing in the skaters. They had two teams, one called the Bombers, the other the Renegades. Atkinson coached the Bombers with his son Sean Atkinson, Sam Washington, Juan Milano, Debbie Garvey, Vicki Steppie, Allie Atkinson and Candi Mitchell while the Renegades were coached by E.G. Miller with Ronnie Rains, Larry Lewis (who is very ill thus not up to par), Frank Macedo, Georgie Fernandez, Diane Syverson, B. J. Peterson, Colleen Rains (Murrell) and Willie Ryan (the only Northern California skater). Joan Weston and Don Drewry did the announcing. Schaeffer claimed the show already has syndication in 33 percent of the country come January but most believe he'll actually start to try and sell the show in January. The TV people made a point they didn't want anyone old or fat involved in the game. Supposedly Rains stole the show.

The RollerGames on television has been fading in the ratings. There is a lot of internal chaos there as well, as the sponsors don't like the commentary job done by David Sarnms (who is producing the thing) and are threatening to pull out and the episodes are going way over budget. The show is a copy of the Titan wrestling with high-gloss production values but the characters just aren't getting over. They had hoped this would spawn a fad are had all these merchandising deals ready, but I just don't hear anyone talking about this and mainly, the characters themselves aren't interesting enough. Got an advanced copy of their yearbook magazine put out by Craig Peters (of Pro Wrestling Illustrated) and I got more into the different characters reading the magazine than by actually seeing them.

The ratings opened decent for the two-hour special, not what they expected, but decent for a curiosity show, however they've fallen sharply since then. Talk is the show will have a 13-week run, and it's touch and go if a second run of 13 episodes will be ordered, and even if they are, it's expected the TV stations will move the shows to death time periods because the shows aren't delivering and the stations are paying money for these shows, unlike wrestling programming in which it is either given away by the promotions or the promotion itself actually pays money to the stations to run the programming. The rights fees are why the RollerGames felt they could do these $700,000 TV shows, despite having no apparent incoming income as they aren't even trying road shows yet.

There is also some heat about the usage of the alligators, which some have claimed was needed to get such a strong syndication network. Some close to RollerGames don't believe the Schaeffer product will be able to clear stations for a few reasons 1) It won't be as high tech; 2) No alligators which they felt were needed to sell it to TV stations; 3) The first RollerGames itself on the market isn't knocking anyone dead.

An interesting note to wrestling fans is the RollerGames team called "The Rockers" has their clothes designed by Zubaz, which is a company owned by the Road Warriors.

As for American Gladiators, this show doesn't seem to be going anywhere. So the programs that were designed to capture and compete for the "pro wrestling audience" aren't getting off to a fast start. My own belief is that the rules are too complex for the average fan to really understand and the alligators and commentary turn the thing into a sideshow. They need marketable characters and while the production values are great, and I wish the NWA could do shows produced to this level (but they'd run so deep in deficit spending it's ridiculous to do shows that cost $700,000 per episode to produce), they haven't gotten over the individual personalities well because of a lack of interviews with the skaters and are instead focusing on the managers, all of whom are playing cliche roles but don't have enough personality on their own. The best of the heels is Georgia Hase, but her act wears thin fast even though it's

pretty strong because of her delivery and facial expressions but no good material. The guy Skull looks evil visually but past the look, there's nothing there.

THE READERS' PAGE

WYATT VS. COBB

Due to the continuous number of calls and letters that I've been receiving concerning the situation between myself and Harvey Cobb of the infamous Pro Wrestling Enquirer, I've decided to write about the happenings.

It started with a show I promoted in which Cobb was supposed to guarantee me a certain amount of money as a sponsor for that particular show. To make a long story short, he came up $1,533 short of the guarantee. I tried to work things out with him on a payment plan but he simply refused to pay. At that point, we had to go to the courtroom route and the judge decided in my favor and ordered Cobb to pay me the $1,533 that, by signed contract, he owed me.

The next day, after the hearing, Cobb phoned my lawyer and informed him that he was not working so he couldn't afford to pay me. He asked my lawyer to see if I could accept $800 cash and call it even. I wouldn't accept that because after the Lawyer received his share, I'd only receive $500 and that's $1,000 less than he owed. I made a counter offer of $1,000 and I 'd drop the remaining $533 and figure that as a loss. Out of that, I'd at least get $700 which is better than nothing. Cobb agreed to pay the $1,000 and drop it there.

That was three weeks ago and still no money. We've since been forced to bring Cobb back to court. It looks like it is going to be a long time, maybe never, before I receive what is lawfully owed me by Cobb.

Ron Wyatt
Suffolk, Virginia

NWA IN NEW ENGLAND

Overall the 9/27 NWA show in Worcester, MA was a decent show despite significant problems. First, the 4,000 seat building had about 700 fans in attendance although the box office claimed that 2,000 tickets were sold. This was the first NWA show promoted by a Boston UWF station. The local Worcester station has been carrying the NWA for a few years but has continually changed the time slot. Ch. 56 in Boston, 40 miles east of Worcester, has televised the NWA for only three weeks, the last two having advertised the 9/27 card adequately. But holding this card in the middle of the state during the middle of the week was a losing combination.

Second, the card didn't lineup with the local advertising. Billed were Flair vs. Funk, Luger vs. Rich, Muta vs. Sting, Midnight vs. Freebirds and Warriors vs. Militia. No-shows were Luger, Hawk, Jim Garvin and Stan Lane. Any relatively new NWA fan, especially if he had driven from Boston, would have felt ripped off.

Third, the workrate was well below par, especially when compared to the phenomenal 7/8 card in Boston. The NWA suffered in comparison because of the departure of Ricky Steamboat, the no-shows, The SST being on vacation, no Missy Hyatt, Robin Green or the Steiner's. It is absurd to expect any promotion to run an outstanding card every night, but the NWA Worcester show on 9/27 lacked the high standard of action that is the NWN's trademark

As we left the building after the show, many of us mused over the fact that "MWA" was printed on our ticket stubs. Someone explained that it is the "Muta Wrestling Alliance".

Tony Amara
Boston, Massachusetts

The NWA show in Syracuse on 9/29 was quite good. The crowd wasn't bad considering there was no advertising at all, no newspaper ads, no radio ads, no posters, no nothing. The crowd was really into the show and were a lot louder than I've heard at the local WWF shows, even though they had larger crowds.

Flair vs. Funk was superb. Funk's antics are outrageous and Flair was his usual self. All the matches were at least good, although Sting vs. Muta was less than expected although I expect that injuries played a part in that.

David and Nannette McCormick
Watertown, New York

I just attended the NWA debut card here (10/1 in Rochester) and was extremely impressed with both the card and the people involved. The crowd was small but extremely vocal and enthusiastic. The card was plugged quite well locally including Jim Cornette appearing on the top morning radio show the previous Friday. Ric Flair got the best reaction of the night and everyone popped big when it was announced that Terry Funk had been reinstated and would wrestle tonight.

All in all, I feel the night was a success for the NWA. As people were leaving, they were anxiously awaiting a return date to be announced. I think they have solidified a strong base here and hope they continue to build on it.

Dan Petronio
Rochester, New York

AWARDS

I would like to suggest two new fields for the annual awards. First would be the coveted "Slowest Man in Wrestling" award. This could be broken into two groups. The Totally Obese Division with nominees like Andre the Giant and Akeem, the Steroid Freak Division with nominees like Butch Reed, Dino Bravo and the Ultimate Warrior along with Jim Duggan, and last and certainly least, Zeus.

The second category would be the funniest man in wrestling. I'd nominate Jim Cornette, Paul E. Dangerously and Rick Steiner, but the hands down winner to me would have to be Jerry "king of comedy" Lawler for his appearance on the Rasslin' radio show in Philadelphia in which he called the WWF a circus, which it may well be, while in his own promotion at the same time they were having matches including wrestlers Freddy and Jason and other kids movie tie-ins. Obviously this comment from Lawler had to be meant as a joke, and because of that, I'd say he has to be one of the funniest wrestlers today.

Joe Reckner
Philadelphia, Pennsylvania

DUSTYMANIA

Inside sources have leaked the surprise news story of the year. Dusty Rhodes is the new booker for the WWF. All new feuds have been lined up leading to the big event in April 1990, 'Dustymania I.'

The line-up will be as follows:

1) Dusty Rhodes vs. Red Rooster: During the match Dusty bleeds from the top of his head so he and Terry Taylor have matching red stripes. Finish sees Dusty fry the Rooster in a large skillet.

2) Dusty Rhodes vs. The Brainbusters: Dusty beats both guys by himself to become the WWF tag team champion. This is solely for revenge for Blanchard and Anderson walking out on him. After the match, Dusty gives himself a new nickname, 'Dust-Buster.'

3) Dusty Rhodes vs. Ted DiBiase: Dusty wins. As part of the pre-match stipulations, "Virgil" is forced to change his name to "Ted Turner."

4) Dusty Rhodes vs. Zeus: Dusty pins Zeus to prove that Dusty Rhodes is bigger than any god.

5) Dusty Rhodes vs. Rick Rude: Dusty beats Rude and wins the right to give the "Rude Awakening" to a young lady. This lady turns out to be Miss Atlanta Lively, which confirms what we 've thought all along.

6) Dusty Rhodes vs. The Ultimate Warrior: Dusty defeats Warrior to become the new Intercontinental champion. The fans appropriately give Dusty a new nickname, "The Ultimate Blob."

7) Dusty Rhodes vs. Akeem: Dusty wins this two ring War Games cage match with Russian Chains and barbed wire on top of a scaffold. Dusty wins when this contraption collapses and he's the only one left standing.

8) Dusty Rhodes vs. Hulk Hogan: The finish sees Hogan go for the leg drop, land on Dusty's belly, bounce to the ceiling of Trump Plaza and knock himself out. After the match, Dusty flexes for the adoring crowd. Unfortunately, Dusty flexes so hard that he explodes and kills 13 people in the first three rows.

At the card the hot new item at the concession stand is

the Dusty Doll. Actually it's just a Cabbage Patch Kid that bleeds from the head and if you leave it in a parking lot, it will get attacked by other Cabbage Patch Kids with baseball bats.

In response to your comments about the Robin Green-Scott Steiner skit on the NWA shows. I had the opposite reaction as you. I felt the skit was less violent than the plastic bag on Ric Flair's head. In comparison to the Dusty Rhodes-Horseman angle when Dusty got his hand broken with the baseball bat, this skit was mild. I'm not saying it wasn't distasteful, because it surely was. Violence of this new nature isn't necessary to attract wrestling fans today. In fact, if the NWA is interested in attracting new fans and a younger audience, angles such as this are downright irresponsible.

As for the. plastic bag, I feel that entire angle was way out of line. Not only was this an act of violence, it was attempted murder. Even though Gary Hart and Terry Funk are acting responsible by encouraging kids not to try this stunt at home, the act was unnecessary. I feel that a booker can build heat in a feud without having a person attempt to murder another.

While I feel both skits were tasteless and unnecessary, the skit with Robin and Scott was much less offensive.

Hal Moore
Marietta, Georgia

VINCE MCMAHON

I was once a harsh critic of Vince McMahon. Although he made wrestling popular again, he also turned it into a circus. But if one really thinks about it, a question comes to mind. Has Vince McMahon turned wrestling into a circus, or has it always been a circus?

When I was growing up in the late 50s and early 60s, I can remember watching wrestling with Ray Morgan. We had the Fabulous Kangaroos with their boomerangs, Lou Albano and Tony Altomore as the Sicilians with their black suits and fedora hats, and who could forget Skull Murphy, Brute Bernard and Kurt and Karl Von Hess. I always get a big laugh out of Ricki Starr with his playful slap to the opponents' face.

While Bruno Sammartino is off criticizing Vince McMahon and while so many others are on the same bandwagon, need I remind these people of GLOW, the most ridiculous form of wrestling ever put on television. The NWA has a slogan, "We Wrestle", yet I remind McMahon bashers that Dusty's Midnight Rider gimmick, Norman the Lunatic and the Scott Steiner-Robin Green skit are not products of Vince McMahon. If the CWA had national syndication, we could see Frankenstein, The Undertaker and the Zombie, who enters the ring in a coffin. Would McMahon stoop to such ridiculous tactics as this? I doubt it. The trouble is the small promotions aren't syndicated nationally so many fans who

are so critical of McMahon don't get a chance to see this stuff. If they did, maybe McMahon bashing would cease.

The point I'm trying to make is this. Wrestling isn't meant to be serious. It's a work and has always been a work and will always be a work. Results of matches have, are and will always be pre-determined in all promotions. The nonsensical, illogical and downright stupidity of pro wrestling is what makes it fun to watch.

Vince DiPalma
Copiaque, New York

JAPAN

I know that all the wrestling in Japan is influenced by Maeda's UWF but to me, watching most of the

New Japan guys and some of the All Japan guys is much more exciting. What can one say about Jushin

Liger. I hate the horns, but that's the only complaint I've got. His work is unreal and I never thought I'd say this but I believe he is on the same level as Satoru Sayama. His matches are all exciting and his matches with Naoki Sano should take top honors for match of the year.

I was somewhat disappointed in not seeing any coverage on the anniversary of Brody's murder. I was shocked by Verne Gagne's comments that Frank deserved what he got in Puerto Rico. It angers and sickens me beyond any word description. And problems Frank had with Verne were undoubtedly caused by the worst, most unscrupulous penny-pinching promoter.

Steve Munari
St.Louis, Missouri

TERRY FUNK

Terry Funk is a lot better looking than most 44-year-old men I know, though how old someone looks is largely a matter of the looker's age. To the large part of the population that is pushing 40, Terry Funk isn't old. He may look like he hasn't slept for a week at times, but that isn't too uncommon among that age group either. Terry Funk should be quite an attraction to an audience that says that wrestling today is all sizzle but no steak. I suspect that many people who don 't buy tickets use that as a reason. They should pay to see Funk. He is, after all, the real thing.

Betsey Anderson
Brighton, Massachusetts

NWA

Until the NWA vastly improves its production and presentation of its product, it will always be a distant second to Vince McMahon's WWF freak show. Very few people in wrestling audiences today care too much on how great the work rate is, but instead, rely simply on a visual impression of what the promotion wants it to look like. You commented on the idiotical Roller Games revival show. It's the same absurd crap the National Skating Derby in Los Angeles peddled in the 60s and 70s. Now it is reincarnated again, along with glitzy video tricks, rock 'n' roll, crowd hysteria, babes prancing around in tight leotards posing as cheerleaders and disgusting shenanigans, Wally George and disparaging commentary on its entire proceedings. Whether you like it or not, in pro wrestling, as in life, it is often style over substance. The WWF has the glitzy style. The NWA does't.

Carlton Lee
San Francisco, California

MADISON SQUARE GARDEN
I attended the first WWF card at Madison Square Garden since May. The place was packed and it was a typical WWF card - lots of hype, little action and tremendous heat. The opening match, Koko B. Ware vs.

The Genius had more heat than the Ric Flair vs. Terry Funk main event at the last NWA card in New Haven. During the Warrior vs. Andre match, despite the fact that both men missed moves left and right, the place was on its feet. I knew it was a terrible match, but I couldn't help but enjoy it with all the excitement generated by the crowd. Later, during the Piper vs. Rude match, every time Rude opened his mouth the whole place booed so loudly you couldn't even hear him. Piper looked almost as bad as Andre but it didn't matter. During the Garvin vs. Valentine match in which Valentine took about 30 stiff chops, some fan behind me asked his friend, "Isn't that the referee guy?" to which his friend replied, "No, that guy's not allowed to wrestle." It was bad enough they didn't know who the wrestlers were, but they had no idea what was going on in the promotion either. Despite encouraging signs from the most recent Clash, this card made me realize a little more just how far back the NWA is trailing the WWF. No matter how hard the NWA tries to shun the image that they are a Southeastern regional promotion, they are.

John Kapon
Wesleyan University, Connecticut

NEWSLETTERS
I'm writing in response to Lance Levine's letter of 9/18. I wasn't referring to his bulletin but rather was commenting on a rather ugly trend that has erupted of late. When I referred to promoters as the enemy, I was using the term as meaning adversary. I believe Levine read things into my argument that simply don't exist, such as giving it a moral connotation. Suffice to say that no promoter would exactly shed a tear if all bulletins ceased publishing. In the final analysis, promoters are part of wrestling and must be studied and reported, however, they do see the sheets as the enemy.

This is my point. It is fine to review another newsletter as

long as an objective perspective is maintained. However, the one thing I've noticed about this current trend is that these reviews cannot be done without frequent recourse to the ad hominem. If one criticizes another form of publication or an aspect of wrestling, the criticism can be accepted as part of the style, now matter how shrill. If one uses the same technique in regard to their peers, or other bulletins, it comes off as being mean-spirited, petty, envious and boorish.

I have a strong dislike for typos and bad grammar. I find typos annoying and bad grammar indicative of careless proofreading. I would often mention these items when reviewing newsletters in Wrestling Eye, but I also kept a sense of proportion. Many editors work at other jobs and literally have to make the time to crank out their bulletins. While this does not excuse typos and bad grammar, it may provide some understanding into why they occur. Also remember that no one is immune to typos and grammatical errors. I've spotted them in the New York Times and Washington Post. A friend of mine spotted a grammatical error in Jane Austen's Pride and Prejudice.

As to the comments about bland and outdated news, beauty lies in the eye of the beholder. What, exactly, is outdated news. Regarding outrageous prices, leave it to the marketplace to correct that. That is why I have always suggested purchasing a sample copy.

When I was with the Eye, the reason I didn't push a bulletin I didn't find interesting was my responsibility to both the writer and the rader. If the bulletin was a rip-off, I said so. If it was decent but not my cup of tea, I merely kept my mouth shut. Suppose I was reviewing Lance Levine's bulletin and didn't like it? Would I be justified in panning it? Applying his standards, I would be for what would be the use of having a column if you can't say what you honestly feel? As it so happens, I think Levine's bulletin is one of the better ones around and I would gladly subscribe. There is a large difference between a rip-off and individual taste.

Ed Garea
Irvington, New Jersey

I've been a long time reader of the Observer back to when it was a monthly publication. Recently, however, I've noticed the quality of the bulletin seems to be slipping. It seems that there are a lot of loose ends and news without a conclusion. For example, in the 0/2 issue, you reported five WWF wrestlers who are thinking of leaving the WWF and they are all 'name' wrestlers. Who are they? The story just stops. If you have no intention of revealing the names, then don't print the story. Readers want to know the details, not to be teased with a piece of information. This is just one example of something that seems to be happening more often in an otherwise excellent publication and it makes it very frustrating to read.

Ted Field Jr.
Woburn, Massachusetts

AWARDS FAVORITES

Once again, it's time to look at a few more categories for the awards that will be voted on in the yearbook. The awards balloting, which technically is to include action from the time period of December 1, 1988 through November 30, 1989, will take place during December and the results will be listed in the Observer yearbook which will be published in late January. A complete listing of categories will be in the Observer in late November or early December.

MOST IMPROVED: The two names that get brought up the most when it comes to this category are Rick Rude and Lex Luger. Deservedly so in both cases.. Both are having better matches now than in years past, and in Rude's case, it's even more impressive considering his opponent for much of the year. Luger has steadily improved since arriving in the NWA a few years back but in recent months has improved to a point where nobody calls him overrated anymore, either in ring work or ring persona. Still, plenty of others also come to my mind. Akira Nogami and Naoki Sano in New Japan have come out of the woodwork and are turning into excellent performers. Ron Simmons is finally showing signs that his wrestling career may live up to the potential everyone saw in him when he started. Doug Furnas isn't completely "there" yet, but is becoming more of a worker to go along with his great athletic skills with his frequent trips to Japan. Dan Kroffatt has gone from being one of the more underrated wrestlers around and a solid talent to a top-10 talent, though still underrated. Wayne Bloom and Mike Enos have come a long way in one year. Great Muta has always been a good wrestler and a top talent, but for a few months this year he was on a level just below the best in the game. He's cooled off a tad, but is still far more impressive than he was in previous years.

MATCH OF THE YEAR: Okay, this is the biggie. The one everyone talks about this year although that hasn't been the case in years' past. Let's face it, there are at least a half-dozen or more matches this year that, if held last year, would have easily captured the spot. Everyone pretty well knows that a Ric Flair vs. Rick Steamboat match is going to win, just not which one. With two genuine classic encounters of pay-per-view, and a 55 minute match which was the equal or better than any match ever televised live in the United States, at least in this decade, there is a lot to choose from. Many of their arena matches could qualify as well. If it wasn't for a routine finish, I saw a house show match between the two that was every bit as good as the three "famous" matches the two had. From a pure emotion standpoint, the first match was the best. From a pure wrestling as art state-

of-the-art standard of work, desire and athletic endurance, the match from New Orleans tops anything I've seen in this country. The Nashville match was good enough to win as well. Because of the quality of these three matches, matches like Flair vs. Funk from Baltimore and Flair vs. Luger from Starrcade '88 in Norfolk probably won't get strong consideration, even though they are candidates to be sure. As far as matches not involving Ric Flair, a few come to mind: Rockers vs. Brainbusters from the Saturday Night Main Event from Hershey, PA; Genichiro Tenryu & Toshiaki Kawada vs. Stan Hansen & Terry Gordy in the finals of the All Japan tag team tournament in December of 1988; Tenryu & Foot Loose vs. Jumbo Tsuruta & Yoshiaki Yatsu & Masa Fuchi was a definite five star match in February; Tenryu & Kawada vs. Tsuruta & Yatsu had two or three matches which were definite candidates. Of Late, the two matches on June 5 - Dan Kroffat & Doug Furnas vs. The Foot Loose and Tsuruta vs. Tenryu have been talked about. The best girls match I can recall was a brawl from Bangkok, Thailand with the Crush Gals vs. Bull Nakano & Kumiko Iwamoto from mid-December of last year. The first Naoki Sano vs. Jushin Liger match is also a candidate. I'm not really a fan of the UWF, but for that style, the Bob Backlund vs. Nobuhiko Takada match was tremendous.

WORST TELEVISION SHOW: As far as something that is truly bad, from what I've seen, Southern Championship Wrestling is really bad. Bad matches. Bad wrestlers. Bad production. Awful announcers. I can't find much good to say about it, particularly in those TV shoots from the lots of the car dealerships. I haven't seen a lot of ICW but what I 've seen has been pretty bad. AWA at least has decent production values but the wrestling itself is snore city. The CWA show, for years right at the top, has plummeted this year and is very hard to watch.

OCTOBER 23, 1989

Topping off the news this week is the stabbing of wrestler-turned-politician Antonio Inoki on Friday. Inoki, 46, was at a concert in Aizuwakamatsu, Japan, and was called in front of the crowd to be a guest speaker when in the middle of his speech, a man, who it was later found out was a former mental patient, jumped onto the stage and quickly slashed Inoki on the side of the head opening a cut from Inoki's ear to his neck. The news made several newspapers in the United States and the CBS network news because of Inoki's status as a member of the Japanese House of Councilors. As it turns out, the injuries apparently weren't as severe as reported in this country. In fact, after receiving emergency medical aid, Inoki returned to the concert and went back on stage to assure the people in the concert that he was okay, and he made his scheduled appearance on Saturday with the Japanese Foreign Exchange Student Olympics after being hospitalized overnight. As I'm writing this, the reports are still sketchy as to his recovery, but it was thought that he would be all right quickly, although nobody was speculating whether the injuries suffered would cause him to cancel his return to the ring scheduled for Dec. 6 in Osaka.

The first Saturday Night's Main Event of the fall season aired on 10/14 after being taped last month in Cincinnati. It was the normal slick production, and as usual for these NBC shows, the wrestling is far above the normal Titan standards. Really, every SNME thus far in 1989 has had at least one outstanding match, with the Rockers vs. Brainbusters match (which is the best WWF match I've seen all year) in February, the Hogan-Bossman cage match and last time out, the Savage vs. Beefcake match with the Zeus angle. This time, the outstanding match was the Tito Santana vs. Rick Martel match. Anyway, a quick rundown of the televised events:

1. Randy Savage pinned Jimmy Snuka. Snuka now barks like Bruiser Brody before and during his match. Too bad he can't work like Brody. Savage had his working shoes on and carried Snuka to a better than average match. Savage took a lot of good bumps to make Snuka look good, and Sherri Martel at ringside created her normal havoc. The finish saw Sherri give Savage the purse, and after Snuka went after Sherri, Savage hit him from behind with the purse and pinned him using the tights in 5:38. After the match, Savage missed his elbow off the top rope and Snuka made his comeback. As he went for his splash off the top, Sherri jumped to "protect" Savage and Snuka didn't jump. Snuka did give Savage a head-butt to chase him away and then chased Sherri around the ring before she left. ** ½

2. Hulk Hogan pinned Ted DiBiase in the WWF title match. They showed highlights of Zeus and never acknowledged the pinfall at SummerSlam, so that pinfall never occured and those of you who thought you saw it, please purge that thought from your mind because the event never took place. I was surprised they used some canned crowd noise since the crowd during a Hogan match should be loud enough. Zeus freely interfered early to give DiBiase the early edge. Jake Roberts came out at 2:30 with the snake and Virgil came out a minute later and stole Damien and Jake chased him away. At the four minute mark, DiBiase clotheslined Hogan over the top rope and they went to the commercial break. Hogan looked very slow and tired during the second half of the match. The overall execution and timing wasn't good during the second half despite the presence of DiBiase. After DiBiase hit a knee drop and Hogan kicked out, it was time for the superman comeback. Hogan did a few punches, then Zeus came in to hold Hogan, DiBiase went for the clothesline but Hogan moved and Zeus got hit. Hogan then cradled DiBiase from behind at 8:00 for the pin. The match itself was a typical Hogan story, but even with DiBiase, the quality was average at best. After the match DiBiase jumped Hogan, Zeus twisted his neck, DiBiase put on the Million Dollar Dream until finally Roberts came back out to make the save using the snake. Somehow in a post-match interview DiBiase blamed Roberts for not winning the title, but I couldn't figure out the connection since Roberts wasn't even at ringside except for one minute and not at the finish. **

3. Roddy Piper pinned Haku with a belly-to-belly suplex in 3:02. Of that, one minute was spent with Bobby Heenan distracting and no action between the wrestlers. The other two minutes were fast-and-furious by Piper. He looked a lot better here than the reports I've been getting on him from the house shows and he really lacked fire and his usual speed (probably caused somewhat from his rib injuries) at the MSG show I saw on tape. * ½

4. Rick Martel and Tito Santana went to a double disqualification. Both guys' Survivors teammates were at ringside for the match which ended up as the finish with everyone involved. The first segment went 3:40 until Santana hit the flying forearm and everyone jumped in but nobody touched and they went to the commercial. They came back and it was one excellent match on both men's parts. Martel is turning into a strong personality as a heel to go along with the fact that he's always has great ability (even though he rarely shows that ability of late). Everyone jumped in at 8:40

and they had an eight-way afterwards. *** ½

5. Bushwackers beat Rougeaus in 3:15 when they did the double stomach breaker on Jacques. The high points of the match were the Bushwackers walking to the ring and the second high point was when they pulled Jimmy Hart's pants off. Nothing happened during the actual match itself, but it still beat the pants off their match at WrestleMania. Rougeaus' best move of the match was Lip syncing their entrance music. ½ *

When most of you read this, it'll be about one week until the NWA's Halloween Havoc PPV event from Philadelphia. As with every PPV show, there are a lot of different factors going into the promotion of the event and things to look at whether the show will be either a financial or aesthetic success. This card offers a lot of things to think about:

*Will the much publicized "plastic bag" incident at the Clash and Scott Steiner parking lot attack and black eye bring in more PPV orders for revenge than the promise of great matches did at previous NWA PPV events?

*Does the public understand, care, or is it excited about the Thunderdome cage and the stipulations, terminators and referee (Bruno Sammartino)?

*Will the excellent commercials that TBS has prepared for this event, particularly the ones with Elvira, actually bring in more orders?

*Can the NWA sell a PPV event without a World title match in the main event and instead concentrate on a weird gimmick as the main selling point?

My own thoughts going in is that this will be the lowest buy rate for a pro wrestling PPV event with the exception of the AWA's Superclash show last December. While the announcers are talking up the card like crazy and the commercials are better produced than anything Titan has done in similar situations (except I still believe Titan's commercials are more effective selling devices simply because they give you the matches and the whys of the matches instead of very clever rhymes) I just don't see much interest in any of the matches. While the Thunderdome cage is not a bad idea in itself, they've added so many different stipulations that most fans probably can't even keep up with all of them. Also, my own opinion is that the company wastes the value of the World champion and the title belt by putting on a big show and having the champion involved in something of this nature. The NWA tag title match means nothing as no matter what they do, nobody respects Michael Hayes & Jimmy Garvin as a championship-calibre team, nor respects the Dudes as a challenger-quality team. The only intrigue in this match is the possibility that the title may change hands Leading to a Dudes vs. Midnight Express feud. The build-up for that angle has been fun, but I'm still wondering if both teams haven't been squashed too many

times so that fans won't really care too much about their matches. The Lex Luger-Brian Pillman match has been built up about as well as it possibly could be. The NWA needs to create new young stars and Pillman does have both the look and the athletic ability. The lack of experience in this situation doesn't bother me because when you create new stars, especially right now when the smaller promotions aren't emphasizing work skills, you aren't going to get a polished worker for this "new star" status. When I first heard about the Luger-Pillman marriage, my main concern was if fans would buy it because of the size difference between the two, but they've done just about a perfect job on television in making Pillman appear to be more than able to overcome that disadvantage.

The Road Warriors vs. Skyscrapers should mean something. It's a natural feud and one you would think people would want to see. But the house shows they've had that match at, haven't drawn as well as the "normal" house shows in the same cities have drawn so, and I'm not blaming these guys because the whole promotion isn't drawing, but this match isn't exactly selling too many tickets. As for the Steiner brothers vs. Doom, the best thing I can say is they are very smart not to let anyone know beforehand who Doom is, because then there would be absolutely no interest in this program. I don't know this for a fact, but one would assume they'll have Doom dressed up with masks or some sort of gimmicks so fans won't know it is Butch Reed & Ron Simmons, because if they can figure it out, there won't be any interest in these matches. The six-man (Steve Williams & Midnight Express vs. Samoan Swat Team & Samoan Savage) is just action underneath and nobody expects or insinuates it is there to sell tickets. Even though the SST are a great tag team and Sam Fatu can be a good worker, I don't see where three Samoans managed by Oliver Humperdink is going to help the NWA in any way, shape or form. Of course, I also thought the last PPV event the NWA did would have its worst buy rate, but underestimated the reaction to all the hype for Flair vs. Funk. As it was, the last PPV event, while TBS claimed a 2.0 plus buy rate, probably legitimately did around a 1.4 or 1.5 which is about as good as the NWA could have expected at the time. If this PPV does anywhere near that figure, and Starrcade holds up decently, I'd say that the worries about the NWA holding too many PPV events would be without merit, but I'm not expecting that will be the case.

Next up for the NWA after Philadelphia (and don't forget the thumbs up/ thumbs down and reader responses to the card for the following week's Observer) will be the Clash of Champions on 11/15 from the RPI Fieldhouse in Troy, NY. The line-up for this free TBS special will be headlined by Ric Flair vs. Terry Funk in an I Quit match for the NWA title, Freebirds vs. Road Warriors, Luger vs. Pillman for the U.S. title, Steiner s vs. Skyscrapers, Midnight

Express vs. Dynamic Dudes, Doom vs. Tommy Rich & Eddie Gilbert, Z-Man (Tom Zenk) vs. Super Destroyer (Bill Irwin) and Steve Williams vs. Cuban Assassin. Not a bad card for a free TV special. As for the host city, that's another story. The NWA's first appearence in Troy, just two weeks back, didn't draw well and the arena is not lit well for television purposes. Another problem at the last show in Late September was that it is freezing inside the building. Imagine if that's the case, what it will be like in November, as they have ice underneath the floor since the facility is mainly used for Ice Hockey. That's not a big deal on television, because really only the spectators live will be cold and in that part of the country in November, they're used to it. But it doesn't make those bumps and chops sting a lot more when it's cold and on a TV special, the wrestlers do normally put out that something extra. Also, when it is cold, the crowd usually doesn't react as well because their hands are in the pockets of their jackets. On a big special, the crowd reactions and crowd noise play a big part. And after drawing such a small crowd for the NWN s first effort in Troy, getting a respectable crowd is just another problem tacked on for this show. Admittedly the crowd in Columbia, SC wasn't large, and you'd never know it from watching on television, but they were rabid and it did help make the show a success. If you look at these matches on paper, the show should be a good television show and the main event has potential to be great. But they are going in with strikes against them because of the location chosen to originate from.

The WWF's mainline stars spent the week in Europe, running shows in London and Birmingham, England, Brussels in Belgium, Grenoble in France and finishing off Friday night in Paris. I know that both the London and Paris shows were sold out weeks ahead of time and they are already planning a more extensive European swing next year.

The UWF card at the Tokyo Dome on 11/29 will apparently be headlined by Akira Maeda vs. Willy Wilhelm, who captured the gold medal in the European Judo Championships and is billed as 6-4 ½, 280 pounds from the Netherlands. The other outside athletes on the card (I've got the names spelled right and right backgrounds this week) are Glenn "The Machine" Berg, the kick boxing champion of the Netherlands who had a mixed match Last year against Yoshiaki Fujiwara on a martial arts show in Tokyo's Budokan Hall; Maurice Smith of the United States who is the current World Karate Association World heavyweight champion; Chris Dolman, the former sambo wrestling champion who had the mixed match earlier this year against Maeda; Chanphuir Davy, a Thailand kickboxing champion and Duane Koslowski from Minnesota, who placed eighth in the Seoul Olympics as a heavyweight in Greco-Roman wrestling (and his twin brother took the bronze in another

weight class). Koslowski is being pushed more for the fact that he beat Jeff Blatnick (1984 Olympic gold medalist) in the Olympic trials to make the team than his eighth place finish in the Olympics. The ine-up for the matches hasn't been officially announced as of yet.

The next major WWF show is the Survivors Series, but nothing really new on that. Nobody is thinking this event will do anywhere near the PPV numbers of SummerSlam, but it will be considered a success with a three percent buy rate, which isn't out of the realm of possibility. A legit three buy rate would gross $6 million. Last year's show did just under a three, although the inaugural Survivors Series did an announced seven percent buy rate (that figure may not be legit and probably isn't and it's also during a time period when there were only two wrestling PPV events per year). If the past two Survivor Series are any indication, this should be the best overall show for action quality that Titan puts on PPV all year. Still, this is a gimmick show and the gimmick is no Longer a novelty, there is no main event with a strong focus and the prime attraction, the Hogan-Zeus Lock-up, has been seen before even though Titan is trying to keep the actual outcome from being a factor for this show. But still, the audience that would consider buying this show would primarily be the same audience that bought the last one, thus they do all recall the finish and an eight-man tag is even less focused than a regular tag match. In addition, Thanksgiving is actually a terrible night for PPV. Thanksgiving got a reputation in the early 1980s as the best night of the year for wrestling with the big Starrcade cards and the Reunion Arena shows in Dallas. It is also the biggest night of the year for the movie industry. So it was thought that this would be a great night for PPV as well. The problem is, Thanksgiving is one of the worst nights of the year for television viewing. Attending a live show, or a closed-circuit theater broadcast of a live show is going "out, which people want to do after spending most of the day "in" on Thanksgiving. Watching TV or a PPV is still staying "in". It probably didn't hurt Titan one bit the first year because the novelty of wrestling on PPV and the first-time usage of the gimmick made it a must-see event for all wrestling fans. As last year showed, that wasn't the case the second time out. I can't see the third show doing much better than the second, although there is no reason to believe it would do much worse, either.

The WWF ran its fourth annual King of the Ring tournament on 10/14 in providence, RI with Tito Santana winning. Don't have details on the show itself other than the crowd was good, but not packed, and that Widow Maker (Barry Windham) no-showed and most felt he was going to be put over. Anyway, results were Akeem pinning Brutus Beefcake, Hercules going to a double disqualification with Jim Neidhart, Warlord pinned Butch Miller, Santana beat Badnews Brown, Rick Martel beat Bill Woods, Luke Williams beat Nikolai Volkoff, Haku pinnedRed Rooster and Jimmy Snuka pinned The Barbarian in the first round. Second round saw Santana beat Warlord, Martel beat Luke Williams and Snuka beat Haku. From that point forward it was Santana over Akeem, Martel over Snuka and Santana pinning Martel in the finals. I don't have DQ's, COR's and the other screw-job finishes that certainly occured but hopefully will get complete details for next week's issue.

CWA

The 10/9 card in Memphis drew an horrendous $2,000 house which is probably the lowest in recorded history. The headline match was a non-title match in which The Soul Taker (a Larry Sharpe trainee with about four months of training) beat Jerry Lawler in a non-title match. They went all the way with this thing as Soul Taker destroyed Lawler the entire way through for ten minutes and didn't sell one thing the entire way. In fact, Lawler even hit him with two low blows and Soul Taker didn't register a thing. The attempt was to turn him into the monster heel ala Zeus, but even though it was a total destruction job, it didn't work live as fans only reacted once or twice the entire match and there was no heat. Also on the card, Buddy Landel & Dirty White Boy beat Lawler & Dustin Rhodes, Rock & Roll Express kept the CWA tag team titles beating The Blackbirds via DQ when they threw Gibson over the top rope and after the match the Blackbirds' new manager, Reggie B. Fine, pulled out a file and messed up Ricky Morton's face with it, Wildside (Chris Champion & Mark Starr) went to a double count out with Dutch Mantell & Bill Dundee in the best match on the card, Soul Taker destroyed Ken Raper, who had to be carried out by Eddie Marlin, Plowboy Stan Frazier pinned Cowboy Kevin Dillinger and Freddy beat Mike Davis via DQ.

Spike Huber is out of action with a neck injury.

Referee Frank Morrell is out of action after suffering a heart attack.

At the TV tapings on 10/14, Lawler & Mantell beat White Boy & Davis via DQ when Dirty White Girl interfered and Rock & Roll Express beat Wilds ide via DQ when Blackbirds interfered.

Lawler did several interviews saying how embarrassed he was that as the World champion he couldn't hurt this newcomer trying to build up the rematch.

Dream Weaver (Trevor Austin) is back.

10/16 in Memphis they are trying a gimmick to bring back crowds offering $15 for a family plan in which parents can bring as many kids as they want and they'll be given seats in a special section and in that section there will be no alcohol allowed and no abusive language allowed from the spectators or there will be immediate ejection. At least this is an attempt to bring kids back to the Coliseum although the real problem is the kids who used to pack the Coliseum and the girls who used to pack the Coliseum in the early

80s either have no interest in the wrestlers currently in the promotion, or if they are interested, consider the NWA and WWF as the major leagues and aren't interested in the local promotion.

Monday's line-up has Frazier vs. Tommy Lane, Ken Wayne vs. Dillinger, Freddy vs. Champion, Rhodes vs. Davis, Starr vs. Mantell, Dundee vs. Landel, Dirty White Boy defending the CWA title against Jeff Jarrett, Rock & Rolls defending the CWA tag titles against Blackbirds once again and Lawler defending the USWA title against Soul Taker with a 20 man Battle Royal added on.

In an interview, Dirty White Girl was talking about Jarrett and Kerry Von Erich and said that Jarrett was "cute" but Von Erich looked like a horse and White Boy got mad when she called Jarrett cute.

OREGON

Rex King captured the Pacific Northwest title from Scotty the Body on 10/7 in Portland in a major surprise. Other results on the card saw Steve Doll beat Jonathan Boyd, Al Madril beat Carl Styles via DQ, Beetlejuice pinned Moondog Ed Moretti and The Grappler drew with Rip Oliver in the main event. 10/14 in Portland had a tournament for the long-vacated Northwest TV title with first round pairings having Moretti vs. Bill Francis, Madril vs. Brian Adams, Doll vs. Styles and Beetle juice vs. Boyd plus King vs. Scotty for the Northwest title and Oliver vs. Grappler in a stretcher match.

They've been pushing on TV for fans to vote for a dream match and all the faces are trying to get the fans to vote for Grappler vs. Nord the Barbarian (both heels and tag team partners) and Grappler keeps trying to get the fans not to write that match in.

TEXAS

The Punisher (Mark Calaway) was awarded the Texas title on 10/5 in Brownsville, TX when champion Eric Embry missed the match due to the blinding angle the previous Friday night in Dallas. USWA rules are that if a champion no-shows a title defense that the title is to change hands, although when the Von Erichs were champs and they no-showed title defenses, sometimes the belts changed (when they were supposed to) and other times they didn't (when they weren't). I guess the real rule is that if/when they want to get the strap from a face and they don't want the face to do the job, then this rule is implemented, but if a guy who is champ no-shows out of nowhere, then the rule is forgotten.

The big news is that Killer Tim Brooks' first TV taping on 10/10 at the Longhorn Bar in Dallas drew nearly 900 fans, which is about triple what the recent Friday night Sportatorium shows have been drawing. It's hard to figure out what is drawing the crowds since the group's television didn't even start until Saturday night, and with the exception of John Tatum, it isn't like they've got any talent that could go anywhere right now. Brooks' group had a problem at its first taping, however, in that about 40 percent of the crowd left before the taping was over because the show lasted so long and it was on a Tuesday night. Top matches saw Tatum & Brooks beat Kenny the Stinger (a Sting knockoff) & Johnny Mantell, Steve Casey beat Botswana Beast via DQ and Scott Casey also beat Beast via DQ while Steve Cox (who got the best crowd pop of the card) and Brian Adias debuted for the group. The top newcomers from Brooks' training classes are Kenny the Stinger and Bullman Downs, both obviously quite green but have some presence. Bill Mercer and Doyle King handle the television. Mercer didn't make any of his famous misstatements on the first taping, but King had a classic where he talked about how Kenny the Stinger's goal in wrestling is to either team up with or feud with Sting.

10/13 at the Dallas Sportatorium saw Jerry Lawler beat Uncle ELmer via DQ in the main event to keep the USWA title. The only other results I've got are Steve Williams (the rookie from Chris Adams' school, not Dr. Death) beat Sheik Scott Braddock via DQ when all the Devastation heels ran in and Punisher kept the Texas title beating Kerry Von Erich.

Frogman LeBlanc was buried on TV at the 10/14 tapings as they made a big deal about how he was afraid to wrestle Punisher, although in reality LeBlanc had been fired for working a Brooks show earlier in the week.

Kevin Von Erich is billed for an upcoming show in EL Dorado, AR.

Bill Dundee did an interview and talked about how he was going to bust up Gary Young and Cactus Jack. Only problem is that Cactus Jack hasn't been around in almost two months.

Not sure of the status of the USWA tag belts. Jeff Jarrett & Matt Borne were the last champions, but Borne left after losing the fall in the Loser leaves town match to Braddock & Ron Starr on 10/6 in Dallas, but apparently that was a non-title match. When Braddock & Starr wrestled on TV on 10/14 and lost against Jarrett & Jimmy Jack Funk, there was no mention of the tag team titles at all.

10/20 in Dallas has Lawler vs. Elmer in a title rematch, Punisher vs. Kerry for the Texas title, Jarrett & Terry Gordy vs. Starr & Taras Bulba, Eric Embry vs. Billy Joe Travis, Chris Adams vs. P. Y. Chu Hi, Funk vs. Braddock and Dundee vs. Young.

The next day in Mesquite they are holding a show called "Wrestlewreck" with a Demolition Derby involving the wrestlers before the card as a speedway. Top matches are Punisher vs. Gordy with the winner to get a title shot at Lawler, Bulba vs. Kerry in a cage and Travis & Scandor Akbar vs. Embry & Percy Pringle in a match where the loser gets painted yellow.

JAPAN

Still slow on news from here.

Frontier Martial Arts Wrestling promotion opened on 10/6 in Nagoya before a sellout crowd announced at 4,500 at the Tsuyuhashi Sports Center with tickets priced from $10.50 to $42. The main event saw Atsushi Onita, who is the main star for the group (a former junior heavyweight champion for Baba's promotion in 1983-84 and a protege of Terry Funk) lose in a lumberjack death match to karate ace Seiji Aoyonagi in a bloodbath when Onita's second threw in the towel. Also Masanobu Kurusu (who was a prelim wrestler for both All Japan and New Japan) beat the masked man called The Sambo Kid in what was billed as a pro wrestling vs. sambo wrestling match. The Witch Woman, who I believe is from Vancouver, Canada and worked for JWP, beat three girls from Japan and after the match Witch Woman was attacked by another woman in a Batman outfit billed at Bat Girl and challenged Witch Woman to a match on 10/10 in Tokyo. Mitsuhiro Matsunaga (karate) beat Billy Mack (wrestler) and Jimmy Backlund from Florida beat Mitsuteru Tokuda (judo). The promotion is more Americanized than the other Japanese groups with heavy emphasis on run-ins, juice and gimmicks. Still, it was a success since they drew a sellout for the debut card without any television.

Genichiro Tenryu kept his triple crown beating usual tag team partner Toshiaki Kawada in 11:59 on 10/8 at Tokyo's Korakuen Hall.

New Japan booker Seiji Sakaguchi is already hyping the February Tokyo Dome show. There has been talk of bringing back Shota Chochyashivili (the judo gold medalist from 1972 who headlined against Inoki at the last Tokyo Dome show) and Sakaguchi has talked with Giant Baba about letting them use Tenryu for one match.

Terry Gordy's nephew Richard Slinger is working in prelims for Baba.

It was announced in Japan that Keiji Muto (Great Muta) will return and work the Tokyo Dome card for New Japan.

New Japan's tag team tournament will be 11/24 to 12/7 with Inoki originally scheduled to work the final two nights of the tour. They will also hold a special card on 12/19 featuring some sort of junior heavyweight showdown with Naoki Sano, Jushin Liger and Akira Nogami.

Mitsuko Nishiwaki & Madusa Maceli won the tag team tournament ALL Japan women had been running.

Ryuma Go's independent group has a show 10/26 in Tokyo and will introduce five new trainees to make debuts on the card.

As part of the 30th year anniversary of Baba's pro debut, Baba is back in main events this month. On 10/7, Baba & Tsuruta & Kenta Kobashi lost to Tenryu & Stan Hansen & Samson Fuyuki. 10/8 saw The Can-Am Express (Dan Kroffat & Doug Furnas) beat Hansen & Joel Deaton.

Japanese girls Kaoru Maeda & Mika Takahashi are billed

as the "Honey Wings" tag team.

Madusa Maceli has a poster out in Japan and will have a record out in December.

New Japan is billing Brad Rheingans, Steve Williams, Buzz Sawyer, Manny Fernandez and Rick Steiner as coming in for the tag team tournament but I doubt the NWA will allow Williams and Steiner to go to Japan.

Tatsumi Fujinami is coming to Los Angeles to get more advanced medical treatment for his back. If his back doesn't respond soon (he's been out of action since July), then it is expected Fujinami will be forced to announce his retirement. Fujinami's retirement has been freely speculated in Japan since August.

A few of the recent moves in the Sano vs. Liger matches. Liger tried a superplex off the top rope but Sano reversed the move and they both tumbled backward outside the ring. Actually that move sounds better in print than it looked. What looked better than it sounds was when Liger came off the top rope outside the ring with a flying bodyblock and Sano leaped up from the floor and drop kicked him. Liger also did the Chavo Guerrero backward splash onto Sano but with Sano outside the ring and Sano reversed a superplex by Liger off the top rope and did a face first gordbuster type drop on Liger (similar to the famous Lioness Asuka vs. Jaguar Yokota move in 1985). Geez, the best thing in the photos from Owen Hart vs. Sano was Sano giving Hart a double arm superplex with both guys standing on the top rope.

Koji Kitao was in Atlanta recently taking some training photos with six-time Mr. Olympia Lee Haney at Haney's Animal Kingdom Gym. A reporter from Sports Illustrated was there and they are doing a story on Kitao's switch from the sumo wrestling world into pro wrestling.

OTHER NOTES

Jimmy Valiant is working some shows for Nelson Royal's Atlantic Coast Wrestling.

Lia Maivia is promoting a card 10/20 as Blaisdell Center in Honolulu with Don Muraco vs. Bob Orton, Dynamite Kid & Davey Boy Smith vs. The Samoan Connection (LeRoy Brown & Farmer Boy IPO), Bam Bam Bigelow vs. Nikolai Volkoff plus Rocky Johnson and Steve Strong will appear.

Hawaii has quite a television Line—up as you can see New Japan (tapes are about six months behind) , USWA, NWA, WWF, Glow and Polynesian Pro weekly.

Memphis Cablevision is talking of starting up its own wrestling promotion. Big Al Greene is working in Florida for Professional Wrestling from Florida (PWF, formerly FCW), The Monster Factory is going to open up a second school in Marion, OH, hometown of Charlie Fulton. Address will be Monster Factory, Box 172, Pruyant, OH 43342.

David Isley & Mike Hart beat The Russian Assassins for the ACW tag team titles. Brad Armstrong is headed to the CWF.

Inside Edition did a segment on the Dusty Rhodes/Steve DiBlasio case, focusing the attention of the story on DiBlasio's remarks exposing the business and Rhodes' admission under oath that it was 100 percent show business. The show acted Like they had uncovered a major scoop that wrestling wasn't worked, similar to when 20/20 laughably used the same approach in its 1985 story.

Sgt. Slaughter was on Geraldo Rivera when Geraldo did a segment on pro wrestling and the RollerGames. They had a psychologist on saying that studies have proven that pro wrestling leads to violent behavior in kids.

Killer Kowalski ran a TV taping on 10/6 in Hanover, MA drawing 420 with Mike Sharpe and Nikolai Volkoff on the card. John Studd may work some shots next year for Kowalski.

Paul Orndorff will definitely be coming out of retirement and has confirmed he's working the November card in Cleveland against Kerry Von Erich plus the TV taping for Heritage Wrestling in Mississippi and I believe is working a charity show in Miami as well. Wendell Cooley and Jerry Stubbs have left CWF for Ron West's new group called North American Championship Wrestling which debuted last week.

Beauty, or Terrence Garvin, has also Left CWF after losing a loser leaves town match when he & Beast Lost to Adrian Street & Todd Morton.

Danny Davis is also going from CWF to NACW and NACW will be running a tag team title tournament on 11/23 in Gainesville, AL with The Nightmares (Ken Wayne & Danny Davis), Mr. Wrestling I & II (no idea who will be Wrestling I) and Bobby & Jackie Fulton. NACW will also be running regular house shows in Birmingham. Did you catch Nick Busick as one of the guys building the Thunderdome cage on the TBS commercial? 10/15 in Orlando, FL for PWF drew 149 as Dennis Knight beat Powerhouse Parker DUD, Lou Perez beat Terminator via DQ **, Ron Slinker beat Tyree Pride to win the Bahama Islands title when Kendall Windham hit Pride twice with a chair ** ½, Steve Keirn beat Jumbo Barretta ** and Nasty Boys kept the Florida tag belts going to a double count out with Windham & Knight (subbing for Blackjack Mulligan) ** ½.   Ron Bass and Dory Funk were announced as coming in on the television show this week and they were still pushing Eddie Gilbert and Missy Hyatt as coming in. There will be a Lucha Libre show on 10/20 in Santa Ana, CA. Charlie Norris beat Ricky Rice for the PWA title on 10/4 at George's in Fridley before a sellout 325. Also on the show included Kenny Jay, Jeff Warner and newsletter editor Kris Pope.

Al Madril won the Northwest TV title tournament on 10/14 in Portland while Nord the Barbarian turned babyface and will feud with The Grappler.

There will be a wrestling tour of Singapore and Malaysia starting 10/24 with Kerry Brown, Gama Singh, The Nasty Boys, Brian Blair, Jim Brunzell, Frenchy Martin, Moondog Moretti and Pat Brady.

10/6 in Calgary saw Davey Boy Smith go to a no contest with Larry Cameron for the Latters' North American title, Great Gama beat Biff Wellington, Bruce Hart pinned Skull Mason, ArchAngel (Curtis Thompson) beat Steve Gillespie and The Derringer brothers beat Ken Johnson & Kim Schau.

For those in the Los Angeles area, Slammers Wrestling Gym in Sun Valley has open ring time for fans wanting to see what it's really like in the ring.

A few weeks back I mentioned the craziest bump I've ever seen was when Dynamite Kid climbed to the top of the ringpost and dove three rows into the aisle with a diving head-butt on the arena floor (with no padding) onto Bruce Hart back in 1981. Forgot to mention what the end result of that was. Dynamite Kid blew out both his knees and Bruce Hart suffered a concussion. Don't try moves like that at home, even if you are a professional.

Scotty the Body regained the Northwest title from Rex King on 10/14 in Portland.

WWF

This item from the Los Angeles Times on 3727 in regards to Gov. George Deukmejian signing the bill to strip the state athletic commission from controlling wrestling come January 1st. Assemblyman Richard Floyd of Gardena, who was on Nightline with Lou Albano and Frank Deford a few month back, sponsored the bill and said, 'it ain't a sport. it aint an athletic contest.' Floyd also said that it was ridiculous to have physicians present at pro wrestling matches. 'it would make more sense to have them at rock concerts. There's more violence there.' Somehow, my impression that the injury rate among rock 'n' roll stars would be quite a bit lower than the injury rate among pro wrestlers, particularly in the NWA Of late.

Hillbilly Jim blew out his knee again this past week and was replaced in a few cities by Bob Orton. Orton worked as a face against Ted DiBiase on Thursday night in Springfield, IL. Orton is scheduled to have a job interview with Titan when they do their TV taping in Topeka, KS on 10/31. That will also be a Saturday Night Main Event taping and tickets aren't moving well at all since the main event is Hulk Hogan vs. The Genius. Obviously this is a ploy to get into the Hogan vs. Mr. Perfect feud but Lanny Poffo on top isn't a good way to draw fans.

All-American and Prime Time Wrestling both did 2.4 ratings on 10/8 and 10/9 respectively. The NFL continues to knock a huge chunk out of the ratings of both NWA and WWF programming that opposes it.

Hogan vs. Mr. Perfect on 11/22 in St. Paul, MN.

The last Madison Square Garden card officially did a $299,104 gate which is one of the 15 largest Live gates in the history of pro wrestling in the United States and the third largest ever at the Garden (behind WrestleMania I and SummerSlam 88).

WWF has a new policy at TV tapings. At the tapings last time, they had posters in front of the building saying that any banners that interfered with the taping of the television show could not be brought into the building. They also checked all banners, not only for anything related to the NWA, but also if the banners said anything derogatory about any of the babyfaces. As far as I'm concerned, if the sign is posted outside the building, they are well within their rights at that point to confiscate banners because they are warning people ahead of time. Paranoia runs rampant.

One of our readers set out to prove the NWA would do the same thing and went to the Johnstown, PA taping with a Roddy Piper shirt in the first row and nobody said a word or cared. Went to the Titan taping with a Four Horseman shirt in the first row and ironically, when WWF officials were checking for NWA shirts, they overlooked him (thought it was a Metallica shirt) so he had to tell them and they took the shirt off. That shirt business has become a work by fans at all the tapings because people know that if you come into the building at a WWF taping with an NWA shirt and sit in the first few rows that they'll give you free WWF shirts.

10/12 was a free show at the Arizona State Fair as Dusty Rhodes beat Big Bossman, Tugboat Thomas (Fred Ottman) beat Barry Horowitz, Bushwackers beat Powers of Pain via DQ, Ron Garvin pinned Greg Valentine and Rick Rude beat Roddy Piper via count out.

The King of the Ring tournament in providence on 10/14 drew 4,500 fans.

10/14 at the Spectrum in Philadelphia drew 15,126 and $186,130 which is the largest crowd and gate in several years as Thomas beat Horowitz (dud), Rude beat Piper via DQ (real good heat early but a horrible match), Garvin pinned Valentine (lots of stiff chops but little heat), Genius beat Jose Luis Rivera (dud), Demolition beat Tully Blanchard & Arn Anderson via DQ (interesting here since there is a wrestling radio show in Philadelphia that had reported Tully & Arn losing the titles and said that to show how ridiculous the WWF was, that they would be announced as champs anyway so what happened was Tully & Arn came out with the belts but they were never introduced as champions – by the way, this was the best match on the card), Warrior beat Andre in 17 seconds and Roberts beat with DiBiase via DQ. Most of the crowd Left during the Roberts-DiBiase match.

10/7 in Lincoln, NE drew 2,907 and $38,000 as Tugboat beat Brooklyn clothesline Brawler (Steve Lombardi), Badnews Brown pinned Bossman, Perfect pinned Beefcake, Demolition beat Anderson & Blanchard via count out and

Roberta beat DiBiase via DQ.

10/6 in Salt Lake City drew 3,900 and $45,000 as Tugboat beat Brawler, Hercules beat Jerry Monti (subbing for Volkoff), Brown pinned Hart, Rhodes pinned Bossman, Perfect (Hennig) pinned Beefcake, Demolition beat Anderson & Blanchard via DQ and Roberts beat DiBiase via DQ.

NWA

At least for right now, Bruno Sammartino's appearance as ref on a PPV show is a one-time thing according to an article that will appear in Pittsburgh later this week. Jim Herd was quoted as saying that the NWA did ask Sammartino to work as a color commentator on television but he didn't want to travel weekly. There is still talk that Sammartino may be brought in for a future Clash or PPV card as a color commentator, but it would be a special thing rather than a regular thing. Apparently David Samnartino isn't being considered to come in and that was never talked about as part of the deal with Bruno doing the ref spot.

Ricky Santana will be back in November.

I was amazed that the NWA announcers acknowledged Sammartino's two reigns as WWF champion, although if you think about it, it shouldn't be amazing in the least. What I was more amazed at was two weeks back on TBS, when plugging the I Quit match at the Omni, Jim Cornette brought up that Flair submitted against Ricky Steamboat in the second fall in New Orleans. That's certainly more honesty than one expects from wrestling commentators, especially when it concerns a wrestler who is no longer with the group and in fact, is on bad terms with the group. I guess it's hard to ignore something that six million people saw ive, though. They are also acknowledging Tom Zenk as the Z-Man, which is an about-face from a few weeks back.

Ricky Santana returns in November.

Kazuo Sakurada (better known in the United States as Kendo Nagasaki) will debut at the TV tapings on Tuesday night in Marietta, GA as "The Dragon Master". His gimmick will be a shaved bald head, shaved eyebrows and he walks to the ring backwards and leaves his back to his opponent and when the foe attacks, he does a quick spin kick to nail him. Yes, he'll be managed by Gary Hart and team with Muta and basically is getting the spot Dick Slater lost as it appears he won't be returning here after going on the Japan tour. Those of you who thought Slater shouldn't have been pushed should be really thrilled at his replacement. Anyway, they will bill Dragon Master as a gangster-type who was banned from wrestling in Japan because of bad connections but Gary Hart somehow got him into the U.S. as a wrestler. Power Hour on 10/6 drew a 1.8 rating (headlined by Animal vs. Jack Victory), World Championship Wrestling on 10/7 drew a 2.3 (peaking at a 2.7 for the Luger vs. PilLman match) and Main Event on 10/8 drew a 2.1 (Skyscrapers vs. Rich

& Gilbert). The only promising sign of the weekend is that the TBS Saturday show actually delivered roughly as many households as Titan's two shows and the audience grew throughout a two-hour period. On the other hand, unlike Titan, it didn't buck NFL programming and a 2.3 rating for that show, even of Late, would only be described as decent.

10/10 in Orlando, FL drew 1,600 as Tom Zenk beat Cuban Assassin ½ *, Steve Williams pinned Mike Rotunda * ½, Brian Pillman pinned Eddie Gilbert ** (Gilbert played full-fledged heel), Steiners double count out with Skyscrapers ****, Freebirds bbat. Pillman & Johnny Ace **, Sting beat Muta via DQ ½ *, Lex Luger pinned Tommy Rich * ½ and Ric Flair pinned Terry Funk *** (advertised as a Texas Death match everywhere but turned out to be a regular match - how can they continue to do things like that?).

10/14 in Baltimore drew 4,500 as Rich pinned Cuban DUD, Zenk put Bill Irwin to sleep * ½, Midnight Express beat New Zealand Militia ** ¼ (lots of apparent heat with Cornette and Stan Lane throughout the match), Funk pinned Pillman when Gary Hart was supposed to brush PilIman's foot off the ropes at the finish but Gary didn't get there on time and Pillman had to move his own foot off the ropes *** ¼, Skyscrapers beat Road Warriors via DQ when Paul Ellering got the key from Teddy Long and hit Dan Spivey with it **, Lex Luger double count out with Sting in 19:25 *** ¾, Freebirds beat Steiner's in 17:30 when Hayes pinned Scott after a clothesline * ¾ and Ric Flair beat Muta via DQ when Muta blew the mist in 24:00 when caught in the figure four leg Lock **. They had the same results match-for-match the next night in Greensboro but drew just 2,200 fans, which is horrendous considering the line-up.

I realize, as the Mr. Mike saying goes, that Jesus Christ with an Etch-a-sketch couldn't draw in the NWA right now, but these well-below-average houses even with Warriors vs. Skyscrapers, Flair vs. Muta and Luger vs. Sting does not bode well for the direction the NWA is going in.

Sting isn't going heel. That was a misprint last week when I was speculating about a possible Flair-Tully-Arn vs. Slater-Muta-Funk feud and mistakenly put Sting instead of Slater in there. It was purely my speculation, not the result of anything I've been told about future plans. Truthfully, I have no idea what's coming up next.

10/6 in Norfolk drew 2,700 as Ranger Ross pinned Brad Anderson DUD, Zenk put Irwin to sleep * , Norman the Lunatic pinned Rich * ½, Dudes beat Militia ** ¼, Skyscrapers beat Midnight Express ** ½, Pillman pinned Cuban * ½, Steiner s beat Freebirds via DQ *** ¼, Sting beat Muta via DQ *** ¼, Luger pinned Williams ** ½ and Flair beat Funk in a deathmatch when Funk couldn't answer the bell for the seventh fall *** ½.

9/30 in Buffalo, NY drew 7,000 as Eddie Gilbert beat Cuban, Zenk beat Norman, Sid Vicious beat Johnny Ace, Rotunda pinned Gilbert (sub for Williams who was in

Lakewood, CO at his high school homecoming football game being honored by his school), Warriors beat Militia (surprisingly good), Sting beat Muta via DQ, Luger pinned Rich, Freebirds beat Midnight and Flair pinned Funk.

The Flair-Muta matches are totally scientific until the last four minutes, with them exchanging technical holds similar to UWF style minus the kicks. From what I was told, for what they are trying to do in the ring, the matches are excellent, just that the fans aren't educated to appreciate exchanging holds so they are disappointed with the matches. They want to see a match of brawling by Flair and flying by Muta since "holds" aren't over with today's public. They can be if pushed correctly, as Dusty Rhodes got the Weaver Lock over huge and it's nothing special, simply because it was pushed so hard but without the announcers explaining the holds to the fans, it's hard for them to mean anything at the arenas.

TBS digitalized Flair's face (since he was bleeding) on the Friday night Power Hour match with Slater (good action but cheap walkout count out finish) so they are serious about no blood on television. Luger and Williams had a damn good TV match on Sunday taped from Salisbury, MD. Luger DQ'd for hitting Williams with a chair.

THE READERS' PAGE

DISCLAIMERS

With all the controversy surrounding the plastic bag incident, the time has come to ask a question. Should a disclaimer be put on the TV screen before each wrestling show begins, informing the viewers that what they are about to watch is not an athletic contest and the violence shown is staged.

Years ago, Vince McMahon would begin his wrestling programs by saying, "The following wrestling exhibitions require discretionary viewer participation". This warning was quickly dropped. Why? Was it too much for the viewers to handle? or was it too much for the promotion to admit?

The vast majority of the American public as well as the vast majority of wrestling fans know that pro wrestling is a work and the violence is simulated. By informing the public that what they are about to see isn't real, it sends the kids a message. It's not okay to do to their friends or their enemies what the wrestlers do to one another. The disclaimer can go something like, "The following program should be viewed for entertainment purposes only. An even stronger added message could be, "It is not presented as literal content. The station can also mention that parental discretion is advised. Is the viewing public ready for this? Is pro wrestling ready for this? I think the answer to both questions has to be,"Yes"

Vincent DiPalma
Copiague, New York

Dave Meltzer: Nearly ten years ago, shortly after Bearcat

Wright and Ron Pope testified to the California State Athletic Commission claiming racist and discriminatory business practices by promoter Roy Shire in San Francisco, on the local wrestling show the local stations would start out with, "The following wrestling exhibitions are for entertainment purposes only". The winners and losers have been predetermined by the promoter. Disclaimers such as this would meet with a ton of resistance among all wrestling promotions. The only reason they did it here, or would do it elsewhere would be if a TV station demanded it and the promotion had no other choice of TV station in the market, or because of insistence by the local state athletic commission. Although there are exceptions, most commissions don't like to buck the big promotions since a large chunk of commission revenue comes from taxing the live gates of the wrestling shows, and if a disclaimer of this type were to lower crowds, it would also lower commission revenue.

LARRY CAMERON

I disagree with you that Larry Cameron is overrated. He has perfected a gimmick, knows its boundaries and won't deviate from it. He also gives tremendous interviews which border on scary but can be funny as well. One of the problems critics face is that the majority of our opinions comes from gossip, tapes and hard news, not through actually watching a performer over a lengthy period of time. I believe if the world was given that opportunity with Cameron, they'd find him to be a Road Warrior, Badnews Brown, Stan Hansen and Chris Champion all in one. In my opinion, the All Japan promotion recreates live action on television better than any other promotion. Actual tension can be felt even watching their matches on television. New Japan and the NWA, when they have Clash cards are close. If we could figure a way to give a TV fan half the action fans see and feel at a PWA match at George's in Fridley, MN, we could all retire now, because the fans go nuts. I agree with Ed Sharkey. Newsletters can't hurt the wrestling business, but they do enhance it. They allow wrestlers to make proper career moves, give honest accounts of gates and how territories are doing, and keep rip-off artists accountable for their actions. Sharkey says, "They're written by fans and all they do is tell us what they want to see."

Ray Whebbe
WWTC Radio and PWA promoter
St. Paul, Minnesota

DUSTY RHODES

I find it very ironic that the WWF bills Dusty Rhodes as "The American Dream" and that every time he got touched in the ring in Tulsa, he shouted out, "Oh Shit", for the promotion that prides itself on entertaining the kids.

Name withheld by request

TOO MUCH COMPLAINING

After reading the Observer for the past four years there is one thing that I've noticed about your readers. They are always picking apart the promotions and the wrestlers and comparing the WWF to the NWA.

You can't compare apples to oranges. They are as different as night and day and always will be. I get the feeling the majority of your readers only follow wrestling so they can pick it apart. In every PPV event that is talked about, we hear how the lighting was bad, the camera work was bad, the wrestling was bad, etc.

We can't today's fans just watch the show and enjoy the soap opera. I've been a fan for over 30 years and I've learned that's the most enjoyable way to do it. Today's fan wants to be in the know. Why? If they would just enjoy the product instead of finding fault with the product they would have more fun. And if you don't like what you see, why not take up a different hobby.

The WWF and the NWA and all the other promotions provide entertainment for the fans. You have a choice. Take it or leave it. If you don't like what you see or pay for, don't buy it in the future. I would be the first to admit wrestling is different today than in years past, but I still enjoy it. My advice to today's fans is, don't try and be smart, just enjoy the show. You'll have more fun.

George Schire
St. Paul, Minnesota

NWA

Please keep on the NWA so they can get their act together. They always seem to go forward one step and immediately retreat two. The Halloween show looks good on paper. The NWA was very good for wrestling in Houston and I wish they would return. The AWA is a joke. My Emergency Volunteer group has contacted them for a fundraiser and we didn't even get a thank you but no thank you letter. Have you heard anything about the NWA doing fundraisers?

Al Tyner
Houston, Texas

Dave Meltzer: Haven't heard of any plans for the NWA to get heavily into fundraiser type shows. Those are generally done in small towns and communities and NWA is still trying to mainly run larger cities.

In the past you have documented the biggest problem of the NWA, which is how the public perceives the promotion. It is useless to even compare Ric Flair with Hulk Hogan simply because the general public thinks Hogan is better. The reason is obvious. Hogan makes Flair look Like a dwarf. I realize people think if Flair had any promotional muscle behind him the NWA would shoot past the WWF in popularity but that is a ludicrous view. Ric Flair has been

on top of the NWA for the past 10 years and has proven that he is nothing more than a regional draw. So what does the NWA do? They give Flair supreme power as far as talent pushes and angles. The first thing he did was bring in Dick Slater and form the dreaded J-Texas corporation. Just because his name is Ric Flair, everyone overlooks that Slater and Gary Hart are getting big pushes and Paul E. Dangerously was fired. Flair's first weeks as booker are strongly reminiscent of Dusty Rhodes' years at the helm but because of Flair's technical ability in the ring, people overlook his faults. The future Of the NWA lies in Lex Luger, Sting, Muta and Sid Vicious, but the future won't be here until Ric Flair realizes he isn't the franchise that everyone has built him up to be. The NWA can't seriously challenge the WWF until Jim Herd can get a booker who doesn't make decisions only to satisfy the booker and his friends.

John McMullen
Haddonfield, New Jersey

I was just recently fortunate enough to see the Baltimore Bash and would like to thank all involved for putting this show together. The whole event was superb and shows what a great promotion the NWA is capable of being.

Does the NWA have any intentions of promoting outside North America in the near future? In this country, ex-promoter Steve Rickard (who promoted NWA shows here before 1986) appears in the newspapers from time-to-time claiming to be negotiating with the NWA for upcoming tours, but since this isn't accompanied by publicity for the NWA and its stars, I assume this is more an exercise in self-promotion than a genuine attempt to bring the NWA here.

Frank Shanley
Uptter Hutt, New Zealand

Dave Meltzer: Haven't heard of any plans for the NWA to promote outside of the United States.

The NWA rolled into town last night, but it was more like open mic night at the comedy club. It was a great card, but I 've never seen a card where nearly every match went for comedy at some point. I'm really sick of the "peanut-head" chant. Tommy Rich went to the mic twice to get the crowd to chant. The Skyscrapers vs. Midnight Express was as good as both of the Express vs. Fantastics matches they had last year in Pittsburgh. The Freebirds came out with only one title belt. Now I know that one of the belts was stolen, but that was more than a month ago. They should have replaced it by now. How can you believe that there might be a title change when there isn't a belt to change hands. It's little things like this that makes the NWA look like a minor league. The last Sting-Muta match in Pittsburgh was terrible, but this one more than made up for it. In the suicide move of the show, Muta mounted the top rope to do the moonsault press, Sting sprang up from the mat and threw a vertical standing dropkick at least seven feet high. He caught Muta in the butt, who grabbed the top rope just before falling over the top rope and crotched himself. The finish saw Muta use the mist and ref DQ'd him. That was controversial since Muta has never been disqualified for using the mist before. Still, it was the best match I t ve ever seen live.

While this was the best live card I've seen since they came here for the 1988 Bash, there are still a lot of things that make the NWA look second-rate. First, the sound system was terrible. They had a guy at the timekeepers desk with a cassette player and a box of tapes. Not only was it terrible to watch this guy changing tapes for the wrestlers, they didn't even have the box wired into the sound system. The guy just held the mic up to the speaker and let it play. Entrance music is a major ingredient in a wrestler getting heat from the crowd. When you can hardly hear it, or when it sounds so horrible that you can't tell what it is, it defeats the purpose of using it.

A second problem was the chairs they had at ringside. They were these flimsy looking orange plastic chairs and didn't look a bit dangerous. The wrestlers tried to use them, but since they wouldn't fold, they weren't effective. Terry Funk got so frustrated he tore the leg off one of them and tossed the rest of the chair aside. Since chairs and other ringside props are frequently used in matches, you'd think they would have an appropriately lethal looking chair at ringside. I know they have them in the building. I guess none of the road guys thought it was important enough to check. That's just one more little thing that makes the NWA house shows look second rate.

I'm not as enthused about the NWA today as I was in June. The Flair-Funk feud has held up very well but the real test is when Flair has to fight someone other than Funk. I know that Funk will retire in May and Flair will probably feud with Luger, but I don't know if his current popularity will hold up.

The upcoming Dudes vs. Midnight feud bothers me. It's obvious Cornette will go with the Dudes. After being the Express' manager for six years and being so vehement about not breaking up the act that they left the NWA earlier in the year, that he would leave them for a minor talent like the Dudes bugs me, especially since it's probably his idea. There was definite hostility toward the Dudes here, since the Midnight Express is the most popular tag team in Pittsburgh, even though ShanenDouglas is from Pittsburgh and is something of a local hero, he was still getting a lot of hostility. If there was a Dudes vs. Midnight match, I believe the crowd would be heavily booing the hometown hero.

Andy Stowell
Pittsburgh, Pennsylvania

It's taken me a long time to admit this, but I've grown to dislike the WWF, especially over the last year. From the advent of Brother Love to Hulk Hogan's Oscar-winning performance at Elizabeth's bedside to the recent coronation of the Macho King, the WWF has become nothing more than a glorified and slickly packaged carnival side-show. Terry Taylor, Barry Windham and even Dusty Rhodes ought to be ashamed of themselves and the product they try to pass off as wrestling. It's unfortunate that these once-great wrestlers have traded in their own personalities in exchange for cheap cartoon symbols who act and react to every whim of Vince McMahon.

I had hoped, since I've become an NWA fan in the last year, that I would be able to enjoy wrestling as I had once known it. I think early in the year, during the Flair vs. Steamboat encounters, this was the case. However, with the recent turn of events in the NWA, I wonder if they are going the way of the WWF. What do you think? I 'd hope not, but am interested in your comments.

Name withheld by request

Dave Meltzer: Wrestling is always going to be changing because if it weren't to change, it would become stale and predictable. Some of the changes aren't always good. Some of them people won't like, and if the promotions pay attention, they'll recognize which work and which don't and act accordingly (except in the case of the WWF which markets so well that really brainwashes because of excellent usage of propaganda that the rest of the promotions haven't mastered that it can get over most of what it wishes to and McMahon controls the direction of the fans rather than the fans controlling any direction the promotion goes). NWA can't turn into the WWF because to get that over, you have to have a big production budget to use those same brainwashing techniques to get them to work. But " story-lines" are going to be a part of wrestling in the next decade, as are exaggerated personalities.

AWARDS FAVORITES

Before getting into this week's categories, I want to mention a little about the plans for the upcoming yearbook. The yearbook will hopefully be completed by mid-January and be back from the printer in early February. I expect it will be in the neighborhood of 100 pages. I don't want to list a price because I'm not sure the length it will wind up being, but it will be part of the subscription plan as in years past. All of the regular yearbook features will be there, such as a rundown of all the major news stories of 1989, the awards, a list of all major title changes for the year, the annual ratings and a directory of all major active wrestlers with heights, weights, ages, real names, years pro and hometowns. In addition, the Observer will present "Decade Awards" in a few categories and have lengthy features on how pro wrestling has changed during the 1980s, several lists, including the 100 best matches of the decade and personality profiles of the biggest name wrestlers of the decade. I'm looking for outside contributions for the yearbook and if anyone has ideas for feature stories, either on trends that have changed wrestling, predictions on where wrestling is going, comedy pieces or anything else of the sort, please contact me.

A major portion of every yearbook is the awards section. Each week here through the end of November we'll be running down a few categories. Balloting for the awards is open to all subscribers during the month of December and we run down a complete list of categories at that time.

MOST UNIMPROVED: This is for wrestlers whose work and match quality has dropped significantly over the past year. Some people come to mind here. Stan Lane's decline has been noticeable since the Midnight Express as a team seems to have lost a step. They've gone in a lot of people's eyes from being the clear-cut best tag team in the business and one of the best teams of the decade (Tag Team of the year 1986-88) to just another tag team this year. George Gray was a decent big man as One Man Gang, but a pathetic one as Akeem. Jim Duggan used to be fun to watch, but he may be one of the worst performers to watch nowadays. Jerry Lawler seems to rely almost exclusively on shortcuts, at least in his matches in Dallas, even though he's one of the most knowledgable working heels around.

Barry Windham is still one of the better workers in the business, but he is not anything close to what he was at the beginning of the year. In January, many would argue that Windham was the best performer in the business. With the added weight, he appears slow and sluggish even though he is still one of the better wrestlers around. Tatsumi Fujinami was No. 1 in last years' ratings but declined steadily in 1989. Now, due to a back injury, his career is in grave jeopardy. Dick Murdoch hasn't been so hot in this country, except on rare occasions, in a few years although he's always been good to great in Japan. His recent Japan stuff hasn't been anything special. Owen Hart declined greatly in the WWF, but once he got out of the WWF his work picked up again. Biff Wellington seemed to be one of the best young workers around last year, but his progress seems to have stifled. Jake Roberts has lost a lot, some due to his injuries, and in fact from a work standpoint, the injuries are probably the main reason for his decline. Roddy Piper's actual work in his comeback has been disappointing. Maybe on interviews it isn't fair to compare him to his old work since that is quite a high standard, but in the ring his recent stuff has been pretty bad, although again, he's working when he's far from 100 percent, but he also lacks the fire in the ring he once had. Hiroshi Hase was one of the top 10 in the world 18 months ago. He's still good, but now he's just another face in the New Japan crowd.

ROOKIE OF THE YEAR: The two that stand out in my mind are Wayne Bloom in the AWA and Dustin Rhodes. Both have had some exciting matches despite being short on experience. By the way, the definition of rookie here is someone who hadn't worked full-time for a regular promotion prior to September of 1988. Rhodes started in September, while Bloom had worked some independent shots before that but his first "real job" was in the AWA this year. Salman Hashimikov became the first rookie to capture a major World title that I've ever heard of when he beat Big Van Vader in Japan and lost the title later in the year to Riki Choshu. For "success" and "push" he should win. He's still not smooth and doesn't do high spots, but his suplexes are hot and he has had some good matches, albeit with top notch guys. Victor Zangiev is a better worker than Hashimikov and actually has potential to be another Hiro Hase, but hasn't gotten as big of a push. Forget the rest of the Soviets.

WORST MANAGER: Mr. Fuji is still around to be kicked around. Fuji has won this thing four times in the past five years and was a close second the other year. His main competition, Paul Jones, has disappeared. Fuji's main WWF proteges, the Powers of Pain, are also probably the least over-pushed act in the WWF despite their massive size and ominous look. And to make it worse, the duo was over a whole lot more before being put with Fuji. And think of how much more over Demolition is now without Fuji? As far as Fuji's challengers, while Tojo Yamamoto cracks me up every time he opens his mouth he is really bad. Percy Pringle as a babyface is too much to take. That televangelist delivery on a babyface is really annoying. Gary Hart is far from the worst, but he's being pushed way too hard. I still haven't figured out what Abdul Wizal adds, well I have, but that's another story.

OCTOBER 30, 1989

Before starting out this issue, I'd Like to sincerely thank all of you that showed so much genuine concern the past few days in how everything went with the earthquake here on Tuesday. We were literally flooded with phone calls, even more so than the week after WrestleMania from people from all over the country and from five foreign countries as well concerned with what happened here. I know that many others tried to get through at various times but the phone company blocked most phone calls in and out of here until late in the week. Anyway, things are fine out here and aside from some minor inconveniences, the earthquake didn't have much affect on myself personally. I feel very fortunate because others in the area weren quite so lucky.

Campbell, California, where I live, is located about 15 miles from the epicenter of the earthquake. Tuesday's are usually the easiest days here, since the issue normally is completed on Monday afternoons (except on holiday weekends or weekends of major shows like this coming weekend) and comes back from the printer on Wednesday and is mailed out that afternoon. Ironically, since the temperature was in the high 80s and sunny, my plan was to do just the typical bookkeeping work and head to the beach in Santa Cruz around noon, but I had one fairly important business call to make and was told I'd be called back soon. Well, luckily I wasn't called back, and worked here most of the afternoon and caught up on some recent videotapes when the earthquake hit. Most Likely I'd have been returning from Santa Cruz on Highway 17 at about the time the quake hit. In retrospect, being on a mountain highway right about at the epicenter of an earthquake of that magnitude isn't the most appeteizing idea. As it was, I was home on the phone when the thing hit. For anyone who has lived in California for any length of time, earthquakes are no big deal. They occur with decent regularity, give you a little shake, sometimes they knock the stacked boxes in the grocery store over but usually they are relatively harmless. This jolt was tons more powerful than any earthquake I can recall, and in fact was the biggest since 1906. The shaking was so strong that I did expect our building to go down, but in reality it was basically unharmed. About the worst thing I can say is that my cabinet of videotapes was knocked over so I wound up with a few hundred tapes on the floor, many of which were unmarked. But if having to reorganize a videotape collection was the worst thing that happened, especially considering how serious the damage was in communities in close proximity to here, then I've got no right to complain.

Even though the earthquake was so powerful and did a lot of property damage and resulted in loss of lives for some, I'd bet most residents of this area would tell you that the aftermath was a lot worse than the actual earthquake. Between the power outages and water line breakages and constant threat of fires, along with telephone calls being blocked so one couldn't check on friends and loved ones, that was the real scary part of the ordeal.

As it turns out, even though the property damage was in the billions of dollars, from phone calls here and also from later articles in the newspaper locally, the consensus seems to be that the national media caused somewhat of an over-panic from the rest of the country, and in fact, the rest of the world, with its earthquake coverage. I mean, I was really touched at the concern of so many people from over the world who were glad to hear that I was alive. But in reality, the vast majority of the area's residents were slightly shaken up, but fine. Those who called, after seeing the harrowing news footage of the broken bridge and the highway collapse thought this place was like Hiroshima after the bomb was dropped. There were places where things were leveled of course, but at the same time, I don't know very many people in Charlotte, N.C. , but most of those I talked with after Hurricane Hugo had some fairly serious damage to their homes or certainly far more inconvenience than most people did here. I know a lot of people here, and don't know anyone with serious home damage.

Still, between a few days during the week where it was impossible to do anything related to gathering information, and very limited mail service through the weekend, this isn't going to be one of the stronger issues when it comes to news content.

For those in the area, the earthquake forced cancellation of Titan's card Friday night at the Cow Palace in San Francisco. The card will be rescheduled for 11/28, which is a Tuesday night. The reason it is being moved to a midweek date (since, with the exception of television tapings, Titan has cut down on midweek shows) is with no other major shows booked that night, Titan will be able to bring virtually the same card advertised into town with the Roddy Piper vs. Rick Rude main event. The advance for the card as of Tuesday was more than 7,000 tickets so the gate probably would have been in the $120,000 range. Interestingly enough, Titan also has a show booked two nights earlier at the Oakland Coliseum Arena, which is the same market and primarily serves the same fans and is promoted off the same television.

With the earthquake postponing the World Series until this coming Friday night, it means that Game Four of the series will go head-to-head with the NWN s "Halloween Havoc" pay-per-view show on Saturday night from Philadelphia.

Between competition already with the Miami vs. Florida State football game on ESPN, things don't look good for the PPV success of this show. I was of the opinion that even with the weak Line-up for a PPV show, that the success of the previous PPV shows and just the fact the show has been hyped so strongly on television and that the TV ratings at least haven't declined and that the Clash drew a good number, that they'd be able to pull a one percent hardcore fandom even against the college football game and with what many are saying would be the disadvantage of running PPV on a Saturday night when many people won stay home. With the added competition of the World Series, which starts at 8:35 p.m. Eastern time (PPV runs from 7-10 p.m. Eastern), not to mention competition from their own World Championship Wrestling show during the first hour on TBS, all bets are now off. Yes, some of this can now be chalked up to horrible luck, but I hope that if the number is abnormally low, that they use the World Series game as a complete excuse for a lack of success. If they do decent, and by decent, I'm talking one percent, they should breathe a sigh of relief and do cartwheels all next week. But if it's less than an 0.7 or an 0.8, yes they can blame the World Series for some problems, but they'd better blame themselves for a lot of other problems.

The trial of Hawaiian-based pro wrestling promoters Lia Maivia, Larry Heiniemi (Lars Anderson) and Ati So'o on charges of extortion began last week in Hawaii. Maivia, 58, is the widow of Peter Maivia, and took over as the main wrestling promoter in Hawaii several years back. Heiniemi is the Secretary-Treasurer of Maivia's Polynesian Pro Wrestling promotion while So'o is the vice president. The three were charged with attempting to extort money from John Wakayama (known in pro wrestling under the name Dunbar Wakayama, who at one time worked with Maivia's promotion as a television announcer) when he promoted shows of his own in Hawaii last November. Assistant U.S. Attorney Michael Burke told the jury on the first day of the trial that Wakayama received a threatening phone call on his business phone recorder and recognized the voice as So'o's. The call, riddled with expletives, told Wakayama to stay out of the wrestling business and threatened Wakayama s children. So'o's name was later mentioned by Maivia when she and Heiniemi later demanded $5,000 from Wakayama. The three defendants had differing stories. They simply claimed that Maivia and Wakayama had a business dispute and that he was making this up to force Maivia out of the wrestling business in Hawaii and claimed Wakayama was using the threat as an excuse ahead of time because he knew he'd lost a ton of money promoting. According to figures in the trial, Wakayama lost $66,000 promoting a series of cards in Hawaii using lots of big-name talent from the United States and Japan including the Funk brothers, Stan Hansen, Jerry Blackwell and Michael Hayes. So'o's attorney

told the jury that he would present an expert witness who would prove that the voice on the recording machine wasn't that of So'o. So'o's defense is at odds with the defense that Maivia and Heiniemi are making, as they are claiming So'o made the call but without their authorization. So'o claims the call was made by Faasamoa Mausali (a wrestler and referee for Maivia's group known as Sam Samson). The prosecution is expected to call Mausali to testify on its behalf during the trial. It is well known within wrestling circles that every promotion that has run shows in Hawaii, including the Japanese groups and the NWA has worked with Mai via and used her wrestlers on the undercard. Not so coincidentally Maivia promoted a show on Friday night in Honolulu, during the trial, in which the proceeds would go to fighting drug abuse on the island.

The WWF announced on Sunday night that the 1990 Royal Rumble PPV card would take place on January 21st in Orlando, FL, which would be Titan's first-ever PPV show from the Southeast. Titan insiders are expecting that show will be its weakest in terms of buy rate. Last year's Rumble was Titan's weakest PPV buy rate ever, gathering about a 1.5 percent of potential viewers or a similar rate to the NWA' s most recent PPV show from Baltimore. The original Royal Rumble in 1988 was a USA network special and still holds the record for the highest cable television rating ever, garnering an 8.2 rating which is the highest rating of any kind for the USA network. Royal Rumble will be part of a series of almost monthly PPV events. The NWA runs this coming Saturday in Philadelphia, WWF follows on Thanksgiving night from the Rosemont Horizon with Survivors Series, NWA follows on Dec. 13 with Starrcade from the Omni in Atlanta, WWF back on Dec. 27 with the Hogan vs. Zeus match which will probably be a taped match, WWF back with Royal Rumble on Jan. 21, NWA will run WrestleWar '90 on Feb. 25 (site yet to be determined) and WWF returns on April 1 with WrestleMania (Latest word is that the Los Angeles Coliseum has the inside track to be the live venue although Toronto is still in the running. Contrary to what may have been printed elsewhere, the decision has yet to be reached).

Qintex, the Australian-based company that was responsible for bankrolling the RollerGames in syndication, filed for bankruptcy this past week according to sources both in Australia and also an article in Saturday's Los Angeles Times. No word on how this will affect the future of the Roller Games. Qintex was also sued recently by MGM when it was claimed Qintex misrepresented themselves when it came to a proposed purchase of the company. The RollerGames were banking on becoming a trendy hit in syndication with the high-gloss production values and attempting to copy the success of Titan Sports in merchandising deals. However, the show just isn't making any kind of a major splash and the group has been completely unsuccessful in marketing any of the skaters' names or the show itself to the public to the level necessary for major merchandising revenue. No word yet on whether a second 13-week cycle of shows will be taped. Even if they are, it's expected they'll have their time slots downgraded by many of the stations because ratings were nowhere near the 7 rating stations had been projecting for the show.

To say the future of the NWA doesn't look good right now is to state the obvious. After nearly one year of ownership by Turner Broadcasting, the NWA is in major turmoil. Right now, there is no indication that anything on the horizon looks bright. Sweeping changes are expected to be made, although what those changes will be is anyone's guess. All sorts of figures are bandied around as far as the money that the World Championship Wrestling company lost during its first year. I don't want to list any figures because nobody who knows for sure is going to give out an honest figure anyway. Some figures could be pure propaganda either by competitors to lure wrestlers away or make them concerned over the future, propaganda to satisfy wrestlers to not worry about their future, or propaganda to talk them into taking a pay cut when the contracts start expiring early next year. The major sources of revenue are house shows, television advertising revenue and PPV revenue. Without question, house shows for the most part have been a disaster this year. It's hard to get a figure on television ad revenue. It is generally based on TV ratings, which have been fair. The numbers are down from last year, but in no greater proportion than the WWF ratings have fallen. Still, on the NWA shows, you see the same basic ads over-and-over, which makes me think that, like virtually all wrestling snows including the WWF, the shows don generate the advertising income and can't charge ad rates for a similar show like a sitcom or drama or movie that would deliver the same-sized audience because advertisers still believe wrestling's primary audience is a lowbrow audience with less spendable income. The NWA's PPV shows have been about as well as could be expected given its TV ratings at the times of the specific shows, although I'm sure TBS expected to generate more income from P PV this year.

Given the costs of running house shows around the country with dozens of high-salaried performers and high-salaried executives, coupled with these house shows not drawing, one has to believe that the losses are in the millions even factoring in PPV and TV ad money.

So, what about the future? To keep going in the current direction without major changes isn't going to change anything. Anyone who thinks that continuing down the same path that put Jim Crockett out of business and put this company in a shambles when it comes to live events will eventually reap profitable results is only kidding themselves. Perhaps my personal greatest frustration in looking at the NWA over the past year was, like during the Crockett regime, the company continually made excuses rather than dealt with the problems at hand and corrected the problems that needed correcting. Virtually all the same mistakes over the fall quarter of 1988, when Dusty Rhodes nearly totally sabotaged this group and left it for dead, are occuring today. Constant no-shows at the house shows without explanation. The same non-satisfying finishes month-after-month at the house shows. The same wrestlers being pushed month-after-month with little influx of new talent pushed to the top of the card. Terrible syndicated television shows. Poor local promotion of house shows. Angles on television having little to do with line-ups at the house shows. And advertised line-ups not taking place as promised, with gimmicks changing and matches changing with no explanation to the fans. That's just the problems with the live shows.

This has been written before here a few months back but bears repeating. Those in charge of the NWA have to decide exactly what they want to be and go in that direction. If they want to be major league, that is a very risky proposition and one that will cost them millions before they will see a profit, if they ever see a profit. But the only way to succeed to the point that PPV is a viable alternative and promoting national is an alternative is to be perceived by fans as major league, which right now they aren't. If they want to be minor league, then realize right now what that means. They can provide cheap programming for the superstation and maybe run a few localized syndicated shows. TV ad money will be cut down, but so will be expenses of paying big money for time slots in major markets. Salaries will have to be sliced for the big names, and the number of wrestlers will have to be cut back. The result of this will be even fewer fans at the house shows then they now have. Figure most gates just slightly above the level of the failing groups in this country, like $5,000 to $10,000 and maybe pop a $20,000 or $30,000 house every now and then. If they can't survive with gates like that, then perhaps most house shows will have to be eliminated.

I see four options right now. Option No. 1 is to continue the same course. We already know where that leads and it's simply throwing good money after bad. The general public will not support what it perceives as minor league wrestling. At least not to a great enough extent that it can be profitable carrying huge salaries and running nightly house shows. Option No. 2 is to fold up right now. That isn't going to happen. Short term economically one can argue that it could be justified, given the fact that this company being profitable in the foreseeable future is unlikely under any circumstances.

Option No. 3 is to scale back and keep the promotion going as a regional minor league promotion. Let's be realistic about what that means. First off, even with cutting back the big salaries, a company of this type isn't going to be profitable. Every small promotion in this country is losing money right now and in its weakest state in history, save perhaps Don Owen in the Pacific Northwest and they are hardly doing any great shakes either. The small promotions survived in the pre-1984 era, and many flourished because they were, for the most part, monopolistic businesses, not because they were run by geniuses that booked better cards or anything. With competition from a group with more glitz, everyone crumbled away. Their flaws became apparent to the fans who never saw the flaws before because they had nothing to compare them with. The prime benefit of taking this option is that the money losses wouldn't be as great, the risks aren't high in comparison with options No. 1 or No. 4 and at least it would provide fairly cheap weekly programming which would deliver ratings for the Superstation and in some syndicated markets in fringe time slots. The ratings would be down from what they are now, but they'd still probably get fair ratings from the type of viewer who will watch any wrestling that's on television. Most of the top stars will leave for Titan. Not all, because Titan can't or won't absorb them all, but anyone who gets hot is going to leave, just Like what would happen if a phenom gets hot in one of the smaller groups right now. Forget PPV at this point. The horses won't be there to get people to get hyped enough to spend money on wrestling like this. They'll watch for free, but they'll spend their money on the major League. In fact, running a large number of house shows, even in a small regional market, would be anti-productive because they aren't going to draw.

The final option is the most risky. It's the best one for the wrestling fans and for the wrestling business and certainly for the wrestlers. Guaranteed it will lose money at the beginning. As much, if not more than the NWA did this year. Its chances of success aren't good, particularly over the short haul. Over the long haul, if successful, this company could be quite profitable. That, of course, is to compete as a major league. Major league office. Major league promotion of live cards. Major league promotion of PPV cards (which is the one area that I would say they are very strong in already). Major league syndicated television. The one factor which could make this risk worthwhile is PPV television. By next year, there is a good chance if TCI has its way, that the number of homes that have PPV availability will increase to 20 million (it's around 12.5 million right now)'. If buy rates stay the same, or even if they drop slightly, that still means a lot more revenue with basically the same expenses. If, as predicted, by 1995, the number of PPV homes is 40 million, then all of a sudden a one percent buy rate and $20 price tag per show will generate $8 million, and if that can be done three or four times per year, even with the splits with cable companies, you are talking about enough money to make wrestling profitable. If, for some reason, the NWA achieves major league status and could do a two percent buy

rate for three PPV events per year, you are talking about a $48 million gross or probably profits on PPV in excess of $20 million. And if all things stay equal, this is the one area that will make Titan Sports in the next decade because even within the company they are saying that over the next year or two that the number of live events will be less. By major league, that means compete on a major league basis. Since the NWA is world's behind the WWF in every aspect except presentation of PPV shows and actual house show product, they've got to improve all the weak areas. They need to be better than the WWF when it comes to marketing the big shows and television content. I'd suggest cutting back the number of live shows first off, since they are a money loser to begin with. Maybe run three house shows per week (Friday-Saturday-Sunday) and a mid-week TV taping. Use the days off to promote in the weekend cities. Get wrestlers into town early and into the media, or at least on the phone with the local radio stations. The TV could focus more clearly on the shows. Localized interviews for the specific markets could be done because there are fewer shows. Run towns with regularity, so one show follows another logically (which means the booking must be done several months ahead), announce the main matches for the next card at the house show so you can the advance off decent. These aren't radical ideas. They are just what Titan does and it's the difference between a promotion which doesn't offer the best product, but appears to the public to be major league and totally organized, and what the NWA appears to be.

In last weeks 'Matwatch', Steve Beverly wrote some ideas, many of which I agree with, some of which I don't, on the future course of the NWA. Some things go without saying. The NWA needs a better front office staff. Both bigger and better. But right now it's impossible to justify acquisitions and new jobs with as much red ink as the company is running into. That's why the present course is a loser and decisions have to be made. An active performer shouldn't be booking for a national promotion. First off, the long-term plans for everyone need to be focused and developed for months in advance at a time. A full-time wrestler, let alone Ric Flair, the World Champion, is constantly on the road, needs to keep in the best condition year-round because there is no off season, and there just isn't time to be on the road daily, deal with the natural headaches being a booker entails, and maintain the work rate in the ring and do the detail work necessary as booker. The best angles, particularly the PPV angles, are the ones that slowly develop. Randy Savage and Hulk Hogan had been set up for one year before WrestleMania. Hogan and Zeus had five months of build-up before SummerSlam. Starrcade is supposed to be the big show of the year. It is now six weeks away, and nobody even knows what the line-up is and there is nothing that has had that long-term build-up necessary for the main event on the big show of the year. That isn't the fault of the bookers, because the very idea of doing a PPV this close to the big show made it impossible to do long-term building up. But at the same time, WWF got their card to the public on television for a Thanksgiving PPV show earlier than the NWA did for a show in late October. In most cities the NWA runs in live, the live fans usually don't even know the card until two to three weeks in advance while with Titan it's usually a solid five week build-up and the shows are promoted tons better in each of those five weeks. An administration is needed to remove the cut-throating which has killed any progress. All I hear about is how this guy doesn't know anything and that guy doesn't know anything. Well if that's the case, then teach them, don't complain and try to back-stab. There are so many things the NWA did this year that Ray Charles could have seen were disasters, from booking the Silverdome, the Superdome for a TV special, this Clash in Troy, NY, etc. People in the NWA knew about it. But instead of rationally making the change and avoiding the mistake, the shows were and will be run. Wrestlers have to have respect for the authority in the company. They don't have to agree with them, but they have to respect the orders. If a wrestler doesn't do a job, can him. And when a big name is canned, the rest of the names will know that following the bookers' orders has to be respected. When Bob Orton argued about a finish, he was canned. But when Sting wouldn't do a finish, the finish was changed and from that point on, the finishes to appease the wrestlers rather than to draw money on future cards became the result. Wrestlers lost respect, at least some of them, when Sting got away before the Baltimore Bash with not putting Terry Funk over, even though it was necessary before that card to have Funk over as the ultimate heel for Flair's return. This hurt Funk, who quite frankly needed fans to think he was a killer heel from results in the ring more than most because of the age and size factor working against him, thus he had to do it all with nothing but talking. At the same time, Ricky Steamboat put Lex Luger over every night, which was the right thing for the company since Luger needed to get over as the big heel for down the road. But when it was over, Steamboat's contract wasn't renewed. Admittedly, a lot of factors went into this but more than one person in the group and many outside made the connection. Sting didn't do the job and wouldn't help the company when the company needed help and he's still on top. Steamboat would, and he's gone. So much for doing jobs and helping the company.

Right now the NWA is somewhat divided into two camps. The bookers vs. The management. The bookers feel management doesn't know anything about wrestling. They become resentful of the mandates, such as on the blood, the plastic bag angle or whatever. There is a belief among the wrestlers that anyone who isn't a wrestler is a mark, and so the complaint goes, they are managed by marks. Of course one can argue that Vince McMahon Sr., Vince McMahon

Jr., Sam Muchnick, Frank Tunney and Hisashi Shinma combined don't have 30 seconds of in-ring experience, and they all did quite well in producing and directing over the long haul. Of course, there is no Hisashi Shinma running the NWA today. Tiger Mask and the Ding Dongs might seem like a similar gimmick to someone on the outside, but for anyone who actually watches wrestling, the only similarity is both wore unique costumes.

A quick update on Antonio Inoki. We had sketchy reports last week, but Inoki was stabbed by someone who jumped out of the crowd while he was giving a speech on Saturday in Aizuwakamatsu, Japan. Inoki's condition turned out to be more serious than I was originally led to believe. Inoki was given a six centimeter stab wound from underneath his ear across and down to his throat. Inoki suffered a severe loss of blood (2,000 cc's) and while the condition is not life threatening, he's been ordered to stop work and cancel his current commitments for one month. I will assume that means he won't be able to return to wrestling in December as was originally planned. The stabbing of Inoki was reported as the lead news story in most forms of media in Japan.

ALL JAPAN

Jumbo Tsuruta won the triple crown (United National, PWF and International titles) by pinning Genichiro Tenryu in 22:38 in the main event of the 10/11 card in Yokohama before 5,200 fans. The rest of the card saw The Can-Am Express (Doug Furnas & Dan Kroffat) retain the Asian tag team titles beating Kenta Kobashi & Joe Malenko in 23:20 when Kroffat pinned Malenko; Stan Hansen & Toshiaki Kawada downed Yoshiaki Yatsu & Shunji Takano, Masa Fuchi beat Shinichi Nakano submit, Giant Baba & Rusher Kimura & Mitsuo Momota downed Motoshi Okuma & Haruka Eigen & Akira Taue, Dick Slater & Joel Deaton beat Yoshinari Ogawa & Samson Fuyuki, Mighty Inoue & Isamu Teranishi & Goro Tsurumi won the opener from Akio Sato & Tsuyoshi Kikichi & Richard Slinger (nephew of Terry Gordy who made his debut two weeks earlier).

The next major All Japan show was on 10/20 in Nagoya with Tsuruta & Yatsu defending the World tag team titles against Hansen & Tenryu, Can-Am Express defending the Asian tag belts against The Foot Loose and Giant Baba vs. Tiger Jeet Singh.

UWF

The complete line-up for Wednesday night's card in Sapporo (10/25) which is the next show has Yoshiaki Fujiwara vs. Nobuhiko Takada, Akira Maeda vs. Masaharu Funaki, Kazuo Yamazaki vs. Tatsuo Nakano, Yoji Anjyo vs. Minori Suzuki and Shigeo Miyaoo vs. MacDuff Roesch. The next show after that is the 11/29 card at the Tokyo Dome which apparently is going to be a huge success. The card will be televised live throughout Japan. The complete line-up will probably be announced later this week, but the best guess right now is that Maeda will headline against Willy Wilhelm (European judo champion), Fujiwara will face Chris Dolman (former world champion in sambo wrestling) and Takada will face Duane Koslowski, who represented the U.S. as a heavyweight in Greco-Roman wrestling in the 1988 Olympics in Seoul, Korea and placed eighth.

10/1 in Tokyo's Korauken Hall before a sellout 2,400 saw Minoru Suzuki beat Jumbo Barretta in 10:53, Kazuo Yamazaki beat Bart Vail in 11:11 and Akira Maeda beat Shigeo Miyato in 6:15 so they had another card with less than a half hour of actual wrestling.

FMW

This new group run by Atsushi Onita ran its second show on 10/10 in Tokyo's Korauken Hall and drew a sellout 2,400 fans. Atsushi Onita finally defeated karate star Seiji Aoyagi in the fifth round of a hair vs. hair match, The masked man called Boat People Joe beat Billy Mack and unmasked, revealing Tarzan Goto who formerly worked for Baba and was touring the U.S. and lost his job working in Tennessee where he was teaming with Akio Sato after he married former girl wrestler Despina Montaguas against the wishes of certain people. In other matches, Bat Girl beat the Witch Warrior, Mitsuhiro Matsunaga (karate) beat the masked Sambo Kid, Jimmy Backlund beat are Mitsuteru Tokuda (judo) and Masanobu Kurusu (who worked prelims for Baba & Inoki) beat Monkey Magic Wakita. They will run a few more shows in December and Dick Murdoch will be switching to this promotion. This card went over good because the gimmickry is new in Japan and also because the work was stiff, so the wrestlers were respected by the fans. Onita brought the house down after his match, giving the fans a speech.

CWA

10/16 in Memphis before another crowd of less than 1,000 saw Plowboy Stan Frazier (Uncle Elmer) beat Tommy Lane, Cowboy Kevin Dillinger (Alan Martin) drew with Ken Wayne, Freddy (Tommy Gilbert) went to a double disqualification with Chris Champion when both Mark Starr and Dutch Mantell interfered, Mike Davis pinned Dustin Rhodes, Dutch Mantell beat Mark Starr via DQ when Champion interfered, Bill Dundee beat Buddy Landel, Jeff Jarrett beat Dirty White Boy via DQ so DWB kept the CWA title, Rock & Roll Express went to a double count out with The Blackbirds in less than three minutes for the CWA tag team titles but they brawled all over the Coliseum for nearly a half hour after the match, Jerry Lawler kept the USWA title beating The Soul Taker via DQ when Nate the Rat and Ronnie Gossett both interfered and Ricky Morton won the Battle Royal.

On TV on 10/21, as Dirty White Boy was wrestling Kelvin Austin (younger brother of former wrestler Norvell Austin, who had worked as Dream Warrior in previous weeks), Dutch Mantell ran in and they had a similar brawl to the one Brian Pillman and Lex Luger had on TBS a few weeks back. Mantell and White Boy will wrestle for the CWA title at all the house shows this week except in Memphis, where White Boy defends against Kerry Von Erich.

Mark Starr wasn't at TV and Ronnie Gossett came out with Chris Champion and the two started arguing over where Starr was, which is the beginning of the turn of Wildside to baby faces. As it is, they're already getting as many cheers as most of the faces.

Also on TV, Reggie B. Fine, the new manager of the Blackbirds came and told Ricky Morton to pay him $250 because Morton ripped up his shirt the previous Monday and when Morton wouldn't pay, The Blackbirds came out and held Morton while Fine hit him with a baseball bat.

The Lawler-Soul Taker match on Monday ended when Gossett and Nate intteffered but Lawler beat both of them up. Mike Davis and Kevin Dillinger ran in so Lawler was then beating up on five people until the Wildside came out and held Lawler and Soul Taker hit him in the throat with a chair and Lawler took a backwards first bump over the top rope.

Lawler came out on television with a neck brace and Nate the Rat (Nathaniel Whitlock) started harassing Lawler saying that since Lawler was hurt, he couldn't do anything about it. Nate started hitting Lawler and Lawler ripped off the neckbrace and started beating on Nate and when Soul Taker came in, Lawler threw fire at him.

The 10/23 card in Memphis had P. Y. Chu Hi (Phil Hickerson) vs. Ken Wayne, Dundee vs. Dillinger, Brian Lee (who originally was going to return here full-time but reconsidered and is staying in the CWF) vs. Rhodes, Mantell vs. Davis, Wildside vs. Jeff Jarrett & Master of Pain (who works in Dallas as The Masked Punisher), White Boy vs. Kerry for the CWA title, Rock & Roll vs. Blackbirds for the tag title in an explosive match (falls count anywhere in the building) and finale is a lumberjack match for the USWA title with Lawler vs. Soul Taker.

OTHER NEWS NOTES

Chavo Guerrero is now working in Mexico and turned heel recently and is feuding with Rayo de Jalisco Jr. in Mexico City. Eddie Guerrero, who is one of the big stars in Mexico, is still working as a baby face.

Ken Timbs & Mike Stone & Rick Patterson beat Los Brazos for the Mexican version of the World 6-man tag team titles.

Bob Luce is running a card on 11/11 in Hammond, IN and he and Buddy Roberts will have their own television show starting on Ch. 66 in Chicago (replacing USWA in the

Chicago market) starting this week.

Even though Matt Borne lost a loser leaves town match and left the area, he & Jeff Jarrett remain USWA tag team champions.

Bruce Hart beat Great Gama on 10/14 in Lethbridge, ALTA to win the Commonwealth title. Davey Boy Smith beat North American champ Larry Cameron on 10/20 in Calgary in a non-title match. The current tag team champions are The Black Harts, but that is in limbo since no beat Black Harts are in the territory and they are looking to bring two new ones in.

The Samoans are running a card on 11/18 in Philadelphia with John Studd & Junkyard Dog vs. The Samoans on top (a match which truly has to be seen to be believed) plus Ken Patera vs. Kamala and Samoan Kokina vs. Yukon Jack. The WWF will be running a card in the Spectrum on the same night.

Apparently Jonathan Holiday told the police in Canada that it was Jerry Morrow and Dynamite Kid who beat him to a pulp in a dressing room attack in Calgary some weeks back. Morrow is now in Puerto Rico while Dynamite is back in Calgary but not working for Stampede. Right now Dynamite Kid, Johnny Smith, Owen Hart and Steve DiSalvo are living in Calgary, but none of them are wrestling. Don't know if charges were filed against Kid and Morrow.

Most of the Americans working in Puerto Rico were fired as Angel Acevedo (Cuban Assassin from Canada) is the new booker so expect lots of wrestlers from Stampede wrestling to become regulars in Puerto Rico.

Nasty Boys lost the Florida tag team titles to Dennis Knight & Jumbo Baretta on 10/17 in Tampa. Nasties have left the promotion for now and will be headed to Singapore and Malaysia on tour.

Akira Maeda has been in the U.S. of late trying to negotiate for a match with Mike Tyson. Nothing is close to happening except word is he's got a better shot at putting the thing together than Bam Bam Bigelow because of his greater drawing power and the money it's guaranteed to make. Funny, because the biggest money fight Tyson could do now in Japan would be against Maeda and the biggest money fight Tyson could have in the U.S. would be against Hulk Hogan, which I guess says something about the heavyweight division in boxing.

Seiji Sakaguchi will come to the U.S. in November to try and book NWA talent to appear for one night in February on the Tokyo Dome show.

Ch. 52 in Los Angeles is now broadcasting Red Bastien's Lucha Libre tapings.

This past Sunday in Mexico City (10/22) saw one of the bloodiest matches of the year as Jerry Estrada (face) beat Javier Cruz in a hair vs. hair match. Said to be one of the best matches of the year anywhere including Estrada doing a suicidal dive through the ropes with a full flip on the way

out. Mexico has a wrestler called Freddy Kruger, who stinks. El Cobarde was paralyzed after doing one of those suicidal moves while famous wrestler El Gran Markus is seriously ill. Markus was a big name in Texas circles in the early 1970s feuding with Jose Lothario.

They are setting up a feud between Larry Cameron and Arch Angel (Curtis Thompson) which would probably result in Cameron being the one to turn baby face.

The current issue of Playboy has a segment on the women of wrestling which includes Mimi Lessos (Magnificent Mimi) and Trudi Adams (Brandi Mae). Told the girls look 75 percent better in the pictures as in real life, not that they look bad in real Life.

10/20 in Honolulu on Lia Maivia's card to benefit drug abuse groups saw Don Muraco pin Bob Orton, plus Nikolai Volkoff, Rocky Johnson and Steve Strong appeared. The Samoan Connection (Farmer Boy Ipo & LeRoy Brown) were to face the British Bulldogs, but the Bulldog team turned out to be Dean Hart (another of the Hart brothers) and an unidentified person.

I'm told the TSN Wrestling shows (Stampede and Pro Wrestling Plus) have been horrible of late.

New manager in Florida is Reverend Billy Wirtz, who does a Brother Love type gimmick and is said to be pretty bad. Dallas Page is doing TV commentary and has gotten a lot better, but sidekick John Heath still puts people to sleep. Kevin Sullivan's name continues to be mentioned on TV by Ron Slinker each week. Slinker is feuding with Steve Keirn - 10/22 in Orlando, which probably didn't draw anyone since Titan was in Orlando and drew 9,000 fans the same night with Hulk Hogan, saw Keirn beat Slinker via DQ to keep the Florida title, Tyree Pride beat The Terminator (Marc Laurinidas) via DQ, Kendall Windham beat Mike Awesome and Barretta & Knight beat Rock Hard Rick & Powerhouse Parker to keep the tag titles.

10/21 in Dothan, AL saw Dixie Dynamite (Scott Armstrong under a mask) beat Downtown Bruno in a match where if Dynamite lost, he'd have to sit in a cage during the main event tag team title match without his mask and if Bruno lost, Sylvia would have to sit in the cage during the main event tag match wearing a negligee, Todd Morton beat The Beast, Jerry Stubbs beat Cactus Jack Manson via DQ, Adrian Street beat Beauty in a loser leaves town match, Brad Armstrong beat CWF champion Dennis Condrey via DQ and Jimmy Golden & Brian Lee kept the CWF tag titles beating The Southern Boys in an Alabama Football Classic match.

GAT promotions ran shows on 10/14 in Riverside, CA and 10/20 in Santa Ana using Bobby Bradley, Mercenary #1 (Billy Anderson), Louie Spicoli, Mario Valenzuela and Carlos Mata. Black Gordman will appear on a show 10/28 in San Bernardino.

10/20 at the Sam Houston Coliseum before 650 fans

saw Tiger Conway Jr. win a 16 man Battle Royal billed for $50,000, Chavo Guerrero beat Tug Taylor via DQ, Kevin Von Erich beat Kimala via DQ, Conway beat Killer Tim Brooks, Charles & Scott Casey double count out Texas Assassins and Shotgun Danny Gage beat Gary Young.

Jose Perez, younger brother of Miguel Perez Sr., who wrestled in Puerto Rico in the 1970s and wrestled and refereed on independent wrestling shows in Alaska in the 1980s passed away in late August at the age of 37.

NWA

The TBS shows for this Saturday and the following Saturday were taped on 10/17 in Marietta before a full house of 1,800 fans. Gordon Solie did the commentary during the first show since they "went to Jim Ross" live in Philly during the show. The show consisted of 24 squash matches. The only new stuff was the introduction of the Dragon Master (Kazuo Sakurada), Doom (with Kevin Sullivan and Woman) and Marc Laurinidas. Laurinidas came out during a match with Ranger Ross vs. Cuban Assassin and beat up on Ross with Cuban cheering him on, then he beat up on Cuban. Doom wore masks similar to the mask Big Van Vader wears in Japan. I'm told everyone in the building knew one was Ron Simmons and most, but not everyone, thought the other was Butch Reed. They didn't Look bad, but they didn't look as menacing as they needed to with that name and gimmick and some fans laughed at them. Apparently even the marks started looking to the back when Gene Anderson would come out knowing it was the signal to go to the finish.

Upon executive orders, TBS has eliminated all blood on television, whether it be TBS, syndicated shows or even PPV shows. Ric Flair does an interview that airs on Saturday on TBS guaranteeing the blood and sweat of his opponents at the PPV.

Ole Anderson just doesn't cut it anymore. I don't know why. But every time he comes out, that thought becomes obvious when the crowd doesn't pop Like one would expect.

Teddy Long came out to ringside during Steve Williams matches so I guess Doc will face either Dan Spivey or Sid Vicious down the line.

In Marietta, Rikki Nelson got his ribs messed up by a Rick Steiner bely-to-belly suplex, Thad Clark blew out his knee against Tom Zenk real bad and Greg Evans was throttled by the returning Samoan Swat Team.

Ric Flair vs. Terry Funk on 11/12 in Amarillo, TX which should sellout.

Most of the early November line-ups at the house shows are Flair vs. Funk in cage matches, Lex Luger vs. Brian Pillman for the U.S. title, Road Warriors vs. Skyscrapers, great Muta vs. Sting for the TV title, Steiners vs. Doom, Freebirds vs. Midnight Express for the NWA tag team title, Tom Zenk vs. Mike Rotunda and Eddie Gilbert vs. Norman

the Lunatic.

They keep hinting of a Norman turn to face and eventual feud with Teddy Long. Angle very similar to the one last year with Kevin Sullivan and Rick Steiner.

NWA off from Dec. 17-24. Return to Detroit at Cobo Arena will be Dec. 16.

The Christmas week schedule is Dec. 25 in Charlotte and Greenville, Dec. 26 in Knoxville and Columbia, SC, Dec. 27 in Philadelphia, Dec. 28 in Baltimore, Dec. 29 in Richmond and Dec. 30 in Greensboro and Asheville.

NWA Main Event was the highest rated wrestling show on cable drawing a 2.6 rating with the Lex Luger vs. Steve Williams hitting a 3.1 which is the highest rating anyone in either federation has done this year opposite the NFL. World Championship Wrestling was a 2.2 while Power Hour was a 2.1. The two-hour WCW show had a different trend. Usually wrestling shows have their largest viewing audience in the final 15 minutes, but this thing peaked early in the show and plummeted in the second hour, losing 30 percent of its audience by the time it was over.

10/20 at the D.C. Armory drew 1,800 as Johnny Ace pinned Rip Morgan ¾ *, Zenk pinned Bill Irwin ½ *, Brian Pillman pinned Cuban Assassin *¾, Sid Vicious beat Scott Steiner via DQ when Rick interfered DUD, Luger pinned Steve Williams when both collided and Luger fell on top ** ½, Freebirds double count out Road Warriors for the tag title ¼ *, and Flair & Sting beat Funk & Muta via DQ in 17 minutes when Gary Hart interfered *** ½. Told it was one of those nights when Flair and Funk almost saved a bad show, but the weak main event finish of a simple run in with no build-up hurt what to that point had been an excellent match.

Tim Willet of the Dallas office went to Mexico to do a piece with Friar Tormenta, who is the priest who wrestles and uses his wrestling earnings to fund an orphanage in Mexico. The piece will air on either TBS or one of the syndicated shows. Tormenta, who is 5-foot-3, will be wrestling on an NWA card in Corpus Christi, TX against another guy he's bringing in from Mexico. From what I'm told from those who follow Lucha Libre, he's absolutely terrible.

Chris Cruise debuted as an announcer on Worldwide Wrestling. His voice is certainly good. I didn't notice anything at all wrong with his performance, not anything spectacular, but Jim Ross pretty much overshadowed him on the first show. It'll be different when he's on his own, which is the plan starting shortly, or at Least put him with another wrestler as color guy. Cruise's background is not in sports announcing, but in doing anchor work for a CNN division and working for the Armed Forces News Service.

On the TV show this Saturday, the announcement is made that the Midnight Express will face the Dynamic Dudes on 11/15 in Troy, NY and that Stan Lane negotiated the match "behind Jim Cornette's back." The following week Cornette announced that he was going to stay neutral during the match and watch it from ringside. The Midnigh-Dudes feud seems to be the only "fresh" thing on television here.

10/22 in Chicago drew 2,742 and $35,000 as Jacko Victory pinned Johnny Ace when Rip Morgan shoved Ace's foot off the ropes during the pin DUD, Zenk pinned Irwin * ½, Pillman pinned Rotunda with a double pin but Pillman raised his shoulder **, Vicious beat Scott Steiner via DQ when Rick interfered ** ½, Road Warriors beat Freebirds via DQ when Birds were DQ'd for making a save on a pin attempt **, Luger pinned Williams with his feet on the ropes for Leverage *** ½, Sting beat Muta via DQ for using the mist *** and Flair pinned Funk in a cage match ***. NWA won't be running any more cards in Chicago for the rest of the year as Ch. 66 has canceled World Wide Wrestling due to bad ratings. That afternoon, the same crew drew 2,000 fans in Rockford, IL.

Shane Douglas missed all shows over the weekend so he's apparently still injured. Other no-shows over the weekend were Captain USA in Chicago (and nobody has a clue who he was to begin with). Dick Slater (the main event at the DC Armory was supposed to be a six-man with Flair-Sting-Pillman vs. Funk-Muta-Slater but instead Pillman was moved to the undercard) who has been in Japan for weeks and Dan Spivey.

WWF

Referee Joey Marella was seriously injured in an auto accident with a ruptured spleen. He was on the critical list in a New Jersey hospital for much of the past week but was upgraded from critical to serious over the weekend. Marella, as most of you know, is the son of TV announcer Gorilla Monsoon.

Barry Windham has missed every date booked over the past two weeks. No word on what this is about but he hasn't been fired, and isn't injured. I guess that means he was suspended.

Koko B. Ware was fired after a hotel room brawl with executive Jim Troy. Troy, a former ice hockey enforcer, got into it with Ware in Brussels but Ware came out the better of it. Trouble always seems to happen when the WWF goes to Europe. The Rockers were also fired in Europe, but were re-hired the next day.

Ticket prices in London ranged from $18 to $45 for the 12,000 seat building which sold out for the Hulk Hogan vs. Randy Savage main event.

WWF found itself having to use English wrestlers on the undercard. There was some obscure law in England that matches can't be held between two non-citizens of the British Commonwealth (in other words they could have gotten away with using Canadians) although I guess they had to pull strings since Hogan vs. Savage doesn't exactly qualify under those rules. They did use local guys in prelims

to satisfy Local authorities.

Roddy Piper will work against Rick Rude next month in Portland, OR, which is only significant because in years past Piper used to no-show bookings in Portland because he vowed he'd never work on a card against Don Owen.

The top ticket prices in the major markets will all follow the lead of Madison Square Garden and be raised to $18 and underneath prices also raised $3 across the board.

There will be a three-hour SummerSlam preview show on the USA network on 11/12 and repeated again the next night.

Widow Maker is booked on upcoming shows . Ironically, some bookings have him against The Genius (Lanny Poffo) which would certainly make him a face.

Big John Tenta has bookings under the name Earthquake Evans, although maybe they'll change the name because of the earthquake in the Bay Area.

All-American Wrestling and Prime Time Wrestling both drew 2.4 ratings on 10/15 and 10/16 respectively.

10/20 at the Nassau Coliseum drew 11,000 and $160,000 as Boreus Zhukov pinned Tim Horner DUD, Tito Santana pinned Haku ½ *, Nikolai Volkoff panned Paul Roma DUD (hear Volkoff really looks awful on his return), Hulk Hogan pinned Badnews Brown * (Brown gave Hogan the Ghetto Blaster before the bell and Left, taking the belt. Ref Earl Hebner with broken wrist called him back and said there must be a match and Brown beat on Hogan the whole way until the superman comeback and leg drop finish), Rockers beat Rougeaus in 65 minutes *** (slow first half but some excellent spots and great selling by Michaels), Rick Martel beat Brutus Beefcake -*, and Dusty Rhodes pinned Big Bossman ½ *.

10/22 in Orlando drew 9,200 as Zhukov pinned Horner *, Martel beat Beefcake DUD, Haku drew Santana -*, Hogan pinned Brown **, Rockers beat Rougeaus *** ½, Volkoff pinned Roma -** and Rhodes pinned Bossman ** ¼.

10/22 in Edmonton drew 5,500 as Tugboat Thomas beat Brooklyn Brawler * ½, Genius pinned Sam Houston (who will replace Ware full-time as a designated prelim loser to Poffo) * ¼, Bret Hart drew Dino Bravo ** ½, Mr. Perfect pinned Jimmy Snuka -* ½ (didn't lock up for eight minutes) Demolition Smash & Jim Neidhart beat Tully Blanchard & Arn Anderson in a non-title match (Tully & Arn billed as champs with belts) ** Jim Duggan beat Randy Savage via DQ * and Warrior beat Andre in 12 seconds. They made an NWA-like blunder on their TV, which airs Sunday, which kept saying "tomorrow in Edmonton" when it was really that night and thus killed the walk-up.

No Survivor Series in Canada because SummerSlam bombed badly in Western Canada on closed-circuit and did pretty bad in Ontario as well. Closed-circuit wrestling is something that's time has passed with PPV, but Canada has no PPV.

Piper vs. Rude drew 14,500 and $170,000 in Los Angeles on 10/22 going against a Rolling Stones concert.

Some interesting matches upcoming including some Santana vs. Bret Hart bouts, Hart Foundation vs. Rockers.

SNME to be taped on 10/31 in Topeka with Hogan vs. The Genius, Warrior vs. Andre, Piper vs. Rude, Savage vs. Duggan and Rockers vs. Blanchard & Anderson in 2 of 3 falls.

A lawyer for Andre the Giant asked for a change of venue in the civil suit by cameraman Ben Hildrebrandt of KCRG when Andre roughed him up while he was filming. Andre's defense is that the federation doesn't allow filming of its matches and Andre claims he was trying to enforce that policy with "misguided zeal". Hildebrandt claims he wasn't filming Andre's quickie loss, but filming the crowd reactions during the main event.

10/11 in Springfield, IL saw Red Rooster beat Conquistador #1 (sub for Windham), Brown pinned Hercules, DiBiase pinned Bob Orton, Warrior beat Andre in 19 seconds, Perfect pinned Suka and Demolition beat Brainbusters via DQ.

After Anderson & Blanchard leave but before Andre's feud with Warrior is finished, Demolition will work a few matches once again with Powers of Pain.

10/20 in Montreal saw Tugboat (Fred Ottman) beat Brawler, Genius beat Houston, Warrior beat Andre via DQ, Bravo pinned Hart, Neidhart & Smash beat Blanchard & Anderson, Perfect pinned Snuka and Savage beat Duggan via count out.

Demolition Axe (Bill Eadie) missed a few shows with an injury.

Ratings: 1. Ric Flair; 2. Jushin Liger; 3. Genichiro Tenryu; 4. Dan Kroffat; 5. Toshiaki Kawada; 6. Nobuhiko Takada; 7. Terry Funk; 8. Naoki Sano; 9. Curt Hennig; 10. Shawn Michaels; 11. Arn Anderson; 12. Kazuo Yamazaki; 13. Akira Maeda; 14. Ted DiBiase; 15. Randy Savage; 16. Great Muta; 17. Jumbo Tsuruta; 18. Tully Blanchard; 19. Shiro Koshinaka; 20. Bret Hart; 21. Terry Gordy; 22. Owen Hart; 23. Barry Windham; 24. Rick Steiner; 25. Tommy Rogers; 26. Rick Rude; 27. Scott Steiner; 28. Hiroshi Hase; 29. Bobby Eaton; 30. Yoshiaki Fujiwara; 31. Brad Armstrong; 32. Masaharu Funaki; 33. Super Astro; 34. Marty Janetty; 35. Lex Luger; 36. Masa Saito; 37. Pat Tanaka; 38. Mike Rotunda; 39. Negro Casas; 40. Mark Rocco; 41. George Takano; 42. Big Bossman; 43. Shinya Hashimoto; 44. Bam Bam Bigelow; 45. Road Warrior Hawk; 46. Chris Benoit; 47. Rick Martel; 48. Steve Williams; 49 . Tim Horner; 50. Riki Choshu

Teams: 1. Rockers; 2. Blanchard & Anderson; 3. Foot Loose; 4. Steiners; 5. Road Warriors; 6. Kroffat & Furnas; 7. Tsuruta & Yatsu

THE READERS' PAGES

WWF

As a recent convert to your newsletter, let me start off by complimenting you on the excellent job you are doing. I've always been a pro wrestling fan, but the Observer has taken me to new heights.

Much time in the Observer is spent comparing the NWA and the WWF. Here is a quick comparison from my point of view. For the past several years, our station has been doing WWF ticket giveaways. I've always been treated nicely by the Titan folks in Connecticut (Mike Weber and Steve Plenamenta) as well as by Jerry Brisco in Tampa and our local arena show people. The WWF folks always take time to chat about the business and basically go out of their way to be helpful, whether it be extra tickets, interviews or whatever for station people. In fact, when I've forgotten to call in advance, they've always been accommodating, even on the day of the event.

My one experience with the NWA was not at all pleasant. I find the Crockett people rude and was told flatly that without a two week written notice, no tickets or passes could be handed out and there were no exceptions to that policy. Now perhaps I caught somebody on a bad day and hopefully things are better under Ted Turner, but that one bad experience really turned me off. Say what you want about Vince, he runs a professional organization with lots of good people working for him.

Charlie Mattos WNWS Radio
Miami, Florida

The WWF rolled into Springfield, IL Wednesday night. They promoted the card as a TV taping but didn't follow through. The crowd was poor and even the section of freebies was empty. This was easily the worst show here. The best match was Ted DiBiase vs. Bob Orton. Barry Windham's absence was not announced or explained although a sign was posted at the ticket office stating that Hillbilly Jim wouldn't be appearing. Nobody but Orton and DiBiase did anything but stand around, choke or punch. Four body slams and one dropkick was the whole card. The matches were so full of pathetic clowning and stalling that many fans were yelling out "NWA, We Wrestle" during the show. People were really upset this night and I expect it'll be a long time before they return.

Chris Martin
Springfield, Illinois

I never thought I'd truly be offended by what a heel would say until Monday night. Did you catch Prime Time Wrestling? Bobby Heenan made several extremely tasteless and crass remarks about the kids that died in the school bus accident in Texas. Now, I know a heel is a heel, but that was totally uncalled for and would be grounds for being thrown off the tube on any other television show. Don't these dips know how to edit bad material?

Teresa DeMarie
Tuckahoe, New York

QUESTIONS

Does FNN/Score have any future plans when it comes to wrestling programming? The last show I saw on FNN was ICW wrestling, which put me to sleep on a weekly basis. But there are smaller promotions like Oregon and Stampede that a lot of fans are unable to watch and would love to see.

Second, has the NWA made any attempt to improve its syndication in the Bay Area? The NWA show we get is on at midnight on a San Jose station that nobody watches. I like the show a lot, but not enough to watch it at midnight.

Sam Nord
Walnut Creek, California

Dave Meltzer: From what I understand, FNN has, or will drop all sports programming and so wrestling is out the window and there are no current plans for a change in that way of thinking. The NWA has talked with Ch. 20 in San Francisco and a deal was close, but when negotiations started to sell the station, the deal was put on hold and I haven't heard any talk of it in a few months.

Why did the NWA never acknowledge the Ric Flair-Harley Race title changes in Singapore and New Zealand? Don't you think it could be used to their advantage to show that the title was truly a World title. Also, did Antonio Inoki ever win the WWF title?

Greg Vanden Heuvel
London, Ontario

Dave Meltzer: The Flair-Race series took place in early 1984. Race beat Flair in a two of three fall title match in New Zealand, and two days later in Singapore, Flair regained the title. I'm not sure of the exact circumstances, but believe it was a referee error as the title wasn't supposed to have changed hands, all the wrestlers on the tour were told never to let anyone know that it did and it was never acknowledged that it did afterwards. Inoki beat Bob Backlund in 1979 for the WWF title in what I believe was a double-cross on Backlund who didn't know they were going to count his shoulders down. They held a rematch one week later which was a no contest, however Inoki, in Japan, "gave Backlund back the belt" pending a rematch. The entire escapade happened because TV-Asahi in Japan was going to televise the January, 1980 Madison Square Garden card with inoki, Fujinami and some of the others on the card.

Inoki wanted to pressure Vince McMahon Sr. into putting a Backlund vs. Inoki match as the main event so Inoki could prove to the Japanese fans that he was a superstar in the United States, which is one of those things Inoki always wanted to be but never was able to be. It should be noted that the figure-head president of the WWF at that time was Hisashi Shinma, who also ran New Japan and was Inoki's personal business manager, which is why perhaps they felt they could pull this off. McMahon had been building up Bobby Duncum for the title shot at MSG and as it turned out, Inoki was brought in and as a compromise, was billed as WWF World Martial Arts champion and he defended the title on that card and beat Iron Sheik. Backlund wrestled and beat Duncum on the card, but as part of the compromise to explain things in Japan where the title was billed as being held up, Backlund didn't enter the ring wearing the title belt nor was he announced as champion in the ring, even though to all New York fans watching the show and in the commentary in English, he was referred to as champion while on the simulcast to Japan, it was said the belt was held up.

OAKLAND 2

I'm afraid that those who are criticizing the Oakland 2 may be more susceptible to Vince McMahon's mind-control than you or they realize. It appears they believe that Mr. McMahon's right and authority to produce television supercedes the rights of the spectators and that of the United States Constitution.

George Maranville
Lexington, Kentucky

I believe that the purpose of the Readers Pages is to voice opinions and not to berate fellow fans. As such, I will try to refrain from sardonic personal attacks that seem to be rampant lately. One impetus for the mud slinging is the Oakland 2 issue. Thank goodness for people like Eric Krol, Elyse Zois and Walter Kurelis who realize that Vince McMahon's purpose in the Coliseum was to produce his wrestling television show and not a documentary. It is his product, and the Oakland 2 are not Crispus Attucks, but rather local brats who would hurl insults and then stick their tongue out from behind the locked screen door. Perhaps they shouldn't have been ejected, but their actions must be construed as smart-ass and not smart. If the Oakland 2 have such disdain for the WWF, let them exercise the option that I do in my preference for the WWF, do not attend the opposing promotion.

The NWA slant to the Observer is certainly annoying. A friend thinking of subscribing, an 18-year veteran such as myself said, "Is Meltzer paid by the NWA? He should be." I Love the informational content of the Observer, but your preference is all too obvious. When the NWA ran a show in Nashville in May, you spent your time at the NWA mall autograph session instead of the Titan show. In Chicago, you couldn't find friends to go to the WWF show. My friends don't attend NWA cards, but we aren't in charge of widely-read newsletters. If a WWF wrestler gains weight, it is because of the Titan diet (8/21 issue). Is Dusty Rhodes' girth the result of all his years on the NWA diet?

WWF fans differ from NWA fans. But to stereotype WWF fans as Pavlov's Dogs (8/21), marks or proponents of total predictability is unfair. I believe Titan fans go to matches to have fun, hence their reaction to musical introductions. NWA fans, in my opinion, are more rabid fans and more serious fans. The difference makes no group better nor worse. The self-righteous NWA letter-writers should be cognisant of this fact.

Brian Smith
New London, Connecticut

Dave Meltzer: First off, my personal preference is any wrestling in which the wrestlers appear to be working to the best of their abilities and are skilled performers. I don't care which group it's in. When the WWF has a match that around the horn has been getting rave reviews (such as Brainbusters vs. Rockers) I will be the first to purchase a ticket for that show. My personal preference is hardly the NWA, although in this country it would be, simply because they have a lot better matches with a lot more frequency than the WWF. I'm a fan of good wrestling, and should be allowed to be a fan, because if I'm no longer a fan, there would be no Observer. I enjoy the in-ring product of the NWA and the live shows of the NWA quite a bit more than the WWF, by and large. But I enjoy the promotional work of the WWF and overall organization far more than the NWA. To set the record straight. I left the NWA mall show to attend the WWF show in Nashville. I went to Chicago to see a football game and to do some visiting. Nobody I knew wanted to attend the WWF show and it was a poor line-up and I hardly feel like I'm obligated to attend a poor card from any group. Had anyone that I was with wanted to see the show, I'd have gladly attended. As it was, I missed half of the NWA show that was in town the same weekend. The only reason I even attended the NWA show was because Ric Flair was in the main event and I will go out of my way to see Flair live if he's appearing anywhere near where I am. If WWF had run a hot card, or even a lukewarm card, I'd have attended (In February, when I went to Chicago specifically to see an NWA PPV show, I attended the WWF show two days earlier, in Nashville also attended both groups card even though the WWF line-up didn't promise much in the way of good wrestling). If both groups ran shows on the same night and I felt they were of equal calibre, I'd attend the NWA show because by and large the wrestlers put out more and across the board are better workers..

If the NWA show had been a major show, I'd have skipped the football game in Chicago and gone to the

wrestling show. As for Titan diet, everyone knows that is in reference to steroids. While usage of steroids is abundant in every promotion, it is far greater in Titan than in any other promotion because anyone with half a brain can see muscular size is the most important factor when it comes to getting a push in the WWF and you cannot get the muscular size and physique that nearly every top WWF star has (with exceptions like those unnaturally huge like Big Bossman or Andre or someone like Dusty Rhodes who doesn't fit into any category) without steroids. Because that is the case, most wrestlers who join Titan immediately start hitting the roids hard, hence a rapid weight gain, hence Titan diet is a nice way of putting it. This is not to say other promotions don't push steroid freaks with little ability, because that's a lie. However, a truly talented wrestler using moderate dosages of steroids, or perhaps in the case of a super talent, no steroids at all, can go to the top in every other promotion and that same wrestler, when he goes to Titan, immediately will go heavy into the juice because without it, they will wind up like countless other "great wrestlers" who become jobbers in Titan. To stereotype Titan fans as marks is not only unfair, but it's stupid. Pavlov's Dogs?

That thought came to me at a television taping a few years back when a babyface won, using his big move, and there was no crowd reaction at all, despite the fact it was a heavily pushed and seemingly over act. When the music came on, late, because of a backstage screw up, the place went bonkers, but the crowd reacted to the music, not to the wrestling, and to the music immediately throughout the night. I've later seen this same thing happen dozens of times. Recently at a Titan show, a heel cheated to beat a face and when they announced the winner, they played the face music and everyone cheered on cue. As far as being proponents of total predictability, all fans are to a certain extent because they have to be "taught" what move or strut or whatever is important, but it is not unfair to say Titan fans are generally proponents of greater predictability .

VIOLENCE
Wrestling is violence, along with a touch of athletics and glitz. But it's primarily violence. Keeping this in mind, how can anyone get too excited about the recent incidents with Ric Flair and Scott Steiner? I was not offended in any way by either of these, but I did recognize it was a mistake to run the plastic bag angle only because it will hurt PPV sales. Many potential buyers of the PPV show will shy away from it saying they don't want their kids watching something worse than a plastic bag angle, which is implied when the PPV is labeled with parental discretion advised.

I don't see why we have this sudden uproar over something that happens daily. I've seen Hulk Hogan, the All-American law-abiding idol of millions of kids using wires of a house mic to choke his opponent. What about Roddy Piper using his belt to whip his way to victory against Adrian Adonis at WrestleMania III. These are two of the top faces in the WWF right now, yet I've seen both do things much worse than what Kevin Sullivan, Butch Reed and Ron Simmons did to Scott Steiner. Anyone remember when Ricky Steamboat was hung by Mr. Fuji and Don Muraco? What about Randy Savage driving the bell into the throat of Steamboat?

The point is, the plastic bag angle wasn't too far, it was simply just a bad idea. Flair should have been humiliated on TV , but not nearly murdered. Flair has to be under tremendous pressure as booker. He is human and he made a mistake. Let's look at the overall job he and the rest of the NWA are doing rather than nitpick and bitch at every single mistake.

Mark Bennett
East Lansing, Michigan

If one compares pro wrestling with any other televised spectator sport, it is bound to offend someone at every turn. Even the youngest kids watching the last Clash at my house felt Ric Flair was completely safe since the bag was open in front of his neck at all times. None of the NWA stuff bugs me although what bugged me most was Scott taking the punch from Rick. Why not stick with make-up?

What offends me more than anything the NWA has ever done is the manhandling of women and treatment of women by Titan. Last week we saw Randy Savage choke, push and force his will on Sherri as well as Hulk Hogan putting his mitts on her at SummerSlam. This sinking to new lows began at WrestleMania when Savage pushed and shoved his own wife. This stuff bugs me enough to want a respite from female valets in wrestling. Robin Green is visibly great, slightly below Missy Hyatt, but doesn't come across well in interviews. Simply awful. Let Kevin Sullivan speak for her.

Dr. Mike Lano
Alameda, California

NWA

Needless to say Ric Flair vs. Terry Funk was the best match I've ever seen live and the best match in Rochester in years. Flair threw some amazing chops that had Funk's chest bleeding in around seven minutes. This was a total breath of fresh air.

They didn't give too much away on the first time in town, but still every match was still a lot better than anything the WWF has ever put on here. All the matches were with New York State Athletic Commission refs and at some point every one of them looked totally lost. Teddy Long and Paul Ellering were wasted as managers live. Jim Cornette was incredible live, and now is a semi-hero locally from his stint on a morning radio show on the local No. 1 station in the market. He had the DJ's cracking up non-stop and

everyone at the station said afterward that he was the best guest on the station since Sam Kinison, which is quite a compliment as they have a special guest comedian every Friday. Too bad the Clash is in Troy. Rochester would have been a better location due to the fact we are easily accessible from Buffalo, Toronto and Syracuse.

Sean Hendrick
Rochester, New York

One aspect of the problems with the NWA that has been overlooked is geography. Both the Crocketts and Ted Turner have shown usual East Coast bias against anything west of the Mississippi. Since 1986, when the first NWA show came to New Mexico, it has been very apparent. At first the NWA drew well here, more than 5,000 per show. They had a lead over the WWF at the beginning yet months would go by before a follow-up show. When they Lost good television time in Los Angeles, the whole West Coast was ignored. Albuquerque, with 450,000 people, was outdrawing Los Angeles, yet somehow our money wasn't good enough for them and without California they felt it wasn't worth coming out here.

During the Western swing in June, Albuquerque's turnout was only 1,400. Yet that was still better than Oakland, Reno or Detroit. The card was awful and many of the wrestlers didn't show up. Those of us in this part of the country have been hurt since Bill Watts sold out to the NWA. If those in charge would work on cities that are strong for them and quit trying in glamour areas like New England and California where the WWF is too strong, they might build back the base that is needed. Everyone's money is the same color.

John Martinez
Albuquerque, New Mexico

AUSTRALIA

Got to see the Baltimore Bash with the four sensational main events, one right after another. It was the best wrestling show I've ever seen. Powerhouse characters, tremendous sports entertainment in the ring, funny lines and comedy (Samoans chewing and punching away at each other while Freebirds were trying to do an interview; Doc Williams surfing across the screen during Stan Lane's interview; the bit with Paul E. and Hayes outside the cage, etc.) Just total entertainment. Although the three final matches were technically better, I have a soft spot for the Sting vs. Muta match. Tremendous spots in that one.

Also saw SummerSlam. I've got an enormous tolerance for the WWF, but even my patience has a termination point. Wrestlemania V was largely crap, outside of the Rockers vs. Twin Tubbos match, but this was worse. I Like everyone in the six-man, but the match was slow and weak on high spots. They left the hot tag for too long. Highlights were

Honkey's "Elvis has now left the building" bit and Gene Okerlund rapid-fire ad Lib.

Julian Licht
Melbourne, Australia

AWARDS FAVORITES

Time to run down a few more categories for the yearbook awards. Once again, we have voting in more than 40 categories in December for the annual Observer readership awards. We run down a list of all the categories in November.

BEST ON INTERVIEWS: This is one of those categories in which year in and year out most of the same names top the list, specifically Ric Flair, Jim Cornette, Jerry Lawler, Michael Hayes and others of that type. Cornette has finished first the past four years and going into this year as hot as he was on the mic, one would figure him a lock for the award. I wouldn't even call him the favorite this time out. One problem is that of late, Cornette's work as a television commentator overshadows what got him his fame, managing and talking in interviews. As the weeks go on, I'm beginning to think Cornette's quickness of the mind and mouth and knowledge and ability to explain points logically in a basically illogical business have made him surpass, or at least equal Jesse Ventura, whose main attributes are his voice and personal charisma. Anyway, that's another subject. Cornette's interviews are still among the best, but it's hard to have people waiting to hear a Cornette interview after you hear him for three hours doing commentary each week. Terry Funk was incredible when he came back to the NWA, and his best work of the year is stuff nobody saw in Florida when he was feuding with Dusty Rhodes. Randy Savage's interviews are excellent, primarily in the delivery aspect. Ric Flair's delivery is great, but it seems like he has nothing new to say in the traditional screaming Flair promo. But Flair's "serious" interviews, such as while he was off, and his promos when he first returned, were without peer. Jerry Lawler in Dallas does the old-time heel insulting the city stuff better than anyone. I think the appeal of that sort of thing is outdated except in the small-time regional promotions, but since that's what he's working for in Dallas, it is classic material. Rick Steiner is not a great interview per set but some of the stuff he does on interviews is some of the most memorable stuff around. Roddy Piper isn't what he once was, but he's still a good interview. Paul E. Dangerously was the best heel manager interview this year, but like Bobby Heenan and Cornette, when you hear someone talk so much each week, it takes a big punch out of their interviews.

MANAGER OF THE YEAR: Another Jim Cornette gimmee award for the past four years. Certainly this year won't be a landslide for Cornette, if he even repeats. Baby face manager is basically a no-win job and although Cornette has been as good as one can be, which basically means hot for a few months and then it goes downhill. Once the thing with Paul E. got old, Cornette really had nothing he could do as a face and for some reason the pairing with the dudes, while good to give the dudes attention, is hard to take seriously. If it was just for work at ringside, Sherri Martel would be a clear cut winner this time. She's the only manager I can recall who works harder during the matches than both wrestlers do in the ring, and I don't mean on this night or that night, but almost every night. Her interviews are better since they're scripted and Savage carries them, but she's still no talker. Bobby Heenan is real good. Paul E. Dangerously is good, but the chemistry with the SST was awful. Scandor Akbar had a whole promotion revolving around him and he carried the weakest crew of heels you'd ever imagine. He was the most important manager to any single promotion to be sure, but to even be mentioned in the same paragraph as the rest of these names for quality of his work as a manager is an insult to the rest of them. Jimmy Hart is fine. Same old stuff. Nothing wrong with it, but nothing particularly good about it either.

WORST MATCH OF THE YEAR: Some years there are big matches, like Andre the Giant vs. Hulk Hogan at WrestleMania III or Roddy Piper vs. Mr. T at WrestleMania II that were so obviously winners. This year a few baddest of the bads come to mind. Since our award period technically starts on December 1, 1988, the classic hand-tied-behind-the-back match from the Clash in Chattanooga with Paul Jones vs. Ivan Koloff has to come to mind. An awful idea for a match to begin with, made worse by the competitors and the fact it was televised live. Speaking of televised live, while more of a TV squash, for just plain awfulness, my pick is the Ding Dongs debut from the Clash in Fort Bragg and I can't even remember off hand who they were against. All those missed moves. The bells flying everywhere. The crowd reaction. As it turned out, the Ding Dongs were two hard-working but undersized guys who were doomed by the dumbest gimmick around, but that first night was just horrid. Speaking of horrid, that horrid show of the year, Wrestlemania IV had two matches that stood out. Rougeaus vs. Bushwackers and Andre the Giant vs. Jake Roberts with John Studd as referee. Dusty Rhodes vs. Honky Tonk Man at SummerSlam was of that calibre. What about any match with Hillbilly Jim? Or that Sid Vicious vs. Scott Hall match on TBS in which they had to put about a dozen post-produced crowd shots into the match to hide the missed moves? Some of the bouts with the Russians in New Japan were pretty bad but I don't recall any that were so pathetic they hurt to watch as the ones mentioned here all did. Almost any match with Percy Pringle or Uncle Elmer has to hurt to watch. Giant Baba is one of the worst active wrestlers around, but somehow the guys in the ring with him make up for it because I can recall one of his matches that I'd pick here, although I'm already thinking his upcoming singles match with Tiger Jeet Singh may be a winner. Two Live matches I saw that stood out were a Rougeaus vs. Bushwackers match from Chicago, and Honky Tonk Man vs. Hillbilly Jim from Nashville.

WOMEN IN TODAY'S WRESTLING BY JEFF BOWDREN

I really thought that Steve Beverly was kidding when he told me about the angle that never was. Down Continental way, some genius decided that a great angle would be to have Linda Street "get pregnant, run the skit over a few months and then have her attacked by various heels and "lose the baby. Beyond the initial distaste that any well thinking human must feel, I found it sort of funny that CWF would even consider an angle that wouldn't be resolved for months since it seems like this promotion is always on the verge of shutting down.

But let's look at the angle. Not only is this idea the sign of a desperate booker, but shows someone who always has a truly sick mind. The conception of such an idea would seem to indicate someone who has a genuine hatred of women. What makes this even worse is that in pro wrestling, this doesn't seem to be an isolated way of thinking. In Texas we saw Toni Adams get mugged on television. Hulk Hogan, the hero to millions of kids, gave Sensational Sherri an atomic drop at SummerSlam. In some arenas, after the Hogan-Randy Savage matches, Hulk would physically restrain Sherri while Elizabeth slapped her in the face. A few weeks ago, during a match between Savage and Jim Duggan, Sherri got up on the ring apron in order to distract Duggan. This of course, led to Savage sneaking up behind Duggan for the victory. During the tape replay of the finish, Vince McMahon and Jesse Ventura were arguing over the result. Ventura stated that the reason Duggan had lost was because he had physically grabbed Sherri for a prior distraction. Vince's replay was that Sherri got what she deserved. Now the good folks of the NWA have created the character of "Woman".

Let's examine this. What we really have is a scheming bitch who used a man and then dumped him. Then she "hires" two other men of seemingly less intelligence to beat up his brother. Can you just wait for Rick Steiner to get revenge? What's he going to do? Give her the Steiner line? And what about this name "Woman", What's the idea? For the predominantly male audience of the NWA to have Nancy represent all women? Are they actually trying to say that all women will stab you in the back and break your heart?

Enough is enough. Are we telling our kids it's okay to slap women around? What other impression are kids supposed to have when the No. 1 babyface in the whole wide world seems to be doing it? What happens when a 12-year-old kid punches out a classmate who is a girl and says, "Hey, the Hulkster did it?"

The unfortunate part of this whole trend is that the only way for this stuff to stop is when it fails at the box office. America is eating up the Sherri-Elizabeth angle and the other promotions must look at this and feel that the wrestling fans are ready to see women get physically abused. We have some seriously sick puppies out there.

NOVEMBER 6, 1989

The National Wrestling Alliance's string of excellent pay-per-view events ended on Saturday night in Philadelphia. "Halloween Havoc" was far from the worst pay-per-view event in history, But from a live perspective, the card came off like just another ordinary night of NWA wrestling. There just wasn't the aura of specialness to the card. While the promotion put together the most creative batch of television commercials ever for a major show, the backbone of the NWA, the great wrestling action on the big shows, wasn't there. Usually in a situation where a major event doesn't live up to expectations, it is criticism time. But really, I don't have any criticism other than the NWA simply wasn't ready to do a PPV card on October 28. I don't think the fans were ready, and the buy rate will be the answer to that one. But the feuds and grudges and storylines weren't ready on October 28 to peak. So to make up for this, the promotion built a cage. Or should I say three strange men somewhere in a blacksmith shop high in the mountains put together one of the most bizarre cages ever and a unique Thunderdome match was made the selling point. Before going any farther, let's take a look at the action itself:

1. The Z-Man (Tom Zenk) pinned Mike Rotunda in 13:23 when Rotunda did a cross bodyblock off the middle rope and Zenk reversed it for the pin. Zenk got a lukewarm reaction as he was booed almost as much as he was cheered, which is a better fate than some of the faces later in the card. They did nothing for the first three minutes and no sustained action for the first half of the match. Zenk caught an elbow in the eye and his eye watered up at five minutes. Rotunda got Zenk in a head scissors and the "boring" chants started. The fans were cheering when Rotunda worked Zenk over although they also cheered the finish when Zenk won. I think they were cheering more just because the match was over. The last two minutes were good, anyway. ¾ *

2. The Samoan Swat Team & The Samoan Savage beat Midnight Express & Steve Williams in 18:16 when Jim Cornette collided with Stan Lane and Lane was pinned by the Savage (Sam Fatu). Before the match started, they had two of the Samoans throw a large stick that was on fire back and forth during the intro. Oliver Humperdink was in as manager, billed as "The Big Kahuna" looking like a clone of Lou Albano right down to the big belly and opened Hawaiian shirts. It was two minutes before a lock-up, and Williams had a lot of stiff clotheslines and tackle spots on all three while they got out of the ring to recover. They alternated between hot tags by the faces and then getting heat on the faces. The most impressive stuff was when Bobby Eaton was in, particularly after Savage blocked a bulldog and Eaton flew by himself into the turnbuckles and was later tossed out of the ring and crotched on the guardrail. Eaton stuck up his knees when Savage went for his finisher (a front splash) and tagged Doc at the 17 minute mark. Doc threw Savage from a military press into the other two and tagged in Lane. Lane had Savage down for the count, Humperdink jumped on the apron, Cornette then hit Humperdink with the tennis racquet as Lane cheered which allowed Savage to come from behind and knock Lane into Cornette and pin Lane. Lane and Cornette argued after the match. The match was very good in spots but disjointed in other spots. ** ¾

3. Tommy Rich pinned Cuban Assassin with the Thesz press in 8:26. The fans booed Rich and were chanting "boring" quite a bit. Actually, they chanted boring before the match even started and never gave it a chance. Following the previous match with a match nobody wanted to see wasn't too smart. Actually, and this is not a statement of Rich's work or anything, but people just don't want to see him anymore. DUD

4. The Freebirds retained the NWA tag team titles beating the Dynamic Dudes in 11:28. Finish saw the Dudes go for their double slingshot back suplex on Garvin, but Hayes tripped Johnny Ace's leg on the move and Garvin fell on top of Shane Douglas for the pin. The fans cheered the Freebirds vehemently and booed everything the Dudes did. The better the Dudes looked, the more they booed. My impression was that it was more the fans hated the Dudes, and more to the point, hated the idea that Jim Cornette was with the Dudes, more than they liked the Freebirds. Jim Garvin was loving it because all he had to do was look at the crowd and they would go crazy. Douglas was actually working with his right arm broken in two places and hadn't worked in two weeks (since re-injuring an already injured arm). Considering he had to do some moves left-handed, which created timing problems, it explains the missed moves. The match had a lot of noise because the crowd got totally into booing the Dudes and cheering the Birds, but there was no actual heat for the match. The Dudes never had a chance here even though, considering Douglas' condition and the fact he still had to carry the team since Ace is green, they did well. ** ½

5. Doom (Ron Simmons & Butch Reed under masks managed by "Woman") beat Rick & Scott Steiner in 15:26 when Reed got a foreign object from Woman and put it

in his mask and head-butted Rick and got the pin. They opened fast with Rick & Scott doing simultaneous german suplexes and simultaneous clotheslines over the top ropes. At 1:47, an eight-year-old in front of me told his friend that they were Butch Reed & Ron Simmons under the mask and everyone in the building probably figured it out shortly thereafter. Doom won't get over, but the fans really get into the Steiners. The match went too long and contained too many holds for what was put over on television as such a major grudge . A fight broke out in the crowd during the match and nobody watched the match and the match lacked in heat during the middle. They got heat on Scott for a while until he made his comeback after kicking out of a stuff piledriver. The place popped big when Scott did the Mata headscissors move (somebody should come up with a better name for it than that) and Rick tagged in and did a powerslam and belly-to-belly on Reed before Woman gave him the object which led to the pin. ** ¼

6. Lex Luger pinned Brian Pillman with a hotshot in 16:48 to retain the U.S. title. Both guys were cheered in this match. Luger got some boos but they were drowned out by the much louder cheers. Pillman's cheers weren't as loud, but he got no boos at all. In contrast with the Ricky Steamboat matches, the crowd was far more vehement in the Steamboat matches (those who cheered and booed Steamboat and Luger in those bouts did so with a passion), while the Tommy Rich matches, nobody cared at all about the matches and only reacted to what Luger did. My biggest complaint came during this match, or more precisely, just before the match started. When Luger came out, they played a taped chant of "Luger, Luger" that was taped a few days earlier in another city, and also put a huge sign which said "Luger, Luger, Luger" facing the crowd in the back (but behind the TV cameras) in order to get the crowd to chant his name. The crowd didn't chant his name anyway although he still got a very big and predominantly positive reaction. What is the logic in this? First off, the guy is a heel that no matter what they do, they can't get the fans to boo. So then they try special effects and brainwashing to get the fans to cheer him to make the people at home think he's even more of a face than he is when the object they've been trying is to get people not to like him. This match was put together to be a four-star match with all the near falls and a hot finish, but it didn't quite make it. The first 10 minutes weren't good. A few spots, some well timed and others not-so-well-timed interspersed between armlocks by Pillman. The last six minutes, after Pillman missed a splash off the top ropes, was all hot action, some of which was excellent and some still with timing problems. There wasn't much heat during the first 10 minutes and people didn't seem to care, but this was the only match on the card that really built up to its finishing minutes and had several exciting near falls

at the end. The crowd popped big for Luger's win. *** ¼

7. Road Warriors beat Skyscrapers via DQ in 11:39 when the ref caught Danny Spivey using the key. Crowd was very much into this match and it was better than it sounds on paper. They mainly got heat on Hawk during most of the match. I think seeing Vicious in the ring next to the Warriors and seeing just how much bigger he was than everyone else gets him over just that much more. He's the most impressive"monster" specimen in the business and he's every bit as poor in working a match as he is impressive just standing there. After Animal got the hot tag, it broke loose. Teddy Long hit Paul Ellering with the key and Spivey got the key and hit Hawk for the DQ and they doubled on Animal using the key until Hawk did a flying clothesline to break it up, then Hawk got the key and hit both guys with it. Ironically, since this is the complaint made here about WWF crowds, when it was announced that the Warriors had won, there was no crowd pop, but about 30 seconds later when the music hit, the crowd popped for the music. ** ½

8. Ric Flair & Sting beat Terry Funk & Great Muta in the Thunderdome cage match in 21:55. Bruno Sammartino was the ref and Ole Anderson and Gary Hart were the 'terminators.' The rules were that the only way the match could end is if one of the terminators threw in the towel, signifying surrender for his team. The cage, without a door, was lowered onto the wrestlers and seconds. The cage looked awesome with tree branches, a Tarzan swinging rope inside, dragons facing outward, cobwebs and a mailbox on one side (I was at least expecting an address of 1313 Mockingbird Lane). The cage was so visually impressive that it took your concentration away from the match. Given the parameters of the match, all four guys did about as good a job as humanly possible. Check that, Flair, Muta and Sting did as good a job as humanly possible. Funk was inhuman, and completely stole the show and turned it into a spectacular match live. From the comments I 've heard, this match didn't translate well on PPV and watching it live, I didn't think it would, but it was about as good as it could have been. Before the match started, the dragons started breathing smoke and somehow the smoke caught some cloth on the side of the cage near the top and a fire broke out. This wasn't planned, and poor Tommy Young had to climb up the cage and put the fire out with his hand (ouch) and a guy with a fire extinguisher running behind Young in case he didn't get the job done. After the fire was out, Muta blew the mist, but apparently on TV it looked like it was just a spot for Muta to blow the fire out with the mist. Flair was chopping like crazy on Funk. There was no blood in this match (save for Funk's hand which bled quite a bit for a hand cut) by orders not only from TBS but also from Pennsylvania state law. When the commission was dropped,

a law was placed in the books that any blading could result in loss of license for the promotion. While nobody has called anyone on it yet, and they've done blood on every NWA show in Pittsburgh of late without the commission jurisdiction, apparently there was a warning before the show that the law would be enforced tonight, and if violated, the implied threat was the penalty (loss of license by the NWA for the state of Pennsylvania) would be enforced. Still, in pre-match publicity, a bloodbath was strongly suggested and I'm sure many fans watching on PPV were disappointed no matter how good the match would be with no juice. Still, Flair and Funk traded ramming each other's heads into the cage. There was a lot of climbing the cage, particularly by Funk. One highlight was with Flair and Funk both battling while holding onto the side of the cage, Flair started doing the stiff chop while Funk held on with one hand. There were spots in which both teams looked to be beaten with submission holds but the terminators refused to throw in the towel. When Muta used the indian death lock chinlock combination submission (which fans haven't been educated so they don't know it's a finisher yet), that was the spot where Ole got over that no matter what he wasn't throwing in the towel. Finish saw Funk use a role to tie Sting by the ankle into the cage high in the air and then Funk got down and they gave Flair a stuff piledriver. Ole Anderson climbed the cage to untie Sting and Sting did the move of the night, flying from the top of the cage with a cross bodyblock onto Funk, which for a moment I thought was going to do in both of them for good. Sting caught Funk with the move in a manner which appeared to take out Funk's already crippled knees and Funk got up like the knee was out, but the guy works an injury better than anyone (I guess since he's got more experience in what it feels like to have the knee out). Muta climbed up to the top rope for the moonsault and Sting dropkicked his butt (actually Sting just grazed him) but Muta crotched himself on the top rope. Flair put Funk in the figure four with Muta incapacitated. Sting then twice leaped off the top ropes with a splash onto the legs of both men when Flair had Funk in the figure four but Hart continually refused to throw in the towel. Muta got back up and shoved Sammartino, who decked Muta and while Sammartino's back was turned, Anderson decked Hart and Hart's towel flew in. Sammartino saw the towel and raised Flair's hand in victory. I guess for some, the sight of Sammartino raising Flair's hand had some historical significance. But I think the majority of the crowd and audience were lost on the significance of Flair, Sammartino and Funk in the same ring for the first time. ****

No pay-per-view numbers in yet, although some companies did report brisk late orders. According to the commission, the show drew 9,562 paid and $137,244, but from being there live, no way that is the case since, with equipment, the place was to be a sellout at 9,300 tickets. An NWA source gave me 7,300 fans and $110,000, which looked legit since it appeared to be about 2,000 tickets shy of a sellout. Either way, it's the second largest live gate of the year for the NWA (behind Baltimore) and one of the larger paid crowds of the year.

Having not seen the television production as of this writing, I can't comment much on the technical aspects. From what I've been told, aside from spectacular missed shots in the main event (which was bound to happen since the match was basically a tornado match and too much was going on at once for a TV camera to get it all in), the show was very good from that aspect.

Comments with fans after the matches basically had the same theme. There were no great matches except the main event. They were expecting more from such a major hyped show. The card was basically the quality of an average NWA house show, just with more impressive ring introductions thrown in. In fact, the last time I was in Philadelphia for the July 22nd house show, that "normal card" was much better than this PPV show.

The ring introductions, while more elaborate than at a normal house show, were not as spectacular as in the three previous NWA PPV shows. Overall, the entire aura of the card, even from the start, was nothing compared with the previous PPV shows that I've attended live. During the Luger-Pillman match, they had cheerleaders come out with Pillman and during the match they ran around the lower deck trying to get fans to cheer for Pillman and all it did was take fans "out" of the match because they were watching the cheerleaders. That may be why there was no intensity in the crowd during the build-up phase, and even a "boring" chant during that match before they went to the hot last few minutes. Results of the Observer poll of phone calls through Monday night:

Thumbs Up : 77 (40.3 percent)
Thumbs Down: 111 (57.5 percent)
In the middle: 4 (2.1 percent)

Some comments :

"Pretty disappointing. They were billing an electric cage and one shock and that was it."

Mike Kachel
Rockville, MD

"Apprehensive thumbs up. The final match almost blew it. I loved Warriors vs. Skyscrapers. Why did they even use Tommy Rich on the card? His match was horrible. I wasn't real impressed with Doom. "

Peter Thiele
Fridley, MN

"Zenk and Rotunda sucked. Rotunda worked like he was bored with life. The 6-man was a terrific match with a good ending. Rich's match was a dumb idea. Why put such a terrible match on a PPV? Even worse was it followed such a good match. Freebirds vs. Dudes was a good match, not great. Steiners vs. Doom was good and thought the ending was strong enough to get Doom over. Luger vs. Pillman was great. Road Warriors vs. Skyscrapers was better than I expected. Not great, but good. Main Event was almost hard to watch. At times it was good. Too much climbing on the cage. Overall I didn't find the match that good. It was a gimmick that didn't get over as well as it should have. The finish was just okay. Overall thumbs down because even the matches that were good didn't interest me because I just couldn't care about them. It just didn't seem like a major PPV card. Why was Robin Green put in an outfit that made her look like Jane Wyman on Falcon Crest? On Saturday's TV, they put her in something that accentuated the greatest body in the United States today. To cover it up was the biggest mistake of the card."

Fred Curtaz
Daly City, CA

"I was very disappointed with the show. It was my first live NWA show in a long time. The work was sloppy. The main event was real good. Road Warriors match was also good but the entire card was too predictable."

Dave Koss
Pennsauken, NJ

"Very marginal thumbs up. Nowhere near as good as the last two NWA PPV shows. It was like comparing a week in Disney World with a night at Busch Gardens. Maybe it isn't fair to compare it with the previous PPV shows . It was a decent show. I hope Starrcade is a whole lot better."

Chris Zavisa
Plymouth, MI

"Thumbs down. The only thing I liked was Jim Ross' comment about Sting's partner in the Blade Runners having not made the progress Sting made."

Steve Parker
Providence, RI

"Incredible. The best PPV show I've seen. Booking and execution were excellent. No flaws at all. Best match was the main event, followed by the six-man. The only bad match was Zenk vs. Rotunda. Everything else was two stars or better and the main event was five stars."

Scott Hudson
Atlanta, GA

"Thumbs up. Not a great show but pretty good action all the way through."

Mike Gunter
Raleigh, NC

"Thumbs up very slightly . I didn't like the way the heels were cheered so much and didn't like that only three faces won."

Sam Nord
Walnut Creek, CA

"I hope they never run a gimmick match like that again. Your average fan hearing about an electrified cage to see them climbing all over the cage would have felt ripped off. The best match was the six-man. It would have been a good PPV show for the WWF but it was the second worst one the NWA has done. This was a totally unnecessary show and they should have used the time to push Starrcade instead."

Jeff Bowdren
Plantation, FL

"Thumbs down. They had a cage match with no blood. They advertised parental discretion advised and didn't do anything violent . The only good match was the six-man tag . "

Dave Rubin
Island Park, NY

"Kind of disappointing, especially compared to the other big NWA shows. Luger vs. Pillman was the best match as far as I was concerned. No crowd reaction for the cage match and it was a real disappointing match."

Rick Carter
Las Vegas, NV

The next big thing on the agenda for the NWA is the Clash from Troy, NY on Nov. 15, which has a whole slew of problems built into it just from the choice of live venue. An interesting note to the Ric Flair vs. Terry Funk "I Quit Match" main event is that it will probably be Funk's final match, as he's scheduled to retire after the match and become the color commentator for World Wide Wrestling working with new host Chris Cruise. This is not to say that a coming out of retirement feud is an impossibility, but for now, nothing is in the works. Ironically, at 45, with a broken down body, Funk was far and away the most impressive performer on the PPV card. And thinking about it, for night-after-night consistency probably the only wrestlers in the United States this year who you could put ahead of him would be Ric Flair and Ricky Steamboat. As far as getting the most out of his physical ability, even Flair and Steamboat have to take a back seat to Funk.

The card for Starrcade '89 on Dec. 13 from the Omni in Atlanta, which is the NWA's next PPV event, will be two

"King of the Hill" round-robin tournaments. The singles tournament will have Ric Flair, Sting, Lex Luger and the Great Muta. The tag team tournament will have the Road Warriors, Skyscrapers, Steiners and Doom. The rules are that everyone has to wrestle everyone else, so it ensures unique match-ups like Flair vs. Sting, Luger vs. Muta, Warriors vs. Steiners that fans would normally never get to see. It also ensures the first Flair vs. Luger match, although it will be non-title. I think this would be a great idea— if this was Japan—or if this was held on a Clash. My own thoughts is that for Starrcade, the biggest show of the year, is you need a main event with a long build-up, more focusing on individual matches than this idea will allow, stronger grudges than this format will allow and the key titles on the line, if nothing else, to get the importance of the titles over. Those will be, as it stands now, the only matches on the card, so you'll have an NWA PPV event without The Freebirds, Midnight Express, Pillman, Dr. Death, Tully Blanchard or Arn Anderson (who I believe will be starting up on Christmas day in Charlotte as babyfaces).

The latest on the trial of Lia Maivia and company in Hawaii on extortion charges were that John "Dunbar" Wakayama, the promoter who claims to have been extorted, testified that he immediately recognized the voice of Ati So'o (who worked in the front office with Maivia's Polynesian Pro Wrestling promotion) when a man threatened him and his family if he didn't pay a $5,000 "tribute fee" to Maivia before promoting a series of three live shows in Hawaii in November of last year. So'o is Vice President of Maivia's company. Wakayama reported the threatening call to the FBI, which later wired him for sound during a meeting in a restaurant with Maivia and Anderson several days before the cards. The meeting continued in Wakayama's office, with Wakayama wired for sound, and Wakayama paid Maivia and Anderson $1,800 and promised to pay another $3,200 later. The FBI arrested Maivia and Anderson immediately upon their Leaving Wakayama's office. So'o claimed he had nothing to do with the extortion and claimed another person, one of Maivia's referees, made the call. Wakayama testified he had talked with So'o many times on the phone before (Wakayama was formerly the TV announcer for Maivia) and had no doubts he was the caller. The FBI has talked with other wrestling promoters who have run shows in Hawaii, both from the U.S. and Japan, to ask them if they faced similar extortion attempts.

Got a copy of the brochure for the proposed "Superpowers Wrestling" promotion that is attempting to start up in January. The brochure claims Superpowers Wrestling will be a combination of pro wrestling, amateur wrestling, karate, sambo and judo. They claim it has the same rules as pro wrestling, but it will be real and without gimmicks and theatre antics. The claim is they have eight teams, a U.S. team, Soviet team, Japanese team, Canadian team, West German team, Italian team, South Korean team and New Zealand team and expect eventual teams from Australia, France, England and China. The promotion is headed by Earl Greenburg, who according to the brochure, was Vice President of Compliance and Practices and later Vice President of Daytime Programming for NBC, producer of the Regis Phil bin Show, Fantasy and Life's Most Embarrassing Moments. This may not be correct as much of the info in this brochure regarding the wrestlers is incorrect. Greenburg is billed as Executive Producer of the TV show, Steve Edwards is Marketing Director, and his background includes Director of Marketing for Major Video Superstores, Antonio Inoki is the promoter, Tor Berg is Director of operations (Berg is from Alaska and the brochure claims he was nominated three times for the Promoter of the Year award by the Professional Wrestling Writers Association— is there such a thing?) and Brad Rheingans is the trainer. They list line-ups for three teams— Japan (Masa Chono, Riki in brochure as World champion as the brochure was printed up before he lost the IWGP title to Big Van Vader, Tatsumi Fujinami, Hiro Hase, Shinya Hashimoto and Masa Saito); United States (Bam Bam Bigelow, Jeff Blatnick, Brad Rheingans, Buzz Sawyer, Leon White and Steve Williams) and USSR (Vladimir Berkovich, Shota Chochyashivili, Wahka Eveloev, Salman Hashimikov, Andrei Slushaev and Victor Zangiev). Credentials for some are misrepresented in the brochure, with minor mistakes (Choshu and Saito are said to have been Olympians in 1976 and 1972 respectively when it was 1972 and 1964, Hase is said to be 21 years old when he's actually 28) to outright lies (Bigelow is billed as a former NCAA champion when he never even went to college). Other claims include "On April 14, 1988 in Hamilton, ONT pro wrestling set a record for the Largest crowd for any Canadian sporting event of 64,938."

Such an event never happened and the largest crowd for wrestling in Hamilton is about 16,000. "Wrestling consistently sells out Wembley Stadium in London." Obviously not true, wrestling never even plays Wembley Stadium. "In Paris, pro wrestling is the second highest rated TV show behind Dallas." Not true at all. "Pro wrestling in Australia is the No. 2 ranked spectator sport in terms of attendance." In reality, pro wrestling, except for a few shows at the smallest club level, is dormant in Australia. Some other claims are closer to legit, claiming a $3.2 million gate for the Tokyo Dome (actually $2,781,000 but that isn't far off) and using WWF figures for other claims of wrestling's popularity in the U.S. The plan is for Cable TV within the United States in January plus international syndication, a U.S. tour in May with a PPV event in May from Las Vegas which will be broadcast in Japan, South Korea and Taiwan, U.S. TV syndication in September, a full international schedule starting in October and a full U.S. schedule starting in 1991 and the first world-wide PPV in April of 1991. Of course, the odds are slim that even fractions of these plans will ever materialise.

Qintex, the Australian-based company that financed the RollerGames on syndicated television, with its bankruptcy, does threaten future plans of RollerGames. As of now, with Qintex out of the picture, the Roller Games has to find a new backer. They have television shows taped to last through February, but would need new money to continue past that point. They are going ahead with the pre-planned marketing ideas for now. Apparently, they have until Dec. 20 to find the new backer and tape a new set of episodes, or the venture will be phased out because of lack of funds, rather than through bad TV ratings. As it is, the ratings for the show have been decent, hovering just under a 4 rating nationally for the weekly syndicated shows. Many stations took the RollerGames as counter programming for NBC's Saturday Night Live and Saturday Night Main Events. Don't know how the SNL ratings have done against the RollerGames or if they've even made a dent, but against the first Saturday Night Main Event a few weeks ago on NBC, the competition of RollerGames didn't even dent the pull of Titan's show. The first SNME drew a 9.5 rating and 28 share, which is above the average for an SNME.

A more clear business evaluation of pay-per-view for the NWA should come when the numbers are in for Saturday's show. My interpretation of the numbers would be:

1) Anything below an 0.9 means not only that the concepts used in selling the show didn't work (i.e the Thunderdome cage gimmick and slick commercials without emphasis on the matches themselves) and they are doing too many PPV shows;

2) An 0.9 to 1.2 means the selling of the show didn't bomb and if the numbers remain constant at Starrcade, then doing five PPV shows next year is feasible as long as the promotion doesn't lose anymore ground;

3) 1.2 to 1.4 I'd say the selling of the show worked, Saturday night isn't a bad night for PPV, and the quality of the previous four excellent PPV shows probably got marginal fans to buy this one hoping for the same;

4) 1.5 or better – don't worry about a thing on PPV except to try and improve the quality of the next show. Five a year is just fine for now. Particularly if it holds up for the next show.

Useless trivia uncovered thanks to the earthquake: While cleaning up tumbled down bookshelves at a friend's house, I saw a baseball book written in 1953 and noticed several nicknames of old-time baseball players. The original "Nature Boy," was not Ric Flair, as most everyone knows, or Buddy Rogers as most had assumed. The original Nature Boy was Napolean Lajoie, a baseball star at the turn of the century. The original "Flying Dutchman" wasn't Dutch Savage, but baseball star Honus Wagner of the early 1920s

(actually that isn't an unknown fact). The one that many of you will know, but some younger readers might not, is that the original Dusty Rhodes was also a baseball player, a pinch-hitter for either the Brooklyn Dodgers or New York Giants in the mid-1950s and that wrestlings Dusty Rhodes took his name because that was his favorite baseball player while growing up.

AIL JAPAN

Four of All Japan's titles changed hands on the 10/20 card in the Aichi Gym in Nagoya before 4,120 fans. In the top match, Genichiro Tenryu & Stan Hansen captured both the PWF World and International tag team titles from Yoshiaki Yatsu & Jumbo Tsuruta in 22:28 when Hansen pinned Yatsu. The Foot Loose (Samson Fuyuki & Toshiaki Kawada) regained the Asian tag team titles beating the Can-Am Express (Dan Kroffat & Doug Furnas) in 16:36 when Fuyuki pinned Kroffat while Masa Fuchi regained the PWF World jr. heavyweight title pinning Joe Malenko in 19:15. The remainder of the card saw Giant Baba pin Tiger Jeet Singh, Abdullah the Butcher & Joel Deaton downed Akira Taue & Kabuki, Shunji Takano, Mighty Inoue pinned Akio Sato and Tsuyoshi Kikuchi pinned Richard Slinger (nephew of Terry Gordy).

All Japan announced the line-up for the tag team tournament from 11/17 to 12/6 with Tenryu & Hansen, Tsuruta & Yatsu, Foot Loose, Can-Am Express, Giant Baba & Rusher Kimura, The Nasty Boys, Abdullah & Tiger Jeet Singh, Kabuki & Shunji Takano, Bill Irwin & Terry Gordy and Dynamite Kid & Davey Boy Smith. No Fantastics or Malenko brothers.

Shamrock, according to the Japanese Wrestling Journal, is good for a rookie and has even used the moonsault press.

Hansen & Tenryu just aren't as impressive as a tag team as the team sounds.

Can-Am Express vs. Kenta Kobashi & Joe Malenko is said to be around a 4 ½ to 4 ¾ star match which says a lot for Can-Ams since Kobashi is still green. Kobashi will be a superstar in Japan in a few years but isn't there yet, but fans like him because he's a super-hard worker. The Tsuruta vs. Tenryu match where Tsuruta won the title was slow paced but the crowd gave it super heat for every spot. JWJ called it "great, but not nearly on the level of their previous match which is a match of the year candidate."

JWJ also called the most recent Liger vs. Sano match on 9/20 a match "second to none."

NEW JAPAN

They are billing Steve Williams, Buzz Sawyer, Rick Steiner, Manny Fernandez and Brad Rheingans for the tag team tournament from 11/24 to 12/7. Will be interesting to see whether the NWA lets Williams, Sawyer or Steiner go although I believe Jim Herd has a meeting scheduled with

Seiji Sakaguchi in the near future. Also in the tournament will be Soviets Hashimikov, Zangiev, Berkovich, Chimur Zarasov , and Slushaev.

10/20 in Niigata saw Riki Choshu & Shiro Koshinaka & Masa Chono beat Big Van Vader (Leon White) & Kokina the Samoan & Tony St. Clair (From England) in the main event, IWGP tag champs Shinya Hashimoto & Masa Saito went to a double count out with Kengo Kimura & Osamu Kido, Super Strong Machine & George Takano beat Matt Borne & Darryl Peterson, Jushin Liger beat Osamu Matsuda, Naoki Sano beat Hirokazu Hata and Kuniaki Kobayashi pinned Tom Prichard.

STAMPEDE

The promotion, which has fallen on hard times both in terms of ring action and crowds recently, should have at least a good short-term pick-me-up with the return of Owen Hart, Chris Benoit and Johnny Smith over the last week. All three, when they are "on," are among the top workers anywhere in the world and Hart has always been a good draw here.

Hart returned on 10/14 in Lethbridge, ALTA beating North American champ Larry Cameron via count out. He made his return to Calgary on 10/20 when his brother Bruce was wrestling Angel of Death and after Angel of Death was DQ'd, he kept pounding on Bruce until Owen ran in from the back and the two brawled back to the dressing room. Earlier in the card Bruce had his "ribs broken" during an interview with Brett & Matt Derringer who are doing a fake cowboy gimmick similar to the one Cowboy Tony used to do in Dallas except not combining it with a gay act. They used a hobby horse they were riding on Bruce's ribs. The next week they attacked Bruce again and shoved chewing tobacco down his throat. The only problem with the Derringers is that they've done two hardcore angles with Bruce, but when they work the grudge matches at the house shows, all they're capable of is doing comedy spots. Also on 10/20, Davey Boy Smith beat Cameron in a non-title match.

With the return of Owen Hart, the 10/27 show in Calgary picked up to 1,200 fans as Hart pinned Angel of Death when Larry Cameron's interference backfired. A gimmick for the show was all tickets would be $1 off to any fan who comes to the building with a Halloween costume. During the co-feature of Smith challenging Cameron for the title, someone in a Halloween costume interfered and cost Smith the title and it turned out to be Johnny Smith (billed as Davey's brother but in reality the two are no relation except that both are originally from England).

They are expecting a sellout this Friday with Cameron vs. Hart for the title and Davey vs. Johnny.

Abdul Wizal is back as a manager tho lord knows why.

10/28 in Edmonton drew 220 as Benoit returned and pinned Skull Mason ** ¼, Arch Angel (Curtis Thompson) pinned Biff Wellington * (Thompson doesn't show much) , Derringers beat Bruce Hart & Sumu Hara via DQ when Hara dropkicked one of them over the top rope ** , Owen Hart pinned Angel ** and Davey Smith beat Cameron via DQ when Johnny interfered and Owen Hart made the save *¾.

Talk of Bob Emory, the muscular jobber who worked a lot earlier in the year for TBS, coming in as one of the Black Harts, who as of now have disappeared.

Great Gama left for a tour of Singapore.

Expect Davey Boy Smith to be injured by Johnny since he's leaving for the tag team tournament.

D. J. Peterson is heading in and will get a big push as a babyface.

Also apparently coming in are Mando Guerrero and Konan the Barbarian (the top heavyweight heel in Mexico).

Bulldog Bob Brown was fired.

The top quality work may be short lived since Johnny Smith and Benoit are both being pursued by the World Wrestling Council since Cuban Assassin, who worked here extensively, is doing the booking in Puerto Rico.

CWA

Lots of changes here. Don't know if they are for the better, but the way business has been of late, they couldn't possibly be for the worst. Jerry Lawler was replaced as booker by Dutch Mantell, who is using Ricky Morton as his assistant. There was heat about the switch, but Lawler is kept pacified because he's allowed full control of his own matches.

Robert Gibson and Buddy Landel both quit the promotion because the money was so sparse. The full-timers are only earning around $30 to $40 per night, and with the driving from Memphis to Louisville and down to Nashville and all around through the week, you can't possibly survive.

Soul Taker captured the USWA title from Lawler on 10/23 in Memphis although the title change isn't recognized in the USWA where Lawler is still champion even though the USWA program plays in every market the CWA runs in. This must add tons of credibility to both programs and I guess continues to explain why this group has so many problems.

Finish of the Lawler-Soul Taker match saw Nate the Rat use his cane on Lawler, Mantell then ran in and Soul Taker went after him. Lawler got up from behind and held Soul Taker in a full nelson and Soul Taker broke the hold as Mantell got Nate's cane and swung it, hitting Lawler and Soul Taker pinned Lawler for the strap.

In other results, Freddy beat P. Y. Chu Hi via count out, Bill Dundee beat Cowboy Kevin Dillinger, The Violator (6'5, 265, flabby physique, not green but not good either) pinned Dustin Rhodes (who is leaving for USWA), Mantell pinned Mike Davis, Jeff Jarrett & Master of Pain (who works as Punisher in USWA) beat Wildside and after the match Ronnie Gossett fired Mark Starr from the team, Kerry Von Erich beat Dirty White Boy via DQ and Morton & Dundee beat The Blackbirds (Iceman King Parsons & Brickhouse Brown).

10/28 in Jonesboro, AK drew 250 as the New York Brawler (Lou Fabbiano doing a direct rip-off of Steve Lombardi's WWF gimmick) drew with Shawn Regal, Freddy beat Davis, Dundee pinned Dillinger, Mantell beat Dirty White Boy via DQ when Soul Taker interfered and Soul Taker pinned Lawler to keep the title when Nate used the cane (Lawler carried it okay but Taker real green and Lots of missed moves and the fans not into the match). Best match was Mantell-White Boy which was a good brawl.

They are now doing the bit with the losing streak with Dillinger which is a Dutch Mantell original idea as he came up with the gimmick several years back when Jack Hart (now Barry Horowitz) did it with Titan. On TV on 10/28, Dillinger went against debuting rookie Regal and lost again. They are building up some sort of an angle between Dirty White Boy and Dirty White Girl over a letter to White Boy from a girl in Georgia. On TV, White Boy was to defend the CWA title against Freddy, and White Boy destroyed Freddy easily and pinned him in the middle when another guy in a Freddy mask (the original—Tommy Gilbert) ran in and the two Freddy's got into it.

Gossett is still managing Chris Champion although they continually harp that the "fired" Mark Starr is Chris' brother.

Eddie Marlin "suspended" The Blackbirds for one week for hitting Morton with the baseball bat on TV the previous week.

The best skit they've done in many moons occurred after they showed the tape of Lawler losing the title. Mantell came out to apologize for costing Lawler the match but Lawler wouldn't accept the apology and then Bill Dundee came out to smooth things over and Lawler got nasty with Dundee as well. Lawler told both of them to mind their own business and that he just as soon would have both of them just leave the building before his main event match starts at the house shows. Lawler came off as a heel. It is no secret the promotion has long felt Lawler needed to turn heel since he meant nothing anymore as a face but Lawler balked because he probably made more money from public appearances and softball games than he did as a wrestler and he needed to stay face for the endorsement income. Some have also hinted that Lawler has political aspirations.

10/30 in Memphis had another family plan (two adults can bring as many kids as they want for $15 total and they sit in a special section with no alcohol allowed and no profanity allowed) night plus one adult could bring one kid free as they are desperate to at least get bodies into the Coliseum. Card is Mike Davis & Dillinger vs. Regal & King Cobra, Ken Wayne vs. New York Brawler, Violator vs. Frankie Lancaster, Real Freddy vs. Imposter Freddy, Bobby & Jackie

Fulton (as heels) vs. Morton & Dundee, White Boy vs. Mantell for the CWA title, Soul Taker vs. Lawler for USWA title and a blindfold Battle Royal.

USWA

10/20 in Dallas drew 450 as Jimmy Jack Funk beat Sheik Scott Braddock, P. Y. Chu Hi pinned Chris Adams in a Lumberjack strap match when Billy Travis hit Adams with the kendo stick, Jeff Jarrett & Terry Gordy went to a double count out with Ron Starr & Tarras Bulba, Eric Embry beat Billy Joe Travis via DQ when Gary Young and Chu Hi interfered but Eric beat all of them up, Gary Young beat Bill Dundee via DQ when Dundee had Young pinned but while the pin was going on, Young put a chain in Dundee's boot that Travis had handed to him and told the ref that Dundee used a chain and when the ref checked the boot he found it and reversed it and Jerry Lawler pinned Uncle Elmer in the main event when Travis gave Lawler a chain and he used it on Elmer for the pin and after the match Gordy ran in and decked Lawler and the main event saw Kerry Von Erich beat The Punisher to win the Texas title.

10/27 they let kids in free to combat the low crowds and brought Kevin Von Erich back for one shot and the result was the biggest crowd apparently in recent months although no word on how much was paid. Kevin & Kerry headlined against Bulba & Punisher plus Embry vs. Travis and a blindfolded Battle Royal.

Buddy Landel and Dustin Rhodes are announced as coming in but Landel probably won't now since he had the money problems with Jarrett.

Solomon Grundy returned on 10/21 as tag team partner of Uncle Elmer, but before they could get enough matches under their belt to clinch the worst tag team of the year honor for the yearbook, Grundy accepted Scandor Akbar's money and turned on Elmer and instead they are going after the worst feud of the year award.

Terrence Garvin (Beauty) is also back, thus far only doing color commentary and he was pretty bad at it the first time out.

Travis broke a guitar on Percy Pringle's head on 10/28's TV show.

Killer Tim Brooks drew 1,200 fans to his TV taping on 10/25 with the only thing major that is happening being Johnny Mantell turning heel on tag team partner Kenny the Stinger in the main event match against Brooks & John Tatum.

Matt Borne will return here after his Japan tour is over and he and Jeff Jarrett will remain tag team champions upon his return.

11/3 in Dallas has Jerry Lawler vs. Terry Gordy for the USWA title that Lawler doesn't even own, The worst tag team of 1985 reunites to try and do it again as Uncle Elmer & Cousin Junior face Solomon Grundy & Sheik Scott

Braddock, Travis & Young vs. Embry & Dundee, Steve Williams (not Dr. Death but a rookie) vs. Punisher, Jarrett vs. Chu Hi, Starr vs. Adams and Bulba vs. Funk.

Embry hasn't been pushing himself as much of late.

OREGON

The first match with new babyface Nord the Barbarian headlining against The Grappler took place on 10/21 in Portland. With Grappler down, Nord pulled up a shopping cart and was hitting Grappler with different items in the cart when all the heels ran in and attacked Nord and tied him up in the ropes and Grappler pulled out scissors and shaved off Nord's beard.

Headed in are Jonathan Holliday as a wrestler/manager and a new valet, name unknown, for Scotty the Body. The new valet will feud with Ginger, the former valet for Scotty who is now the face valet for Steve Doll.

10/24 they had a special show in Portland to commemorate the 21st anniversary of pro wrestling in the Portland Sports Arena headlined by Nord vs. Grappler in a hair vs. hair cage match. Nord pulled out a chain but Grappler got it and used it first but couldn't get the pin. Then Grappler tried to use powder but Nord got the powder and threw it at Grappler but couldn't get the pin. Grappler then tried to use the green mist but Nord moved and didn't take it. After a ref bump, Nord pulled out another object but Grappler got it and it wound up with both guys juicing (which is illegal in Oregon but that's another story for another day) and with Grappler knocked out, Brian Adams climbed into the cage and started cutting off large amounts of Nord's hair before Rip Oliver got into the cage to make the save. Also on the show, Al Madril kept the TV title beating Jeff Warner via forfeit when Warner accepted Grappler's money to leave the ring and turn heel plus Steve Doll & Rex King beat Col. DeBeers & John Boyd and Scotty the Body beat Bill Francis.

Even with Nord vs. Grappler on top, the crowds of late have been only a few hundred in Portland and barely 100 on the road.

THIS AND THAT

Raymond Schwartz, who was convicted in the Jim Leon (Ricki Lawless) murder was sentenced last Monday to 30 years in prison, of which the first 15 years he'll serve and the second 15 years will be suspended. He will also serve three years concurrently for carrying a dangerous weapon and Schwartz is still awaiting trial on a burglary charge.

The independent show in Manteca, CA scheduled for 10/21 was postponed due to the earthquake to 11/10 with Alexis Smirnoff, Ray Stevens and others appearing.

10/14 in Lakehurst, NJ drew 425 as Jules Strongbow double count out with Nikolai Volkoff and Cousin Luke beat Joe Daniels via DQ plus Linda Dallas and Kat LaRoux underneath.

10/21 in Woodbury, NJ drew 725 as Patty O'Brien beat Daniels for the WWA title and Big Hoss & Chief Thunder Mountain Lost the WWA tag team titles to the new Motor City Mad Men (Mike Moore & Al The Sledge Hammer) plus Kimala double count out with Strongbow and Cousin Luke appeared. WWA has shows 11/11 in South Philadelphia and 11/18 in Gloucester, NJ with Volkoff vs. Mike Sharpe.

Heritage Championship Wrestling ran its second TV taping on 10/25 in Vicksburg, MS using The Fantastics (as heels), Buddy Landel, Jerry Stubbs, Manny Fernandez and Robert Gibson. Paul Orndorff called ahead and canceled the date claiming an injury. Since this was to be Orndorff's return, some are wondering whether Orndorff is going to really make this comeback or not after all. The top match on the show saw Terry Gordy pin Dustin Rhodes which I'm told was an excellent television match with Gordy carrying Rhodes to a Japan calibre match.

10/29 at William Patterson College in Wayne, NJ drew 350 as Larry Zbyszko kept the AWA title pinning David Sammartino and Ken Patera beat Volkoff.

Kendall Windham beat Ron Slinker on 10/29 in Orlando to win the Caribbean title. Iceman King Parsons & Brickhouse Brown have some dates in Florida this week against Florida tag team champions Dennis Knight & Jumbo Barretta so the Blackbirds will be in as baby faces.

Parsons & Brown are also working every weekend in November for Edward Faulk's independent group in Louisiana.

Red Bastien's WIN promotion taped 10/28 in San Bernardino before 70 fans. A Mexican wrestler called Super Boy wowed the crowd with Owen Hart calibre flying. Also on the show included Konan, Mando & Eddie Guerrero and The Mercenaries (Billy Anderson & Louie spicoli & Riki Ataki).

Watch for Spicolli as an NWA jobber and Bobby Eaton lookalike.

11/10 in Mexico City will have Dos Caras defending the WWA World title against Konan.

Angelo Mosca has been campaigning in the press to get the soon to be vacant job of commissioner of the Canadian Football League. Mosca said he'd use pro wrestling marketing techniques to bolster the financially distraught league. Being that Mosca had such a long successful run as a promoter one would think that would make him qualified to run a football league. How many shows did Mosca promote? I think it was one very successful show, then a year later two unsuccessful shows and never again.

Phone Programs Inc. will be starting a wrestling trivia line with Bruno Sammartino and Lou Albano.

Universal Wrestling Superstars is billing TV tapings on 11/8 at the Regina Center in Brooklyn and 11/9 at Farrell High School in Staten Island with Bruno Sammartino and Craig DeGeorge billed as announcers plus Big John

Studd, Bam Bam Bigelow, David Sammartino, Kimala, Stan Hansen and Lou Albano as a manager.

10/13 in Knoxville saw The Southern Boys (Tracy Smothers & Steve Armstrong) beat Jimmy Golden & Brian Lee but the CWF tag titles didn't change hands since there was outside interference from Dixie Dynamite (Scott Armstrong), Robert Fuller, Jerry Stubbs and Sylvia. Also Dennis Condrey kept the CWF title beating Davey Rich in an I Quit match, Adrian Street & Todd Morton beat Beauty & The Beast, Stubbs beat Fuller via DQ and Dynamite drew Cactus Jack Manson.

USWA on 10/21 in Mesquite, TX saw Eric Embry & Percy Pringle beat Billy Travis & Scandor Akbar, Terry Gordy beat Punisher to earn a title shot at Jerry Lawler, Kerry Von Erich beat Taras Bulba in a cage match, Jeff Jarrett beat Ron Starr, Chris & Toni Adams beat P. Y. Chu Hi & Tojo Yamamoto, Bill Dundee drew Gary Young and Uncle Elmer beat Sheik Braddock.

Terry Gray's Southern Wrestling Federation ran a show on 10/15 in Ft. Lauderdale with Rock & Roll Express (Rick Morton & Robert Gibson) teaming with Grey to beat The Mighty Yankees (Bob Cook and someone else) & The Moondog plus Bugsy McGraw beat Kendall Windham via DQ.

Lia Maivia's card on 10/20 in Honolulu drew nearly 5,000 as Rocky Johnson beat Dave Friend, The Samoan Connection (Farmer Boy Ipo & LeRoy Brown) went to a double disqualification against Mando Guerrero & Konan the Barbarian (Last week I incorrectly reported that it was Dean Hart and someone else), Steve Strong beat Lightning Leilani and Don Muraco beat Bob Orton in the main event.

Texas All-Pro Wrestling has a show on 11/25 at the Sam Houston Coliseum headlined by Kerry Von Erich vs. Kimala.

AWA has a TV taping on 11/18 in Rochester, MN with Larry Zbyszko defending the title against Nikita Koloff, Destruction Crew defending the tag title against The Fantastics (Fultons), Pat Tanaka returns vs. Paul Diamond plus they are also advertising the return of both Doug Somers and Jerry Blackwell.

Chris Love's show on 10/10 in Peru, IN drew 750 as Ricky Steamboat teamed with Zebra Kid to beat the Kansas Outlaws (Roger Ruffin & Sam Cody). It was Steamboat's first match since leaving the NWA in July.

10/14 in Warsaw, IN drew 800 as the Nightmares beat Flying Tigers.

Wayne Coulter's Professional Wrestling from Florida promotion is trying to put together a public stock offering to raise capital. PWF officials are working with Tampa underwriter American Wall Street Securities, Inc. to get Securities and Exchange Commission approval. Coulter is hoping to raise between $500,000 and $2 million in capital to keep the promotion going and make it more competitive

with the larger organizations. The only other promotion which sold stock to the public that I know of was Global in Florida, which went out of business within one year.

NWA

Expect to see these matches on television over the next few weeks as part of the ratings sweeps: Freebirds vs. Steiners for the NWA tag team title, Ric Flair vs. Bobby Eaton (which will be the first time these two have ever worked a singles match), Steve Williams vs. Sid Vicious and Great Muta vs. Tommy Rich.

With Terry Funk being retired after the 11/15 Clash card, his spot in Gary Hart's Army will be taken by Buzz Sawyer. Sawyer can be one of the best workers around, but his track record shows that it's quite a risk using him, particularly in such a key position over the long haul.

The Dragon Master (Kazuo Sakurada) was at the PPV and came to the ring with Muta but nobody in Philadelphia even knew who he was and I don't think he was even acknowledged on the PPV either.

To correct a mistake from last week. NWA didn't lose its World Wide Wrestling slot in Chicago. The slot was simply moved as NWA is scheduled to have a 10 a.m. to noon time slot with both syndicated shows on WGBO in Chicago on Saturday. The reason the NWA isn't promoting Chicago for the next few months is simply because they canceled November so as not to compete with Survivor Series and with the week off in December, other cities were scheduled so it's not like they are out of the market, but still no live shows until next year.

Kangaroo Athletic Wear will be doing a major promotion with the NWA besides coming out with the new shoes bearing the names of Ric Flair, Sting, Road Warriors, Rick Steiner and Lex Luger. They will have life-sized posters of the six wrestlers on display at sporting goods stores throughout the country plus will be marketing Sting make-up kits, Ric Flair combs, Lex Luger sunglasses and Road Warrior spiked bracelets. The contract with the NWA specifies that Kangaroo gets 10 days per year with each of the wrestlers for promotional work and they'll have a party for the Kangaroo execs and have the company bigwigs in attendance at the 11/18 St. Louis card. They'll see a lot of empty seats since only 250 tickets were sold for that card as of Monday.

NWA had its best ratings weekend in many moons the weekend before the PPV show, which may bode well for the PPV doing better than anticipated. World Championship Wrestling on 10/21 got a 2.6 rating, which is the highest since March, while the Power Hour on 10/20 set a new record with a 2.6 rating and NWA Main Event on 10/22 got a 2.5. The World Series on 10/28 probably didn't hurt the PPV as bad as anticipated either since the ratings for the Series finale were no better than normal programming would have done in the same slot.

Seven wrestlers were fined $1,000 apiece for missing a show in Charleston, WV.

The Skyscrapers missed one or two shots as well and have talked with Titan. Titan isn't as thrilled as you would think about Sid. Everyone knows he's going to be one of the biggest stars of the 90s, but he hurts people in the ring and that's the last thing they want.

10/27 in Richmond, VA drew 4,500 as Dynamic Dudes beat New Zealand Militia, Zenk beat Irwin, Pillman pinned Rotunda, Steiners double count out with Skyscrapers, Sting double count out with Muta, Luger pinned Williams (best match on card), Freebirds beat Road Warriors via DQ and Flair pinned Funk.

They've talked with Stan Hansen about coming in.

WWF

Some personnel notes The actual story about Barry Windham (Widow Maker) is that he had an operation to remove a benign tumor underneath his breast bone and should be back in a few weeks. Several at Titan continually denied there was an injury but that's the case.

Bret Hart was hospitalized after Sunday night's card in Toronto when he took the guard rail wrong in a match with Dino Bravo. He had to be stretchered out of the building and spent the night in a Toronto hospital before being flown home on Monday to Calgary. The Toronto newspapers reported a ruptured spleen, but I'm told that report was incorrect and that he's got badly bruised ribs but is in pretty severe pain.

Tim Horner was also injured Saturday night at Madison Square Garden but don't know the extent of that injury.

Supposedly Koko B. Ware will be back early next year after being fired in Europe.

Apparently Jim Troy, the Titan VP in charge of international affairs and lying on PPV buy rates was the instigator of their fight in Brussels. Troy officially has resigned from the company in order to work more in boxing, although he's still working out of the same office and is still a consultant to Titan.

The Niagara Falls building is claiming a Hogan vs. Zeus match for 12/11, which may be taped for the PPV on 12/27.

Fred Blassie made an appearance on Prime Time Wrestling on 10/23. That Prime Time show drew a 2.8 rating, which is the best since football season started and highest rated cable show of the week, while All American on 10/22 drew a 2.4.

The match where Demolition beats Brain Busters (Tully Blanchard & Arn Anderson) for the tag team titles will air on the syndicated Superstars of Wrestling show this coming Saturday.

TV tapings Tuesday night in Topeka (Superstars & SNME for November) and Wichita on Wednesday (Challenge).

10/29 in Colorado Springs, CO drew 1,600 and $20,000 as Honky Tonk Man pinned Jim Neidhart, Tugboat Thomas pinned Barry Horowitz, Rockers beat Rougeaus, Paul Roma pinned Ted Danz, Haku pinned Red Rooster, Rick Martel pinned Brutus Beefcake and Jake Roberts beat Ted DiBiase via DQ.

10/22 in Los Angeles drew a $170,000 house as Hercules pinned Akeem -** ½, Greg Valentine pinned Ron Garvin ** ½, Al Perez beat Horowitz * , Rick Rude beat Roddy Piper via DQ * ½, Bushwackers beat Powers of Pain via count out - * , Honky Tonk pinned Rooster * ¼ and Roberts beat DiBiase via DQ ½ *.

10/21 in Winnipeg drew 4,000 as The Genius pinned Sam Houston, Thomas beat Brooklyn Brawler, Ultimate Warrior beat Andre the Giant in 20 seconds, Demolition Smash & Neidhart beat Arn Anderson & Tully Blanchard (in the newspaper before the card it was written that Demolition had won the belts in Wheeling and would be defending, and the crowd was confused since Tully & Arn entered the ring with the title belts - by the way, best match on show), Hart drew Bravo, Mr. Perfect pinned Jimmy Snuka and Jim Duggan beat Randy Savage via DQ in a bad match.

All sorts of rumors about guys leaving after Thanksgiving, but the only ones I know of are Rougeaus and Blanchard & Anderson. Where would anyone else go? With the exception of Hart, apparently NWA hasn't seriously talked with anyone and they are nowhere near a deal. And the way the business is now, unless you are like the Rougeaus who simply want to go home and quit traveling, you don't quit Titan until you've got a firm deal with the NWA or Japan or you stand a good chance of winding up with nothing.

THE READERS' PAGES

OLD TIME WRESTLING

I read something in a letter that I didn't agree with and felt I had to write. It was that entrance music is a major ingredient in a wrestler getting heat from the crowd. In my opinion, nothing could be more wrong . If a main event wrestler needs entrance music to get heat, then he doesn't belong in the main events.

In the 1960s here in Northern California, Pepper Gomez didn't need any entrance music but the fans loved him and let him know it by their loud and Long applause. The same for Ray Stevens. The fans actually hated the heels Like Kenji Shibuya, Pat Patterson and Dr. Bill Miller. How many of today's heels are actually hated by the fans? As a kid, I remember going to see the matches every other Wednesday in San Jose. The main event was always two out of three falls and 90 percent of the time the first two falls were split. By the start of the third fall, the fans from the balcony were down on the main floor and were 10 feet deep all around the ring, clapping and cheering for the babyface to make his comeback. All this heat was generated without any entrance music. I went to the WWF's last card in Arco Arena in Sacramento and the music was so loud and you couldn't hear a thing after the music stopped. Do you think maybe they give everyone music and turn it so loud because if they didn't you could hear a mouse squeak when the wrestlers came to the ring? I know that with Tommy Rich, Hercules Hernandez and I'm so with many others that there is no fan response at all, just noise from the music.

Not only is the music ridiculous but the outfits some of the guys are wearing are as well. You see jobbers in the first match of their careers in patent leather boots that come up to their knees, multi-colored spandex wrestling tights, sequined jackets and bleached blond hair. All this and they get beat up in less than two minutes. What is wrong with having most of the guys on the card where black boots and trunks like they do in Japan? That way, when a guy like Ric Flair or Sting comes out with a colorful outfit, it means something . The same thing with the music. Save it for a few special wrestlers, like the Road Warriors, whose music matches them perfectly.

Rich Frisk
Sacramento, California

Dave Meltzer: We can debate forever the positives and negatives of pro wrestling in the 60s and 70s as compared with today. But the audience is totally different and the product is different for a whole slew of reasons, some differences in society, some differences in promotion and some the difference that happens when so much wrestling is available on free television which forces promotions to go farther and farther out to gain attention and attract viewers. But this letter reminded me of growing up and attending wrestling every other Wednesday in San Jose and I talked with my best friend in those days and realized a few points. One is, the number and percentage of kids that attended the live shows then was probably comparable to what the WWF draws, because the crowds were loaded with kids in those days and older people, but seemed to be missing the ages 15-25. There was tons more heat derived from the matches but that was because there was a greater believability factor and because with only one promotion on television, there were very few stars in comparison with today than one would have to be familiar with and you became exceedingly familiar with the main eventers. I can think of a lot of positives about territorial wrestling. More live shows. More wrestlers able to make a living. More movement of wrestlers when they became stale. There are just as many negatives as the business was less competitive and more like a big oligopoly, who got pushed was probably as much if not more politically determined because a promoter could get just about anyone over when he controlled all the wrestling the viewer had the chance to see, the big names didn't have the opportunity to make money on the level of today's big stars

unless they were lucky enough to get regular Japan work. The actual quality of the work and shows were primitive compared with today. But the emergence of promotions with national television exposure began to make territorial wrestling somewhat obsolete, and while territories still exist and will exist for years to come, they won't ever be the same as they were as long as a dominant promotion has national exposure.

WRESTLEMANIA

Over the last few weeks, in talking with several other readers, one topic that comes up in each conversation is the upcoming WrestleMania. We all agree that Titan seems to have no big money match coming up. It's too early to turn either the Warrior or Roddy Piper and with Piper's Hollywood career, I don't think he wants to be a heel anymore, anyway. Barry Windham hasn't gotten enough of a push, and with his family history, he may be considered too unreliable for the main event. Although Hogan vs. Windham could be a real good match, that is of course, irrelevant to Titan.

I've come up with an idea. I know that Vince McMahon probably wants badly to do the mixed match (Hogan & Elizabeth vs. Savage & Sherri). But Elizabeth probably doesn't want to wrestle. Randy Savage probably doesn't want her to wrestle and why would Sherri want to wrestle Liz, because there is nothing she could do with her? Here's a way around it. Have Sherri injure Liz, then have Hogan look for a partner to get revenge on Sherri (although after SummerSlam, they could always book Hogan vs. Sherri) and this gives them the perfect chance to bring back Wendi Richter. I know she left on bad terms, but so did Barry Windham and Jimmy Snuka. The main event could be a huge money maker with the most popular women wrestler ever in the U.S. teaming with the most popular wrestler ever against Titan's two best heels, with Elizabeth still in the corner.

Steve Friedlander
Bronx, New York

Dave Meltzer: The consensus within wrestling is that it'll be Hogan vs. Warrior in the main event at WrestleMania, but I don't think the actual decision will be made for another month or so and it should be obvious by sometime in January where things are headed.

RATINGS

You should have given the No. 1 spot to Jushin Liger. No. 2 should be Naoki Sano. Bobby Bradley is the best worker on the WIN show. He's one of the best fliers around and is only 18 years old. Hopefully he'll be in Japan in a few years.

David Hannah
Studio City, California

HARVEY COBB

Over the past few months you have heard a lot about myself and Pro Wrestling Enquirer . First, I would Like to say PWE hasn't anything to do with the lawsuit Ron Wyatt has against me. The letter in the 10/16 issue of the Observer by Wyatt is full of lies meant to hutr me and tarnish the reputation of PWE.

Wyatt says he tried to work out a payment plan with me. Not true. I haven't spoken to him in more than three months. Last time we spoke was July 29th and no deal was made.

We did not go to court and there was no hearing because the case was settled out of court for $1,000 and I have yet to pay it.

Since there was no hearing, I didn't call his lawyer and try to work out a deal for $800. That was my grandfather who called and wanted to settle for $800. Wyatt says I'm not working and that is not true. If Wyatt is taking me back to court, I don't know anything about it.

Harvey Cobb
Norfolk, Virginia

TAPES

I'm sending this letter as a warning to fans who may have seen an ad recently on television regarding a series of four wrestling tapes for sale. The tapes were advertised by VCA Wrestling of New York, titled, "Battle Royals," "Caged Madness," "Monsters of the Mat" and a bloopers tape called "Crazy Cuts."

On the surface, this looked great. The matches were all vintage classic early 70s stuff. I paid over $110 for the set. They are a big rip-off in my opinion, except for the tape called "Crazy Cuts."

The first three tapes contain such people as Bruiser & Crusher, Bockwinkel & Stevens, Ox Baker, Ernie Ladd, Superstar Graham, Wahoo McDaniel, Bobby Heenan, Pepper Gomez, Dick Murdoch, Dusty Rhodes, Baron Von Raschke, Blackjacks Lanza & Mulligan, Jimmy & Johnny Valiant, The Sheik, Bobo Brazil, Bruno Sammartino, Chris Taylor, Mad Dog Vachon, Moose Cholak, Haystacks Calhoun, Verne Gagne and others. The matches are filmed from a typical low-tech early 70s view, and that's okay. It's expected and it doesn't hamper the fact that these matches are almost all great stuff. Where is the rub?

The original soundtrack was taken out and Bob Luce overdubbed the announcing. Words cannot describe how inept Bob Luce is. He destroys the enjoyment of these three tapes. He makes the Ultimate Warrior and Andre the Giant sound like William F . Buckley. The guy can't talk. He stumbles over words and everything is "the best ever" or "can 't get any better" and he wanders on and babbles about things totally alien to what's going on. He really ruins a great series of matches. There's plenty of blood and lots of super action, but his announcing will make you beg for Rod Trongard or Bill Mercer. If they would re-issue these tapes with the original soundtrack, I'd pay another $110 to see them as they are that good, but with Bob Luce, they are very close to torture to view.

The last tape is worth ordering because it is all studio raps and interviews so we get to hear the original soundtrack. No matches, but lots of great studio stuff with Crusher, Bruiser, Gomez, Kim Duk, Mitsu Arakawa, Cholak, Jimmy Valiant, Heenan, Ladd and Lots of Baker and Rhodes.

Richard Kunkel Akron, Ohio

RODDY PIPER

I want to comment on Roddy Piper's inclusion in the Most Unimproved Wrestler section. I have an ethical thing about putting guys in this category who are injured. That doesn't just go for Piper, although he's a good example, because there's plenty of fodder coming from the uninjured ranks.

It was always my impression that this award was based strictly on ring work, not interviews. While, I do admit Piper is far better as a heel interview and being a face in his current WWF role is difficult for him, he is still good. His work on Prime Time has improved tremendously. I think it is perfectly fair to compare his current interview skill with his old interviews., but i'm not sure this is the right category for it.

However, it is completely unfair to put him in this category based on ring work. It doesn't seem possible to me that a guy who is barely back in the ring full-time for two months, much of it working with a major injury, can be evaluated as being unimproved. That doesn't take into consideration a two-and-a-half year layoff. Piper's SNME match was filmed prior to his injury and compare that with his match at Madison Square Garden, which appears to be the best match he's had with Rick Rude so far, should give you an example of how much this injury has affected his work. It is hardly typical of Piper to have trouble sustaining heat and getting to his feet off the mat, taking long restholds, blowing up easily, working slow and lacking his usual hand speed and not displaying intensity of fire. With Piper, his intensity is a state of being. It's a combination of his natural presence, vocal inflection, facial expressions, and deliberate body language. When he feels like hell, it's the first thing that goes. From what I've seen and heard, he's struggling to get through his matches with his ribs intact and is working on automatic pilot more or less. If I had to describe his matches with Rude, it would be disjointed. He seems to hit the wall after about 2 minutes of working near normal speed. I also don't discount he's had a similar injury before but managed to work for six weeks before he just had to stop and take some time off.

Unfortunately, he appears to be going down the same road again. Maybe this time he'll get lucky. The thing I don't like is that even after the intercostal nerve blocks, he's still evincing a lot of pain and breathing difficulty, which suggests he's in rough shape. I wouldn't be surprised if he limped along with his injury well into December as working a full schedule doesn't leave much time for healing. I just hope he'll be able to pull himself together by thanksgiving because he's going to have to carry his team, as well as his opponent if he feuds with Snuka, and right now he's in no condition to carry anyone.

It's shaping up to be the toughest year of Piper and his WWF career, but if he can hang on without another major injury, his eventual heel turn should be well worth waiting for, since he's more over as a face this time round. His feud with Snuka should be hot, although the matches may not be. Other than his injury, he looks to be in good shape and appears to be around 220. He lacks any sag to his physique, no doubt because of all those years without a tan and not being overly pumped up. His various orthopedic problems (back/hip/knee/wrist) seem to have healed decently.

I've not been too crazy about Ric Flair's booking. Being a hardcore wrestler, hes booking way too hardcore. Some of the angles he comes up with smack of Dusty Rhodes which is pretty frightening in itself. He seems to have fallen into the trap of feeling he must come up with an angle that is more fantastic, and often more absurd, than the previous one, which is not necessarily the best thing. Flair getting possibly replaced gives grave predictions to his future with the NWA. I think he needs to step out of his role as the No. 1 wrestler in the promotion and look at the promotion as a fan, rather than as a wrestler. His personal decisions haven't been the best, either. I do realise it's hard to pilot a boat that is already full of holes before you get on board. Working with the brass at TBS can't be much of a pleasure either.

Teresa DeMarie
Tuckahoe, New York

BACKGROUNDS

Could you provide some background on Robin Green? How she got into wrestling and what she was doing previously. Also, what positions did Brian Pillman and Lex Luger play in the NFL and USFL and for how long?

Ken Capps
St. Louis, Missouri

Dave Meltzer: Robin Green (Nancy Daus) has been with Kevin Sullivan the past few years. She formerly was Sullivan's valet "Fallen Angel" on several smaller promotions and on independent shows but I don't know any other background on her. Brian Pillman was a noseguard in college football at the University of Miami of Ohio and was the Mid American Conference Most Valuable Player as a junior and a senior in 1982 and 1983 and was second team All-American on the Playboy squad in 1983 and honorable mention on most

other squads.

Interestingly enough, the first team All-American on the Playboy squad that year was William "Refrigerator" Perry, and you couldn't find two more diverse body types than that playing the same position. Because of his lack of size (which is also why he was an unrecruited walk-on in college), he wasn't drafted by the NFL but made the Cincinnati Bengals in 1984 as a free agent linebacker and mainly was on the suicide squad that year before being traded to Buffalo before the 1985 season. He was injured and wound up playing for the Calgary Stampeders before an ankle injury ended his football career and he turned to pro wrestling in Canada. Luger (Larry Pfohl) played college football at Penn State in 1976 and either was kicked off the team or transfered to University of Miami (in Florida) in 1977 and was kicked off that team. Because he couldn't even try out for the NFL until his senior class had graduated, he went to Canada and I believe played for the Montreal Alouettes and was a starting offensive tackle at the age of 19. He was in camp with the Green Bay Packers and played pre-season games with them, but never made the team, and wound up with Memphis in the USFL before the league folded and he drifted into pro wrestling.

GENIUS OF MCMAHON

Over the past few weeks, with all the talk centering around Tully Blanchard and Arn Anderson's defection back into the NWA, and rumors of other WWF stars doing the same, I've realized the true genius of Vince McMahon.

While McMahon obviously creates his gimmicks to make money and add color to otherwise bland wrestlers, I believe he also creates them to prevent talent from leaving. The most obvious example of this would be Terry Taylor, who at this point has humiliated himself to a point where he cannot wrestle outside of the WWF because fans of no other organization would take him seriously. Some less obvious examples would be Ted DiBiase, Curt Hennig and Randy "Macho King" Savage.

Assuming Titan Sports had a copyright on the "Million Dollar Man" gimmick, DiBiase would have to go back to the basics if he were to join the NWA. That would look mighty silly, going from being a millionaire to being an average Joe. Fans would not simply forget that Curt Hennig was Mr. Perfect if he were to follow Blanchard and Anderson. Ignoring that gimmick would be too confusing to the average fan. Is it not a coincidence that Savage became Macho King around the same time Blanchard and Anderson gave notice? While some might see it as a renewed push given to Savage after two losses on the last two PPV events, a more critical viewer sees it as a brilliant ploy devised by McMahon to make Savage Look like a pathetic cartoon figure. As big of a star as Savage has become, he'd have a heck of a time trying to get NWA fans to take him seriously.

Sam Nord
Walnut Creek, California

Dave Meltzer: McMahon has the gimmick names trademarked, not copyrighted, but yes, another group in theory can't use the gimmick names (although most wrestlers who have left the WWF have used their gimmick names with little effort by Titan to stop them – "Adorable" Adrian Adonis in the WWF, JYD, Uncle Elmer, Cousin Luke, Cousin Junior, Dynamite Kid and others were all trademarked names as well as was John Studd and virtually every name except Ricky "The Dragon" Steamboat that has been with Titan in recent years and used a name other than their real name). If Taylor were to come to the NWA, he'd have problems at first from catcalling fans and it would be hard to push him past a certain level, but more because Titan has established him as a prelim talent in combination with the moniker. DiBiase, Hennig and Savage could jump, forget the gimmick names, and do just fine. But Savage is the only one who would really draw.

STEINER SKIT
While I'll admit the Scott Steiner skit was hardly the best skit of the decade, it sure wasn't as bad as you thought. I guess I was lucky, but I picked up on the "I'm going for help" line immediately. Put me down as one who really enjoyed the skit. The only problem with the whole thing now is Nancy Sullivan's acting ability, or lack of it. True, she is stunning, but her delivery reminds me of Ron Garvin. This angle is one of my favorites of the year.

My award favorites in some categories are: Rookie of the year—Dustin Rhodes; Most Improved—Scott Steiner; Most Disgusting Promotional Tactic—Jose Gonzales' babyface return in WWC following his acquittal; Most Unimproved and Worst Wrestler—Jim Duggan; Feud of the year—Ric Flair vs. Terry Funk; Card of the year—Wrestle War in Nashville with the Baltimore Bash a close second.

Scott Hudson
Atlanta, Georgia

A few months back, I had given up on wrestling. It had gotten to such a bad state. Then, totally by surprise at an NWA card in Philadelphia, I saw the light at the end of the tunnel. The wrestlers from the top to the bottom of the card performed like never before, and the powerful personalities of the talent seemed to be exploding. The Freebirds, Steiner s, Muta and Sullivan are all capable of the highest in wrestling showmanship. They can stink, also. But the most impressive is Terry Funk. He is the only person in the NWA who can tear up a crowd without even getting into the ring. Hate him or love him, he's the best there is. The complaints about the plastic bag are missing the point. Funk

is there to stir up trouble and hatred and to push Ric Flair as a baby face and make fans interested. I thought the plastic bag and Steiner assault and Robin Green into Woman were all great. Much better than Norman's keys, the Ding Dongs or Ricky Steamboat, the family man.

Wrestling should be wild, crazy, violent and border on the taboo. Anyone who doesn't like that should watch the WWF.

Joel Shipley
Philadelphia, Pennsylvania

Dave Meltzer: There's a thin line, often hard to distinguish, between good heat and bad heat, even though both appear to be the same at the house show. Good heat draws fans. Bad heat, which gets fans every bit as mad, maybe worse, makes them not come to the show. Whatever any of us personally think pro wrestling should be, when it crosses a certain line where more people decide not to go to the show from an angle then decide to attend the show because of that same angle, no matter what I or anyone else thinks of the angle, it is not a good angle because it defeated the purpose of why it was put there. The only exception I would have to using that as a rule is any character that teaches and reinforces in people dangerous stereotypes. That has nothing to do with being good or bad for wrestling, but being bad for society, which is a much more important factor than gates at a pro wrestling event. Wrestling should never be the place kids look to for role models (they do, but they do with other people who are no better) but it isn't good for society as a whole to reinforce ancient, sometimes outdated in the real world and certainly dangerous stereotypes of foreigners, blacks and other minorities.

AWARDS FAVORITES
Time to run down some of the last few categories when it comes to the Observer awards. Next week we'll finish this up and start getting on with the balloting for the awards. The awards are an annual part of the Observer yearbook, which will be released hopefully by the end of January. This year's book will be the biggest, and hopefully the best as we'll not only have annual awards but decade awards and hopefully lots of other interesting features to boot.

MOST CHARISMATIC: This is for the guy who has to do the least to get the most. Somehow, I think this describes the Ultimate Warrior almost to a T. Second place would be Hulk Hogan. If Zeus was a wrestler full-time, I'd be tempted to give him third. If Elizabeth was anything full-time, I'd be tempted as well. Chigusa Nagayo has retired. Sting was like a rising comet last year but I don't see anything more charismatic about him than anyone else getting pushed in the NWA right now. I guess Akira Maeda belongs on this list near the top as well.

BEST TELEVISION ANNOUNCER: Jim Ross won big last year and he's been even better this year, for the most part. He clinched it in my book on February 20th with his call of the Ricky Steamboat-Ric Flair match, which was better on television than it was live, and it was one hell of a match live. I recognize he's got his detractors who would say his energy live is too high for an entire show (while others would argue that is one of his strongest points) or he hypes too much on television and doesn't call the match enough (more a function of the difference between calling wrestling and calling a sporting event today, and this criticism is voided on any major event where nobody calls a match better). Anyway, taking everything into consideration that I've seen this year, whomever is second would not even be a close second. As for second, Lance Russell is not anywhere as good out of the Memphis environment as he was in it. Tony Schiavone is very good. Vince McMahon does what he's supposed to do, which isn't hard since he's the guy who decides what the announcer is supposed to do. But he doesn't exactly spend his time calling the action and not hyping or keeping his energy level low, either, and doesn't impart nearly as much into a broadcast or bring any sense of realism to the show in comparison with Ross. Lee Marshall has a good voice, but since SuperClash was still technically in this year's period and that was about the worst announcing job I've ever seen on a big show, that's a big demerit. Not his fault because the supervisors must have told him to lie to the level he did during the show, but he appeared to be so dishonest and uninformed at times that I've never been able to take him seriously since. Admittedly, he has never been that bad since, but awards are won and lost on the big show.

WORST FEUD: Let's see, who worked programs with Andre the Giant this year? Why, of course, John Studd. Do you remember that feud? you don't? It headlined all over the country. Plus, it was a rehash of the legendary Andre the Giant vs. John Studd feud of 1984, which, not so coincidentally, was the worst feud of that year as well. Eric Embry vs. Scandor Akbar was actually a great feud, considering the limited appeal of these two, for a long time. But not this long. It's gotten silly and ridiculous at this point and if crowds are any indication, this was over a long time ago. It's just that some people haven't found out yet, and they are the ones in charge. Col DeBeers vs. Derrick Dukes get a mentions for pure bad taste and the fact that nobody came out to see the paint matches to begin with.

NOVEMBER 13, 1989

After a WrestleMania-like response of 420 letters or phone calls over the past week, the response to Halloween Havoc was the closest and probably the most varied since we've started doing the polls after the big shows.

HALLOWEEN HAVOC

Thumbs up: 202 (48.1 percent)
Thumbs down: 209 (49.8 percent)
In the middle: 9 (2.1 percent)

A couple of trends to note about these results. First off, the response was significantly more positive among those who viewed the show on PPV as compared with those there live. From those live, we had a 57-16-1 response with the 57 being negative. If you take those 74 responses away, you wind up with a somewhat positive, although not overly so, from those viewing on PPV A second trend is that those who voted on the phone were a lot more negative than those who wrote letters. The only reason I bring this up, because I don't know if it means anything and what it would mean if it did, is because this was a definite strong trend in both directions which when put together, almost equalled out to a total stalemate.

Just to set the record straight, officially the live show drew 7,300 fans to the Philadelphia Civic Center and $104,234. The figures listed last week which were incorrect, although we did write that we knew they had to be incorrect, were not from the commission but from a non-NWA source who simply lied about the gate to my normal contact.

The biggest news pertaining to the show is from all reports this week, the show did a 1.7 percent buy rate on PPV, which is a lot higher than I, or even the company for that matter, expected. Keep in mind right away that both companies (NWA and WWF) have been known to not sometimes, but almost always, exaggerate PPV figures. For example, the last NWA PPV show (Baltimore Bash) was reported by the Turner people as doing a 2.1 percent buy rate, but a random check of companies by us indicated about a 1.4 percent buy rate, a similar check by another indicated about a 1.4 percent buy rate, a similar check by another a 1.4, and finally two different NWA sources told me a 1.5 figure, which is at least believable. However, this 1.7 figure was reported to me by two different sources that have been honest in the past and the basic word within the company is the show did better than Baltimore. Now this 7 percent figure was

not reported to me as a definite total, but as the preliminary estimate the company had as of Wednesday. Legitimate figures aren't available until two weeks or so after the show. If the preliminary figures are taken from companies mainly from the Southeastern area, this Legitimate estimate could be well above a national average anyway since the NWA's appeal is regionally based. But if the 1.7 figure holds up to about 175,000 to 195,000 orders, you are talking about gross PPV revenue of somewhere between $2.6 million and $3.2 million (figuring the list price was $14.95 for the show and the late price was $19.95 and PPV is traditionally a late buy). Even if this 1.7 is either an exaggerated figure, or a figure based on early returns from stronger regions, even if this thing winds up at around a 1.3 percent buy rate, which all indications are that it will, then it has to be labeled a success. This show being a success with somewhat of a weaker line-up then previous NWA PPV outings can be attributed to a few factors. First off, several within the NWA have suggested the surprising success is due to the surprising and sudden ratings increase the two weeks prior to the show. With more people watching the show in the last two weeks than at any time since the early part of the year, that is more potential buyers being reached at a time when the hype for the show was at its strongest. Another factor is that while many of us thought Saturday night wouldn't be a strong night for PPV for psychological reasons (you know, people want to go out on Saturday while on weeknights one would think they are more apt to stay home), it appears the night of the week doesn't matter. Some have even suggested that on the West Coast, going on Saturday is a plus since the 5 p.m. West Coast starts make it hard for people to be there on time and psychologically, people don't like to order the replay show as much. The competition from the World Series turned out to mean less than we had thought here, simply because there was less interest in this World Series, due to the Earthquake and subsequent delay, than any Series in recent memory and the TV ratings for that game were below the other network's normal programming. One also has to think that the vast majority of those who purchased four previous PPV shows had to be happy with the shows, which could be a factor with a marginal buyer who wasn't totally thrilled with the line-up but figured if it's a PPV show, it's going to be hot.

The reason I brought up the difference in the results of those who saw the show live vs. those on PPV is because I was one of the fortunate ones who got to see it from both perspectives. As a live show, I thought it was a decent house show, but I felt disappointed overall with the feeling that a PPV should be better than decent. However, after viewing the show on PPV, I enjoyed the show quite a bit more. It had its obvious weaknesses to be sure, and still wasn't as good as the last Clash (which was a freebie) and may not be as good as the next Clash. There are so many variables between the live show and PPV, but the funny thing is, most of the time, seeing something live is the more enjoyable of the two. In Chicago for the PPV, I enjoyed the card overall more live than on PPV (although the Flair vs. Steamboat main event was definitely better as far as drama and story-telling on PPV although the chops had to be seen live to be appreciated). Nashville was excellent live and excellent on PPV. Baltimore was easily the best PPV to date and equally as good live.

The difference in Philadelphia as to live vs. Memorex stems from both crowd factors and show factors. The Tom Zenk vs. Mike Rotunda match live was ruined because it was a late arriving crowd and people were coming in during the match (which explains why the WWF always advertises its starting times for its house show as 15 to 30 minutes earlier than the PPV starts and gives a non-televised prelim match) and because those who were there didn't care about the match. Zenk was booed as much as he was cheered and even though the crowd got on Rotunda a few times, they were cheering him later when he was throwing Zenk around. The 6-man tag match (Samoans vs. Dr. Death & Midnight Express) deserved close to 3 ½ stars. Just a very good match and Bobby Eaton was excellent. Freebirds vs. Dudes seemed the same either way. It was even more apparent live, the crowd being 100 percent cheering the heels and vociferously at that. Steiners vs. Doom was better on tape. Live, a few things were apparent. First, since almost everyone in the building knew who Doom was, there was a "let down" feeling in the crowd once they got past the hot opening sequence. Woman has gotten the biggest push of any heel Woman in wrestling in a long time, and she's great to look at, but that's where it ends. She didn't even attract close to the heat that regular female valets with nowhere near the push normally get. It took away from the match although watching the "work" itself on tape, it was certainly an above average match .

Luger vs. Pillman was much better on PPV than live. One problem live was the cheerleaders running around the floor distracted the fans from the match. Another is simply that it was an impatient crowd, and the chants of "boring, boring" in the first half were noticeable live even though the match built as well as any match of the night and the final few minutes were hot. As bad as Rich vs. Cuban seemed on PPV, it was even worse live. They should have opened with that match and maybe the arriving crowd wouldn't have been so distracting during Zenk vs. Rotunda (which still should have been a better match than it was, but I wouldn't call it bad or anything). Road Warriors vs. Skyscrapers has two distinct connotations when you say it to fans. A lot of people ooh and aah about the big monsters going against each other and envision it as a fantasy-type war. Others think of a bunch of guys not selling for each other and it would be terrible.

The truth, as always, is in between. The Warriors are a good tag team as far as working. Nowhere near their image of the greatest tag team of the decade or all-time, but quite good nonetheless. Dan Spivey is a better than average big man. Sid Vicious doesn't have to be in the ring much. So there was nothing bad about the match except that there wasn't going to be a finish.

Really, whether one liked or disliked the show in many cases came down to the main event. Strictly based on what the guys did, it was an excellent match. Based on what had been advertised and promised, it was a flop saved only by the fact that the action was good. There is only one finish to the old Coward Waves the Flag rules match, and that was it. But on tape that finish looked like the screw-job that it was. Live, the crowd was ready for the finish when it came and popped big for it. But if you were paying to see how brutal it would get before someone throws in the towel, you'd feel ripped off even though the babyfaces won. And the whole electrified cage angle which had been so loudly hyped was a flop. There were gimmicks set up to where if you touched certain parts of the cage it would make your hair stand up on end, but the electricity to those special effects were turned off when the fire marshall ordered the plug pulled on the cage after the pre-match fire. And one was promised the most violent match ever and with the blood ban, the effect of what they were selling wasn't there. There was no logical reason for all the cage climbing. Anyway, it' s easy to understand why a lot of people were not happy with this main event, and equally easy to see why a lot of people were happy with it.

As a technical production, I've got few complaints. The interviews (which were done live rather than pre-taped earlier in the day, for which I've got no idea as to why) didn't have the spark of previous shows. In the prior major cards this year, the interviews with Steamboat and Luger in Chicago; Flair and Steamboat in Nashville and Flair, Sting and the War Games teams in Baltimore added drama to those matches beforehand (and in the case of Steamboat in the locker room in Chicago, added to the match afterward). That spark wasn't there in these interviews. Not that there was anything wrong with them, but there was nothing memorable about any of them. The camera work, which was so bad it was annoying at the Clash in Columbia, SC, was just fine here. The only thing missed underneath of note was the Lane/Cornette argument after losing the 6-man match. There were missed shots in the main event, but in a tornado match with so much going on it would be impossible to catch everything and they didn't miss a lot. The entrances were more spectacular at previous shows, but were still better than those at WWF big shows. An interesting note is that a lot of people commented, based on the "special effects" ring entrance of Lex Luger (they played a tape of fans chanting "Luger, Luger" while he came in to give the effect that the fans were actually chanting his name, which they weren't, even though they were being led to do so with the large banners and the soundtrack chant being piped into the building) that Luger was the most over personality and should replace Flair as champion (which is subject for a completely different story at another time). Actually, while Luger got a great reaction, Flair's was far more impressive, as was the reaction to the Warriors and Sting and Luger's was maybe the same as the Freebirds, who got a better babyface pop. But the special effects and the message they were designed to get across worked on television, and that is that Luger is the top star in the promotion. Jim Ross was excellent announcing, giving all the bio info and getting a story into the matches to make one overlook the slow spots. Bob Caudle stayed with him, but Ross is so "on" on these big shows that he kind of overshadows everyone else. Only point I could see live that they missed were two spots during the main event where they put the tension on whether the flag would be thrown in (when Muta had Flair in the combo indian deathlock and chinlock submission and when Funk was hanging upside down by the ankle in the cage and Sting was holding Muta overhead in a press and threatening to drop him over the top rope for a long time and Sting eyed Hart for him to throw the towel and Hart wouldn't and Sting finally disgustedly dropped Muta into the ring - the effect of that spot live was lost on the PPV audience) and I didn't get that effect watching the PPV. So to the TV audience, the entire terminators thing was useless except for a way out to not have an ending.

We'll be doing polls on the 11/15 Clash of the Champions TBS special from Troy, NY and for the Survivor Series on Thanksgiving night on PPV. For those in the area, we will be having get togethers for both these shows (Thanksgiving will be at 8 p.m. Pacific time for the replay show rather than live so as not to have anyone's family disown them) and most likely for Starrcade as well.

The Universal Wrestling Federation's big show on 11/29 at the Tokyo Egg Dome (capacity 56, 000) billed as U—Cosmos, will almost certainly be one of the two largest live gates in the history of pro wrestling. Tickets for the show are priced at 30,000 yen ($210) for ringside, 20,000 yen ($140), 10,000 yen ($70), 7,000 ($49), 5,000 ($35) and 3,000 ($21). The complete line-up, all of which will consist of pro wrestlers against top athletes from other sports, was announced this past week. Matches are: 1) Pro Wrestling vs. Judo——Akira Maeda vs. Willy Wilhelm (Netherlands, former European Cup heaqyweight champ in judo) ; 2) Pro Wrestling vs. Amateur Wrestling -- Nobuhiko Takada vs. Duane Koslowski (United States, eighth place at a heavyweight in Greco—Roman wrestling in 1988 Olympic Games in Seoul) ; 3) Pro Wrestling vs. Karate: Minoru Suzuki vs. Morris Smith (United States, World Karate Association World heavyweight champion) ; 4) Pro Wrestling vs. Kick

Boxing——Yoshiaki Fujiwara vs. Glenn Berg (Netherlands, Netherlands heavyweight champion in kick boxing) ; 5) Pro Wrestling vs. Sambo Wrestling -- Kazuo Yamazaki vs. Chris Dolman (Netherlands, many—time World champion in sambo wrestling) ; 6) Pro Wrestling vs. Thai-style Kick Boxing——Yoji Anjo vs. Changphuir Davy (Thailand, ranked 4th ih the World in the junior welterweight division). The mixed match gimmick has always been a big draw in Japan including setting pro wrestling live gate records (which have since been broken) when Antonio Inoki had matches against Muhammad Ali, Chuck Wepner and Later Leon Spinks. The UWF already holds the second spot in the all-time gate record (behind the New Japan card on April 24th at the Tokyo Dome) with its $1,714,000 house on May 6, 1989 for the Maeda vs. Dolman match in Osaka.

I've got a quick comment to make about a subject that has received quite a bit of comment in other newsletters, namely the comment by Verne Gagne as it relates to the death of Bruiser Brody. While the initial response to most was that Gagne is somewhat lower than the lowest specie in the food chain for those remarks, some have defended Gagne saying that at least he was honest in his comments. I think that's the problem. He was honest in his comments. If it was just some sort of a work to hype a grudge match, all would be forgotten. But in his deluded world, Brody got what he deserved by being murdered simply because Gagne held a grudge against Brody for walking out in the middle of a match once and in the middle of a program the second time. And Gagne was no angel in his dealings with Brody, either. But the comment truly reveals what a sick individual Gagne really is for thinking that a man deserves to be murdered simply because he had a few business disagreements with the man.

The WWF was in Madison Square Garden on 10/28 (same night as the NWA PPV show, which believe it or not was a coincidence since the Garden dates are booked months in advance) drawing 16,000 fans and approximately $250,000. For all the compliments you may give the WWF for the quality of its television production and promotional hype, to say these house shows leave something to be desired is understating the obvious. I've seen plenty of bad WWF house shows over the past year, but this card, with the exception of the main event, ranks among the worst house shows I've seen from any group aside from nights when promotions and wrestlers simply go in the tank because there are no fans.

1. Tito Santana pinned Bore-us Zhukov in 12:48 with the flying forearm. This was the second best match on the card, only because of a few nice near falls at the end. Match itself consisted of stalling, tests of strength and nerve holds with an armdrag thrown in at the six minute mark. *

2. Al Perez beat The Conquistador (Jose Luis Rivera) in 10:16 after the alley-copter. Timing was really bad between the two and no heat at all since the crowd doesn't know who Perez is yet. I'm still trying to figure out what anyone sees in Perez. Good-looking guys with nice physiques are a dime a dozen in the business today, and unless you have the charisma or ability to go with it, it means nothing. The only crowd noise were the boring chants. Rivera doesn't sell moves good enough to make Perez' offense look effective. – ½ *

3. Bret Hart went to a 20 minute draw with Dino Bravo in a match which lasted 18:18. Bravo must be real bad because Hart missed three moves in the first six minutes which either means he doesn't have excellence of execution or his opponent makes it impossible to have it. Of course, Gorilla Monsoon still repeated that phrase ad nauseum during the match. Bret did sell a few early power moves great, but 90 percent of the match was either stalling or slow spots. Hart seemed to be working at less than 100 percent so the injury he suffered the next night with Bravo in Toronto was probably building up. There was no crowd reaction when Bravo put on the bearhug, which he held for 2 ½ minutes before Hart pulled off a few two counts just before the bell rang. DUD

4. Brooklyn Brawler beat the unmasked Jose Luis Rivera, who proved to be equally terrible without the hood in 7:35. This was like an independent match with two guys with no experience, but these guys do have experience. Everything both guys did looked bad and no heat at all. This might as well have been intermission because I'm sure there was better execution of moves at the hotdog stands than in this match. -* ¼

5. Randy Savage pinned Jim Duggan to keep the crown in 16:03. Sherri Martel, who had half her face painted black and her hair frizzed out that she looked like an alien from Star Trek, carried the early part of the match. As the bout got going, Savage took some spectacular bumps and carried it to a good match. After a ref bump, Duggan had Savage pinned after a few stationary clotheslines (like the kind Dusty Rhodes used to do to Ric Flair). No ref. A few more pin attempts with no ref until Sherri gave Savage the purse and hit Duggan with it. When they finally revived ref Danny Davis, he made an ultra-slow count and Duggan kicked out. A moment later, Savage pinned Duggan with his feet on the ropes and Sherri holding his feet. Duggan looked terrible but this was like the old Flair-Rhodes matches where one guy was good enough to make the match by himself. *** ¼

6. Hercules beat Akeem via count out in 11:20. Words cannot describe how bad this match was. If this was on a PPV show it would win worst match of the year. Akeem missed a tackle and wound up on the floor and was counted out. - ** ¼

7. Mr. Perfect (Curt Hennig) pinned Jimmy Snuka with the fisherman supLex in 10:37. Not one move until the 5:00 mark when Hennig used the hotshot. The only action up to the point was an exchange of chops at the 3:00 mark and Snuka using two or three thumbs to the throat. Snuka was stationary most of the way and Hennig did very Little. ½ *

8. The Ultimate Warrior defeated Andre The Giant in 21 seconds after three clotheslines. They played the music the entire match and afterwards and by the time the music stopped, Warrior was long gone. It was still better than if they actually tried to do a match with these two. DUD

9. Bushwackers beat Powers of Pain via DQ in 7:54. Gorilla Monsoon called Warlord and Barbarian brothers, which goes against the WWF cardinal rule of acknowledging relatives, except it was okay because it was within the WWF parameters for announcers of never telling the truth. Your basic midget match. Mr. Fuji jumped in with the cane and the ref saw it for the finish. ½ *

Next MSG card is 11/25 with Savage vs. Duggan with two referees, Jake Roberts vs. Ted DiBiase, Brother Love interviewing Elizabeth and Sherri (they are bringing this act around the horn), Hart Foundation vs. Rockers, Bravo vs. Hercules and Bad News Brown vs. Santana.

UWF

The 10/25 show in Sapporo at the Nakajima Taiiku Sports Center drew a sellout 5,600 fans and just under $200,000 as Nobuhiko Takada downed Yoshiaki Fujiwara in the main event in 17:11 after Fujiwara was knocked down five times and the match was stopped; Akira Maeda beat rookie Kiyoshi Tamura in 2:19 when the ref stopped the match; Kazuo Yamazaki beat Tatsuo Nakano in 7:22, Yoji Anjyo went to a 30 minute draw with Minoru Suzuki and Shigeo Miyato also went to a 30 minute draw against MacDuff Roesch from Florida.

Maeda was originally scheduled to face Maaaharu Funaki, however Funaki suffered a legit shoulder separation about a week before the match.

Maeda was in New York earlier this month to tape parts of a television special on him which will air on Fuji-TV network. During his stay he met with a few independent promoters and made preliminary negotiations for a UWF show in New York City, which I still feel is a huge long shot to ever actually come off.

NEW JAPAN

Only results are on 10/26 in Kochi before 1,230 fans saw Riki Choshu & Masa Chono beat Darryl Peterson & Kokina the Samoan in the main event, Big Van Vader pinned Masa Saito, Shinya Hashimoto pinned Matt Borne, Hiro Saito & Norio Honaga & Tatsutoshi Goto upset Hiroshi Hase & Kantaro Hoshino & Kuniaki Kobayashi, Naoki Sano & Black Cat beat Jushin Liger & Osamu Matsuda, Super Strong Machine & George Takano beat Shiro Koshinaka & Kengo Kimura, Osamu Kido pinned Tony St. Clair, Takayuki Iizuka pinned Tom Prichard and prelims.

OTHER JAPAN NEWS

The independent Pioneer promotion (run by Ryuma Go) ran its second card on 10/26 in Tokyo's Korakuen Hall before a poor crowd of 1,200, which is the smallest crowd for a card in Tokyo in recent memory. Go beat Fumihiro Niikura in 22:02 in the main event. Niikura is best known as Hiroshi Hase's first partner in Calgary as the original Viet Cong Express, but he suffered a heart attack two years ago and this was one of his first matches back. Masahiko Takasugi, who used to work for Baba as the masked Ultra Seven about six or seven years ago, beat a karate guy in the fourth round by submission and the rest were all matches involving Go's new proteges having their pro debuts. Go will promote his next show on 1/4 in Osaka and claims that they will bring in foreign wrestlers for the first time and martial arts guys as well for a 2/24 card in Korakuen Hall.

Koji Kitao will make his pro debut on the February 10, 1990 card in the Tokyo Egg Dome against Bam Bam Bigelow while Keiji Muto (Great Muta) returns from the United States for that night as well.

Atsushi Onita's Frontier Martial Arts Wrestling will run seven shows between 12/1 and 12/10 bringing in Dick Murdoch (whose contract with New Japan wasn't renewed), Jos LeDuc and women wrestlers Despina Montaguas (who is married to FMW wrestler Tarzan Goto) and Delta Dawn (who formerly worked with the All Japan women's group as the tag team partner of Madusa Micelli).

FMW will promote cards in South Korea from 11/22 to 11/27 and plan to promote cards in California, working with Red Bastien, in late December and have a big show planned for January 7, 1990 in Tokyo Korakuen Hall.

USWA

The 11/3 card at the Dallas Sportatorium drew about 350 as Jerry Lawler went to a double disqualification with Terry Gordy in the main event for the USWA title, which Lawler holds in some cities, but not in others. Other results saw Eric Embry & Bill Dundee over Gary Young & Billy Travis, Jeff Jarrett beat P. Y. Chu Hi, Uncle Elmer & Cousin Junior beat Sheik Scott Braddock & Solomon Grundy in a dream match, Jimmy Jack Funk beat Taras Bulba and Dustin

Rhodes beat the Dog of War. Earlier in the night, Chris Adams was in a squash match when Travis & Young ran in and handcuffed Adams to the ropes. Then the two grabbed Chris' wife Toni Adams and pulled her in the ring, pulled her skirt up over her head and spanked her bare bottom (no underwear, only a G-string) as Chris watched. This was all taped for television but the whole angle was digitized.

Ironically, Adams isn't wrestling against Travis on the 11/10 card in Dallas. Last week Travis broke his guitar over the heads of Embry and Percy Pringle so they had Travis vs. Embry booked on 11/10. On the 11/4 TV tapings, Adams asked Embry to step aside so he could wrestle Travis but Embry refused and the two wound up getting into an argument over it.

This won't be the Eric Embry show any longer as he's no longer the booker, with booking now being done by a committee of Jerry Jarrett, Bill Dundee and Gary Young. Word I got was that Embry voluntarily removed himself from the booking spot because he had run out of ideas.

Terrence Garvin (Beauty) is now doing color commentary on television with Mark Lowrance but apparently some legit heat because the two won't work together. Lowrance tries not to acknowledge anything Garvin does.

The 11/10 card in Dallas has Lawler vs. Kerry Von Erich for the USWA title (which Lawler technically will probably even hold by the time the match takes place), Jarrett vs. Chu Hi, Travis vs. Embry, Bulba & Jeff Gaylord & Young vs. Adams & Funk & Steve Williams plus Punisher vs. Dustin Rhodes.

Killer Tim Brooks' promotion debuted a babyface tag team called TNT who are twin brothers who I'm told pulled off some nice moves in their pro debut.

CWA

The 10/30 card in Memphis saw The New York Brawler (Lou Fabbiano doing a rip-off of Steve Lombardi's act) beat Ken Wayne, Shawn Regal & King Cobra beat Mike Davis & Cowboy Kevin Dillinger, Brawler went to a double count out with Frankie Lancaster, The Real Freddy went to a double count out with The Imposter Freddy, Ricky Morton & Bill Dundee beat The Fantastics (Bobby & Jackie Fulton), Dirty White Boy pinned Dutch Mantell to keep the CWA title, Soul Taker beat Jerry Lawler via DQ so Soul Taker retained the Tennessee version of the USWA unified World title and Cobra won a blindfolded Battle Royal.

They continued to hint at Lawler going heel this week. At the 11/4 television tapings, Lawler called Mantell out after showing clips of the Memphis match. The finish in Memphis saw a ref bump, then Dirty White Boy jumped in the ring and Mantell (who Lawler had asked the previous week to stay away during his match) made the save and grabbed the cane away from the White Boy but the ref got up and saw Mantell with the cane and DQ'd Lawler for the outside interference . Lawler once again told Mantell to stay out of his business and Mantell asked the fans if he was in the wrong and the fans all cheered for Mantell. Later in the TV show, Lawler did another interview putting down several local radio personalities saying that they were all guys frustrated because they wanted to be television stars and later asked the fans if they thought Mantell was right and most cheered again and Lawler responded, "I wish you'd all shut up when I'm trying to do an interview. "

They continued to build upon an angle where Dirty White Boy gets a mysterious letter from a Lady in Georgia and Dirty White Girl doesn't know what it's about.

Ronnie Gossett was apparently fired as he's no longer around. Chris Champion & Mike Davis came out to be a tag team and Champion said that he got rid of Gossett because he found out that when he and Mark Starr were sending their money back home to their mother that Gossett was intercepting the letters and said when he found out, he put Gossett in the hospital. Davis, who was with him, started defending Gossett and the two got into it with Champion chasing Davis away so Champion is on the way to turning face.

The 11/6 card in Memphis has Davis vs. Lancaster, Regal vs. Hoss Deaton, Cobra vs. Dillinger, Dundee & Morton vs. Champion & Brawler, Lawler vs. Dirty Rhodes (a really fat Local DJ who is not Roger Smith who formerly worked here under the same name), Freddy vs. Freddy with the mask at stake, a double pole match with Dutch Mantell's whip on one pole and White Girl's S&M whip on another pole as White Boy wrestled Mantell and Lawler vs. Soul Taker for the title inside a cage and Lawler will probably regain his title on the card.

How's this for an interesting twist of events? On 10/23 in Memphis, the night Soul Taker won the title from Lawler, it was a day or two after the booking switch from Lawler to Mantell, however Lawler was given the authority to book his own programs. Mantell told Soul Taker that he was too green and that they were going to get rid of him, and less than a half hour later, Lawler came in and went over the finish with Soul Taker and dropped the title to him, so he went from being fired to being World champion in a few minutes time.

OTHER NOTES

Brickhouse Brown is headed to the CWF. No word on the next destination for Iceman King Parsons but he won't be returning to Tennessee (money is horrendous there now).

Bob Geigel will be running a show on Thanksgiving in Kansas City with Mike George defending the WWA title in the main event against the return of Bulldog Bob Brown. Run, don't walk, to your nearest ticket outlet for that one, folks.

Ivan Putski and his wife are talking of starting a promotion in South Texas.

Jerry Blackwell's Southern Championship Wrestling has had a promotional split. Larry Oldig, who was the producer-director for Blackwell's television show, has started a new group called Georgia All-Star Wrestling and basically took almost every wrestler away from Blackwell after getting the key TV slot on Ch. 69 in Atlanta. Most of the wrestlers made the switch because their dream is to be "discovered" by the NWA. Jimmy Powell and Ted Allen (Nightmare) are bookers and they are using Rose as Bob the & Brad Lead Armstrong heel.

Gordon Clements, who owns Alpharetta Auction Barn where Blackwell was running regularly, stayed with Blackwell because he didn't want to make the switch against Blackwell after all the personal heartbreak Blackwell has gone through this year (he lost a son to cancer and nearly died himself) but they are running without television and ran a show on 10/22 with John Michaels and Steve Lawler as the only hold-overs and using Bobby Fulton as booker.

Mark Starr did an interview on the Florida television show challenging Steve Keirn for the Florida title as a heel.

11/5 in Orlando drew 134 as Ron Slinker beat Mike Awesome DUD, Keirn beat Jimmy Backlund ½ *, Kendall Windham pinned Tyree Pride * ½, Lou Perez beat Jumbo Barretta * and Keirn beat Terminator (Marc Laurinidas, who is leaving for the NWA) **.

Heritage Championship Wrestling on 10/28 in Greenwood, MS saw Rock & Roll Express go to a double disqualification with The Fantastics, Terry Gordy double count out with Dustin Rhodes, Mr. Olympia (Jerry Stubbs) pinned Buddy Landel, Jimmy Valiant beat Manny Fernandez via DQ plus Steve Pritchard, Joey Maggs and Jimmy Powell worked underneath.

Pat Tanaka, Doug Somers and Scott Norton all returned to the AWA for its TV taping on 10/28 in Minneapolis.

10/27 in Manatee, FL saw Bam Bam Bigelow beat Jerry Lawler via DQ in a match billed for the USWA title that Lawler held in some places and not others, Keirn beat Kendall Windham, Fantastics beat Scott McGhee & Ron Bass, Jumbo Barretta & Dennis Knight kept the PWF tag titles beating Vern Henderson & Lou Perez plus Wendi Richter worked a prelim.

OREGON

New valet Veronica Lane debuted on the 10/28 Portland show with Scotty the Body and Scotty agreed to let her be his valet only if she helped him get back a girl he once dated and agreed that their relationship would be platonic. Later in the show when Ginger (Scotty's old valet) came to the ring with Steve Doll, Scotty gave her a box of candy and she wouldn't take it. Brian Adams then beat Doll via DQ. Ginger then came to ringside with Rex King and Scotty brought her flowers and she wouldn't take them. Jonathan Holliday (who does one hell of a good interview and is a Roddy Piper lookalike which by itself should draw him heat here added to the heat he seems to draw by just being in places) then wrestled King and pinned him using the ropes but Carl Styles told ref Sandy Barr and he reversed the decision. Bill Francis then comes out for an interview and told Scotty he could beat him with one hand tied behind his back. They have the match and Francis is pounding on Scotty with his right forearm but eventually Francis accidentally hits Barr with the forearm. Jonathan Boyd comes out and ties his other hand behind his back and puts the snake around his neck before Beetlejuice made the save and challenged Boyd to a Snake Box match on 11/4. Stips for this match are if Beetle juice loses then the "Little Juicer" (a young child who seconds Beetlejuice in Portland) has to go into the box with the snake and have the box locked. And you thought they'd already scraped the bottom of the barrel this year as far as angles went. Rip Oliver beat The Grappler via count-out. Kids were admitted free to this card and the crowd was about triple what it had been in previous weeks.

WWF

Sketchy details on the television tapings this past week in Topeka and Wichita. They taped the Saturday Night Main Event in Topeka that will air on 11/25, or two days after Survivor Series. The key angle saw The Genius beat Hulk Hogan via DQ which didn't exactly thrill a lot of the guys wrestling here who have had to put Hogan over strong. Somehow Mr. Perfect took a hammer and smashed up the title belt to heat up their impending feud, although Hogan wound up chasing both guys away and posing at the end. The only other things I heard at the SNME was that Hennig beat Red Rooster clean and that the Rockers beat Tully Blanchard & Arn Anderson in two straight falls with Bobby Heenan firing Tully & Arn between falls. Heard it was a great match and that Vince doesn't miss a trick, does he? Supposedly Tully & Arn were forced into jobbing themselves out on television because they had a contract with Titan and Vince held the contract over their heads and threatened not to release them from the contract if they didn't job themselves out. In Wichita, Blanchard was supposed to put Warrior over as part of the Prime Time special which airs Sunday on USA network but don't know if he did it or not as I didn't get details from that taping. Rick Martel did a TV segment where he was modeling clothes.

They also are going to do their own version of the Robin Green angle with an overweight black woman, who I believe worked as a wrestler in the early 70's, having a crush on Dusty Rhodes.

No newcomers at the tapings although Bobby Jaggers worked as a jobber.

10/30 in Kalamazoo, MI drew 2,000 as Hercules beat

Akeem via count out, Perfect pinned Snuka, Rhodes pinned Bossman, Demolition beat Brainbusters and Savage pinned Duggan.

Unconfirmed report is that Ron Garvin broke his leg on 11/3 in Erie, PA. He was injured, but don't know for certain how serious. Even though most of the WWF guys have Tuesday, Wednesday and Thursday off since Titan books few shows mid-week unless it's TV week, they are doing the double shots once again on weekends and just like last year, guys are dropping like flies.

All American Wrestling on 10/29 drew a 2.5 rating and Prime Time on 10/30 drew a 2.8, while syndicated ratings are down about 1 ½ points from this time last year.

Koko B. Ware definitely returning in January.

Bob Orton was told that everything is booked through January but they'd consider him when there was an opening.

Expect Hogan vs. Zeus as the WrestleMania main event. Just my speculation, but Warrior isn't turning.

GQ had an article this week on the WWF.

11/3 in Denver drew 5,000 and $63,000 as Tugboat Thomas beat Boreus Zhukov (horrible), Perfect pinned Snuka, Santana beat Conquistador, Rick Rude beat Roddy Piper via DQ (best match), Powers Of Pain beat Bushwackers (negative stars), Genius beat Paul Roma and Jake Roberts pinned Ted DiBiase (Jake mainly kept pulling Ted's trunks down).

10/29 in Toronto drew 9,000 and $110,000 as Nikolai Volkoff beat Rivera, Hercules beat Akeem via count out, Demolition beat Brainbusters, Rhodes pinned Bossman, Savage pinned Duggan and Warrior beat Andre via DQ.

10/27 in Auburn Hills, MI drew 7,000 as Hercules beat Akeem via count out, Bravo pinned Hart, Perfect pinned Snuka, Tim Horner pinned Volkoff, Demolition beat Brainbusters, Piper double count out with Rude and Warrior beat Andre via DQ.

Ann Bojack was announced as the new Vice President Of International and PPV operations for Titan Sports, replacing Jim Troy, who resigned after his brawl with Koko B. Ware in Europe. According to Titan's press release, Troy left to pursue opportunities as an independent consultant for PPV and international television sales.

WWF had a major fiasco on 10/28 for its afternoon show in Springfield, MA. Card was set for a 1 p.m. start, however the wrestlers were for the most part arriving from Detroit the night before and the plane wasn't even due to arrive until 1:50 and didn't until 2:30 so the card started one hour late, with the main event of Savage vs. Duggan (who worked in Syracuse, NY the previous night) on first as they were among the only ones at the building on time. They did a three-star match and stalled for 23 minutes with a five minute ref bump in between. Second saw Bushwackers beat Powers of pain via DQ in 20:10 ½ *. Then a 23 minute intermission followed by Volkoff going to a 20 minute draw with Rivera — *, Perfect pinned Snuka in 17 minutes * (Hennig stalled ala Zbyszko most of the match), Tim Horner collapsed in his match with Bret Hart with a legit injury after four minutes (to correct what I reported last week that Horner was hurt in MSG, actually he was hurt here and missed MSG), Hercules pinned Akeem ½ * and Warrior beat Bravo via count out *. No-shows were a Roberts vs. DiBiase match and Widow Maker (who still hasn't returned).

10/10 in London, England saw Roma beat Brawler, Hart beat Bravo, Duggan beat Honky Tonk Man (who is still booked after Thanksgiving which dispels rumors that he's leaving after Survivor Series), Rockers beat Rougeaus, Ware pinned Zhukov and Hogan pinned Savage plus prelim matches involving WWF wrestlers against British wrestlers.

10/13 in Paris saw Horner beat Brawler in 14:00, Hart beat Honky in 15:25 via DQ, Duggan pinned Bravo, Rockers beat Rougeaus, Roma pinned Zhukov and Hogan pinned Savage. Only wrestler who even looked decent in Paris was Hart. Told the fireworks and laser effects and confetti throwing and balloons made it a great "show" in London and Paris but very weak performances in both cities. Why am I not surprised?

NWA

TV ratings were way up last weekend with the NWA Main Event show on 10/29 (Ric Flair vs. Mike Rotunda which was a better match than anything on PPV save the main event) drawing a 3.5 rating which is the highest rating for the NWA in that time slot since a Sting & Luger & Windham vs. Flair & Anderson & Blanchard 6-man tag in April of 1988 drew a 3.7 rating. World Championship Wrestling on 10/28 drew a 2.5 (misleading because first hour drew a 2.7, then about 200,000 homes tuned out second hour but that's about the same number of homes as tuned into the PPV) while power Hour did a 2.1 on 10/27 (tied for second best rating ever). That Sunday show probably had the highest NWA rating in competition with the NFL in years.

Forgot to mention last week that Kevin Sullivan was pulled from the "Woman and Doom"angle by order of Jim Herd the day before the PPV show. Reason I was given was they (not the booking committee, which had its hands tied at this point, but management) felt Sullivan would remove heat from Woman, so his TV appearances with Doom this past weekend will be his last although he will work in prelims at the house shows starting next month.

Tommy Rich suffered a broken eardrum and needed 30 stitches after a miscue in a match with Lex Luger on 10/30 in Gainesville, GA at the TV taping. Because of that, the announced Muta vs. Rich TV title match on TBS this Saturday won't take place and instead Muta beat somebody else with Rich in the corner.

Steve Williams wrestled Sid Vicious ending with Williams

via DQ when Dan Spivey interfered and Norman made the save for Doc. Norman turned face earlier in the show when Doc gave him a large teddy bear.

Rick & Scott Steiner took the NWA tag belts on 11/1 at Center Stage in Atlanta but acknowledged it won't air until until that 11/18 weekend on TBS.I don't know this as a fact, but I'm assuming the change won't be acknowledged until that weekend and they'll bill The Freebirds vs. Road Warriors match on 11/15 Clash as a "title match." Speaking of which, if you saw the WWF tag title change this past weekend, you saw the "promise" that the finish would be presented as controversial due to pinning the wrong man reneged upon. It all evens out. Blanchard and Anderson when they gave notice claimed they were leaving because of a Japanese offer, not to go to the NWA and Titan folks still swear they aren't NWA bound as they were still claiming to office staff they weren't going as late as this past week but they are.

Lord Littlebrook (Roger Brooks), the former midget star, is coming in as manager of the New Zealand Militia.

Flair vs. Muta on TBS on 11/25 and Flair vs. Bobby Eaton on the following weekend.

TBS signed a four year contract for $400,000 per year with USA Wrestling (amateur wrestling) and will broadcast at least six events per year, not that this has anything to do with pro wrestling because it absolutely doesn't.

Was amazed to see Starrcade ads all over TBS this weekend with the complete line-ups and everything. The "Iron Man" concept is a great one, but I still think Starrcade should be the big card with World title matches and focus on settling feuds and this concept is better to fill another PPV slot or to be put on a clash.

Love the line in billing the Flair vs. Funk I Quit match, "It began with a handshake, it'll end with a handshake," as the loser must shake hands with the winner, although nobody in the human race should have any questions on who is losing.

Can you name one masked act that has gotten over since the 'new era' began? Doom won't either. Todays fans equate masks with jobbers, a fact reinforced both by WWF and NWA for the past five years and these guys aren't good enough to change that perception.

THE READERS' PAGES

HALLOWEEN HAVOC

Overall, thumbs up, mainly for the ring work since story-wise, the show wasn't very satisfying. The hot move was Sting's dive off the cage. Heel fans' delight was the "wrong" crowd reaction in the Freebirds vs. Dudes match. I don't know how it sounded on television, but the house was very pro-Freebirds and anti-Dudes, which isn't so astonishing if you live in Philadelphia. Did you know that Santa Claus was once booed at an Eagles game? Seriously. Shoot of the night. On the opposite side of the cage, one of the burlap decorations was set ablaze by smoke. Yours truly pointed it out to an NWA crew guy who politely brushed me off. Several seconds later another NWA crew member realized what was going on and ran for the fire extinguisher. In the meantime, Tommy Young put out the fire by climbing the cage and tearing off the burning burlap. The funniest thing people didn't see. The intro music was loud and blared from a speaker off to the side of the stage where Lance Russell and Joe Pedicino were doing the hotline call. Evidently the feed into their headphones was pretty close to the actual sound level in the house. I just wish I had a camcorder on Lance to tape his facial expressions when the Guns 'n Roses song blared into his headphones.

Granted, the phyiscal layout of the Civic Center is limiting but I thought they could have come up with fresher, more varied entrances considering the magnitude of the show. The Samoans flame routine was flashy but Oliver Humperdink's Lou Albano imitation is hurtin' for certain. Tommy Rich's music ought to be "Exodus" considering the way he had the fans scurrying for the concession stands during his match. It's been too soon since the Russian Assassins to let Doom use the loaded mask gimmick. The main event was very entertaining live but it was wrestling's version of a circus. Somehow I suspect it may not have come off as well on television. However, as they continually stressed the electrified roof in the pre-show hype and then well, you know the complaint well by now. And what about the Van DerGroff generator? If it was operational and threw static sparks to the cage, that would have been a cool effect. But if it was attached simply to imply it was charging the cage, then that was lame. Some technical screw ups resulted in the malfunction of the generator.

My biggest problem was with the finishes. It's bad enough that they were all so predictable, but to make matters worse, half the matches were first run and the finishes used were to set up house show rematches. That's great for your basic house show, but PPV is perceived as a special event. The biggest surprise in the show was that there were no surprises on the show.

After the show, four friends and I went out for grub. All four are hardcore fans who follow both Titan and the NWA. One had decided to quit watching wrestling after paying for the PPV of WrestleMania V but planned to attend occasional NWA shows until his Observer subscription expired. It did and this was officially his last card as a fan. He was not particularly impressed with the show, since he was uneducated as to the current storylines. One thought the show was just okay but wondered why there was no blood in the cage match nor any title changes. When I brought up my biggest gripe about the NWA, the lack of continuity from the end of one feud to the beginning of another, another friend said, "They always screw up. Always." He remarked

about dropping four bucks for a program which listed the card wrong (Editors note: The line-up sheet inserted in the program had the matches correctly but inexcusably failed to list two of the main events). Another one said, "Everytime they take one step forward they take two back." He also had a pretty funny idea about giving the Cuban Assassin a red-headed valet named Lucy who keeps trying to break into wrestling. I must say most of the comments from the fans were enthusiastic. I've got a feeling that the balloting on this one is going to be closer than for any card in the recent past because NWA fans have been spoiled by so many good freebie shows and the exceptional quality of the previous PPV events. That's not really fair. A Titan card the quality of Halloween Havoc would have been considered an overwhelming success.

Ernie Santilli
Drexel Hill, Pennsylvania

Thumbs up, even though the NWA has set too high of a standard for itself with its recent PPV and Clash shows. Halloween Havoc delivered good action for most of the card. Lex Luger vs. Brian Pillman was super and epitomized the in-ring excellence the NWA has showcased on its big events during the past 11 months.

Luckily the workrate overall was decent because Havoc perfectly described other aspects of the show.

The finishes of Steiners vs. Doom, Warriors vs. Skyscrapers and Thunderdome were dreadful. Cuban vs. Wildfire belonged on syndicated television. The Dudes push backfired when the fans treated Jim Cornette and the Dudes as backstabbers of Lane & Eaton. And Bruno Sammartino was asked to do the impossible and the illogical, keep law-and-order in a no DQ, no pinfall, no rules gimmick match where his real role was basically to be the special guest towel catcher.

Tony Amara
Boston, Massachusetts

The show was quite disappointing. I enjoyed the 6-man tag match the best. Expected a lot more from Luger vs. Pillman and the main event was a waste of time. The juice doctrine hurt that match considerably. I hope TBS will ease up on the juice as I feel a reasonable amount of juice is needed in certain grudge and cage matches.

David McCormack
Watertown, New York

Thumbs up on the show but thumbs down on the main event. Why was the match in a cage? Why was it electrified? Why were they climbing up the cage? To get electrocuted? The entire premise of the match was ridiculous. The ending was pitiful with the terminator concept and the white towels ludicrous. Funk was his usual daredevil self but he couldn't salvage the silly set-up. Too bad about the Dudes. Only a return of Paul E. Dangerously as their manager can save their careers. Pillman vs. Luger was terrific and the 6-man tag was awesome. Doom & Woman have good potential. The show was solid but where do they go from here?

Dan Reilly
Enfield, Connecticut

I thought it would be impossible to put on a show as bad as I witnessed at the Civic Center. With all the talent and an excited crowd, they somehow found a way. I would have thought they would have wanted to start the show off hot, but instead we got Mike Rotunda stalling almost an entire match. I didn't have a problem with who worked the first match, but how they worked. After the 6-man, which Steve Williams looked great in and the fans loved, what idiot decided to put Sierra vs. Rich out. It was unfair to the crowd and unfair to the two wrestlers. The crowd was starting to get really into the show when this bomb was dropped. With all the new outfits everyone is wearing, couldn't they get a new tag belt for Michael Hayes to wear? Just one more thing to make the tag title seem unimportant. It must have been more than a month before I read the belt was stolen and nobody seems to think it is important to replace it quickly.

From being there live, I missed quite a bit of the action in the main event due to all the junk attached to the side of the cage. I realize the match is for the PPV audience more than the live crowd but it would have been nice to have a better view.

I have some good things to say, especially about Terry Funk. He gave his all in the main event. Unbelievable bumps and great action from the oldest guy on the card. The NWA will probably reward him the same way they rewarded Ricky Steamboat. I also enjoyed Freebirds vs. Dudes. I loved Johnny Ace's shock as the crowd chanted, "Freebirds, Freebirds." Luger vs. Pillman was the best match. Great action and most importantly, a clean win. Just because Pillman was pinned didn't diminish in any way his effort and performance in this match or his ability in the eyes of the fans. If all the wrestlers in the promotion could understand how to do this then all the championships would be more respected. But with all the stupid finishes in title matches of the past few years, fans don't think much of any of the belts. On the line-up sheet, the Steiners vs. Doom and Luger vs. Pillman matches were both missing. The NWA— "We Wrestle but we don't think."

Ron Townsend
Philadelphia, Pennsylvania

After viewing Halloween Havoc, I realize the NWA is the best circuit in terms of putting on good shows. With the talent, it had to be a blockbuster event and it was. With the exception of Rotunda vs. Zenk and Rich vs. Cuban,

the card was strong. Luger vs. Pillman was the best match and close to four stars as was the Thunderdome match. An observation I made is that every wrestler interviewed before the start of their match ended up winning the match

Michael Tolaney
Arcadia, California

I wasn't happy with Halloween Havoc. A gimmick like the Thunderdome match didn't belong on PPV. The only way they could give the fans what they were promising is for someone to be maimed or killed, and they can't even bleed. Every fan knows there is only one finish to that kind of a match, and that was the finish we got.

They've dragged Terry Funk out for too long after misusing him from the start. Nobody believes he can beat Ric Flair. Once he couldn't beat Sting or Steamboat, they already killed him for Flair.

They've got to get to Flair vs. Luger. That's their money match and if they save it for too long, there won't be an NWA. Luger is the star of the promotion and it's time for Flair to step down.

I'm not too impressed with Sid Vicious. I don't think he can work an NWA main event. Maybe he'll improve like Luger, but I think it would be best for all concerned if he was traded to the WWF for Ted DiBiase and the Hart Foundation.

I've gained a lot of respect for Danny Spivey from Japan tapes. He looked great as a killer heel but he's missing something. They should let him use the DDT. I liked Doom. Too bad the guys weren't new to the territory. They could get over better if everyone couldn't figure out right away who they are. It's really now like just doing another Jack Victory angle. I hope they know what they've got in Scott Steiner. He can do the power gimmick, the flying gimmick, has good looks and does good interviews. Hope the NWA gets Furnas & Kroffat soon. They're unbelievable. Another move to improve the NWA's image would be to book a mixed match against a famous boxer. Maybe not a champion, but someone in the top ten. If the boxer won't work it, let them do a shoot and have the wrestler be Steve Williams. Win or lose, it would make news and make the NWA seem like a legitimate organization.

Steve Yohe
Alhambra, California

I enjoyed the show very much. Jim Ross was superb as usual. I can only hope he never gets throat problems. He adds so much to any wrestling event. This time had also had lots of background information on all the wrestlers which I found both enjoyable and informative. Technically the show was far superior to the last Clash. Far less crowd shots and therefore far less missed shots. I enjoyed all the matches. I think they should have done more with the impending feud with the Express vs. Cornette. They had a prime opportunity after Stan Lane hit his head on Cornette's tennis racket. They should have argued in the ring (editors note: They did argue in the ring but those at home missed it because they were showing a replay of the finish and an interview). Why is there still only one tag team title belt? Inexcusable. Robin Green looked fantastic. I guess I'm in the minority but I think her interviews are great. The one with Cornette where he spilled the champagne was hilarious. Finally, the Thunderdome was great. I don't go much for gimmick matches as a rule but really got into this one. The guys made good use of the cage by doing all the climbing. I know that TBS said no blood, but I feel a match of this type really calls for juice.

As for the plastic bag incident, I'm glad to see you received some letters that stated my feelings so well. I think everyone has overreacted to that whole thing. Violence in wrestling isn't new. I've been going to wrestling since the late 50s and I've learned to never be surprised by anything. When I was a child, the thought never entered my mind to try and duplicate what I saw in the ring and kids today are a lot more sophisticated about wrestling than I was. Give them credit. They know what's going on. My only fear is that excessive violence may keep the NWA away from a mainstream wrestling fan which would make them more popular and more successful. I personally enjoy everything about the NWA but I realize people with children might feel differently.

The NWA and WWF offer two completely different forms of entertainment and there should be room in this country for both. They appeal to different crowds but both these crowds have money to spend for the product they want .

Karen Shehorn
North Hollywood, California

Overall a thumbs down. The entire show was routine, mundane and uneventful and the finishes were all disappointments. One thing I admire about the NWA is their willingness to try new and different kinds of gimmicks, like the Tower of Doom and Thunderdome, but they don't fully commit themselves to them and the matches end up falling flat. This main event could have been a classic, but instead came off like an embarrassing three-ring circus. Bruno Sammartino might just as well have been a cardboard poster. The finish was worse than boring or predictable. It was downright irritating. Luger. vs. Pillman was passable because of Luger's improvement as a performer and Road Warriors vs. Skyscrapers was the most exciting match of the night, even though I knew neither team would do job. Spivey & Vicious may not be great wrestlers, but they are a convincing menace.

Zoogz Rift
Canoga Park, California

RADIO

In the world of radio, Titan Sports has to be the worst promotion to work with. I've dealt with the NWA and the AWA plus the smaller promotions. Most promotions love free publicity. Titan doesn't care.

The only person who has worked with us in the WWF in the last two years has been Jesse Ventura, who is a fabulous guest.

Peter Thiele
KSTP Radio, St. Paul, Minnesota

UWF

I'm amazed by people who hate the WWF and yet tell me that the best promotion in wrestling is the UWF. The last four UWF cards have been rip-offs. I've never heard of the WWF putting on a show with less than a half hour of wrestling. And doesn't anyone remember that Kazuro Horiguchi died on March 31st from a brain haemorrhage. He suffered that injury while training to wrestle for the UWF. That is enough for me to conclude that the promotion is nowhere near the best.

Michael Connors
Waltham, Massachusetts

Dave Meltzer: Hey Mike, whatever happened to Gail Fisher as Peggy?

T-SHIRTS

The reason why I wore the opposing T-shirts to the NWA and WWF TV tapings held in the Pittsburgh area was out of curiosity and greed, to acquire a free T-shirt . However, you misinformed your readers about the Wheeling situation to suit your focusing on the WWF's paranoia. I got a free Rockers T-shirt out of the generosity of the WWF. They mistook my Four Horsemen T-shirt for a Metallica one. I took off my Four Horseman shirt and wore my WWF logo shirt and cap proudly. I was not forced to remove my NWA shirt. I got a free shirt without causing any ruckus. You also failed to mention that the group I was with sat in the front row facing the cameras and were solidly behind the heels. We booed the faces and not once did WWF officials complain to us. It seems to me the only paranoia I can recognize is your distorting the facts to downgrade the WWF

John Lanigan
McKeesport, Pennsylvania

Dave Meltzer: Okay John, here are the facts. I've gotten plenty of phone calls and a few letters saying that if someone wore a WWF T-shirt to an NWA taping that the NWA would behave exactly like the WWF does at their tapings. Whether your motivation was simply to get a free T-shirt from the NWA or not, you inadvertently proved my point when no NWA officials cared what you wore.

As for Wheeling, I received a phone call the day after the Toledo taping (two days after Wheeling) from a WWF official complaining to me about the people who came to the tapings in the first few rows wearing either NWA or Pro Wrestling Illustrated T-shirts and how nice they were to take them off in exchange for free WWF t-shirts and how it was all a work by fans, not to show loyalty to the NWA but to get free t-shirts. You also mentioned to me in a phone call the day after the show that before you were allowed to bring a banner into Wheeling, they checked to make sure what was on the banner. You also mentioned in the same phone call that the guy who was checking to make sure nobody was wearing the wrong shirts in the front row didn't notice your Horseman shirt, so you pointed it out to him and he thanked you for doing so because he would have gotten in trouble for letting it go, then you voluntarily removed the shirt. You know as well as I do the WWF policy, had they seen an NWA or PWI shirt in camera view, would be to find a way to have the person remove the shirt. I didn't distort any facts and never once implied a ruckus was created. In fact the WWF official who complained to me about people coming up with the idea from the Observer told me that everyone is very nice about removing their shirt, once they get the free shirt from the WWF. As for no officials complaining because you cheered the heels, that means the WWF is one better than the Dusek—Embry World Class group. But that's hardly a germane point, since Titan has the capabilities and often changes the crowd soundtrack to suit their purposes anyway, so if any noise had come out on tape, they could have easily removed it in post-production.

WOMEN

I have a difficult time finding the medium ground between a scheming bitch (Woman) and a subordinate female (Elizabeth). If the portrayal of both characters is considered misogynistic, where does that leave women in the business, save actual female wrestlers? This smacks of feminist paranoia. In a world inhabited by horror movie icons, limp-wristed ambisexuals, asylum rejects, redneck jailors, etc. isn't it the most sexist attitude of all to say that women shouldn't have the opportunity to portray a variety of characters? If wrestling today encourages violence toward women, that it must forever be encouraging violence, period. Or perhaps, neither. Maybe it's just a form of cathartic entertainment. Honestly, how much more real does wrestling purport to be than most other TV fodder? It's generally accepted that the plastic bag was a bad idea, but I'm not convinced that because little Johnny will beat a bobo doll after being subjected to hours of viewing similar actions in a laboratory environment that he'll stuff his sisters' head into a hefty bag. Our social consciousness might be getting the best of us. As tasteless as the proposed miscarriage angle was, I have to dig pretty deep to find a distinguishable difference between wrestling and soap operas, where women are constantly "losing" babies. And many soaps are written by women. In an attempt to shield women from exploitation, are we narrowing their avenues for opportunity in the wrestling business and being more sexist than we realize?

George Maranville
Lexington, Kentucky

NWA

As sick and tired I am of hearing about the NWA, I thought the 10/30 issue was great. Your points were right on and you put them very well. The NWA is in need of a big change in one direction or another. The problem is they keep saying they are going in a new direction, but it's more like 50 different directions at once. I agree they should cut back on arena shows, staying in their strongest markets.

Run the full crew three or four nights. This would give them more rest. They should perform better.

And it should help morale. Use the extra days to do special localized interviews in every city. The seven-day-a-week schedule they've been running has really hurt the work of late where the NWA house shows are really just minor league versions of the WWF but with a little better work rate. I've seen enough NWA house shows where the workrate stinks and is just a little better than WWF when it should be a lot better.

Another big problem is perception at the house shows. From what I've seen live, the NWA comes off as minor league when it comes to the ring, lighting, entrance music, souvenirs, etc. One reason I love Japan wrestling is that everything comes off so major league like it is a major sporting event. Someone at the last NWA show I was at said that no matter how crummy the matches are, everything else in the WWF looks great. If they claim their own niche and were major league in doing so, they could make it as an alternative promotion because as slick as the WWF is, they are still seen by many as just one big commercial with no substance where the NWA could provide action that viewers want.

SMM
East Coast

NOVEMBER 20, 1989

The box office magic of Akira Maeda and the Universal Wrestling Federation has been one of the biggest stories in wrestling since the group's reformation in the spring of 1988. But never has this magic been more apparent.

On November 4th, the UWF held a press conference to hype ticket sales for the November 29th "U-Cosmos" show at the Tokyo Egg Dome, which would go on sale the next morning. At the press conference, Maeda said that when the UWF originally reformed, they had hoped they would simply be able to keep the promotion alive and fight the style of wrestling they wanted to use for three years. Maeda did say that when they decided to reform the group, after Maeda had been fired from the New Japan promotion (which may go down in wrestling history in hindsight as a blunder equivalent to when the Boston Red Sox sold Babe Ruth's contract to the Yankees), they had hoped to be able to promote a card at the Tokyo Dome. Shinji Gin, the president of the UWF then said the UWF would prove something to the wrestling world on Nov. 29 by selling out the Tokyo Dome (56,000 seats) and setting a gate record that no other group would be able to break (the house was scaled at approximately $3.2 million-the current live gate record is $2,781,000 set by New Japan when it nearly sold out the Tokyo Dome with 53,800 fans in May—U.S. record is $1,628,000 for this past WrestleMania at Trump Plaza).

Tickets went on sale the next morning at 10 a.m. The ringside tickets were sold out (priced at $210) at 10:04 a.m. The $140 tickets were sold out by 10:30 a.m. The advance had topped $1.5 million in the first half hour, which totally destroys every record for quickest selling tickets in the history of pro wrestling. The old record for quickest sale was set by the UWF last year for its Ariake Coliseum card which sold out 12,000 seats and $500,000 in six hours. In comparison, for the biggest U.S. event ever in terms of attendance. WrestleMania III from the Pontiac Silverdome, tickets were on sale for one week before they had surpassed 20,000 seats. I never did hear how many tickets were sold that first day before the box office closed, but assume the card has sold out by now. They also announced nine closed-circuit locations to go on sale on 11/5, with showings in Sapporo, Sendai, Niigata, Shizuoka, Nagoya, Osaka, Hiroshima, Tokushima and Fukuoka. Sapporo, which had sold out the UWF's previous house show on Oct. 25 the first day tickets went on sale, also sold out for the closed-circuit showing in a matter of hours.

It's almost as if the card itself, which will feature six mixed matches with UWF wrestlers taking on stars of other martial arts sports, is anti-climactic to the records that will be set at the gate well before the card even takes place. In the history of pro wrestling, there have been, before this event, six $1 million gates in history, three in the United States (WrestleMania III-IV-V) and three in Japan (UWF shows at the Osaka Baseball Stadium and Yokohama Arena this year and the New Japan Tokyo Dome show in April). Now there are seven, three of which have been from one promotion during a seven month period.

At the same time the UWF is gearing up for its big show, its rivals New Japan and All Japan are gearing up for the annual big tournaments, which start in a matter of days. New Japan surprised everyone with the announcement that it will not be holding a tag team tournament, as it has every year since the late 70s (last December New Japan instead held a six-man elimination tag team tournament rather than the standard four-man tournament which had become a tradition with the two established promotions for each December), but instead be holding a complicated singles tournament. The tradition based All Japan group is sticking with the tag team tournament, even though with the field much weaker than in any previous year, the anticipation going into the tournament is nothing compared with years past.

New Japan will be running a larger and more complex tournament with the same basic principles as the one-day tournaments the NWA will be running for Starrcade '89 (more on that later). The tournament, which starts on 11/24 in Gunma, will have four round-robin (everyone wrestles everyone else) brackets, which last through 12/4 in Hakata. The top two finishers in each of the four brackets will then advance to a single elimination tournament, with the quarterfinals to be held on 12/5 in Nagoya, the semifinals on 12/6 in Osaka and the finals on 12/7 at the Sumo Hall in Tokyo. Tournament rules within the four brackets will have all matches with a 30 minute time limit, with November 20, 1989 a pinfall or submission victory worth five points, a count out victory worth four points, a disqualification victory worth three points, a draw with two points for both wrestlers and any kind of a loss worth zero points. The Nagoya matches and Osaka matches will have 45 minute time limits (in the case of a draw, I've got no idea what criteria decisions will be used) and the final in Tokyo will have no time limit. Bracket "A" is scheduled to be Riki Choshu, Kengo Kimura, Buzz Sawyer, Rick Steiner and Victor Zangiev. However, because of his recent signing with the NWA, I don't expect Sawyer to fulfill his commitments and I'm pretty sure Steiner won't be allowed to attend either, in fact just about sure since he and his brother captured the NWA's tag team title on 11/1 in Atlanta. Bracket "B" has Shinya Hashimoto, Masa Chono, Manny Fernandez, Timur

Zarasov and Andrei Sulsaev (a former Olympic medalist who will make his pro debut during the tournament). Bracket "C" has George Takano, Hiroshi Hase, Tatsutoshi Goto, Brad Rheingans and Salman Hashimikov. Group "D" will be Osamu Kido, Shiro Koshinaka, Super Strong Machine, Steve Williams (who is definitely appearing) and Vladimir Berkovich.

For those of you who collect Japanese tapes, they will be taping television shows on 11/24 in Gunma (Choshu vs. Sawyer, Chono vs. Zarasov, Hase vs. Hashimikov and Williams vs. Berkovich), 11/29 in Ishikawa (Sawyer vs. Zangiev, Fernandez vs. Sulsaev, Takano vs. Hashimikov and Williams vs. Kido) and the final three nights. To project the tournament out, the way the 12/5 quarterfinals look are the winner in Group A (probably Choshu) vs. second place in Group D Machine?); winner of B (Hashimoto) vs. second in C (Hase), winner of C (Hashimikov) against second in B (Chono) and winner of D (Williams) against second in A (Zangiev or Kimura, unless Sawyer or Steiner do appear and dependent upon if they don't, who replaces them).

All Japan's tag team tournament goes from 11/17 with the finals on 12/6 at Tokyo's Budokan Hall. Shows that will be taped for television are on 11/17 (Stan Hansen & Genichiro Tenryu vs. Dynamite Kid & Davey Boy Smith, Jumbo Tsuruta & Yoshiaki Yatsu vs. Abdullah the Butcher & Tiger Jeet Singh, The Foot Loose vs. Doug Furnas & Dan Kroffat); 11/19 (Hansen & Tenryu vs. Terry Gordy & Bill Irwin, Tsuruta & Yatsu vs. Giant Baba & Rusher Kimura, Kabuki & Shunji Takano vs. Nasty Boys); 11/25 (Hansen & Tenryu vs. Butcher & Singh, Tsuruta & Yatsu vs. Kid & Smith, Furnas & Kroffat vs. Nasty Boys); 11/29 (Hansen & Tenryu vs. Baba & Kimura, Tsuruta & Yatsu vs. Furnas & Kroffat, Kid & Smith vs. Butcher & Singh, Foot Loose vs. Kabuki & Takano); 12/4 (Tsuruta & Yatsu vs. Gordy & Irwin, Hansen & Tenryu vs. Nasty Boys, Baba & Kimura vs. Kroffat & Furnas—that will be an interesting match to watch and see just how good a worker Kroffat really is if he can make that one passable); and the finals on 12/6 in Tokyo which will almost certainly come down to Hansen & Tenryu vs. Tsuruta & Yatsu for first place, Kid & Smith vs. Furnas & Kroffat for third, Gordy & Irwin vs. Butcher & Singh for fifth and Baba & Kimura vs. Foot Loose for seventh).

New Japan also has officially announced the first pro wrestling event ever in the Soviet Union on New Years Eve in Moscow, which will be televised back to Japan (this may be something for those of you with satellite dishes to look out for, as perhaps they'll have to go through a U.S. satellite to get the signal from the Soviet Union to Japan, perhaps not also). Three wrestlers from the United States will be part of the big event. Bam Bam Bigelow, Brad Rheingans and scheduled to be Buzz Sawyer (though you can't be sure with his NWA deal). All of the Soviet amateur greats-

turned-professional will appear, of course, along with Black Tiger (Mark Rocco from England), plus the return to the ring of Antonio Inoki, who is currently a member of Japanese parliament and is now recovering from stab wounds in an attack of several weeks back. New Japan will also be bringing Choshu, Hashimoto, Chono, Jushin Liger (Keiichi Yamada), Masa Saito, Hase, Kuniaki Kobayashi and Takayuki Iizuka to this card.

On the U.S. scene, the biggest news of the past week is that the World Wrestling Federation fired Tully Blanchard just weeks before he was scheduled to finish up. No official reason was given for the move, which took place after the TV taping on 11/1 in Wichita which included a taping for the WWF Prime Time Wrestling special which aired on the USA network both on Sunday and Monday nights. Blanchard had a match on the show scheduled against the Ultimate Warrior, and no doubt they wanted the clean job on television and we had received word before the taping that no way Blanchard was going to do it. It wound up with Blanchard in the position of being pinned but a DQ finish when Arn Anderson ran in, and Warrior wound up making his own comeback on both guys anyway and held his own when Haku ran in until Andre came in and he needed help from his Survivor Series teammates at that point. It had been assumed that the reason both Blanchard and Anderson, who will start appearing on NWA television shows the first week of December, stayed on with the WWF was because Vince McMahon wouldn't release them from their contract unless they stayed through the PPV show, and also because they wanted to stay through the same show and get the big one-day payoff from it (pay-offs last year for Survivor ranged from $2,500 to $7,500, with no doubt Hulk Hogan and maybe Randy Savage getting significantly more). Whether it was because he didn't do the job (and he did everything but), or more likely, because the WWF simply wanted Blanchard out of its dressing rooms because it was well known that he was a major influence in getting WWF wrestlers to look into going to the NWA (an exodus of which never materialized because the NWA heads. Jack Petrik and Jim Herd didn't want to start up a raiding game that would escalate salaries of all the major wrestlers plus McMahon refused to let others out of their contracts and nobody was willing to test contracts), Blanchard was gone and will be replaced by Haku in most of his scheduled arena show appearances the rest of the way against Demolition. Nobody has been officially announced as replacing Blanchard in his match in the Survivor Series, although the best speculation from this end is that Bobby Heenan will wrestle on the card in his place.

Even though the NWA's "New York Knockout" on 11/15 will have been held by the time you read this, it came after our press time. Don't know how it all came out, although barring a last minute injury (in which case the main event wouldn't have taken place), the show marked the final match, at least for now, of Terry Funk, who headlined against Ric Flair. I cautiously use the term final match, because both in 1983, and again late in 1987, I'd assumed that Funk's career was over, only to have him come back. He received possibly the greatest career sendoff in Japan in 1983 with a big show headlined by his retirement match, and he did actually stay retired until late 1984 when he had a few tune-up matches in the United States and came back in December for the tag team tournament in Japan. Funk mainly worked independently in North America and toured Japan frequently for the next few years, but it appeared that an injury suffered from a bad fall in Puerto Rico, which led to Funk barely able to work even months later in the 1987 tag team tournament in Japan (and even barely able to work he had a few good matches) and that was going to be it. But after a few months rest. Funk worked a few more independent dates with the back injury from Puerto Rico not appearing to bother him as much. When he wasn't invited back for the tag team tournament in 1988 with the feeling being in Japan that he was too old, based on his injury-riddled performance the previous year. Funk responded by getting into the best shape of his life and returned to the wrestling mainstream in the NWA this past May. To say Funk put on the comeback performance of the year would be to grossly underestimate his performance. Despite so many factors going against him, between age, recurring injuries because he wouldn't compromise his crazy working style or take shortcuts even though common sense and self preservation would have told anyone else to, and the perception of many that he was simply too old to be headlining, on a nightly basis he performed better than almost every wrestler in the country and was able to get more heat than any other heel in the NWA. Every show the NWA did this past year that drew more than $70,000 was with Funk opposing Ric Flair in the main event, either in singles matches, or in the tag team match on the PPV event from Philadelphia. Both Pay-per-views he headlined were financially successful, at a time when the NWA wasn't so successful. Yes, there was a lot of criticism in the decision to keep him at the top against Flair for so long. Personally, I think they went too long with it as well. And despite its box office success and Funk's great interviews, he never was able to get across to the fans the belief in fans' eyes that he really could beat Flair, which somewhat limited the box office success of the feud after the first meeting in most cities. Television ratings did rise, with Flair vs. Funk being the key issue during the rise. Maybe Funk had little to do with all this, that it was just a promotion rising from rock-bottom, and truthfully is still nowhere near where it needs to be to be profitable. Maybe he had a lot to do with it.

I fully expect to see Jim Cornette surprise everyone and turn heel Wednesday night as well, and rejuvenate the Midnight Express as the heel tag team which dominated our awards balloting for several years.

From the WWF side, the newest issue of the WWF magazine confirms what we've had hinted this way for a few weeks, that the original idea of having a Hulk Hogan vs. Zeus cage match for the WWF title in conjunction with a PPV showing of the movie "No Holds Barred (or Used)" on Dec. 27 has been changed. In its place, the match which will be part of the movie PPV special will be a tag team rematch of Hogan & Brutus Beefcake vs. Zeus & Randy Savage in a cage, which means one of two things. Either Zeus has progressed so little that they are simply afraid to put him in the ring in a singles match with Hogan, even though the match will be taped and they will have more than a week to re-edit the actual match before airing it "live." The other alternative is the match was changed so that the first Hogan-Zeus singles meeting can be saved for WrestleMania. The match will be billed as occurring live, although in reality the match will be taped, although I'm not sure of the site other than it will be at a television taping in Florida in December.

As for other upcoming PPV events, the WWF has just about made the decision that WrestleMania will be from the Sky Dome in Toronto on April 1, 1990. I'm told it's not "official," but a virtual certainty at this point. If the show isn't held in Toronto, then it would almost surely be held at the Los Angeles Memorial Coliseum, which would seat nearly 90,000 for wrestling. The NWA is also working on booking its Feb. 25 PPV show. Cities I've heard mentioned were St. Louis, at the Fox Theater (Theater was already booked that date and refused to make a change, this was the NWA's first choice and would have been a bad choice because the acoustics for sound in wrestling are hideous since the place is built for all crowd noise to be muffled and all stage noise is magnified—a few years back Bruiser Brody ran a show there and even when the wrestlers whispered spots, you could hear it all over the building), Richmond (which would get great heat as its a lively crowd and one that used to resoundingly boo Ric Flair when he was a heel even tho he was half-cheered everywhere else, in other words, if they are concerned about the "wrong" reactions and they are, this is the safest site), Baltimore (best to draw a big gate, but they may be wary of running too many big shows there), Tampa or New Haven (the only reason I could think of they would even consider this one is because it is so close to the headquarters of Titan Sports).

A correction from last week. We reported that Ron Garvin broke his leg in a match in Pennsylvania, but I've later heard that he was simply limping leaving the ring.

The Atlanta Constitution reported on Wednesday that the NWA had signed up Jorge Gonzales, a 7-foot-6, 380-pound former member of the Argentinian national basketball team. Gonzales was originally a draft choice of the Atlanta

Hawks, but was deemed to be neither in good enough condition nor tough enough under the boards to survive in the NBA. Jim Ross of the NWA had been pressuring the group to sign the guy and try and market him as a new, and much taller version of Andre the Giant (Gonzales' 7'6 height is legit whereas Andre's announced 7'5 is in reality closer to 6'9 or 6'10 and several wrestlers have sworn that when both stood up next to each other that 6'9 ½ Ernie Ladd was taller than Andre). Andre was the biggest box office attraction in the United States for a one-time shot during the 70s (although as actual drawing cards for the long haul, Andre was nowhere near the draw of either Bruno Sammartino or Dusty Rhodes, although looking at pre-1985 history to determine what would work today isn't valid given the total change in both the audience and the attitude of the audience in what they are seeing. Gonzales was actually signed nearly two months back, but it was kept hush-hush because the NWA feared the embarrassment in case the guy never progresses to where he even wrestles, and those close to the organization are said to be pretty unhappy the story leaked. Gonzales was signed to a three-year contract and is training in Florida with Hiro Matsuda, and may also be doing some training in Virginia with Lou Thesz. The hope is that his debut could be a last minute surprise at the NWA's February PPV show.

Gonzales, who is scheduled to wrestle under the ring name, "El Gigante," is a definite crap shoot. Looking at this business realistically, size is a major, major factor. People believe the big guys can beat the little guys, and all things being equal, that is the case. Freakish size, as far as weight, used to be an attraction, such as Haystacks Calhoun (450-500 pounds, billed at 601 pounds) in the 1960s through the early 70s, who was a major attraction before he was more or less made obsolete by a combination of age and health problems and more so by the emergence of Andre. In recent years, the freakish size has somewhat been replaced by infatuation with freakish sized muscles, rather than enormous poundages, witness today's leading attractions mainly being musclemen, while the freakishly massive guys in the WWF (Tugboat Ottman, Earthquake Evans Tenta, Akeem) aside from Andre and Bossman (who has survived on top mainly because he's a great worker) are in prelim matches and get little heat on the cards. Another factor with Andre's fame in the early 70s has to be looked at. While Andre was never a great worker, when he started in wrestling he was just a large wrestler (6'7, 240) in Europe and the glandular disease freaked him out. He was first discovered in the "modern" world by the late Isao Yoshihara, who brought him to Japan when he was still well under 300 pounds. Verne Gagne spotted him in 1971, at which time he'd already been working four or five years and he was maybe 335 pounds, and Gagne first tried to get him into boxing and sold him on the idea of fighting Ali. Andre

then went to Montreal and hooked up with Frank Valois, who became his business agent and the old Montreal group. At first, he was a big draw, and set a Montreal record gate for a match with Don Leo Jonathan and drew big money for subsequent rematches. After a while, Andre, who was then called Jean Ferre, had a harder and harder time drawing as a main eventer. That's when Valois introduced him to Vince McMahon Sr., and Sr. decided that if Andre stayed in any territory for any length of time that he would kill the territory, but if he traveled as an attraction from territory to territory and maybe appeared twice a year in each city, he'd remain fresh and a big drawing card for the long haul. Many in wrestling have suggested that if territories had stayed strong, this same thing could have kept the Road Warriors as big attractions in the same way, as their drawing power when they appear in Japan hasn't diminished, but they appear infrequently. Their drawing power in the U.S., where they are on TV weekly, is virtually nil. But the point being, which means little as it relates to Gonzales because the world is different, is that Andre as a great attraction was more because he never stayed in any area for any length of time. Late in his career, in the WWF after he quit touring for others, Andre remained somewhat of a draw as a face through infrequent appearances in each city, and the heel turned revived him and he wasn't overexposed as a heel because of the injuries when he was at his hottest, but Andre was one of the great attractions in the history of the business. But again, Andre had about six years of experience before he ever set foot in the United States, whereas this guy will debut in a troupe which up and down the roster has the best working talent around. Giant Baba had a similar experiment in Raja Lion, a 7'2 legit guy from India, and it was a definite failure. But this could work. It all depends on whether or not Gonzales wants it bad enough and if the fans want it and if they can find ways to use him, which won't be easy either since he's got nine inches on Sid Vicious.

Some facts as it relates to pro wrestling on cable during the third quarter (July-August-September) of this past year. The Clash of the Champions on Sept. 12 turned out to be the seventh highest rated show on cable television during the three-month period. The Clash, emanating from Columbia, SC and headlined by Ric Flair & Sting vs. Dick Slater (replaced injured Terry Funk) & Great Muta match plus Luger-Rich, Road Warriors-SST, etc. drew a 4.7 rating. The highest rated show during that time period was an NFL pre-season game with the Chicago Bears against the Kansas City Chiefs on Aug. 27 which drew an 8.8 rating. Other shows that topped the Clash were two USA network first-run movies, two other pre-season NFL games on ESPN and the Pittsburgh-West Virginia college football game on Sept. 30. The WWF's Prime Time Wrestling show, buoyed by those high numbers for the first few weeks of Roddy

Piper, was the fourth highest rated show on cable for a continuing series with a 3.1 rating, trailing NFL exhibition football and College Football on ESPN and the Sunday Morning movie on TBS. All American Wrestling was 10th with a 2.5 average. Since the regular TBS wrestling ratings were in the toilet at that point, its highest rated show during that period was the Sunday NWA Main Event which was 13th with a 2.2 average. But even at the point when the wrestling ratings were down, with the exception of movie programming, pro wrestling is still the highest rated regular programming on TBS. The WWF wrestling on the USA network ranks along with the Saturday night "Hitchhiker" series and Thursday night boxing as the USA network's top show, while AWA wrestling is nowhere near the top of the ESPN ratings.

While on the subject of other sports, somebody noted something in Dick Vitale's Basketball Weekly when talking about Detroit Pistons center Bill Laimbeer. Laimbeer was described as "a typical WWF wrestler." While the moniker was probably given because he's rough under the boards, the same evaluation also said, "He doesn't work on his game. He has no offensive technique, plodding, slow and can't move well or jump." So the moniker was probably even more accurate than the writer even knew.

Special thanks to Joan Ryan of the San Francisco Examiner for the nice write-up; congratulations to Jon Talaugon for his marriage on Sunday and to Lance "Chokehold" Levine and wife Jan on the birth of daughter Amanda Marie on Monday.

This isn't confirmed as I write this, but I was tentatively scheduled to appear on the wrestling segment on WFAN radio in New York this coming Saturday night/Sunday morning at 3 a.m. New York time.

CWA

Jerry Lawler regained the USWA title (recognized here) from The Soul Taker on 11/6 in Memphis. Soul Taker's manager Nate the Rat tried to interfere in the match from the top rope but Lawler threw him onto Soul Taker and pinned both of them. After the match the Dirty White Boy jumped into the cage and started beating up on Lawler when Dutch Mantell came in to make the save. The heels then moved their attention to Mantell and started beating on him while Lawler simply walked out of the cage, rather than help Mantell, who had to be helped out of the ring. At the television show on Saturday (they still do it live here), Mantell came out for an interview and asked Lawler why he walked out on him after he had saved Lawler. Lawler told Mantell that he just doesn't like him and slapped him a few times. Mantell then asked Eddie Marlin to sign for the title match and Marlin agreed to it. At least for this week, Lawler is a heel in Memphis and by the time the television show ended, Lawler was 100 percent booed. Later in the show, Chris Champion was doing a squash match and Mike Davis and the New York Brawler (Lou Fabbiano) banged his leg with a chair. As Champion came out later limping, Lawler moved in on his interview and called him a crybaby and started insulting the crowd which started chanting, "We Want Dutch."

Cowboy Kevin Dillinger signed up Boss Winters as his new manager to try and end his losing streak, but in a television match against Frankie Lancaster, Dillinger lost again.

Dirty White Boy got another letter from "the girl from Georgia." No idea where that one is going.

Also on 11/6 at the Mid South Coliseum, during a match with Bill Dundee & Ricky Morton against Brawler & Davis, Champion jumped into the ring and attacked Davis which caused the faces to lose via DQ. After the match. Champion apologized to Morton and Dundee about causing them to lose the match and shook hands with all of them, completing his babyface turn.

Freddy (Tommy Gilbert) is history.

11/13 in Memphis had Lawler vs. Mantell for the title in the main event, White Boy defending the CWA title against Dundee, Tracy Smothers vs. Soul Taker with the winner getting a shot at the winner of the Lawler-Mantell match, Champion vs. Davis, King Cobra & Todd Morton vs. Brawler & Dillinger and Lancaster vs. Black Jack.

NEW JAPAN

Hiro Saito returned to New Japan on 10/20 as a complete heel. Saito said that he was tired of the amateur wrestling style that everyone in New Japan has been using and said he was going to change the style to a rougher style. He then hooked up with prelim wrestlers Tatsutoshi Goto and Norio Honaga and formed "The Wild Trio." Saito & Goto pulled several major upsets in prelim matches.

Masa Saito won't be appearing for the tournament because he and Brad Rheingans will be putting the finishing touches on Koji Kitao, who will make his pro debut on 2/10/90 at the Tokyo Dome against Bam Bam Bigelow. New Japan has offered Titan Sports $200,000 to get Hulk Hogan for one night, which is by far, with nothing ever coming even close, the largest offer ever made by a promotion to get a wrestlers' services for one match. And I'm sure it'll be turned down since McMahon will never risk Hogan being put in an environment that McMahon himself isn't in complete control of.

IWGP champion Big Van Vader is defending the title in Mexico from 11/12 through 11/20. Then on Dec. 22, as Leon White, he defends the CWA version (Europe) of the World title against Otto Wanz. Supposedly, after the Tokyo Dome show, White will go to the NWA as Big Van Vader.

Jushin Liger (Keiichi Yamada) will miss the tournament as he's going to tour Mexico from 11/23 to 12/15. Liger, Naoki Sano and Akira Nogami are all being kept out of action in Japan until Dec. 19 as they are doing a special big card in Tokyo with those three headlining for Sano's IWGP jr. heavyweight title. Hiro Saito will likely be added as well and they'll do a one-night junior heavyweight tournament. Saito will wrestle CWA jr. heavyweight champion Steve Wright (England) in West Germany on 12/8 and may return to Japan holding a version of the title.

Tatsumi Fujinami appeared at the 11/3 card in Tokyo and announced to a cheering audience that he would return to wrestling once his back improves. Fujinami hasn't wrestled since suffering a major back injury in July and it's been strongly speculated, since the injury hasn't responded to treatment, that he would be forced to retire from wrestling.

With Inoki out of action because of his retirement into politics and Fujinami out with an injury, the two long-time top draws for New Japan, the crowds for spot shows have been at an all-time low with just Choshu and a lot of the younger wrestlers who are over big in cities like Tokyo and Osaka but not nearly as well known in the towns.

Goto & Saito pulled upsets over Hiroshi Hase & Takayuki Iizuka in their debut on 10/20, then lost their match two nights later against Shiro Koshinaka & Hase. The next night Saito used a foreign object to bloody up Kuniaki Kobayashi (who teamed with Kantaro Hoshino) and left him laying with a 12-stitch cut. On 10/25, Saito teamed with Honaga against Sano & Hirokazu Hata with Kobayashi in the corner and Kobayashi attacked Saito, however Goto then interfered and they managed to get rid of Sano & Hata and tripled on Kobayashi once again. To make this undercard feud seem more real, after the card on 10/25, New Japan president Seiji Sakaguchi said that he wanted Saito, Honaga and Goto to stay at a different hotel on the road with the rest of the New Japan wrestlers and they were no longer welcome on the New Japan "Japanese" tour bus and instead had to travel in the foreign tour bus.

On 10/26 in Kochi, the Wild Trio had a six-man against Hase & Koshinaka & Hoshino and the latter team brought Hata (who they had knocked out the night before in the attack) to ringside with them. Hata started using all sorts of profanity at Saito and they juiced Hata. Goto then got a keg of beer from the concession stand and brought it to the ring and knocked Hoshino out with it.

11/1 in Toki, drew a sellout 2,140 (hometown of Hashimoto) as Riki Choshu & Masa Chono & Jushin Liger beat Big Van Vader & Tony St. Clair & Tom Prichard, Hashimoto pinned Kokina the Samoan, Saito & Goto beat Hase & Kobayashi when Honaga interfered and caused Hase to get pinned, Sano pinned Honaga in an excellent match, Kengo Kimura & Osamu Kido beat Takayuki Iizuka & Shiro Koshinaka, Super Strong Machine & George Takano beat Matt Borne & Darryl Peterson and prelims.

11/3 at Tokyo's Korakuen Hall was the final night of the last tour which drew a sellout 2,300 with Hashimoto

upsetting Vader via count out in the main event of a brutal match, Choshu & Chono beat Koshinaka Kimura when Chono pinned Koshinaka, Liger pinned Iizuka, The Wild Trio beat Hase & Kobayashi & Sano when Saito pinned Sano, Kido pinned Peterson, Machine & Takano beat Borne & Kokina, Black Cat & Hoshino beat Prichard & St. Clair and prelims.

Chono and Hashimoto have a big feud going after Hashimoto gave Chono a DDT on the arena floor and Chono juiced.

Sounds like they are bringing out the blade and turning up the violence mid-card to combat stale crowds after the Russian gimmick wore off. This group should do well starting early next year nonetheless when Kitao starts up because the early curiosity should lead to incredible TV ratings. For example, Wajima's pro debut a few years back drew double the rating that the WWF did when it was on NBC for its last Prime Time special and basically triple what All Japan is getting weekly now.

OTHER JAPAN NOTES

All Japan started a campaign for victims of the San Francisco Earthquake starting at the 10/28 card. During the last tour, fans were given autograph placards of either Butcher & Singh or Kroffat & Furnas for $3.50 with all the money going to the Red Cross in San Francisco. During the tournament they will be doing that with all the teams in the tournament.

Kiyoshi Tamura, who worked with Akira Maeda on the 10/25 card in Sapporo, suffered a broken bone underneath his right eye from a kick. Ironically, this was the same injury Riki Choshu suffered a few years back from the shoot kick by Maeda which led to everyone that has happened in Japan in the last two years.

Red Bastien's group in Southern California is getting lots of publicity in Japan as Atsushi Onita will work for them in December. Onita's Frontier Martial Arts and Wrestling Promotion has shows on 12/1 in Osaka headlined by Onita vs. karate star Mitsuhiro Matsunaga and the first chain match in Japan in more than a decade with Dick Murdoch vs. Crusher Dennis (?). Matsunaga will face Tarzan Goto on 12/7 in Kumagaya.

12/10 in Tokyo's Korakuen Hall has Onita & Goto vs. Matsunaga & Seiji Aoyagi in what is billed as the first tag team karate vs. wrestling match plus Murdoch vs. Jos LeDuc in a Street Fight and a women's strap match with Despina Montaguas vs. Delta Dawn.

All Japan's Kenta Kobashi and Abdullah the Butcher are regularly seen now in national TV ads.

Giant Baba, Jumbo Tsuruta and Rusher Kimura have been on game shows of late.

USWA

Lots of new things going on with Bill Dundee as booker.

Jeff Jarrett & Matt Borne were stripped of the USWA tag team titles for failure to defend the titles (Borne lost a loser leaves town match and toured Japan). Ironically, the announcement was made just as Borne returned to the area and the tournament will be 12/1 at the Sportatorium.

Former college football All-American Jeff Gaylord is back, under the management of Scandor Akbar.

I don't know if this is an angle, but assume it must be. Eric Embry came on TV wearing a cast on his hand and when asked about it, said that Percy Pringle accidentally shut a taxi door on it when they were getting out of a cab.

Kevin Von Erich returned as well and appears to be motivated for the first time in years. Von Erich looked really good in a television match (when was the last time he looked good in a match?), wasn't dazed or lost and spoke clearly in an interview. Kevin said that people always ask where he is, since he never wrestles anymore. Usually whenever Kevin drifts back for a week or two before no-showing begins and he drifts away just as quickly, when he returns they always say on TV that Kevin has been fighting for Christianity in foreign countries that Kevin has been fighting for Christianity in foreign countries when in fact, he's usually home asleep. Kevin admitted in this interview that he's been doing nothing for all this time and said that he hasn't been motivated for years, ever since he found out one day in Texas Stadium that Kerry was the more popular brother and he'd always be the star. Kevin then said he's motivated and would face anyone, even Kerry or Eric Embry, to gain titles or whatever.

The 11/10 card at the Sportatorium drew 300 fans as Jerry Lawler beat Kerry Von Erich in the main event. The only other result is that Billy Travis beat Eric Embry via DQ when Chris Adams interfered and attacked Travis. Embry then broke a guitar over Travis' head and tried to shove it up his rear end.

At the TV tapings the next day, all the heels attacked Adams and held him down while Travis spanked Chris.

Lots of furor locally over the incident last week where Toni Adams was spanked and had her dress pulled up and she wasn't wearing underwear. Not sure if the furor was because of what she wasn't wearing or just because of the angle, but as the 11/10 attendance shows, it didn't sell any tickets.

11/17 in Dallas has Embry vs. Buddy Landel, Adams vs. Travis, Jeff Jarrett vs. P.Y. Chu Hi with the strap on the pole, Kevin Von Erich vs. Sheik Braddock, Uncle Elmer & Cousin Junior vs. The Punisher & Taras Bulba, Gaylord vs. Borne, Gary Young vs. Dundee, Jimmy Jack Funk vs. Dog of War and Dustin Rhodes vs. Texas Battleship.

Terrence Garvin and Mark Lowrance are still doing the TV but Lowrance still won't work with Garvin.

Killer Tim Brooks' promotion drew 450 on 11/7 at the Longhorn Ballroom as Iceman King Parsons debuted and teamed with Brooks & John Tatum to beat TNT & Steve Cox on top, plus Johnny Mantell beat Kenny the Stinger and Brian Adias beat Scott Casey.

OREGON

The Northwest tag team titles were held up on 11/4 in Portland after a match where The Southern Rockers (Rex King & Steve Doll) faced Brian Adams & Jeff Warner. After a ref bump, The Grappler came in with a board and gave it to Warner, but King got the board away and somehow the ref saw him with it and DQ'd the Rockers. Not sure why the titles were held up because of this, but they were and it was to be settled on 11/11. Also Doll beat Al Madril via DQ, Scotty the Body drew with Carl Styles, Beetlejuice beat John Boyd and Rip Oliver beat Grappler in a Loggers match.

OTHER AREAS

Mark Starr & Lou Perez won the Florida tag team titles from Jumbo Barretta & Dennis Knight.

Gary Allbright is working in Puerto Rico as the No. 2 heel feuding with Invader #1 (Jose Gonzales). Allbright, who was second in the nation while wrestling for Nebraska, has an offer to fans of $5,000 if they can escape from one of his holds, and thus far nobody has been able to.

After the split of Southern Championship Wrestling and Georgia All-Star Wrestling, it was surprising to hear that most of the new Georgia group's wrestlers worked for Blackwell's group last week in Alpharetta, GA. Blackwell and Gordon Clements are trying to put together a promotion, or I should say keep it going as they lost the TV to the new group and Blackwell offered the guys $40 guarantees to work the show (which is larger than the independent guys in Georgia, ail of whom have other jobs, are used to earning) but turned out for naught without any advertising as only 18 fans paid to see the show.

Steve Strong (Steve DiSalvo) returned to Puerto Rico and shot a big angle where they carried Carlos Colon out on a stretcher to build up for a match on Thanksgiving night. However DiSalvo is trying to hold up the group so he may not come back for the match.

Angel of Death and Gary Allbright are now the top two heels in Puerto Rico.

The anniversary card, after being postponed a few weeks for Hurricane Hugo, drew 17,000 fans and was also available in Puerto Rico on PPV.

Congrats to Ted Robinson, new TV voice of the Charlotte Hornets.

El Canek lost his UWA World title in Mexico to The Killer.

Heritage Championship Wrestling taped 11/8 in Vicksburg, MS with Terry Gordy, Mr. Olympia (Jerry Stubbs), The Bullet (Bob Armstrong), Brad Armstrong,

Fantastics and Rock & Roll Express at the tapings.

11/3 in Calgary saw Owen Hart go to a double count out with Larry Cameron, Davey Boy Smith went to a 60 minute draw with Johnny Smith, Arch Angel (Curtis Thompson) beat Dr. Drago Zhiavago, Chris Benoit & Biff Wellington beat Jason Anderson & Skull Mason, Bruce Hart beat the Derringer brothers in a handicap match and Sumu Hara beat Steve Gillespie before a near sellout 1,300 fans. The spot shows in Western Canada have picked up significantly with the return of Owen Hart full-time as 11/8 in Prince George, BC drew more than 1,000 and others have topped the 1,000 mark as well. They expect to bring back Dynamite Kid in February, while D.J. Peterson starts up this week. Bob Raskin's United States Wrestling Association has a show 11/17 in Irvington, NJ with Sgt. Slaughter, Bam Bam Bigelow, Junkyard Dog and Afa the Samoan.

Ken Dunlop and Bruiser Davis were said to have had the best match so far this year in Australia on 11/5 in Ingleburn before 200 fans. Davis holds the Australian title while Dunlop & Wayne Pickford hold the tag team titles and the current top 10 has Dunlop, Bill Condolian, Davis, Pickford, Mr. Wrestling, Kevin Martin, Blade Runner, David Hart, Lou Marcello and Mike Starr in that order.

A new group in Kentucky called Mountain Wrestling has a TV show with Randy Hales and Bruce Swayze doing the announcing. They seem to be running about four shows per week and averaging about 200 fans, although a few of the shows have drawn pretty well. Bill Dundee and Dustin Rhodes have worked for the group and on TV they are plugging Jerry Lawler, Rock & Roll Express and Jeff Jarrett as coming in.

A new group called Universal Wrestling Superstars ran about six hours worth of television tapings on 11/8 in Brooklyn and 11/9 in Staten Island before about 450 and 600 fans respectively. Bruno Sammartino and Craig DeGeorge did the announcing while Lou Albano did some managing. Killer Kowalski and Dominic DeNucci were both at the shows. The highlight of the first night was Big John Studd using an Oklahoma side roll (used to be the finishing move of Jack & Jerry Brisco). Stan Hansen and Scandor Akbar no-showed while those appearing as wrestlers included Bigelow, Studd, Kimala, Ivan Koloff, David Sammartino, Mike Sharpe, S.D. Jones and Johnny Valiant as a manager. The first night main event saw Sammartino beat Koloff via DQ for using a chain while the second night Bigelow beat Kimala in the main event by DQ in 2:20 of what was described as a terrible match. Heard the best matches were average and most were something a whole lot less than that.

WWF

Crowds have been pretty weak the last two or three weeks. Some are putting the blame on the Survivor Series hype, but then again, crowds weren't weak before the other PPV

events. Some of the feuds have lost their steam while others (in particular Savage vs. Duggan) isn't hot enough to headline a card in a major market. The upcoming Warrior vs. Bravo feud doesn't figure to change this trend, although Hulk Hogan vs. Mr. Perfect, after the SNME angle airs on Thanksgiving weekend, should draw really good. For one thing, everything with Hogan draws anyway. For another, he hasn't had a new foe since Randy Savage, and that was back in late February when the hype started so it's the first new challenger in something like nine months.

Barry Windham and Tim Horner are still out of action. Not sure about Bret Hart. Horner is expected back in about a week.

The Prime Time special, taped on 11/1 in Wichita, saw one match which involved singles matches from opposite teams in Survivor Series. Dusty Rhodes beat Akeem via count out, Mr. Perfect beat Luke Williams, Tito Santana beat Big Bossman when Rhodes interfered, Ted DiBiase beat Demolition Smash when Zeus interfered, Randy Savage pinned Hercules when Sherri used the loaded purse and Warrior beat Blanchard via DQ when Anderson interfered.

11/2 in Altoona, PA and 11/3 in Erie, PA had same results as Warrior beat Andre in 20 seconds, Rockers beat Rougeaus, Hercules beat Bad News Brown via DQ, Hillbilly Jim beat Brooklyn Brawler (worse than it sounds), Rick Martel pinned Brutus Beefcake, The Canadian Earthquake (John Tenta) beat Mark Young and Ron Garvin drew with Greg Valentine. The Erie show drew 3,700. Heard Rockers vs. Rougeaus by far the best match.

11/2 in Rockford, IL drew 1,500 as Al Perez beat Barry Horowitz, Sam Houston beat The Conquistador (Jose Luis Rieera), Savage pinned Duggan, Honky Tonk Man pinned Red Rooster, Akeem beat Jim Neidhart, Rhodes beat Bossman and Demolition beat Anderson & Akeem.

Haku is mainly subbing for Blanchard right now.

11/2 in Omaha drew 3,848 as Tugboat Thomas beat Boreus Zhukov, Perfect pinned Jimmy Snuka, Haku pinned Santana, Rude beat Roddy Piper via DQ (best match and only good match on card), Bushwackers beat Powers of Pain via DQ and Jake Roberts pinned Ted DiBiase.

Prime Time Wrestling jumped to a 3.1 on 11/6 while All American the previous day drew a 2.2.

Survivor Series video hits the stores on 12/13.

11/11 in Boston drew 5,500 as Paul Roma pinned Mike Sharpe, Perfect pinned Snuka ** ½, Thomas pinned Brawler DUD, Savage pinned Duggan ***, Dino Bravo pinned Neidhart - ***, Demolition beat Haku & Anderson and Roberts beat DiBiase via DQ when Virgil interfered **.

NWA

A couple of sellouts that I know of over the last week or so as a show in Springfield, MO on 11/4 sold out (2,800 tickets) and as expected, the 11/12 card in Amarillo headlined by

Ric Flair vs. Terry Funk drew a sellout (told the crowd was 6,500 but I don't think the building holds that much). The crowd booed Flair heavily and cheered Funk.

World Championship Wrestling on 11/4 drew a 2.9 rating which is the highest since a January show which had Windham vs. Gilbert and Steiner vs. Rotunda. NWA Main Event with Brian Pillman vs. Mike Rotunda on 11/5 drew a 2.7 while NWA Power Hour on 11/3 fell to a 1.7.

The NWA program in the Joe Pedicino column mentioned that Ron Simmons was one of the Doom team.

11/2 in Norfolk saw Tom Zenk beat Mike Rotunda, Johnny Ace beat Bill Irwin, Midnight Express beat New Zealand Militia, Lex Luger pinned Brian Pillman, Sting beat Great Muta via DQ, Road Warriors beat Freebirds via DQ, Skyscrapers beat Steiners and Flair pinned Funk.

Gary Hart and Terry Funk got into an argument on TV so perhaps Funk will retire as a babyface.

Impressed with the Starrcade TV commercials, both with content and with the fact they've gotten them on TV so fast. Expect a hard sell for the tournament format starting next week.

Several cable companies reported a significant number of phone calls on Halloween night for Halloween Havoc, so the name did confuse some people into thinking the show was on the 31st.

THE READERS' PAGES

RATINGS
I have several disagreements with your ratings in the 10/30 Observer. I think Jushin Liger and Naoki Sano should have been ranked No. 1 and No. 2. You ranked Ric Flair at No. 1 and Terry Funk at No. 7. How can you possibly rate Flair above Liger and Funk above Sano when the Liger-Sano matches have been better than the Flair-Funk matches. I thought the last Liger-Sano match was the greatest wrestling match of all time. Flair hasn't even had a five-star match with Funk. Why wasn't Randy Savage ranked above Ted DiBiase. You also rated Lex Luger well below DiBiase. We all know DiBiase is a far better worker than Luger, however in recent months, Luger has done much more than DiBiase and should be rated above him. Barry Windham should have been rated much lower than No. 23. He is one of the best workers around but he hasn't shown a thing lately. Rick Rude should also be rated above DiBiase and Windham. I don't think the UWF wrestlers should be rated. Could you imagine how much everyone's performances would improve if they only worked one match a month? Why weren't Akira Nogami or Kenta Kobashi rated? Both have done a lot more than Ted DiBiase lately. There are several Mexican wrestlers who deserve to be in the ratings. I think you should only rate matches and list an exact time period for each set of ratings that you do, that way we'll know what matches are

included in the ratings. Super Boy did the most unbelievable maneuver I've ever seen on 10/28 in San Bernardino at the WIN tapings. He did a rope walk where he stood on the top rope, dropped down to sit on the top rope but instead of flipping backwards after the sitting position, he spring straight up in the air to stand on the top rope again and he executed a backflip off the top rope. For pure skill, that move can't be topped.

David Hannah
Studio City, California

USELESS BASEBALL TRIVIA
The 11/6 Observer reported that Dusty Rhodes got his stage name from a 1950s baseball player. This may be coincidence and is definitely even more useless trivia, but on Sept. 18, 1908, Dusty Rhoades (spelled with an "a") of Cleveland pitched the first no-hitter against the Boston Red Sox. Since most people recognize Mata as a World War I spy, a new name is in order for Scott Steiner's awesome and relatively unique move. A "Power headscissors backward somersault snap mirror off an irish whip into the ropes" would be an accurate but unsuitable description. But a "Suicide Scissors" sounds short enough for both television announcers and newsletter reporters. What has happened to Keiji Muto since July 23rd? Did he mess up his knees beyond the point where we'll never see the moonsault press again? Has he been held back because his principal opponent, Sting, had been injured for a long time?

Tony Amara
Boston, Massachussetts

Dave Meltzer: The baseball player that Rhodes took his name from was a pinch-hitter in the 50s who gained some fame for key pinch hits in a World Series. That player probably got his name from the early century pitcher. Muto's knees aren't in great shape so he saves the moonsault for special occasions, but I've seen him do it a few times since July 23rd. In the context of his matches with Sting and Flair in singles, doing that move doesn't make sense since he's the heel and they don't want people to regularly kick out from the move and obviously he can't use the move to pin those guys, either.

AKBAR FOR MANAGER OF THE YEAR
What about Scandor Akbar for manager of the year? I think about all those managers around, but who else got a near down-and-out promotion going again? I don't know of any other manager that comes close to doing more for wrestling this year than Akbar. It sounds dumb, but I think he's the best man for the award this year.

Larry Saale
Parts Unknown

DANGEROUSLY

To be an aficionado of pro wrestling, it is a necessary prerequisite to become immured to the constant misuse of talent ala Owen Hart by the World Wrestling Federation and the premature departures from a promotion whether of the performers own volition, financial frugality by the promoters or the standard creative differences euphemism. However, I must register my disappointment and frustration at the loss of Paul E. Dangerously from the NWA, the only Western wrestling promotion worth following. Financial and management inadequacies aside, Paul E. had become, in my mind, one of the most valuable personalities to emerge in the business since Roddy Piper broke through the banner of anachronism that had held pro wrestling in thrall. Dangerously had surpassed Jim Cornette, admittedly somewhat negated by his current babyface role, as the best manager in the game. He was right up there with Cornette as a TV personality and most importantly has the state-of-the-art sensibilities of a sharp 24-year-old to keep in touch with the younger fans, but also has a fine knowledge of wrestling history to counterpoint any obstacle he may encounter.

Peter Schroder
Victoria, Australia

BILLY WIRTZ

In defense of the Rockin' Reverend Billy C. Wirtz, he is primarily a musician and quite a talented one at that. He has been doing the fire and brimstone salvation act since at least 1979. He has quite a following on the East Coast and is opening for the Nighthawks in Baltimore on New Years Eve. He was always quite a wrestling fan and he and I would swap stories whenever he blew through the D.C. area. I was in London when the WWF came to town and I saw no sign of wrestling. No newspaper mentions. No newspaper ads (I read six or seven papers a day), no subway ads, no nothing. I was really surprised.

Bill Hanrahan
Baltimore, Maryland

CORNETTE

I haven't agreed with anyone on the readers' pages as much as I agree with Andy Stowell and his assessment of the Cornette-Dudes-Midnight affair (10/23 issue). Cornette and the Midnight Express are an inseparable unit and until months ago, Cornette seemed to have believed this himself. I believe the Midnight Express needs Jim Cornette and vica versa. After the resounding boos received by the Dynamic Dudes during Halloween Havoc, I hope whoever is booking this angle decides to change things quickly and make sure Cornette doesn't go with the Dudes. A Midnight-Dudes feud can't conceivably exist even if the Dudes have Cornette because the Dudes just aren't over. It appears they can't even ride on Cornette's coat tails. I really hated seeing

Cornette with them and more after the match when they were being booed out of the building. The main event at Halloween Havoc was good, but the finish could have been better. I was hoping we wouldn't see an inadvertent towel toss-in. Actually, I was expecting Ole Anderson to turn. The cage gimmick was fun with the electricity idea. I missed the blood, especially after advising viewer discretion. Overall the show is a strong thumbs up and I can't wait for the Clash and Starrcade. The most impressive parts of the show were the ring entrances. The NWA has them down to a science. The entrances of the Samoans, Freebirds, Steiners, Doom and all the main eventers were incredible.

Craig Stambaugh
Clariton, Pennsylvania

SETTING THE RECORD STRAIGHT

Thank you for taking the time, effort and space in the 10/30 issue to explain your preferences and set the record straight. As if often the case in written communication, readers may not always garner the correct message from reading between the lines and your detailed response supplied the reasons behind certain remarks, although I'll never be convinced of a lack of NWA preference, perhaps my own over-reaction to years of McMahon-bashing in every wrestling news source. Indeed, I'm sure that some of my remarks may have come across as more acerbic than intended. The Oakland 2/brats analogy is not name-calling, but simply a result of those fans disrupting production and calling attention to themselves. I don't want to attack their preferences or their personalities, but merely their methods. Brian Smith New London, Connecticut SPORTS ILLUSTRATED ARTICLE The 10/30 issue of Sports Illustrated had an interesting article on banners at sporting events. Some of the incidents they talked about are somewhat similar to the WWF banner incident in Oakland. Personally I'm not opposed to the WWF banning banners at their matches. I do, however, admit to being curious as to why the WWF seems to have also banned wrestling moves at their wrestling matches.

Harry White
St. Louis, Missouri

HALLOWEEN HAVOC

As far as Halloween Havoc goes, thumbs down. To me it just seemed like another house show at the Civic Center. The show certainly wasn't as good as it should have been, but it certainly wasn't as bad as the last WrestleMania either. Although, I at least got to see a World title change hands at the last WrestleMania. I'm not as enthused about the NWA as I was maybe five or six months ago. When I tape on Saturday, I get more excited about taping Titan's television shows. In my opinion, the Thunderdome match was by far the best match on the card and I'd give it 4 ½ stars. The six-man tag was very good as was Lex Luger vs. Brian Pillman. Tommy Rich vs. Cuban Assassin was as bad as the matches at WrestleMania. Prime Time Wrestling has turned into one of my favorite shows of late.

Chris Poulos
Lansdowne, Pennsylvania

I barely gave the show a thumbs up. The 6-man tag was good and the rest of the matches were solid except the Rich vs. Cuban match. Luger vs. Pillman was great. Anyone who thinks Luger is just another musclehead didn't see this match. The main event was terrible. Was the cage electrified? If it was, how come only Muta got shocked? Why were they climbing the cage when the only way to win was by submission. Too many unanswered questions. Until the NWA can put on a big show without confusing fans, they just won't be able to go up against Titan.

Bob Nichandowicz
Union, New Jersey

Thumbs up. While it wasn't anywhere near the level of the previous NWA PPVs this year, several of the matches were excellent, particularly Luger vs. Pillman and the Thunderdome main event while Steiners vs. Doom and Freebirds vs. Dudes were both surprisingly good. Once again to my amazement, Luger was in the best match on the card. Judging from his steady improvements in work and interviews, it's becoming blatantly obvious that he's the future of the promotion. While Ric Flair is an idol to many of us, he just looks too old to cut it as the top man in a promotion that should build itself around its young stars like Luger, Pillman, Sting, Steiners, Muta and Sid Vicious. By letting Flair stay on top, he would serve the same purpose Dusty Rhodes did, holding back younger stars who people want to see. It'll be interesting to see if Flair can swallow his pride and do what is best for a struggling promotion. I would also like to comment on a most unique experience I had following the card. With all the talk about different promotions being kind to the fans, the NWA wrestlers present themselves as class acts by taking photos with and signing autographs for the many fans who traveled to the hotel after the card. I was impressed with the way Lance Russell took time to stop, talk and pose for pictures, but the most impressive guy was Terry Funk. He really worked harder than anyone else on the card and was nowhere near 100 percent, but while in great pain, still took time to pose with fan after fan.

Rob Brownstein
Philadelphia, Pennsylvania

A big thumbs down. It was the first time I've ever felt ripped-off WWF style while watching an NWA card. The Thunderdome concept must go. The idea of terminators in the corners was absurd, since nobody truly expected either guy to call it quits, and if they had, it would have made for a cheap ending anyway. The outside camera work was annoying, as it is in any cage match, and the wrestlers couldn't seem to agree as to which rungs in the cage the electricity started at. Add to this the cobwebs and other junk strewn around the thing, the lack of heat and ultimately that the wrestling itself was subpar at best, and it was like watching a particularly bad installment of "American Gladiators." To see four of the world's greatest workers in a circus side-show atmosphere such as this was utterly depressing. If the NWA wants to promote "We Wrestle," they should leave the hokey gimmicks in the closet where they belong, especially ideas involving alleged life-and-death situations like the plastic bag and electrified cages. Best match by far was Luger vs. Pillman, both for sustained interest and credibility, but all in all, I'm glad I didn't shell out any money for this show. My hosts weren't too happy that they had.

Joe Coughlin
Boston, Massachusetts

November 27, 1989

If there was a Hall of Fame for pro wrestlers, Terry Funk would have long since earned his spot. But the induction ceremony should have been held on Thursday morning.

Funk's "farewell" match (at least for now, because I do expect him to return) on Wednesday night, an incredibly dramatic "I Quit" match with Ric Flair, will go down as one of the great individual performances in recent memory.

Paced by that main event, the Clash of the Champions/New York Knockout from Troy, NY became only the second big show to earn a 100 percent favorable rating in the Observer telephone poll.

As of Monday, between letters and phone calls, the Clash drew: 395 thumbs ups and Zero thumbs downs, with calls coming in at a record pace heaping mountains of praise on not only Funk, but the overall show as well. The only other 100 percent favorable rating was also this year from the NWA, when "Wrestle War 89" from Nashville on May 7th headlined by Flair regaining the NWA title from Ricky Steamboat also drew a 100 percent thumbs up.

Ironically, the Clash started out looking like anything but what it wound up being. Just about everything looked like it was going to go wrong during the first half hour. As expected beforehand, the biggest problem was the location. The live crowd in Troy, NY, which numbered about 4,000 (heavily papered) in the 5,800-seat RPI Fieldhouse, was unresponsive for the first two matches, Which made the matches come off flat on television. Considering the Road Warriors were in one of those matches, things didn't bode well for the card. Truthfully, the card started out looking like a rerun of a WrestleMania from Trump Plaza, something the NWA could ill afford at this time.

But when Shane Douglas did a dive over the top rope onto Bobby Eaton in the Midnight Express vs. Dynamic Dudes match, the crowd suddenly woke up. The finish of that match, with Jim Cornette double-crossing the Dudes and turning heel and going back with the Express by hitting Douglas with the tennis racquet, drew the biggest crowd pop, not only live, but probably in a few million homes watching on television as well.

From that point on, the card sailed. Two outstanding matches with the Steiners vs. Skyscrapers and Lex Luger vs. Brian Pillman preceded the main event, another in the long line Of Match Of The Year candidates for 1989.

Officially the Clash special did a 4.9 rating and a 7.8 share overall, which translates into 2,507,000 homes during an average minute. It was the third highest rating of the nine Clash specials, but since TBS has grown in the number of homes served in the past year, the actual number of viewers was second only to the first Clash (Flair vs. Sting 45 minute draw from Greensboro on March 27, 1988) which averaged 2,560,000 homes. The rating is even more impressive considering the plethora of wrestling on cable during the week, with Titan Sports getting three extra two-hour slots on the USA Network during the week for repeated showings of its "Countdown to Survivor Series" special. Not so coincidentally, one of those showings went head-to-head with the Clash in the Eastern and Central time zones on Wednesday night.

An interesting trend in the ratings of this Clash as compared with past Clashes is that the ratings didn't build in the same manner as in the past. For most Clash specials, the rating starts somewhat low and builds up consistently throughout the show, peaking with the main event. In Wednesday's show, the rating started out comparatively high, with the Freebirds vs. Road Warriors opener drawing a 4.5 rating. But the rating stayed flat for most of the way (varying between a 4.2 and 4.7) until increasing a tad to a 5.0 for the Pillman-Luger match and shooting up to a 6.3 for the Flair-Funk match. The Flair-Funk main event was viewed in approximately 3,216,000 homes, which in a manner of speaking, would make it the most-watched match from the standpoint of an average minute in the history of cable television. The average minute of the Flair-Sting match from the first Clash drew 3,138,000 homes, although the final 15 minutes peaked to 3,431,000 homes so there were more viewers in the final 15 minutes of the Flair-Sting 45 minute draw than during the Flair-Funk match, but during an average minute of the Flair-Funk match, there were more viewers. The USA Network's "Royal Rumble" special in January of 1988 from Hamilton, Ontario also drew about 3.2 million homes for the main event. With about seven million viewers, the final match was very close to, if not the most-watched pro wrestling match ever in the U.S. live with the exception of the two WWF prime time specials on MNBC (and obviously every taped SNME on NBC drew a far larger audience than a TBS cable special could ever come close to). But the match did have more viewers than the far-greater hyped MTV specials "Brawl to Settle it All" and "War to Settle the Score" in 1984 and 1985 during the pro wrestling media boom.

1. The Freebirds beat the Road Warriors via DQ in 5:18. Originally this match was billed as for the NWA tag team titles, however the Birds had dropped the titles to the Steiner brothers on 11/1 in Atlanta. That match didn't air on television until 11/18. Everyone expected they would take the WWF route and pretend the belts hadn't changed hands until the change was viewed on television, thus the

Freebirds would come out with the belts and be announced as champions. Instead, they made an attempt to both "hide" the result of the match that still hadn't aired on TV, but still not lie and bill the Birds as champions. The Birds didn't come out with the belts, nor were they acknowledged by the commentators as champs. There was a graphic during their intro listing them as champs, which was a mistake but the subject of the belts was never brought up by the announcers. This was a bad match. Cold crowd. Decent pacing but bad timing. Too short to develop into anything and a godawful finish. Animal was thrown over the top rope behind the refs back and Hawk was brawling in the ring and tossed down Tommy Young for the DQ. The Warriors then kicked the Birds out of the ring. DUD

Next up was Bill Apter coming out to give Sting the "Most Popular Wrestler" award and Ric Flair the "Pro Wrestling Illustrated Wrestler of the Decade" award. The Sting award, supposedly based on fan response, would have worked better if they had given an address and promoted it for fans to write in. The contest was touched upon a few times in pre-Clash hype, but without the address, it made the contest seem like even more of a work than these things usually are. At least Titan gives an address {which it uses to add names to its merchandise mailers) before it works gimmicks like this. Very little crowd response for either man. Flair was looking totally stressed out. It figured to be a very long night at this point.I was waiting for someone to come out and break the trophies but it didn't happen--yet.

2. Doom (Ron Simmons & Butch Reed) beat Tommy Rich & Eddie Gilbert in 5:15. The lack of heat once again made it seem like a dead match, although everyone was trying and the pacing was decent. Finish saw Simmons hit Rich with a clothesline off the middle rope and Reed held him up. *¼

Then came a "Louisville Slugger" segment with Cornette interviewing the Steiners, Best thing on the show thus far. Rick Steiner cracks me up. The only significant thing out of this was they named the move Scott Steiner does wherehe does the forward flying head scissors and spins the guy over in mid-air (The Raul Mata headscissors) and call it the "Frankensteiner." Now what about that blockbuster suplex?

3. Midnight Express beat Dynamic Dudes in 9:22 when Cornette, who had stayed neutral the entire match, hit Douglas with the tennis racquet and Eaton pinned Douglas. Eaton has dropped 35 pounds since his return and now looks small, but was moving like the old Bobby Eaton. Fans were cold when this thing started but the match was heated at the end. Douglas still has to work left-handed since his right arm hasn't recovered from being broken when Sid Vicious dropped him wrong on a guardrail about six weeks

back. The best sequence was when Eaton tried a superplex, Douglas flipped behind him and got a reverse roll, Eaton kicked him off and Douglas jumped off the middle rope and came back with a cross bodyblock. Fans were behind Midnights all the way, even though they were playing heels. This will probably be the case for at least the beginning of all their matches around the horn because nobody likes the Dudes anymore. Finish saw Eaton pull out a chain, Douglas backdropped him and he dropped the chain. Cornette grabbed the chain, made a quick facial expression acting disgusted at Eaton, threw the chain to the crowd, then popped Douglas from behind with the racquet. One of the best finishes to a match in a long time. ***½

4. Steve Williams pinned Super Destroyer (Jack Victory) in 1:41 with the Oklahoma Stampede. Originally Williams was to face Cuban Assassin and Tom Zenk was to face Super Destroyer, who was to be Bill Irwin (Irwin is the brother of the late Scott Irwin who was a headliner on TBS as Super Destroyer in the early 80s and later Bill & Scott Irwin were tag champs for World Class as the Super Destroyers). Then it was decided to eliminate the Williams-Cuban match, except nobody told Williams, who came to Troy anyway. Irwin left for Japan for the tag team tournament, so the designated sub was that man of 1,000 identities, Secret Service Jacko Russian Assassin Blackmailer Victory, adding yet another: alias to his ever growing resume. Zenk arrived late to Troy and was pulled from the show in favor of Williams. This also gave them a chance to use Norman the Lunatic, who was there apparently without purpose. Norman came out in a Santa Claus outfit and gave Williams a teddy bear. For a short squash, this was good action and served its purpose. *¼

5. Rick & Scott Steiner downed The Skyscrapers via DQ in 6:08 when Doom did a run-in. Rick was in the stands pretending to be a popcorn salesman as Scott came to the ring by himself, and then Rick came in. Rick german suplexed Spivey and clotheslined him over the top rope to open the match, which was heated all the way. Spivey came back with a tombstone piledriver. After getting heat on Rick, he made the hot tag to Scott who used the Frankensteiner on Spivey and the blockbuster suplex on Vicious. When Vicious got back in, Scott took a great bump from a vicious clothesline (Spivey's attempt at a simultaneous dropkick from behind missed its mark). After Rick tagged in and was giving Spivey the belly-to-belly suplex and Vicious was banging Scott into the guard rails, Doom came in with Woman. Woman then hit Rick with a high heel shoe but Rick didn't sell it. Rick was about to go after her when a 7-foot unknown guy jumped into the ring. The Road Warriors came in to somewhat even the odds and they brawled until the commercial break. The 7-footer will be called Nitron and for now will serve

as Woman's bodyguard. He never actually touched anyone. This isn't the Argentinian basketball player, Jorge Gonzales, that we wrote about last week, but instead a wrestler from Canada. I'm not certain about this, but I believe his real name is Darryl Karolet and he worked as Sky Hi Lee in Portland in late 1987 and as masked Barry Gasper (teaming with Bob Orton)with New Japan in March of 1988. During the post-match interview with the Warriors and Steiners, the satellite transmission of the picture went out and we could only hear the audio for about a minute. After the commercial break, all was well. ***½

6. Lex Luger pinned Brian Pillman in 12:38 to retain the U.S. title. This was even better than their match in Philadelphia two weeks earlier. The two still were rough in spots but they worked hard enough, stiff enough and fast enough to where it didn't hurt the match. Pillman did less flying than usual because of his bad knee. He concentrated on Flair-like chops and flying moves where the brunt of the bump would be on his back rather than his knees. Pillman worked over Luger's arm, ramming it into the post and guard rail. Luger's chest was all welted up from the stiff chops. Luger did two press-slams, including one where he dropped Pillman behind him. After a ref bump, Pillman scored twice with cradles and had Luger down for the count by no ref to count the pin. Luger then got a chair and absolutely clobbered Pillman with it and got the pin. After the match, Luger twice hit Pillman in the back with the chair before putting him in the torture rack. Sting came in to make the save and ended up slapping Luger in the face before Luger finally bailed out. Even with the execution problems, the match was awesome. ***¾

7. Ric Flair made Terry Funk say "I Quit" in 18:38 of a one-of-a-kind match. 'The two brawled all over the place the entire way, with the usage of the mic inside the ring greatly adding to the dramatic effect of the match. The effect of the mic was so great that this match had more intensity (aka "silent heat," an intensity of such that the crowd is on its feet and enthralled by the action but stunned into silence at the same time) than any U.S. match in a long time. Flair was his usual self, which is to say, the best wrestler of this and maybe any era. But this was Funk's night and he outshined everyone. Funk's intensity, mic work and bumps stole the show. This didn't have the number of great moves and athletic high spots of your normal Match of the Year candidate, nor was it a typical brawl. It seemed far more brutal , even without a trace of juice. Highlights included Funk piledriving Flair on the floor; Flair twice tackling Funk on the floor; and Flair whipping Funk into the ringside table and Funk sliding across the table, off the table and hitting his head on a chair. Flair finally got Funk to say "I Quit" using the figure four leglock. After the match, Funk went to shake hands with Flair as pre-match hype had promised.

By the way, in an interview just before the match, Flair said that if he were to lose the match, that he'd be "through in this sport," This was too late to mean anything as far as ratings, but would have added another aspect to the match except that any thinking fan would "know" Flair was going to win all along with the Starrcade ads billing him in the tournament and not Funk. Anyway, Gary Hart tried to stop Funk, who then shook Flair's hand. Hart attacked Funk from behind, Flair punched and chopped Hart until the Great Muta and Mr. J (another man of many names, aka Dragon Master, Kendo Nagasaki, Kazuo Sakurada and by insiders as Big Bubba Nagasaki) attacked Flair. Sting did his second run-in and Flair caught Muta in the scorpion while Hart was hitting Funk in the knee with the branding iron. Lex Luger came out for an encore appearance and hit Sting with a chair and then hit Flair with a chair and the heels went to town on the faces, leaving Flair, Sting and Funk all layed out in the ring. Luger then went to the backstage area and broke Flair and Sting's trophies with a chair and the last thing we saw was Luger holding a broken trophy over his head. *****

Gordon Solie and Jim Ross handled the announcing. It was a unique pairing matching the best announcer of the 1970s with the best announcer of the late 1980s. Ironically, the main event was a similar match-up. The chemistry between the two appeared awkward at first. It was the first time they had ever worked together on a play-by-play broadcast. Solie was forced into doing the color, which was somewhat new for him and occasionally they stepped on each others' toes. However, by the end of the show, and in the last match in particular, the pairing jelled, I'm no big Solie fan, but his work added a lot to the main event and he did an excellent job in getting Funk over after in theory he'd been already "blown off" at the house shows on the Friday night prior to this show.

Funk will be "out of action" for a while and then return as a color commentator on World Wide Wrestling working with Chris Cruise. There are no actual plans for Funk to return to the ring as a babyface right now, but I'd be quite surprised if it doesn't eventually happen.

It appeared to me that this show finally established the Steiners as the top babyface tag team in the promotion, supplanting the Road Warriors.

Overall production was excellent. Very few missed camera shots. Those live said the production crew created a genuine miracle in getting the dingy and poorly lit RPI Fieldhouse transformed into a modern well-lit facility.

Ring entrances were top-notch.

I was most impressed with how the wrestlers, through good work and hot angles saved what could have been a very bad show. The place started out like Trump Plaza. It was the wrong location to be doing such a major live special in. But everyone came out smelling like a rose.

I can recall after WrestleMania IV, I was discussing with a key NWA person about the WrestleMania and he was saying the same thing everyone else was saying, about how bad the show was, I said that even so, and it was a terrible show, that if Flair and Sting had been put in that building that they couldn't have gotten any reaction either, The guy told me that Flair was smart enough that he somehow would have found a way to get his match over and that if the wrestlers at WrestleMania had worked hard and smart enough, they could have changed the atmosphere at the building throughout the show until the crowd would have been lively. Maybe yes. Maybe no. But on this night, it was the workrate that made what could have been a bad show and turned it into a major success. . Titan's second replay of its Survivor Series special, which went head-to-head with Clash, drew a 1.4 rating and 700,000 homes. One could say that without the competition of another wrestling show on the rival cable network that this show would have been the highest rated NWA Clash thus far. However, one must remember that the first Clash was going head-up with WrestleMania IV, which was viewed in almost as many homes as the USA network special. By the way, that USA rerun was the lowest rated WWF show on the cable network in prime time in at least a few years. However, the original two showings of the Survivor Series special on Sunday and Monday nights drew a 3.9 and 2.9 rating respectively, both very strong showings.

Normally at this point I'd have some comments from the phone messages, but it would be fruitless with so little diversity of opinion. All thumbs up, most very enthusiastically. very few only marginally impressed. Lots of comments that Flair-Funk should win Match of the Year. An awful lot of comments, in both phone messages and letters, that Funk should win Wrestler of the Year. I wouldn't go that far but it was one hell of a performance. A few other comments, probably more on the money, said that Funk deserved either an Academy Award or an Emmy for his work. The Cornette turn was highly praised, especially since the vast majority couldn't see it coming. Many comments that this show was better than Halloween Havoc and should have been the PPV while Havoc should have been the free TV special. Got to disagree. The big angles should be shot before your largest audience, and for the NWA, the largest audience is the Clash specials. The WWF shoots its biggest angles on NBC, not on its PPV shows.

A quick reminder that we've got another thumbs up and thumbs down poll with comments requested for the Survivor Series on Thanksgiving night from the Rosemont Horizon in suburban Chicago. As of Monday the show wasn't sold out, but the advance had topped $200,000 and was close enough to sold out that the sellout is a formality. Titan also has a SNME on 11/25 headlined by the sizzling confrontation, Hulk Hogan vs. Lanny Poffo.

There's been yet another change in the Tully Blanchard and Arn Anderson situation this week. As of press time, Blanchard is no longer coming into the NWA. Anderson is set to debut at Center stage in Atlanta on 11/28 after finishing up Thanksgiving night for the WWF. His television debut, as Ric Flair's "big surprise" will air on 12/9 and Anderson should be hitting the NWA house shows starting Christmas day.

As for Blanchard, everything is now up in the air. NWA officials are claiming that hiring Blanchard right now could be a potential public relations nightmare so they are backing off. The official reason given by the WWF for dismissing Blanchard was that he failed a drug test (no jokes here about him failing because they couldn't find any steroids in his system). The NWA felt it could put them in an embarrassing position if word got out that they hired someone that the WWF fired for using drugs.

My suspicion is there is a lot more to this story than meets the eye, I believe the drug test was a convenient excuse for the WWF to use because they wanted him out of their dressing rooms. The NWA very likely considers the acquisition of Blanchard & Anderson as a whole lot less of a coup today than it did when they were tag team champions and gave notice back in early September. McMahon was able to successfully "destroy" the two on television leading up to their planned NWA arrival, and did succeed in making it look like the NWA is bringing in two more WWF rejects ala Butch Reed and JYD rather than stealing tag team champions. At the same time, Blanchard has been in the wrestling business for 14 years, many of them in the front lines of promotional wars in Texas. He should have known Titan was going to use him to set an example for other wrestlers who were contemplating making the big jump. And they succeeded in doing so in more ways than one. When people are looking at destroying you, you've got to be careful enough not to give them the ammunition. The last word I've heard is the plan is for Ole Anderson to take Blanchard's place as Arn's partner in the bookings already made starting Christmas. Actually, if Blanchard were to swallow his pride and go through rehab (whether he needs it or not isn't the issue here, this entire game is politics, not dealing with an alleged drug problem), my guess is the NWA would take him. Whatever PR problems this potentially could cause would be averted (even though in reality the odds are very slim any such problem would ever crop up) and the NWA would politically be able to look like the group who is giving someone who has tried to face his problems a second chance.

To update last week's lead story on the UWF's "U-Cosmos" show on 11/29 at the Tokyo Dome, the show shattered an all-time pro wrestling record on Nov. 5 when on the first day tickets went on sale for the show, they sold 40,000 tickets for well over $2.5 million. The old record for first-day sales was set last year by the UWF when it sold out the Ariake Coliseum (12,000 seats and $500,000) the first day tickets went on sale. The 56,000 seat Tokyo Dome sold out in short order, more than three weeks in advance so the UWF has already broken the all-time gate record set by New Japan at the Tokyo Dome on April 24 of $2,781,000 (sellout gate was roughly $3.2 million). I believe that all the closed-circuit locations are also sold out for the show, so this group with a half-dozen wrestlers, no television, and three or four front office employees will gross roughly the same amount of money {and no doubt profit tons more) than the WWF did at its first WrestleMania. As mentioned last week, the ringside ($210) tickets were sold out in four minutes. Apparently those who were in line to buy ringside seats had to be in line by the evening of Nov. 1 (four days before tickets were to go on sale people started camping out to get the ringside seats). It was said that if you weren't in line by Nov. 1, the ringside seats would have been sold out by the time you got to the ticket window. Maybe nobody in wrestling besides Akira Maeda can do this, but Mick Jagger does it all the time.

New Japan, which has booked the Tokyo Dome for a big show on Feb. 10 of next year, now almost "needs" to sell the 56,000 seat building out to save face. After all, the UWF is an upstart promotion with no television comprised of wrestlers who had all worked for New Japan and were never pushed to the top. Even though the card is months away, New Japan bookers Seiji Sakaguchi and Masao Hattori are working hard on pulling this off. Koji Kitao, the former Sumo Grand Champion (Futuhaguro) will debut in Japan on the card against Bam Bam Bigelow (Kitao actually made his pro debut this past Saturday night at an AWA television taping in Rochester, MN) and this event will have widespread general public interest in Japan. Antonio Inoki will wrestle on the card, and perhaps use the big show as a grand retirement send-off and with Inoki now in the Japanese parliament, that also has much general public interest, especially coming back from the stab wound and all.

New Japan also wanted to book "all four World champions," which would have been Ric Flair, Hulk Hogan, Big Van Vader and Larry Zbyszko. As for now, the only hold-up is Hogan, and New Japan, according to Weekly Fight magazine, made a record offer of $200,000 to Titan to get Hogan's services for one night. But there is no amount of money that would get Hogan to appear in a situation that Vince McMahon doesn't have complete control of, let alone on a card which includes Flair with the current political situation being what it is. Flair is to defend the title against the Great Muta, while Zbyszko is also set to defend his title. Sakaguchi is trying to work with Giant Baba to use a few All Japan guys for this show as well, and if that deal comes together (I'd guess it's unlikely, but the two sides are talking)

than Vader will defend his title in a "dream match" against Stan Hansen, and no doubt Genichiro Tenryu would appear in a "dream match" as well.

The appearance of both Flair and Zbyszko would be a first for the New Japan promotion. It would end an association in which the NWA champion appeared exclusively for All Japan (and before that with its predecessor company, the JWA) dating back to Lou Thesz in the 1950s. Relations between the two sides started falling apart last February when All Japan sent Tenryu to Cleveland for the Clash of the Champions and the NWA came up with a scenario where the opponents of Tenryu & The Road Warriors were "locked in the dressing room." This totally embarrassed All Japan in the Japanese media since the match was taped for television and it made Tenryu look like a party to a circus sideshow rather than a sporting event as pro wrestling is treated in Japan. The last vestige of the relationship seemed to be destroyed a few weeks later when the NWA sent Ricky Steamboat to Japan to defend the title. All Japan used Steamboat in the middle-of-the-card against mainly prelim wrestlers except on one night of the tour, instead of as a main eventer. The AWA champion used to appear for the now-defunct IWE in Japan until that group went out of business and Verne Gagne transferred his alliance to All Japan in the late 70s.

Gagne himself, and later Nick Bockwinkel, Rick Martel and Curt Hennig all defended their titles for All Japan and All Japan's Jumbo Tsuruta even held the AWA title for a few months in 1984. New Japan, for years, had been affiliated with the WWF. While Bruno Sammartino never worked for New Japan because of a loyalty to Baba and a dislike of Inoki, subsequent champ Bob Backlund frequently defended his title on New Japan cards as did Hulk Hogan before McMahon and Inoki's relations fell apart over McMahon double-crossing New Japan twice on scheduled tours by Hogan.

More World title trivia. Vader, the IWGP champ, may have accomplished a first in pro wrestling history on 11/12 in Mexico City. Vader defeated El Canek to win the UWA version of the World title before 13,000 fans. This makes Leon White the holder of three different World titles (IWGP in Japan, UWA in Mexico and CWA in Europe) simultaneously in three different continents and under two different names (in Europe, he works without the hood as Leon "Bull Power" White). It's expected that White will drop the CWA strap back to Otto Wanz in Australia when he returns there in late December. Canek must have regained the UWA title just days earlier from The Killer before losing to Vader. It is said that Canek wanted to lose to Vader in the hopes that doing New Japan that favor would be rewarded by being brought back to Japan for some tours in 1990. Canek at one time was a big deal in Japan, but in recent years has meant little and it was thought his career in Japan was over.

After at least two "shoot" comments on recent television interviews, it has become something less than top secret that the No. 1 divisive point right now in the NWA is Ric Flair. The TBS organization has decided it wants to build the promotion around Lex Luger and Sting as soon as possible and Flair may be in the biggest fight of his career to stay on top. This is going to turn into a major issue in 1990 and one where there is no correct answer. It's one of those gut feelings. I can sit here and give you plenty of reasons why Flair should be kept as the top man in the promotion. I can also sit here and give you just as many reasons why he shouldn't be. I've heard arguments from both sides. There are logical reasons for each point of view, and some reasons that probably have as much emotional and personal connotations rather than what would be best for business. There are very few actual facts to this. While quality of work can't be called an actual fact, nobody right now will dispute the statement that right now Flair is the best worker in the NWA. With Funk on the sidelines and Steamboat at home, nobody is even a close second. Facts also: Ric Flair is 39 – he turns 40 on February 25th. Luger is 31. Sting is 30. Facts: Measuring a promotion's success can be determined by house shows, television ratings and PPV buy rates. House shows are poor. TV ratings have rebounded strongly of late. PPV has stayed surprisingly steady. (Before I forget, officially the PPV from Philadelphia drew a 1.77 percent buy rate, which is about 200,000 orders and just over $3 million in gross revenue. I'm told the gross revenue and total buys were slightly better than any previous NWA PPV event, which surprised just about everyone)

Let's look at the arguments for Flair stepping down from the top: 1) The house shows aren't drawing well and Flair is the top attraction; 2) Age – the most frequently cited and really the thrust of the entire argument; 3) Some feel the promotion needs a new image and feel Flair is a part of an old image that has left a bad taste in people's mouth; 4) People want to see the young studs, not the older wrestlers (and those ratings for Flair-Funk last Wednesday sure shoot this argument all to hell); 5) Because of Flair's size, he isn't believable in the era of the monsters; 6) After more than eight years of being on top, it's simply time for something new and that's nothing against Flair in any way, simply that eight years is too long during the modern era to have one guy on top.

Now the arguments for keeping Flair: 1) He is the best all-around performer in the NWA and taking everything into consideration, in the game today; 2) Despite his age, he has shown no signs of slowing down inside the ring. In fact, the best matches of his career have been in 1989; 3) He is still the most well-known wrestler in the group, sells the most tickets and his matches draw the highest TV ratings; 4) While the house shows aren't doing well, when Flair came back in

August, the houses were generally better than in July, during the heavily-hyped and traditionally strong Bash series, with much stronger undercards in July with Luger as the top star; 5) The same shows that didn't draw with Flair on top also had Sting, Luger, Road Warriors, Steiners and the rest at the top of the card as well and the NWA has promoted all of them as near-equals so it's unfair to blame Flair; 6) If Luger was made champion, he wouldn't be able to draw against anyone but Flair--evidence is the Luger-Sting matches thus far have drawn well-below-average houses when Flair was working with Muta (who has no business being the main event heel). In other words, it's the Flair match that draws or doesn't. Luger and Sting make little difference in the crowd; 7) At a house show, there is no match that Flair can't follow. There are few, if any opponents that he can't carry to a main event calibre match. That can't be said for Sting or Luger.

I've got a lot of thoughts of my own on this subject. If business was strong right now, I wouldn't even entertain the notion today of replacing Flair as the top dog. I'd certainly be ready to make the move when necessary, and given the age of Flair, eventual change is an inevitability. But business isn't strong right now. Because of that, you have to consider the move. At the same time, there is a very valid argument I hear over and over again. The NWA can't consistently draw at the house shows because the WWF is the major league. The reason they are the major league is because the general media gives their major drawing cards the status of cult celebrityhood. For the NWA to make it, they need to make their top stars celebrities. Of the wrestlers in the NWA, the only ones whose personalities are strong enough to get over consistently in that environment are Flair and Jim Cornette. What can Luger do on a talk show except take off his shirt, which may get him one invite but there is no reason to invite him back? What can Sting do? Flair is a tremendous representative of the business. He can get himself over in any environment. When the Kangaroos folks had a deal with Steiner, Warriors, Sting, Luger and Flair, the comments of the execs were that the other guys had no personalities and were what they expected as wrestlers. But Flair was different. He impressed them. This is a valid point, but after one year, I haven't seen any progress in this area and if there isn't going to be progress, it's a moot point. If there is going to be progress, it's a point in Flair's favor.

The real subject is age, however. Arguments can be made in two ways about this one. Athletically, today, age is not a factor. Neither Sting nor Luger will be close to Flair as a performer until he shows signs of a decline. Those signs aren't there. As for marketability, that's another story. If you look at the top "performers" in action movies right now, the hottest guys are Chuck Norris, who is much older than Flair; Schwarzanegger, who is older than

Flair; and Stallone, who is around the same age. Hollywood

isn't moving those guys out this year. Nor is the WWF moving out Hogan, who is three years younger than Flair. There are wrestlers who have drawn more money in their 40s than in their 30s. Bruno Sammartino, Nick Bockwinkel, Buddy Rogers, Gene Kiniski, Fritz Von Erich, Lou Thesz and Verne Gagne all pop into my head without any time thinking. At the same time, today's wrestling business is more a youth oriented business than in years past, and anything that worked prior to 1985 is almost irrelevant today.

Based on what I've seen of late, I've got a good deal of confidence in Luger. Not nearly so much in Sting as far as being the No. 1 guy, but I believe Luger can pull it off. Ray Charles could see this weekend that Luger is being groomed for the spot. I say give him the chance, but don't bury Flair in the process. Keep the two as somewhat equals, with Luger as the heel champ, but Flair as the challenger that fans are led to believe could take Luger when the big match takes place. Give Sting the chance to be a challenger for Luger as well. By the time all this is tried, the answers to most of the arguments will become self-evident. If Luger can't draw as well against a guy like Muta, you've got your answer in front of you. If he draws better, you also have your answer. Maybe Luger and Sting can't fill Flair's shoes, and maybe they can. We can argue and list reasons all day supporting either idea, but I say, give it a try. Who knows, maybe Luger will be a great champ. Maybe Flair's semifinals will gain more interest than Luger's title matches. Instead of maybe's, there should be answers come early next summer, which, from a business standpoint, should determine exactly where Flair should be and who should be on top.

It's easy for an organization to blame the guy on top, rather than accept the responsibility that maybe the problem is the weakness of the organization. The reverse is also true. I've heard too much of late saying that replacing Flair with Luger is the answer to the NWA's problems, when the problems themselves run a whole lot deeper than who holds the title belt. At the same time, no matter how great a worker he might be, Flair knows the rules of the game as well as anyone. If someone can draw more money, then they deserve the spot.

Since there is no chance of this ever happening given the current political climate, here's some suggestions on how to set things up for a short run. Put Luger over at Starrcade, since he's going to get the title shot at the next PPV. But have Luger win the tournament in this fashion--he beats Muta and somehow screws Sting but gets pinned by Flair. Flair loses the tournament, however, because he gets DQ'd against Muta and goes to a draw with Sting. Sting pins Muta in the other match, and save Sting vs. Luger for the last match. Luger wins the tournament, but he was pinned clean by Flair. Who is the top guy? That gets answered in the rematch. When Luger wins the strap, and somehow during the interim Sting gets the U.S. strap, you've got two challengers that fans know can win the title--Flair and Sting. At that point the fans will determine, based on the box office, who the top babyface is, If Sting vs. Luger doesn't draw, then it's time to consider Flair. If it does, maybe stay with Luger. Maybe consider Sting. Maybe consider a younger guy like Scott Steiner who may well surpass Sting or Luger. Maybe age will catch up with Flair and everything will be obvious, and if Flair stays in the stressful position that they and he have put him in at the present, the face will look old and that is awfully significant in a business of this type.

WWC

Some line-ups of recent shows. On 10/28 at Juan Loubriel Stadium in Bayamon saw Carlitos Colon vs. Steve Strong (Steve DiSalvo) for the Universal title, Invader #1 (Jose Gonzales) vs. Abbuda Dein (Rocky Iaukea) for the Puerto Rican title in a match with the ring surrounded by fire, Mark & Chris Youngblood defending the WWC tag team titles against Rip Rogers & Chicky Starr, Miguelito Perez & Hurricane Castillo Jr. defending the Caribbean tag team titles against The Mercenaries (Cuban Assassin Angel Acevedo & Jerry Morrow), Junkyard Dog vs. Ivan Koloff, Super Medico (Jose Estrada) defending the jr. heavyweight title against Brett Sawyer and Ron Starr vs. Lec Burke.

1/4 at Loubriel Stadium had Colon vs. Strong with Chicky Starr to be hung in a cage above the ring, Mercenaries defending the Caribbean tag belts against Invader #1 & TNT, Ron Starr vs. Burke, JYD vs. Dein, Medico vs. Sawyer, Castillo vs. Rogers and Perez vs. El Gran Mendoza.

WWF

Jim Duggan and Curt Hennig appeared this past week on the game show "Super Sloppy Double Dare."

Based on a pre-sweeps survey of the top 23 markets in the country, the WWF Superstars of Wrestling was drawing a 3.3 rating in the period of 9/30 to 10/27, Challenge getting a 3.1, while the NWA Pro show was getting a 1.9 and World Wide getting a 1.3. some of that difference is because in the big markets the WWF has the stronger stations and better time slots, but that's a catch-22 anyway. Roller Games did a 2.5 during the same period, which shows it continues to drop, and in the big markets, it's stations and time slots are a lot stronger than the NWA.

Roddy Piper was on Arsenio Hall on Tuesday night plugging Survivor Series.

According to the Montreal newspapers, the Rougeaus are going to take a one-year sabbatical from wrestling before going back to the WWF late in 1990. Their last match is actually 11/27, so they are staying through the end of this weekend.

All-American Wrestling on 11/12 drew a 2.2 rating.

11/18 in Philadelphia drew 7,325 and $90,423 as Mark

Young pinned Bob Bradley, Boreus Zhukov pinned Al Perez (probably a test for Perez to break his "spirit" so he'll be a loyal employee but it also shows what Perez' future looks like), Honky Tonk Man pinned Red Rooster, Dino Bravo pinned Jim Neidhart, Bret Hart (back in action after the rib injury) double count out with Tito Santana, Demolition beat Arn Anderson & Haku (who are billed as the Brainbusters), Dusty Rhodes pinned Big Bossman and Roddy Piper went to a double disqualification with Rick Rude. Told nothing better than two-stars here.

Miller Brewing Company at its national meeting proclaimed its Lite-o-Mania ad campaign was its most successful ad campaign of 1989, citing public response. However, the folks at Miller have no plans of doing anything with pro wrestling in the foreseeable future.

11/12 in Norfolk drew 4,000 as Young beat Conquistador (Jose Luis Rivera), Perez pinned Barry Horowitz, The Genius pinned Sam Houston, Zhukov pinned Hillbilly Jim (another upset but Zhukov is from the area), Mr. Perfect pinned Jimmy Snuka, Demolition beat Haku & Anderson, Rhodes pinned Bossman and Hulk Hogan pinned Bad News Brown.

11/3 in Peoria drew 3,500 as Perez pinned Horowitz, Houston pinned Tom Stone, Demolition beat Haku & Anderson, Rhodes pinned Bossman, Honky Tonk Man pinned Rooster and Randy Savage pinned Jim Duggan.

11/13 in Roanoke for the WWF debut in town drew a very disappointing 2,300 for Hogan as Perez pinned Brooklyn Brawler, Perfect pinned Snuka, Zhukov pinned Hillbilly, Hogan pinned Brown, Genius pinned Young, Bushwackers beat Powers of Pain via DQ, Houston pinned Conquistador and Rhodes pinned Bossman. Hogan got a big reaction but they didn't care about Rhodes. Told the independent VWA puts on better house shows than this. There was a ton of local publicity for the WWF debut and Hogan, but the crowd was less than the NWA averages in that city with no local publicity even during its recent problems.

NWA

TV ratings still on the upswing. Power Hour on 11/10 shattered its old record with a 2.9 rating (previous best was 2.6), while World Championship Wrestling (Sid Vicious vs. Steve Williams main event) drew a 2.9, which ties the previous week and the second highest of the year while NWA Main Event drew a 2.4 (Tommy Rich & Eddie Gilbert vs. Midnight Express).

This is not etched in stone, but there is a good chance the booking committee will have several new additions. The current booking committee is Ric Flair as head booker, with Kevin Sullivan, Jim Cornette and Ole Anderson as assistants. There is talk of adding some or all of the following: Jim Herd, Jim Barnett, Jim Ross and Terry Funk.

The 11/10 Power Hour that set a record had Luger vs. Murdoch as the headline match for the title, Luger's improved a ton this year, but the two matches with Murdoch on TV were a lot worse than Hulk Hogan matches.

Kevin Sullivan did the color with Jim Ross at the TV tapings at Center Stage on 11/16. Told it was a try-out for Sullivan and either he or Michael Hayes will wind up with the spot. It was felt if Cornette continued that it would make it harder for him to get the fans to boo him so he's only on Friday's. They may do a "Louisville Slugger" segment weekly on saturday. Expect some other changes in the announcing line-ups as well, perhaps even a return of Missy Hyatt as a co-host on Sunday.

Promoters Elliot and carl Murnick were fired by TBS and Sandy Scott was demoted from being a promoter to being in charge of the rings getting from city-to-city. Chip Burnham of TBS, Gary Juster and Tim Willett will be the event coordinators for the future. My guess is with Burnham new to the position that he'll make some rookie mistakes early. Long run? Wait and see. Ralph Freed was also dumped which ends the several decade long relationship of Fred Ward promotions in Columbus, GA and the NWA. The demotion of the Murnicks (who are trying to get in with Titan Sports now) ends a long era as well, as their father, Joe Murnick, was the half-owner of Jim Crockett Promotions with Jim Crockett Sr. when the territory was built.

There is no guarantee that you will ever see Jorge Gonzales (El Gigante) in a wrestling ring. Word I get is that if he can work enough to be worth something, he'll get a shot. If not, you'll never hear the name again. The WWF had also been actively recruiting Gonzales, and my guess is that if he had gone with them, work would have meant nothing. NWA is crossing its fingers hoping he can be introduced to the TV audience at the next Clash (February Champion, 6 in Corpus Christi) and maybe debut on the February 25 PPV show (which apparently will be from the Greensboro Coliseum).

At the 11/16 tapings at Center Stage, Flair wrestled Muta in a very good match which airs this Saturday. Finish has Flair getting Muta in the figure four when Mr. J runs in. Flair gets the advantage outside the ring and gets Mr. J in the figure four when Buzz Sawyer runs in and they do a number on Flair once again. This airs on Saturday. The following Saturday Flair swears revenge and says he'll have a big surprise (Arn Anderson) for the following week on television.

The other highlight of the taping was Midnight Express vs. Dynamic Dudes ending with the Express Dq'd when Cornette was caught using the tennis racquet. The Express was cheered early but managed to turn a good percentage of the crowd against them as the match went on.

Love those Cornette & Stan Lane interviews over the weekend.

Sawyer debuted on all the TV's this weekend. The guy is

one incredible worker. I'm not so sure he can get over, and his track record indicates he may not last long, but I'd love to see him against Flair even if it was just a TV main event.

Danny Davis worked as jobber Dan Devine, while jobber Lou Tallafoni from New York is really Louie Spicoli from Puerto Rico who is headed to the USWA.

Lord Littlebrook was said to be hilarious as manager of the Militia.

The Road Warriors agreed to return for the option year of their contract so they are signed with the NWA through December 9, 1990, which should end any rumors of them going anywhere else. From what I'm told, terms were the same as last year, $2,000 per match for each Warrior and $1,100 for Paul Ellering and 250 dates per year, which means they trail probably only Flair and Hogan as the highest paid wrestlers in North America. There had been talk the Warriors wouldn't renew for their option year.

They finally got the second tag belt for the Steiners.

For those traveling looking for a wrestling holiday, NWA will run the Omni on 1/1, Gainesville (50 miles away) on 1/2 and Center Stage in Atlanta on 1/3.

Brian Pillman is out of action with a pretty severe knee ligament injury. He may not be back until January.

11/19 in Pittsburgh drew 3,400 as the three Samoans beat Ranger Ross & Tommy Rich & Eddie Gilbert DUD, Tom Zenk put Iron Sheik to sleep DUD, Midnight Express beat Dynamic Dudes ***¼, Danny Spivey beat Road Warrior Animal via DQ **, Steiners beat Doom via DQ **, Luger pinned Zenk after hitting him with the title belt (almost exact same match as with Murdoch on TV, complete with too much early stalling) *¼ and Flair beat Muta via DQ when Muta blew the mist in 24 minutes ***¾

11/18 in St. Louis drew a $24,000 house with the same results. Steiners-Doom said to be the best match on that card followed by Midnight- Dudes.

11/9 in Knoxville, TN saw Gilbert beat Cuban Assassin, Rich pinned Norman, Mike Rotunda beat Zenk, Midnight Express beat Militia, Steiners beat Michael Hayes & Rotunda, Vicious beat Animal via DQ and Luger pinned Pillman.

Vicious no-showed this past entire weekend, so the Warriors-Skyscrapers matches wound up being Spivey vs. Animal. Hawk made the shots. No word on why Vicious missed the shows as of yet.

MEXICO

Pirata Morgan won the WWF jr. heavyweight title from El Satanico. Apollo Dantes beat Bestia Salvaje in a hair vs. hair match. Big feud going on with Mil Mascaras & Dos Caras against Cien Caras and Mascara Ano Dos Mil. Blue Demon Jr. beat El Matematico in a mask vs. hair match.

On 11/19 in Mexico City the top two matches were Big Van Vader & Cien Caras & Fabuloso Blondie (Ken Timbs)

beating Lizmark & El Faraoan & Satanico in two of three falls with Vader basically indestructible against the guys who were maybe half his weight. Finish saw Lizmark try and sunset flip off the top rope but Vader didn't go over and sat down and squashed him for the pin. Main event was hair vs. hair with Brazo de Plata & El Brazo beating El Verdugo & Hombre Bala in two of three. Last fall was pretty exciting as it was elimination style and each team won a fall and the heels (Verdugo & Bala) got lots of near falls on El Brazo before Brazo got the pin on both of them and the heels got their heads shaved. Plata (the fat Brazo, body like Jonathan Boyd) did a dive through the ropes in the third fall which saw three successive dives out of the ring.

CWA

Jerry Lawler turned heel and used a chain to pin Dutch Mantell in the main event on the 11/13 show in Memphis to keep the title. They did a pull-apart brawl after the match. Even with Lawler's turn, the crowd was still tiny. Other results saw Dirty White Boy keep the CWA title pinning Bill Dundee when Dirty White Girl sprayed hair spray in his eyes plus Soul Taker pinned Tracy Smothers when Nate the Rat distracted the ref, Mike Davis double count out with Chris Champion, Todd Morton & King Cobra beat New York Brawler (Lou Fabbiano) & Cowboy Kevin Dillinger and Frankie Lancaster beat Black Jack.

Fantastics are headed in as heels.

Master of Pain (Punisher in USWA) back as a face.

They had another letter from the girl in Georgia to Dirty White Boy and White Girl grabbed the letter and started to read it when White Boy grabbed the letter back and started yelling at her.

In a cage match from Nashville, Lawler beat Soul Taker but after the match White Boy jumped in and they were beating on Lawler until Dundee made the save. When all the heels started beating on Dundee, Lawler just walked out of the cage.

11/19 in Memphis saw Cobra beat Brawler, Ricky & Todd Morton beat Dillinger & Black Jack, Master of Pain beat Soul Taker via DQ, Champion beat Davis in a lumberjack match, Dundee won the CWA title from White Boy with White Girl handcuffed to Ricky Morton and Mantell beat Lawler in a non-title death match. In the third fall both were KO'd and first guy to his feet wins, Ref was bumped and didn't see Soul Taker interfere and piledrive Mantell. As Lawler, now acting as a face, went to tell Calhoun what had happened, Dundee came in and hit Lawler with a chain and Mantell got up first to win. Lawler did a babyface interview on TV on 11/18.

OTHER LATE NOTES

Eric Embry beat Buddy Landel in the main event on 11/17 in Dallas before 350 fans to earn a shot at Kerry Von Erich's

Texas title in two weeks. Perhaps a turn coming up since on the Thanksgiving card in Dallas (where they always run a big angle} the main event is Chris Adams vs. Billy Travis with Embry as ref and Adams and Embry did have an argument on TV a few weeks back. Kevin Von Erich on his interview said he didn't mean to mislead anyone about him wanting to wrestle Kerry, but that he wanted a title belt and would wrestle anyone to get it.

Nikita Koloff beat Larry Zbyszko via DQ at the 11/18 AWA tapings in Rochester, MN. Masa Saito (in Minnesota to help Brad Rheingans train Koji Kitao) worked the card and beat Pat Tanaka in a martial arts match. Kitao worked a dark match as the Monster Machine teaming with Saito to beat Jim Evans & Randy Fox. Fantastics beat Destruction Crew via DQ when Johnny Valiant interfered and Jerry Blackwell made the save. Later, Fantastics & Blackwell beat Crew & Valiant when Blackwell squashed Valiant. Valiant also managing Doug Somers who is feuding with Tommy Jammer, while Paul Diamond beat Tanaka via DQ when Akio Sato did a run-in.

Paul E. Dangerously booked an ICW TV taping and all sorts of stuff happened. Dangerously wanted to get Tony Atlas to drop the title to Mike Moore and Atlas refused which caused a major confrontation. I believe Dangerously is already through with the group and never appeared in front of the camera. He brought Tom Prichard and Bob Orton to the taping.

Brickhouse Brown & Lou Perez are now Florida tag team champs.

Rex King & Steve Doll regained the held up Northwest tag belts on 11/11 in Portland beating Jeff Warner & Brian Adams when Warner jumped off the top rope intentionally on Adams so Warner is back as a face after doing one of those famous Len Denton three-week turns.

11/18 had Scotty the Body (still the lone bright spot in this group) vs. Doll for the Northwest title and if Doll won, then Ginger (Doll's valet) would get Veronica Lane (Scotty's valet) in a cage and Ginger vowed to rip all the clothes off Veronica's body.

Chris Benoit & Biff Wellington will hold the Int. tag titles beating The Black Harts (Tom Nash & Jason Anderson) before any of you read this.

Owen Hart having 3 to 3½ star matches with Larry Cameron on top.

Arch Angel (Curtis Thompson) showing good improvements.

D.J. Peterson started this past week while Steve DiSalvo headed in and Davey Boy Smith "suspended" so he can tour Japan.

Bob Emory and the Derringer brothers are already gone.

Owen Hart to feud with Arch Angel now.

Saw Jushin Liger vs. Nacki Sano from 9/21 in Osaka and easy five star. Reminded me of the old Tiger Mask-Kobayashi bouts in 1985. Best of the three. Finish saw Liger try a superplex from the top rope but Sano reversed it into a gordbuster. Sano then leaped off the top, flipped over Liger's back to get behind him, and pulled him over in a full nelson into a german suplex for the fall.

THE READERS' PAGES

CLASH

The NWA is back on track and back to business after 18 days. From an unspectacular PPV show to the most thrilling and entertaining free television wrestling show I've ever seen, making Titan's Survivor Series preview look like just another edition of Prime Time Wrestling.

Announcing: Up until the main event, Gordon Solie seemed to slow down Jim Ross. He couldn't keep up with him. Although for some it was a solid dream pairing, it didn't work early. However, in the main event, Solie illuminated some new old history not previously covered by Ross, such as that Dory Funk beat Gene Kiniski with the spinning toe hold. Jesse Ventura, Tony Schiavone and Vince McMahon have never come this close to excellence of elongation as they did in the main event.

Camera angles: Finally, not too many shots were missed. The dives out of the ring were shot with the long angle. For once I enjoyed the crowd shots in the main event because of the reactions.

Only Glitch: The blackout during the Road Warrior interview. Doom is really lame as a team but Robin Green spilled out of her cocktail Joan Collins dress.

It was the best booked television special of the past three years. Great acting by Jim Cornette.

The whole thing was sheer brilliance. With Terry Funk and Paul E. Dangerously gone, the heel side desperately needed a great talker. Pillman vs. Luger was four stars. A great and quick pace illuminating Luger's improvement was tarred only by a few clumsy moves early and Pillman having to help out so much on Luger's second press-slam, Superb pacing, but where does it leave Pillman now that Sting and Luger are wed?

The Steve Williams squash got across quickly exactly what it should have. It was much unlike the boring and slow Tommy Rich squash at Halloween Havoc.

Normally, I hate when promotion's do a self-serving Bill Apter awards ceremony (topped off by the one a few years ago for Mike Von Erich), but tonight it nicely put Sting into upper echelon territory and emphasized Ric Flair in fans' eyes as not just the dominant wrestler of the 80s, but the late 70s and perhaps of the century. It was okay, and, of course, allowed Luger a spotlight in destroying the trophies as every promotion always does. Shouldn't fans have been suspicious that Funk wasn't listed for Starrcade, and shouldn't that have given away the result of the I Quit match? Starrcade is going to take a lot of selling because they are leaving out a lot of guys that fans want to see on a big show.

Woman's unique ala Ric Flair entrance in having costumed guys lead her to the ring showed the NWA isn't sexist and at least is up to the 1960s where all the other promotions are still buried in the prejudice 1950s. Luger's entrance was spectacular. I wish they could have done more with Funk's entrance than having two lame looking cowboys that they didn't even comment on. How about bringing out some horses or Dory Funk with him?

Tommy Young is the most overlooked valuable performer on these shows. He was constantly trying out the mic to make sure it would work at the crucial moment, just as at the last big show he put out the burning shroud.

Terry Funk and Ric Flair put on one of the best matches I've ever seen. Many, many fantastic chops. The reasonably smart people watching the show with me, including my wife, asked at the end of the card "Were the guys in the last match going at it for real?" It was that kind of match. Five stars, even without the post-match brawl.

Roddy Piper on Arsenio Hall the night before was the best WWF guest thus far to date on his show. He did fine until he started shilling so painfully for Vince's Survivor Series, With one of the best mouths in the history of the business, why can't Piper correctly pronounce Albano (Albino), Snuka (Schnuka). His disease has spread to Ron Garvin, who pronounces Valentine as Valentime.

I hope the people complaining about Ric Flair's booking eat crow with this one.

Dr. Mike Lano
Alameda, California

AWA
The AWA's Team Concept is not only conceptually ridiculous, but a complete waste of time on television. How do they expect to get any ratings by showing wrestling matches in an empty television studio? Where is the heat?

Jack Cullen
Burtonsville, Maryland

QUESTIONS
Does Naoki Sano qualify as a rookie? I hope Dan Kroffat soars to the top of the year end awards. He's been great all year. He and Doug Furnas are my tag team of the year and Kroffat has to be in the top three for Most Outstanding Wrestler. Whatever happened to Terry Allen?

Glenn Fox
Seattle, Washington

Dave Meltzer: Noaki Sano has been wrestling regularly since February, 1985 so he's far from being a rookie. This year was just his first one in the spotlight in Japan. He's certainly a candidate for Most Improved Wrestler and would be a

deserving winner, but my guess is since he hasn't had the exposure with readers as much as Lex Luger, Scott Steiner and Rick Rude, that he can't do any better than fourth. Terry Allen (Magnum T.A.) is living in Virginia and got married in September. Ric Flair has wanted to bring him in as part of the announcing crew but right now the NWA has about as many announcers as it needs.

I'm a long-time fan and would love to have information as to the whereabouts of some former wrestlers like Johnny Valentine, Pepper Gomez, Cowboy Bob Ellis, Haystacks Calhoun, Hans Mortier, Don Curtis, The Fabulous Kangaroos and the Tolos Brothers. Also, what happened to The Spoiler, Masked Superstar and Steve Travis? Also, is there any chance of Terry Allen returning to the wrestling ring?

Carl Gessner
Pluckemin, New Jersey

Dave Meltzer: Valentine is living in Fort Worth and is still crippled from the airplane crash of 1975 (the same one in which Ric Flair suffered a broken back and also ended the career of Bob Bruggers). Valentine was 47 at the time but was still one of the top heels in the country. He tried managing but didn't come across well and it was hard for fans to hate a heel manager who needed braces to help him walk. Gomez is living in the San Francisco Bay Area and works at Scoma's Restaurant in Fisherman's Wharf in San Francisco. The last I heard of Ellis was that he's been in and out of legal trouble for allegedly trying to fix horse races. Calhoun is living in McKinney, TX and is very much alive, although he had part of one leg amputated and still follows wrestling closely through the newsletter. Last I heard Mortier was in Europe. Don Curtis was for years the building manager for the Jacksonville Coliseum in Florida but quit the job about a year or two back but as best I know, he's still living in Jacksonville. Roy Heffernan of the Kangaroos went back to Australia and I'm not sure what happened to him, or even if he's still alive. Al Costello resides in Michigan and trains wrestlers and still wrestles on occasion and also avidly keeps up with today's wrestling scene. Don't know about Chris Tolos, but John Tolos lives and works in Southern California, I believe at one of the major studios but several readers know and I'm sure we'll get the correct info within two weeks on him. I saw him in 1988 at the Cauliflower Alley club banquet and even though he's 58-years-old, he looks 35 and has kept himself in great cardiovascular condition. Spoiler is living in Texas, but don't know exactly where. Superstar is wrestling in the WWF as Demolition Ax. Travis career was cut short by an auto accident and don't know anything about current whereabouts.

PIPER

In regards to Teresa DeMarie's letter in the 11/6 Observer, she's absolutely right. To single out a performer, who hasn't been involved in the game for the better part of the year is not fair. Truthfully, Piper is doing quite well considering all the problems he has encountered. She's on target to say it isn't ethical to include Piper as a candidate for this less-than-flattering award. My choices would be Andre the Giant, who continually gets worse, Dusty Rhodes, who hasn't been much for years but is now a sad joke, Jim Duggan and very sadly, Ted DiBiase, a one-time favorite of mine. I disagree with the Hogan vs. Warrior match at WrestleMania. Warrior sells too much merchandise to heel him. Terry Funk is my leading candidate for Wrestler of the Year, Best Heel, Most Improved and a few others. He has kept my interest in wrestling alive in an otherwise lackluster year. The round-robin tournament for Starrcade, while interesting, is also limiting. They can't feature many of the other wrestlers and that's a waste. You can have some intriguing match-ups and some really screwy finishes plus possibilities of turns. Yet, a Starrcade card without a World title match doesn't seem right.

J.D. McKay Jr.
Louisville, Mississippi

NWA

If we had not watched Halloween Havoc on our own, judging by your comments and the phone poll, we may not have ordered it. However, we are glad we did. All of the matches were two stars or better with the exception of Tommy Rich vs. Cuban Assassin, which had no business being on the card.

This may not have been the NWA's best PPV, but when you consider it in comparison with WWF PPV cards, it was outstanding. The crowd popped. The booking was creative, the TV production was the best so far from the NWA. Overall, it was a very entertaining show to watch.

Why are you so prejudiced against the NWA? For the average wrestling fan that likes action instead of hype, it is the best promotion in North America. If the NWA wasn't on television, we wouldn't watch any wrestling.

We would also appreciate more inside information, not theories on how to run the NWA. For example, why are Eddie and Missy Gilbert being phased out? Why is he no longer on the booking committee? Do they not get along with Ric Flair?

Fred Stolaruk
Detroit, Michigan

Dave Meltzer: I agree that by a wide margin, the NWA provides the best actual wrestling action in North America, however this is both a business and an entertainment form that we are talking about. Whether you think the NWA has been really entertaining, and for the most part, I concur and certainly the big shows have been outstanding (in fact, my own belief is that a lot of the negative reaction to Halloween Havoc was because people compare it with so many big shows this year that were more outstanding, rather than taking it for what it was by itself, a better-than-average and fairly entertaining night of wrestling), there are business aspects to look at. The NWA has lost millions of dollars this year, and for it to survive in any form over the long haul, and the No. 1 priority of any business is to survive, even ahead of putting out a great product, changes have to be made or what you will have is simply the Turner people spending millions each year to finance what a core of fans consider to be great entertainment. That won't last forever. Eddie and Missy Gilbert were phased out because of the decision of the booking committee. They felt there were others that would be more marketable to push and didn't decide Gilbert should have a top spot. There were personality conflicts, somewhat because Gilbert's longterm goal is to become head booker, but at the same time those in charge probably also felt they could justify it from a business standpoint.

After having the pleasure of speaking to Jeff Carr of TBS this past weekend, I must retract my statements that the NWA is comfortable occupying the No. 2 seat. From our discussion, I learned that the NWA is well aware of its many problems and more importantly, is in the process of addressing them. It may take time, but it looks like they will eventually rebound. Let's just hope the rebound isn't too far in the future because the fans will benefit when the best product also has a top-notch organization.

Paul MacArthur
Camillus, New York

The points you made about the imminent survival and future of the NWA were both timely and relevant. But in many cases, I don't think such drastic measures are necessary.

The NWA has to be asking, "What are we doing wrong?" and "What are we doing that's right?" They have a good core of a product to rebuild, and it's all in the marketing of the organization. I believe the group should get back to basics and try to copy what Vince McMahon did when he created the rock and wrestling alliance. At that time, Titan wasn't exactly packing them in. Vince used the right connections to bring the group to near overnight fame. Can't the NWA do that also?

If the NWA could hook up with a major celebrity, either musical or otherwise, to tout their virtues and introduce the NWA to a non-fan audience, it could create the same enthusiasm McMahon does. All of McMahon's top stars appear on Arsenio Hall, Regis Philbin and other successful talk shows. Why don't the NWA wrestlers? Why doesn't the

NWA send Arsenio Hall to a big card? He goes to all the Titan shows. They should give him a taste of their style of wrestling. It can't hurt, and he may like it better.

The NWA needs an aggressive media blitz, the same type that Vince McMahon employs to convince the world that he has the only wrestlers that exist in the world today. The NWA should have played up the fact that Terry Funk appeared in movies with Sylvester Stallone and Patrick Swayze. It's certainly nothing to be ashamed of. The cause isn't lost if the group takes a serious look at itself and uses the same techniques used by celebrities the world over to get over. You can't show the world your greatness if you are in the shadows or burying your head in the sand.

J. Paul Sutter
London, Ontario

1989 WRESTLING OBSERVER AWARDS

It's that time for the annual readers awards for the bests and worsts of the past year. Ballots will be accepted from the time you read this. Keep in mind that for our purposes, these awards cover action from December 1, 1988 through November 30, 1989. Anything that happens in December of this year isn't eligible, while events from last year in December such as Starrcade, Superclash III and the finals of the Japanese tag team tournaments all count as part of this year. To be included, ballots must be sent in so they get here by the first week of the New Year. I suggest that readers both overseas and in Canada to please mail by Christmas to make sure your vote gets here in time and for those in the United States to mail no later than Jan. 2. The awards, which will be released in the 1989 yearbook (which hopefully will be mailed out by late January or early February), will, as in the past, be accompanied by comments from readers so you are encouraged to not only list placings, but also make comments on them if you wish.

Our awards get broken down into two categories--category "A" awards you are encouraged to pick a first, second and third place winner for and they will be given points on a 5-3-2 basis. The award is determined by the person, promotion or match that gets the most total points. Category "B" awards you should pick one winner, and the person, match or whatever with the most votes gets the award. You don't have to pick winners for each category, nor have to pick three finishers in Category "A."

CATEGORY A AWARDS

1. WRESTLER OF THE YEAR.....This award should be based on a combination of several different criteria. Work, drawing power, influence, interviews, creativity, value to the promotion, quality of matches should all be considered when coming up with the three places. Last year's top three were Akira Maeda, Ric Flair (who has never finished lower than second and has won six times in the past eight years) and Tatsumi Fujinami.

2, MOST OUTSTANDING WRESTLER.....This is based on who is the best worker, ie. who had the best matches, worked the hardest, had the most ability and even more importantly, made the most use of that ability. The top three last year were Tatsumi Fujinami, Owen Hart and Ric Flair (who had won the previous two years)

3. BEST BABYFACE....Workrate has nothing to do with this award. This is based on box office power and ability to generate positive heat at the matches. The top three last year were Hulk Hogan, Sting and Akira Maeda. Hogan has won the award for seven consecutive years

4. BEST HEEL...Similar to best babyface, The top three last year were Ted DiBiase, Eddie Gilbert and Barry Windham

5. FEUD OF THE YEAR.....This is for the best series of matches over the past year, Quality of the matches is a factor. Drawing power is a factor. How much "heat" for the matches that was built up because of angles and interviews is also a factor, The top three feuds of 1988 were Midnight Express vs. Fantastics, Randy Savage vs. Ted DiBiase and Jerry Lawler vs. Eddie Gilbert

6. TAG TEAM OF THE YEAR.....Generally this award has been for the most outstanding tag team of the past year, the one with the most ability and who has had the best matches. While influence has always been a factor, traditionally the best working tag teams beat the most hyped tag teams in this poll. The top three last year were Bobby Eaton & Stan Lane (Midnight Express), The Fantastics and Arn Anderson & Tully Blanchard. Eaton & Lane were also winners the previous year and Eaton & Dennis Condrey won in 1986.

7. MOST IMPROVED.....This is based on the wrestler whose work in the ring has improved the most over the past year, not for a wrestler who has gotten his first big push but was always good. The top three last year were Sting, Rick Steiner and Biff Wellington

8. MOST UNIMPROVED.....This is for the wrestler whose work has declined the most over the past year. Once again, not a wrestler whose push has gone down, but one whose actual work has declined. The top three last year were Bam Bam Bigelow, Greg Valentine and Steve Williams

9, MOST OBNOXIOUS.....This is for the people involved in wrestling, whether they be wrestlers, managers, announcers, promoters or anything that you simply gag when they appear on your television tube. The top three last year were

Dusty Rhodes, David Crockett and Vince McMahon

10. BEST ON INTERVIEWS.....Top three last year were Jim Cornette (for the fourth consecutive year), Paul E. Dangerously and Ric Flair

11. MOST CHARISMATIC.....The guy who has to do the least to get the most reaction. The top three last year were Sting, Hulk Hogan and Akira Maeda. Hogan had won it the previous three years

12. BEST TECHNICAL WRESTLER.....This is for the ability to display wrestling technique within the confines of a pro wrestling match and make it entertaining, not for someone who has a great amateur background but hasn't adapted into pro wrestling or someone who is necessarily a great shooter. The top three last year were Tatsumi Fujinami, Owen Hart and Hiroshi Hase

13. THE BRUISER BRODY MEMORIAL AWARD..... This is for the wrestler who has had the best brawling style matches of the past year, both in terms of dishing it out and selling. The top three last year were Bruiser Brody, Barry Windham and Terry Gordy. Brody won the award six of the past eight years and finished second the other two years

14. MOST OVERRATED.....The wrestlers that the general public believes are better than they really are; guys who are pushed that don't deserve it (which isn't the same thing, but both are criteria). The top three from last year were Dusty Rhodes, the Ultimate Warrior and Hulk Hogan.

15. MOST UNDERRATED.....Wrestlers who are great but don't get the general recognition for it and wrestlers who deserve a bigger push but don't get it. The top three last year were Tiger Mask, Chris Benoit and Owen Hart

16. BEST WRESTLING PROMOTION,....In terms of both business and product delivered. New Japan Pro Wrestling has won this the past two years. Last year the Universal Wrestling Federation placed second and the World Wrestling Federation finished third

17. BEST TELEVISION SHOW.....Only weekly television shows are eligible. Don't pick a special show like Clash of the Champions or Saturday Night Main Event, Please pick the individual show, not just pick "WWF" or whatever. The top three last year were New Japan Pro Wrestling, WWF Superstars of Wrestling and the Continental Wrestling Federation

18. MATCH OF THE YEAR.....Everyone's favorite category for 1989 since this is the best year for great wrestling matches in anyone's memory. Please pick the match, and the date (if you don't know the date, list city or at least the result so I can figure out which match you mean) because in several cases, Flair vs. Steamboat, Rockers vs. Brainbusters, Flair vs. Funk, Tsuruta vs. Tenryu, Tenryu & Kawada vs. Tsuruta & Yatsu, Steamboat vs. Luger, Liger vs. Sano all come immediately to mind, there are several different matches involving these participants that are all sure to get votes. You can vote for more than one match of the same participants if you wish, since almost everyone is going to anyway. Last year's top three matches were Ric Flair vs. Sting from the first Clash of the Champions in Greensboro, Midnight Express vs. Fantastics from the first Clash in Greensboro (first time ever that two matches from the same card finished 1-2 in the balloting) and Midnight vs. Fantastics on 4/26 from Chattanooga

19. ROOKIE OF THE YEAR.....Wrestlers who haven't had a full-time job with a regular promotion (one that works a regular schedule rather than just spot shows or weekend work) prior to September 1, 1988 are eligible. Ballots with wrestlers who don't meet those specifications will not be counted. Wrestlers who do meet the specifications include Dustin Rhodes, Wayne Bloom, Mike Enos, Salman Hashimikov, Victor Zangiev (and all the other Russians in New Japan as well), Larry Cameron, Steve Gillespie, Jason Anderson and Lee Scott. The top three last year were Gary Allbright (Vokhan Singh), Todd Morton and Ricky Rice

20. MANAGER OF THE YEAR.....Simply put, the best manager and the guy who did the most during the past year. The top three last year were Jim Cornette (for the fourth year in a row), Paul E. Dangerously and Bobby Heenan

21. BEST TELEVISION ANNOUNCER (play-by-play)..... This is for a show host who actually calls the matches. Since wrestlers who do color commentating like Jim Cornette and Jesse Ventura have entirely different duties (to add to the work of the announcers but also to entertain with their wit and get themselves over as personalities), they have their own category. The top three last year were Jim Ross, Lance Russell and Tony Schiavone. Russell had won the previous four years.

22. WORST TELEVISION ANNOUNCER.....In this one, both play-by-play and wrestler/commentators are eligible. The top three last year were David Crockett, Superstar Billy Graham and Ed Whalen.

CATEGORY B AWARDS

1. BEST CARD OF THE YEAR (new category)

2. WORST BIG CARD OF THE YEAR (new category)

3. BEST WRESTLING MANEUVER.....The most mind-boggling and skillful move executed that you've seen over the past year. Keiichi Yamada's shooting star press won the past two years, and it's so mind-boggling that not only has nobody else stolen it, but he doesn't even do it anymore

4. HARDEST WORKER.....Ric Flair has won this five straight years

5. BIGGEST SHOCK OF THE YEAR.....Last year's biggest shock was the death of Bruiser Brody

6. MOST DISGUSTING PROMOTIONAL TACTIC.....Who sank to rock bottom in an attempt to get heat or draw fans over the past year. Last year's winner was when Fritz Von Erich faked a heart attack and the promotion pretended that he may not live the night

7. BEST COLOR COMMENTATOR...Jesse Ventura won this last year

8. STRONGEST WRESTLER.....This is for legitimate power displayed within the confines of a pro wrestling match, not for the guy with the biggest muscles, the guy with the best physique, the guy who "looks" the strongest or even the guy who can push the most weights in a gym. Steve Williams has won this the past two years

9. READERS FAVORITE WRESTLER.....Ric Flair has won this all five times we've had the category

10. READERS' MOST HATED WRESTLER.....Dusty Rhodes had won this the past two years

11. WORST WRESTLER.....First off, rookies aren't eligible since they don't have experience. Jobbers who don't work regularly aren't eligible either. This is for full-time wrestlers, and generally those with pushes who are just horrible in the ring. Last year's winner was the Ultimate Warrior

12. WORST TAG TEAM.....Again, for a pushed tag team that doesn't work too good. Last year's winners were The Bolsheviks (Boreus Zhukov & Nikolai Volkoff)

13. WORST TELEVISION SHOW.....Only weekly shows are eligible. Last year's winner was the AWA show on ESPN

14. WORST MANAGER.....Last year's winner was Mr. Fuji for the fourth time in five years

15. WORST MATCH OF THE YEAR.....Self-explanatory.

Last year's winner was that legendary classic Hiroshi Wajima vs. Tom Magee from Kawasaki, Japan. For a Japanese match to beat out all the U.S. contenders says just how bad a match that one really was

16. WORST FEUD....One with bad matches, or that the public didn't care about, but was still pushed beyond all logic, or one that just simply didn't work. Last year's winner was the Midnight Rider (Dusty Rhodes under a mask) vs. Tully Blanchard

17. WORST ON INTERVIEWS.....Last year's winner was Steve Williams

18. WORST PROMOTION.....Last year's winner was the AWA

19. BEST BOOKER.....The one who made the most use of his talent, drew as much as possible given the circumstances, put together creative and entertaining television. Last year's winner was Eddie Gilbert

20. PROMOTER OF THE YEAR.....Last year's winner was Vince McMahon

21. BEST GIMMICK.....Last year's winner was the Varsity Club and Rick Steiner's act

22. WORST GIMMICK.....Last year's winner was Dusty Rhodes as the Midnight Rider

23. MOST EMBARRASSING WRESTLER.....The wrestling personality who makes you embarrassed to be a wrestling fan. Last year's winner was George Steele.

DECEMBER 4, 1989

What a difference a few years make.

Thanksgiving. Traditionally the biggest day of the year for pro wrestling in the United States. And not only the Thursday night, but the rest of the weekend used to be filled with Holiday spectaculars around the country that packed them in.

The wrestling business has changed a lot in the last few years. Back in 1983, six years ago, which in the wrestling business is several eternities, Thanksgiving night was probably the biggest night in the history of wrestling when it came to live crowds. All across America, pro wrestling was packing them in. World Class sold out Reunion Arena -- some 18,500 tickets -- and turned another 6,000 to 8,000 away to see a loser leaves town match between Kerry Von Erich and Michael Hayes. In St. Paul, the AWA was finishing up the biggest year in its history with a sellout of around 18,000 at the St. Paul Civic Center, and following it up a few days later with a sellout in Chicago to boot. In Florida, Alabama, Tennessee, San Antonio and many other cities, the holiday shows drew more than 5,000 fans in these smaller promotions. In Atlanta, the annual tag team tournament at the Omni drew something like 13,000 fans. The WWF, with Bob Backlund facing his month as champion, drew crowds of 6,000 to 10,000 per night over this holiday weekend. And in Greensboro-- it was Starrcade. The first closed-circuit pro wrestling event ever to cover such a wide territory (three states and into Puerto Rico), with not only a sellout in Greensboro of 15,500 fans to see Ric Flair regaining the NWA title from Harley Race, but some 40,000 more fans watching the event on closed-circuit.

Those kind of live attendance figures are from another era. One when pro wrestling was one year or so away from becoming fashionable. Just a few scant weeks before wrestling as we knew it changed when Hulk Hogan, Gene Okerlund and Roddy Piper joined up with Titan Sports, Bob Backlund was taken from the spotlight, and the World Wrestling Federation became synonymous with pro wrestling.

Four years later, on Thanksgiving of 1987, the last major battle of the wrestling war, which started just a few weeks after what was probably wrestling's biggest day ever, finished. While it was a year later before Jim Crockett had to sell majority interest in Jim Crockett Promotions, the last vestige of the formerly powerful National Wrestling Alliance, many point to Thanksgiving of 1987, and more

particularly the fourth quarter of 1987, as the key period which brought wrestling to where it is today.

The whole story has been covered in "Matwatch" in detail. Crockett, after hearing the figure of $31 million that Titan grossed at Wrestlemania III (the realistic figure was $17 million, by the way), saw those dollar signs dangle in front of his head and figured Thanksgiving night, Starrcade '87 would be the day the NWA became major league. Starrcade, which after four successful promotions on previous Thanksgiving night, starting in 1983, on closed-circuit, would go national this time. Pay-Per-View. The potential income was limitless. The traditional live site of Greensboro, which had sold out well in advance for the four previous Starrcade shows (when it had to share the live card with Atlanta the previous two years), was moved to Chicago. The third largest market in the country. Chi-Town Heat. The battle was lost months before the show ever took place. Titan Sports planned the Survivor Series the same night from Richfield, Ohio on pay-per-view. Coming off the incredible success of Wrestlemania III, its previous PPV outing, McMahon had a lot of leverage in this industry in its infancy. Almost every company which had promised to carry Starrcade backed off when faced with a McMahon ultimatum -- he wouldn't offer his show to any company which carried Starrcade -- nor would he allow those offending companies the right to carry Wrestlemania IV either. Out of about 260 major cable companies which at that time had PPV capabilities, something like six stayed with the NWA, a few in the Southeast, I believe one or two in the Dallas-Fort Worth area (where the NWA had it offices) and a company in San Jose, California, simply because the head of the company refused to go back on his word when he originally agreed to carry the Crockett show.

Thanksgiving weekend of 1989 shows just how much the wrestling business has changed over these past few years. Survivor Series III on PPV was the big show of the weekend. But aside from the one show, business over the holiday weekend was nothing to celebrate.

St. Paul, Minnesota was one of the cities that made the Thanksgiving wrestling tradition. This year, with Hulk Hogan going against local product Mr. Perfect at the St. Paul Civic Center on the day before Thanksgiving, the result was a paltry 3,700 fans. Madison Square Garden, which always sold out, usually in advance, over the holiday weekend, had its smallest crowd (8,200) in over a decade. Given the NWA's problem with drawing fans at house shows this year, nobody would probably be disappointed with the 7,500 that turned out Thanksgiving night at the Omni in Atlanta, but the 3,300 in Baltimore on Saturday night and 1,400 in Philadelphia that afternoon on what is traditionally the best weekend of the year to draw fans, has to be numbing. The rest of the WWF shows drew poorly over the weekend as well, with the exception of California shows, and of course, Survivor Series.

The lone holiday wrestling tradition left and only legitimate box office success of the weekend drew 15,294 paid and $239,917 to the Rosemont Horizon in Chicago. The gate is the third best ever in the Windy City-- trailing an NWA/AWA combined show a few years back at White Sox Park and the live showing of Wrestlemania II from the Horizon with inflated ticket prices which featured a half-dozen NFL players in a battle royal. Some would say that Survivor Series took the edge off the live crowds over the rest of the weekend, and to an extent, there's some validity to that. However, Survivor Series was on PPV the past two years when crowds over the Holiday weekend were a lot stronger than they were this year. And the vast majority of Americans still don't have PPV capabilities.

It's too early to tell about PPV buy rates for Survivor Series, but the earliest most vague estimates were around three percent, which would mean roughly 350,000 orders and a $7 million gross.

Of that, Titan's share would be $3 million, which once again shows where the wrestling business is headed, when in one night the promotion grosses a few weeks worth of normal house shows.

SURVIVOR SERIES '89

Thumbs up: 50 (23.5 percent)
Thumbs down: 117 (54.9 percent)
In between: 46 (21.6 percent)

Based on reader phone calls through Sunday night.

My own response to the show was more of an in between reaction. PPV shows are now too plentiful to expect something great or some major angle to transpire every time out. Like Halloween Havoc, this show really added nothing of significance to the major storylines. If you missed the show, you really didn't miss anything major when it comes to the overall scheme of things. At the same time, if you saw the show, it seemed to be at least decent entertainment.

The previous two Survivor Series were two of the three best overall big shows Titan has put on. The concept of elimination tag matches, allowing guys ample rest time between their stints in the ring, camouflaged one of the key problems with so many of Titan's wrestlers, the lack of cardiovascular conditioning. To me, the message I got coming out of this year's show is that Titan has a handful of the best wrestlers in the business, and we all know who they are. But even when cutting the number of participants down to 40 this year (as compared with 50 the two previous years), the number of top-notch wrestlers were enough to carry eight-man elimination tags into being decent matches, and even a few good ones, but no great ones.

The star of the show, in my book, was Curt Hennig, who single-handedly made it impossible for me to give the show a thumbs down. His performance in the fourth match of the card, which from start-to-finish was the best match, made it the closest thing to a great match. Very close behind were Arn Anderson and Shawn Michaels in the finale, also a good match. The opening match was decent, although Tito Santana (who was eliminated early) and Rick Martel were the only ones who looked like top calibre workers. The second match, which on paper figured to be carried by Bret Hart on the face side and Randy Savage and Barry Windham on the heel side, was the lone bad match of the show. Hart was still banged up from his rib injury from a few weeks back, and while he was still the only top-flight worker on his team, he wasn't in much and wasn't quite up to par. Savage wasn't in enough to carry his side, which needed a bit of carrying since Windham didn't appear and was replaced by the Canadian Earthquake (Big John Tenta). For some reason, it seemed like Dino Bravo was the workhorse of the heel team, and while Bravo did try hard, he just doesn't cut it in the ring. Bravo's immense push remains one of life's great unsolved mysteries. While the third match, billed as the main event, since it featured Hulk Hogan and Zeus, was decent (thanks only to Ted DiBiase as it would have been a dud without him), it seemed to be a big disappointment and was the most criticized match of the show. Hennig single-handedly made the next match, and Anderson carried the heel squad in the finale.

For overall workrate, the card was the best of Titan's four PPV outings thus far this year. Where it fell short, especially in comparison to SummerSlam, was in the booking department. Not only did nothing of importance happen, but the matches were painfully predictable. Far too many of the eliminations ranged from being cheap to being outright lame. While the fast eliminations of Zeus and Andre were the best things possible when it came to producing a good match, the way they were eliminated cheapened both of their matches. And I don't even want to bring up the Bad News Brown elimination. A summer rerun on Thanksgiving weekend. Everyone who was expected to win, did win. No major stars being pushed lost cleanly, even if they could have with some creative story-writing. And there were a lot of complaints about the three no-shows. The three MIA's were Akeem in the opener, Widow Maker (Windham) in the second match and Tully Blanchard in the finale.

The problem, and this extends to every promotion in the U.S., is the way fans are treated when advertised talent fails to appear. One has to expect that injuries will occur on a fairly frequent basis in a business as rough as pro wrestling can be. Even in the WWF, which isn't as rough as some of the other promotions, just the travel schedule alone can wear someone's resistance down to the point where they become more susceptible to injuries. Fans have no right to complain about legitimate injuries provided they are acknowledged and explained. But the promotions today, and this covers all the American ones, don't feel they have to explain the no-shows, which leaves a lot of spectators with the "ripped-off" feeling. This was one of the key things that killed the Von Erichs and the Gagne promotions and was among many factors that killed the Crocketts. To have three no-shows on a PPV show is excusable, especially considering there were legit reasons. However, to not acknowledge the substitutions, nor explain them, is inexcusable for a show which has been so heavily hyped and line-ups that have been publicized for so many weeks.

I've heard two stories on Akeem, one was that he was injured and another that he had an ulcer flare up. Either way, it was a last minute deal and it was too late to change the advertising. As for Windham, he still hasn't returned from having the tumor removed in his chest. No explanation has been given, either at this show, or at any arena that he's no-showed at for two months now, for his absence. Neither of these two were even acknowledged in passing during the show. Blanchard, as everyone knows, was fired by Titan three weeks before the show. As with Windham, Titan knew far enough in advance that he wouldn't be there, but continued to advertise him anyway. I don't know how many times people from Titan complained about how Verne Gagne killed cities by doing this, but they did the exact same thing. The NWA isn't angelic about this either. The Nov. 20 issue of Video Review magazine had an ad for the Halloween Havoc tape, which will be released to video stores in December, and the ad listed the angle leading up to the Havoc main event and listed of Flair & Sting vs. Funk & Muta, but also had a photo of Ricky Steamboat in the ad and listed Steamboat as appearing on the card. Since the angle they were talking about didn't take place until mid-September and the main event wasn't booked until early September and Steamboat was gone from the NWA at the end of July, some major explaining is due from some people over the content of the ad. And the WWF listed John Studd's name for SummerSlam more than three months after he had left the promotion. Anyway, in the case of Blanchard, not only was he billed on television through the last minute, but on the PPV show itself, his name and face was continually shown right until the moment Bobby Heenan stepped into the ring, despite his being fired three weeks earlier (and no doubt the decision made to fire him occurred well before that).

1. The Dream Team (Dusty Rhodes & Brutus Beefcake & Red Rooster & Tito Santana) downed The Enforcers (Big Bossman & Bad News Brown & Rick Martel & Honky Tonk Man) in 22:01. The crowd, which was hot for the open, had pretty well died down after five minutes. Actually this was the case in most every match. There was no sustained heat despite the packed house and even with at least decent work throughout most of the night. Martel pinned Santana with a reverse roll-up off the ropes and holding the tights in

9:15. Santana looked good he was in there. Bad News kept nothing to tag in but finally Rooster slingtshotted him in. Shortly after, Bossman accidentally hit Bad News and Bad News simply walked out for a count out. Exactly the same thing they did on the same show last year. Second fall was 6:11. Third fall lasted 1:58 with Beefcake pinning Honky Tonk Man after a flying knee to the chin. Jimmy Hart at ringside was working harder with the megaphone than any of the wrestlers were in the ring. Fourth fall went 2:49 ending when Martel was using the ropes to pin Beefcake, but the ref kicked Martel's hands and Beefcake caught him in the sunset flip. It took just 47 seconds for the fifth fall when Bossman caught Rooster in the Bubba-Slam. This left Bossman with Rhodes and Beefcake, and Rhodes pinned Bossman with a cross bodyblock in 1:04. After the match, Bossman hit Beefcake with the nightstick (Beefcake didn't see it coming and forgot to sell the first time) and hit Dusty in the stomach. Slick and Bossman handcuffed Dusty to the ropes and beat on him until Beefcake came out with the clippers. Dusty juiced. He must have one hell of a lot of power to be able to juice in the WWF. There was almost no crowd noise when the heels were on top, which was the case most of the way. Martel was the best performer. Rhodes, Honky and Beefcake were all bad-to-worse, though Rhodes did do a dropkick. **

2. The King's Court (Randy Savage & Canadian Earthquake & Dino Bravo & Greg Valentine) beat the 4x4's (Jim Duggan & Bret Hart Ron Garvin & Hercules) in 23:25. You knew things were bad when the faces out with four 2x4's and were throwing them back and forth about two feet apart and they were dropping them. Earthquake squashed Hercules to win the first fall in 3:57. Hercules used to be good. He hasn't been good for years, but in recent weeks he's been so bad you wouldn't have thought it would be conceivable that he once was a good wrestler. He was one of the worst guys on the show aside from the freaks who have no business in a ring to begin with. One of two big pops of the bout was just before the finish of the second fall when Garvin and Valentine traded the hard chops for a few seconds but Duggan clotheslined Valentine for the second fall in 3:35. The biggest pop came next, when Savage and Hart tagged in with each other. Although they were the best on their respective teams, the action when they got in was just okay since Hart wasn't 100 percent. After 30 seconds the pop was already gone. Bravo pinned Garvin for the third fall with the side slam in 3:45. After Hart missed a tackle into the corner, Bravo gave him a shoulder breaker and Savage got the fall after the elbow off the top rope in 7:49. Hart was in and getting pounded on almost the entire fall. This left Duggan with Savage, Earthquake and Bravo. Duggan was "holding his own" until Sherri pulled down the ropes and Duggan, trying to rebound off, fell over the top rope and

was counted out for a cheap finish at 4:19. Duggan hit the remaining heels with his 2x4 after the match. * ½.

3. The Hulkamanics (Hulk Hogan & Jake Roberts & Demolition) beat The Million Dollar Team (Ted DiBiase & Zeus & Powers of Pain) in 27:32. Hogan started with Zeus. Aside from a non-sell shoulder block, they did nothing for 2:02 which was a lot better action than when they actually tried to do something. Zeus doesn't even no sell, well. A few tackles and punches that Zeus didn't sell, then a bodyslam by Hogan and Zeus starts a choke and gets DQ'd quickly at 3:21. It was best for all concerned to get the guy out of there fast but it looked so cheap. There was virtually no heat for the next 20 minutes because of this. The quietest I've ever heard a crowd during a Hogan match. Second fall went at 6:29 when Warlord pinned Ax (Eadie) when Mr. Fuji tripped Eadie coming off the rope. The work was adequate but the lack of heat made it seem boring and it was getting painful to watch by the third fall. Barbian pinned Smash with a flying clothesline off the top rope after Smash gave DiBiase a hotshot but missed seeing DiBiase tag out. One of the only creative finishes to a fall the entire night, time 3:52. This left Hogan & Roberts with Powers of Pain & DiBiase. Roberts was getting pounded on for four minutes until Hogan finally tagged in, but at 6:09 he got caught with a stuff piledriver and the ref DQ'd both members of the Powers of Pain for this. DiBiase then put Hogan in the sleeper for two minutes which eventually did get the crowd going. Hogan finally tagged to Roberts, and Virgil came to ringside from the dressing room. Roberts gave Virgil the DDT but DiBiase immediately gave Roberts a fist drop and pinned him using the ropes in 4:00. DiBiase just shoved Virgil out of the ring off the apron and onto the floor and went to work on Hogan. The match, which was a dud for the first 20 minutes, got exciting at this point. Finish saw Hogan not sell a back suplex, do the superman bit with a foot to the face and legdrop for the pin in 3:41. Booking of this match, with the exception of the one fall, was so predictable and uncreative and no heat until the hot finish. **

Before the intermission, they were interviewing Hogan & Beefcake about their 12/27 PPV match with Zeus & Savage (which will be taped on either 12/12 in Nashville or 12/13 in Huntsville, I believe but it's definitely not live since Hogan is wrestling Curt Hennig in Los Angeles at the same time as the PPV will be on). Anyway, Sherri Martel came out and threw powder in both guys' eyes and Savage & Zeus came out and a bunch of faces and heels (some of whom weren't even on the card) broke it up. Very staged looking.

4. The Rude Brood (Rick Rude & Mr. Perfect & Rougeaus) downed Roddy's Rowdies (Roddy Piper & Jimmy Snuka &

Bushwackers) in 21:27. Snuka pinned Jacques Rogeau with a nice superfly splash off the top rope in 4:01. Piper pinned Raymond Rougeau after a piledriver in 3:29. Perfect pinned Butch Miller in 3:16 with a rolling reverse cradle. Rude pinned Luke Williams in 1:28 with the Rude Awakening. Hennig and Snuka then battled for five minutes with Hennig carrying it to hot action. Finally Piper and Rude got in together and quickly brawled out of the ring for a double count out in 6:21. Piper looked a lot better here than I've seen of him lately but he was never in the ring for any length of time. Rude also wasn't in that much during the match. Perfect and Snuka then traded lots of exciting near falls, and very little heat once Piper and Rude were out of the match. Perfect finally got the pin with the Perfect plex in 3:42. Snuka tried to splash The Genius after the match but Perfect pulled Genius out of the way. ***1/2

5. The Warriors (Ultimate Warrior & Jim Neidhart & Rockers) beat The Heenan Family (Andre the Giant & Arn Anderson & Haku & Bobby Heenan) in 20:30. Warrior clotheslined Andre who fell out of the ring was counted out in 27 seconds. Haku evened things up pinning Neidhart after a thrust kick in 3:05. Haku did a thrust kick on Jannetty and tagged Heenan who got the pinfall in 5:21. Michaels pinned Haku with a flying body press off the top rope in 4:01. Anderson pinned Michaels with the spinebuster in 2:53. This seven minute portion of the match, most of which was Michaels vs. Anderson, was the hottest part of the entire card. Warrior pinned Anderson after a press-slam after Anderson and Heenan collided in 2:32. Heenan then ran from the ring, Warrior brought him back in, Heenan took his two patented bumps and Warrior splashed on him for the pin in 2:11. ***

If that wasn't enough, the WWF also ran its latest Saturday Night's Main Event two nights later on NBC. Easily the worst one of recent memory. My tape ran out during the last match so I missed the third fall, although the Rockers won. Here's how it went:

1. Ultimate Warrior beat Andre the Giant via DQ in 7:47 due to interference of Heenan in an IC title match. Just about every move either guy did looked bad, but still, I was still giving thanks as it could have been worse. When you consider how long they've been working together you'd think the timing would look better. But then when you consider the talent in the ring, just having both guys live through the match makes it a success. Heenan grabbed the belt to hit Warrior but Warrior hit Heenan first and picked him up for the press slam but couldn't get him up, and heaved him at Andre. – ½*

2. Hulk Hogan kept the WWF title, losing via count out

to "The Genius" Lanny Poffo. One-sided early. Poffo went out of the ring and pretended to mathematically figure out how to beat Hogan and hit him with a few moves. Mainly Genius pranced around during the match and stalled most of the way. Mr. Perfect came out four minutes deep and stuck gum on the belt (which was the extent of the so-called hot angle). Genius posted Hogan twice and they were some of the weakest post shots ever. Then he did a backflip press but Hogan kicked out and did the superman comeback. Hogan threw Genius over the top rope and they brawled out of the ring. Hogan threw Genius back in and as he was trying to get in, Hennig hit Hogan with the title belt and Hogan was counted out in 7:44. Hennig and Poffo left with the title belt. What didn't air on TV was Hogan going back and beating up both Hennig and Poffo, getting the belt back and doing his posing routine to make the fans happy at the house show. Smart they didn't air that on TV as it would have killed the angle. *½

3. Dusty Rhodes pinned Big Bossman in 4:47 of one of the worst network matches of all-time.
This was the worst I've ever seen Rhodes look, which is saying a mouthful. Rhodes won with a totally botched up cradle from behind (you have to bend down to do a cradle, don't you?) as Bossman waited for Slick to give him the night stick. Slick was arguing at ringside with the woman who is now Dusty's manager (an angle shot at television earlier in the week). –*½

4. Mr. Perfect pinned Red Rooster with the Perfect Plex in 4:13. Too short for these two and pretty much a squash, but nothing at all wrong with the action. *½

5. Rockers beat Brainbusters in 2 of 3 falls. I'd been told this was two straight, but evidently not. Michaels pinned Blanchard with a roll-up in 1:50 for the first fall. Heenan argued with the Busters and left them (which actually created the angle where Arn is now babyface for the NWA). Blanchard pinned Michaels in the second fall when Michaels did a flying head scissors but Anderson outside the ring pulled him down throat first on the top rope in 2:14. Didn't see the third fall so won't rate the match, however it was one excellent spot after another and from what I saw, both teams looked great.
   Only other comment is that the fake crowd noise (the tinny sound and canned sounding boos when the heels had the advantage-- in fact it sounded like 70 percent of the soundtrack was canned) was more obvious here than in other recent shows.

When New Japan president Seiji Sakaguchi returned from his U.S. tour, he announced at a press conference that he and NWA president Jack Petrik had reached a cooperation agreement on Nov. 8 and that Ric Flair, Great Muta and Sting would all be appearing at the Feb. 10 show at the Tokyo Dome. The February show now has a formidable obstacle in that two days later Mike Tyson will make a boxing title defense in the same city and in Japan, a wrestling show and a boxing show which both are expected to draw 50,000 fans would be competing events for many of the same fight fans. In addition, the WWF has the Tokyo Dome booked on April 13, or shortly after Wrestlemania. This would be the first card by a foreign promotion ever in Japan.
   There is also talk that the NWA wants to do either a Clash or a PPV from Tokyo as well. Actually, there has been talk now for a years of the NWA trying such an event but there is more talk of late. Big Van Vader, the leading foreign star for New Japan, will appear on the NWA's Feb. 25th PPV in return and New Japan would like to get Koji Kitao (who is being groomed for stardom by the promotion) booked in the NWA as well. However, while doing a speech at one of the colleges in Japan (lately it's become the "in" thing at colleges to invite the leading wrestlers to give speeches-- Baba, Inoki, Maeda, Takada, Yamazaki, Tenryu and Jushin Liger have all done so of late), Giant Baba said that he wasn't going to send Tenryu or Stan Hansen to New Japan's show which quells some rumors of Baba helping New Japan for the Tokyo Dome show.
   There was an error last week when I ran down the awards. As the fans of Lucha Libre kept bringing to my attention, I left out the category of best flier in the Category A awards. For those of you voting by the numbers, the Category A stuff is: 1. Wrestler of the Year; 2. Most Outstanding Wrestler; 3. Best Babyface; 4. Best Heel; 5. Feud of the year; 6. Tag team of the year; 7. Most Improved; 8. Most Unimproved; 9. Most Obnoxious; 10. Best on Interviews; 11. Most Charismatic; 12. Best technical wrestler; 13. Best Brawling wrestler (Brody award); 14. Best flier (guy who executes fling moves the best within the context of a wrestling match); 15. Most Overrated; 16. Most Underrated; 17. Best wrestling promotion; 18. Best television show; 19. Match of the year; 20. Rookie of the year; 21. Manager of the year; 22. Best TV announcer (play-by-play) and 23. Worst TV announcer. Pick three in each category.
   In the results of the Clash poll, after all the letters and calls for this week are added in, the final tally was 486 thumbs up and one thumbs down.

CWA
Jerry Lawler made the full-fledged heel turn on television on 11/25. He did an interview with a copy of a recent issue of PWI Weekly in which he read a section where it talked about how fans were turning against him in Memphis. He complained about the fans again for taking Dutch Mantell's side in their feud and kept talking while Mike Davis & New York brawler came out for a squash match. Lawler kept

talking while TV announcer Dave Brown tried to get him to stop so they could watch the match. Lawler wouldn't stop talking and wound up doing color as a heel during the match. After the match Lawler went to two women in the audience (obviously plants) and asked them which one they liked better and both girls said they liked Dutch because he was a better wrestler. Lawler, before asking, asked one of the girls if she was a guy or girl. After they said they liked Mantell better, Lawler started insulting them. It wound up with Lawler doing smart-ass commentary during a Chris Champion squash. Lawler kept asking rhetorically why the fans would cheer Champion (who is the most over face in the promotion right now) since he had greasy hair and worshiped the devil. Champion challenged Lawler to get in the ring but Lawler didn't. Then, after the squash, Dirty White Boy, Mike Davis, Brawler and Soul Taker jumped into the ring and attacked Champion. Mantell and Tracy Smothers came out to make the save and Lawler asked the crowd if he should jump in and help and when they told him to, he slugged Mantell from behind. Then as Soul Taker held Mantell, Lawler hit him with a chair and walked out of the building.

Smothers, The Fantastics and Master of Pain are all headed back pretty much full-time.

Cowboy Kevin Dillinger who is doing the Jack Hart loser gimmick, came out this week with manager Boss Winters and had the name of every CWA wrestler in a fish bowl and was going to pick a name out for his opponent who he vowed he would beat to end his winless streak. He claimed he had a new gimmick which would enable him to win all his matches, and he came out wearing face paint and claimed his name "The Ultimate Dillinger." The name he picked out was Soul Taker, and Soul Taker destroyed him in 29 seconds. After the match Winters and Soul Taker's manager Nate the Rat started arguing and there will be a match down the road between the two managers for the managerial rights to Soul Taker.

Dirty White Boy and Dirty White Girl nearly got into it on television as well. White Boy was about to hit White Girl when Champion came out to save her. White Boy then attacked Champion but when they got in the ring, Champion used the superkick to run him out of there.

Master of Pain challenged both Lawler and Soul Taker.

They are going to have a big show on Christmas night in Memphis with the finals of the CWA tag team title tournament (belts are vacant--last champs were the Rock & Roll Express but Robert Gibson quit the promotion) plus a pole Battle Royal.

11/27 in Memphis had Lawler vs. Bill Dundee on top and if Dundee won the match, he'd get a shot at Lawler's USWA title, Soul Taker vs. Mantell, Ricky & Todd Morton vs. Fantastics (Bobby & Jackie Fulton), Champion vs. White Boy, Smothers vs. Brawler and King Cobra vs. Black Black

Jack (Tommy GIlbert dressed up like he was about five years back when he worked as The Ace of Spades).

Crowds have picked up a tad with Lawler as a heel.

The annual Thanksgiving show in Jackson, TN drew 1,100 as Freddy (Tommy Gilbert) beat Rooster Cogburn, Todd Morton & Frankie Lancaster beat Dillinger & Brawler in a death match (good match, all worked hard), Champion pinned Davis, Soul Taker pinned Smothers (awful), White Boy pinned Cobra and Lawler beat Mantell via DQ when the ref caught Mantell using the chain that Lawler had brought into the ring while the finale was a Turkey Battle Royal (last man in is called "Turkey of 1989" and Dillinger was the last man in and was tarred and feathered).

STAMPEDE

11/18 in Edmonton drew 700 as Great Gama pinned Drago Zhivago *½ , Arch Angel (Curtis Thompson) made Vinnie Valentino submit *¾ (Thompson is making noticeable improvements since coming here), Johnny Smith pinned Sumu Hara *¾ , D.J Peterson pinned Skull Mason **, Chris Benoit & Biff Wellington beat The Black Hearts (Tommy Nash & Jason Anderson) in a non-title match ***½ (all for Benoit & Wellington who worked together like the Midnight Express used to), and Larry Cameron kept the North American title beating Owen Hart via DQ. Main event saw Angel interfere to give Cameron an apparent fall, but Peterson then interfered and Hart pinned Cameron to apparently win the title but heel ref Burton Thomas (Tom Burton from Minnesota) told the original ref that Peterson's interference had caused the win and ordered the decision revered and belt given back. ***

Konan the Barbarian from Mexico (who has a body like a young Kerry Von Erich) starts here in two weeks.

Davey Boy Smith was "suspended" on 11/10 in Calgary (so he could tour Japan for the tag team tournament) for powerslamming ref Thomas after Thomas DQ'd him in a match against Johnny Smith. Also Owen Hart pinned Cameron in a non-title match, Hara pinned an unmasked Jason Anderson (by the way, the reason Tatsumi Kitahara is using the ring name Sumu Hara here is because his favorite wrestler growing up as a kid was Ashura Hara), Bruce Hart pinned Apocalypse, Peterson pinned Nick Flair (Tommy Nash without a mask doing a gimmick where he's the black sheep of the Flair family), Benoit & Wellington beat Zhivago & Anderson and Arch Angel beat Valentino.

11/17 in Calgary saw Cameron beat Owen Hart via count out, Benoit & Wellington beat Black Hearts in a non-title match, Peterson beat Goldie Rogers, Angel & Johnny Smith beat Hara & Valentino and Great Gama beat Steve Gillespie.

Bruce Hart will be feuding with Gama for the millionth time.

There have been talks with Cactus Jack Manson, Trent Knight and Bad News Brown about coming in.

11/24 in Calgary saw Steve Disalvo return and beat Valentino, Bruce Hart beat Mason, Angel &

Johnny Smith beat Ken Johnson & Kim Schau, Black Hearts retained the tag titles beating Benoit & Wellington and Peterson beat Cameron via DQ when Angel interfered.

ALL JAPAN

Stan Hansen & Genichiro Tenryu gave up their PWF World tag team titles on 11/16-- the day before the tag team tournament started because they said the winner of the tournament deserves to be World tag team champions. No doubt it will come down to Hansen & Tenryu vs. Jumbo Tsuruta & Yoshiaki Yatsu in the finals on 12/6 at Tokyo's Budokan Hall.

The tournament opened on 11/17 in Osaka before 4,550 fans as Hansen & Tenryu beat Dynamite Kid & Davey Boy Smith in 18:30 when Hansen pinned Kid with the lariat, Tsuruta & Yatsu beat Abdullah the Butcher & Tiger Jeet Singh when Tsuruta pinned Singh with a backdrop suplex, The Can-Am Express (Doug Furnas & Dan Kroffat) went to a 30 minute draw against The Foot Loose (Samson Fuyuki & Toshiaki Kawada) in the best match on the card, The Nasty Boys beat Akira Taue & Kenta Kobashi, Terry Gordy & Bill Irwin beat Isao Takagi & Shunji Takano, Kabuki & Giant Baba & Rusher Kimura beat Hakura Eigen & Motoshi Okuma & Shinichi Nakano, Masa Fuchi pinned Yoshinari Ogawa, Mighty Inoue pinned Richard Slinger and Mitsuo Momota pinned Tsuyoshi Kikuchi.

11/18 in Tokyo's Korakuen Hall drew a sellout 2,400 as Tsuruta & Yatsu beat The Foot Loose, Singh & Butcher beat Can-Am Express, Kid & Smith beat Gordy & Irwin, Hansen & Tenryu & Ogawa beat Kobashi & Baba & Kimura, Nasty Boys beat Kabuki & Nakano and Taue & Takano beat Eigen & Okuma plus prelims.

All Japan is going to bring in Gene Kiniski for an old-timer appearance early in 1990.

Next tour will be 1/2 to 1/28 with Kid, Smith, Fantastics (Tommy Rogers & Bobby Fulton), Ivan Koloff, Nikolai Volkoff, Randy Rose, Steve Gator Wolfe and Abdullah. This tour will mainly consist of shows in Tokyo itself, with Korakuen Hall booked seven times (Jan 2, 3, 14, 15, 26, 27 and 28) in four weeks. When you add in the FMW, Japanese women and New Japan, there are 14 shows booked over a 28 day period at Korakuen Hall, which is the easiest building in Japan to sellout, but they are going to make it harder with all those shows in that short of a time period.

While Baba was giving a speech at a college in Tokyo, an interesting interplay happened which I guess shows why Baba in some ways is the best promoter in the business right now. One of the students asked Baba "Why don't you book Rip Rogers anymore? " Baba said that he hated Rogers' gay act and felt it was out of place with the style of wrestling they have. He then asked other students what they thought.

The students mainly said they liked Rogers' act and one even said they thought it would be a great match to put Baba vs. Rip (since Baba is a comedy figure in Japan anyway). Baba said while he couldn't understand what the appeal was for Rogers and hated Rogers' in-ring act, that he was going to have to change his opinions if that's what the fans wanted and that he would book Rogers next year.

OTHER JAPAN NOTES

TV-Asahi renewed New Japan's television contract through March of 1991. There was talk that New Japan would lose its network affiliation which would spell complete disaster for the promotion, but the network probably felt that Koji Kitao's name would be enough to build TV ratings. The New Japan show in recent weeks has been preempted on TV-Asahi almost as often as the AWA gets preempted on ESPN in this country, which has resulted in weak crowds in the small town shows when New Japan tours.

Rick Steiner was replaced in the singles tournament by Wayne Bloom. I believe Buzz Sawyer did go to the tournament since he didn't work any NWA shows this weekend and I haven't heard his name mentioned on any house shows until 12/9, and the tournament tour ends 12/7.

Antonio Inoki's new foreign policy will include promoting a boxing show on Feb. 1 in Tokyo which features the debut of six of the Soviet Olympic boxers as professionals. Inoki has also announced that he will be going to Red China to train some of the best Red Chinese martial arts fighters the pro wrestling style and wants to promote next year in Red China.

The UWF held a try-out in Tokyo and had 150 kids try for spots and six were picked after going through several tests of stamina including doing 500 squats with no weight, followed by repetition presses and the likes with light weights to see who would quit first.

On the 11/29 show, Glen Berg, the kick boxer from the Netherlands was replaced with Dick Leon Fry, No idea who Fry is and what his background is. Refs for the Tokyo Dome show are Masami Soranaka (son-in-law of Karl Gotch) and Larry (Professor Boris Malenko) Simon while judges are two kick boxing officials. All the matches have different rules. Maeda vs. Willie Wilhelm will be seven five minute rounds; Takada vs. Duane Koslowski will be one fall, 45 minute time limit, Yamazaki vs. Chris Dolman will be seven five minute rounds, Fujiwara vs. Fly will be seven three minute rounds, Minoru Suzuki vs. Maurice Smith will be seven three minute rounds, Yoji Anjyo against the Thailand kickboxer will be five three minute rounds and the opener between Tatsuo Nakano vs. Shigeo Miyato will be one fall, 30 minutes.

Manami Toyota won the All Japan Japanese Women's title beating Mika Takahashi in Masuda, while Noriyo Tateno of the JB Angels captured the All-Pacific title pinning Bull

Nakano on 11/18 in Ashikaga (Tateno's home town).

All Japan TV on 11/12 drew an 8.1 rating while New Japan on 11/4 drew a 5.9.

USWA

The annual Thanksgiving spectacular drew a disappointing crowd of 600 to the Dallas Sportatorium as Matt Borne pinned Sheik Scott Braddock, Kevin Von Erich pinned The Punisher (Master of Pain), Bill Dundee beat Dog of War (Buster Fowler), Jeff Gaylord beat Jimmy Jack Funk, Scandor Akbar & Tojo Yamamoto won a handicap match over Cousin Junior, Jeff Jarrett beat P.Y. Chu Hi (Phil Hickerson) in a barbed wire match and got to lash him 10 times with a leather belt as a result of winning, Gary Young went to a double count out with Dustin Rhodes and the main event saw Billy Travis beat Chris Adams via DQ. Eric Embry was the ref and they teased a turn but didn't actually do it. Embry totally favored Adams all the way and finally Travis punched Embry, who punched Travis back, then raised Adams' hand. Tony Falk (who in reality is Embry's best friend) then came in and reversed the decision because Embry was acting so biased as a ref and because he had hit Travis. Adams then started arguing with Embry because he had caused him to lose the match by punching Travis and was even madder because Embry wouldn't stand up for his original decision and allowed Falk to overrule him. But they wound up shaking hands when it was over and even agreed to form a tag team for the tournament this coming Friday for the USWA tag belts.

The tournament has Chu Hi & Buddy Landel vs. Rhodes & Funk (an interesting combination considering family and alleged family history), Kevin & Kerry Von Erich vs. Robert Fuller & Brian Lee, Travis & Young vs. Adams & Embry and Jarrett & Borne vs. Punisher & Braddock.

USWA lost its television slot on Ch. 21 for its syndicated show, apparently in part because of complaints about the Toni Adams angles. They still have the key local two-hour show on Ch. 11, which is one of the higher rated wrestling shows in the country on a local basis. Killer Tim Brooks' promotion lost its TV on Ch. 39 apparently because production costs were higher than expected. Brooks drew 700 fans on 11/21.

OREGON

The 11/11 show in Portland saw Steve Doll open the show by throwing out C..W Bergstrom to win a Battle Royal for "$5,000" and earn a title shot at Scotty the Body. When Doll was out doing his interview, Scotty attacked him and stole the money and then claimed that since Bergstrom won the Battle Royal, he deserved the title shot. Scotty easily pinned Bergstrom in less than two minutes to keep the title. After the match Doll came in and knocked the roll of bills away from Scotty, but Scotty's valet Veronica Lane grabbed the

money and put it down her top and ran off. Also on the show, Carl Styles pinned Jonathan Boyd in a terrible match, Southern Rockers (Rex King & Steve Doll) regained the held up Northwest tag team titles beating Brian Adams (called "Big Chris Adams" by ring announcer Dong Owen) & Jeff Warner when Warner turned on Adams, Bill Francis (whose only claim to fame is that he's huge about 6'6 and 300lbs and while not built like a heavy lifter, looks like he'd be one of those big guys you'd never want to mess with but his wrestling is pretty bad, but he's the brother of Russ Francis of NFL fame) beat Al Madril via DQ and Jonathan Holliday beat Beetlejuice.

11/18 in Portland saw Scotty buy Ginger (Doll's valet) plane tickets to Mexico and then kissed her but Veronica (Scotty's valet) attacked Ginger and they did a pull-apart. Doll beat Scott in the main event and because of that, Ginger and Veronica had to go into a cage and Ginger pulled Veronica's shirt and jacket off and got the $5,000 and Veronica ran off in her danskin outfit. However when Ginger gave Doll the money, Scotty jumped Doll and grabbed both the money and the Northwest title belt from him. Also King pinned Madril, Beetlejuice beat Holliday via DQ when Madril rain in with a bucket of water and a towel and he and Holliday wiped the face-paint off of Beetlejuice, Warner beat Boyd via DQ when The Grappler and Adams jumped in and painted the words "Wrecking Crew" on his neck, Grappler pinned Francis and Rip Oliver beat Adams via DQ.

11/25 in Portland saw Doll beat Col. DeBeers, Scotty beat Styles when Veronica tossed in a loaded glove. Scotty then came out for an interview and was going to ask Ginger to marry him when Doll attacked Scotty and in the ensuing melee, Veronica poured a bunch of beer all over Ginger. Rex King won the TV title from Madril, Boyd beat Francis via an over-the-top-rope DQ, Beetlejuice beat Holliday with the winner getting to lash the loser 10 times. Holliday ran out but Styles and Doll brought him back in for the whipping. Finale saw Oliver & Warner beat Grappler & Adams via DQ when ref tyles DQ'd heels when Grappler used his loaded boot.

OTHER NOTES

Nelson Royal's ACW ran a show on 11/15 in Hillsville, VA which drew 65 fans headlined by Royal vs. L.A. Stephens and Colt Steele vs. David Isley.

The big indie show that caused a lot of attention on 11/17 in Cleveland drew 550 fans and Paul Orndorff did work his first match in a few years on the card. Orndorff didn't have his old body, but still had a body. Orndorff worked against Kerry Von Erich in what was billed as a match for the World Class World Title (which doesn't even exist anymore and if it did, Lawler would be champ but you know how that goes). Anyway, Orndorff won on a DQ when, playing heel, he threw Kerry over the top rope behind the refs back. Kerry threw Orndorff over the top in front of the ref. Orndorff then grabbed the title and proclaimed himself new World champion since World Class rules stipulate a belt changes via DQ and they had a big discussion in the ring where it was decided that Ohio rules supersede World Class rules and Kerry retained the title. Told the match was okay. Remainder of the matches were one star or less as Sam Houston beat Zoltan the Great, Krusher Klebanski pinned Psycho Mike when Orndorff ran in and gave Mike the piledriver, Rockin Robin kept the WWF Women's title going to a 30 minute draw with the Fabulous Moolah, Paul Jones pinned Ivan Koloff using the ropes, Jerry Lawler beat Kimala to keep his version of the World title (Kimala was managed by Paul Jones who wore a Bengals jersey to ringside, Manny Fernandez beat Lawler via DQ (Lawler subbed for King Parsons) and Brian Blair & Jim Brunzell as The Killer Bees beat Larry Zbyszko (with Baby Doll) & Fernandez (subbing for Buddy Landel) when Zbyszko was pinned.

Jerry Monti and Alexis Smirnoff ran a card on 11/10 in Manteca, CA drawing 288 fans and $3,600 for Earthquake Ferris & Jim Gorman vs. Alexis Smirnoff & Rex Farmer on top. Originally Ray Stevens was to ref on the show, which was postponed because of the earthquake, but Stevens couldn't make it on this new date. Monti and Smirnoff have a show on 12/9 in Tracy.

GAT promotions ran 11/17 in Riverside, CA drawing 70 fans for a card which included The Mercenary (Billy Anderson), Tim Tall Tree, Super Boy, Pero Aguayo from Mexico, Mario Valenzuela, Carlos Mata and Bobby Bradley.

Col. DeBeers and Mike George worked three shows last weekend for Rocky Mountain group based in Denver.

11/12 in San Bernardino, CA drew 118 for a Lucha Libre show which included Super Boy, Mando Guerrero, Ultraman I & II, Tim Tall Tree, Bobby Bradley, Rey Misterio, The Mercenaries and the main event saw Black Gordman pin Konan the Barbarian.

Ron West's North American Wrestling Federation was billing shows this past week in Cordele, GA, Rainsville, AL and FLorence, AL. The Thanksgiving show in Rainsville had Sika the Samoan (managed by Dutch Mantell) vs. Jerry Stubbs, The Bullet & Brad Armstrong vs. The Storm Troopers, Mr. Wrestling I & II vs. Chic Donovan & Larry Santana, Pez Whatley & Rocky King vs. Don Harris & The Sheik (George Weingeroff) and The Uptown Rockers (Reno Riggins & Sid McCormick) vs. The Gladiators. Ivan Koloff, Manny Fernandez, Nicholas the Czar (Nick Busick) and Junkyard Dog all appeared on recent TV tapings. 11/12 in Kingsport, TN included Nikita Koloff beating Fernandez via DQ, Rock & Roll Express beat Ivan Koloff & Russian Assassin via DQ when Fantastics interfered and attacked Rock & Rolls, Jimmy Valiant beat Paul Jones.

Bob Raskin's USWA drew 742 fans on 11/17 in Irvington, NJ as Sgt. Slaughter beat Bam Bam Bigelow in the main event plus JYD beat Sika the Samoan and also appearing underneath included Larry WInters, D.C. Drake, A.J. Petrucci, Mike Kaluha and Jungle Jim McpHerson.

Former pro wrestler Ernie Ladd was inducted into the Grambling University Hall of Fame last month. Ladd played football at Grambling from 1958-61 before playing eight years in the NFL and wrestling on-and-off for 23 years.

Larry Sharpe and Dennis Coralluzzo's WWA ran 11/11 in South Philadelphia with Tony Stetson losing the jr. heavyweight title to Johnny Hot Body with Coraluzzo as heel ref, Winters beat Kaluha while 11/18 in Gloucester, NJ saw Larry Sharpe beat Nikolai Volkoff and Mike Moore & Al the Sledge Hammer kept the tag titles beating Big Hoss & Chief Thunder Mountain plus Misty Blue and Linda Dallas did their thing.

Heritage Championship Wrestling taped more television on 11/25 in Vicksburg, MS with mainly the same crew including Rock & Roll Express, Fantastics, The Bullet, Ken Massey, Buddy Landel, Mr. Olympia (Jerry Stubbs) and other local wrestlers. No word on when television will start for this group but they've already got eight shows in the can for when they are ready to start the television. The shows are said to have good action and mainly wrestling with lots of interviews.

Ladies Professional Wrestling Association will run four tapings on 12/18 and 12/19 (two sets each day) in Laughlin, NV (about 70 miles from Las Vegas) featuring MIsty Blue, Leilani Kai, Judy Martin, Susan Sexton, Velvet McIntyre, and about five girls brought in from the All Japan women's group including Yumi Ogura and Manami Toyota plus several managers. This group was originally going to do its first TV taping in October in Tokyo but that fell through.

12/11 in Marietta, GA has a show with Stan Hansen, Abdullah the Butcher, Dutch Mantell and Kimala announced.

San Francisco lawyer Jon Karesh is moonlighting as a country-western DJ in Salinas, CA (KTOM-FM) under the radio name Jon Flair, and talks a lot about wrestling in his midnight to 6 a.m Sunday night stint.

I'll be appearing on WFAN on 12/2 in New York. At least that's the current plan, but you know how that goes.

11/25 in Mexico City was headlined by Lizmark (answer to the question, what was Elizabeth before she met Randy Savage) & El Satanico & Rayo De Jalisco Jr. beating Fabuloso Blondie (Ken Timbs) & Pirata Morgan & Cien Caras. See if you can figure out this finish, because if you can, you're a lot better than I am. Morgan came out waving the U.S. flag (in Mexico, that's equivalent to Sheik waving the Iranian flag) for Timbs. Anyway, Timbs and Morgan broke up during the third fall and started fighting. Timbs also started fighting with Caras and ended up getting pinned for the deciding fall.

Since Timbs argued with his two heel partners, that makes him a face, right? As Timbs and Morgan brawled outside the ring, Timbs posted Morgan and left him laying in the ring covered in blood. That makes Morgan the face, right? Then after all that, Lizmark comes out and brawls with Morgan to the dressing room. So Timbs is the face. Not so fast, then Lizmark and Timbs brawl all around ringside.

AWA taping on 12/16 in Rochester, MN has Kokina Maximus vs. Jerry Blackwell in a bodyslam match, Destruction Crew defending the tag titles against The Trooper (Del Wilkes) & Paul Diamond plus a Tag Team Battle Royal with Texas Hangmen, Johnnie Stewart & Doug Somers, and Diamond & Tommy Jammer, Brad Rheingans vs. Wayne Bloom in a Greco-Roman wrestling match plus Masa Saito, Akio Sato, Baron Von Raschke and Nord the Barbarian.

Billy Jack Haynes left Florida after only one week, telling the local promotion that he just got an offer from the WWF to return in January. Then last Tuesday, out of nowhere, he shows up at a boxing match in Las Vegas and is announced to the crowd (which booed heavily the mention of pro wrestling) and challenges Mark Gastineau (The New York Jets lineman who has made noises about becoming a boxer) to a boxing match.

12/2 in Manatee, FL has Lawler vs. JYD for the title, Fantastics vs. Malenko brothers, Nikita Koloff vs. Ron Bass plus Rock & Roll Express vs. Original Midnight Express (Dennis Condrey & Randy Rose managed by Paul E. Dangerously).

11/26 in Orlando, FL for PWF drew 178 as Lou Perez drew Jumbo Barretta **, Mike Awesome beat Bodyguard Mark DUD, Bounty Hunters (Tim Parker & Al Greene) kept the tag titles beating Tyree Pride & Brickhouse Brown via DQ **½ , Ron Slinker beat Florida champ Steve Keirn in a non-title match ½ * and Mike Graham & Bugsy McGraw beat Kendall Windham & Blackjack Mulligan via DQ * (Mulligan has lost a ton of weight)

Bounty Hunters won the tag titles from Mark Starr & Lou Perez when Starr walked out on Perez who had to face both by himself. The masked guys in the title match were Greene & Nick Busick, but now they are Greene & Tim Parker.

Red Bastien's WIN Lucha Libre show airs in the San Francisco market on Ch. 14 at 10:30 a.m. on Sundays.

WWF

News from the TV tapings on 11/21 in Indianapolis: Tugboat Thomas (Fred Ottman/Big Steele Man) finally made his debut in a television match. Toot, toot. Big Bossman tied up a jobber Larry Wilson with a ball and chain and then started yelling at the lady at ringside (called Sapphire--real name is Juanita Wright--used to wrestle in the early 70s as Princess Dark Cloud as a black indian gimmick) and went after her but Dusty Rhodes made the save and

later in the show Rhodes announces that Sapphire is his new manager and she'll be traveling around the horn with Dusty once this airs on television. Originally she was brought in to manage Zeus, so either this will be a Robin Greene thing, or Zeus is going to be history after this coming PPV (I suspect the latter since Zeus originally had been told he was going to work full-time in December against Hogan at the house shows and Titan switched the booking to Hogan vs. Mr. Perfect, which won't draw as well, but the Hogan vs. Zeus matches would be so bad even Titan didn't have the chutzpah to put them on--then again, maybe they are saving Hogan vs. Zeus for Wrestlemania). Earthquake (John Tenta) worked with both Dino Bravo and Jimmy Hart at ringside. Rick Rude beat Red Rooster in a TV squash using the Rude Awakening so Terry Taylor is down to jobber status now. Randy Savage pinned Jim Duggan with his feet on the ropes after Sherri hit Duggan with the purse. The Bolsheviks (Zhukov & Volkoff) were pushed as a heel tag team. Mr. Fuji issued a challenge to the Rockers and they gave him a double dropkick and double fistdrop. What a great way to waste the hottest tag they've got, against the coldest team (Powers of Pain). Rick Martel did some more modeling. He does the gimmick great. Jake Roberts beat Ted DiBiase via DQ. Tito Santana beat Honky Tonk Man via DQ. Most of the taping was aimed at promoting the 12/27 cage PPV match with Hogan & Beefcake vs. Savage & Zeus. Jimmy Snuka fought to a no decision with Greg Valentine when Ron Garvin ran in and stole the shin guard and later in the show Garvin starts using the shin guard and a scorpion deathlock as his finisher. Andre & Haku are now called the Colossal Connection. Martel now puts a tie on the jobbers after he beats them. Finale saw Hogan beat Perfect via DQ when Genius interfered.

11/18 at the Meadowlands drew 5,000 as Mark Young beat Bob Braldey, Zhukov pinned Al Perez, Dino Bravo pinned Jim Neidhart, Demolition beat Anderson & Haku, Dusty Rhodes pinned Big Bossman, Honky Tonk Man beat Red Rooster and Roddy Piper went to a Double DQ with Rick Rude in a lumberjack match.

Zeus (Tiny Lister) appeared for the past two weeks as a guest on "Matlock" with Andy Griffith. Without his stilts he wasn't much larger than Griffith.

Koko B. Ware has already returned to replace Tim Horner. Horner went to Vince McMahon to give notice since he wanted to go to the NWA under a hood as Captain USA. McMahon told him he had a valid contract and he wasn't going to let him out of it, then suspended him without pay to make the point with others considering such a move. NWA is still hopeful of getting Horner but it appears unlikely since McMahon seems intent on enforcing his contracts. The reason he let Blanchard & Anderson go even though they also had contracts appears that Blanchard & Anderson were going to leave whether they had the contracts or not and if need be, try and invalidate the contracts. McMahon instead let them go since it was a good PR move for the rest of the guys at the time (you know, not standing in the way of a good opportunity) and that way his contracts wouldn't be challenged.

Widow Maker (Barry Windham) should be back around Christmas.

Hillbilly Jim also missing all his current dates with a bad knee. Doubt anyone is missing him, though.

Sean Mooney and Sherri Martel have been hosting Wrestling Spotlight as of late.

11/17 in Poughkeepsie, NY drew a full house of 3,000 as Paul Roma pinned Brooklyn Brawler, Beefcake pinned Martel, Genius beat Jim Powers, Duggan beat Savage via count, Earthquake beat Bill Woods, Perfect pinned Snuka and Bushwackers beat Powers of Pain via DQ.

Among those backstage at Survivor Series as potential late replacements were Barry Horowitz, Sam Houston, Tugboat Thomas and Mark Young. I believe Boreus Zhukov pinned Paul Roma in a warm-up match live.

11/24 in St. Louis drew 4,200 and $45,000 as Young beat Conquistador, Tugboat beat Zhukov, Rooster Double DQ against Honky Tonk, Valentine pinned Garvin, Bushwackers beat Rougeaus, Roberts beat DiBiase via DQ and Warrior beat Andre in 30 seconds.

11/25 in Las Vegas drew a heavily padded 3,500 as Tugboat pinned Zhukov, Valentine pinned Garvin, Rhodes pinned Bossman, Bushwackers beat Rougeaus, Honky Tonk beat Rooster, and Piper beat Rude via DQ. Best match was Piper-Rude and it was only *½ at best for that one.

11/25 in Madison Square Garden drew 8,200 and $134,000 as Perez beat Brawler, Bravo beat Hercules, Santana double count with Brown, Roberts beat DiBiase via DQ, Hart Foundation went to a 20 minute draw with Rockers (best match at MSG since January's Rockers vs. Brainbusters match-- about ***½) and Duggan beat Savage via count out when Elizabeth gave Duggan the purse that Sherri threw to Savage and Duggan used it to knock Savage out of the ring. Titan had hoped the Brother Love segment with Liz and Sherri would pack the place, but no such luck. Lots of heat, but not lots of fans. It ended with Sherri slapping Liz and Brother Bruce keeping Liz from fighting back. Duggan runs in and chases Sherri away and Brother Bruce puts the moves on Liz and Duggan runs back and hits him a few times with his 2x4.

Brother Love also wound up in an oversized diaper and dragged around on a rope courtesy of Roddy Piper on TV this weekend.

11/22 in St. Paul drew 3,700 as Tugboat pinned Horowitz, Martel beat Beefcake, Powers of Pain beat Bushwackers, Bravo pinned Snuka clean with the side slam, Perfect beat Hogan via count out, Garvin pinned Valentine, Genius pinned Young and Roberts beat DiBiase via DQ.

NBC Prime Time special set for Feb. 23, 1990.

11/22 in Moline drew a full house of 6,500 as Perez drew somebody, Earthquake beat Tom Stone, Savage pinned Duggan (good), Rockers beat Rougeaus (excellent), Neidhart beat Brawler and Rude beat Piper via DQ.

WWF got a full page ad for Survivor Series in the front of the Sunday comics section in the Chicago Sun-Times on 11/12. You can't ask for better visibility.

11/19 in Detroit drew 3,400 as Tugboat beat Horowitz, Garvin pinned Valentine, Bad News beat Roma, Rockers beat Rougeaus in two straight falls, Roberts beat DiBiase via DQ, and Savage pinned Duggan.

That night in Grand Rapids drew 2,000 as Bad News pinned Roma **, Bravo pinned Hercules, Tugboat beat Horowitz *, Roberts beat DiBiase via DQ **, Valentine pinned Garvin **, Duggan beat Savage via count out ** and Rockers beat Rougeaus in two straight falls **.

Piper vs. Rude in a cage on 12/28 in MSG.

11/25 at the Capital Center drew 6,000 as Perez beat Brawler, Haku pinned Roma, Rockers drew Hart Foundation (***½), Savage pinned Duggan, Roberts beat DiBiase via DQ and Santana beat Brown via count out.

NWA

Very disappointing crowds all week.

11/20 in Columbus, OH drew 2,500 for TV tapings as Ric Flair beat Bobby Eaton via DQ after an excellent 20 minutes when Cornette interfered, and after the bout Flair had Cornette in the figure four when Eaton did the Hemorrhoid hop onto Flair and left Flair laying. I just hope there is a purpose for leaving Flair laying against the Midnight Express somewhere down the road as it's getting too Dusty-ish for these continual leaving Flair layings. Lee Scott set the NWA for highest backdrop in a match against the Samoans. Kevin Sullivan destroyed jobber Alex Porteau so badly that the match will probably never air on TV. Porteau bled like crazy (not the hard way, the hardest way) and wound up taken out in an ambulance. Also Tom Zenk beat Iron Sheik, Steiners double DQ with Doom (very good match. Fans were upset live as Luger vs. Pillman and Skyscrapers vs. Warriors were advertised and neither took place (due to legit injuries) but no explanation was ever made to the fans.

Pillman should be out about three more weeks with medial collateral ligament damage.

Sid Vicious apparently broke a rib at the Clash when Scott Steiner gave him the blockbuster suplex. Three days later, in the St. Louis airport, he collapsed before a show when the broken rib punctured his lung and he's been hospitalized since then. It's touch-and-go whether he'll be back by Starrcade. If he isn't, the Samoan Swat Team will take the Skyscrapers place in the tournament. Jimmy Garvin has been placed on a company-imposed vacation, whatever that means.

Brad Armstrong, The Southern Boys, Scott Armstrong and Cactus Jack Mason were all scheduled for look-sees at the TV tapings on 11/27 in Pensacola, FL.

Thanksgiving at the Omni drew 7,500 as New Zealand Militia beat beat Brad Anderson & Trent Knight ½ *, Mike Rotunda pinned Norman the Lunatic using the ropes ½ *, Zenk pinned Michael Hayes ¾ *, Road Warrior Animal beat Danny Spivey via DQ when Teddy Long interfered *½ , SST & Savage beat Tommy Rich & Eddie Gilbert & Ranger Ross *½ , Steiners beat Doom via DQ (before the match started, Doom stuff piledrove Rick, who was carried out. Scott worked the whole way by himself, mainly against Simmons since Reed was limping badly because he blew out his knee in Columbus, OH three days earlier) but Rick ended up running in ***, Midnight beat Dudes **¾, using the racquet, Sting double count Lex Luger *** and Flair beat Muta via DQ in 30 minutes in a total Japanese style match with crowd into it pretty good. Luger interfered for the DQ and Sting made the savage. *** ½

11/21 in Raleigh drew 2,000 as Militia beat Knight & Anderson *¾ , Zenk beat Bob Emory DUD, Rotunda pinned Norman **½ (can't figure out that result since Norman is supposed to be pushed into a feud with the Skyscrapers in January and Rotunda is going nowhere), Hawk beat Spivey via DQ when Teddy Long interfered **½ , Samoans beat Rich and Gilbert & Ross ***, Rick Steiner pinned Doom Simmons when Nitron's attempt at interference backfired **½ , Midnight beat Dudes with the tennis racquet finish (crowd booed Dudes) ***½ , Sting double count with Luger ** and Flair beat Muta via DQ in 21 minutes when Luger interfered. Flair bled a whole bunch ***½.

11/25 in Baltimore drew 3,300 with the same results as Atlanta except Doom beat Steiners via DQ (same bit with Rick used), Ole Anderson, Gary Hart, Luger and Sting all interfered after the Flair-Muta match and the Luger-Sting finish was the old Dusty finish where Sting throws him over the top rope after a ref bump, then pins Luger, and the ref counts three to win the title and a second ref reverses the decision. Since they haven't done that finish for an entire year, there's nothing wrong with it, but if they start relying on it, they'll destroy the remnants of the business that Dusty Rhodes didn't finish off.

Same crew worked that afternoon in Philadelphia drawing just 1,400 fans (second lowest crowd the NWA has ever drawn in that city since they started coming--only card which drew worse was headlined by Steamboat vs. Iron Sheik and Flair wasn't on the show) while New Haven on 11/26 drew 1,600 with same results as Atlanta except Samu didn't arrive in time so Fatu & Savage beat Ross & Gilbert in a tag and Steiners beat Doom via a pinfall.

World Championship Wrestling on 11/18 (Steiners vs. Freebirds title change) drew a 3.0 rating--the best since January. NWA Main Event on 11/19 drew a 2.7 with Pillman & Sting vs. Militia while Power Hour on 11/17 drew a 2.2 with Luger vs. Murdoch. The Clash replay on 11/21 starting at 10 p.m. Eastern drew a 2.3 rating-by far the largest of any Clash replay. The combined rating of the two Clash shows made it the most-watched Clash ever. Officially, the live showing of Flair vs. Funk went into 3,340,000 homes or about 7.4 million viewers, which depending upon how you look at it, was either the most viewed or the second most viewed pro wrestling match ever on cable. Several changes in the booking were expected to be made at a meeting on Monday night in Pensacola. They are going to appoint different sub committees to handle different aspects of the booking in a way to remove power from Ric Flair without actually removing him as booker. It is expected that Terry Funk is going to wind up with some power out of all this.

The Flair-Muta match on TV Saturday was mainly submission moves for most of the way. Good Japanese style match, but the people watching the match weren't Japanese. Fans have to be educated as to what holds mean by making the submissions work against jobbers before using them in the big matches for long periods of time where they appear to be simply restholds. The match still had good heat, mainly because it was the hottest match-up in Center Stage in a long time. Muta blew red mist in Flair's face to make it look like he was being left laying in blood, where is the ban of blood on television?

A FEW LAST MINUTE NOTES

It appears Survivor Series did right at a three percent buy rate.

Harvey Cobbs and Ron Wyatt settled their problems out-of-court for $1,000 stemming from a guarantee for putting on a show months back.

Sunday's New York Times had an article about the NWA in the business section. It's obvious those in charge at the NWA believe the only way for them to make it is to go WWF-style. A story in AD Age magazine even quoted Jim Herd in saying that it would become more fairy-tale-like. My own belief is that becoming a cheap imitation of the WWF would be even more suicidal than their current course. Actually the current course would be okay if they just totally revised several aspects in how they tour and promote house shows. TV ratings and the PPV's are doing just fine (that is cable ratings). The syndication ratings, which tie in with local promotion of house shows, are poor as are house show crowds.

Kevin Sullivan did the color on TBS this past weekend. In comparing him with Michael Hayes--Hayes is more colorful and more entertaining to listen to, however Sullivan gets across all the angles and ideas that need to be put across and doesn't use the stage as a forum to get his own personality over.

Working against Buzz Sawyer has to be the single least fun job in professional wrestling.

Kerry Von Erich was on a Dallas radio station two weeks back and the host asked him about Ric Flair and Kerry said, "I beat him." When asked about Hulk Hogan, Kerry claimed that Hogan thought he was hot stuff but when they wrestled in Tennessee that I (Kerry) taught him a lesson and beat him. He claimed his father was the one who taught Dusty Rhodes and Bruiser Brody how to wrestle. Said Frank Dusek was gone because he "got beat up in the locker room and just went away." When asked about Japan, Kerry said it was easy money because the little Japanese just kick and scream a little and if you hit them once, you can knock them down.

Eric Embry still giving hints of staying a face for his upcoming match with Kerry as on TV he said that "I need the title for my family (fans of Dallas)."

THE READERS PAGES

AWARDS

Perhaps there should be another category added to the awards; Wrestling Mind of the Year. If so, Jim Cornette wins hands down.

The explanation of his latest Express-Dudes angle leading up to his eventual turn back to heel was pure genius. It all made such perfect sense. Cornette's recap of the entire turn of events ("We took two months off to get our heads together.. teams like us give us the most problems. The Dudes made it easy by asking for help, etc." was beautiful. It was as close to a logical and believable real-life storyline that pro wrestling ever comes. Jimmy even threw in some historical references for good measure (citing Bobby & Stan's feuds with the Fantastics and Rock & Roll Express).

It's a clever angle like this that demonstrates how a good dose of creativity can liven things. Whether or not the Express-Dudes feud gets over, Cornette's proven once again that there are more entertaining and effective ways to build a feud than by taking the easy way out-- that is, relying (sic) on an unprovoked run-in or an illogical turn.

Jeff Sigel
Evanston, Illinois

Hope you get to see Super Boy real soon. The guy is great. For the first time I have a real solid first place choice for rookie of the year.

Skeeve
Walnut, California

I feel that reader Mike Connors confused quantity with quality when he wrote in the 11/13 Observer that "the last four UWF cards have been ripoffs. I've never heard of the WWF putting on a show with less than a half hour of

wrestling." Well, I've seen plenty of WWF cards with less than 30 minutes of wrestling, including just about every Madison Square Garden show over the past year.

As a wrestling fan for nearly 20 years, I believe the UWF offers the most technically sound and proficient, sophisticated, unique and innovative wrestling today. In just 18 months, the UWF has truly rewritten the rules of pro wrestling. Their five knockout rule brings pro wrestling closer to legitimate sport than it has been in more than 30 years. The UWF promotes only monthly cards. Each card is an event, often with only two or three major matches. They still feature a core of less than 10 rigorously-trained wrestlers. There are no title belts. No tag team matches. No costumes. With some 30 minute cards, amateur scientific style wrestling, no high spots, almost no television should be commercial suicide. Tell that to the 56,000 fans at the Tokyo Dome at the end of the month.

I find the UWF's emphasis on a few wrestlers and matches to be most satisfying. It allows the big stars like Akira Maeda, Nobuhiko Takada, Kazuo Yammazaki, Yoshiaki Fujiwara and Masaharu Funaki to shine all the brighter. Maeda, Takada and Yamazaki can stand shoulder-to-shoulder with Ric Flair, Owen Hart and Genichiro Tenryu as the best wrestlers in the game today. David Hannah wrote that he felt the UWF stars shouldn't be rated, because of their monthly schedule. Well, beyond the ability of these men, which I feel deserve to be rated higher than they were, the physical style of the UWF requires more time between appearances like boxing.

I expect many will vote for All Japan as the best promotion this year. Many have never seen the UWF. All Japan is certainly very tough and physical in its own way. But I find the style to be somewhat sluggish, brainless and emphasizing burly power and intense brawling instead of scientific wrestling. The All Japan crew is talented enough, but personally I don't get excited by Jumbo Tsuruta, Toshiaki Kawada, the Can-Am Express or Terry Gordy. I feel these wrestlers aren't the equal of the UWF wrestlers with the exception of Tenryu. I admire Stan Hansen, but he embodies the barroom rough-house style which I characterize All Japan by.

To cite Tenryu vs. Tsuruta on June 6 for match of the year and to ignore Maeda vs. Takada on Jan. 10 is to misrepresent. Of course the UWF runs so few cards that feud of the year, especially with their politeness, seems inappropriate. But if one is to mention Tsuruta vs. Tenryu for feud of the year (even with Baba's uncreative revolving door title changes) then one should acknowledge Maeda vs. Takada for the same award. I'd also mention Takada vs. Yamazaki, as both of these feuds had more diverse and intricate matches than the tired and repetitive Tsuruta vs. Tenryu feud.

Don't think we UWF fans haven't noticed your digs at Maeda. To call Maeda overrated is to ignore his singles matches in 1986 and his matches with Takada in 1987 which were among the greatest matches of the decade. And if these past glories don't speak enough of Maeda's ability, consider his matches with Takada and Yamazaki over the last year and his performance with Chris Dolman on 5/4. How many other wrestlers could adapt to Sambo submission style wrestling? Not only has Maeda's profound knowledge of the art of wrestling schooled every other UWF competitor, his training, authenticity and humility define the UWF philosophy which has helped it become the most successful promotion in the world, not to mention the most unique.

My pick for most underrated is Owen Hart. Of course Vince McMahon held him back. I still felt as Blue Blazer, his flying was spectacular, and he had my favorite WWF singles match of the year until he was jobbed out.

As for match of the year, no doubt the Rockers vs. Brainbusters had some of the year's top bouts. Their SNME match was excellent, but I felt their Jan. MSG match was better. Obviously Jushin Liger vs. Naoki Sano was one of the best singles series of the year. Their first match had heart stopping flying moves, but I prefer Liger vs. Akira Nogami as it had better scientific wrestling along with great aerial moves. Tiger Mask vs. Dynamite Kid from 1982 was better than Liger vs. Sano.

I'm voting for Anderson & Blanchard for tag team of the year. Beyond their ring work, which is the best around, they also had the most out-of-ring impact two years running. Last year when they left the NWA, it seemed to sink the Crockett ship. This year, there are lots of scenarios upon return on everyone's lips.

Clint Freeman
New York, New York.

CHANGE OF SHOES
It's conceivable that one may soon be seeing barefoot fans in the front row at Titan TV tapings after the first of the year. You should be forewarned that this shoeless gathering would not be a meeting of the Hillbilly Jim Fan Club, but rather fans who have been forced to dispense of their footwear in order to enjoy the privilege of WWF ringside seating. The Kangaroo shoe line featuring NWA wrestlers makes its debut in January. If ringside fans have to remove NWA T-shirts for WWF t-shirts at tapings, will a strict sneaker policy be far behind? It's a good bet that Titan would never let fans on television gaze upon front row feet decorated by names of their competition. If so, this could lead to rumors racing around the building. What if the people with Luger and Sting shoes have to remove them but the person with the Flair shoes is told he can leave them on. What would that mean for fans trying to predict who is going to jump.

Harry White
St. Louis, Missouri

XENOPHOBIA
Thumbs down for the xenophobia that flowed from Jim Ross at the end of the Ric Flair vs. Terry Funk match. Please, spare us U.S. vs. Japan rhetoric. World War II ended 45 years ago. Unfortunately, news travels slow in the NWA. This nearly spoiled the final match of one of this sport's all-time greats. Thumbs up for the show for one great match after another once the first two duds were out of the way.

The Steiners are the best tag team in North America. Lex Luger had the kind of night that Riki Choshu used to have in his heyday. He could win Heel of the year coming off this Clash as he came off as a thoroughly contemptible SOB.

I want to thank Terry Funk as a fan for all his work over the years. He gave it his all Wednesday night. I kind of figured he'd wind up as a face when it was over. I can't stress how annoyed I was with hearing Ross during the post-match brawl. If somebody tuned in for the first time, you'd think the Clash was being televised from Pearl Harbor.

Some picks for awards. Akira Maeda for Wrestler of the Year for all the reasons he won the award last year. Best card of the year NWA Wrestle War 5/7 in Nashville. Worst promotion is the WWF. Most disgusting promotional tactic goes to Verne Gagne for his words about Bruiser Brody. Worst match was Rougeaus vs. Bushwackers from WrestleMania. That was worse than seeing a dozen Andre. vs Warrior matches in a row. At least those matches were short.

Paul Hanlin
Philadelphia, Pennsylvania

NWA
For months we've all talked about the NWA and the progress they have and haven't made. Gates, TV ratings and PPV sales are all considered and everyone has a comment to make. But I'd like to comment on an area of the NWA not frequently discussed--the wrestlers.

I think the crew they have now is possibly the best one they have ever had. Not only do these men do a great job in the ring, but their enthusiasm carries over in their attitude toward the fans. Three years ago I can think of maybe two or three NWA wrestlers who would have stopped and signed autographs, much less actually talk to a wrestling fan. Dusty Rhodes and Jim Crockett bred these sorts of people, I guess. In the past six months, I have yet to see even one wrestler who has been rude or impatient with fans. It is almost as if they have suddenly been given their freedom to be athletes who are people and not untouchable superstars. Thank goodness there are no Hulk Hogan attitudes in the NWA.

The people responsible for bringing in Brian Pillman, Tom Zenk, Scott Steiner and Sid Vicious should be given a pat on the back. No finer wrestlers could have been chosen. We need these kinds of stars in the organization right now.

Terenda Sargent
Gainesville, Georgia

It all makes sense now. World Championship Wrestling is nothing more than a large tax write-off for Ted Turner. This summer, when it looked as if the NWA was finally headed in the right direction, Ted said "Hey, this booking committee is working. We better change it now."

I've been a hardcore NWA fan from the beginning. After suffering through the Dusty Rhodes era, I was hit with deja vu. Unfortunately, Ric Flair isn't half the booker that he is a wrestler. I thought the Turner brass didn't want another Dusty Rhodes situation. I guess they didn't learn their lesson the first time around.

The NWA needs to do something drastic to draw attention, and then keep their audience over time. Build a strong product and people will watch. Let Sting turn heel on Ric Flair. Run some heel vs. heel feuds. Make their personalities into crossover celebrities. Just do something.

I believe Starrcade '89 is the case of the right idea at the wrong time. We never had explained to us what a Dragon Shi match was. Most younger fans I talked with had no idea what a Texas Death match was. This round-robin idea is just more confusion. And with the Survivor Series just three weeks earlier, it looks like a rip-off of a WWF idea.

Hal Moore
Marietta, Georgia.

Having read the letters page, there is obviously concern that Ric Flair and his booking committee are getting too violent. I hardly think so. Granted, the plastic bag angle could be taken as too violent for family viewing, but what about the rest of television programming? Last night, "Commando" was on TV and how many people got killed in that movie. Arnold wasn't punished for breaking into a store with a bulldozer and stealing loads of merchandise or for assaulting a police officer or for grand theft auto.

Why do people continually pick on wrestling when half the free world is a mockery to begin with and then say it sets a bad example. It's not like the NWA is marketing Terry Funk plastic bags for Christmas.

The letter by Mike Lano hit the nail on the head when he said that violence takes place in the WWF with no mention by anyone, especially the Savage-Sherri bit. Savage choked her for calling "Macho Man" instead of Macho King.

What a great angle that Piper/Rude was with the mouthwash. It was a classic. Piper's not too hot in the ring but I think his interviews are great, especially the ones for the Survivor Series.

I'm a big supporter of Stampede Wrestling, but I have to admit that Ed Whalen is ruining the show. There is no way they will survive on TSN if they don't show better matches. I can understand if they would blackout the main events on the local show to draw fans in, but it shouldn't be that way for the rest of the country that doesn't get a chance to see them live. They don't even talk about the finishes in the main events anymore.

They don't even show the angles anymore. The show has turned into a showcase of prelim matches that is hard to draw an audience for. I disagree with you on Larry Cameron. Sure, he's green as a wrestler but he has charisma and does a decent interview. Given time, I think he'll be a big draw, if he's given time to develop. He has an athletic background. Look how bad Steve Williams was when he started. Cameron's only problem is he needs a new haircut.

In reference to violent angles, does anyone remember when Bad News Allen punched Dynamite Kid's pregnant wife in the stomach to start up their feud?

Grant Zwarych
Peterborough, Ontario.

December 11, 1989

Officially, the card has taken place and the record was set.

The Universal Wrestling Federation's "U-Cosmos" show which took place on Wednesday night at the Tokyo Egg Dome, was unique in that it was a show in which the real news of the show happened well before the card ever took place.

When the UWF made the ultimate test of its drawing power by booking the biggest stadium in Japan, there were two key questions. Who would they bring in to oppose the Japanese stars in order to make unique match-ups that would pique curiosity enough to fill a big building? And more important, would they be able to fill such a big building without any television exposure? The answer to the first question occurred about two months back when they announced the foreign athletes brought in for the show, former Olympic judo medalist Willie Wilhelm of the Netherlands, Duane Koslowski of the 1988 U.S. Olympic Greco-Roman wrestling team, former World sambo wrestling champ Chris Dolman, Thai kickboxing champ Changpuek Kiatsongrit and World Karate Association World heavyweight champion Maurice Smith from Seattle, Washington. The answer to the second question occurred on 11/5, when tickets went on sale for the Tokyo Dome and within a half hour, the gate had already surpassed $1.5 million and by the end of the day, more than 40,000 tickets were sold. Both marks devastated all existing records for quickest sales of pro wrestling tickets.

I don't have a detailed report as of yet as to the 11/29 card. News of the card was broadcast locally on Tokyo TV news (which airs in the San Francisco area) and the sold out crowd was reported as in excess of 60,000 and the results of the matches saw Akira Maeda force Wilhelm to submit to a knee lock in the main event, Nobuhiko Takada made Koslowski submit to a cross armlock, Dolman made Kazuo Yamazaki submit to a cross armlock, Yoshiaki Fujiwara made Dick Leon; Fly (a kick boxer from Europe) submit with a knee lock, Maurice Smith knocked out Minoru Suzuki with a punch, Yoji Anjyo went to a five round draw with Kiatsongrit and in the only match-up of UWF wrestlers against one another, Tatsuo Nakano beat Shigeo Miyato. I'd been told ahead of time that a full house would be a $3.2 million gate, which breaks the all-time record for largest single- site gate for pro wrestling (set in the same building by New Japan on April 24th of this past year--U.S. record is $1,628,000 set at WrestleMania V at Trump Plaza), although that was for 56,000 seats, With several thousand standing room tickets sold as well, that should push the figure slightly higher. When you add in nine closed-circuit locations plus the amazing concession business UWF does (at their Osaka Baseball Stadium show in May, they averaged $30 per head in gimmick sales--if that figure holds up here, and there is no reason to expect that it didn't--the UWF would have grossed more money through concessions alone than any card, including the WrestleManias, has in ticket sales) and the relatively small overhead (UWF has a front office staff of just a few people), you are talking about possibly the single most profitable pro wrestling event in the history of the business.

The top story in the U.S. of this past week is the folding of the Continental Wrestling Federation promotion. It's been rumored for quite some time that this group was on its last legs, particularly after long-time General Manager Ron West left the group to form his own promotion. The word reached the boys at the 11/25 card in Dothan, AL that owner David Woods had decided against putting any more money into the operation and that it would be closing down after current commitments are fulfilled. Woods said that the promotion was piling up losses of $15,000 per month and that he simply couldn't afford to keep it going. When word reached us that Woods was calling it quits, the story was that Robert Fuller and Jimmy Golden would try and re-start the promotion in January. However, with Fuller and Brian Lee capturing the USWA tag team titles this past Friday night in Dallas, it appears that Fuller himself has decided to go full-time into Texas and work for Jerry Jarrett. As far as the other wrestlers are concerned, Dennis Condrey (who was the CWF's singles champion) has left for the new Heritage Championship Wrestling group based in Mississippi, Tracy Smothers & Steve Armstrong are headed to Mexico (to feud with Los Brazos), Fuller & Lee are going to work for Jarrett, Cactus Jack Manson had a try-out on Tuesday night with the NWA, Ron Starr has returned to Puerto Rico while the remainder of the Armstrong clan (Bob, Brad and Scott) are expected to bounce around the various small Southern independent groups. West's attempt at running an opposition group called North American Wrestling Association also folded its tent up the previous night, and West is attempting to negotiate for a spot in the NWA office.

The final results of our Survivor Series poll of letters and phone calls that have reached here by Dec. 4 are:

Thumbs up: 77 (22.6 percent)
Thumbs down: 208 (61.0 percent)
In The Middle: 56 (16.4 percent)

The response did get decidedly more negative when the letters came in as compared with the phone calls, with the biggest complaint being the lack of angles stemming from the shaw. Most of the other complaints were pretty well covered last week. Ironically, traditionally the letters are more favorable in past polls to the WWF shows, where this one the phone calls indicated it more so (from past surveys, the phone calls usually rate cards more on the workrate itself while the letters usually put more emphasis on storyline). It appears that there was little discrepancy from the view that this was overall the weakest of the three Survivors' shows.

Based on figures I've gotten, the buy rate looks to be around 3.3 percent, which is up from last year's 2.8 for the same show. Other sources are putting the figure at somewhere between 2.8 and 3.0. As for the marketing of the show itself, I kind of expected it to do slightly better than last year because it was promoted better on television, plus all those airings of the "Countdown" show on USA which was a two-hour commercial which aired four times. That made up for the match-ups themselves being a lot less interesting than in previous years. A three percent buy rate with a universe of nearly 12 million homes would indicate about 350,000 orders and upwards of §7 million in gross revenue, The split on PPV is 50 percent for the cable operators, 45 percent for Titan and five percent for Viewers Choice/Request and whomever the syndicator is (that five percent, and Titan's attempt to eliminate the middle-men from the picture is what caused all the furor prior to WrestleMania last year and nearly got Titan's big show knocked off PPV). However, what has happened are a few things in the past that have a small factor in the revenue. While traditionally PPV is late buys (and there is generally a $5 surcharge on the late buys), somehow the extra $5 on the late buys never gets into the pot. Also, there are people who order the show and don't pay when the cable bill comes the next month, although I don't know how much of a factor this really is (but the Crockett NWA had a beef with one of the syndicators in 1988 over this subject and cost them one major cable syndicate for Starrcade '88). Realistically, Titan's revenue from PPV for Survivor Series should be around $3.15 million and costs at around $1.35 million to put on the show so the profit margin should be about $1.8 million. In comparison, the NWA's profit margin for the Halloween Havoc card was said to be $1.25 million although Titan sources dispute that figure saying it couldn't have been that high.

Multichannel News reported in the 11/13 issue when reporting on Halloween Havoc said that systems contacted reported buy rates generally between 1.5 and 2.0 percent for the show, which indicates the figure bandied about within NWA circles that the show did a 1.77 percent buy rate appears legitimate. Steve Chamberlain of Turner Home Entertainment publicly claimed a two percent buy rate which, if nothing else, appears to be the smallest exaggeration of the legitimate figures of any PPV event thus far for either group. Chamberlain, in the article, said that the increase in buy rate when compared with the previous NWA PPV events (ironically Chamberlain claimed a 2.1 for the Baltimore show, now claims a two percent as an increase and they were claiming a ridiculous 2.8 for the Flair-Steamboat Chicago show) was because they wrapped more entertainment around the actual wrestling itself and because of the promotional spots using Elvira. Chamberlain said in in the future "we'll be much more aggressive towards the entertainment marketing of the events" and said that they will try to introduce a new gimmick match on each future PPV event after Starrcade, which he said would be more wrestling-oriented because of its past history and tradition.

In other wrestling-related PPV events, the Thunder and Mud show from several weeks back with Jessica Hahn, where the lure was the mud wrestling and the cheapest PPV event ever offered ($9.95 price tag) did less than an 0.1 percent buy rate which also makes it the least purchased PPV event ever. Another Women's Wrestling PPV event from another company is scheduled for 12/22 which should do similar business. The demo tape sent out to cable operators for the show (which doesn't include any women wrestlers that I've ever heard of) was said to be worse than GLOW ever was. The bottom line here is that it is not wrestling on PPV that is the big draw, it is wrestling that is heavily hyped on television that is the draw. People won't buy a wrestling event on PPV just because it is wrestling, only if it has been hyped to death as something major.

This is the last issue you'll be reading prior to Starrcade on 12/13. The major thing leading up to this will be if any indication will be given on television this coming weekend as to the status of Sid Vicious. As mentioned last week, Vicious collapsed on 11/18 at the St, Louis Airport when the broken rib he apparently suffered three days earlier in the Clash (nobody knows for sure when the injury occurred, speculation is it was when Scott Steiner gave him the blockbuster suplex) punctured his lung. The latest reports I've heard on Vicious is that he was still hospitalized by mid-week and it was doubtful he'd be able to return by the show, but it wasn't ruled out as impossible. The last word I'd also heard is that if Vicious isn't able to appear, that the Skyscrapers would be replaced in the "Iron Team" by the Samoan Swat Team. While this would make for better actual matches, that replacement wouldn't be well received by a lot of people purchasing the event. I don't expect any announcement to be made about Vicious' injury at any time, and instead they'll just have him continually no-show at all the house shows so these Warriors vs. Skyscrapers matches advertised never take place which must thrill the paying customers to no end. That's already one strike against the show if they put in a last-minute replacement team without any advance warning. There is also still a lot of internal disagreement as to how both tournaments should end up and what should be done to get them to that point. If the Scrapers are out, one expects the tag division to wind up being either the Steiners or the Road Warriors. Since everyone has been told over and over again before-hand on television that Lex Luger is going to win the singles thing, I guess that makes him the favorite going in although other ideas have been bandied about.

After the 12/27 PPV event (which I believe will be taped just days after you receive this), which should be an interesting test with a one match plus movie show, the next Titan PPV will be Jan. 21 from Orlando for the third Royal Rumble. The Rumble will once again be a 30 man affair with most of the big names involved and will probably tease the angle which will wind up as the top match at WrestleMania (the angle itself will be shot on NBC in February). The undercard sounds every bit as bad as last year's--already announced are a Brother Love segment with two guests (which will wind up being Sapphire--Dusty Rhodes' new manager and Sherri Martel to set up a feud between guess who and guess who) plus Brutus Beefcake vs. The Genius, Ron Garvin vs Greg Valentine and Bushwackers vs. Rougeaus (don't know what appearance of Rougeaus for this show means as I'd heard they wouldn't be returning until late in 1990--maybe just a one shot deal so they can try and win the worst match of the year in two years consecutively) and possibly Rockers vs. Powers of Pain (this hasn't been announced, but all four were notably absent from the card). Zeus won't be working the card, which seems to indicate that Zeus will be phased out after 12/27. WrestleMania VI on April 1st will be at the SkyDome in Toronto as Titan will attempt (and no doubt succeed) to set the North American record for largest live gate. Titan's 4/13 Tokyo Dome date may set the Titan gate record, however as there is already lots of publicity in Japan about that date.

Two quick corrections from notes in past issues about TV ratings. Last week I mentioned that the the replay of the 11/15 Clash from Troy, NY (on 11/22) which did a 2.3 was the highest rated Clash replay. Actually, it was the second highest rated replay as the Cleveland Clash with that awesome Flair-Steamboat angle drew a 2.6 rating when it aired the second time. Also, several weeks back after the Ric Flair vs. Mike Rotunda match on NWA Main Event drew a 3.4 rating, I said it was the highest rated Sunday NWA ME show since the program's debut show in April of 1988 when Windham-Luger-Sting vs. Flair-Anderson-Blanchard drew a 3.7. Actually it was the third highest rated, as a show in early March of this year which aired an eight minute portion of the Flair-Steamboat title change match from Chicago drew a 3.5.

While we're on the subject of ratings, last week's SNME drew an B.7 rating and a 24 share, which is about a point lower than the previous shows this season had done.

For those on the West Coast, I'll be back on KCBS (740 AM) out of San Francisco on Mike Woodley's Sportsbeat show on Saturday, Dec. 23 reviewing the year in wrestling. It's a phone-in show from 6 to 8 p.m. and at this time of the year, the signal carries from British Columbia down through the Mexican border and we'll talk about anything related to pro wrestling. I'll also be on WALE in Providence, RI on 12/12 at 7 p.m. talking about Starrcade and will be on in Melbourne, Australia this coming Friday night as well.

There was a lot of controversy within NWA circles about the New York Times article on the NWA which appeared in the Nov. 26 Business Section. The article, headlined by, "This isn't real," discussed the NWA's attempts to try and keep solid athletic wrestling while at the same time introduce gimmicks for kids. Within the context of the article it talked about how the NWA has banned blood (I don't know if the article specified they had only banned blood on PPV and television events because they regularly have juice at arena shows) and said that the blood was drawn when wrestlers use razor blades to cut open their opponent (which sounds even sicker than the real story). From a journalism standpoint, it wasn't a good story. Too disjointed. Also, its accuracy wasn't that great. Besides the blood mention, which is of course wrong, they added by saying that the reason they don't have blood anymore is because they've instituted fines for wrestlers who use chairs, tables and other objects which is of course quickly going from reality-reality world into wrestling-fantasy world. Many in the NWA, including several key wrestlers were furious at this piece as a kayfabe violation. But I've got to disagree on this one. The journalism world is based on "herd journalism" (which has nothing to do with the exec VP of the NWA). The only reason the Titan admissions of wrestling as fake in the New Jersey hearings earlier this year got so much play nationally is because the New York Times printed the story on the front page. Once the editors of the Times decreed it was front page news, the rest of the country followed since the Times is a premier newspaper. Likewise, when the Times devotes several pages to the NWA, this makes the herd journalists want to do the same story and the NWA will get a lot of publicity. Sure, in almost every story the subject of fakery will be bandied about. But back in 1984-85, when the WWF was getting its media blitz (again based on the herd journalism since the New York media had decreed their wrestling as a new fad well before there was any facts to back up that claim, and it was the media blitz as much as anything which created the fad) nearly every story also brought up the idea that wrestling was something less than on-the-level sport. But the publicity made the WWF something of an "in" thing and they've managed to ride the crest of that wave since. If anything, the biggest compliment one could say about the WWF is that they managed to use the "fad" press to build a base but never lost the base when the "fad" stories ended (Largely as a result of their ability to garner such good ratings for the SNME's which kept them with network credibility). Almost nobody believes wrestling is pure sport today, and if they do, they sure aren't reading the business section of the New York Times. I know that wrestlers are brainwashed from day one that the single biggest sin is to expose the business, but in recent years, the business has been exposed over and over, and the business exposed the most has been the WWF. Face it. You can't have it both ways. Wrestling can either stay in the closet and reach a hardcore following and not have enough mainstream exposure to do anything but small houses and small PPV's, or it can be an acceptable part of the entertainment industry as a pseudo-sport and get the coverage that its popularity warrants. But that coverage will always either be tongue-in-cheek and somewhat condescending to its audience or somewhat serious, in which case it will assume knowledge and write giving the impression that this is not pure sport we are talking about. The one disadvantage the NWA has when compared with the WWF of five years back is when the WWF made its move, every major media treated them like they were the only wrestling group around. At the time of the stories, in many markets, maybe even in more than half the country, the WWF was actually trailing the established promotions when it came to TV ratings and attendance, but those regional groups were never mentioned. In any story this year or next in a major newspaper or trade publication about the NWA, the subject of the WWF will always come up and the NWA will always be written about as the second place group trying to play catch-up. But just being acknowledged by major media sources as a major player is a significant step. If the NWA can manipulate the media into proclaiming them as a close second place (and if they use recent cable TV ratings, they can even claim right now in at least one factor they have a slight lead), which they aren't, and they are seen as a viable competitor, it is the one thing Vince McMahon has trying to avoid since this thing started, That he has competition. As mentioned here many times, the reality of who is doing what is not nearly as important as the illusion that the groups create to outside sources and to the public. Lots of the WWF's early success was based on media manipulation and illusion, so even though the NWA's house shows are doing the worst in recent memory, that in no way precludes them from making important media breakthroughs.

With the first pro wrestling event ever in the Soviet Union set for New Years Eve at Moscow's Soviet Coliseum, New Japan through Antonio Inoki's new political connections has announced another breakthrough. New Japan is scheduled to promote the first pro wrestling event in Red China in February of 1990 with a card booked in Peking at an outdoor stadium. Inoki has set up a Japan-China exchange program which will also promote a track and field event and martial arts events in Red China during 1990. New Japan will also train the leading martial arts fighters from Red China the pro wrestling style (similar to what was done this year with the Soviets). It is said that after the experiment in Red China is complete that New Japan will before the end of 1990 also get their television and promote live events in South America. With Titan promoting a show in Tokyo in April, it appears that on a world-wide scale, the real wrestling war may be Titan vs. New Japan several years down the road. It's inconceivable that the Japanese group, no matter how strong their wrestling product may get in the future, could ever be competition for the leading U.S. promotion in North America, but as a world-wide entity, that is a different story.

ALL JAPAN

The tag team tournament continues.

11/23 in Tottori saw Stan Hansen & Genichiro Tenryu down Dan Kroffat & Doug Furnas when Hansen pinned Kroffat with the lariat in 9:46, Dynamite Kid & Davey Boy Smith beat The Nasty Boys, Giant Baba & Rusher Kimura & Kenta Kobashi beat Jumbo Tsuruta & Yoshiaki Yatsu & Masa Fuchi, Tiger Jeet Singh & Abdullah the Butcher beat Isao Takagi & Shunji Takano, Terry Gordy & Bill Irwin beat Kabuki & Akira Taue and The Foot Loose beat Mighty Inoue & Shinichi Nakano plus prelims before 2,800 fans.

11/24 in Fukui drew a sellout 3,400 as Hansen & Tenryu & Toshiaki Kawada won the main event over Tsuruta & Yatsu & Fuchi, plus Kroffat & Furnas beat Gordy & Irwin, Baba & Kimura beat Takano & Kabuki, Singh & Butcher beat Taue & Takagi, Kid & Smith beat Kobashi & Nakano and Nasty Boys beat Samson Fuyuki & Yoshinari Ogawa plus prelims.

11/25 in Fujiyoshihara saw Tsuruta & Yatsu beat Kid & Smith in 12:48 when Tsuruta pinned Kid with a back suplex, Hansen & Tenryu beat Singh & Butcher in 11:22.

11/27 in Iwate before 2,700 saw Singh & Butcher beat Foot Loose in the main event, Tsuruta & Yatsu & Nakano beat Hansen & Tenryu & Ogawa, Gordy & Irwin beat Nasty Boys, Kobashi & Kid & Smith beat Baba & Kimura & Puchi (this must have been an "interesting" match to see how it was done) and Furnas & Kroffat beat Takagi & Kabuki plus prelims.

As of 11/27, the standings were: 1, Tsuruta & Yatsu (10), 2. Hansen & Tenryu (8), 3. tied with Kid & Smith, Singh & Butcher and Baba & Kimura (6), 6. Gordy & Irwin (4), 7. Furnas & Kroffat (3), 8B. Nasty Boys (2), 9. Foot Loose (1), 10. Takano & Kabuki (0).

Baba was very impressed with the effort shown by the Nasty Boys thus far in the tour and will book them regularly in 1990. Part of this also is because of the need by Baba to develop new foreign attractions because with the major talent signed up with WWF and NWA, Baba is left with a small stable of foreign attractions (Can-Am Express, Gordy, Hansen, Kid & Smith, Butcher) who come so frequently that they get stale.

Hansen & Tenryu nearly split up in their TV match on 11/19 against Gordy & Irwin. After Tenryu pinned Irwin for the win, Gordy attacked Tenryu and was thrown outside the ring. Gordy was pounding on Tenryu outside when Hansen jumped in and tried to punch Gordy, who ducked and he hit Tenryu. The two shoved each other after but wound up shaking hands before leaving. Baba announced this week that because of the comments by students at the college he was speaking at, that he's contacted Rip Rogers and is adding him to the January tour.

Gene Kiniski will also be on the tour from 1/26 through 1/28 at Korakuen Hall doing question and answer sessions with the fans during intermission from mid-ring.

NEW JAPAN

The Japan singles World Cup tournament started on 11/24 in Gunma before 4,500 fans as Super Strong Machine & Shinya Hashimoto beat Riki Choshu & Shiro Koshinaka in the main event. In tournament matches, Masa Chono (who is getting a huge push) pinned Soviet Chimur Zarasov, Salman Hashimikov pinned Hiroshi Hase and Steve Williams beat Vladimir Berkovich. The Blond Outlaws (Hiro Saito & Norio Honaga & Tatsutoshi Goto with bleached blond hair) beat Kuniaki Kobayashi & Naoki Sano & Kantaro Hoshino, Wayne Bloom & Brad Rheingans beat Osamu Kido & Kengo Kimura, Manny Fernandez pinned George Takano and Akira Nogami & Takayuki Iizuka beat Hirokazu Hata & Osamu Matsuda.

Buzz Sawyer didn't appear for this tour as many of you saw by his appearance on TBS this weekend. He didn't cancel on time so no substitute was brought in to take his spot.

11/25 in Numazu before a sellout 2,170 saw Choshu & Chono & Kido beat Hashimikov & Victor Zangiev & Berkovich when Choshu lariated Berkovich, Hashimoto pinned Fernandez, Kimura pinned Bloom, Koshinaka pinned Machine and Rheingans pinned Takano in the tournament plus Hase & Iizuka beat Honaga & Hiro Saito via DQ and Williams pinned Goto.

Jushin Liger (Mexico) and Masa Saito (Minnesota helping with the finishing touches on the training of Koji Kitao) aren't wrestling on this tour.

11/26 drew a sellout 2,200 at Korakuen Hall to see the grudge match as Chono pinned Hashimoto in 20 minutes in the main event. Also Choshu & Kimura & Hashimkov beat Williams & Rheingans & Bloom in 6:38 when Hashimikov gave Bloom the Northern Lights suplex (this match had some interest in Japan because it was the first time Williams and Hashimikov would oppose each other in the ring), Goto pinned Hase, Kido beat Berkovich, Kobayashi & Koshinaka beat Saito & Honaga, Fernandez pinned Zangiev and Sano pinned Hata.

11/27 in Sendai drew a sellout 3,140 as Choshu pinned

Kimura with the lariat in 7:48. The pro debut of Soviet amateur star Andrei Sulsaev was in the semi-main however Bulsaev put over Chono in 6:49, Kido upset Koshinaka while Rheingans pinned Hase plus Williams & Fernandez & Bloom beat Machine & Takano & Hashimoto when Williams stampeded Machine, The Blond Outlaws beat Kobayashi & Nogami & Hoshino plus prelims.

Antonio Inoki officially canceled his planned comeback matches on 12/6 in Osaka and 12/7 in Tokyo since he's still recovering from his stab wounds suffered in an assassination attempt about a month back. However both Inoki and Tatsumi Fujinami will be in Osaka and they will be doing a live press conference with questions from the fans for both of them for 30 minutes during the card. Also Habieli Victashev of the Soviet Union (sambo wrestling champ) will work in Osaka against Takayuki Iizuka. Some months back they had this match and even though Iizuka lost, that loss propelled him into a small degree of the spotlight and made him a "name" performer and he later won the tag title with Choshu.

Inoki did announce he would make his wrestling comeback on the 12/31 card in Moscow.

Hidekazu Tanaka (the young ring announcer for New Japan) is promoting a show on 12/19 at Tokyo's Korakuen Hall with the Hashimoto vs. Chono grudge match on top plus the spotlight on the young guys with Nogami vs. Iizuka, Jushin Liger returns vs. Takeshi Misawa, Sano vs. rookie Hiroshi Ohtori and Hada vs. Matsuda.

Sakaguchi has been meeting with Baba more concerning the Tokyo Dome card in February. Even though Sakaguchi is either very close to, or already has inked a deal with Jack Petrik of TBS (Petrik is said to be going to Japan for the Tokyo Dome show), several of the NWA wrestlers had signed exclusive Japanese contracts to work for Baba and they are trying to work out a deal. Sakaguchi is particularly interested in Tom Zenk and Sting for the Tokyo Dome but no word if Baba will let them do the show. Right now the only NWA talent officially booked for the Tokyo Dome is Ric Flair and Muta. Sakaguchi is also going to negotiate with Verne Gagne about "buying" the AWA belt (either for short term or even permanently) to allow either Chono or Hashimoto a vehicle to superstardom when they capture an American "World" title so if the deal goes through then Zbyszko will drop the strap in Tokyo.

UWF

The 11/29 Tokyo Dome was said to be a "slight thumbs up" as far as the quality of the card itself, UWF is pushing 12/29 as the day that tickets for the 1/16 card in Tokyo's Budokan Hall (15,000 seats) and 2/9 in Osaka (7,000 seats) go on sale.

The Tokyo Dome card will air on television in Japan in mid-December.

OTHER JAPAN NOTES

12/12 in Japan will be declared Rikidozan Memorial Day (Rikidozan was the most popular wrestler in Japan and the "Babe Ruth of Japanese wrestling" from 1954 until his death of a stab wound in a mob related incident in 1963) and among those speaking at the celebration will be former Japan prime minister Yasuhiro Nakasone (equivalent in U.S. to a position somewhere between President and Speaker of the House), Baba, Incki, Sakaguchi, Dick Beyer (The Destroyer--one of Rikidozan's leading rivals at the time of his death), Shinji Jin (President of UWF), former wrestlers Toyonobori (big star in the 60s) and Kojika and the president of the sumo association.

Several of the Japanese papers picked up that Koji Kitao worked with a mask on at the AWA tapings in Rochester, MN which was supposed to be kept secret. New Japan was trying to promote that Kitao (who I'm told in Rochester, MN locked like just another green rookie) would debut at the Tokyo Dome. Told it made the papers on the 27th after the Observer hit Japan the 26th (which is the day before that issue reached the East Coast which says something about the US Mail but I don't know what).

USWA

The USWA tag team title tournament was on 12/1 in Dallas before 500 fans (with kids prices lowered to $2) and ended up with Robert Fuller & Brian Lee (The Tennessee Stud Stable) beating Jeff Jarrett & Matt Borne in the finals. The tournament opened with Billy Joe Travis & Gary Young beating Chris Adams & Eric Embry when Adams was holding Travis, Embry came off for a clothesline, Travis ducked and Embry clotheslined Adams and Travis pinned him.

They are doing this break-up of Embry and Adams slowly. I'm told Embry is still the most "over" face in the territory, but I expect he's the one turning heel since Adams has so many marketing ideas (wrestling school, calendars, promoting "sold" shows with his wife, etc.) which seems to require him to be a face. Then Fuller & Lee beat Kerry Von Erich & Bill Dundee when Kevin no-showed (didn't take long, did it?) and Sylvia hit Dundee with the kendo stick to set up the Studs win. Dustin Rhodes & Jimmy Jack Funk beat P. Y. Chu Hi & Buddy Landel via DQ and Jarrett & Borne beat The Punisher (now Master of Pain in CWA) & Sheik Braddock. Second round saw Fuller & Lee beat Rhodes & Funk when Sylvia hit Funk with the kendo stick. Jarrett & Borne beat Travis & Young via DQ when Scandor Akbar interfered and the faces lost, but second ref Tony Falk ran into the ring and told Bronko Lubich what happened and he reversed the decision and it led to the finals in which Sylvia, for the third time, used the kendo stick, this time on Jarrett, to set up the winning fall.

Second quote of the week (quote of the week by Hillbilly Jim later in the issue) by Kerry: "The USWA accidentally booked Kevin in two places last night. Since the Houston date was signed first Kevin had to go to that one. Because if a Von Erich signs a contract to be somewhere, he's there."

Color commentator Terrence Garvin continually tried to get Kerry to say that he and Kevin aren't getting along.

When Eric Embry pulled down his strap ala Jerry Lawler Garvin had his best line since starting with the color: "I don't know why he does that. It makes him look pregnant."

They are doing an angle where Garvin (who does a flamboyant act and does the commentary at ringside wearing a dress) "has a crush" on Jeff Jarrett.

12/8 in Dallas they are letting kids in free in order to get some fans out with a card headlined by Fuller & Lee defending against Jarrett & Borne, Dundee & Adams & Embry vs. Travis & Young & Akbar, Kevin Von Erich vs. Chu Hi and Landel vs. Steve Williams.

Ch. 21 has put the syndicated TV show back on the air after taking it off for a few weeks, at least in part due to the Toni Adams incident.

Killer Brooks gave up his TV on Ch. 39 because he couldn't afford the production costs.

12/15 in Dallas will be Lawler vs. Kerry with both the USWA and Texas titles up in a unification match.

CWA

11/27 in Memphis saw King Cobra pin Black Jack (Tommy Gilbert), New York Brawler (Lou Fabbiano) pinned Tracy Smothers due to outside interference from Nate the Rat (who has to be a contender for worst manager honors), Dirty White Boy pinned Chris Champion when DWB acted like he was going to punch Dirty White Girl, Champion tried to save White Girl and White Boy cradled him from behind, Ricky & Todd Morton beat Bobby & Jackie Fulton, Dutch Mantell beat Soul Taker via DQ when Nate interfered and afterwards Boss Winters attacked Nate and the main event saw Jerry Lawler beat Bill Dundee via count out when after a ref bump, Lawler piledrove Dundee on the floor after hitting him with a chain. Mantell ran in after Lawler but Soul Taker attacked Mantell and Lawler and Soul Taker both did a number on Mantell.

Lawler is still coming out of the face dressing room and had an argument on TV Saturday with Mantell. Mantell claimed that Lawler and Soul Taker were working together and Lawler said Mantell was making it all up so the fans would boo him. When Lawler said these fans (in studio) were his fans, they booed, and then Lawler said that it didn't matter, because the millions of people watching on TV were his fans and when the few in the studio wise up it'll be too late because he won't let them cheer for him anymore.

Lawler's mic work in this feud are far and away the best talking in wrestling of late. Only thing close is Flair and Funk just before their "I Quit" match.

New to the area are the Million Dollar Babies (Mark Sampson & G.Q. Stratus) who I believe worked independently in Virginia. Both Boss Winters and Nate the Rat want to manage them.

They announced a match on 12/25 in Memphis with Nate vs. Winters with the winner getting Soul Taker's contract. I believe Winters will win since there is personal heat between Soul Taker and Nate.

They also announced Lawler must defend his title on 12/25 or be stripped of it and Lawler said that all the babyfaces must have told on him because they all want title shots now.

This week Dirty White Girl got a letter, unsigned, saying something like why do you put up with the abuse from White Boy (White Girl came out with a "black eye" and they hinted she'd been punched by White Boy). White Boy blamed Chris Champion for the letter. Then in the stupid remark of the week, Champion came out for his interview and said that the way White Boy was treating White Girl was "all bullshit." Since the Memphis show goes on the air live, this went out loud and clear over the air. Both announcer Dave Brown and later Champion had to apologize for it after the fact on the air.

12/5 in Memphis has Lawler & Soul Taker vs. Mantell & Master of Pain on top, Champion vs. White Boy in a street fight, a four-team four-corners tag match with Ricky & Todd Morton, Brian Lee & The Grappler, King Cobra & Frankie Lancaster and Mike Davis & New York Brawler plus Mortons vs. Davis & Brawler, Lee vs. Lancaster and Cobra vs. Grappler.

Louie Spicoli starts up here next week as a heel (a few weeks back I said he was from Puerto Rico---actually San Pedro, CA).

Some talk that if Eddie Gilbert doesn't have his contract renewed in the NWA that he'd return here.

THIS JUST IN

A federal jury last week acquitted Hawaiian wrestler promoter Lia Maivia of Polynesian Pacific Wrestling and business partners Larry Heiniemi (Lars Anderson) and Ati So'o of attempting to extort $5,000 from rival promoter Dunbar Wakayama last October. The jury didn't believe it was So'o who left a threatening message on Wakayama's answering machine and believed that the $5,000 that FBI agents had videotaped Maivia wanting from Wakayama simply constituted, as Maivia claimed, a booking fee rather than attempted extortion. The jury believed there simply wasn't enough evidence for a conviction.

The defense had maintained that Sam Samson (one of Maivia's referees) had left the threatening message on Wakayama's machine, although Samson denied the allegation on the witness stand. The jury heard the tape over-and-over again and heard both So'o and Samson testify. The jury said that they didn't believe So'o left the message. The trial had lasted nearly two months. The jury deliberated for two days before coming in with the verdict.

HERITAGE

This group based in Vicksburg, MS is scheduled to start full-time on Jan. 8 with a five-day per week schedule. The crew of regulars is said to be Ricky Morton & Robert Gibson, Bobby & Jackie Fulton, Junkyard Dog, Buddy Landel, Dennis Condrey, Tim Horner (that's a surprise since last word I got was Vince McMahon wasn't going to let him out of his contract), Steve Pritchard, Joey Maggs, Brett Sawyer, Mr. Olympia(Jerry Stubbs) and Mr. Nasty (Ken Massey). Also working spot dates will be The Bullet (Bob Armstrong), Brad Armstrong, Terry Gordy (between Japan tours), Joel Deaton (between Japan tours), Bob Orton (until he goes, if he goes to WWF) and Manny Fernandez. Denny Brown was also in for some shots and there is talk of bringing in Bam Bam Bigelow to feud with Terry Gordy when it gets going. The territory will be Mississippi and Northern Louisiana. The last taping before it gets started is 12/6 with some TV's starting up in Mississippi and Shreveport and they may try and get the TV slots that will be vacated in Alabama by the folding of the CWF. They are hopeful of doing tournaments in March for singles and tag team belts. Kelly Keith manages Landel, who is feuding with JYD. Other feuds are Morton & Gibson vs. Fantastics, and Bullet vs. Mr. Nasty and they are hopeful of putting Brad Armstrong & Horner together as the Lightning Express.

STAMPEDE

Several of the guys have taken off over money problems including D.J. Peterson (who just got there and was being primed for title shots at Larry Cameron) and Tom Nash of the Black Hearts who was half of the tag team champions.

No word on what will happen with the tag title although speculation is they'll do a phantom title switch to Chris Benoit & Biff Wellington.

Steve DiSalvo is back, but only working weekend dates

The top three singles guys will be DiSalvo, Cameron and Arch Angel (Curtis Thompson) who are all heels right now so somebody will be turning.

11/17 in Gibbons, ALTA drew 160 as Arch Angel beat Wellington DUD, Great Gama & Johnny Smith beat Bruce Hart & Jesse Jackson (a new jobber) *½, Cameron pinned Benoit when Angel interfered ** and Benoit & Wellington & Bruce Hart & Jackson beat Cameron & Gama & Angel & Smith in 25 minutes ****

OTHER NOTES

Jerry Blackwell's latest in a long list of bad breaks was on 11/22 when his house burned down. The wrestlers, most of whom had left Blackwell for a rival group, got together on

11/26 and did a benefit show in Alpharetta, GA which did a $1,000 gate and all the money was given to Blackwell so the wrestlers worked free and Gordon Clements (who owns the auction barn) gave the building for free.

Latest on the AWA team thing is the standings have Baron Von Raschke's team in first place with six wins, one loss and two draws for 15 points, Zbyszko's team in second with a 5-4-1 record and 11 points and Slaughter's team with 5-5-1 and 11 points. Of course, that's all bogus because how can there be three teams and none have a losing record?

Miguelito Perez won the Caribbean title from Rip Rogers on 11/4 in Bayamon. The Universal title was held up between Carlitos Colon and Steve Strong (DiSalvo) and it was settled on 11/23 in Bayamon with either Colon retiring or Strong leaving town and Colon captured the title in Strong's last night in. Koko B. Ware worked here while he was gone from the WWF. Harley Race is also working here. It is said that Tully Blanchard will work here a little bit until everything with the NWA gets smoothed over although there is no guarantee he'll be going to the NWA. Just that everyone expects that when everything cools down, that is where he'll wind up being.

Bam Bam Bigelow and Larry Sharpe have met on a settlement as Sharpe won a judgement against Bigelow some time back over non getting his percentage of Bigelow's earnings as part of the deal when Sharpe trained Bigelow for free.

An indie show in Gloucester, NJ with Sharpe vs. Nikolai Volkoff did a $10,000 house.

Georgia All-Star Wrestling is doing a show in Marietta, GA on 12/10 with Ken Patera, Kimala, Junkyard Dog and others as a TV taping.

ESPN won't be airing any AWA tapes during the month of December. Expect some changes when the contract comes up for renewal early next year which could put another nail in the coffin.

Emilio Charles beat El Dandy for the Mexican version of the World middleweight title on 12/2 in Mexico City.

Expect lots of indie shows in California in January when the commission no longer regulates wrestling.

Rob Russen ran a show on 12/2 in Manatee, FL drawing 890 which included Nikita Koloff going to a deathly 20 minute draw with Ron Bass, The Fantastics (Rogers & Fulton) beating "The New Midnight Express" (Dennis Condrey & Doug Gilbert) when Paul E. Dangerously tried to interfere but was stopped by Diamond Dallas Page and the phone fell in and Rogers hit Gilbert with the phone for the pin, Steve Keirn beat Ron Slinker and Junkyard Dog beat Jerry Lawler via DQ in a match which had no action at all, it was simply Lawler doing a long interview over the house mic. Dangerously was brought down as ref. Early in the show they did a Danger Zone with Dangerously and Page which ended up with Page attacking Dangerously but

getting ambushed by Condrey & Gilbert.

Billy Jack Haynes showed up in Portland on 12/2. Now to me, that's one of the biggest shocks of the year.

Mr. Pogo, Bob Orton, Doug Gilbert and Tom Prichard booked for upcoming ICW tapings; Orton was turned face on TV. Joe Savoldi quit the promotion which says something when it's his brother, Mario Savoldi, that runs the promotion. . .

Bruno Sammartino was speaking over the weekend in Slippery Rock College against steroids. Sammartino's son Darryl Sammartino throws the javelin at the school.

Windy City Wrestling drew 325 in Berwyn, IL on 11/11 and 500 in Chicago on 11/12 for shows which included Jim Brunzell, Col. DeBeers, Rich Lupkes (who beat Scott Norton in arm wrestling and is a real World champion in that sport. Buddy Roberts and Bob Luce are also doing indie shows in the Chicago area and are said to have put together the worst TV tape anyone has ever seen.

Bob Geigel's Thanksgiving show in Kansas City drew 328 and included Ric McCord, Rufus Jones, Bobby Jaggers, Akio Sato, Curtis Hughes, Steve Ray. Main event saw WWA champ Mike George beat Bulldog Bob Brown via DQ. Geigel is doing a show on 12/28 with Larry Zbyszko vs. either George or Harley Race as the main event.

A correction to a question in the letters page – well, really an update. Al Costello sold his home in Detroit just a few weeks back and is now living in St. Petersburg.

Western States Wrestling ran 12/1 in Riverside before 100 using Tim Tall Tree (John Renesto, about 160 pounds but stole the show), Billy Anderson, The Mercenary (Louie Spicoli), Tim Patterson and Bobby Bradley who won the Americas title from Black Steel in the main event.

12/22 in Bloomington, MN has Ken Patera & Steve O vs. The Terminators managed by Sheik Kaissey, Nord the Barbarian vs. Kevin Kelly plus Kenny Jay underneath.

NWA

They did tapings on 11/28 at Center Stage for the next two weeks on TBS. The show that airs 12/9 is headlined by Ric Flair's surprise for Gary Hart, which turned out to be Ole & Arn Anderson.

It got a big pop live, but whether cards with the double feature of Flair & Andersons vs. Muta & Buzz Sawyer & Dragon Master (Kazuo Sakurada) and Sting vs. Luger will do any business at all is questionable.

The Midnight Express announced they would work three times and give any jobber team $5,000 if they could last five minutes. They beat the first two teams, then the third team of Bruce Wayne & Dick Grayson came out and it was the Dudes under the masks and they beat the Midnights in 20 seconds.

Danny Davis worked under a hood as The Galaxian and lost to Tom Zenk.

Kendall Windham returned as a heel, even lighter than before, and interfered in the Mike Rotunda vs. Tommy Rich match.

They are now doing a bit where Norman has a crush on Woman and takes photos of her at ringside.

On the 12/16 show was the debut of Cactus Jack Manson (this may not air as it was a try-out match) as a jobber with Rick Fargo against the Steiners and after Fargo got beat, Manson attacked him. All the interviews were backstage so no talk about Starrcade, which would be over, in front of the fans. Norman beat Cuban and Zenk beat Samoan Savage via DQ. Teddy Long has put up a $350 bounty on Norman.

Flair is now chairman of the booking committee but not "the booker" anymore. Basically a way to strip him of power without stripping him of position.

Why do they keep saying the Steiners are the first brother team to be tag champs since the Andersons? Jack & Jerry Brisco held the title more recently than the Andersons.

TV ratings set another new high last week. World Championship Wrestling on 11/25 drew a 3.1 rating with Flair vs. Muta on top. That rating was the highest WCW has done going back well over one year. Even more impressive is the rating was achieved going head to head with the Miami-Notre Dame college football game which was the highest rated college game in two seasons. NWA Main Event (Luger vs. Pillman) also did a 3.1 while Power Hour with the Flair vs. Mike Rotunda replay on top did a 2.5. Over the past weekend the NWA cable shows outranked the WWF cable shows by a full three points.

11/30 in Meridian, MS drew a sellout 2,100 as Cuban Assassin pinned Danny Davis ***, Iron Sheik beat Alex Porteau DUD, Hawk beat Dan Spivey via DQ **¾, Dudes beat Midnight when Cornette accidentally hit Eaton with the racquet **** and Sting double count out with Luger ***¾.

Others during the week weren't so hot. Memphis was said to have drawn terribly on Friday, TV in Pensacola on Monday drew 1,100 and Columbus, GA on 11/30 drew 1,900.

11/25 in Philadelphia drew 1,400 as Tom Zenk beat Michael Hayes, Animal beat Spivey via DQ, three Samoans beat Ranger Ross & Tommy Rich & Eddie Gilbert, Midnight beat Dudes, Steiners beat Doom, Sting double count out with Luger and Flair beat Muta via DQ.

Correction on Flair-Eaton TV match. They didn't leave Flair laying. Flair got up after being hit with the leg drop off the top rope after Cornette's interference caused a DQ, then ducked the racquet and Cornette hit Eaton with the racquet. Match went 13 minutes and Eaton was really "up" for it bumping like crazy. Both guys sold great, and sold the holds great, but until they are "educated" (which takes time, may not even catch on, but you can't complain about the process

because it has to start in so-called big matches) to those leg holds, right now it makes the match not seem so not. Well, that portion of the match, anyway, because it was at least 3 ½ stars in any book for the stiffness of the work and the hot bumps by Eaton, who trimmed down some 35 pounds mainly for the match and the heel turn.

Midnight-Dudes on TV Saturday was a blistering pace but Dudes' timing is off when the pace is that hot. Johnny Ace always seems a step behind.

WWF

Quote of the week: Hillbilly Jim, after the 11/25 Hart Foundation vs. Rockers tag match in Madison Square Garden: "What a match, Gorilla, How long did they go? 30, 45 minutes?" Gorilla: "The match had a 20 minute time limit." Hillbilly: "Well, that was the fastest 20 minutes I've ever seen. What a match, Gorilla." Actually, it was about 3 ¾ or so. Best match in MSG in several months. . .

Oakland on 11/26 was a disaster. WWF had run Fresno earlier that day (drawing 3,000 fans--main event saw Warrior beat Mr. Perfect) and had 6,000 in attendance in Oakland--but no wrestlers. Fresno to Oakland is a 3 ½ hour trip no matter how you slice it, but holiday traffic and making the guys drive it saw none of the guys there when the card started. After sending out a jobber match, sending Warrior (who did make it somehow--must have been allowed to fly) vs. Andre (who wasn't in Fresno) for nearly 30 minutes (of what was said to be the worst match of all-time), a 45 minute intermission, a Battle Royal with local guys, an attempt at a Bobby Heenan interview segment which went over really bad, they finally canceled the rest of the show and offered either refunds or allowed you to use your stub for the 11/28 show in San Francisco. Right after the announcement, then seven guys showed up.

SF drew 7,000, but 4,000 of them were from the show two nights earlier getting in free.

Jake Roberts is working on a broken foot.

With the exception of Hart Foundation vs. Rockers, the last MSG show was every bit as bad as the one the previous month. Hercules vs. Bravo rivalled Hercules vs. Akeem in the worst match category.

Prime Time Wrestling did a 3.0 on 12/27 while All American did a 2.4 the previous day.

That Rick Martel as "The Model" stuff is so bad that it's good.

11/24 in Sacramento drew 3,500 as Canadian Earthquake (John Tenta) beat Barry Horowitz, Mr. Perfect pinned Jimmy Snuka, Koko B. Ware pinned Jerry Monti, Martel pinned Brutus Beefcake, The Genius pinned Sam Houston, Roddy Piper beat Rick Rude via DQ when Mr. Perfect interfered and Demolition beat Powers of Pain via DQ.

11/27 in Daytona Beach drew 5,100 as Haku pinned Paul Roma **, Bravo pinned Hercules - **, Warrior beat Andre in 20 seconds DUD, Rockers drew Hart Foundation **** ¼ , Al Perez beat Brooklyn Brawler DUD, Tito Santana beat Bad News Brown via DQ * and Jim Duggan beat Randy Savage via count out ½ *.

12/3 in Miami drew 2,900 as Roma beat Horowitz (good), Tugboat Thomas beat Conquistador (real bad), Savage pinned Duggan (negative stars), Bret Hart beat Honky Tonk Man, Snuka pinned Bad News Brown, Piper beat Rude via DQ and Andre & Haku beat Demolition via DQ (horrible).

12/2 in Daytona Beach drew 4,800 as Roma beat Horowitz ½ *, Snuka pinned Brown DUD, Andre & Haku beat Demolition via count out * (for Heenan, dud for match), Hart pinned Honky Tonk Man DUD, Tugboat beat Conquistador -*, Savage pinned Duggan ½ * and Piper beat Rude via DQ *.

Duggan vs. Bossman added to the Royal Rumble undercard. Rockers and Powers of Pain will be in Rumble so won't work underneath.

Tony Schiavone back on TV this week.

Late word: Talk of Dan Spivey & Nitron as Skyscrapers in Starrcade. Sid even more doubtful for the show than before.

THE READERS' PAGES

CWA

The CWA is such a small promotion that it has received very little mention on the letters page. It is dying quickly in terms of crowd appeal, talent and money. One could write this off as merely the result of the monster promotions and a lack of talent in the small promotions. But I disagree. During the past year both Sid Vicious and Scott Steiner were in the CWA, didn't get a big push, yet proved to be quite marketable in the NWA. The Rock & Roll Express, Bill Dundee, Master of Pain, Dutch Mantell, Dustin Rhodes and Jeff Jarrett are there now, and all have considerable talent and local name recognition. My feeling is that these are the problems:

1) Inflexibility. When Jerry Jarrett took over World Class, there was the feeling that he was going to have a larger talent pool. Instead, it seems like he has less talent. Some of the more prominent World Class wrestlers (Michael Hayes, Samoan Swat Team, Al Perez) departed. Instead of pooling his talent and running fewer shows in each city but better shows, Jarrett continued to run every show he could and weekly shows here. The difficulty of maintaining fan interest by having to run new angles weekly with so few personalities is now too much.

2) Scuzz-appeal. I can take my seven-year-old to a WWF card, but not to a CWA card. Obscene gestures, cursing and inappropriate behavior are the rules at CWA cards. Even a recent attempt at sanitizing fan behavior and banning cursing from the crowd was ruined by Brickhouse Brown grabbing the house mic and shouting, "Get those sons of

bitches back here. I want to kick their asses." Jerry Lawler typically kicks his larger opponents in the groin and looks to the crowd for approval. Mark Starr would frequently mouth obscenities to the disapproving crowd to get heat.

Jarrett has made no attempt in the last nine years, apart from his TV, to appeal to the mainstream fan. No attempt at public relations. No anti-drug messages. No visits to schools to encourage achievement. The only attempts to increase crowds are limited to lowering ticket prices, which is something known only to those who pay attention to the TV show.

3) Champ or Chump. Jerry Lawler became the unified champ and potentially the CWA had a great opportunity to encourage recognition of its and Lawler's credibility. Instead, Lawler rarely acts like a champ. Whereas Hogan usually pins his opponents and now so does Flair, Lawler only pins jobbers on television. Lawler's arena matches usually either see him lose in non-title matches or have fluke DQ endings. CWA fans have been denied the chance to boast that Lawler could stand up to Hogan, Flair or any other top performer. Lawler's house show matches are also filled mainly with either stalling or comments into the mic. Punches have become his only maneuver in the ring. It even appears that Hogan is a better worker.

4) No finishes. Major matches rarely have a finish with a pinfall or submission. In fact, submission holds are unknown in the CWA. Run-ins, foreign objects and manager interference are all a part of wrestling entertainment, but they dominate not only the main events, but even the undercard matches. Talking to fans going home after a house show indicates that they feel ripped off at these finishes.

In my opinion, the CWA must either change or die. Pay days are so poor now that they can't keep the talent that they have. While no longer major league, the CWA has even recently been both an entertaining and credible promotion. As a Louisville resident, I hope the changes are made so they remain in business for a long time.

Bob Brenan
Louisville, Kentucky

HALL OF FAME

Don't you remember Slammers Wrestling Gym houses the World Wrestling Museum and Hall of Fame? It starts with the Gorgeous George Private Collection, through to the Pro Wrestling Photo gallery. Starting with our opening awards ceremony on Sept. 22, Slammers gives out the Legends of Wrestling award. Next year, Terry Funk will be inducted. Actually this was determined long before the Clash, as you wrote, he has long since earned his spot.

For the record, the inductees so far have been Gorgeous George, John Tolos, Mike and Ben Sharpe, Vic Christy, Mike Mazurki, Maria Bernardi, Art Abrams, Gene LeBelle, Shirley

Montgomery, Mae Young and Lillian Ellison (Moolah).

Verne Langdon
Slammers Wrestling Gym
Sun Valley, California

How about starting up a Wrestling Observer Hall of Fame with this upcoming yearbook? Each year a wrestler would be elected and nominated by readers. A profile on his life and wrestling career would appear in the yearbook each year. I'd nominate Terry Funk as the first member.

Pat Higgins
Culver City, California

USELESS TRIVIA
Some useless information:

It's a little bit after the fact at this point, but people might like to know that Terry Funk's entrance music was the theme to Sergio Leone's "Once Upon a Time in the West," a great 1968 Western.

Kevin Sullivan is actually from Cambridge, Massachusetts, not from Boston.

Does Jason Hervey subscribe? I interviewed him in 1988 and at the time he had never heard of the observer or any newsletters for that matter.

Paul Sherman
Brookline, Massachusetts

Dave Meltzer: Jason Hervey doesn't subscribe to the Observer, but he does know about it as we met and talked about it after the Baltimore PPV show.

NWA
Don't you think Bobby Heenan's ratings during the second and third falls of the Brain Busters WWF swan song were a bit overdone? It was obvious to me that this was intended to be a very strong warning to other Titan wrestlers who had entertained thoughts of leaving. While I don't know if it will have its desired effect, it also could backfire and cause some good wrestlers to think twice before going to Titan.

Didn't the NWA brass miss a great chance to blow the WWF's ship right out of the water on the whole issue? Imagine if back in October Gordon Solie would have announced on his news spot that the WWF World tag team champions have given notice that they are quitting and returning to the NWA. Vince would have been caught. Everything he would have done over the next two months to buy Tully and Arn wouldn't have worked since it would have been taken with a large grain of salt because many fans would know what it was all about. The whole wrestling world would have known the Busters had quit the WWF and they were tag champs when they did, not the way it looks to the fans today. If you are going to have a wrestling news spot, you may as well use it to your complete advantage.

Is there any chance Eddie Gilbert may be kept around for another year? What are the chances of the NWA using some of the Mexican and Japanese wrestlers and creating a lighter weight division?

Chris Zavisa
Plymouth, Michigan

Dave Meltzer: I think that Gilbert will be given the opportunity to stay around. Whether they'll renew his contract for the same money is something else. That I doubt, but if they come up with a role for him or a role for Missy Hyatt, then there would be a chance. Right now I'd say there is no chance of the NWA creating a lighter weight division and using Mexican or Japanese stars in it. There has been talk of reviving a junior heavyweight division, but never to the point of it being seriously considered as anything more than it used to be with Les Thronton or Nelson Royal.

With the NWA returning to Buffalo next week, it looks like they are doing another great job of keeping the show one big secret again. Actually, you don't notice just how poor a job of promoting the NWA does until you watch them promote shows when Titan has a same show in the market at the same time.

In the last two weeks, the only promos I've seen are two spots that do nothing but quickly list the matches. The Joe Pedicino segments have been promoting Clash IX, and now Starrcade. Those are important of course, but wasn't that segment supposed to be the NWA's answer to the WWF's Events Center? I won't even get into how the two compare.

Why on the NWA big shows does Jim Ross talk about how Mike Rotunda represented Buffalo in the NFL's Punt, Pass and Kick contest and how Brian Pillman played with the Bills. The Bills are big news in Buffalo, so wouldn't it not be good business to promote these facts to their advantage in Buffalo. Green Bay quarterback Don Mankowski is a native of Western New York. Whenever the media here talks about the Packers, they are quick to harp on that fact that he's a local player who has gone onto success. I bring this up because the man who the NWA wants to be its top star of the 90's is a native of Orchard Park, NY. When the NWA came to town the first time, this point was never brought up. Yet during Lex Luger's match on the card, you could hear chants of "Larry, Larry, Larry," from the crowd.

In closing, I'd like to act like a real mark for a second. If the NWA would spend less time in-fighting and instead devoted time and energy to improving the promotion of local shows, then when they take those big steps forward, they wouldn't be followed by lots of little steps backwards.

Charles Hodgkisson
Toronto, Ontario

In July, I wrote to you about the poor quality of the

concession items at the NWA shows. A few weeks later you made note of it and said that you would be embarrassed to purchase such items for friends. Well, as bad as they were then, they are worse now. The only two T-shirts sold at the last St. Louis card were of Sting and Ric Flair, with awful renderings of their likeness. Actually, the Flair shirt looked exactly like Terry Taylor. Maybe they could save some money by hiring him. They did have some excellent posters of Tom Zenk, Woman, the Road Warriors and Skyscrapers.

Another item is promotion on the day of the event. The day of the last St. Louis card, I picked up both the Post-Dispatch and the Sun. Neither paper had an ad for the card, or even a mention of the card in listings in either the sports or entertainment section of the paper. Oddly enough, I did find an ad for the WWF show that was going to take place the next week at the Arena.

Not that this is a scientific method of measuring, but I scanned the St. Louis radio stations as much as possible during my trip down and listened regularly during the week and never heard an ad or a mention of the card. Titan runs light about two weeks in advance of the show and heavy the last week on radio here.

Not actually living in St. Louis, I don't want to say they did a bad job of promoting outside of TBS (and most likely their local KDNL which I don't get here) but it doesn't seem like they are covering all their bases. It's not a complicated procedure and seems like very basic promotion. It's going to be extremely difficult for the NWA to get over to the mainstream without the simplest efforts that make such things successful.

Chris Martin
Springfield, Missouri

BLANCHARD

The NWA has hired cannibals, butchers, assassins, people who mug opponents in the parking lot, people who hit people with branding irons and baseball bats, people who brag about killing other wrestlers, guys who brag about having sex with every good looking women in the world and guys with bodies built from frequent trips to the pharmacy. Every kind of violent pervert has been on an NWA TV show. So now they worry about hiring a wrestler who has failed a drug test. Who cares? Nobody but those who read the sheets would ever know about it.

Ric Flair doesn't draw as champ even though he's the greatest wrestler in the world and has the best matches because he's been seen over-and-over again hitting Nikita Koloff, Sting, Lex Luger, Dusty Rhodes, Hawk and Animal with his super chops and they don't sell a thing. Not only did they not sell his best move, but they mainly chased him around for 30 minutes until there was a DQ or a stupid finish. Flair doesn't draw because he lost his title to Kerry Von Erich, Ron Garvin, Rhodes and Ricky Steamboat, lost

many rematches to them and after winning the title back, it seems to marks that he never gave them rematches. While he wasn't champ this year, he lost to Sting and Luger and never gave them title matches when he came back. He doesn't draw because we marks can turn on ESPN any afternoon and watch him sell for every turkey on World Class Wrestling and watch him one million times lose to Kerry Von Erich.

Are we supposed to forget all of this and still accept him as the greatest wrestler in the world?

The NWA has misused Flair and misused the World title for years. You can't overcome those mistakes. To smart fans, Flair's past doesn't mean anything because they know wins and losses don't mean anything and that the guy is great. But to a mark, a wrestler isn't the same after you've seen him lose again and again. If Hulk Hogan were to have been beaten as many times as Flair, his following would have long since disappeared. Flair's been beaten by everyone, even Ricky Morton, for years.

My point is, make Lex Luger the champ. It's the only way to go. Keep Ric Flair strong, but let Lex Luger be champ. Luger should be made superior to everyone, just like Hulk Hogan. A fan should know that when he pays to see Luger, the champ is going to win clean or lose clean. Some people will cheer him, but he should remain an egotistical heel. Don't worry if they cheer him and boo his opponent as long as they buy tickets to see him.

I gave Clash a big thumbs up, Survivors a smaller thumbs up (but the previous two were a lot better) and the SNME was terrible. This past Saturday I found at least a few picks for the worst match of the year.

Steve Yohe
Alhambra, California

December 18, 1989

Since you will all be reading this after Starrcade '89 has taken place, and this is being written several days before, my comments obviously won't be reflective upon whatever happened that night.

Whether this tournament concept for Starrcade is a good or bad idea from a business standpoint should be answered when the PPV figures come in. Since the TV ratings are the highest they've been in a long time, more people know about the show than for any PPV this year. The show has been well advertised through the cable medium, not only on the wrestling shows but I've seen ads for Starrcade On CNN and on other cable channels. While certain specifics should have been better publicized, for example, nobody ever answered the question of how one goes about winning the thing, the general idea of what matches and what is going to take place seems to have been hyped well.

Whether the public will buy a PPV event without specific personal issues is the question that will be answered . If this show does decent business, it's probably a decent idea to make it an annual thing. Running a gimmick PPV allows your specific angles to be geared toward the house shows Without the duplication of PPV and house show cards which makes the house show cards appear meaningless. If the show doesn't do as well as the NWA's two most recent PPV events (both hyped on shows which didn't have nearly as many viewers), then the NWA should stick to specific personal issues on its PPV events for the time being. The WWF has twice tried tournaments on PPV. The first one was back in 1985 in Chicago, which was one of their better overall PPV shows, but was a financial disappointment. The second was WrestleMania IV, which was an aesthetic disaster and didn't do nearly the business it figured to do, but it's hard to call a record-setting show a financial flop. But I bet it is a long time before we see a tournament on a WWF PPV show. The NWA audience is somewhat different, and because the tournaments didn't really work on the WWF cards doesn't mean they won't work or will work. But the buy rate should answer the question.

The only other comment I've got about the show is that I was disappointed in the NWA the way they've handled the Sid Vicious injury. They had several weeks to come up with some excuse, even if they didn't want to say Vicious was injured (one can argue legitimately that saying he's hurt would detract from his superhuman aura, and without that aura he's got absolutely nothing), or at least somehow

announce the Samoans as being on the card. It's only true in advertising. The way they handled it was a real Verne Gagne way to promote things. They knew full well when the television shows that aired this past weekend were taped that Vicious wouldn't be a part of the card, but continued to hype and advertise himanyway. Of course this is no different from what the WWF did at Survivor Series.

What could potentially turn into a major story was released two weeks back when Titan Sports publicly said that it wouldn't distribute its PPV events in the future, starting with the Royal Rumble in January, through Viewer's Choice and Request and will instead offer the events directly to the cable companies. This had been in the works for almost a year, and is a repeat of what Titan tried to do last year before WrestleMania V but had to back out of it because cable companies, standing behind Viewer's Choice, got the NWA to agree to do a PPV head-up with WrestleMania and the vast majority of systems weren't going to carry WrestleMania. When Titan backed down and went with Viewer's Choice, these same companies then asked the NWA to cancel its PPV event and the NWA instead ran the New Orleans Clash of Champions special on TBS instead Of a PPV event that day.

The reason Titan decided to try again to ace Viewer's Choice and Request out of the picture at this time was because the company felt that if it had to sacrifice one PPV event to get the point across that they were doing this, it might as well be the one which would damage them the Least financially since Rumble was the least bought of the four WWF PPV events thus far in 1989. Originally Titan sources felt that Viewer's Choice and Request, which are the middlemen between the promoters and the cable companies and get 10 percent of the gross revenue on these events, would be able to limit Royal Rumble to a potential universe of just two million homes (in comparison, the recent NWA and WWF PPV events have had universes of nearly 12 million homes). However, of late, Titan has expected this universe for Rumble to be closer to five million. It is felt that if they can get away with putting this show on without any backlash (and nobody expects the NWA to get involved this time in an attempt to sabotage a smaller event like Royal Rumble), that faced with the prospect of losing WrestleMania,one of the most profitable PPV events of the year with no competing event on that day, that the majorlty ot the cable universe sign up with Titan and break the stranglehold of Viewer's Choice on the PPV market. The real story if there is one would be if or what Viewer's Choice does in retaliation, and if this gamble fails at the Royal Rumble, where will that leave WrestleMania. But with this smaller universe it would appear that Royal Rumble would need approximately a 2.7 percent buy rate to break even, or more than double (because of the additional universe) what a normal WWF PPV's break-even point would be. Last year's Royal Rumble delivered approximately a 1.5 percent buy rate. If Titan clears less than five million homes for the Rumble, the odds are long that the show can be profitable, in which case they will be putting on the event strictly as a loss leader to attempt to gain additional profits for WrestleMania if they are successful in breaking the stranglehold.

Speaking of PPV, it appears our estimates last week on the Survivor Series buy rate were a tad low. While Titan's claim of a 5.8 percent buy rate for the Thanksgiving show can be dismissed as fiction, KBLCOM Inc. reported a systemwide buy rate of four percent. Since they have a more heavy base in the Northeast (which traditionally does well above the national average for Titan PPV events), that figure is no doubt above what the actual buy rate was, but based on figures here, the number appears to be between a 3.3 and 3.4 percent buy rate, which is significantly up from last years 2.8 percent buy rate for the same show. That would be an estimated 385,000 orders at a suggested price of $18.50 or roughly a PPV gross of $7.12 million On the event (of which Titans share would be about $3.2 million).

The next WWF PPV event will be the No Holds Barred movie and match which airs on 12/27This will be an interesting test of Titans PPV power. They will be charging $11.95 for the right to see a movie which anyone can rent for $2 at any video store (and the movie isn't renting well according to three local stores I've asked) and adding a one-match wrestling card, a cage match with Hulk Hogan & Brutus Beefcake vs. Zeus & Randy Savage. The price tag is less then Titan charges for its normal PPV events, but considered outrageous considering most PPV movies nowadays go for around $6.95 (and those movies generally haven't been released on video at that point). Logically one would say that this one is going to lay an egg, but I'm betting against that. There is simply too much television spending too much time effectively hyping this event for it not to do business. Now you can't sell what people really don't want to see, but this is a match people want to see, and on most WWF house shows and most of its PPV events, what sells the tickets is the main event. This has a main event people went to see, and for a cheaper price than usual.

The next NWA PPV event will be on Feb. 25 in Greensboro headlined by Ric Flair vs. Lex Luger. There has been some talk that this will also be a cage match but officially the card hasn't even been booked.

Don't have details as of yet, but the tournaments in Japan ended this past week. The All Japan tournament ended on 12/6 in Tokyo's Budokan Hall with Stan Hansen & Genichiro Tenryu beating Jumbo Tsuruta & Yoshiaki Yatsu to win the thing when Hansen pinned Yatsu after the lariat. Both teams went into their final tournament match having scored victories over every other team in the tournament setting up this meeting that was scheduled on the final day. What a neat coincidence, huh? Hansen & Tenryu also captured the PWF World tag team titles, which they had vacated going into the tournament. New Japan's singles tournament ended the next night at the Sumo Hall in Tokyo with Riki Choshu pinning Shinya Hashimoto to win using the sleeper hold. Choshu used Tatsumi Fujinami's finisher, which he had never used before, to capture the final match.

A few notes on the Universal Wrestling Federation's card on 11/29 at the Tokyo Dome. The ring magazines in Japan wrote that none of the matches were particularly good. That's pretty much expected since every match but one consisted of a worker vs. a non-worker that was an outstanding performer in a combat sport, but had never worked before. In reality, for these matches to be exciting is almost to ask for a miracle (although Don Nakaya Neilsen, a kickboxer, did prove on three occasions to be a miracle worker). Two of the matches turned into outright shoots. One was the Yoji Anjyo vs. Changpuek Kiatsongrit match (UWF wrestler vs. Welterweight champ of Thai style kickboxing) which went to a draw. Don't know which was the other one other than the UWF guy took a serious beating.

As for box office records. As mentioned previously, the 40,000 tickets in one day (Nov. 5, first day tickets went on sale) and $2.5 million first day sale destroyed all pro wrestling records for one-day advance sale. The crowd of 60,000 (58,000 paid) was the third highest in the history of pro wrestling and the largest ever in Japan. The record, of course, was WrestleMania III at the Pontiac Silverdome which drew 90,817 followed by a Hulk Hogan vs. Paul Orndorff match at Toronto Exhibition Stadium on August 28, 1985 Which drew 69,300. The live gate of about $3.3 million broke the old record of $2.78 million set on April 24th of this year when New Japan booked the same building. The only actual figure I was given as for the gate is a combination of live, closed-circuit (nine locations) and concessions totalled $5.6 million. In comparison, throwing in concessions (which normally aren't figured into this equation), this figure is probably slightly higher than WrestleMania I (which had 138 closed-circuit Locations) and maybe a tad lower than WrestleMania II and obviously far greater than anything the NWA or any other Japanese promotion has ever done for a single show. WrestieManias III through IV grossed more dollars because of PPV. If you take out PPV revenue, WrestleMania III, which was the most successful of all the WWF cards, grossed $6.8 million live and closed-circuit, not including concessions (which should have totalled at least another $1.5 million). WrestleMania IV would have totalled $3.6 million live and closed-circuit, while V did about $4.6 million. Profit-wise, this UWF show certainly did better than the early WrestleManias because expenses of nine closed-circuit theaters is obviously far less than 138, not to mention far less advertising costs and no celebrity Involvement. Because of PPV revenue, these recent WrestleManias grossed far more money than this UWF show. It's hard to ascertain how much more profitable, or if they were more profitable, because there are too many variables we don't know about.

With these kinds of dollar figures mentioned on these big shows indicates the trend pro wrestling is taking going into 1990. This is turning into primarily big show business, whether it be in the United States or in Japan. The nightly live event crowds are down for groups, including WWF, but because Of PPV, the revenue generated from presenting wrestling events should continue to grow next year. I expect both the NWA and WWF to go more and more into hyping one PPV event after another, as has been done in recent months. The WWF will probably cut down on the number of house shows in 1990, but even if crowds continue to fall, they should remain profitable at the houses at least as long as Hulk Hogan is working a semi-regular schedule. While the other headline babyfaces can draw on an irregular basis, only the Ultimate Warrior appears to be able to draw fans on name value alone except for Hogan. WWF cards have always drawn based almost exclusively on the strength of the main event (except in smaller cities where they run infrequently where the crowd is drawn primarily through the novelty of having the major leagues of wrestling coming to your town). Dusty Rhodes has been removed as a headliner, but may get another chance next year. I expect this will be Jim Duggan's last chance as a headliner. Roddy Piper drew well upon his return. but of late, his series with Rick Rude has sputtered at the gate. Even Warrior's drawing power has to have some question marks on it next month with Dino Bravo as the foe. It 's already apparent that the Hulk Hogan vs. Mr. Perfect (Curt Hennig) matches are going to do good business everywhere, as Hogan does no matter who he's against. However, the past two weekends, after the SNME angle aired, have also shown this isn't a strong enough match to draw sellouts in the big cities either, which at one time the name of Hogan alone could do.

For the smaller groups, the prognosis for 1990, is more of the same. Which in reality means less of the same. The decline of regional wrestling promotions has steadily occurred since 1983, and right now, two or three groups appear to be on life support systems and the final plug may be pulled before the weather warms up. The CWF is already history. If ESPN doesn't renew the AWA's contract which expires in February, and it appears that they won't, that could finally be the death knell of a group many have said really has been dead for a few years already. USWA will survive simply because the costs of operation are low and they make money through television syndication and advertising. Whether the CWA, which in many markets Jarrett is pulling in favor of the USWA, survives is more questionable. Portland Wrestling will probably continue as

long as the TV station in Portland continues its tradition of carrying the Saturday night matches on a three-and-a-half hour tape delay that same night. Stampede has lost a lot of wrestlers this year over payoff problems and recent problems between the producers of the TV show and the promotion have made it virtually impossible for the group to gain any ground.

Which brings us to the NWA once again. Christmas week is going to be a big test for the NWA. With Ric Flair vs. Lex Luger a s the headline match in all its major cities, which a year back could draw on a pretty consistent basis (right now, except for Atlanta, none of the cities draw) and what is traditionally one of the two best weeks of the year for the wrestling business, if these shows don't significantly pick up business then TBS had better get the message. The message is, at least until they've somehow changed the public perception of them as the feeder system to the WWF (or Triple-A wrestling). They can't make money promoting house shows. They've proven in recent months that they can get television viewers and they can sell PPV events. But the nightly house show business is in a shambles and if a Flair vs. Luger series can't revitalize it, there is no other match they can promote that will and that facet of the operation should face some sort of restructuring.

For readers On the Rest Coast, my appearance on KCBS radio (740 AM in San Francisco) On Mike Woodley's "Sportsbeat" phone-in show has been moved up to this coming weekend, Dec. 16 at 6 p.m. pacific time. The show can be heard pretty well from British Columbia to San Diego.

Special congratulations to former Sportsbeat host Ted Robinson, now ba ed in Minnesota, who was nominated by the San Jose Mercury News over the weekend for Bay Area Sportscaster Of the decade along with Hank Greenwald, Bill King, Lon Simmons and Wayne Walker, which is some pretty heavy company. Brad Muster was also nominated for Bay Area college football player of the decade by the same newspaper along with John Eiway, Ron Rivera (who also plays for the Chicago Bears) and Mike Perez former San Jose State quarterback).

With kind of a dearth in wrestling news this week, it gives me a chance for a quick update on what's going on in Roller Sports. The syndicated RollerGames show is now airing re-runs. The future of the show is in limbo pending a series of court proceedings by two sides wrestling for control of the company——— David Samms of Samms/Miller, the company which put together the new concept and sold the syndicated package to so many stations, and Qintex, the recently bankrupted Australian-firm which has now decided it wants control of the show. Bill Griffiths, the long-time Roller Sports promoter is in the Qintex camp as Griffiths and Samms have gotten along like Vince McMahon and Verne Gagne would from the very start of this thing. There will be a court ruling on Tuesday to decide about the current injunction which prevents Samms from having anything to do with the show. Samms himself also has a restraining order out on Griffiths to prevent him from taking the RollerGames on a national tour. The syndicated ratings have fallen steadily from the first week, and are nowhere near what Samms had promised the stations he'd be able to deliver, but they are still considered decent ratings in most markets. The next ten weeks of reruns should be a real test of the show's following. Most of the stations that signed up for the show signed up for 26 weeks. Whether the show will continue or not depends upon who winds up with control when the legal hassles are over, if that group then gets the financial backing to continue taping new shows (apparently Qintex now wants to stay involved with the group, provided Samms is out—— Samms claims he has new investors for his own group and a recent TV Guide article which largely praised him as a Vince McMahon clone did nothing to hurt his attempts in that veneer) and if enough stations will renew. Either way, it appears Samms will be out as TV announcer and that some of the ideas like the alligator pits and celebrity with the rock bands will be history because the former never made any sense to stare with (but those close to the RoilerGames maintain the alligators were a key factor in getting such a strong syndicated line-up) and the latter as a cost-cutting measure. If Qintex gains control, they will attempt to send the Roller Games on the road (provided someone else puts up the money for the tour) and all the glitz will be removed. Chet Forte, the former producer Of ABC's Monday Night Football, would be retained. They would tentatively tape another 13 weeks worth of shows in mid-January.

Another group, headed by Patrick Schaffer, which taped a pilot show similar to the old Los Angeles Roller Games of the early 1970s is taping some more pilots in this area on Jan. 23 and 24 at the San Jose Civic Auditorium and Jan. 26 and 27 at the Alameda County Fairgrounds in Pleasanton. My guess is these tapings will be scrapped as Schaffer can't line up enough of a syndicated line-up at the NATPE convention in early January. A complete failure by the Roller Games would be bad news for Schaeffer's outfit because it's unlikely television stations would be quick to try a Roller Derby Like show so shortly after a failure of the same gimmick.

SOUTH KOREA

Munhwa Broadcasting Company, one of the television networks in Korea, aired a pro wrestling show on 11/25, which featured several of the wrestlers that work for the Frontier Martial Arts and Wrestling promotion in Japan. The Only North American grappler that appeared on the show was Jos LeDuc, who started the show ranting and raving a few expressions in Korean and saying that he ran

Kintaro Oki out of the wrestling business. Kintaro Oki is the most famous wrestling name in Korea, but the problem LeDuc made is that in Korea, he's known as Kim III (and after his retirement from wrestling became a key political figure in South Korea because of his wrestling popularity) so nobody knew what he was talking about. Ultra Seven (Masahiko Takasugi, a former Japan prelim wrestler) worked in the opener teaming with Wakitahiro Hito (who I believe works for FMW as Monkey Man Wakita) and beat two Koreans. Then Korean Bak Yoo Gun beat Japanese kickboxer Seiji Aoyangi (the one who feuded with Onita of late) while Masanobu Kurusu (a former prelim wrestler for both All and New Japan) beat Dennis Ray Kennet of the U.S. (I believe he is working in Japan for FMW right now as Crusher Dennis, don't know what name or if he's worked in the U.S.). Atsushi Onita went to a double count out with a Korean wrestler and after the match Onita laid the Korean wrestler out with a piledriver on the floor onto a chair . The main event saw LeDuc team with Hoagie Wooing losing to a Korean team of Yi Byohg Pil & Yok Bal San (Riki Bassan in Japan, original Strong Machine #2 of 1984 fame) flying all over the ring when LeDuc did the job.

USSR

The line-up for the New Years Eve card at the 9,400 seat Soviet Coliseum was announced this past week. The card will be televised to Japan on Jan. 6 in TV-Asahi, so the original plan to closed-circuit this event has been dropped. The main event will be Antonio Inoki & Shota Chochyashivili (1972 Olympic gold medalist in judo) vs. Brad Rheingans & Masa Saito, Vladimir Berkovich vs. Bam Bam Bigelow, Jushin Liger vs. Black Tiger, Riki Choshu vs. Victor Zangiev, Salman Hashimikov vs. Manny Fernandez, Shinya Hashimoto vs. Andrei Sulsaev, Takayuki Iizuka vs Kuniaki Kobayashi, Masa Chono vs. Wahka Eveloev and Hiroshi Hase vs. Habieli Victashev in a sambo match. Typical main event booked for ego. Since Chochyashivili is the only one of the Soviets that was an Olympic gold medalist, they used him in the main event even though he's the least developed of all the Soviets who have worked in New Japan this year. Inoki was put in the main event because he booked the show. Rheingans was there because he's an American who competed in the Olympic games and Saito is there to carry the other three since he's about the only guy good enough to cover for the other three .

NEW JAPAN

New Japan has Korauken Hall booked on 1/5 and 1/6 but won't be using any foreign wrestlers on that show. The foreign wrestlers will appear from 1/11 through 1/31 with Big Van Vader, Owen Hart, Kokina the Samoan, Steve Armstrong, Tracy Smothers, Black Tiger and Biff Wellington booked for the three week tour.

ALL JAPAN

Only thing I've got from here are results of a television taping on 11/29 in Sapporo before a sellout 4,800 fans as Stan Hansen & Genichiro Tenryu downed Rusher Kimura & Giant Baba in 20:22 when Tenryu pinned Baba which is the first time Baba has ever done a job for a Japanese wrestler so this was fairly major news, Jumbo Tsuruta & Yoshiaki Yatsu beet Dan Kroffat & Doug Furnas in 18:04, Dynamite Kid & Davey Boy Smith beet Tiger Jeet Singh & Abdullah the Butcher when Smith pinned Butcher in 8:23, plus Kabuki Shunji Takano beat The Foot Loose in 17:02, Terry Gordy & Bill Irwin beat Shinichi Nakano & Isao Takagi, Nasty Boys beat Akira Taue & Kenta Kobashi, Masa Fuchi beat Yoshinari Ogawa, Mighty Inoue beat Richard Slinger and prelims.

FMW

This group started its first actual tour on 11/29 in Osaka before 1,500 fans as Atsushi Onita beat Mitsuhiro Matsunaga with a power bomb, Dick Murdoch pinned Crusher Dennis in a chain match, Tarzan Goto beat Jos LeDuc via forfeit when LeDuc no-showed claiming a stomach ache and several prelim matches including a couple of Women's matches which would be a rare occasion in Japan where men and women appear on the same card.

SOME U.S. NOTES

The Orlando newspaper did a story last week about former pro wrestler Ed "The Bull" Gantner, who started out at about the same time as Lex Luger in Florida. Gantner disappeared from the wrestling scene in 1987 due to kidney problems, which can be traced to problems from childhood. When he disappeared the word in wrestling was that he nearly died due to kidney problems related to steroid usage. Last August both his kidneys shut down and he was close to death several times and was kept alive for more than a year being constantly hooked up to dialysis machines. Finally his older sister donated a kidney when doctors told him he had two months left to live.

Former pro wrestler Cocoa Samoa was arrested last week after being identified as the enforcer for an alleged cocaine and heroin ring in the Portland area. Samoa, whose real name is Ulualogaiga Emilio, 45, was arrested on charges of drug conspiracy after being arrested in Honolulu. Samoa was being held without bail after police testified that he had threatened agents working on the case. Samoa has claimed to be the brother of WWF wrestler Jimmy Snuka and has worked in Japan under the ring name of Jack Snuka.

CWA

Jerry Lawler apparently turned back face, on Monday night in Memphis, but by Saturday, was still firmly implanted on the heel side.

The 12/4 card in Memphis drew 1,800 fans, which is the largest crowd in a while, with the main event of Lawler & Soul Taker against Master of Pain & Dutch Mantell ending with no decision. Master of Pain turned on Mantell and he, Soul Taker and Brian Lee all jumped Mantell until Lawler finally made the save for Mantell and wound up getting tripled on as well and both were left laying in the ring. On television this past Saturday, it was announced that the main event for 12/11 would be Lawler & Mantell against MOP & Soul Taker, however Lawler on television said that he hated Mantell and wanted nothing to do with the match and said he wouldn't wrestle. Finally Bill Dundee stepped in to be Mantell's partner for the Memphis matches while Lawler agreed to defend his USWA title against Ricky Morton on the same card. Lawler still acts like a complete face on his local "Jerry Lawler show" talk show on Sunday mornings, even though he's a heel on the wrestling show the day before.

Billy Travis is headed back as a heel, probably just for a few shots while Dustin Rhodes is also coming back in.

Also on 12/4, Ricky & Todd Morton won a four-team elimination match over King Cobra & Frankie Lancaster, New York Brawler (Lou Fabbiano) & Mike Davis and Brian Lee & The Grappler (Kevin Dillinger). Lee turned on Grappler after he had dropped the fall. Also Mortons beat Davis &n Brawler, Chris Champion beat Dirty White Boy, Cobra beat Grappler and Lee beat Lancaster.

The remainder of the 12/11 card will have Dundee vs. Lee for the CWA title (good shot at a title change), Champion vs. Dirty White Boy in a first blood match, Mortons vs. Billion Dollar Babies and Lancaster vs. Louie Spicoli.

USWA

Chris Adams and Eric Embry finally had their split-up on 12/8 in Dallas. The main event was Adams & Embry & Bill Dundee against Gary Young & Billy Joe Travis & Scandor Akbar and Adams kept getting worked over for nearly 15 minutes and continually tossed over the top rope behind the refs back. Whenever he would get tossed over, Embry would throw back in the ring. Finally Toni Adams at ringside told Eric to stop and throw in the towel but instead Embry shoved down Toni Adams. Chris Adams then jumped Embry and they went at it. The fans at the Sportatorium, at least the vast majority, cheered Embry even though they were supposed to be cheering Adams. On television the next night, both guys acted like faces when they did their interviews for the Embry vs. Adams main event on 12/15. Adams said he had to win the match to defend his wife's honor while Embry said he had to win the match to defend the honor of his "family" (the Dallas fans). In other matches On Friday, Robert Fuller & Brian Lee kept the USWA tag team titles beating Matt Borne & Jeff Jarrett when Travis interfered and hit Jarrett with guitar,

The Medicine Man (Chris Youngblood) debuted as a heel beating Steve Williams, Kevin Von Erich beat: P. Y. Chu Hi via DQ and Chico Torres pinned Tojo Yamamoto.

On the 12/9 TV show, Akbar tried to get Torres to sign with him but Torres turned him down and now Akbar is claiming he has to teach Torres a Lesson.

12/15 in Dalllas has Embry vs. Adams, Jerry Lawler vs. Kerry Von Erich with both the USWA and Texas titles at stake, Dustin Rhodes vs. Gary Young, Fuller & Lee defending the tag team titles against Jarrett & Borne and Travis vs. Jimmy Jack Funk.

Even with kids free on 12/8, the Sportatorium crowd was dismal with just a few hundred.

INDEPENDENTS

12/3 in Orlando drew 144 as Jimmy Backlund beat Mike Awesome (who worked under a hood as The Pro on a few NWA tapes that aired over the weekend) ½ *, Lou Perez & Tommy Rogers (of Fantastics fame) beat Bounty Hunters via DQ *½ , Awesome beat Grizzly Bear Ray - ****, Steve Keirn beat Ron Slinker to keep the Florida title * and Mike Graham & Bugsy McGraw beat Blackjack Mulligan Jumbo Barretta in a bunkhouse match * ¾ .

No more PWF wrestling in Orlando as they lost their television slot.

George Michael Sports Machine will be doing a feature sometime in the next month or two on Japanese sumo wrestler turned wrestler Koji Kitao.

An independent show on 12/1 at the Sam Houston Coliseum included Shotgun Danny Gage, Kevin Von Erich (this was the same night as the USWA tag team tournament in Dallas where he no-showed), Jeff Gaylord, Scott Casey, Tug Taylor, Tiger Conway Jr., Junkyard Dog, Chavo Guerrero and the main event had Ricky Morton & Robert Gibson beating John Tatum & Johnny Manteli via DQ.

Interesting that many of the guys who appeared, work for Tim Brooks' independent group in Dallas while Kevin Von Erich also worked the show.

Veteran TV jobber Chris Curtis was on the Pat Sajack show on 12/5.

Larry Hamilton is promoting independent shows in Jacksonville, Florida.

Wellington Wheatley and Kevin Kastelle who are based in Minneapolis will be working on the Jan. 16 Card in Tokyo's Budokan Hall.

Wendi Richter quit the AWA after her lawyer sent a note to the AWA trying to get her contract voided with the claim that she's unfit to wrestle any longer because of a bad back.

Candi Divine is now the champ after beating Judy Martin on 12/6 in Toronto before 200 fans in the 10,000 seat Coliseum. Divine was billed against Richter on the card. The main event was scheduled to be Larry Zbyszko vs. Sgt. Slaughter and former area big draw Angelo Mosca was the guest ring announcer.

AWA will be taping 12/16 in Rochester, MN with Mike Enos & Wayne Bloom defending the tag team titles against Paul Diamond & The Trooper (Del Wilkes), Jerry Blackwell vs. Kokina Maximus in a bodyslam challenge, a tag team Battle Royal has the Texas Hangmen, Jonnie Stewart & Doug Somers and Diamond & Tommy Jammer, Trooper vs. Enos with former Minnesota Viking Bob Lurtsema as ref, Zbyszko vs. Unknown Soldier plus also billed are Tokyo Bullets, John Nord, The Top Guns (whomever they may be) and Masa Saito.

Windy City Wrestling on 12/15 in Oak Lawn, IL has Super Maxx (Sam DeCero) & Rich Lupkes vs. Col. DeBeers & Steve Regal on top. They also have a show 12/16 at the Pavek Community Center with DeBeers while on 12/17 at the Vic has Steve Regal vs. Ken patera on top.

Complete results of Rob Russen's show on 12/2 in Palmetto, FL before 890 fans saw Junkyard Dog beat Jerry Lawler via DQ when Lawler hit the ref with a foreign object given to him by Paul E. Dangerously, Steve Keirn kept the Florida title beating Ron Slinker, The Fantastics (Tommy Rogers & Bobby Fulton) beat New Midnight Express (Dennis Condrey & Doug Gilbert with Dangerously in the corner), Nikita Koloff beat Ron Bass via DQ, Mike Graham beat Kendall Windham via count out, Lou Perez beat Hard Rock Rick and Keirn won a Battle Royal.

Billy Jack Haynes returned on 12/2 to Portland.

The Grappler Brian Adams had just beaten Carl Styles & Jeff Warner when Adams used Grappler's loaded boot on Styles.

Haynes then ran in and knocked Grappler out of the ring and started talking with Adams (it was explained to the fans that Adams and Haynes were best friends from way back) and Adams went to hug Haynes, then gave him a belly to belly suplex. Also Bill Francis beat Jonathon Holliday via DQ, Al Madril beat Beetlejuice thanks to help of Holliday and Scotty the Body pinned Steve Doll.

WWF

The NBC Prime Time special will be on Friday, Feb. 23, which just so happens to be two days before the NWA's PPV show from Greensboro is probably purely coincidence since Titan has to take whatever NBC is going to give them when it comes to a prime time slot).

The angle for WrestleMania will be shot there. No word at all on what it will be, although the best bet appears to be Hulk Hogan vs. Ultimate Warrior.

Hogan & Warrior will team up in a few cities in early January against Mr. Perfect (Curt Hennig) & The Genius (Lanny Poffo).

Next Saturday Night Main Event will be taped Jan. 3 in Huntsville, AL for 1/27 air date.

Hulk Hogan made the cover of TV Guide this past week

as one of the 20 biggest television personalities of the decade.

11/25 in Los Angeles drew 9,500 and $134,000 as Canadian Earthquake (John Tenta) pinned Barry Horowitz, Genius pinned Sam Houston, Koko B. Ware pinned The Conquistador (Jose Luis Rivera), Rick Martel pinned Brutus Beefcake, Mr. Perfect pinned Jimmy Snuka, Demolition beat Powers Of Pain and Warrior beat Andre the Giant via DQ. Told all the matches were bad.

Barry Windham continues to miss advertised matches as of this weekend. Two different sources from outside the organization have said that Windham won't be returning, nor is he NWA bound, although WWF officials insist he'll be back after Christmas. We'll have to wait and see.

12/1 in Austin, TX drew 13,500 and $154,000 for the WWF debut in the market. The house, the most impressive WWF house in a while (Survivor Series was a bigger house on Thanksgiving, but it was also expected while this was a pleasant surprise since house show business by and large has been off) was drawn for a combination of the WWF's debut, Hogan's debut and the return of Dusty Rhodes who grew up in Austin, TX and was the subject of a tremendous amount of local media attention.

Results saw Red Rooster beat Dale Wolfe, Rick Martel double disqualification with Brutus Beefcake, Rhodes pinned Big Bossman, Genius pinned Tito Santana, Rockers beat Powers of Pain via DQ, Ware pinned Al Perez and Hogan pinned Perfect with the legdrop. The same crew with the same results drew 6,000 In San Antonio on 12/2 and 3,800 in Little Rock on 12/3.

Quick correction, a card in last week's Observer on 12/2 which it stated was In Daytona Beach was actually in Lakeland, FL.

Prime Time Wrestling drew a 2.9 on 12/4 while All American drew a 2.5 the previous day, once again with both shows trailing both TBS weekend programs.

While the Rougeaus have come off the road, they will appear on occasional PPV events putting guys over so they'll be at Royal Rumble, but it'll probably be their only appearance (except perhaps a show or two in Montreal) for a while.

12/3 at the Nassau Coliseum drew 11,000 and $150,000 as Mark Young beat Conquistador DUD, Dino Bravo pinned Santana DUD, Genius pinned Houston DUD, Ron Garvin drew Greg Valentine *½, Bushwackers beat Bolsheviks DUD, Dusty Rhodes pinned Bossman ½ * and Perfect beat Hogan via count out.

12/9 in Springfield, drew 5.800 and $70,000 as Young beat Conquistador DUD, Bravo pinned Santana *, Bushwackers beat Bolsheviks *½, Rhodes pinned Bossman ***, Valentine pinned Garvin **½, Genius pinned Houston ½ * and Perfect beat Hogan via count out ***½.

12/9 p.m. show in Boston drew 8,700 and $114,000 as

Young beat Conquistador DUD, Bravo pinned Santana *, Bushwackers beat Bolsheviks **, Rhodes pinned Bossman **, Valentine pinned Garvin ½ *, Genius pinned Houston ½ * and Perfect beat Hogan via count out **½.

The Hennig-Hogan matches have been going 15 to 17 minutes, although that includes two minutes before locking up and a three minute resthold midway through the match. Hennig is said to have looked real good in all three bouts. Hogan looked good in Springfield, but was his normal self in the other two spots, or just fair.

Next tapings after Chattanooga/Huntsville on Jan. 2/3 are in Florida on Jan. 22/23 after the Rumble in Orlando.

PUERTO RICO

They are doing a big show on 12/16 with some sort of a War Games on top with Carlos Colon & Abdullah The Butcher (Abby just turned face there) & TNT & Mark Youngblood & Invader #1 (Jose Gonzales) against Chicky Starr & Leo Burke & Harley Race & Manny Fernandez & Kimala plus Colon vs. Burke for the Universal title, Invader vs. Fernandez, Mercenaries vs. Youngbloods for the tag team title and Race vs. Ricky Santana.

12/9 in Guaynabo saw El Gran Medoza beat Victor Jovica, Super Medico beat Abbuda Dein, Miguelito Perez Hurricane Cast-illo Jr. beat The Mercenaries (Cuban Assassin & Jerry Morrow) via DQ, Invader pinned Gary Allbright and Colon & TNT went to a double DQ against Starr & Burke.

THIS JUST IN

Former top pro wrestling attraction William "Haystacks" Calhoun passed away on 12/7 in Richarsdon, TX. He was buried the next day. Calhoun had been in poor health for some time due to complications brought on by diabetes and was living in a trailer home in McKinney, TX for a few years. Calhoun was one of wrestling's biggest attractions in the 1960s as the 601 pound country boy with the lucky horseshoe and overalls until the emergence of Andre the Giant made his gimmick somewhat obsolete.

OREGON

Wrestling's big wedding of the year is scheduled on 12/16 in the Portland ring between Scotty the Body and babyface valet Ginger/ It started 11/25 when Scotty was about to pop the question but Steve Doll beat him up before he could get the words out of his mouth. On 12/2 Scotty did pop the question and Ginger said she'd give him his answer next week. On Saturday, Ginger accepted on the condition the wedding was the next Saturday at the wrestling card and that Steve Doil was the best man, which Scotty accepted. But lo and behold, there are already problems. Seems later in the card on 12/9 when they had a "hot legs" contest between Ginger and Veronica, Scotty came out and covered Ginger up and said he didn't want his old lady parading around like that. Veronica threw water in Ginger's face and they went at it again. Main event saw Billy Jack Haynes & Jeff Warner beat The Grappler & Brian Adams via DQ when Warner was hit with the loaded boot and all the heels in the area attacked Haynes until Rio Oliver (Haynes' long-time rival) made the save. Haynes & Oliver tag up on 12/16. Also Rex King beat Jonathan Boyd to keep the TV title and Boyd's snake now has to leave town but Boyd beat King up with the title belt after the match, Doll beat Al Madril via DQ, Francis no decision with Beetlejuice when after ref bump, Jonathan Holliday knocked Juice off the top rope and Francis pinned him but when Francis found out what happened, he refused the win and Cari Styles pinned Holliday but after the match Holliday used Veronica's loaded purse to KO Styles and put a dress and lipstick on him.

NWA

Arn Anderson's return finally aired on television this past Saturday. Some of the suspense about Ric Flair's mystery was removed when during promos for upcoming dates on the Power Hour and earlier in the show on WCW when both Arn & Ole Anderson's names were announced for late December shows. Big pop for the return. Whether it'll translate into box office is something else. My guess is no because the heel threesome isn't strong enough. Muta should be a face as he's ineffective as a heel. Sawyer is an effective heel but it 's too early in his stint for him to be a headliner, if he should ever be one, while Dragon Master (Sakurada) just shouldn't be there at all. Christmas shows are scheduled to be Ric Flair vs. Lex Luger, Road Warriors & Steiners vs. Wild Samoans (Fatu Samoan Savage) & Doom, Andersons & Sting vs. Muta & Sawyer & Dragon Master, Midnight vs. Dudes, Tom Zenk & Brian Piliman vs. Freebirds, Mike Rotunda vs. Tommy Rich and Eddie Gilbert vs. Kevin Sullivan.

Samu is history, at least for now, so Fatu & Tama are billed as the Wild Samoans instead of the Samoan Swat Team. Officially they are saying Samu wanted to be taken off the road, but that sounds fishy.

World Championship Wrestling on 12/2 (Midnight Vs. Dudes) drew a 3.6 rating – highest of the year and 1.9 million homes which is the most homes ever to watch a regular WCW or GCW show. Main Event on 12/3 (Flair vs. Eaton) drew a strong 3.3, while Power Hour on 12/1 (Steiners vs. Doom) drew 2.2. NWA Main rating was the third highest of the year behind Flair vs. Steamboat and Flair vs. Rotunda.

12/1 in Memphis drew 1,000 as Kevin Sullivan pinned Brad Anderson, Mike Rotunda pinned Norman, Midnight beat Dudes, three Samoans beat Hector Guerrero & Ranger Ross & Eddie Gilbert, Zenk pinned Jim Garvin, Hawk beat Dan Spivey via DQ, Steiners beat Doom and Flair beat Muta via DQ.

Sid Vicious won't be back until mid-January at the earliest but still being billed everywhere.

12/5 in Dayton for a TV taping drew 2,000. All three advertised main events (Steiners vs. Doom, Warriors vs. Scrapers and Pillman & Zenk vs. Freebirds) didn't take place. Main results saw Animal beat Spivey via DQ, Ole & Arn Anderson (who got the best reaction of the night) beat State Patrol, Steiners & Norman beat Spivey & Doom via DQ, Sullivan pinned Gilbert, Andersons beat Freebirds with a clean pin on Hayes, Rotunda pinned Rich in a lumberjack match when Kendall Windham hit Rich with a loaded glove, Arn Anderson pinned Rotunda, Steiners beat Freebirds via DQ (Woman came down and interfered and Steiners lost, but Norman at ringside shooting the photos showed the photo of Woman interfering to the ref who reversed the decision –Birds were originally announced as new tag team champions) and Rich & Gilbert beat Sawyer & Dragon Master via DQ and heels destroyed faces after until Ole & Arn made the save. I believe this was originally to be a singles match with Sawyer vs. Gilbert but some backstage heat over the proposal that Sawyer destroy Gilbert and be left laying until getting saved.

12/6 in Gary, IN canceled due to no advance.

12/7 in Buffalo drew 2,000 as Sullivan pinned Brad Anaerson *, Rotunda pinned Norman ½ *, Samoans beat Rich & Gilbert *½ , Pillman & Zenk beat Freebirds **, Animal beat Spivey via DQ ½ *, Midnight beat Dudes ** ½ , Luger pinned Zenk (Sting no-showed) **, Steiners beat Doom *** and Flair beat Muta via DQ **½

TBS taping 12/10 in Greensboro (air dates 12/22 and 12/29). Dudes challenged Midnight for a no DQ match wIth the $10,000 (which they won as Bruce Wayne & Dick Grayson) at stake. Cornette accepts and signs only it's a Cornette vs. Douglas match for the second show. Sting beat Luger via DQ when Lex used a chair and it wound up with Flair, Muta, Sawyer, Dragon Master and Andersons involved in a brawl and Sting unofficially became the Fourth Horsemen. Later Sting beat Dragon Master with Andersons at ringside to keep anyone from interfering. In Doom's squash, Norman came out with roses but Woman wasn't there. Cactus Jack Manson (who starts full-time in mid-January) teamed with jobber against Rich & Ross and after losing, Manson beat up the jobber and gave him the elbow on the floor of the ice-covered hockey-rink floor, Zenk & Pillman beat Freebirds via DQ, Midnight Express beat Fantastics, Flair beat Muta via DQ, Rich DDQ Rotunda and Terminator (Marc Laurinaitis) debuted. Crowd was very small due to the ice storm. In fact, WWF canceled its competition show the night before in Winston-Salem because of weather.

12/8 in Norfolk, VA saw more than a dozen no-shows because of weather conditions but fans were offered a choice of either refunds or free tickets to the next NWA show in Norfolk because of it. Results of a makeshift show saw Sullivan beat Brad Anderson, Samoans beat two local guys, Freebirds beat Gilbert & Rich, Sullivan won a Battle Royal to get a match with Sting (since Luger couldn't appear), Sting beat Sullivan and Flair beat Muta via DQ.

12/9 at the D.C. Armory in Washington, DC drew 1,000 as Rotunda pinned Norman, Samoans beat Rich Gilbert, Midnight beat Dudes, Pillman & Zenk beat Freebirds, Steiner beat Doom, Sting double count out with Luger and Flair beat Muta via DO.

In the TV match on Saturday between Rotunda and Rich, there were two unscheduled occurrences. First off, the Tommy Young ref bump was real (in fact, Tommy Young still hasn't returned to action after his neck was whiplashed and he still has numbness in his arm and isn't expected back for a while) and then the generator blew in the building (through no fault of the promotion but somehow these things always seem to happen to the NWA) so they had an unscheduled legitimate lights out match with Rotunda winning using the trunks.

Kendall Windham looks tremendously improved upon his return. His work itself is great as are his mannerisms. The only thing holding him back is that he looks so skinny next to the monsters. In reality, Kendall looks normal, in fact, much larger than normal (he's 6'5 and probably 215ish) for a normal human being but the standards for size of a wrestler are so ridiculous because of chemical bloat that normal looks like a scarecrow inside a wrestling ring.

THE READERS' PAGES

TIMES ARTICLE

I picked up the New York Times article and agree with your analysis that Jim Herd wants to take the NWA into WWF territory with the kids. The idea of a rage meter and a slam meter is right up there with the Ding Dongs and could have only come from Jim Herd. Personally, I don't care too much if they try to outsick Titan in the looks department. I wouldn't even care if they put Ric Flair in a Galactic Warrior costume provided that he could still wrestle like Ric Flair. Same goes with all the other guys.

Chris Zavisa
Plymouth, Michigan

QUESTIONS AND ANSWERS

In your last newsletter, one of the readers asked about Roy Heffernan. Roy is still alive, he's 64-years-old and fit as a bull. He has had both his hips replaced. He still promotes wrestling in the clubs in Sydney. He trained both myself and Wayne Pickford some years back and has a great wrestling mind.

The shows here have picked up a bit lately. Finally the promoters are seeing the light and pushing the younger guys. We have six good young guys. The older guys are jealous and treat these guys like crap, but the promoter is stick with them.

Ken Dunlop
Sydney, Australia

Why should the NWA worry about Tully Blanchard? They should just put him over and forget about it. After all, Puerto Rico has a murderer as one of its top babyfaces and look at Jim Duggan. Fans will buy whatever they're told.

Do jobbers get paid extra when Jake Roberts puts the snake on them? How about some background on Diamond Dallas Page?

Bruce Ciangetti
Manahawkin, New Jersey

Dave Meltzer: I don't know if jobbers get paid extra for working against Jake Roberts, but do know they get paid extra for working with Brutus Beefcake and getting clipped. Dallas Page was the head guy at a nightclub I believe in Fort Myers, FL before getting into the wrestling business with the AWA last year.

I have a few questions about the yesteryear of wrestling that others may find interesting as well. When Ivan Koloff won the WWWF heavyweight title, did he have any title defenses, and if so, against whom, before losing to Pedro Morales? The same question concerning the Iron Sheik. After beating Bob Backlund, did he wrestle as World champion and defend the title before losing to Hulk Hogan? What are Haystacks Calhoun, Man Mountain Mike and Cyclone Negro's real names?

Name withheld by request

Dave Meltzer: Don't know the answer to the first question, but assume Koloff must have defended the title during that brief period between the first Bruno Sammartino title reign and the Morales reign. Sheik did defend the belt against guys like Tito Santana and Bob Backlund during the period between the Backlund reign and the Hogan reign. Haystacks Calhoun's real name is William Calhoun, Man Mountain Mike I believe Is Jerry Fletcher and Cyclone Negro has a hispanic name but I can remember what it is.

We were recently discussing wrestling rumors and family ties, and had a few dubious ones we thought you might be able to shed some light on.

Is George Steele really a professor of philosophy at Rutgers? How about University Of Michigan? If the latter, did he ever teach Rick Steiner or The Genius? What is the relationship between Hulk Hogan and Brutus Beefcake? How are The Model and Queen Sherri related? Is Elizabeth really the illegitimate daughter Of the Fabulous Moolah? Is Al Hayes really a lord, Or just a jester? Are the WWF aIbums available on CD? We can't find them anywhere. And most importantly, and we know you know the answer to this one, who was the guest supposed to be on the Brother Love segment at SummerSlam '88 and what happened ?

Harvard University Wrestling Fan Club
Cambridge, Massachusetts

Dave Meltzer: How come you didn't ask me if Paul Orndorff was dead? What a scary letter. Next thing you know someone will tell me George Bush is a wrestling mark. George Steele was never a college professor. He was a high school football coach and phys ed teacher in Detroit and wrestled over the summer until McMahon talked him into going into wrestling full-time about four years ago and now he's a road agent for the WWF. Neither Rick Steiner nor Lanny Poffo went to the high school he taught at. Hogan and Beefcake are twin sons of different mothers. Seriously, they are childhood friends and grew up together in Florida, but are not brothers even though they began their careers wrestling as a brother tag team. The Model and Queen Sherri aren't related at all. Rick Martel is a stage name because when he got started in wrestling as a teenager, the promotion in Quebec brought him in under the guise that he was the younger brother of Frenchy Martin (which he wasn't) who at the time was using the ring name Pierre Martel. Queen Sherri's real name is Sherri Martel. Don't you guys ever study genetics in school? If you did, you'd realize there is no way genetically for Mooiah to have an offspring that looks like Liz. Hayes is McMahon's jester. I don't know if the WWF albums are on CDs. The WWF originally wanted Brother Love's guest as Summer Slam to be Ric Flair, but Vince wouldn't give Flair a guaranteed contract and with the Turner purchase and the ouster of Dusty Rhodes as booker, Flair stuck with the NWA in 1989.

WWF TAPING
I attended the 10/31 WWF taping in Topeka, which of course, resulted in the SNME show on Thanksgiving weekend. I don't normally go that far to attend a wrestling card (two hours each way) but when I read It was going to be an SNME taping, a couple of friends and I decided to do it for the novelty of it since we'd never been to a taping before. It was interesting for the experience, although I don't think I'd do It again. certainly not on a weeknight. It doesn't surprise me at all that they have to dub in crowd noise and some of their matches. Sitting through several hours of squash matches with only a few decent bouts thrown in with almost no breaks would put even the heartiest wrestling fan to sleep. What really got me was the $12 ticket price. With it all taped for TV, you would think they would at least discount the tickets. Maybe if they had

done so, they could have sold the place out.

Robert Garrison
Raytown, Missouri

CLASH/ SURVIVORS
From the MIdniqhts vs. Dudes match on, it was a great show. The Steve Williams match was a painless enough squash. Midnight—Dudes was good, despite some execution problems from the Dudes, with a great surprise finish as I'm sure many thought Cornette would remain a face. Hopefully it will inject renewed vigor into the Express. Again, a big problem at NWA shows is the strong crowd reaction to the heels, although that's not the case when Ric Flair retires. Steiners vs. Skyscrapers was good and short enough to hide Sid Vicious' lack of ability. Lex Luger was impressive as he really stood out as the star of the show in the post-match angles.

The biggest compliment I can give the Flair-Funk match is that while I knew it was a work, the drama and physical nature Of the match got to me, especially the incredible bumps by Funk. Jim Ross and Gordon Solie were excellent on commentary, particularly Ross, and I loved his line about how critics of pro wrestling should appreciate the level at which Punk and Flair were performing at. The entrances were great as well. Now if only they could build from it.

Bruce Colon
Chicago, Illinois

Even though I knew the ending, I haven't felt this much tension since the Flair-Steamboat matches.

As far as I'm concerned, the Flair vs. Funk match was exactly what pro wrestling should be all about. If they have to throw in Norman and his teddy bear. to appeal to the so-called mainstream, I can tolerate it as long as a product like that is delivered in the main event.

Is it my imagination or has Luger turned into one of the better wrestlers in selling and putting over his foe. I don't know if my eyes were out of focus, but Luger was taking some bumps like Bobby Eaton and that ain't bad.

Howard Kesner
Pikesville, Maryland

Despite a rather uninspired first half, the latter matchups at Clash were amazing enough to make the whole show a thumbs up. Luger and Pillman worked great together. Scott Steiner seems to have become one of the five best workers in the NWA. The Cornette turn was both fun and unexpected. Doom wasn't quite as lumbering as they've been. The run-ins weren as telegraphed as run-ins usually are and the show worked pretty well to promote the Starrcade card.

Flair was top-flight as always. Does the guy ever have an off night? Funk clinched my vote for Wrestler Of the Year. He could work with a fruit fly and still make it a three-star match. Let's hope that once he's healed that he won't discount another return to the ring. All in all, a better show than Halloween Havoc to be sure.

Sure, Verne Gagne's comments on Bruiser Brody were tasteless and unwarranted. But since when does anything Gagne say account for anything of importance? Not in my lifetime.

I gave Survivors a marginal thumbs up for the same reason as the previous Survivors shows. The good workers (all seven of them) were a few steps above their typical performances. The rest of the bunch weren't in the ring long enough to resthold out and seemed to actually exert a modicum Of effort.

What a concept? Consequently, the show showed the WWF workrate at its collective annual best.

Some minuses. The no-show situation should have been handled better . But this is Titan Sports, were you expecting honesty? Randy Savage was unusually mediocre for a big show. That standard Hogan finish has got to go. The first two matches were ho-hum. A Jimmy Snuka turn would have perked up Piper's match. Gino Monsoon's cliche spewing was even heavier than usual. I'd like to see hrm hanging from the rafters above a capacity crowd. Chuggin' Duggn, the Ultimate Pharmacy and the Mighty Jerkuies and the Eighth Wonder were actually worse than expected. paying for a show while getting hit with numerous plus for another PPV show was also most unwelcome.

The plusses. Arn Anderson. I liked the Bad News Brown heel character without heel friends . Jesse's work was pretty good, especially the first and last mention of the anatomically off—color "nuts" on a WWF broadcast. The cameras seemed to be covering the right stuff at the right time. The booking wasn't half bad, although a surprise or two would have been nice.

Steve Prazak
Atlanta, Georgia

The Survivor Series left me confused. On the one hand, the wrestling was decent for the WWF and on a one-to-10 deserved about a 6 ½. The final match was the best, with Arn Anderson really putting out in his swan song .

However, what was hyped never materialized. Nothing happened with Piper-Snuka . Jesse Ventura continually hinted at dissension within the Heenan family but nothing really happened there. The crowd didn't seem to pop for Hogan like usual. His act has become tiresome. I remember when WWF PPV shows would offer at least one surprise. This time, nothing happened at all.

Vince Dipaima
Copiague, New York

Solid thumbs down. I generally prefer the WWF over the NWA but this show really sucked. I had expected they would set up some good angles for the future, but instead all we got were endless plugs for another PPV show. No good new angles. No new angles at all. No good work, either. I thought I was watching the NWA with the screw-jobs, count outs and DQ finishes. The angle in the dressing room was totally worthless. Give Arn Anderson and the Rougeaus credit for doing the job even though they were leaving. I guess I expected a little action, which I got, but felt cheated by the lack of angles and quality of the production.

They are out of their minds if they think I or anyone will pay $15 see "No Holds Barred" when it can be rented for $2 and I already paid $5 to see it. I'm not sure I'd watch it again as a free TV movie. I haven't missed a WWF PPV in three years, but this next one is a definite pass.

Ron Hickey
Falls Church, Virginia

I need to comment about the Flair-Funk match. I've always been a big Funk fan and after his performance I think there can be no doubt that he has always given more than 100 percent of his efforts to the business. With all his injuries and his age, he still outworked everyone else on the card. He still took his crazy bumps and absorbed those super-stiff chops by Ric Flair. He also made his submission look very much real. I watched this Clash with several members of my family. They don't like wrestling and didn't like any of the other matches on the card. During the Flair-Funk match they had their eyes glued to the screen. Even though none of them care for wrestling, each one of them told me they really enjoyed that match. To me, this IS the biggest compliment one could ever give Ric or Terry Funk. For one match, they turned some wrestling-haters into wrestling fans. These people wouldn't be caught dead watching wrestling, but they had great respect for the performance of both men.

Tony Johnson
Chesnee, South Carol ina

AWARDS

This is a quick late reminder about the Wrestling Observer awards balloting. For readers in the U .S. please mail in the ballots by Dec. 30 and for readers in other countries, by Dec. 24 to make sure it reaches us on time.

Awards will be broken down into two categories. Category "A" awards you can vote for a first, second and third place. You don't have to vote in all categories or for three in Category A, but you can, and points will be awarded on a 5—3—2 basis with the winner being chosen by whomever gets the most points. Awards will be listed in the following categories: 1.. Wrestler of the year: 2.. Most Outstanding wrestler; 3. Best babyface; 4. Best heel; 5. Feud Of the year; 6. Tag team Of the year; 7. Most improved; 8. Most un—improved; 9. Most Obnoxious: 10. Best on interviews;

Il. Most charismatic; 12. Best technical wrestler; 13. Best brawler ; 14. Best flier; 15. Most Overrated; 16. underrated; 17. Best promotion; 18. Best TV show; 19. Match of the year; 20. Rookie Of the year; 21. Manager Of the year; 22. Best TV announcer; 23. Worst TV announcer.

Category "B" awards, in which you vote for only one entry and the winner is determined by the total votes are: 1.. Best major card; 2. Worst major card; 3. Best wrestling move; 4. Hardest worker. 5. Biggest shock; 6. Most disgusting promotional tactic; 7. Best color commentator; 8. Strongest; 9. Readers favorite wrestler; 10. Readers most hated wrestler; 11. Worst wrestler; 12. Worst tag team; 13. Worst TV show; 14. Worst manager; 15. Worst match of the year; 16. Worst feud; 17. Worst on interviews; 18. Worst promotion; 19. Best booker; 20. Promoter of the year; 21. Best ginÄick; 22. Worst gimmick; 23. Most embarrassing wrestler.

DECEMBER 26, 1989

Before getting started on the final issue of the decade, I want to say a special thank you to all of you who have supported this endeavor so well. Also, special thanks for all the nice Christmas cards and kind words during this holiday season. This past year has been a great deal of fun, particularly being able to travel and meet so many readers at the big shows. It's really a nice feeling to be able to go into any city in the country and find so many friends.

Any decade in pro wrestling is going to be monumental. This past one was probably more so than any before. It's hard to believe that such far reaching changes in the industry could occur in the next ten years as compared with the past ten years, but they will happen. It's hard to predict exactly what form they will take. As this year comes to a close it appears this next decade will bring about changes in the same direction as this past decade. Fewer regional offices. Wrestling on this continent will be dominated by a few, at least one and no more than three, promotions. It's hard to believe a company would be able to compete with Titan Sports in this country for the economic top spot. But ten years is a long time and even the most ardent Titan supporters will readily concede that Ted Turner is in the wrestling business for the long haul. As long as the NWA has PPV capabilities to draw a decent buy rate, as the number of homes wired for PPV increases, the potential income increases To the point the promotion would almost be able to run on PPV and advertising and marketing income alone. They'll need to, because as PPV gets stronger, house shows will become less and less important and become harder and harder to turn a profit on. Right now I see no conceivable way that the NWA would be able to consistently turn a profit on house shows in the foreseeable future, particularly with their current salary structure. But the potential PPV income, particularly down the road, may make the latter face insignificant anyway. Even Titan is finding it harder and harder to draw at the houses and wouldn't surprise me that in a year or two the house show business would become hard for even them to turn a profit on, but PPV barring any serious problems. is going to be a goldmine for Titan for at lease a few more years.

We'll be running more from big show to big show. Over the last few months, it seems that is what the business has turned into anyway. Between Bashes, Clashes, Wrestle Wars, WrestleManias, SummerSlams, Starrcades and Survivors, we'll have had ten PPV events, a half-dozen NBC specials and five TBS Clash specials in 1989. Prediction for 1990 is more of the same. That's 20 television spectaculars with the "super matches," which almost by necessity, will make house shows seem less and less important.

I'll be getting into this more in the yearbook. The book is coming along well. We been flooded with awards ballots. We've got lots of different writers contributing special stories. We'll have awards for both the year and the decade. A review of the top stories. profiles on the key personalities. Comedy features. The 100 best matches of the decade. The ten best matches of the decade that never took place. And a lot more. There won't be an Observer next week for two reasons. The main one is the main promotions are all shut down during this coming week so there will be little to report. It also gives me time for the yearbook production . So we'll be back with the regular Observer in two weeks, and run bi-weekly until the yearbook is taken care of.

STARRCADE '89; FUTURE SHOCK

Thumbs up: 171 (76.3 percent)
Thumbs down; 36 (16.1 percent)
In between: 17 (7.6 percent)

Based on phone responses to the Observer poll through Monday morning.

Before getting into comments on the show itself, let's take a look at the show. Starrcade, traditionally the NWAs biggest spectacular of the year, dating back to 1983, was composed this year of an "Iron Man" and "Iron Team" tournament. The tournaments each had four participants or teams that would have round-robin matches against one another (which creates unique face vs. face and heel vs. heel matches). The victor would be determined by a point system, which was never released publicly until the day of the event. It was similar to the New Japan point system for its tournaments, with 20 points for a pinfall or submission victory, 15 points for a count out victory, 10 points for a disqualification victory, five points for each man for a time limit draw (or I suppose, a double count out or double DQ although that was never specified). Losers would get zero points. The New Japan system (five for a pin, four for count out, three for a DQ win, two for a draw) was also considered but it was felt that it would be psychologically more impressive to fans to have winners with 40 points than winners with ten points. This was a first of its type that I know of in the United States (Japan has similar tournaments, but with larger fields and they take place over a few week period).

The live event drew about 6,000 fans to the Omni in Atlanta on Wednesday night (12/13). About 5,200 were paid for a gate of $70,000. No PPV figures are available at press time. Even with the excuse that a Wednesday night isn't the best night for wrestling, the live gate has to be a major disappointment. Regular shows at the Omni in recent months have drawn upwards of 10,000 fans. While I didn't expect a sellout because the tournament concept doesn't allow for hyping specific grudge matches (which is what draws – impulse buys not logical buys) I still felt the idea of it being a heavily hyped PPV event and Starrcade to boot, would be good for at least 10,000 fans again. Also, because of the 7 p.m. starting time (Omni shows traditionally start at 8 p.m.), this was a late arriving crowd and when the card started there were barely 2,000 fans in the building. This caused the early matches to lack in heat and make the event look "cheap" on camera because of all the visible empty seats at ringside.

1. Rick & Scott Steiner beat Doom via count out in 12:24. With fans arriving, there was no big crowd momentum early and the bout started slow. It picked up after Scott took a bump over the top rope and Nitron (Woman's bodyguard, billed at 7 foot plus, apparently 6 '10 or so legit) pounded on him. Butch Reed threw Scott over the top rope again near the 10 minute mark. The ref was distracted and missed Scott's comeback near fall on Reed and then after a belly-to-belly, he tagged Rick. Rick popped Reed with a major potatoclothesline but Nitron tripped him from outside the ring. Rick jumped out and clotheslined Nitron and all four brawled outside and it looked like a double count out but Rick snuck into the ring to beat the count. It should be mentioned that in this match, along with in many other matches, they were "shaving" time. They made the 10 minute call at a legit 7:30, and they were calling four minutes to go and three minutes to go with 2:30 shaved off real time. In other words, they gave the appearance that this was going to be a time limit draw (same appearance throughout most of the card) because time was running out when they went to the finish.**¼ .

2. Lex Luger pinned Sting in 11:31. They started with a hot high spot. The time shaving reached its most embarrassing here. At the two minute mark Terry Funk, doing color with Jim Ross, said that was the hottest first minute he'd ever seen. Just seconds later, ring announcer Gary Cappetta called five minutes. They made the ten minute call at 6:00. Sting flipped over when Luger attempted a suplex at 9:30 and apparently legitimately hurt his ankle (while Sting returned for his matches the rest of the card, he missed the rest of the week's shows). Sting made the superman comeback, but missed a few moves, one of which brought out a groan from the crowd. The two were brawling on the apron and both went over the top rope with Luqer falling on top of Sting and pinning him using the ropes for leverage. Because of the time shaving, this match again "went down to the final seconds" before the finish. In fact, since they had four minutes shaved off, they even went past the "worked" time

limit to reach the finish. There were good spots here and the heat was better than in the opener, but nowhere near what the heat should have been with these two. However there were a lot of missed moves and at times Sting looked lost in the ring and the finish looked bad. **¼ .

3. Road Warriors beat Doom in 8:31 by pinfall. Woman changed her dresses between each appearance similar to Elizabeth at the 1985 Wrestling Classic in Chicago where Randy Savage worked four times. They called five at 2:45 this time. Hawk missed a shoulder block and went to the floor and they tried to get heat on Hawk. The crowd never even made a peep, let alone a pop on near falls on the Warriors which makes it very hard to get heat on them because people don't "buy" them selling. They didn't even pop for a near fall when Reed did the elbow drop off the rope onto Hawk and went for the cover. They called ten minutes at 6:50 . Hawk gave Animal the hot tag at 7:48. Finish saw Reed about to pick up Animal for a piledriver when Hawk clotheslined him off the top rope and Animal got on top for the pin. **

4. Ric Flair pinned The Great Muta in 1:55. Ole & Arn Anderson came down to ringside with Flair. The match started out furious (it was obvious it was going to be a quickie) and got the first real heat of the show. Buzz Sawyer and Dragon Master ran in and the Andersons brawled with them outside the ring. Muta went for the moonsault but Flair got his knees up and then cradled him for the win. This was the most excitement on the card except for the final match, but too short to be rated higher than **.

5. The Steiners beat the Road Warriors in 7:27. This unique match-up had good action, but surprisingly little crowd response. Was told by those live that the crowd was into the match, just didn't pop big because they were confused as to how to react. This bout would have gotten over real big in Japan. Again no peeps, Let alone pops, when the Steiners put winning moves on the Warriors. The hot move of the match was Scott giving Hawk a belly-to-belly superplex off the top rope. Wasn't a picture perfect executed move, but still creative. Finish saw Animal have Scott up in a back suplex and Hawk came off the top rope to clothesline him (the old Choshu & Hamaguchi finish) but both Scott and Animal had their shoulders down when they hit the mat and Scott raised his at the count of two, clearly, for a rare pinfall loss by the Warriors. Big surprise that the Warriors lost (which made it obvious they were going to win the tournament as they'd never have agreed to it if they weren't getting the payoff in return). While the double pin finish has been done too often on NWA big shows in 1989, the fact that the Warriors did a job made it less objectionable as if someone else was involved. ***.

6. Sting pinned Muta in 8:41 with a superplex. Again, no heat at all for this one. The match was a combination of some decent action and restholds until an excellent finish. Muta went for the moonsault, Sting got up, Muta landed on his feet and gave him a karate kick. Muta went back up to the top rope, Sting dropkicked him, Muta crotched himself and Sting pulled him off with the winning superplex. **¾ (mainly for the closing sequence).

7. The New Wild Samoans Fatu – Solofa Fatu and Samoan Savage – Sam Fatu, who are actually brothers) beat Doom in 8:22. No heat at all for the entire match. The work itself was actually quite good but the match never had a prayer. The Samoans were subbing for the Skyscrapers who had been advertised for the past month even though Sid Vicious had been hospitalized with a punctured lung back on 11/18. The live crowd was given no explanation for the substitution (and they had several weeks on TV to announce the change and didn't, but that's all been said before). On PPV Jim Cornette said it was a last minute injury and wasn't sure of the severity and the Samoans got the nod to come in earlier in the day. Ross then followed by saying that Sid had a punctured lung from a match with the Steiners (which is actually the truth) and it was touch-and-go if he'd be released by his doctor to compete. Contradictory stories since the Steiner match was a month ago and Cornette said last minute and Cornette didn't know the injury but Ross did. Still, this was a lot better than Titan handled similar situations as their PPV so no matter what one might say about the two promotions, one is far above the other when it comes to honesty to the public (although that far ahead is more by default than any great honesty by the NWA). Samoans tried to work as faces but fans didn't notice. Finish saw Fatu and Reed collide head-on-head. Reed went down and Fatu stumbled backward to the ropes. The Big Kahuna (Humperdink) then pushed Fatu who fell on Reed for the pin. For work this was a three star match but no heat. **

8. Ric Flair went to a time limit draw with Lex Luqer at 17:01. Unlike the previous matches in which they shaved time, in this one they gave them more time. I'm not complaining or anything about this match going long, but they didn't lock up for two minutes. Flair went with the hard chops and working on the arm early. They started a bit slow for the short time limit match and really didn't open up until the nine minute mark. From that point on the match was excellent with one great spot after another. Luger worked over Flair's throat and Flair was actually coughing. Flair got the figure four on just as they were counting down time but Luger held on for the draw. This match turned the card around. While the work in every match prior was at least decent and generally good, the heat was subpar except for the Flair-Muta quickie. The heat was great for this match

and the crowd stayed hot most of the rest of the card. ***¾.

9. Samoans beat Steiners via DQ in 14:05. They stalled for several minutes before even starting the match and stalled for the first three minutes of the match. Scott missed the Frankensteiner and was thrown out of the ring and they got heat on him. They crotched Scott on the guard rail and head-butted the groin and he was thrown over the top rope behind the refs back. Scott was in, getting heat (and they did get heat) for six minutes before making the comeback and hitting the Frankensteiner. They were shaving one minute off on the time calls (five minutes came at 4:00, ten minutes at 9:00) and were counting down the minutes. Scott flipped Fatu over the top rope and ref Lee Scott (subbing for Tommy Young who is still out of action from that bump he took in the Tommy Rich vs. Mike Rotunda television match) had his back turned–but he wasn't supposed to. And they had also passed the "work" time limit but Scott still acted like he saw Scott (does this read confusing or what?) throw Fatu over and made the DQ call. ***.

10. Luger beat Muta via DQ in 11:48. Lex walked down the aisle slowly, still selling the effects of the figure four from the match with Flair. Lex spent the entire match selling the knee and did a great job. Muta spent the match working on the bad leg with unique holds. They called five at 3:00 and ten at 7:00. Luger sold most of the way. Surprisingly, the live crowd cheered Muta slightly more than Luger. Surprising since Luger has gotten cheered more than a lot of the faces he's been in with, but when he's in with a heel (who should be a face himself, but that's another story) he didn't get the majority of cheers (although it was something Like 55-45 percent pro-Muta). Finish saw Muta blow the mist in Luger's eyes for the DQ just "seconds" before the worked time limit was going to expire. The match was very good and very intense, but the finish defied all logic as Muta was creaming him almost the entire way, it was just before the time limit would be called for the draw, and he blows mist right in front of the ref for no reason for the DQ. ***¼ .

11. The tag team tournament came down to Warriors vs. Samoans. At this point, the Steiners have 35 points, Samoans have 30, Warriors have 20 and Doom has nothing. I'll ask Doom the 20 point bonus question and if you get right you're in the lead but if you miss it, then it's last place. The question is, Who is Doom One? One masked guy says, "Ron Simmons." Lee's see what your partner said, now hold up the card, "Butch Reed." Last place for you guys. Road Warriors, you've got 20, if you get this one you'll be in the lead but if you miss it, then it's third place. Here's your question——What are you thinking right this minute? Hawk answers, "We don't do any stinkin' jobs on any stinkin' game show." The answers match. Samoans, if you get this right

you're in the lead but if you miss it, then it's third place. What happened to Samu? Fatu answers, "It's a secret." Let 's look at the card, Samoan Savage's card says, "He went home." Judges, do we have a match? Our distinguished panel of judges by the way are the 6-time World champion out of St. Louis, Lou Thesz, the only man from New Zealand ever to win the title, Pat O'Connor and one of the only brother combination to each win the NWA title, Terry Funk. They say no match. Steiners, it's down to this. If you get this right then you're our grand prize winners but if you miss it, then it's second place. The question is, Whatever happened to Alex? Scott answers, "I came in and they dropped the gimmick?" Now, let's see the card, Rick. Hold the card up, Rick says, "We changed bookers again." No match, Road Warriors, you are our grand prize winners today . Anyway, a 1970s game show was better than this final match. The guys were missing moves left and right and even screwed up the finish but Hawk wound up clotheslining Fatu from off the top rope for the pin at 5:18 so the Warriors win the tournament. Very little reaction. -*

12. Its now down to the singles finals. Lex Luger is already in the clubhouse with 35 points while Muta has zero. Ric Flair has 25 while Sting has 20. If it's a draw, Luger wins. If Flair wins by a pin or count out, he gets the whole thing. If he wins by a DQ, then he's tied with Luger and we have a wrestle-off (which we already know is impossible because we're running out of time on the PPV) If Sting wins on a pin, he's got the whole thing. If he wins via count out, we've got a tie, but if he wins by DQ, then Luger gets the thing. Flair and Sting enter to about an equal number of cheers. Those live said Sting had slightly more boos but really nobody booed either guy. This was the old Ric Flair, playing vintage heel and doing the same type of spots he did in most of his matches prior to this year when working with Ricky Steamboat and Terry Funk totally changed his "normal" routine. He carried Sting to an excellent match. Still wasn't booed but turned Sting into a favorite. The match was excellent all the way through with them adding instead of shaving time, giving the guys an extra minute to do their thing. They passed 15 and it was announced "one minute to go" and they went to all the near falls and with just seconds remaining, Flair went for the figure four, Sting caught him in an inside cradle and got the pin at 15: 54. ****¼

I'd give the thing a thumbs up. Given the restraints of the tournament, the booking was excellent. The winners did jobs (such as they were) earlier in the show, which the tournament allowed for. They went down to the wire with three possible tournament winners in both divisions going into the final match. Sting's win in the singles tournament came as a complete surprise since they spent the last six weeks telling everyone that Luger was going to win and they teased the draw. Out of 12 matches, 11 of them had at least a decent level of work and several were pretty good. The only bad match was kept short and those guys had each worked twice earlier. And that wasn't bad work rate, just missed moves. The crowd heat was disappointing early on, but once Flair-Luger started the crowd was with it as good as it deserved the rest of the way. They had winners in matches nobody thought they'd come up with winners in (Flair vs. Sting and Warriors vs. Steiners) and both had the underdogs win.

Still, this was a show for the hardcore wrestling fan. I don't think a casual fan would get into seeing the same guys wrestle three times. The scoring system was great if you were really following the show closely but if you weren't following closely, or were and had no concept of simple mathematics, the show went over your head. Really, aside from Flair, and to a lesser extent Luger, the guys don't have enough versatility to give you three different matches. I mean, how many clotheslines and power slams do you need in one night? I think the people who ordered the PPV show should have been happy. Maybe not ecstatic, but happy. Those live, for the most part, thought it was a good show, although the comments seemed to think it wasn't a Starrcade-calibre show. Unless the buy rate proves me wrong, I still maintain that the tournament itself was a good idea, but not for Starrcade. There was almost too much wrestling with nothing else. Just one match after another, albeit mainly solid matches.

I don't want to harp on problems since the show was basically good, but they needed trophies for the winners and presentations made because after the Warriors won the thing, when it was over, it was like they hadn't won anything of significance. I won't say that for Sting, because just beating Ric Flair made it something of significance for him. Just before the finishes of every match they were exploding the dry ice backstage for the next entrance so the fans would all start looking backstage (like they were anticipating a run-in — fortunately there weren't any major run-ins on the show) just before the finish of most matches. They sometimes had entrance music and sometimes didn't. No consistency. I would have thought all that screwing with the times of the matches would be no big deal, but there were several complaints about it. The Skyscraper deal, which has been gone over enough, but is still inexcusable.

Out of seven Starrcade shows, I'd rate this one no higher than fifth (ahead of 1984 and 1987). And of all seven, it had the least Starrcade-like atmosphere about it.

No major technical complaints. This wasn't the best announced NWA PPV show, but considering Jim Ross was working under some adverse conditions (he had a root canal the next day and was in major pain), no complaints. There was nothing wrong with Ross' work and until I was told after the show, I had no idea anything was wrong but there was a special zip of enthusiasm not quite there. Jim Cornette was more serious than he is on the TBS shows. He wasn't playing the strong heel doing commentary as he does on Power Hour and did well in the tag tournament. Terry Funk worked with Ross on the singles and got over the key points but it was nothing you could call better than expected. They had a snafu at the end when before they went to Sting's post-match interview, the show just went off the air. Boom, the credits rolled and the show was history, with no sign-off.

I certainly don't sense this show, good as it may have been, as any kind of a turning point for the NWA. The singles matches were exciting, but they also gave away the first Flair-Luger meeting which takes away from the house shows. The tag tournament didn't seem to have the interest overall except the curiosity for Steiners-Warriors and heat for Steiners-Samoans (only because it was a good match following a hot match).

Speaking Of PPV, the WWF taped its No Holds Barred main event match on 12/12 in Nashville which airs on 12/27 as part of a PPV with the movie . Titan officials are predicting between a two and three percent buy rate for this package, which sounds overly optimistic to me, but it's been hyped too well to flop. The one-match card with Hulk Hogan & Brutus Beefcake vs. Zeus & Randy Savage in a cage saw the heels come in first. Beefcake came in to his music and then Hogan comes down to his music but they slam the cage door on Hogan's head before he gets in the cage. Beefcake gets doubled on for a while until Hulk gets in and they turn the tables. Sherri Martel climbed the cage to give Savage a foreign object (something from the cage door like a bolt or something) but Beefcake gets the thing and uses it on Savage who does a major league juice job. Somehow Beefcake and Savage end up going over the cage together leaving Hogan in with Zeus. Zeus does some choking inside while Savage and Beefcake try to take fans' eyes away from what's not going on inside the ring by continuing to brawl all around the cage. Somehow Beefcake got back in the cage to help Hogan. Hulk does the superman comeback, bodyslam, legdrop and 1-2-3 and Zeus is history.

The future of Ric Flair and the NWA title: A few weeks back I got into a key power struggle that had turned into a major divisive issue within the NWA and remains so today. What is the future of Ric Flair and what is the future of the NWA title. You can add what is the future of the NWA right along with it. When Flair was made head booker a few months back, I thought it was a bad move. Not a bad move because I thought Flair couldn't do the job. A bad move because the best thing the NWA had was Ric Flair and I didn't want anything to tamper with the NWA's biggest asset, those great final matches on the big shows and even the one match which saves a iot of lackluster house shows.

The stress factor in being booker is a killer. Take one look at Flair's face. It reminds me of Jimmy Carter when he was President. Between trying to keep the wrestlers happy when you are trying to get them to put people over and trying to keep management and second-guessers happy it is a no win situation. The NWA has so many holes that even the best booking isn't going to do house show business these days, and when the house shows don't draw, the booker is under fire and when he's under fire, the stress gets even greater. With Flair, the problems are doubled. Not only does he have to take a certain amount of responsibility for not drawing because he's the booker, but also because he's in the position where he's the leading draw. It's like being both coach and quarterback at the same time on a team with good talent that is losing way more often than it should. It's no secret that the powers in management want to replace Flair as World champion with Lex Luger and replace Flair as top babyface with Sting. They want to push young guys. While phasing out Flair may be putting it too strongly, phasing him down is certainly accurate. Points and counterpoints were all gone into a few weeks back.

I wanted to wait until Starrcade to give my own point of view on the subject, more so then just to give Luger a chance. I thought it would answer some questions. Starrcade is over. Flair is clearly the best wrestler in the NWA. Luger is good – very good, but not really close at all to Flair. Sting can do good high spots and has a lot of charisma, but is very limited in what he can do when he's not being carried. He even gets lost in matches. Ric Flair is not a drawing card anymore. Maybe it's because of age. Maybe it's because he's been around too long on top. Maybe, and I'm kind of convinced of this one, it is simply because nobody at this point can be any kind of a drawing card with the NWA with all its flaws. However, Luger, for all his improvements and his physique, is also not a drawing card. Sting, for all his charisma, is not a drawing card. No matter which of these three men holds the title, none will draw big crowds consistently in 1990. Really, no matter which is champion, the NWA will be hard pressed to draw any kind of crowds except for a few big shows without major changes being made in television and advertising which have nothing to do with the charisma or drawing power of any of the competitors or how they are booked. As a fan from a personal standpoint, which has nothing to do with business, I came out Of Starrcade "wanting" Flair to stay as champion because when Luger and Sting, the two big stars, were in there together, the match didn't get nearly the heat it should have, and it wasn't that great a match. Flair had three matches. All different. They were the three most heated matches on the card. He had the two best matches of the card and his bout with Muta would have been the third best if it had gone longer. For all the criticisms some may have of Flair as being perhaps no longer the best wrestler on this side of the ocean, he still can carry an opponent better than anyone else, has the best ring psychology, and even with the stress and age, is in better condition than almost anyone around. But the face shows age. It can't be ignored. It can't be denied. Physical age is not a factor, because even if Flair declines in the ring over the next five years (and we've got Terry Funk in a sense as living proof that someone 44 who has the desire and ring psychology can still get over more and work better than just about anyone in the business) it is doubtful Luger will ever surpass him in ring work, barring a major injury or change in Flair's own desire. Sting never will. Nor does it appear either of the two will be the "team players" that Flair was at Starrcade, putting someone over cleanly, or submitting to Ricky Steamboat as he did in New Orleans to try and sacrifice himself to re-educate the public to holds. And while physical age may not be a factor, cosmetic age is in this business. And at the same time, the NWA's lone advantage in its competition is the superior wrestling and the superior big shows. In every big show this year, from Starrcade '88 with Lex Luger, through three matches with Steamboat, a tag match in Columbia,   a flawed Thunderdome match in Philadelphia, a pair of Funk matches, through Starrcade '89, who was involved in the best match on the card? In fact, some of the best matches of the decade. Luger and Sting can have good matches, and in fairness, if both were pushed as the top guys, their singles matches should be better than Wednesday and have more heat. But finishing every card with those matches of the year will be a thing of the past. But also inevitable, there will come a day where the change has to be made. Some may argue that Funk is living proof that it may be several years away, when the guys nipping at Flair's heels may not be Luger and Sting at all, but maybe guys who are just breaking into the spotlight today. And you almost feel sorry for Luger when and if the move is made this year. When Luger doesn't draw, and he won't, and it won't be his fault, there will be second-guessers everywhere. The first time Luger headlines against anyone but Flair, and if the match is anything less than excellent, it will come again. Two years from now, it may get worse. Legends get better as time goes on and Flair's reign as champion will become legendary when it is over. All the greats in this business are a lot better in long-time fans' eyes and remembrances than they are when you see videotapes of them.

Tully Blanchard cocaine and wrestling: It's not the most political position to try and defend someone who has a drug-user rap on him. But I feel sorry for Tully Blanchard, Granted, part of his current situation is self-created. He put himself in a position where those who wanted to use him to set an example were able to. But the hypocrisy on both sides can't be ignored. On one side you have a promotion that does test for cocaine usage, and has suspended wrestlers in the past and even fired wrestlers for repeated positive testing,

and at the same time has blatantly promoted wrestlers for no other reason than chemically-altered physiques. But Blanchard did put himself in the position where an example could be made of him.

On the other side, we've got a promotion that doesn't test for drugs. There are wrestlers under contract who have been arrested on drug charges in the past. The usage of steroids, while not as prevalent as in the WWF, is still significant.

The business of wrestling breeds drug usage. Wrestling is not alone in this. Some quasi-sports, bodybuilding for one, breeds it even more. Other totally respectable sports, like pro football, breeds it to a significant degree as well. Wrestling breeds steroid abuse. The emphasis from both the promoters and to the public is on freakish looking physiques. Wrestling breeds usage of downers. These guys are usually in some form of pain from the punishment they take. They abuse their bodies in the ring, they have to combat almost daily jetlag, have to get to the gym several times per week for hard workouts in the morning and still have enough to put out and perform athletically almost every night. I can sit here and be moralistic and say how bad this all is, but looking at the subject from a realistic point of view, the drug usage is simply a byproduct of the demands of the profession. Wrestling isn't the only profession that drug usage is a byproduct of. And it isn't the worst, but it is a significant part of the business.

At the same time, there has to be common sense and there has to be limits. When drugs start negatively affecting your health and your life, it's time to face another form of reality. There are more important things in life than getting over and staying over. That is something each wrestler has to evaluate personally. When drugs start negatively affecting your performance at work, then it is something your employer has every right to do something about. There are wrestlers whose drug problems have killed them, and those whose drug problems have taken them from potential superstar status to guys struggling in the minor leagues and never reaching their potential. Things like bad work, bad conditioning and no-showing can be a product of excessive cocaine usage. There are many wrestlers whose ringwork, showing up for matches and the like have been negatively affected by cocaine. I dare say that nobody would even hint for a second that Tully Blanchard's name should be on that list. He's one of the better workers in the business. Not the best, but in the top echelon. Shows up and works hard each and every day. And whatever he does in his spare time is his own business, provided it doesn't affect his work negatively, especially when you consider that both promotions have guys whose outside habits do negatively affect their work to sizable degrees.

A lot of sports drug test now. A lot of non-sports professions do as well. The NFL and NBA drug test mainly for public relations reasons. The NFL got a rep as being a league loaded with cocaine and steroid abusers and it put the credibility of the game with a segment of the public into question. So out come the tests, which those close to the field will tell you are a joke. It is no secret what to take, when to stop and how to mask so you can beat a steroid test. A Local doctor here who worked with about two dozen local Olympic athletes that were using steroids prior to the Seoul games had zero positives in steroid testing even though some were on the stuff up through the final weeks of preparation. One NFL coach described the steroid testing as comparable to an IQ test. If you are smart and you follow what to do, you can take the stuff and pass the test. If you are stupid and you take the stuff, you'll fail the test.

With pro wrestling, the tests came right after the WWF had its own PR scandal, when Jim Duggan and Iron Sheik were traveling together and made the second page of the New York Post because there was cocaine in the car. Tests weren't made for steroids, which some doctors will say are more dangerous, and are far more abused in the WWF, because that wasn't the PR problem at the time.

Since nothing the NWA does will make page two, they haven't had the PR problem to bring on drug testing. That doesn't make NWA wrestlers any more or less abusive, and as a fan, it's really nobody's business provided it doesn't affect the product —— the wrestling.

Blanchard was fired by the WWF because he tried to recruit wrestlers to join the NWA. Failing a drug test was a convenient excuse. One wrestler doing the same stuff Blanchard was doing is headlining right now with the WWF, and probably a lot more than one. Blanchard wasn't signed by the NWA because those in the organization, when it came time to sign the contract, felt it wasn't nearly as big a coup to get him as it was when the promises were made. Or maybe just because there was a public relations fear from the reasons Titan gave for firing him. Yeah, he made his bed by giving everyone an excuse to do what they did. But a failed drug test wasn't the reason. It was an excuse. And those in charge are to blame to a significant degree for what pro wrestling breeds. I feel sorry for a guy when a business that breeds abuse uses that abuse as an excuse for someone whose alleged problems have hardly hampered his ability to do his job.

ALL JAPAN

The tag team tournament ended on 12/6 in Tokyo's Budokan Hall before a near sellout of 14,800 fans paying $620,000. It was the second largest crowd in the history of the All Japan promotion, trailing only the crowd for the super show on June 5th with the Tsuruta vs. Tenryu main event. As mentioned last week, Stan Hansen & Genichiro Tenryu captured the tournament beating Jumbo Tsuruta & Yoshiaki Yatsu in 28:57 when Tenryu gave Yatsu the enzuigiri and Hansen pinned him after the lariat. In other matches on the card, Dynamite Kid & Davey Boy Smith downed Dan Kroftat & Doug Furnas in 17:50, Tiger Jeet Singh & Abdullah the Butcher beat Terry Gordy & Bill Irwin, Giant Baba & Rusher Kimura beat The Foot Loose, Shunji Takano & Kabuki beat The Nasty Boys, The Wild Bunch (Haruka Eigen & Motoshi Okuma & Masa Fuchi) beat Kenta Kobashi & Shinichi Nakano & Yoshinari Ogawa, Isao Takagi & Akira Taue beat Isamu Teranishi & Goro Tsurumi plus prelims.

12/5 in Yamagata drew 2,200 as Hansen & Tenryu & Ogawa beat Baba & Kimura & Fuchi, Tsuruta & Yatsu beat Kabuki & Takano, Gordy & Irwin beat Foot Loose, Kid & Smith & Kobashi beat Nakano & Kroffat & Furnas, Singh & Butcher beat The Nasty Boys and Richard Slinger (Terry Gordy's nephew) won his first pro match pinning Tsuyoshi Kikuchi.

Final tournament standings saw Tenryu & Hansen finish first with 18 points, Tsuruta & Yatsu with 16, Baba & Kimura with 14, Kid & Smith with 12, Singh & Butcher with 10, Furnas & Kroffat with 7, Gordy & Irwin with 6, Foot Loose with 3, Nasty Boys with 2 and Kabuki & Takano with 2.

Tenryu Hansen also captured the PWF and International tag team titles which they had vacated going into the tournament in order that the tournament winner would also get the titles. After the tournament was over, they presented a series of awards to the different teams entered and also some All Japan annual awards. Tsuruta & Yatsu were awarded the Most Outstanding team prize. Kid & Smith were voted Best Technical tag team. Kroffat & Furnas were voted New Wave prize (which means most innovative tag team with their moves), Gordy & Irwin were voted Hardest Workers, The Foot Loose were voted best new tag team and Most fearless (in other words were awarded for doing the most high-risk moves).

Tenryu was voted All Japan's Most Valuable Wrestler which comes as no surprise with Tsuruta as the runner-up.

The tournament itself was something of a letdown compared to years past. It was obvious all the way through which two teams were going to the finals and there were no big upsets or any kind of surprises. The audiences in Tokyo and some of the larger cities even booed Hansen when he worked against guys like the Bulldogs and Can-Am Express because he couldn't keep up with them and they wanted Tenryu in since he could. However there was substantial heat and interest in Hansen vs. Gordy and that tag match was one of the better bouts in the tournament.

NEW JAPAN

The singles tournament ended on 12/7 at the Tokyo Sumo Hall before a near sellout crowd of 9,850 when Riki Choshu beat Shinya Hashimoto with the sleeper in 15:32. Because of the win, Choshu was announced as being the opponent of Big Van Vader on the Feb. 10 card at the Tokyo Dome for Vader's IWGP World title. In other matches the final night, Steve Williams & Brad Rheingans beat Salman Hashimikov & Victor Zangiev when Williams stampeded Zangiev (interesting since all four have superior amateur backgrounds – Rheingans as an NCAA Division II champ and Greco-Roman Olympian, Williams as NCAA runner up, Hashimikov as five-time World Cup winner and Zangiev as a World champion), Hiroshi Hase won a mixed match in 8:15 making Habieli Victashev (Soviet champion in sambo wrestling) submit with the octopus hold, Masa Chono pinned Manny Fernandez, Kengo Kimura & Osamu Kido upset Super Strong Machine & George Takano, Kuniaki Kobayashi & Naoki Sano beat Tatsutoshi Goto & Norio Honaga, Akira Nogami pinned Black Cat and prelims.

Hashimoto was named Most Outstanding in the tournament, Williams as Best Technical Wrestler and Chono as Hardest Worker.

The Wild Blonds (Hiro Saito & Honaga & Goto) on television issued a challenge to Choshu saying they wanted to work in the main events but thus far Choshu hasn't responded.

The Blonds do some good brawling but Goto has the most ridiculous looking haircut of 1989 with the blond hair (barely beating Dino Bravo's blond locks and Johnny Smith's punk hairdo).

12/6 in Osaka drew 5,910 for the tournament semifinals with Choshu making Chono submit to the scorpion in 11:36 and Hashimoto beating Williams via count out in 14:08. Victashev beat Takayuki Iizuka in a mixed match by submission in the fifth round, Kido pinned Zangiev, Hashimikov pinned Rheingans, Goto & Honaga beat Shiro Koshinaka & Kantaro Hoshino, Kimura pinned Fernandez and Machine & Takano beat Hase & Kobayashi plus prelims.

12/5 in Nagoya drew 7,910 for the quarterfinals as Hashimoto pinned Hashimikov, Choshu pinned Kido, Williams pinned Zangiev and Chono pinned Rheingans. Also Hase & Kobayashi beat Goto & Honaga via DQ, Kimura pinned Koshinaka, Machine & Takano beat Fernandez & Wayne Bloom, Sano & Hoshino beat Nogami & Hirokazu Hata plus prelims.

New Japan has bee heavily publicizing the Tokyo Dome show. They had a giant-sized ad in the newspaper on Dec. 1 (two months before the card) with photos of Ric Flair, Muta, Larry Zbyszko, Vader, Koji Kitao, Antonio Inoki (who comes out of retirement for this card and the Soviet Union show), Tatsumi Fujinami (scheduled to return on that card) and Choshu. Tickets are priced at $350 for ringside (which is the most expensive ticket ever for pro wrestling), plus $210, $140, $70, $35 and $20 which means a full house would break the gate record set on 11/29. The Flair-Muta match is somewhat in jeopardy because Muta

doesn't want to do it after Starreade because he felt that finishing with zero points and with the fans in Japan reading about Starrcade in the newspapers and magazines that he wouldn't be viewed as a legitimate contender for the title. Muta had a problem getting over in Japan because he was viewed as too much of a pretty boy and not tough even though he had awesome moves. Because he did so well in the U.S., he thought he could return without the "heat" but with Starrcade, he was afraid that they would view him as the same Keiji Muto who left as a guy with good moves who wasn't "tough."

WWF

Nothing else major at the TV tapings on 12/12 in Nashville and 12/13 in Huntsville. Other bouts from Nashville besides the NHB main event saw Dusty Rhodes beat Bossman, Ultimate Warrior over Dino Bravo, Mr. Perfect over Ron Garvin and the Colossal Connection (Andre the Giant & Haku) over Demolition via count out. Prime Time Wrestling drew a 2.9 on 12/11 while All American did a 2.2 the day before which was its second lowest rating of the year. Once again in the cable ratings the NWA clearly outdistanced the WWF again.

12/16 in Philadelphia drew 8,126 and $83,000 (second lowest Hogan gate ever in Philly) as The Genius pinned Paul Roma, Bad New Brown pinned Mark Young, Bravo pinned Tito Santana, Brutus Beefcake double disqualification with Rick Martel, Hart Foundation went to a 20 minute draw with Rockers (excellent match), Jake Roberts pinned Ted DiBiase and Mr. Perfect beat Hulk Hogan via count out.

At the Huntsville tapings Beefcake used his scissors and chopped up one of Martel's sweaters. How did I know that was going to happen?

The Friday night prime Time special on 2/23 will be taped out of Joe Louis Arena in Detroit. Coliseum video will be releasing 11 tapes in 1990 as compared with 21 in 1989 with more non-television footage on each tape.

Titan dark until 12/26.

Other weekend dates were nothing special with nothing over about 6,000 people but a card in Dallas this week drew less than Killer Brooks' card a few days earlier although way more than USWA did.

MAJOR NEWS ITEMS OF THIS WEEK

More sources, including some at ESPN continue to say that the AWA will be dropped after its contract expires in February. Word has it that ESPN isn't interested in dealing with pro wrestling after that date. With so much time and money invested in baseball starting in the spring, they don't even have enough time on the air for fringe programming as they consider wrestling. Without ESPN, there is a good chance that the AWA may not survive the year, although the Obituaries for the AWA have been written on a regular basis for the past few years. If the AWA is to fold, expect Larry Zbyszko to drop the title at the Tokyo Dome.

Another promotion in some jeopardy is CWA. Jerry Jarrett continues to mainly be concerned about the USWA (which isn't drawing, but Jarrett can make money off selling ads because of its 100+ station syndication line-up). The gate this past Monday in Memphis of $3,000 was one of the lowest ever. The CWA show this week contained a lot of USWA clips and the Memphis card this week with Jerry Lawler vs. Dustin Rhodes on top is practically designed not to draw any fans. When Jarrett met with David Woods about acquiring rights to the dozen or so TV markets Woods' now-defunct Continental Wrestling Federation had, Jarrett told Woods that he was going to operate everything out of Dallas and would run a big loop with shows in Tennessee and Alabama with a Dallas-based crew. That doesn't bode well for the CWA. I've been concerned about the CWA ever since Jeff Jarrett went full-time to Dallas because it's obvious when Jeff quit working shows where his father's priorities were.

Some breaks on the CWF front. Eddie Gilbert wound up acquiring TV rights for the dozen stations Woods had his CWF in. This geets confusing since Gilbert is still under contract to the NWA and he's not going to walk out on his contract. Even more confusing is that Missy Hyatt will start as co-host of the Sunday NWA Main Event show on TBS starting with the 1/2 taping in Gainesville, GA (for airing on Jan. 14). For a long time everyone assumed that Gilbert's NWA contract wouldn't be renewed since he's been buried there ever since Ric Flair took over as booker, however the NWA didn't give Gilbert a 90-day termination notice this month which means in theory, his contract, by the wording, should be automatically renewed for another year. Still, it appears Gilbert will leave the NWA to get a chance to run his own territory based in Alabama. Paul E. Dangerously is flying down to Alabama this week to tape wrap-arounds of a series of eight to ten old CWF shows (shows from last year when Gilbert was booking) to build up to a return of the CWF with the same guys when it was hot planned for February. Dangerously is trying to put together investors in New York (and we all thought that was a gimmick) to fund the group. If it qets started, Tom Prichard will be the CWF champion (Dennis Condrey was the last champ and there will be a phantom title change) and Austin Idol, Ken Wayne and Danny Davis will also return. There will be negotiations with Rob Russen to sell shows for this group similar to what Russen did with the AWA and have the group promote either some or very few shows on its own, depending upon what gets worked out. Gilbert will try and put together a working relationship with other independents and maybe even try and put together a booking agency for independent talent such as Bam Bam Bigelow. But this is all very much still in the formative stages, but Gilbert and Dangerously

seem to be looking to this as a challenge to be able to repeat the work they did last year.

Some details on the death of former top wrestling attraction William (Haystacks) Calhoun who passed away on 12/7. Calhoun, 55, who gained wrestling fame as the 601 pound country boy from Morgans Corner, Arkansas (he was in reality from McKinney, TX) passed away suddenly on the 7th from a massive heart attack while talking at home with his mother. Calhoun had just had an artificial leg put on and was starting to get up and around after several years of basically being confined to a trailer home nearly destitute in McKinney.

Those close to Tully Blanchard are saying that he's ready to call it quits on wrestling, although some speculate that may be a negotiating ploy. Blanchard is telling friends he has a firm job offer from Coca Cola to work in marketing. Some speculate whether after all these years of being a wrestling star whether Blanchard, still one of the better workers around, cansettle down to a 9-to-5 job. Blanchard has to make the decision one way or another by Jan. 1 as to whether he's going to accept the job or not.

Jerry Blackwell appears to have regained control of the Georgia independent territory once again. Don't have details right now but apparently Blackwell convinced David Oldig and Randall Brown, who were running things, to give him another shot at control. Even though Blackwell's business sense hasn't always been praised, he's remained well liked by the wrestlers and with all his personal tragedies of late, he somehow managed to get back in control.

Bam Bam Bigelow's attorney made a $10,000 settlement offer to Larry Sharpe over a $21,000 judgement Sharpe gained in a breach of contract suit against Bigelow. Sharpe had trained Bigelow for free for a percentage of Bigelow 's earnings and since the two had their split, Sharpe hadn't gotten his percentage. Bigelow's attorney told Sharpe that Bigelow would work off the remaining $11,000 by working a series of independent bookings for Sharpe's WWA but Sharpe refused the offer and they are going back to court.

USWA

The 12/15 card at the Dallas Sportatorium drew just 130 paid as Jerry Lawler beat Kerry Von Erich in a USWA title vs. Texas title match so Lawler now is also the Texas champion, which makes lots of sense that a World champ would also hold the Texas title. Terrence Garvin, who is the color commentator on the TV show, threw a chair into Lawler who used it on Kerry for the pin. Lawler was on Memphis television the next day with both belts and did an interview in Tennessee saying he was going to throw the Texas belt down in an outhouse. Chris Adams went to a double DQ with Eric Embry as they brawled all over the building in the co-feature. While the promotion sort of tried to get Adams over as the face, the fans cheered for

Embry in this match and Embry and Adams both tried to get fans support with Embry succeeding. On television in Dallas the next day, not only was Embry not even on television, but his name wasn't even mentioned. Supposedly he'll be gone at least until the New Year. The other major match saw Robert Fuller & Brian Lee keep the USWA taq belts going to a no decision with Matt Borne & Jeff Jarrett when P.Y. Chu Hi ran in and hie Borne with a chair and the ref ruled that since Fuller Lee didn't ask for the help that the faces wouldn't win via DQ which in USWA would have also meant a title change.

Soul Taker is headed in.

Billy Travis dressed up as Santa Claus on television and hit Jeff Jarrett with a garbage can.

Scandor Akbar is still trying to sign up Chico Torres.

Killer Brooks' independent shockingly sold out the Longhorn Bar (1,600) on 12/12 and he's moving his shows to the larger Bronco Bowl in Dallas. Some feel this is a mistake because the bar atmosphere is part of the reason this group is drawing a steady crowd without television.

This group is dark until 12/25 in Dallas with Gary Young vs. Dustin Rhodes in a strap match, Chu Hi vs. Borne and Travis vs. Jarrett as the triple feature On the "Christmas spectacular."

CWA

The reason Jerry Lawler apparently turned face on 12/4 but was a heel again on television the following Saturday is because he turned face on his own in Memphis and Jarrett told him that he'd better be a heel on television Saturday or else. So Lawler turned himself twice in the same week.

The Christmas Chaos card in Memphis will actually be on 12/30 because the Coliseum workers didn't want to work on Christmas night.

Lawler spent much of the TV show insulting Dusty Rhodes, since his main event on 12/18 is a title defense against Dustin Rhodes. The rest of the card has Bill Dundee defending the CWA title against Billy Travis, Chris Champion vs. Dirty White Boy and if Chris wins, White Boy gets handcuffed to the corner and Chris gets to kiss Dirty White Girl ten times but if White Boy wins, Champion gets handcuffed and White Boy gets to whip him 10 times, Dutch Mantell vs. Master of Pain, Ricky & Todd Morton vs. Soul Taker & Brian Lee and Steve Austin (Steve Williams, the rookie from USWA) vs. Black Jack (Tommy Gilbert).

Lawler did heel commentary on TV and rated the matches. He called a black kid in the crowd "Dutch Mantell's son" and a fat guy in the crowd "Dusty Rhodes" and said that Dusty had T.B. – Twin Bellies.

Mike Davis and Kevin Dillinger are gone.

OREGON

Nothing special at the big wedding on 12/16 in Portland.

Luke Brown (who used to be Grizzly Smith's tag partner as The Kentuckians in the 1960s) was the preacher and some of the faces and heels were in the ring dressed up. Steve Doll brought Ginger down the aisle with the wedding march song and then they stopped the music and started playing Scotty the Body's music. Instead of going to the ring for the wedding Scotty took the flowers and gave them to Veronica (his valet) and said the wedding was all a hoax and told Ginger she should be more like Veronica and Ginger was left crying in the ring. Later in the show as Scotty was wrestling Bill Francis, Doll asked Francis to step aside and started pounding on Scotty. After a ref bump, Veronica hit Doll with a loaded purse. Ginger jumped in and knocked Veronica down and jumped On Scotty's back. Veronica then hit Ginger with the purse and Scotty picked Doll up for a superplex but instead gave him a piledriver off the middle ropes which was the hottest move in the territory in some time and left Doll and Ginger laying. The main event saw Billy Haynes & Rip Oliver beat The Grappler Brian Adams via DQ when several of the heels ran in, Beetlejuice beat Al Madril via DQ when Jonathan Holliday interfered, Holliday pinned Carl Styles in a match where if Holliday lost he'd have to kiss the rear end of a pig while if Styles lost he'd have to wear a dress to every city for one week. After a ref bump, Madril poked Styles in his good eye and Holliday gave him a DDT for the win and Holliday powdered Styles' face and put him in a dress while Rex King pinned John Boyd to keep the TV title.

Boyd will be through by the end of the year while D. J. Peterson is headed in.

Grappler & Adams won the Northwest tag team titles from Doll King On 12/14 in Salem.

Christmas card is headlined by a cage match with Haynes & Oliver vs. Grappler & Adams while 12/23 regular card is headlined by Beetlejuice & Jeff Warner vs. Madril & Holliday.

Crowds for the spot shows are generally poor (50 to 100 most nights) but the Portland cardsstill draw several hundred and often more than 1,000.

OTHER NOTES

There was a hair vs. hair match on 12/10 in Mexico City between Sangre Chicana and Pero Aguayo but don't know result yet. Ken Timbs beat Pirata Morgan on 12/9 in Mexico City to win the Mexican lightheavyweight title while El Hijo Del Santo beat All Star on the same card in a mask vs. mask match.

Caught reader Bryan Dorfler on the Ch. 2 News at Noon show on the afternoon Of Starrcade showing his expertise in wrapping Christmas gifts.

Bob Emory is feuding with Larry Cameron on top for Stampede wrestling right now.

An independent show on 12/10 in Marietta, GA drew a

$10,000 house for a card with Junkyard Dog vs. Terry Gordy, The Bullet & Brad Armstrong vs. Dennis Condrey & Randy Rose in a cage, Ken Patera vs. Kimala, Jimmy Powell vs. The Nightmare in a cage, Mike Golden vs. Chic Donovan and Big Foot (billed as 7-foot-7 and 500 pounds) against Big Red Reese for the superheavyweight championship Of the world.

Larry Sharpe and Dennis Coraluzzo drew a $10,000 house on 12/16 in Camden, NJ for JYD vs. Samu the Samoan, Mike Sharpe vs. Jules Strongbow plus Jim Mcpherson won the WWA jr. title from Johnny Hotbody.

Paul E. Dangerously got into an altercation at Gleason's Gym in New York on 12/12 on an ICW card. Dangerously was doing a Danger Zone in the ring when the mic went out so he started shouting the Danger Zone (maybe 300 fans at the show) and threw down the ring mic and the owner of the gym got the mic and started saying testing 1-2-3 over the mic while Paul E. was shouting his thing in the ring. Afterwards the owner wanted $200 from Dangerously to fix the broken mic and said he was going to have it taken from Dangerously's hide. It wound up a standoff between the security force at Gleason's (a bunch of semi-pro boxers) and the wrestlers and Tony Atlas collared two of the guys before everyone cooled down.

Art Barr (Beetlejuice) will be going to trial in January on the rape charge.

ESPN replaced World Class legends Monday through Thursday of this week with current AWA tapes.

NWA

Japanese girl wrestlers Toshiyo Yamada & Manami Toyota will come in to work a series against Bull Nakano & Kumiko Iwamoto in February. Even though these girls all work hard, Bull, the heel, is going to wind up being cheered by the fans I'd bet unless they all just go to the concession stands and don't care about the match.

Sid Vicious has dropped 25 pounds (so he's "only" 280) since being out of action. He's expected back sometime in January.

Tommy Young expected back in about one month.

Next PPV called "The Wild Thing" on 2/25 from Greensboro.

Rock & Roll Express to return in January while Cactus Jack Manson also starts then on the road. Manson was in an auto accident in New York on 12/14 in the backseat on the passenger side and had 120 stitches taken in his face. The gash was so large he could stick his tongue out through his chin.

Bob Seegar's people complained about the theme music for Woman so we won't be watching her strut to that song anymore.

They were still airing Starrcade commercials on ESPN four days after the event took place during basketball games

and also on TBS during the wrestling show on Saturday after the event.

Apparently the promotion will cut back to four shows per week early next year.

Expect some changes in the booking committee shortly. If those changes are made, there will be a lot to say.

World Championship Wrestling on 12/6 drew a 3.4 rating for the return of Arn Anderson while Power Hour the night before fell to a 2.0 for a pretty weak show and Main Event drew a 2.4 with Samoans vs. Steiners On 12/7.

12/14 in Peoria drew 3,500 fans but mainly papered for a TV taping as the house was $11,000 though the -110 temperature outside didn't help any. This stuff will air the first weekend of 1990. Sting wasn't there (missed everything this week after Starrcade) but Ole & Arn Anderson did two interviews asking him to come out and become the official Fourth Horseman and he never came out. Norman drew a picture of Woman and she threw it down and Norman and Nitron started fighting and Woman and Nitron both tried to break the portrait over Norman's head and it didn't break so Kevin Sullivan had to get the job done and the red coloring on the painting ran all over Norman's head to make it look like blood (since no blood is allowed on TV they are being clever between red mist and running red paint to get a bloody-like appearance without violating the rules). Ric Flair beat Eddie Gilbert on Worldwide with Gilbert playing heel in a good, but nothing special match while Flair pinned Bobby Eaton on NWA Main Event in 17 minutes of an excellent match. They held a match to fill a hole in World Championship Wrestling for 12/27. This is a long story but at the WCW tapings in Greensboro they held a match with Shane Douglas vs. Jim Cornette after the Dudes "trick" Cornette into signing a contract. The match winds up with the Midnights attacking Douglas for the DQ and leaving him laying . Douglas was booed during the match against Cornette even though Cornette did everything to turn the crowd including throwing powder. Anyway, Douglas went to Jim Herd and complained that he couldn't even beat a manager on TV and wanted to quit, Herd then told the booking committee that the Greensboro match will never air on television and that he wants another match between the two taped with Dougles beating Cornette. So the match was supposed to be taped but Cornette came out with his arm in a sling and had a note from his doctor saying he couldn't wrestle for another eight months and Douglas wrestled Stan Lane and it wound up with Cornette in the ring and getting pinned. The way it turned out may not have been so bad but it would have been stupid this early for Cornette to get beat up so soon after turning, and certainly not on free television, that should be for the arena or PPV. Also Ole & Arn Anderson beat the Militia (who now have Beefeater Gin outfits with Lord Littlebrook), Tom Zenk & Brian Piliman beat Freebirds, Pillman beat Kendall Windham and

Dudes beat Militia. Fans were pretty upset since Warriors vs. Skyscrapers was advertised as the main event, Skyscrapers weren't there and Warriors, while there, did one interview but never even did a squash match while Doom vs. Steiners also billed never took place because Steiners were no-shows for no apparent reason. Sting and Muta also didn't appear.

12/15 in st. Louis drew 1,300 and $14,000 as Gilbert double count out with Sullivan in 2:15, Militia beat Tommy Rich Ranger Ross, Midnight beat Dudes, Hawk beat Dan Spivey via DQ when Teddy Long interfered, Ric Flair pinned Lex Luger clean in 21 minutes with Flair juicing like crazy, Zenk & Pillman beat Freebirds and Steiners beat Doom. They canceled the next date in St. Louis since they took out two quarter-page ads and headlined with Flair vs. Luger and didn't draw any fans.

Rich broke two ribs when Militia stomped him with new boots that weren't broken in.

12/16 in Detroit drew 2,500 and $30,000 as Sullivan pinned Gilbert in 2:00 (Sullivan accidentally stepped on Gilbert's ankle and he suffered a hairline fracture of the ankle, then fell out of the ring and landed on his shoulder and messed up his rotator cuff and was hospitalized that night but he will probably be back by Christmas anyway), Victory pinned Ross * (Rich didn't work 'because of the broken ribs), Midnight beat Dudes *** with Express cheered by most of the crowd and Dudes heavily booed when Lane pinned Ace after Eaton used the racquet, Hawk beat Spivey via DQ when Long interfered **, Flair pinned Luger in 22:30 with an inside cradle **** (Flair juiced like crazy and Luger's chest was red from the chops), Andersons beat Samoans when Arn pinned Savage and Steiners beat Doom *** with Nitron and Woman teasing a pplit up afterwards.

Jim Herd offered Sam Muchnick $5,000 to do a series of television interviews endorsing the NWA today but Muchnick turned it down because he wouldn't endorse the current product.

Terry Funk will take over as Executive Producer of the syndicated TV shows starting in January.

NWA starts back up on 12/25 in Greenville and Charlotte.

NWA will probably be viewing tapes of Jushin Liger and Flair will get to see him live in Tokyo in February but it's premature to say there's much of a chance right now of them bringing him in. Morton & Gibson start at the TV tapings on 1/2 in Gainesville, GA.

Stampede
12/15 in Calgary saw Angel of Death return and beat Jason Anderson, K.C. Houston beat Desiree Peterson in a women's match, Bob Emory pinned Skull Mason, Bruce Hart kept the Commonwealth title beating Johnny Smith, Arch Angel (Curtis Thompson) beat Konan the Great (Konan from Mexico) and Larry Cameron kept the North American title beating Steve Disalvo.

12/16 in Edmonton saw Anderson beat Konan, Angel Of Death over Chris Benoit, Mason Houston over Biff Wellington & Peterson, Bruce Hart beat Great Gama, Owen Hart beat Arch Angel and Cameron pin Bob Emory.

QUICK WWF STUFF

TV tapings in early January in Chattanooga and Birmingham, then in Florida in late January and in Arizona in mid-Feb.

Bob Orton to return early next year.

12/15 in Montreal saw Bad News Brown over Mark Young, Rick Martel over Brutus Beefcake, Hart Foundation drew Rockers, Bravo over Santana, Genius over Roma, Roberts over DiBiase via DQ and Perfect over Hogan via count out. Same crew was in Hamilton, ONT the previous night with same results except Beefcake over Martel and Genius and Bad News switched to beating Young and Roma respectively.

THE READER PAGES

CLASH/ SURVIVORS
While your coverage of Clash was up to its usual high standards, you did overlook two important news items. First, you failed to point out a directorial flaw. Viewers missed the action that followed the original, unique and never-been-done-before angle where Lex Luger trashed the trophies. That's right, immediately afterwards he pushed Bill Apter's face into a birthday cake.

Second, as every subscriber to the Runnels News Service knows, the NWA has been begging for Dusty Rhodes to return as the booker. What didn't make the Observer was that Jim Herd actually gave Dusty a booker tryout to book the finish of the Flair-Funk I Quit match. Here's how Dusty 's finish went. After a ref bump, Gary Hart picked up the mic and imitated the voice of Ric Flair surrendering. A second ref, who was blind, came to ringside, heard the announcement over the PA and awarded the match to Funk. Tommy Young then came to ringside and he and the second ref argued until they agreed that the only fair solution would be to award the title to Dusty Rhodes.

At that point, Lee Scott ran in, put a spike in Dusty's eye, broke his leg, showed the secret photos that Baby Doll had, and hit Magnum T.A. with a baseball bat. The skit would set up a Dec. 13 main event at the Omni with the card modestly renamed "Starrdustcade 89."

Ernie Santilli
Drexel Hill, Penn sylvania

Did any big card this year besides the Clash from Troy have four or more 3 ½ star or better matches?

Gary Collina
Minneapolis, Minnesota

Dave Meltzer: The Baltimore Bash had four (Sting vs. Muta, Steamboat vs. Luger, War Games and Flair vs. Funk). All Japan's June 5 card in Tokyo may have had more than that. Tsuruta vs. Tenryu and Foot Loose vs. Kroffat Furnas were both close to five stars. Hansen Gordy vs. Dynamite Kid & Davey Boy Smith was 3 ½ stars and Sting vs. Danny Spivey was close to 3 ½ stars. The only other match I saw on the card that was televised (Mitsuo Momota vs. Isamu Teranishi) was three stars, and according to Japanese Wrestling Journal, that was the worst match on the card.

Overall the Clash was better than Halloween Havoc. I was elated by Jim Cornette turning on the Dudes. Steiners vs. Skyscrapers was great. Flair vs. Funk was at least 4 ¾ stars, if not five stars. The match was non-stop action all the way with an incredible post-match brawl. The show kept my interest all the way through.

The same can't be said for Survivors. A half-hearted thumbs down. The Hogan match was a total screw job. Roddy's Rowdies vs. Rude Brood was surprisingly decent. The Ultimate Warrior show was disgusting, but the match was decent. Bobby Heenan worked better than most of the wrestlers. Biggest disappointment was the Earthquake.

Eddy Beeson
High point, North Carolina

Thumbs up for Survivors. It was solid, but not spectacular. The booking was smart as they kept Zeus and Andre to a minimum and a few messages were delivered. Mr. Perfect is still perfect and now set for title shots at Hogan. Dino Bravo survived so he's worthy of title shots. And Hogan and Warrior are still the top two wrestlers in the WWF. This was the only WWF PPV that didn't end with a Hogan posedown.

What's the story On the Iron Sheik 's NWA contract? Does he just get paid even though they rarely use him on cards? Do you think we'll see the British Bulldogs back in the WWF now that the Rougeaus are gone and the WWF is short in the tag team ranks?

Recently Matwatch is making it obvious that you're not giving the full inside story on some things that I have to assume you know the details on. Matwatch seems to give the complete story but you seem to hold back on giving the whole story

Joe Mannion
Prospect Park, Pennsylvania

Dave Meltzer: The WWF did a 1985 PPV called The Wrestling Classic in Chicago and Hogan didn't pose at the end of that show. I think JYD barked at the end instead. Sheik gets paid $2,000 or so per week for staying home as he signed a six-figure one-year contract with the NWA when George Scott was booking. It probably expires around February and it certainly won't be renewed. The Bulldogs

want to return to the WWF and it may happen, but the morale of a lot of the wrestlers is a lot better with them gone because of their propensity for ribbing.

Everyone knows that the Survivor Series is generally the best WWF PPV card because the dead wood only gets moments of exposure in multiple member elimination matches. However, as McMahon should realize by this turkey, when the organization is made up of mostly dead wood, that the only significant thing that came out of the show was an insight into McMahon's booking policy. put all the heat on the upcoming PPV show and run no other angles to confuse the fans.

If that wasn't enough, I watched the SNME. This was the first time I actually turned the show off. The first two matches were among the worst matches I've ever seen on television. While nobody expected Andre vs. Warrior to be good, and the commercials between the match had better wrestling in them, I never expected Hogan vs. Poffo to be that horrible. Rhodes vs. Bossman was decent watching with the speed search on, which probably doesn't say much for the regular version. Perfect vs. Rooster was a waste. Rockers vs. Brainbusters was good, but I didn't like what the WWF was trying to accomplish with it.

Needless to say, the Clash was a much better show. But I have to disagree on Flair vs. Funk. I didn't find it a very good match. It was very slow, even prompting a comment from someone viewing with me that Flair and Funk looked like they were making Love instead of wrestling. I gave it three stars, but only for the angle at the end.

Teresa DeMarie
Tuckahoe, New York

WRESTLING TALK

I'd like to make you aware of our show, "Wrestling Talk." We're a two-year-old talk show which began on local cable and is now seen monthly on WHLL-TV, Ch. 27 in Worcester, MA, which has a signal that carries all over southern New England. We've had the likes of Bruno Sammartino, Lou Albano, Johnny Valiant, Don Muraco, Larry Sharpe, Madusa Miceli, Misty Blue, Terry Funk, Ricky Steamboat, Toru Tanaka, Iron Sheik and others as guests.

We try to let our viewers see a more personal side of pro wrestlers and their likes and dislikes both in and out of pro wrestling. We feel that the fans enjoy knowing personal tidbits about their favorite stars that they won't find out on television.

We are aiming for find a sponsor or advertisers so the show can air weekly on Ch. 27 instead of just monthly. We are seen weekly, without.advertising, On 28 cable systems in Massachussetts.

Leonard Caplan
Producer-Host Chelsea, Massachusetts

QUESTIONS
Please comment on the decline of legitimate women's wrestling in the United States. I personally feel that the women need their own promotion modeled after the Japanese promotion. It is the only way to keep women's wrestling from degenerating into GLOW and POWW.

Michael Pell
Los Angeles, California

Dave Meltzer: My own belief is that currently the wrestling climate conditions aren't right for a women's promotion to make a go of it economically in this country. I wish that wasn't the case, but even the men's promotions, with the exception of the WWF, are having a tough time making it economically. The Japanese promotion has declined significantly since it peaked in late 1985, mainly because of the retirement of the Crush Girls, Dump Matsumoto and to a lesser extent Jaguar Yokota. At its peak it was in many ways the best promotion going. But there are cultural differences between the U.S. and Japan. The Japanese promotion was supported mainly by teenage girls who looked to the wrestlers as role models and heroes because they represented something different than the cultural norms (Japanese women traditionally are submissive to men culturally, although that is also changing). While the work rate, at its peak, was the best in the world, the traditional wrestling fans of Japan still didn't attend the live shows with any frequency (although they did watch the television because at its peak, it did better TV ratings in fringe slots than did here in Prime Time on NBC). At its peak it had a large "closet-fan" viewership because it was considered somewhat unacceptable for males to admit to being fans of women's wrestling. Anyway, for whatever reason, the cultural differences make it unlikely, more like impossible, that teenage girls are going to rally behind female wrestling strong enough to support a promotion in this country. GLOW and POWW weren't economically viable either, witness their inability to run house shows for any length of time and I believe both are out of business right now (GLOW is still on TV but these are old tapes and will be out of syndication when this TV season ends). And male wrestling fans aren't going to support female wrestling, no matter what the work rate, for the same reasons most professional female athletics (tennis being an exception) have a hard time making a go economically.

Could you please give me some information of the backgrounds of the Ultimate Warrior and Sting. I had heard that they started out as part of a foursome called Power Team USA out of California . They went on as a duo called The Freedom Fighters. If this is true, could you also tell me what happened to the other two wrestlers in Power Team USA. Are they still wrestling? Also could you give me some background on Sid Vicious. Did he ever play pro football

and what federation did he start out in?

Greg Manning
Staten Island, New York

Dave Meltzer: Warrior and Sting were both Southern California-based bodybuilders when a guy named Rick Bassman was going through the bodybuilding gyms looking for four massively muscled and good-looking guys that he envisioned would be brought into wrestling, under his management, to be babyfaces to feud with the Road Warriors, who were the rage in wrestling at the time. After very little actual wrestling training, the two started out in Memphis in late 1985 under their real names of Jim Hellwig and Steve Borden as Power Team USA as babyfaces. After about a month, then booker Bill Dundee turned them heel, painted their faces like the Road Warriors and called them the Blade Runners. Shortly thereafter they went to Bill Watts' UWF and broke up there. Watts became insistent that the guys lay off the steroids and drop weight and learn to work before putting the weight back on. Hellwig, then known as Blade Runner Rock, instead quit the promotion and went to World Class as the Dingo Warrior and then wound up in the WWF as the Ultimate Warrior. Sting stayed in the UWF and worked his way from the bottom to main event status after the UWF was purchased by Jim Crockett. None of the other original Power Team members made it in pro wrestling, although one, Magic Schwartz, appeared in the wrestling movie "Grunt" and another, Mark Miller, occasionally works independent shows in Southern California. Sid Vicious started wrestling as Lord Humongous in Memphis in 1987, and also worked under that name in the CWF before taking off the hockey mask gimmick as Sid Vicious in Memphis in late 1988. He never played pro football although the story is he could hit a softball farther than anyone in West Memphis, Arkansas.

Years ago there were three great high flyers —Antonino Rocca, Edouardo Carpentier and Argentina Apollo. I know Rocco is dead. What happened to the other two?

Al Stichter
New York, New York

Dave Meltzer: Carpentier is retired and living in Montreal. He last worked in wrestling doing French commentary for the WWF syndicated shows that would be sent to French speaking markets in Canada and overseas. Apollo died several years ago when he was in his late 40s.

NWA
Despite the NWA's prominence on TBS, cable is still cable, which is why I pose the scenario for Ted Turner to spike an unlikely alliance with the FOX Network to try a prime-time "Bash" preview show next spring, similar to the NBC

prime time WWF show. I know that broadcasting magnates are uncomfortable working together, but if they could work things out, it would be relatively cheap programming for Fox that would draw ratings and a boost for the NWA.

Jeff Cohen
Great Neck, New York

Printed in Great Britain
by Amazon

34414021R00203